Changing European Identities

INTERNATIONAL SERIES IN SOCIAL PSYCHOLOGY
Series Editor: Professor W. Peter Robinson, University of Bristol, UK

Adolescence: From Crisis to Coping (Gibson-Cline)
Assertion and its Social Context (Wilson and Gallois)
Children's Social Competence in Context: The Contributions of Family,
School and Culture (Schneider)
Emotion and Social Judgments (Forgas)
Game Theory and its Applications in the Social and Biological Sciences
(Colman)
Genius and Eminence, 2nd edition (Albert)
Making Sense of Television: The Psychology of Audience Interpretation
(Livingstone)
The Psychology of Gambling (Walker)
Social Dilemmas: Theoretical Issues and Research Findings (Liebrand)
The Theory of Reasoned Action: Its Application to AIDS Preventive
Behavior (Terry, Gallois and McCamish)

To obtain copies of any of the above books approach your bookseller or, in
case of difficulty, contact the Sales Department, Butterworth-Heinemann,
Linacre House, Jordan Hill, Oxford OX2 8DP, UK. If you wish to contribute
to the series please send a synopsis to Matthew Deans, Commissioning
Editor, at the same address.

For order or further details you may also contact Butterworth-Heinemann
on e-mail: matthew.deans@bhein.rel.co.uk.

Changing European Identities: Social Psychological Analyses of Social Change

Edited by
GLYNIS M BREAKWELL and EVANTHIA LYONS
SPERI, University of Surrey, England

International Series in Social Psychology

Butterworth-Heinemann
Linacre House, Jordan Hill, Oxford OX2 8DP
A division of Reed Educational and Professional Publishing Ltd

 A member of the Reed Elsevier plc group

OXFORD   BOSTON   JOHANNESBURG
MELBOURNE   NEW DELHI   SINGAPORE

First published 1996

British Library Cataloguing in Publication Data
Changing European identities: social psychological analyses of social
  change/edited by Glynis M. Breakwell and Evanthia Lyons.
  p.   cm. – (International series in social psychology)
  Includes bibliographical references and index.
  ISBN 0 7506 3008 6
  1 Group identity – Europe.   2 Social change – Europe.   3 Social
  psychology – Europe. I Breakwell, Glynis M. (Glynis Marie)
  II Lyons, Evanthia.   III Series.
  HN373.5.C468   96–13486
  303.4′094–dc20   CIP

ISBN 0 7506 3008 6

Library of Congress Cataloguing in Publication Data
Changing European identities: social psychological
  analyses of social change – (International series in
  social psychology)
  1 Group identity – Europe   2 Social psychology – Europe
  I Breakwell, Glynis M.   II Lyons, Evanthia
  302′.094

Composition by Genesis Typesetting, Laser Quay, Rochester, Kent
Printed and bound in Great Britain by Hartnolls Limited, Bodmin, Cornwall

CONTENTS

PART THREE CONSTRUCTING A EUROPEAN IDENTITY

PART FOUR   COPING WITH SOCIAL CHANGE

Contributors

VIERA BACOVA, Slovak Academy of Sciences, Slovakia

MARTYN BARRETT, SPERI, University of Surrey, Guildford, England, UK

DENNY E. BENSON, Department of Sociology, Kent State University, Kent, Ohio, USA

MICHAEL BILLIG, Department of Social Sciences, University of Loughborough, Leicestershire, England, UK

GLYNIS M. BREAKWELL, SPERI, University of Surrey, Guildford, England, UK

JONATHAN CHASE, SPERI, University of Surrey, Guildford, England, UK

XENIA CHRYSSOCHOOU, Université de Paris V René Descartes, Institut de Psychologie, Laboratoire de Psychologie Sociale, 28 rue Serpente, 75006 Paris, France

MARCO CINNIRELLA, Department of Psychology, Royal Holloway & Bedford New College, University of London, Egham, Surrey, England, UK

SUSAN CONDOR, Department of Psychology, Lancaster University, Lancaster, England, UK

MARK DERMOT, Department of Psychology, University of East London, Romford Road, Stratford, London, England, UK

ANNAMARIA SILVANA DE ROSA, Dipartimento di Psicologia dei Processi di Sviluppo e Socializzazione, Università degli Studi di Roma 'La Sapienza', Via dei Marsi 78, Italy

PATRICIA ELLIS, School of Applied Social Studies, University of Luton, Luton, Bedfordshire, England, UK

HANS-PETER ERB, University of Mannheim, Germany

DENIS J. HILTON, Ecole Supérieure des Sciences Economiques et Commerciales, Cergy-Pontoise, France

NICK HOPKINS, Department of Psychology, Dundee University, Scotland, UK

GABRIEL HORENCZYK, School of Education, The Hebrew University of Jerusalem, Mount Scopus, Jerusalem 91905, Israel

MARY HORTON, Department of Psychology, University of Hertfordshire, College Lane, Hatfield, Hertfordshire, England, UK

KARMELA LIEBKIND, Department of Psychology, University of Helsinki, PB4 (Fabianinkatu 28), 00014 Helsinki, Finland

EVANTHIA LYONS, SPERI, University of Surrey, Guildford, England, UK

UWE KANNING, Westfälische Wilhelms-Universität Münster, Psychologisches Institut IV, Fliednerstrasse 21, 48149 Münster, Germany

ROSEMARIE MIELKE, Westfälische Wilhelms-Universität Münster, Psychologisches Institut IV, Fliednerstrasse 21, 48149 Münster, Germany

DAVID J. MOLIAN, Imperial College, School of Management, London, England, UK

AMÉLIE MUMMENDEY, Westfälische Wilhelms-Universität Münster, Psychologisches Institut IV, Fliednerstrasse 21, 48149 Münster, Germany

MARK F. PETERSON, Texas Tech University, USA

STEVE REICHER, School of Psychology, University of St Andrews, St Andrews, Fife, Scotland, UK

CARLO E. RUZZA, Department of Sociology, University of Essex, Wivenhoe Park, Colchester, England, UK

MARGARITA SANCHEZ-MAZAS, Faculté de Psychologie et des Sciences de l'Education, University of Geneva, 9 rte de Drize, 1227 Carouge, Switzerland

PETER B. SMITH, CRICCOM, School of Social Sciences, University of Sussex, Falmer, Brighton, East Sussex, England, UK

ELISABETH S. SOUSA, Instituto Superior de Psicologia Aplicada (ISPA), Rua Jardim do Tabaco, 44, 1100 Lisboa, Portugal

VELINA TOPALOVA, Institute of Sociology, Bulgarian Academy of Sciences, 13a Moskowska Street, Sofia 1000, Bulgaria

JOSÉ R. TORREGROSA, Universidad Complutense de Madrid, Madrid, Spain

KAREN TREW, Department of Psychology, Queens University of Belfast, Belfast, Northern Ireland, UK

MICHAEL WENZEL, Westfälische Wilhelms-Universität Münster, Psychologisches Institut IV, Fliednerstrasse 21, 48149 Münster, Germany

MARISA ZAVALLONI, Department of Psychology, Université de Montréal, Canada

Part One

Towards a Social Psychological
Analysis of Social Change in Europe

1

Changing European Identities and Social Change in Europe: A Challenge for Social Psychology

EVANTHIA LYONS and GLYNIS M. BREAKWELL

SPERI, University of Surrey, England

Background to the Book

Attempts to unify Western Europe and the collapse of communism in Eastern and Central Europe have given rise to a number of phenomena such as the resurgence of strong nationalist feelings, the creation of new social categories with which European peoples are asked to identify, the restructuring of value systems and the need for both individuals and groups to adapt to different cultures. These phenomena of social change have provided a dual challenge for social psychologists. The first challenge is to explain these phenomena and predict their development, using social psychological theories and methodologies. The second challenge is to examine the extent to which existing theories are supported when tested in naturalistic settings and the extent to which existing methodologies are adequate for investigating these phenomena (Moscovici, 1990; Breakwell and Canter, 1993).

In May 1993, the Social Psychology European Research Institute (SPERI) at the University of Surrey organised a conference on *Changing European Identities: Social Psychological Analyses of Social Change* at Farnham Castle, Surrey in order to examine these issues. The conference provided a forum in which researchers discussed the growing body of social psychological research in this area and focused the debate on the extent to which current research can respond adequately to these challenges and the direction social psychological theory and enquiry in this field should take in the future. The interest of SPERI's members in this area reflects their long-term theoretical and research interests in identity processes (e.g. Breakwell, 1986; Breakwell, 1992; Lyons and Breakwell,

3

1994; Chase, 1992; Stephenson, Breakwell and Fife-Schaw, 1993; Barrett and Short, 1992; Millward, 1993a and *in press*), group processes (Brown and Millward, 1993) and history and social psychology (Chase, 1994; Chase and Uzzell, 1991; Uzzell, 1992, 1993). Their interest also stems from the realisation that recent events in Europe provide an ideal opportunity to build social psychological theory and carry out research in accordance with certain concerns which underlie the research carried out at the Institute and for which members of SPERI have argued on previous occasions.

The first of these concerns is that there is a need to develop explanatory theoretical models which stipulate the relational rules predicting interactions between societal, interpersonal and individual processes in the production of action (Doise, 1986; Breakwell, 1994). Breakwell in this volume discusses in some detail the concept of relational rule and the value of such a model for building a social psychological theory of social change.

Second, it is necessary to develop theories which are relevant and valid in real-life situations (Israel and Tajfel, 1972; Sampson, 1991). However, ensuring that social psychological research is of relevance to social problems is not enough. It is also important to point out the relevance of social psychological analyses of social phenomena such as those occurring in Europe to both policy-makers and researchers in other disciplines (Jahoda, 1979). Indeed this is essential for the survival of social psychology as policy-makers control, at least partially, the provision of research resources. A social psychological perspective is also a vital ingredient in understanding social change since this is the key level of analysis in explaining the nexus between the individual, the group and society (Giddens, 1984).

Third, drawing attention to the need for methodological rigour, it was argued that social psychological theory and enquiry may benefit from the development both of new technologies (e.g. desktop video and non-linear audio and video editing) which enable the effective and manageable analysis of rich data and of multivariate statistical techniques which can be useful in modelling the relationships between the large number of factors we need to take into account if we are to understand complex social phenomena.

Fourth, it was argued that there is a need to use multiple-methods for studying a phenomenon and to develop ways to integrate data obtained from different methods (Breakwell, 1993; Sotirakopoulou and Breakwell, 1992; Breakwell and Lyons, 1993; De Rosa in this volume).

The recent social, political and economic developments in Europe provide a useful natural context in which factors involved in identity and social change processes can be studied. Indeed, understanding the phenomena involved in the recent restructuring and upheaval in Europe requires the modelling of complex relationships between different factors and the way these relationships change over time. It also requires the integration of different levels of analyses. Furthermore, the lack of a social psychological contribution to the public debate about the formation of new identities and the entrenchment of "old" national identities among certain groups renders the need to make the value of social psychological analyses of these phenomena known to policy-makers urgent. Similarly it seems that there is very little dialogue between social psychologists and other social scientists who are concerned with analysing phenomena such as changing identities which social psychologists have been studying for some time.

The contributions to the academic programme of the conference were selected to reflect different epistemological, theoretical and methodological approaches. Researchers from twelve European countries, the USA and Canada, presented over thirty-five papers which examined the concept of nationalism in the European context and covered empirical work on the processes involved in the construction and reconstruction of national identities in Eastern and Western Europe; the processes of identification with Europe as a new social category and the processes of acculturation of immigrant groups.

The present volume comprises a selection of the papers presented at the conference and aims to provide a useful handbook for the student of identity and social change processes by providing a collection of the work of a number of researchers who are exploring these issues across Europe. It is also hoped that it will provide a useful reference text, showing what social psychology can contribute to the understanding of these issues for researchers in other disciplines and others who are interested in policy-making in this area.

Recent Changes in Europe and Consequent Social Psychological Phenomena

In the last decade there have been two major series of events which were related to a number of social changes in Europe that strongly invite investigation. First there have been the moves towards greater political and economic integration among members of the European Union. Second is the collapse of communism in Eastern and Central Europe.

The move towards greater integration in Western Europe began with the signing of the European Single Act in 1986 which increased the powers of the European Parliament and set the conditions for the implementation of the 1992 European Community Programme which aimed to create a Community-wide unified market by the end of 1992 by eliminating all the remaining trade barriers. The Maastricht Treaty which was negotiated in December 1991, and was finally ratified by all member states by late 1993, provided for the gradual creation of a single currency, a European Central Bank and Community-wide citizenship.

The mid-1980s also saw Gorbachev come to power in Moscow which signalled many changes within the Soviet Union and relaxed its control over the other Eastern European countries of the Warsaw Pact. This allowed the establishment of non-Communist governments in these countries in 1989–90. The Berlin Wall "came down" in 1990 and German unification was achieved. Gorbachev also sought rapprochement with the West which resulted in the end of the Cold War. The apparent collapse of the communist system and the dissolution of the Soviet State in December 1991 resulted in the transformation of the map of Eastern Europe with the appearance of a number of "new" nations. The federation of Yugoslavia started disintegrating in 1991 with conflicts in Croatia and Bosnia-Hercegovina starting in 1991 and 1992.

With the applications by a number of both these "new states" and the "older" states to join the European Union, a new debate about how to define Europe and Europeanness was inaugurated.

These changes have happened at the time of significant advances in both the technology and availability of information. The globalisation of information has had the effect of both increasing the amount of information to which people have access and also producing a more homogeneous world news culture. It can be argued that these developments have led to a much greater consciousness of the degree to which problems and events have global or regional rather than purely local significance. This globalisation is also mirrored in the growing mobility of capital leading to truly transnational business entities.

The events of the last decade have also brought about the resurgence of nationalist feelings which have sometimes led to intergroup conflicts, wars, or intensification of racist feelings. At the same time, these changes involve the creation of new social categories by political élites and/or the media with which European peoples are asked to identify. The contributions in this volume are concerned with theoretical analyses and empirical studies of some of these issues.

The book is divided into four parts. In addition to this chapter, Part One also includes a chapter by Breakwell in which she discusses social change in Europe in more detail and puts forward a generic model for building an explanatory and predictive social psychological theory of these changes, raising some of the questions we may all need to address.

Part Two includes chapters discussing issues of construction and reconstruction of national identities in the context of on the one hand the relinquishing of national sovereignty by members of the European Union and on the other the reclaiming of specific regional identities by the peoples both of the ex-communist countries as well as the people of ethnic/cultural groups which were previously submerged in the nation states of Western Europe. The third part deals with issues involved in the construction of a new social category of "European" and the process of identification of people with this new European identity. The final part of the book is concerned with the strategies individuals and groups use either to cope with or to bring about social change.

Changing National Identities?

Part Two of the book includes chapters concerned with processes of national identifications, expressions of national identities and the significance of national identities for understanding socio-political actions in different spheres. They emphasise the importance of placing the constructions of and changes in national identities in a historical context. However, it is also recognised by some of the authors that histories can themselves be reconstructed and that this process is influenced by identities. Questions about the role of national identities when financial and/or political interests are multinational and the media has become globalised are also raised.

The chapters by Lyons and Condor are concerned with the construction and expression of national identities. Lyons shows how identity processes influence the representations of national identities by guiding a group's social memories. Condor examines the English national identity and discusses different explanations for the lack of significance attached by the English to the concept of Englishness. In discussing how history can be used to explain constructions of national identities, she draws our attention to questions of social influence; how do social representations of politicians and the media shape individual consciousness?

The importance of adopting a historical approach is also shown in Torregrosa's chapter which examines the relationship between Spain, America and Europe. Its importance lies in its location of current trends in Spanish nationalism within the context of the history of the connection between Spain and its American colonies. It shows how the loss of the American colonies generated in Spain a re-orientation towards Europe at the turn of the century. It turned towards the notion of European supra-nationalism, the European nation and state. The weak Spanish national identity is simultaneously replaced by strong "peripheric" nationalities (Catalan and Basque) and a strong European identity. Importantly, he thus locates current nationalism in a historical framework. In the context of European change, we often forget this: we are sometimes dealing with ancient nations and old alliances.

Hopkins and Reicher are concerned with how social categories are developed and in particular how national categories are constructed in the context of argumentation. They explored how the Scottish National Party (SNP) tried to make the concept of Scottishness relevant to the people while undermining the relevance of Britishness and how the Conservatives attempted to make Britishness relevant while rendering Scottishness irrelevant.

Trew and Benson introduce a symbolic interactionist approach. They emphasise identity theory and the question of authenticity, particularly the authenticity of public identities which has not been previously explored. They use Northern Ireland as the venue for their examination of this question of authenticity. They examine the relationship between nationalist and religious identities. They emphasise the ambiguities of identity choice in a changing political and social climate. They show quite remarkably how low the overall salience of these public identities are compared to the salience of private identities. Of course they have a problem in that they are dealing with a sample of students. But there is a link between the findings from this study and that of Condor. She found that the majority identity was less salient, less well articulated, less clearly identifiable. Here too we find that minority group members show greater identification with this aspect of their identity than majority group members. It is interesting that the authenticity of the identity of Protestants is low: the question is why. The authors suggest that public perception of contradictory dimensions for this identity leads to a lack of authenticity.

The Bacova and Ellis chapter discusses some of the methodological issues involved in cross-national research in this area. They have an interesting argument that scaling is a better approach to the collection of data in cross-cultural research since there are inestimable problems in translating ideas and concepts in methods which are less numerically based. Even here, however, there is an acknowledged lack of comparability in the targets which are used for scaled responses; for instance, there is a lack of equivalence in concepts in the British and Slovakian societies, classically illustrated by the problems in self-categorisation for ethnic identity terms which is experienced by the British sample.

Topalova sets her chapter in the context of changes in Eastern Europe. This chapter represents a major contribution to our understanding of what changes are actually occurring in the former Soviet Bloc countries. As an approach, it is valuable, telling us to look at the dimensions of social differentiation which ordinary people use in mapping the social structure and the political arena. It is also of tremendous value in giving us a method for examining this form of social differentiation.

Another major theme which emerges from the chapters in this part of the book is the effect of the internationalisation of political and financial interests on the construction of national identities. Billig discusses nationalism as an ideology which is not internal to a nation state but rather as an ideology which is transglobal and normalises the existence of national states and legitimises and perpetuates them. He argues that the socio-psychological aspects of nationhood are constituted within familiar discourses. He suggests that this form of nationalism is a new phenomenon which provides new forms of identity. He argues that the socio-psychological aspects of nationhood are constituted within familiar discourses. For instance, by imagining the ingroup in terms of its particularity and the symbols of ingroup membership, for instance monarchy, and also, by eliding distinctions between the self, nation and party. Also these familiar discourses generate the image of the outgroup; "we" are defined in contrast to "them". Particularity for new nations is gained against given dimensions on accepted symbols (e.g. flags, anthems and so on). However such an analysis of nationalism seems to ignore the fact that nations have a material component such as political structures, history and territory as well as the fact that they are able to act as discrete political entities. Therefore there is a sense in which nations, even if imagined, once they are imagined, do exist outside of discourses.

In contrast, Ruzza discusses the movement of Lega Lombarda which was founded in 1982 to promote cultural, economic and political self-determination among the peoples of Northern Italy, as an example of the new move away from national towards regional identities. Ruzza's chapter is written from a political sociological viewpoint and raises very clearly the problem of what is an ethnic identity, what is a collective identity and at what level a collective identity exists. Like Billig, Ruzza argues the role of the other, the enemy, in defining, promulgating and generating strengths of identity. In this case, it is the Southerners or immigrants who are used as the enemy or "outgroup" in order to provide a counterpoint in the definition of Lombard identity.

The emphasis on language as a defining property of an identity is very important but it also illustrates the weakness of language as a means of generating identity when this language is artificially highlighted or artificially created. Where the language is parochial and can be ridiculed for an emphasis simply on differences in dialect, it can be a hazardous means of generating identity salience. It is notable that in the case of Lega Lombarda the original emphasis on dialect has been replaced by street talk which is crude and direct.

The chapter also provides a good summary of common tactics of social movements in their efforts to bind members to themselves. It emphasises the importance of symbolism. There is clearly too little social psychological research on the importance of symbolism as yet in relation to national identity.

Pointing out that the responses of different nations to several of the socio-political problems we face today have transnational implications, Chase examines the implications of national identities for action at a number of different levels. He provides an illuminating discussion of the importance of national identity processes for broader socio-political and economic issues, especially in relation to ecological and environmental issues. Chase introduces an analysis of the way in which a theory of threats to identity can be used to predict responses to socio-political and environmental problems.

The two final chapters in this part of the book examine how minority immigrant groups adapt in new social contexts. Liebkind examines identity processes involved in the acculturation of a minority ethnic group. Her analysis shows that one cannot examine one identity irrespective of others. For example she shows how intergenerational conflict impinges on gender identities. Horenczyk looks at processes of identity reconstruction among Russian immigrants in Israel. He shows that, although immigrants and host Israelis share a rhetoric of integration, there is a discrepancy as to the extent to which immigrants would like to assimilate (language and culture) and what they think is expected from them, while the majority see less discrepancy between what they would like to happen and what the immigrants want.

Constructing a European Identity

Part Three examines issues involved in the creation of new social categories and the processes and factors which influence the psychological signifi-cance of these categories. It raises questions about the way the relationship between different social categories should be conceptualised and emphasises the significance of the affective component of social identification. A dominant theme in these chapters is the need to integrate different theoretical paradigms such as social identity theory and social representations in order to explain fully the processes involved in the construction of European identities.

For instance, Cinnirella is concerned with how social representations of European integration inform the construction of national and European identities among a sample of English and Italian students. He uses his data to raise some interesting questions about the limitations of Social Identity Theory, social representations and socio-cognitive theories of self and attempts to integrate these approaches. Hilton and his colleagues examine the extent to which different social representations of history lead to different attitudes towards European integration. They draw parallels between history and group identity and biography to individual identities. Unlike Cinnirella, Hilton *et al.* suggest that comparisons of a group with its past along some meaningful dimension are as important for gaining positive self-evaluation and an awareness of an identity as comparisons with an outgroup.

Chryssochoou discusses some of the necessary conditions for the construction of a social identity. She argues that group beliefs are a necessary and prior condition for the construction of a social identity. She uses interview data from a small group of Greek and French people to show that though each of the two groups shared beliefs about their national group, they did not share such beliefs for Europe. Also she shows that individuals did not feel they participated or could influence any decision-making at the European level. These two aspects she claims make the creation of Europeans as a meaningful psychological group very difficult.

Sousa draws attention to the multidimensional nature of social identifications and argues that the affective components of the national and European identifications are associated with different conceptions of European identities. Those people who identified highly with both social categories displayed ethnocentrism. Those who identified highly with the national category, but identified low with the European, favoured competitive identities. Those who identified low with both social categories adopted a more individualistic discourse. Those with low identification with the national category but who identified highly with Europe saw European identity as inclusive. Sanchez Mazas's chapter shows a sophisticated conceptualisation of nested identifications and the ways in which they may be experimentally examined.

Barrett examines the development of national and European identities in children. He argues that there is a shift in children's self-categorisations between the ages of six and ten years. At ten years old, children tend to categorise themselves as Europeans as well as English. This shift is associated with an increase in geographical knowledge of Europe. Barrett also looks at children's perceptions of, and affective responses to, other national groups showing that the older children tend to recognise that Europeans have more variable attributes than the six year olds who ascribe univalent attributes to European people. Furthermore there is a decline of negative affect with increase in age.

Barrett's work is a valuable contribution to the book as it attempts to understand the origins of the evaluations of national identities and outgroups. However, it raises questions about measurement and definitions. Is simple knowledge that you belong to a geographical region and labelling enough to argue that someone possesses a specific social/national identity? This is specifically pertinent in the case of children whose responses cannot necessarily be taken at face value. More questions about group beliefs and evaluations are perhaps necessary.

Unlike most of the work presented in the previous chapters which are concerned mostly with the processes of self-identification with the social category of European, Smith and Peterson look at the extent to which a specific group of people (managers) share certain practices and therefore the extent to which one can talk about the "European" manager.

The study of the phenomena of social change occurring in Europe involves a number of methodological problems. De Rosa provides an interesting discussion on the relationship between identity and social representations. She makes the case for the use of multi-methodological approach to study social representations, describing two instruments she used for her international study of the representations of European identities.

Coping with Social Change

Part Four comprises two chapters looking at the strategies individuals and groups use to cope with social change. Mummendey and her colleagues provide a lucid analysis of the options for change in the context of Eastern Europeans who can be seen to have a negative social identity. This analysis explains the types of strategy available in relation to the type of intergroup condition. It tests the traditional models of social change and social mobility strategies postulated by the Social Identity Theory and finds them markedly in predictive power. Most particularly, it shows that there is poor prediction of cognitive strategies from structural variables. Perhaps, if individual differences (particularly self-concept predictors) were introduced there would be greater predictability.

Horton argues that the Social Identity Theory should be combined with the Alienation theory in order to understand social change. Such a model would deal with the relationship between individuals and institutions and conceptualise processes of social change as a function of different dimensions of the relationship between the self and other members of the group and between the self and the system/institution.

References

Barrett, M. D. and Short, J. (1992). Images of European people in a group of 5–10 year old English school children. *British Journal of Developmental Psychology*, **10**, 339–63.

Breakwell, G. M. (1986). *Coping with Threatened Identities*. London and New York: Methuen.

Breakwell, G. M. (ed.)(1992). *Social Psychology of Identity and the Self Concept*. London: Surrey University Press/Academic Press.

Breakwell, G. M. (1993). Integrating paradigms, methodological implications. In G. M. Breakwell and D. V. Canter (eds), *Empirical Approaches to Social Representations*. Oxford, Oxford University Press.

Breakwell, G. M. (1994). The echo of power: a framework for social psychological research. *The Psychologist*, **17**, 65–72.

Breakwell, G. M. and Canter, D. V. (eds)(1993). *Empirical Approaches to Social Representations*. Oxford: Oxford University Press.

Breakwell, G. M. and Lyons, E. (1993). A jigsaw puzzle with missing pieces: an argument for the systematic explanation of the relationship between processes of representations and identity. *Papers on Social Representations*, **2**, 44–7.

Brown, R. and Millward, L. J. (1993). Perceptions of group homogeneity during group formation. *Social Cognition*, **11**, 126–49.

Chase, J. (1992). The self and collective action: Dilemmatic identities. In G. M. Breakwell (ed.), *Social Psychology of Identity and the Self Concept*. London: Surrey University Press/Academic Press.

Chase, J. and Uzzell, D. (1991). Setting an agenda for social psychology and history. British Psychological Society Social Psychology Section Conference, University of Surrey, Guildford.

Chase, J. (1994). Historical analysis in psychological research. In G. M. Breakwell, S. Hammond and C. R. Fife-Schaw (eds), *Research Methods in Psychology*. London: Sage.

Doise, W. (1986). *Levels of Explanation in Social Psychology*. Cambridge: Cambridge University Press.

Giddens, A. (1984). *The Constitution of Society: Outline of the Theory of Structuration*. Cambridge: Polity Press.

Jahoda, M. (1979). The impact of unemployment in the 1930s and 1970s. *Bulletin of the British Psychological Society*, **32**, 309–14.

Israel, J. and Tajfel, H. (eds)(1972). *The Context of Social Psychology: A Critical Assessment*. London and New York: Academic Press.

Lyons, E. and Breakwell, G. M. (1994). Self-concept, enterprise and educational attainment in late adolescence. *British Journal of Education and Work*, **6**, 75–84.

Millward, L. J. (1993a). Situating female sexual identity: social representations of gender and heterosexuality. Annual conference of the Women's Section of the British Psychological Society, Brighton.

Millward, L. J. (in press). Contextualizing social identity in considerations of what it means to be a nurse. *European Journal of Social Psychology*, **25**.

Moscovici, S. (1990). New problems for social psychology in a new Europe. *European Bulletin of Social Psychology*, **2**, 2–10.

Sampson, E. E. (1991). The democratization of psychology. *Theory and Psychology*, **1**, 275–98.

Sotirakopoulou, K. P. and Breakwell, G. M. (1992). The use of different methodological approaches in the study of social representations. *Ongoing Productions on Social Representations*, **1**, 29–38.

Stephenson, N., Breakwell, G. M. and Fife-Schaw, C. R. (1993). Anchoring social representations of HIV protection: the significance of individual biographies. In P. Aggleton, P. Davies and G. Hart (eds), *AIDS: Facing the Second Decade*. London,: The Falmer Press.

Uzzell, D. (1992). The interpretation of the past: reconciling personal memories and collective representations. L'Entreprise de Patrimonie: Institutions et Pratiques dans le Contexte Européan, European Culture Research Centre, Florence, Italy.

Uzzell, D. and Blud, L. (1993). Vikings! Children's social representations of history. In G. M. Breakwell and D. V. Canter (eds), *Empirical Approaches to Social Representations*. Oxford: Oxford University Press.

2

Identity Processes and Social Changes

GLYNIS M. BREAKWELL

SPERI, University of Surrey, England

The Social Psychological Analysis of Social Changes

This chapter depicts one approach to developing a social psychological analysis of some of the social changes which have been happening across Europe. The economic and political processes underlying these changes have been subjected to extensive analysis. The social psychological processes now require some attention.

The sort of social changes to be considered include for instance: the redrawing of state boundaries with the dissolution of the Soviet Bloc; the redefinition of national sovereignty with the agreement on the Maastricht Treaty establishing the European Union; and, the restructuring of employment and training prospects with the evolution of "human capital mobility" as labour laws are rewritten and financial and trade free markets are created, particularly in the context of rapid innovation in information technologies. These social changes have been tied to a wide variety of consequences (directly or indirectly). There has been the resurrection of old ethnic rivalries and, in some cases, this has led to outright physical conflicts, even wars. Of course, there has been the revival of fascism, notably linked to racism. More prominent still has been the rekindling of nationalism and the re-examination of religious allegiances and their significance.

Of course, there is no justification for arguing that nationalism, fascism, or religious and ethnic conflicts are somehow novel phenomena. They are certainly not new or unique responses tied to the recent changes in international relationships and reordering of political regimes. Not at all. These are endemic aspects of social life. It would not be a human society without them. It is the particular form they are assuming which is tied to recent political and economic

13

changes. It may even be more realistic to argue that they are an integral part of such changes.

The disintegration of earlier national and international social orders has simultaneously offered both the hopes and the fears of freedom. It provides space for "social creativity". Individuals and groups can take part in a process of re-definition and re-evaluation of social norms, belief systems and the power structures. The other side of this opportunity is that it also threatens "social chaos". Previously accepted social absolutes begin to melt into insignificance, though they may linger in memory enough to cast doubt upon any new rules which are generated. The communal sense of continuity and permanence is challenged.

A caution may be valuable here: it is obviously possible to overestimate the importance of the current social flux in Europe. Seen against the backdrop of several centuries, the scale of contemporary changes come to seem less dramatic. Economic and political change in Europe has been continual throughout recorded history. The upheavals of earlier centuries were often no less precipitate and often involved greater disruption of everyday life than those of the last two decades. Wars, revolutions and doctrinal schisms (religious and political) are the hallmarks of Europe. Spasmodic unification of erstwhile independent states is also typical (whether through conquest as in the Roman era or through dynastic alliances as in the Hapsburg empire). Nevertheless, it has to be acknowledged that federation by democratic consent, as in the European Union, is a somewhat unique experience. It also has to be noted that, while the exploitation of technological innovation has been characteristic of European cultures, the rate of change over the last two decades in information and biochemical technologies has been unparalleled previously. Furthermore, the potential accumulated environmental costs of industrialisation have only begun to be appreciated over these years.

In fact, the technological developments which have occurred, especially those which make simultaneous mass communication over infinite distances feasible, mean that the social significance of political and economic changes is altered. The character of these changes may be little different in substance from many such in the past but the speed with which they become public knowledge and can elicit some response is changed beyond recognition.

In this context, how should a social psychological analysis proceed? What type of theory do we need? What can social psychology offer beyond the historical or political science analysis? The answers to these questions depend in many ways on precisely what one decides to analyse. The simplest distinction would be between analysing the reasons for specific changes and analysing the consequences of those changes. This is not to ignore the logical possibility that the consequences of one change can be the causes of another change. The distinction merely points to two alternative focuses for analysis. It emphasises that a starting point for the analysis must be chosen and that this can be after an identifiable change occurs or in anticipation of potential changes. Given its concern for the social influence processes which shape individual thought, feeling and action, social psychology has mainly focused on the consequences of macro-social changes at the level of individuals and groups. It has been rare for social psychologists to try to explain the processes which bring about macro-social changes, though social identity theory as originally formulated by Tajfel and social representation theory are exceptions to this generalisation.

If one wishes to elaborate a social psychological analysis of social changes which offers an explanation of both their aetiology and their aftermath, a comprehensive, inclusive approach to theory-building is necessary. A social psychological analysis of these changes—if it is to be comprehensive—will need to examine: their socio-historical context; their physical-environmental context; the ideological and social representational structures which carry them; the institutional and interpersonal affordances for action and influence which they offer; the normative pressure they generate upon action; and, their relationship to cognitive, conative and oretic processes at the level of the individual.

Figure 2.1 represents what could be argued is a generic model for social psychological theorising (Breakwell, 1994). That is to say, it summarises the constructs which any social psychological theory should have. There may be constructs which should be included that have been omitted. That is open to debate. However, none of those included can be sensibly ignored, although their salience may vary according to the specific forms of individual action to be explained or predicted.

The lines connecting each construct have no arrowheads indicating direction of influence. That is unnecessary at this level of outlining a generic framework

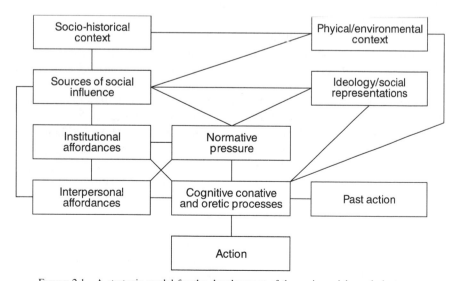

FIGURE 2.1   A strategic model for the development of theory in social psychology

for theorising. In certain theoretical formulations the arrows will go one way and in others, the reverse. The point here is that our research efforts should be directed at understanding the nature of the "relational rules" which characterise the social psychological processes involved in the interactions of these constructs.

This approach to theory-building encourages us to explore both the origins and effects of change in social structures and institutions. In the context of the current argument, it is perhaps important to reiterate that the flow of influence can operate from top-down or bottom-up. That is to say, change at the level of, for instance, the physical environment can push towards change at the level of individual action but the reverse can also be true. Thus, in using this approach to analyse social changes, the change can be in any construct at any level in the model. It is possible to start with the assumption that the change to be understood lies, for instance, in a modification in ideology. The relational rules to be tested might then postulate that some change in the physical environment (say, the availability of a communications technology) alters the relative salience of two sources of influence (say, the ruling political party and the dominant religion); this change in influence then affects how they represent their ideologies, altering the normative pressure they bring to bear, and ultimately changing the relative significance of the two ideologies. This set of relational rules might then be accompanied by others which specify that the change in the salience of ideologies will bring about changes in motivations at the individual level.

As suggested above the interaction of constructs can be specified in what can be called "relational rules". What is a relational rule? The simplest would probably be: $a = f(b)$. That is, variable "a" is some function of variable "b". The relational rule specifies the nature of that function. It could be that when "a" diminishes, "b" increases. The relational rule could be more precise: "b" increases 5% for every 10% decrease in "a". Alternatively, the relational rule could be couched in probabilistic terms. Thus, it might be: 95% of the time when "a" decreases, "b" increases. The relational rule does not have to entail quantification, it simply has to specify how change in one construct is related to change in another.

Many theories in psychology do not contain true relational rules. Such theories are largely taxonomies. Sometimes they taxonomise types of behaviour: at others, types of people. They provide a framework for interpreting behaviour systematically. They do not provide predictive theories of behaviour. To predict, a theory must contain specific relational rules. To be predictive in social psychology the relational rule must be complex. It must be hierarchically nested, calling upon constructs lying at different levels of analysis: minimally at the intra-psychic, interpersonal and societal levels (cf. Doise, 1986).

Many of the constructs in Figure 2.1 are self-evident. Two need further clarification. First, the socio-historical context construct. This is a different order construct to the rest. Since the socio-historical context could be conceived of as nothing more than the sum of the movement of the other constructs through time, it could be signified in the framework by iterating the other boxes. The discrete socio-historical construct box is retained for diagrammatic clarity. It is also retained because it is a construct so frequently omitted by social psychology theories which treat it as outside their remit. Consider the box present as at least a reminder. Of course, recent historical social psychology studies show how the socio-historical context is itself a product of active reconstruction driven by known social psychological processes. Such processes of social memory are increasingly a target for research in their own right and again make the presence of this box in the generic framework reasonable.

The second construct requiring some comment is the box labelled "cognitive, conative and oretic processes". Conceiving of the intrapsychic processes in this tripartite way is to follow McDougall (who used the terms to refer respectively to thinking, emotion and will). In practice, this probably entails careful analysis of emotional states as they relate to decision-making and intention besides the more usual analyses of action-relevant schema (that is, information matrices) and goal-relevant evaluation (that is, the strength of purpose and its associated cost-benefits analysis). It should be noted that from the research evidence, it appears that cognitive, conative and oretic processes are somewhat individualised. Individuals acquire through their lifespan a recognisable style (what might be called processing habits). This fact requires social psychological theorists to take individual differences (whether characterised in terms of personality or cognitive traits) seriously. Social psychological analyses cannot work with relational rules that posit that individuals are somehow cognitively, conatively or oretically homogeneous. It sounds preposterous that they might try to do so and yet this has been characteristic of many social psychological theories. Such theories tend to occupy one level of analysis and studiously ignore variance attributable to other levels.

From the point of view of providing a social psychological analysis of social changes, the approach as outlined above has at least one serious weakness. The action construct needs further clarification. Any single act in reality is embedded in complex action systems. No act is independent of either earlier patterns of activity on the part of the individual concerned or coterminous action on the part of others involved either directly or indirectly. Put simply, each act is not independent of coaction. The action construct, when it comes to analysing social changes, has to be particularly carefully defined. Often, in understanding social changes, the most interesting action is not that of the discrete individual but the action of collections of individuals (whether groups, communities or whole nations). Figure 2.1 does not include collective action as a discrete construct. There is a logical problem in doing so: collective action is subsumed in other constructs which are included, for instance in normative pressure, and in interpersonal and institutional affordances, not to mention the socio-historical context. The decision to omit collective action, therefore, is deliberate and seen as justified since collective action is subjected to a more fine-grained analysis as part of other constructs. However, for a specific analysis, there is no reason why collective action should not be treated as a discrete construct with its relationship to individual action being specified. For example, this may be necessary when analysing the genesis of civil unrest, perhaps manifest in an inner-city riot. The approach represented in Figure 2.1 is not suggested in order to constrain but rather to encourage a more comprehensive orientation in social psychological analyses of social changes.

Given the title of this chapter, it might be expected that Figure 2.1 would include an identity construct. It rates no explicit mention in Figure 2.1 because, like collective action, identity processes are subsumed in several of the other constructs. Elsewhere in this volume, Lyons explores how Identity Process Theory may be used to explain how individuals and groups respond to macro-social changes. In doing so, she illustrates how identity processes, at the individual and group levels, have a superordinate role in organising cognitive, conative and oretic processes and directing the evolution of social representations. The rest of this chapter is an attempt to look at how identities are currently changing in the context of the social changes created by the evolution of the European Union. In doing so, it will return at points to the generic framework for social psychological analysis.

Change that Challenges National Identities

Modelling the relationship between changes in identities and patterns of social change requires extensive long-term programmes of data collection. It requires cross-disciplinary collaboration and must be multi-national. Preferably, it needs cross-sequential designs to trace cohort, age and time effects. Such concerted research is expensive and has not been done. The research by social psychologists conducted so far has been spasmodic, relatively small-scale and rarely allows change over time to be examined systematically. Of course, some of the best studies are represented in this volume. Nevertheless, it is evident from them that the available data on changes in identities is limited. One way around this problem is to use data not collected specifically to explore changing identities but which is relevant. In fact, the *Eurobarometer* surveys provide a valuable source of relevant material.

The data reported in the *Eurobarometer* No. 38 (December 1992) will be used here to present an argument about the processes which may be involved in the development of a so-called "European identity". The current development of a European identity cannot be easily explained within our existing social psychological theoretical frameworks. Standard social psychological theories have considerable difficulty in encompassing any analysis of the impact of large-scale political and economic change upon either individual or group identity processes. Consequently, we rarely systematically collect data which would allow us to develop theories of large-scale change. There is something of a vicious circle involved here: no theory, no data, no theory-development. Hence the need to resort to the *Eurobarometer* surveys.

Eurobarometer surveys are conducted for the Directorate General Audio Visual, Information, Communication, Culture of the European Commission each autumn and spring and have been collected since the autumn of 1973. The sample comprises representative samples of 15+ year olds, *n* = 1000 in Belgium, Denmark, Greece, Spain, France, Ireland, Italy, The Netherlands, Portugal and the UK. In Germany there is a sample of 1000 taken from the former West Germany and a sample of 1000 taken from the five new landers (previously East Germany). A sample of around 500 is taken from Luxembourg and of around 300 from Northern Ireland. In the presentation of data in the *Eurobarometer* reports, percentages are presented weighted for population size. These *Eurobarometer* surveys have generated over the last twenty years an enormous complex and elaborate data bank on public opinion. It is unfortunate that the *Eurobarometer* administration does not present any multivariate modelling of data. It does, however, present very useful analyses of trends over time and it is these which are used to support the arguments below.

Figure 2.2 (derived from *Eurobarometer* 38) illustrates changes in support for the unification of Western Europe and the Community (i.e. the Union as comprising twelve states) which have occurred in the period 1981 to 1992.

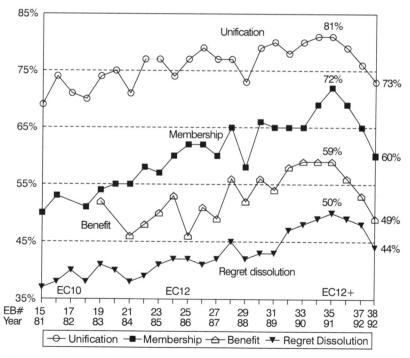

FIGURE 2.2   Support for European unification and the Community (EC12) 1981–92
Source: Taken from *Eurobarometer*, 38 (1992).

The most interesting feature of this graph is that as unification in reality has approached more closely with the advent of the Maastricht Treaty, it is evident that opinion across the Community has shifted away from whole-hearted support for unification. Across all samples, 73% are in favour of efforts being made to unify Western Europe by 1992; 60% say that their country's membership of the Community is a good thing, 23% say it is neither good nor bad and 12% say it is a bad thing. Just less than half (49%) see their country benefiting from Community membership. It is consistent then to find that 44% say they would be very sorry if they were told that the Community was to be scrapped, 34% are indifferent and 12% would be very relieved.

The most significant falls in support for European unification and the European Community during this period are registered in the United Kingdom and in East Germany. The survey, it should be remembered, took place shortly after Black Wednesday and the withdrawal of sterling from the Exchange Rate Mechanism, while the East German result appears to signal a definite end of post-revolutionary euphoria which is assumed to have followed the fall of the Berlin Wall. But major reductions in support for unification were also experienced in Italy, where support for the Community has been, in many measures, traditionally the strongest; in other southern EC member states, Spain, Portugal, Greece, and in Ireland declines are all significant. In several cases this may reflect the effects of austerity measures perceived to be in preparation for monetary union as well as the exchange-rate crises experienced in both Italy and Spain just prior to the survey.

Remarkably, given its reaction to the Maastricht Treaty, which it initially failed to ratify, Denmark was the only country which increased support for European unification in this period. It seems that since 1986 more and more Danes have systematically supported the principle of the European Community while remaining deeply sceptical about the political European union.

There is a very real question as to how far these sentiments about the increasing unification of Europe are related to fears concerning a loss of national identity or a potential for the development of a European identity. The increasingly discussed topic of possible tensions between a new European identity and traditional national identity was addressed in two different questions in this *Eurobarometer* survey.

People were asked whether they thought their sense of national identity would end up disappearing and being replaced by a sense of European identity if all the countries of the European Community came together in a European Union, or whether they thought one could have a sense of national identity as well as a sense of European identity at the same time. Figure 2.3 presents the findings.

With a proportion of almost three to one, EC citizens believe that a national and European identity are compatible. Absolute majorities everywhere see compatibility as possible. Nevertheless, there are considerable proportions in most of the states which expect that their national identity, would, indeed, be replaced by a European identity.

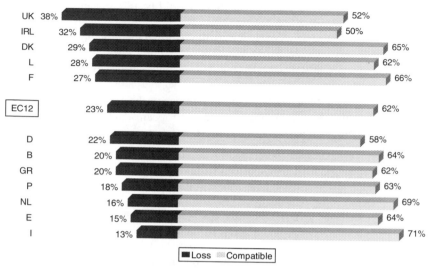

FIGURE 2.3 Loss of national identity or national identity/European identity compatible?
Source: Taken from *Eurobarometer*, 38 (1992).

In a further question, the samples were given two possible options as to how this issue might evolve within the Community: whether a real European Union would mean the end of national cultural identities and their diversity; or whether the only way to protect national cultural identity and their diversity is through the countries of Europe becoming a real European Union.

A seven-point scale was used. Respondents were asked to choose a number on the scale corresponding to their point of view: one (European Union will end national cultural identities) to seven (European Union is the only way to protect national cultural identities in the future). Four is the mid point between the two views. Absolute or relative majorities in nine countries indicate confidence in the European Union protecting national cultural identities and their diversity. Ireland (36% to 35%) and the United Kingdom (39% to 42%) are borderline, while only in Denmark (32% to 45%) are substantially more people found to be fearful of losing their national cultural identities.

Comparing Figures 2.2 and 2.3, there is some evidence in these data that the decline in support for the European Community is associated with a fear that national identity and national cultural identity or diversification will be lost as a result of unification. But equally, it is notable from Figure 2.3 that there are considerable national differences in the amount of fear or rather, to be precise, since the intensity of fear is not recorded, the proportion of people expressing a fear that national identity will be lost. This raises the question: why?

There are two obvious reasons why there should be this variation:

1. Nations differ in the status of their existing national identity. For instance, the existing identity may be particularly strong, having been stable over many years, or particularly weak, having been subject to multiple alterations previously.
2. Nations differ in their social representations of the developing European identity. For instance, some may see the European identity as very closely allied to their national identity; others may anticipate it will be very different.

With regard to the first reason, it is tempting to postulate a relational rule: if the socio-historical context favours a stable national identity, the sample will report lower perceived threat from unification. Yet, it is really not so simple. The nature of the relationship of the status of national identity to the extent of fear of loss of national identity is somewhat difficult to anticipate. There are reasonable arguments in both directions. For instance, one might choose as a UK national acting in a relatively ethnocentric fashion to interpret the finding that the UK sample expresses a great fear of losing of their national identity by saying that the stronger and better and more positive an identity is, currently, the more fear the possessors of that identity will have about the prospect of losing it. Alternatively, if one were being less ethnocentric, the UK analyst might argue that the weaker an identity is, the more fearful those who possess it will be that it can be eroded easily. Of course, the more analytical approach will admit that both processes may be at work simultaneously since in a large sample of people there may be individuals on both sides of this divide. The relational rule would need to be less specific in the absence of more data. It might legitimately state: current status of national identity will affect the perceived threat from unification. The research task is then to refine the rule.

The point which this concern about the status of national identity serves to highlight, and which needs to be stated even though it is remarkably obvious, is that there is no such thing as "national identity" in an absolute sense. Every nation has many national identities since each individual, in social context, negotiates what the meaning of his or her national identity is and can renegotiate it moment by moment. Being British is not simply different for different subgroups (the Scots, the Welsh, the English) but also for different individuals within each subgroup. The significance and salience of a national identity for an individual depend not only on the social processes forming it for all fellow nationals but also upon the intrapsychic processes adjusting it for the specific person.

This dynamism of the national identity of the nation and the national identity of the individual is something which needs to be considered when modelling how identities are currently changing in Europe. At the national level, for example, fear of the loss of a national identity may also be associated with its longer-term history than with its current immediate status. For instance, countries with a very elaborated and extended track record of adaptation to change may be less fearful of the loss of a national identity since they have in the past found that even quite radical changes do not erode the value of their national identity in fulfilling what are potentially its prime functions: motivating allegiance and cohesiveness and explaining relative power.

What European Identity?

There is also the influence of the prevalent concept of European identity to consider. Currently there is little evidence to indicate how different countries vary in their social representations of a future European identity. It is not possible to formulate a relational rule that states why representations of the European identity might differ from one country to another because we have only the most slender knowledge of the facets which potentially comprise these representations.

The *Eurobarometer* contains no explicit questions about the perceptions of European identity but one of the indicators which might be indicative of the social representations of the prospective European identity involves feelings about which countries should be considered part of the European Community. The data collected for *Eurobarometer 38* included a question which asked respondents to indicate which countries should be members of the Community in the year 2000.

Figure 2.4 shows the results. Patterns across countries in this image of the EC in 2000 are remarkably similar. There are, of course, illustrations of existing national rivalries in this pattern. While in the majority of countries, around 40% would accept Turkey as a member of the EC by 2000, in Greece, only 19% of respondents would accept Turkey's presence in the EC. While geographical distance from the existing states of the EC seems to be somewhat predictive of acceptability, this is certainly not the sole criterion operating in this putative image of the EC in 2000. For instance, Cyprus, which is at least as far away as Moldavia, is accepted by many more in the sample. It is, of course, evident from this rank ordering that many ethnic, religious and historical factors are at work in moulding the image which people have of the future development of the Community and, presumably, as a corollary of its identity.

In considering the European identity, we are really talking about the generation of a new identity in the context of the European Union. It is not possible to talk about a European identity which currently exists. If one were to do this, it would be necessary to preface the concept with putative or potential. There is a potential European identity. There may indeed be many potential identities for Europe. Furthermore, any evolving European identity cannot ignore the fact that it has roots stretching back into cultures long dead and disappeared. The contemporary process cannot be totally separated from its historical soil. To continue the metaphor, it is now artificially cultivated, designed by bureaucrats and politicians for rapid consumption through the mass media.

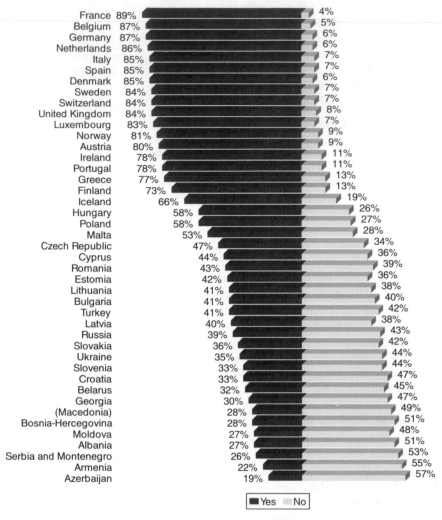

France 89% 4%
Belgium 87% 5%
Germany 87% 6%
Netherlands 86% 6%
Italy 85% 7%
Spain 85% 7%
Denmark 85% 6%
Sweden 84% 7%
Switzerland 84% 7%
United Kingdom 84% 8%
Luxembourg 83% 7%
Norway 81% 9%
Austria 80% 9%
Ireland 78% 11%
Portugal 78% 11%
Greece 77% 13%
Finland 73% 13%
Iceland 66% 19%
Hungary 58% 26%
Poland 58% 27%
Malta 53% 28%
Czech Republic 47% 34%
Cyprus 44% 36%
Romania 43% 39%
Estomia 42% 36%
Lithuania 41% 38%
Bulgaria 41% 40%
Turkey 41% 42%
Latvia 40% 38%
Russia 39% 43%
Slovakia 36% 42%
Ukraine 35% 44%
Slovenia 33% 44%
Croatia 33% 47%
Belarus 32% 45%
Georgia 30% 47%
(Macedonia) 28% 49%
Bosnia-Hercegovina 28% 51%
Moldova 27% 48%
Albania 27% 51%
Serbia and Montenegro 26% 53%
Armenia 22% 55%
Azerbaijan 19% 57%

■ Yes ▨ No

FIGURE 2.4   EC in the year 2000: which countries should be members?
Source: Taken from *Eurobarometer*, 38 (1992).

The most interesting question from the point of view of developing theory within social psychology must be how is this potential European identity actually being developed? What actually is actually happening in what is such a multi-national enterprise? Of course, we do not know. There are no adequate data which have been collected by social psychologists over the last ten or twenty years which would enable us to trace the development of conceptions of a European identity. The *Eurobarometer* information, while interesting, is often inadequate for the purposes of social psychological theoretical development.

It does seem likely, however, that this new European identity or this multi-faceted variety of new European identities will be created in accordance with the principles guiding standard identity processes. Identity Process Theory would suggest that the European identity will be developed in accordance with the needs to maintain continuity, to achieve distinctiveness, to establish efficacy and to maintain esteem. Lyons explores these issues in the next chapter in relation to national identities; here they can be explored briefly in relation to what we see happening in the context of the development of a European identity.

It may be better in this context to talk more precisely of a European Community identity rather than a more inclusive European identity. It is possible that both could be evolving simultaneously but with quite separate conclusions. In the case of the European Community identity, if it is to be developed in accordance with the principles of continuity and distinctiveness, it faces considerable difficulties. For one thing the European Community is changing with the addition of new member states. This certainly challenges its continuity but also challenges its distinctiveness: since the boundaries between European Community and non-European Community are known to be subject to change, the characteristics which differentiate between member states and non-member states cannot therefore be held as simple or constant. A non-member state in one year may be a member state in the next. It is however interesting that there are extended and very lengthy procedures (what might be called initiation procedures) that transform a non-member state into a member state. There is a lengthy period of waiting for acceptance, of checking credentials and only then a virtual probationary acceptance into the Community. This may have the effect of encouraging and protecting the perceived continuity and distinctiveness in what is inevitably a world of changing boundaries.

The efficacy and esteem principles are clearly pursued avidly by the European Community. The European Community identity has attached to it the assumptions that membership and unification will generate higher levels of wealth, power and civil liberty. Efficacy is evidenced directly in the control of financial markets and is symbolised in the attempts to create a Euro-army. It is ironic, but perhaps inevitable, that the very things that create the strong European Community identity, such as the creation of the single market, are exactly those features which are perceived by citizens of the member states to erode national identity. The *Eurobarometer* shows that the loss of national identity is the third highest reason for being afraid of the advent of the single market. The second highest reason is that the single market will result in too much immigration associated with the loss of jobs for native workers. This finding leads to a question concerning the implications of economic policy for national identity. The single market should entail greater labour mobility. This is inevitably associated with migration. While the ideal of the compatibility of a European Community and a national identity may be acceptable to around two-thirds of EC nationals, the reality of the economic changes it involves may stimulate hostility, not because national identity is attacked, but because individual self-interest is in conflict with allowing nationals from other member states to compete with oneself in one's home labour market. Fears for the loss of national identity then could be argued to be merely a rather compact way of saying that one prefers to compete with one's own nationals rather than nationals from other states.

In arguing that the development of the European Community identity is paralleling known processes at the level of individual identity—continuity, distinctiveness, efficacy and esteem—it should also be emphasised that this is an identity which is being negotiated by nation states. Powerful individuals may be steering these negotiations but the process of building a new pan-national identity is essentially operating at the level of power elites who provide a template European Community identity for individual citizens. As yet, the template is relatively lacking in detail and ill-defined. Citizens find identification with the version of the European Community identity promulgated in their countries (and the version does differ by country) difficult, or rather pointless. Identification, after all, depends on motivation. The factors influencing motivation to actively identify oneself with a group (or other collectivity) are well known. One which may be central in the case of European Community identification is likely to be the perceived importance of an out-group. Europeans wishing to distinguish themselves either from non-Europeans or from non-EC members are likely to be motivated to assume what they think is the accepted Euro-identity.

Formulating Relational Rules

Of course, given that the image of European Community identity is currently blurred, and it is still novel, now is the time to research it. The failure so far to catalogue these transitions will be regarded by future social psychologists as horrendous. To persist in the failure would be inexcusable. Given the social psychological approach to theory-building suggested earlier, the target for this research should be to test a series of hypothesised relational rules. One key set of relationships would be between social representations of the EC and EC identity, normative pressures from institutions (e.g. legal or political sources), and the significance of identification with the EC upon individuals' decisions. Another set of rules would focus on what factors influence the sort of constituents that are accepted into the Euro-identities firstly by power elites and secondly by individual citizens. A third set of rules would be concerned with the nature of the relationship between national identity, Euro-identity and other types of identification (for example, religious, racial or gender identities).

It is evident that people can use the concept of national identity with great ease. It is one of those concepts which is regarded by the general population as unproblematic. It needs to be made problematic by social psychologists if we are to use it as an explanatory concept in predicting the behaviour of individuals and most particularly if we are to use it in predicting the behaviour of groups. We require internationally comparable longitudinal and time series data on the development of the European Community identity and the European identity in a broader sense. To make this viable in terms of resources, we have to start by agreeing as a research community upon at least a few questions that we will address. This requires some consolidation of definitions of terms and some, even if tentative, decisions about which relational rules we will attempt to specify.

References

Breakwell, G. M. (1994). The echo of power. *The Psychologist*, **7**(2), 65–72.
Doise, W. (1986). *Levels of Explanation in Social Psychology*. Cambridge: Cambridge University Press.
Eurobarometer (1992). No. 38. Brussels: Commission of the European Communities.

Part Two

Changing National Identities?

3

Coping with Social Change: Processes of Social Memory in the Reconstruction of Identities

EVANTHIA LYONS

SPERI, University of Surrey, England

This chapter outlines a theoretical framework within which we can study and understand how groups maintain and reconstruct their social memories. In particular, it addresses the question of why certain memories are maintained over time as well as how these may be reconstructed over time. The focus is on the processes involved in the maintenance and reconstruction of those social memories which are used by members of a national or ethnic group, to describe and define the identity of that group. For example the way in which memories of Dunkirk are used as a symbol for the ordinary Englishman's characteristic of defiance in adversity, reconstructing a defeat as a victory.

In recent years we have seen the restructuring of European space both in terms of the redrawing of the boundaries on the map of Europe and in the redefinition of memberships of different ethnic and national groups. The collapse of communism in Eastern and Central Europe and the attempts to bring Western European countries closer have resulted in uncertainty as to how national and ethnic groups are defined and hence how the European map should be redrawn. Social scientists have identified the processes of remembering and forgetting as playing a central role in the processes of social change that we are witnessing (Schlesinger, 1991; Moscovici, 1990). If we are to understand how the societies emerging from the former Eastern and Central European socialist states will organise themselves and how national and ethnic groups will relate to each other, we will have to understand the processes involved in the maintenance and reconstruction of the social memories. Individuals and groups will make sense of the uncertainties of the present by those memories they choose to employ in constructing their past. Their construction of the past will also determine their aspirations for the future. At the same time, however, the reconstruction of the past will also be a function of the present conditions groups find themselves in.

The Social Nature of Memory

Recently there has been a revival of interest and debate as to what memory is and how psychologists should study it. The debate between proponents of Discourse Analysis and others held in *The Psychologist* (October 1992) and the concern of cognitive psychologists to study memory processes in ecologically valid situations (Neisser, 1978, 1988) have drawn attention to the social nature of memory processes and functions.

For the purposes of this chapter it is sufficient to accept that while individual memory is the capacity to store and retrieve information, and to that extent memory is information processing, the processes of inputting information, remembering and forgetting are social. Firstly the recollection of information is not a simple passive retrieval of an image stored in an individual's mind, rather recollection is an active process of reconstruction. Bartlett in his book on *Remembering* stated "when a subject is being asked to remember, very often the first thing that emerges is something of the nature of an attitude. The recall is then a construction, made largely on the basis of this attitude, and its general effect is that of a justification of the attitude" (1932, 206–7). Second, remembering can take place collectively, either through conversation or in public commemorative ceremonies and rituals. Thirdly the functions of these processes are social. At the individual level, memory allows us to perform everyday activities, such as eating, writing, riding a bicycle etc. Personal and social memories enable a person to construct their identity, to make sense of present events and to act in an intelligible manner. Most theories of the self and identity are indeed based on the assumption that people have the capacity to remember and to reconstruct information (Markus, 1977; Breakwell, 1986). Our memories will define who we are and enable us to act, at least most of the time, in a way which is consistent with our identities, at the same time enabling us to understand other people's actions. At the societal and group level, what we remember and the way we remember it enables us to constitute and sustain a certain kind of social order (Shotter, 1990; Connerton, 1989). Our memories and the way we communicate them either in private (such as the way we behave when we are alone or the way we think) or by public actions such as social conversations, public commemorative ceremonies and rituals or as they are embodied in symbols and other artifacts will sustain different social and power relationships and ideologies (Middleton and Edwards, 1990; Billig, 1990; Connerton, 1989).

As was mentioned above, this chapter focuses on those memories that are used by members of a group to define that group's identity, for example, the way in which memories of the Cypriot bishops and Archbishop Kyprianos martyred by the Turkish occupiers in 1821 are maintained in Greek-Cypriot memory as a means to constitute the distinct "Greek-Orthodox Christian" identity of the group. Although one would expect that such memories are shared by all or the vast majority of the members of the group, a functional definition is employed in order to avoid having to consider an arbitrary level of commonality at which a memory can be considered the property of a group. This is a problem similar to the one of "how many people" should share a representation before it can be called a social representation; a criticism over-rehearsed by the critiques of social representations theory. Furthermore, this definition can be distinguished from a discourse-analytic perspective although they both use a functionalist approach.

For although it is acknowledged that the study of "how everyday *versions* of events (including persons, things, states of affairs) are *constructed* and *occasioned* in talk and text" (Edwards *et al.*, 1992, 441, his emphasis) could be a legitimate exercise, it leaves a number of questions unanswered, and its value is rather limited. For example, the issue of veridicality of memories and the explanation of the genesis of these discourses are not addressed in this paradigm. Most importantly for the purposes of the argument presented in this chapter, discursive processes of remembering are only one mechanism for maintaining group memories. In addition, group memories are not only located in conversations, they can be private, non-linguistic/semantic, they can be embodied in other forms of social activity, national symbols and so on.

The theoretical framework suggested here is based on the work of a group of social psychologists at the Social Psychology European Research Institute (SPERI) which attempts to integrate social representational and identity processes involved in the production of action drawing on Identity Process Theory (Breakwell, 1986). It is proposed that, first groups have collective identities which are more than just the summation of the identities of its individual members. Second, one can conceptualise collective identities in a similar way to that employed to conceptualise individual identities. In particular, it is claimed that Breakwell's Identity Process Theory (1986) is a good starting point in conceptualising group identity. Third, one can hypothesise about processes of social remembering and forgetting on the basis of what is known about the memory processes involved in remembering information about the self. Fourth, it is argued that social/group remembering is not being carried out in a vacuum. Therefore social/group remembering can only be understood by taking into account the interaction between group identity processes and contextual social influences.

Conceptualising Group Identity

Group identity refers to the identity content and processes that the members ascribe to a group which do not necessarily reflect their individual identities or at least do not reflect them in the same degree. For example, Guzzo *et al.* (1993) discussed the concept of group potency which refers to the collective belief in a group that it is effective and efficacious which differs from the self-efficacy of individual members. Similarly Crocker and Luhtanen (1990) talked about the concept of "collective self-esteem"; the extent to which members of the group evaluate the group positively. Although these studies refer to small group situations, it is suggested that these concepts can be applied to larger groups such as national and ethnic groups. However, group identities, especially where large groups such as nations are concerned, should not be considered static constellations of attributes and valuations. I think Schlessinger was quite apt when he observed that "'National characteristics' are not given. National cultures are not repositories of shared symbols to which the entire population stands in identical relation. Rather they are to be approached as sites of contestation in which competition over definitions take place." (1991, 174)

As was mentioned above, it is suggested that a conceptualisation of a group identity could be developed by drawing on Breakwell's Identity Process Theory (1986). In summary, within Identity Process Theory, identity is seen as the outcome of the interaction between the biological characteristics of memory, consciousness and organised construal and the physical and societal structure and process along a temporal dimension. Identities are articulated through thought, affect and action in a context of personal and social power relationships. In the case of group identity, identity would be the outcome of the interaction between the capabilities, limitations and identities of its individual members, the structure of the group including the network of social and power relationships it entails, and its position in relation to other groups.

At the individual level, the structure of identity has two dimensions; the content and value dimensions. The content dimension comprises the information about the person that makes that person unique. This will include attitudes and belief systems, behavioural styles, self-ascribed attributes and belief systems, as well as group memberships. The value dimension comprises the values attached to each element of the identity.

One can see how these concepts can also be applied at the level of group identities. The content dimension would include the members' beliefs about what the group stood for, the social representations held by the group as a whole, styles of operating as a group and so on. Similarly, members of a group will be likely to have opinions as to the value the group as a whole attaches to different elements of its identity.

Individual identity is also conceptualised in terms of two processes; assimilation-accommodation and evaluation. The assimilation-accommodation process refers to the absorption of new information and restructuring of the existing identity structure to accommodate such information. The evaluation process refers to the apportionment of value to the new information assimilated into the identity.

The processes of identity are guided by four main principles which determine which endstates are desirable for the structure of identity; self-esteem, continuity, distinctiveness, and self-efficacy. Self-esteem refers to the desire to be evaluated positively. Continuity refers to a person's desire to give a consistent account of their self-conception over time. Distinctiveness refers to the person's desire to be unique. Self-efficacy refers to the strive to be competent. These principles are historically and socially defined.

At the group level, the processes of assimilation-accommodation and evaluation are likely to be negotiation processes among the members of the group and among institutions, the media and so on. It is likely that these processes would be guided by the same principles that govern individual identity processes as well as by the principle of cohesion, as some degree of cohesion is vital for the group's existence. However, it is likely that the importance of the historical and social specificity of these principles is even greater for the group identity than the individual identity.

Such a conceptualisation of group identity is useful because it encompasses both concepts of identity as structures and process, is succinct in describing group identities as the product of social forces and has built into it the temporal dimension which is very important in understanding the development of identity processes and yet is very often omitted from social psychological theorising on identity.

Identity and Social Memory Processes

Previous research has shown that certain characteristics of large-scale events influence the formation and development of collective memories. For example in a series of studies Pennebaker and his colleagues showed that events such as political upheavals which represent significant long-term changes to people's lives are likely to be collectively remembered. Also, collective memories are likely to be formed if people actively talk and think about events to a high degree (Pennebaker and Banasik, 1992; Pennebaker and Harber, in press; Pennebaker and Polakoff, 1990).

It is argued that it may also be reasonable to assume that the same principles which guide the processes of accommodation and assimilation of new information guide the processes of selective memories and reconstruction of memories and that we can rely on what we know about processes of remembering information about the self to form hypotheses about processes of social remembering of the kind I have been talking about here.

Indeed there is some evidence from earlier experimental work which suggests that information about the self which helps to maintain a high self-esteem and is consistent with the knowledge of self will be more easily accessible (Fiske and Taylor, 1991; Greenwald, 1980; Greenwald and Pratkanis, 1984). For example, Kuiper and his/her colleagues have shown that most individuals tend to recall positive personality information easily whereas negative information is difficult to recall (Kuiper and Derry, 1992; Kuiper and MacDonald, 1982; Kuiper et al., 1985). Also most people tend to recall better information related to success than that related to failure (Silverman, 1964) and tend to recall their task performance as more positive than it actually was (Crary, 1966). Second, it was shown that memory can be distorted in order to maintain perceptions of consistency. Kulik and Mahler (1986) found that extroverts tended to recall that they spent more time talking in a "getting-acquainted conversation" than introverts did.

It is argued that in a similar way groups are also likely to sustain memories and reconstruct them in such a way as to show their continuity, collective self-esteem, distinctiveness, efficacy or potency and cohesion. Continuity can be said to guide our memories when we attempt to explain the group's present identity with the consistent constructions of the past. For example, for Cypriots to assert our "Greekness", we construct our past with memories from the history of mainland Greece; in fact, about twenty years ago the history syllabus in elementary and secondary schools devoted eleven and a half of its twelve years to Greek history and only six months to the history of Cyprus. Now after the 1974 Turkish invasion, there is an attempt to construct a Cypriot consciousness and there is much more Cypriot history in the syllabus.

The desire for self-esteem can be seen at work for example in the process of claiming famous scientists as members of one's own ethnic or national group. As Einstein said "If my theory of relativity is proven correct, Germany will claim me as a German and France will declare that I am a citizen of the world. Should my theory prove untrue, France will say that I am a German and Germany will declare that I am a Jew" (address in the Sorbonne, *New York Times*, 16.2.1930).

Distinctiveness may guide the processes of remembering the uniqueness of Jews as God's chosen people as they are embodied in the rituals of Passover.

The way in which memories of sporting victories such as the World Cup of 1966 for the English, or the Berlin Olympics of 1936 when Hitler was humiliated by the victory of a non-Aryan athlete for African Americans endure while defeats are forgotten can be said to be guided by the group's desire to be efficacious as well as to enhance their collective self-esteem.

Groups would also be likely to construct their past in ways that would emphasise its unity rather than divisions. For example, Englishness will be presented in memories of royal events and ceremonies such as the coronation rather than say the General Strike of 1926 which is itself used to stress the unity of the labour movement.

However, it is not enough to show that these principles will guide group memory processes. We also need to specify the conditions under which one principle will dominate the others.

It could be hypothesised that when a group's identity is threatened by challenges to its values and what it stands for, then the continuity and cohesiveness principles will dominate and therefore there will be an emphasis on the past and an entrenchment of identities. Where the group's identity is threatened in terms of recognition of its existence by others, then the distinctiveness principle will dominate because what makes a group distinct is likely to provide the rule of inclusion and exclusion for the group. When there is a need to empower the group, the efficacy principle will dominate. Of necessity this is not an exhaustive list of the type of situations where each of the principles may dominate the processes of maintenance and reconstruction of memories. Indeed such a list could only be constructed if we developed a complete typology of context and understood more about the processes of interaction between context and group identity.

Some theorists have pointed to the conflict between the need to reconstruct the past in order to cope with social change and the need for continuity. For example, Halbwachs (1941) and Mead (1929) have argued that we construct the past in a way that will serve the needs of the present, whereas Durkheim (1965) claimed that societies need to remember to reproduce the past as it was so that "society renews the sentiment which it has of itself and its unity" (p. 420). Schwartz (1990) in his study of the reconstruction of Abraham Lincoln over time has shown how these needs can be resolved since, although there is some social change, it is still the same society and therefore their constructions of the past will reflect the change but also the continuity of the society.

Social Memory Processes in Context

It is important to take into account that group remembering and forgetting do not take place in a vacuum. So the freedom of maintenance and reconstruction is constrained both by internal and external influences on the group. Firstly, although a group may want to forget something, other groups with whom they must interact will wish to emphasise or keep alive that memory. Secondly, the mass media both acting as a challenge to certain constructions of the past and as reflecting the constructions of powerful groups in society, either by censorship or propaganda, play an important role in determining both what groups remember and how they remember it. Also the way we reconstruct our memories cannot be unconstrained. The need to maintain societal continuity, the group's existing social representational systems, other groups's constructions of the past, and the physical/material artifacts of the past will constrain the extent to which we are free to reconstruct the past. Unlike the world described by George Orwell in *1984* societies are not free to reconstruct the past in an arbitrary and self-serving way. The emergence of nationalistic fervour among the peoples of the former Soviet Union illustrates the constraints and limitations of attempts to reconstruct national identities as part of a monolithic Soviet whole.

Finally, it is suggested that using this theoretical framework outlined above, one could go beyond description towards developing a theory of processes of collective remembering and forgetting which specifies the rules that describe the relationship between certain individual process and contextual factors which lead to the construction of group identities. This in turn will enable us to work towards the prediction of certain individual and collective actions.

The processes of remembering and forgetting and their role in constructing group identities could be studied in contexts where social memories are located. Everyday conversations within the family, peer groups and so on will be one of the ways groups memories are maintained. Here discourse analysis may be useful in describing how certain memories are used. However, one would need also to explain how these discourses are generated and why certain groups would use one discourse to construct their past rather than another. In addition memories are embodied in national symbols and artifacts, social activity, rituals, commemorative ceremonies, public holidays, educational syllabi and media.

References

Bartlett, F. C. (1932). *Remembering: A Study in Experimental Social Psychology.* Cambridge: Cambridge University Press.

Billig, M. (1990). Collective memory, ideology and the British Royal Family. In D. Middleton and D. Edwards (eds), *Collective Remembering.* London: Sage Publications.

Breakwell, G. M. (1986). *Coping with Threatened Identities.* London and New York: Methuen.

Connerton, P. (1989). *How Societies Remember.* Cambridge: Cambridge University Press.

Crary, W. G. (1966). Reactions to incongruent self-experiences. *Journal of Consulting Psychology,* **30,** 246–52.

Crocker, J. and Luhtanen, R. (1990). Collective self-esteem and ingroup bias. *Journal of Personality and Social Psychology,* **58,** 60–7.

Durkheim, E. (1965). *The Elementary Forms of the Religious Life.* New York: The Free Press.

Edwards, D., Potter, J. and Middleton, D. (1992). Toward a discursive psychology of remembering. *The Psychologist,* **5,** 441–7.

Fiske, S. T. and Taylor, S. E. (1991). *Social Cognition.* New York: McGraw-Hill Inc.

Greenwald, A. G. (1980). The totalitarian ego: fabrication and revision of personal history. *American Psychologist,* **35,** 603–18.

Greenwald, A. G. and Pratkanis, A. R. (1984). The self. In R. S. Wyer and T. K. Srull (eds), *Handbook of Social Cognition* (Vol 3). Hillsdale, New Jersey: Lawrence Erlbaum Associates, Publishers.

Guzzo, R. A., Yost, P. R., Campbell, R. J. and Shea G. P. (1993). Potency in groups: articulating a construct. *British Journal of Social Psychology,* **32,** 87–106.

Halbwachs, M. (1941). *La topographie légendaire des évangiles.* Paris: Presses Universitaires de France.

Kuiper, N. A. and Derry, P. A. (1982). Depressed and nondepressed content self-reference. *Journal of Personality,* **50,** 67–79.

Kuiper, N. A. and MacDonald, M. R. (1982). Self and other perception in mild depressives. *Social Cognition,* **1,** 233–9.

Kuiper, N. A., Olinger, L. J., MacDonald, M. R. and Shaw, B. F. (1985). Self-schema processing of depressed and nondepressed content: the effects of vulnerability to depression. *Social Cognition,* **3,** 77–93.

Kulik, J. A. and Mahler, H. I. M. (1986). Self-confirmatory attribution, ego-centrism, and the perpetuation of self-beliefs. *Journal of Personality and Social Psychology,* **12,** 344–52.

Markus, H. (1977). Self-schemata and processing information about the self. *Journal of Personality and Social Psychology,* **35,** 63–78.

Mead, G. H. (1929). The nature of the past. In J. Coss (ed.), *Essays in Honor of John Dewey.* New York: Henry Holt.

Middleton, D. and Edwards, D. (1990). Conversational remembering: a social-psychological approach. In D. Middleton and D. Edwards (eds), *Collective Remembering.* London: Sage Publications.

Moscovici, S. (1990). New problems for social psychology in a new Europe. *European Bulletin of Social Psychology,* **2,** 2–10.

Neisser, U. (1978). Memory: What are the important questions? In M. M. Gruneberg, P. E. Morris and R. N. Sykes (eds), *Practical Aspects of Memory.* New York: Academic Press.

Neisser, U. (1988). New vistas in the study of memory. In U. Neisser and E. Winograd (eds), *Remembering Reconsidered: Ecological and Traditional Approaches to the Study of Memory*. Cambridge: Cambridge University Press.

Pennebaker, J. W. and Banasik, B. (1992). Looking back: monuments, movies and books as commemorative data. Unpublished manuscript. Dallas, TX: Southern Methodist University.

Pennebaker, J. W. and Harber, K. (in press) A social stage model of collective coping; the Persian Gulf war and other natural disasters. *Journal of Social Issues*.

Pennebaker, J. W. and Polakoff, R. (1990). The effects of the John F. Kennedy assassination on Dallas. Unpublished manuscript. Dallas, Texas: Southern Methodist University.

Schlesinger, P. (1991). *Media, State and Nation: Political Violence and Collective Identities*. London: Sage.

Schwartz, B. (1990). The reconstruction of Abraham Lincoln. In D. Middleton and D. Edwards (eds), *Collective Remembering*. London: Sage Publications.

Shotter, J. (1990). The social construction of remembering and forgetting. In D. Middleton and D. Edwards (eds), *Collective Remembering*. London: Sage Publications.

Silverman, I. (1964). Self-esteem and differential responsiveness to success and failure. *Journal of Abnormal and Social Psychology*, **69**, 115–19.

4

Unimagined Community? Some Social Psychological Issues Concerning English National Identity

SUSAN CONDOR

Lancaster University, England

My interest in English national identity was first aroused a couple of years ago on a trip to the USA. The immigration card asked for details of my "nationality" and "country of birth". After a good deal of hesitation, I filled in the card with "British" as an answer to the first question, and "England" to the second. My friend who was travelling with me responded "British" and "Scotland" respectively. On arrival, my friend's card was accepted without comment. My card was snatched by an irate official who overscored both of my answers with "UK" in thick blue ink. Somewhat bemused, I pondered a number of questions. If the authorities had wished to know my citizenship, why had they instead asked about my nationality? Why was it apparently legitimate to claim an identity as Scottish and British, but not as English and British? Why had it taken me so long to answer these apparently simple questions? Why had it not even occurred to me to answer "UK" to either of them?

These commonsense questions translate quite easily into a social scientific problem. How can it be, in an age of increased international contact, when national distinctions are of such personal and political significance (Anderson, 1983; Gellner, 1983; Giddens, 1985), that a relatively well-educated, experienced traveller is unable to answer apparently straightforward questions concerning national identity and citizenship to the satisfaction of North American immigration officials?

41

When I began to consider questions concerning English national identity from a more academic perspective, I came across a relative absence of contemporary social scientific literature on the subject. There has been a wealth of work in the humanities on issues such as "English architecture", "the English novel", "the English character" and so forth. Most of this scholarly work adopts what Tajfel (1978), would term an "objective" perspective: discussing "The English" from the viewpoint of an external observer. It is from this sort of perspective that scholars have, for example, developed their well-known analyses of English individualism (Macfarlaine, 1978; Stone and Stone, 1984), and of the English way-of-life (e.g. Blake, 1982; Langford, 1989; Porter, 1992). What is lacking from many of these accounts is any analysis of how English folk perceive and represent *themselves* as a national group. There is, of course, some work on cultural representations of the English, focusing on a range of phenomena including images of the physical terrain and representations of national character and social life. However, these analyses tend to rely on political speeches or on published documents representing dominant voices from various sites of cultural production (such as the cinema, literature, children's comics, newspapers, design, advertising and the "heritage" industry). It is, of course, possible that texts such as these may be more prescriptive than they are descriptive of popular consciousness. However, with few exceptions (e.g. Coetzee, 1992), authors have tended to assume a simple correspondence between the "contents" of these media and the consciousness of ordinary folk (e.g. Bommes and Wright, 1982; Colls and Dodd, 1986; Hobsbawm and Ringer, 1983; Porter, 1992; Strathern, 1992). Furthermore, existing analyses have tended to focus on those particular historical periods during which English national self-construction has been self-conscious and transparent, including the periods 1740–1830 (Newman, 1987); 1880–1920 (Colls and Dodd, 1986), 1920–40 (Samuel, 1989a).

Social scientific work which might be expected to shed some light on contemporary constructions of Englishness is, however, lacking. Considerable efforts have been expended in examining the claims to national identity on the part of peoples from Scotland, Wales and Northern Ireland, and there has been much concern for the "marginal" national identities of ethnic minorities in the UK (e.g. Feldman, 1989; Gilroy, 1987; James, 1989; Kelly, 1989). However, there have been few parallel analyses of the indigenous English,[1] and extant discussions have been based almost entirely on the intuition of the author. Nevertheless, some of the existing "theories" (if they can be accorded such a title) suggest that the issue of English national identity may be worthy of greater theoretical and empirical consideration.

A number of writers have commented on the confusion that people (including academics and government officials) may face concerning the distinctions between the terms "English", "British" and "UK citizen" (e.g. Crick, 1991). It has been suggested that the inhabitants of Great Britain accept the label British when it is applied by outsiders, but tend to prefer to label themselves as English, Welsh or Scottish (Kearney, 1991). Others, however, suggest that the English may not identify themselves as a distinct national group. This claim is usually warranted with reference to the assumption that English folk equate the terms "English" and "British".[2] The failure on the part of social scientists to consider distinctive English identities (and their own tendency to slip between usage of the terms "English" and "British") is attributed to the belief that the English themselves act in this way. Less commonly, an absence of work on "English" national identity is justified with reference to the comparative lack of authorised public symbols of Englishness (see Nairn, 1988; Samuel, 1989a). Today, the only significant cultural icons specifically designated as "English" are the national sports teams. The English flag and the red rose are seldom used as popular symbols. There is no English national costume and no distinctive English national anthem.[3] In England, public holidays have no national significance, and most English people do not even know the date of St George's day. The recent revitalisation and re-invention of English "heritage" has been aimed almost entirely at the tourist market.

With few notable exceptions (e.g. Nairn, 1977), this lack of public symbolism or celebration of Englishness, and the assumed tendency of the English to identify themselves as Britons, has led theorists to regard English national identity as simply "unproblematic", and to focus instead on the "problems" caused by the English tendency to co-opt the term "British". However, in a world of proliferating national and regional identities (Marquand, 1991) this apparent absence of Englishness is itself a phenomenon worthy of consideration. In this chapter I shall explore, from a social psychological point of view, the question of how "ordinary" English people in the 1990s may represent themselves in national terms.

National Self-Identification

I start this section of the chapter with a disclaimer. A comprehensive analysis of national identity would have to take account of complex contextual variation. This would include variation due to the social location of individual subjects (in concrete social networks, family structures); geographical, historical and ideological variations in the significance and meaning of national identity, and the intersections of national identities with gender, generational, ethnic and class identities. Such analyses would have to consider context-specific norms in the expression of national identity and contextual variations in salience. A full analysis of national self-identity would have to take account of the various ways in which identity may be symbolised (visually as well as verbally), and the possibility that, for the individual subject, national self-identification may exist at varying levels of consciousness. I shall be alluding to some of these issues in the course of discussion. However, it is beyond the scope of a single chapter to engage fully with the subtleties of national identification. Rather, I shall confine myself to discussing (as is usual among social psychologists) a set of data drawn from a few rather specific research contexts.[4]

I noted earlier that although there has been plenty of scholarly speculation concerning the national self-definition of the English, there exists little empirical data on this subject. As an initial point of departure I conducted two studies which simply involved asking English people direct questions concerning their national identity and their feelings about their nationality. The first study used semi-structured interviews with 50 adults (25 men and 25 women) from the North-West of England. Interviews opened with questions concerning identity and self-perception in general, and then went on to focus on more specific issues pertaining to national identity and sentiment. The respondents were all attending adult education classes. They were aged between 21 and 68 (mean age was 45 years), and were mainly skilled or semi-skilled workers. All were white, with English parents. The interviews were conducted in the respondents' colleges after classes, and lasted between 25 and 95 minutes (the average duration was 40 minutes).

The second study used self-report questionnaires which were administered to students from Lancaster University. The questionnaires, which consisted of a series of open-ended questions concerning national identity, were distributed to students in their rooms on campus, and were collected approximately one hour later. In the following pages I shall consider only the responses of 170 students who had been born in England of English parents. All of these respondents were white, 99 were female and 71 were male. Ages ranged from 17 to 27 (with a mean age of 19.5 years). Although insufficiently detailed information was obtained to classify the respondents accurately according to social class, the majority of respondents came from professional or managerial families.

For the purposes of this chapter, I should like to extract four aspects of the results of these studies for particular consideration.

Hesitancy in National Self-Definition

The manner in which my initial (straightforward) questions concerning national identity were answered in the interview study confirmed suspicions that English people may experience, and certainly express, difficulty in categorising themselves in national terms. There was a marked tendency for respondents to hesitate before answering the question, "What is your nationality?" (the average latency period was just under four seconds) which was not apparent in their answers to other questions on a range of issues concerning identity and self-perception. Only a minority of the respondents (N=10) gave an unqualified answer to this question (eight of these defined themselves as "English"). Typically, responses were qualified by expressions of uncertainty or ambivalence:

Well, British I suppose, although [. . .] yes, British

English or Brit [. . .] British. English probably

Hmmm [. . .] I think English

or by various rhetorical attempts to distance themselves from their answers:

> I suppose you could say I was British

> I have a British passport, so I suppose that means I am British.

Written answers to questions are less likely to yield information concerning uncertainty or prevarication. Nevertheless, a sizable number of the respondents in the questionnaire study avoided answering the question, "What is your nationality?" (see below), and a small minority (N= 10) appeared to have misunderstood the question, giving "inappropriate" answers such as, "a student at Lancaster", or, "a WASP".

Self-Identification as "British"

There was a good deal of evidence that, in general, respondents were confused by the distinction between "English" and "British" (no respondent in either of the studies ever used the term "UK"), and in many contexts they tended to use the terms interchangeably. For example, it was common for the students in the questionnaire study to refer to "British" sports teams.[5] However, there was very little evidence that respondents used these labels thoughtlessly or treated them as synonymous in all rhetorical contexts. In particular, the respondents in the interview study rarely applied the category "British" to *themselves* in a thoughtless or straightforward manner. Rather, they seemed uncomfortable with the category "British" as being self-descriptive, but were unsure about using the term "English".

Of the thirty-four respondents who initially identified themselves (although possibly hesitantly and prefaced by expressions like "I suppose") as "British" in the interview study, the majority (N=30) in some way qualified this, either by also specifying their English identity, or by using various strategies to distinguish between their "knowledge" of their (official) British nationality and their "feelings" of "really" being English:

> Well, I'm British, I suppose. But when people ask me where I come from, like, when I'm on holiday, I always say "England". I mean, I've lived in England all my life. I've never even been to Scotland or Wales. I would say that I feel more English.
>
> (woman, aged twenty-seven)

Another common feature of the respondents' talk was a tendency to present Britishness as non-authentic, an alien identity imposed by external forces rather than emerging from within the individual:

> In conversations like this, I have to keep reminding myself that I am from "Britain". It doesn't come naturally. It doesn't sound right, and I usually say "England", and then correct myself.
>
> (man, aged twenty-seven)

> It's just that sometimes you're sort of forced into it, you know. Like when you see the news on telly, and it's "Britain" this, and "Britain" that. Then you have to pinch yourself, and say, "yes, that means me". But, in general, I just don't think like that.
>
> (man aged fifty-three)

A few of the respondents in the interview study alluded explicitly to a form of linguistic hygiene, which they saw as restricting their ability to use the term "English":

> British [. . .]. Yes, British. Well, it's not done to say you're English nowadays. I don't know why, but you just don't, you know.
>
> (man, aged sixty-four)

> I suppose I'd say I was British. That's what you say on forms, isn't it? That's what you are meant to call yourself if you are English, I think.
>
> (woman, aged forty-five)

Refusal of National Identification

The majority of the respondents in the interview study ($N = 32$) at some stage denied the personal significance of national identity:

> Well, I don't really think about being English. But I suppose, if you ask, I'd say I was English, but it's not something I often think about, to be honest.
>
> (woman, aged fifty-two)

> I do not see England as "my country". It is just a piece of land as other countries are, and anyone should be able to enter it.
>
> (woman, aged twenty-nine)

This form of denial was particularly marked among the students who participated in the questionnaire study. This study did not allow the respondents the opportunity for discursive digression or qualification accorded by the interview study. Nevertheless, in answer to the opening question, "What is your nationality?", nearly a fifth of all respondents ($N = 33$) "refused" the question, denying any personal sense of national identity:

> My national identity is virtually zero.
>
> (man, aged twenty)

> My national identity isn't important to me.
>
> (woman, aged twenty-one)

In response to the subsequent question, "What are your feelings about your nationality?", almost 70% of respondents denied any strong sense of national affiliation:

> I have, a very weak sense of national identity. I do not really have any feelings because I tend not to think about it. I think about my nationality at only the most basic level that I was born here and have always lived here. It is nothing more than a nationality to write down on forms and a place to live.
>
> (woman, aged nineteen)

> I think that my description of my national identity is more of a classification than a reflection of a feeling of solidarity with my country. I will certainly support the English in sporting activities but identity wise I tend to feel closer to smaller groups like the student population or people round my age group. My national identity I think I save for special occasions, mostly when I am abroad.
>
> (man, aged nineteen)

Respondents in both studies often stressed that their feelings of national identification were confined to particular contexts, especially when viewing sport or when abroad on holiday. The rejection of nationality as a basis for self-definition was largely expressed on the grounds of commitment to more local social identities, or to values of individualism:

> I don't think that, left to myself, I think about being British or English or anything really. I'm just me.
>
> (interview, woman aged nineteen)

> I don't really think about being English. I don't think it is nice that people should be nationalistic like that, because we are all individuals.
>
> (interview, woman aged thirty-two)

Respondents did not simply deny the salience of their national identity. They often displayed a positive resistance to national self-identification. This was often expressed with reference to a sense of "embarrassment" at being so categorised by others:

> I find it embarrassing to be identified as English when I am abroad. As a homosexual I find it hard to be patriotic and have any national identity.
>
> (questionnaire, man aged twenty-one)

> I only really think about it when I am abroad on holiday. And then, sometimes I pretend that I am not from Britain, because it can be embarrassing.
>
> (interview, woman aged thirty-one)

National Pride and Shame

It was rare for respondents to express an unqualified sense of national pride. Only seventeen respondents to the questionnaire study and four of the respondents in the interview study made any reference to feelings of national pride, or any statements which might be interpreted as reflecting national pride, which were not immediately qualified:

[Question: "How would you describe your country?"]

> I would say that I am proud to be English. It is a country respected by foreigners. I am proud of our traditions and heritage, and the beautiful countryside.
>
> (questionnaire, woman aged nineteen)

> Britain is a nice, stable country. Its democratic institutions and monarchy are respected throughout the world.
>
> (interview, man aged forty-five)

More commonly, expressions of national pride were muted or qualified:

> I'm very proud of the beauty of the countryside but I'm ashamed of the way Britain is becoming overdeveloped. I suppose I'm proud of the land and ashamed of the flag. The behaviour of British people abroad is embarrassing as is the politics. I don't think I have a tremendously strong National identity but I do feel a bond to many areas of Britain, because it's home.
>
> (questionnaire, woman aged eighteen)

Such expressions of "qualified pride" were identified in the accounts of thirty-eight of the respondents in the questionnaire study, and twelve respondents in the interview study. Often, however, the nation (whether "Britain" or "England") was discussed with explicit reference to "shame" (interview study: $N = 9$; questionnaire study: $N = 31$), or in terms which implied a sense of shame on the part of the respondent (interview study: $N = 12$; questionnaire study: $N = 26$). Shame was often expressed in the context of a particular representation of history which focused on national decline. This was especially prevalent among the students who completed the open-ended questionnaires, and may be illustrated by two (not untypical) responses to the question, "How would you describe your country?":

> A country in decline in terms of military and economic power and cultural influence.
>
> (man, aged twenty-three)

> A country and a nation in decline. We are a nation confused about our own standing in the world, while other countries overtake us. In many respects it is our country's past glories that carry us through modern day difficulties.
>
> (man aged nineteen)

Explicit reference to national decline was also apparent in the accounts of a large minority ($N = 16$) of the respondents in the interview study:

> It is a once powerful nation, slipping from its position of glory.
>
> (woman, aged forty-five)

A number of respondents in both studies presented national pride as an anachronistic throwback to the days of Empire:

> I perhaps feel a little embarrassed sometimes because of the notion of superiority among the British seems a little misguided—more a reflection to days when Britain was colonising the rest of the world. The time of the British Empire. Britain is not as "Great" as it makes itself out to be. I am not really proud to be British. It seems to me, as a country, Britain has little to be proud of.
>
> (interview, woman aged twenty-seven)

A sense of "shame" was often articulated in terms of a sense of inherited guilt. British or English national pride was commonly constructed in association with "prejudice":

> I find it hard to identify with the nationalism and intolerance of others that seems to be part of being British. I often feel ashamed to say that I am British because in the past, and indeed the present, the British have seen themselves as so self-righteous and superior.
>
> (questionnaire, man aged nineteen)

There was some evidence from the interview study that these sorts of sentiments were more likely to be expressed by respondents under forty years than those over forty.

In both studies respondents showed a tendency to differentiate self from "other people", who espoused a strong sense of English or British national identity:

> National identity is not something that is very important to me, not something I think about very much. I don't go around thinking of myself as a Brit. Sometimes I see people doing this, and it looks very strange, like cheering to Rule Britannia, or waving Union Jacks. But it all seems rather strange and distant to me.
>
> (interview, man aged twenty-nine)

And compatriots who openly exhibited national pride were described as shaming:

> Although Britain used to be a great world power, it isn't any more. But, people still act as if it is, and think that Britain has a lot of standing in the world. Sometimes that makes me ashamed with foreigners.
>
> (interview, woman aged 45)

Although these sorts of sentiments were often expressed with specific regard to English or British national sentiment (which were, after all, the focus of the questions), many of the respondents expressed more general antipathy towards patriotism or nationalism:[6]

> OK, I support England in Football, and cheer on the British [sic] athletic team, but that about sums it up. The whole idea of being proud to be English or British is scary, as are the implications involved in patriotism and nationalism. With the rise of nationalism in Europe as well as in Britain, to be nationalistic involves a degree of "we are better than you", and is the most terrifying prospect.
>
> (questionnaire, man aged twenty)

> The term national identity makes me uneasy – it reminds me of fascism. So I like to think that my national identity is not very strong.
>
> (interview, man aged forty-five)

Images of National Character

In social psychology, analyses of popular images of a nation (or any other social category) tend to focus on "stereotypes": the characteristics (usually the personality characteristics) associated with a "typical" category member. Although social psychological work initially focused largely on images of national groups (e.g. Buchanan, 1951; Buchanan and Cantril, 1953; Katz and Braly, 1933), very few studies have considered stereotypes of the British or the English. Moreover, existing work has apparently used the category labels "English" or "British" without any principled rationale, and has occasionally confused the categories.[7] In this section of the chapter I shall discuss briefly three studies on English autostereotypes (these studies are presented in greater detail in Condor, in submission).

Stereotypes of the English and the British

Social psychological analyses of (national) stereotypes typically employ some form of adjective check-list or rating-scale. As an initial step in analysing popular images of the English, I conducted a standard adjective rating-scale study. The scale consisted of 100 adjectives, selected from a review of existing studies of national stereotypes. Two versions of the scale were used. In one version respondents were asked to indicate how "typical" each adjective was of "English people", and in the other version respondents were asked to rate the adjectives for their typicality of "British people". The scales were administered to two groups of respondents. One group consisted of 100 students from Lancaster University

(48 males, 52 females), who were approached in campus cafeterias. The other group consisted of 98 adult holidaymakers (40 males, 58 females) who were approached in cafeterias at Blackpool Pleasure Beach. In each group, half the respondents completed the "English" version, and half completed the "British" version of the scale. All of the respondents were white and had been born in England. The two groups differed on a number of dimensions, including age (student mean age was 20.3 years; holidaymaker mean age was 42.5 years); social class (the majority of the students were from professional or managerial backgrounds, the majority of the holidaymakers worked in skilled or partly-skilled manual occupations); and region of origin (all but five of the holidaymakers were from the North of England; 40 of the students were not originally from the North).

A summary of the focused stereotypes (Williams and Best, 1982), the ten adjectives most frequently attributed to the two categories, is shown in Tables 4.1 and 4.2.

TABLE 4.1 Stereotypes of "English people" (Percentage of respondents rating a characteristic as either "very typical" or "typical"

Characteristics	% Students (N = 50)	% Holidaymakers (N = 49)
Nationalistic	80	76
Patriotic	78	76
Proud	76	74
Tradition-loving	76	76
Conservative	76	74
Polite	74	70
Good-mannered	70	70
Sarcastic	66	72
Reserved	70	64
Educated	68	64

TABLE 4.2 Stereotypes of "British people"

Characteristic	% Students (N = 50)	Holidaymakers (N = 49)
Aggressive	72	68
Arrogant	72	82
Competitive	70	76
Materialistic	68	76
Nationalistic	90	88
Patriotic	82	86
Proud	80	72
Quarrelsome	70	64
Stubborn	68	64
Xenophobic	80	60

The first thing to note is the extent to which the two rather different groups of respondents concurred in their attribution of adjectives to the categories "English people" and "British people". A second point of interest concerns the differences between responses to the two category labels. The English stereotype appears in many respects to parallel popular images of the South and the British stereotype to parallel popular images of the North (see Howkins, 1986; and Weiner, 1985). This is particularly interesting given that all of the respondents were currently living in the North and that the majority of the Holidaymaker group were indigenous Northerners. For both groups of respondents, English stereotypes appear more feminine than British stereotypes (cf. Eagly and Kite, 1987; Hall, 1992; and MacKay and Thane, 1986). In particular, the stereotype of the British (but not the English) seems to have aggressive (war-mongering?) implications, which is consistent with the rhetorical use of "British" identity in the mobilisation of the population during the Falklands (Chambers, 1989) and the Gulf (Reicher, 1991) conflicts.

There are obvious problems in trying to "read off" evaluative orientation from simple lists of adjectives (Condor, 1990). However, it may be noted that the focused stereotypes of the English and the British do not, on the face of it, appear overwhelmingly positive in tone. Some of the most positive traits on the list provided (e.g. "intelligent", "truthful", generous") were considered distinctly atypical of either category. Although many of the characteristics of the focused English stereotype are somewhat ambiguous, it would appear that the stereotype of "British people" is generally less positive than that of "English people".

While these data are interesting in their own right, they fail to address a number of important issues. Studies which extract adjective ascription from rhetorical context can tell us little about the meaning (or possible constellations of meaning) associated with these characteristics. I have noted the difficulties involved in assessing the favourability of stereotypes taken out of context. More generally, data such as these do not allow us to distinguish between those characteristics which are seen to be (stereo)"typical" of a national group, and those which are seen to be desirable or "normative" aspects of group membership (cf. Turner, 1987). One particular limitation of check-list studies is their in-built assumption that people necessarily regard the members of a social category as a single "type" (Clifton *et al.*, 1976; Deaux *et al.*, 1985). Bearing these issues in mind, two further studies were conducted in order to gain a more detailed, qualitative understanding of stereotypes of the English.

English Stereotypes and English National Characters

Social psychological research has demonstrated that stereotypes generated by open-ended questions may differ markedly from those generated through the use of adjective scales or check-lists. The interview and questionnaire studies of national self-identification described above did, of course, yield some data concerning images of the English. However, since respondents were free to define their "nationality" and "country" in any way, it was not always clear whether their remarks were directed towards the English, the British or both. Moreover, the questions used in these studies did not directly invite description of "national character", and remarks pertaining to this tended to be made incidentally as part of an answer to a more general question concerning national identity or sentiment.

In order to collect some more systematic information concerning stereotypes of the English in a less constrained context than that afforded by an adjective rating-scale, small discussion groups were set up, and their transactions recorded. Respondents were adults from Lancaster and the surrounding areas who were attending evening classes (generally in craft subjects) at two local institutions. Fifty-seven respondents took part (37 women and 20 men), all of whom were white, and had been born in England. Respondents took part in groups of three or four members. The groups were asked to discuss the topic of "the English" for fifteen minutes, and then to produce a written description. For the purposes of analysis, only the discussions were considered.

There were some clear similarities between the stereotypes generated in this study and those elicited by the adjective rating scale. Descriptions of the English commonly included reference to nationalism/patriotism; lack of emotional demonstration ("stiff upper lip"); insularity and unsociability; conservatism and traditionalism. Also, in line with the findings from the studies of national self-identity, respondents also often referred to the English "Empire mentality" and "delusions of grandeur". However, in this study, adjective phrases accounted for only 19% of all descriptions. More commonly, respondents alluded to "typical" English habits and appearance or styles of dress. One especially common theme concerned food and eating habits (this accounted for nearly 25% of all responses), including: "eat fried breakfasts", "always drinking tea", "eat roast beef" and "like fish and chips".

Another interesting finding was that these discussions of the English were overwhelmingly negative in tone. This is, of course, consistent with some of the findings from the studies on national self-identification. Quite often descriptions of English life, habits or character were associated with rhetorical flourishes such as "the worst in the world" ("the worst food in the world", "awful clothes sense— must be the worst in Europe", "the people must be the ugliest in the world"), or were spontaneously compared negatively with equivalent habits or practices from other countries ("really disorganized industry—not like the Germans", "not at all friendly. Very reserved not like Italians and Spanish who are more fun and like a laugh"). Only eight of the respondents' contributions were, on balance, more positive than negative in tone. Moreover, English traits and habits which might be regarded positively (e.g. "polite", "sense of humour", "animal lover") were often, in practice, presented in a manner which suggested that they should not be taken altogether seriously—for example, they were often associated with humorous caricatures, or were presented ironically through juxtaposition (e.g. "They're great animal lovers, and they really enjoy hunting").

Respondents in this study did not, in general, allude to a *single*, homogeneous, English national character (cf. Diehl and Jonas, 1991). Rather, in the course of discussion, respondents were drawing upon a range of "stock characters" (MacIntyre, 1981). These were sometimes expressed as "types" ("City gents", "football hooligans", "English roses", "Girls in stilettos") and sometimes expressed in terms of particular iconic figures ("The Queen", "Winston Churchill", "Bertie Wooster", "Ma Larkin"). It was clear that the majority of respondents were attempting to incorporate variety or balance in their description of "the English": it was very rare for a respondent to describe "the English" with reference to a single "type" or style of life. One noteworthy factor, apart from the simple fact of variety, is that almost all of these stock characters, habits, and ways of life, are marked in terms of social class.

Stereotypes and the Description of Individuals

The studies described above required respondents to generalise about the English as an abstract category. A third study was conducted to see how constructs of Englishness might be employed in the description of individuals. Specifically, it looked at the ways in which people may deploy notions of Englishness in making decisions about whether any particular individual is (or is not) "English", and the ways in which individuals identified as "English" may be described. In this study, respondents (50 university students and 36 adults from Institutions of Continuing Education from the North West of England) were presented with a set of 40 black-and-white photographs of faces. The photographs were selected from a pool held at Lancaster University Psychology department. For the purposes of the present study, all of the stimuli used were pictures of white faces, as pilot research suggested that the inclusion of pictures of black people led respondents to conclude that study was a covert test of racism. Respondents were asked to sort the photographs into piles according to whether or not they "seem to be English", explaining their choices as they went along. The photographs selected by the respondent as "seeming to be English" were then laid on a table, and the respondent asked to consider the ways in which the people in the photographs might be similar to, or different from, each other. Respondents were then asked to select from these subcategories the one which was, in their opinion, "most typically English". Finally, they were asked to select the single photograph which seemed to them to be "most typically English". Respondents were tested individually, and the entire transaction was recorded with their knowledge. The interventions of the interviewer were restricted to occasional prompting for more information (e.g. "why do you think that?").

Again, it was clear that social class constituted a central axis around which respondents organised their images of "English people". In this study, class distinctions were often explicitly mentioned by the subjects themselves—in fact class was the third most often specified basis for distinguishing between the "English" pictures, after gender and age. This fact is all the more noteworthy given the very limited information available in the photographs with which respondents were working.

This study revealed more positive images than did either of the studies which elicited descriptions of "the English" as an abstract category. The photograph most often selected as "the most typically English" was of a smiling elderly man, who was generally described as "nice", "gentlemanly", "a decent sort of chap", "kind-looking", "thoughtful" and "educated". The derogatory images of English national character apparent in the previous studies were also apparent, however. The second most often selected photograph was of a scowling middle-aged man, who was generally described as, "thick", "prejudiced", "a yobbo", and, "thinks British is best".

The Janus-Face of English National Character

The second and third studies, which allowed for some appreciation of the discursive contexts in which reference may be made to particular "English" traits or habits, suggested that the various (and sometimes apparently contradictory) images of the English tend to be applied in two broad constellations:

Gentleman/woman	Hooligan/lager lout
Manners	Rudeness
Tolerance	Prejudice
Fair-minded	Small-minded
Educated	Ignorant
Nice	Lazy
Stiff-upper-lip	Patriotic/nationalistic
Love of justice	

Generally, it seems that rather than assume a homogenous national character, respondents constructed a two-sided English national identity. One side represents the "normative" social image (in Turner's 1987 sense of the term). The other side represents the "grotesque" other (Stallybrass and White, 1986), the "black sheep" of the ingroup (Marques, 1990) reminiscent of the "other" so often deployed by respondents in the national self-identity studies. These two constellations of characteristics are partly class-specific. However, it would be a mistake to suppose that what is revealed here is simply a representation of English middle-class decorum as opposed to English working-class crudity. Rather, it was clear from the respondents' construction both of subcategories and of individuals that these constellations could cut across class lines. For example, the "Gentlefolk" constellation could (with the exception perhaps of "education") be applied to the plucky, mannerly working class (as stereotypically depicted in Ealing comedies). Similarly, the "Hooligan" character could be applied to the middle class ("Yuppies", "the Estate-agent type", "the Blue-Rinse Brigade") or the aristocracy.

In the course of discussion, either the Dr Jekyll or the Mr Hyde side of the English national character could be used to characterise the English-in-general, and it was common for a single respondent to use both images as prototypes at different times:

> English people are a real embarrassment. When you are abroad, if there is someone who is loud and noisy and drinks too much and is disturbing other people, you know they will turn out to be English.

> One distinctive thing about the English, above all, is their reserve. Especially compared with some European countries where they shout and scream all the time. English people are more quiet and reserved, and keep themselves to themselves.

> (picture-sorting study, woman aged forty-five)

Englishness: Social Context, Social Representation and Social Display

If one were to take the results of these studies at face value, they appear to suggest that, in a world in which it is difficult to conceive of a "man without a nation" (Gellner, 1983, 6), these English people were experiencing difficulty in conceiving of themselves in national terms. They lacked glib answers to straightforward questions concerning their nationality, and often indicated that they were conscious of their national identity only in unusual circumstances. Other aspects of the results suggest not so much the chronic non-salience of national identity, as the possibility that respondents were motivated to dis-identify with the national category to which they "objectively" belonged. Respondents often voiced a sense of shame in their nation, and distanced themselves from compatriots who exhibited national pride. There was little general evidence of the sort of ethnocentrism which is usually seen to accompany social identification. In a "world obsessed with national pride" (Brennan, 1990, 44) these respondents seemed to prefer to stress the negative characteristics of England and the English. Moreover, in a world in which nationalism represents an "international ideology" (Billig, this volume), these members of the "oldest nation in the world" apparently rejected the value of nationalism.

A number of questions arise concerning the status of these findings. First, as I noted earlier, expressions of national identity are likely to be context-dependent, and one has to bear in mind the local contexts in which these data were gathered. There is no reason to suppose that these same respondents would necessarily respond in the same way in other settings, nor should it be assumed that all English people would have behaved in the same way in these studies. However, the case remains that these studies do seem to have identified a set of phenomena which are characteristic of some English people at least some of the time.[8] Second, is the issue of whether we, as social psychologists, *should* accept these accounts at face value. Some perspectives in social psychology treat subjects' self-descriptions, and their responses to measures of stereotyping, as reports of covert mental processes. However, other perspectives might be more inclined to treat these accounts as forms of strategic self-presentation (e.g. Potter and

Wetherell, 1987). For the time being I shall maintain an agnostic stance concerning the status of respondents' accounts. In the following pages I shall consider some possible explanations for the behaviour observed in my studies. To this end I shall adopt (although not uncritically) perspectives from social identity approaches to intergroup behaviour (e.g. Tajfel, 1978) and group membership (e.g. Turner, 1987).

Social Context: the Structure of the British State and Nationalist Discourse

One important consideration to be borne in mind when considering responses to the studies on national self-identification is that the British State developed historically before the advent of modern forms of "nationalism". Since the break-up of the Soviet Union, the United Kingdom of Great Britain and Northern Ireland is anomalous in constituting a multi-national state. As Nairn (1988) suggests, Britishness:

> "makes no sense" according to the standard concepts of today's nation-state politics. . .But that's because it dates before the formation of these concepts . . .
>
> (p. 259)

The confusion that some of my respondents apparently experienced over their national identity may be seen to reflect contemporary assumptions concerning the "naturalness" of the nation-state. However, this observation alone is not sufficient to explain respondents' lack of confidence or spontaneity in describing themselves in national terms. Rather, it simply raises the question of why these (and presumably other) English Britons had not learned "answers" to such questions. There is no *a priori* reason why the status of the UK as a multi-national state should not be popularly recognised.

Along with its multi-national character, there are other distinctive aspects of the British State, and of England, which render difficult the application of contemporary notions of nationalism. Plamenatz (1973) distinguishes two forms of modern nationalism: "Eastern" nationalism (based on notions of ethnic homogeneity) and "Western" nationalism based on liberal values of self-determination). Neither of these constructs is easily applicable either to Britain or to England. Both Britain and England have, historically, been constructed in terms of ethnic diversity (see below), although there have been some attempts on the part of the Right to articulate a notion of Englishness in terms of "race" (Condor, forthcoming (a); Nairn, 1977). In contrast, the peoples of Scotland, Wales and Northern Ireland may, on occasions, construct national unity through reference to ethnic distinctiveness (see Hopkins, this volume, for an example). The "Western" construct of nationalism also is not readily applicable either to England or to Britain although, again, it may be used as a basis for nationalist sentiment and action or the part of the "minority" nationalities of the UK. Nairn (1988) argues that the identification of the British state with the crown (rather than "the people") precluded the development of popular British or English nationalism. Certainly, the English British have traditionally demonstrated antipathy to popular Nationalism:

> The received wisdom is that . . . Popular nationalism is the vulgar face of other peoples, some because they are oppressed and need it, and some because they just like that sort of thing. The English do not need nationalism and do not like it; they are so sure of themselves that they need hardly discuss the matter.
>
> (Colls and Dodd, 1986 preface)

Some of the responses in my studies on national identity and stereotyping might be interpreted as reflecting this legacy. A rejection-of-popular-nationalism does not seem to figure as part of the current (conscious, or articulated) English autostereotype—indeed, respondents described both the English and the British as "nationalistic" and "patriotic". Nevertheless, in many respects, the respondents' own behaviour (their association of nationalism with "prejudice", their construct of the grotesque patriot) may be seen as an enactment of this (distinctively English?) norm. This observation raises the question of the necessary role of consciousness in determining social action (see Condor, forthcoming (b)). Whereas social identity theorists conceive of group-typical action as the consequence of an individual's awareness of group membership and the self-application of recognised group stereotypes, it is on occasions possible for individuals to enact group-specific norms without conscious awareness of the fact that they are doing so (e.g. Bourdieu, 1984).

An Invisible Nation? The Conceivability of the English

There are a number of reasons to suppose that the English may be particularly likely to take their nationality for granted. Kohn (1940), for example, suggested that, due to the early unification of England in the eleventh century, "It became so deeply ingrained in the English mind that nationalism lost its problematic character with the English." However, other commentators, most notably Colley (1992) suggest that an "English" identity actually developed relatively late historically, after the development of the identity of "Briton". Others warn against anachronistic attempts to attribute "nationalism" to medieval England, suggesting instead that "by some definitions of nationalism, the English . . . never properly experienced it at all" (Best, 1982, 12).

A second possibility is that the non-salience of Englishness may be attributed to the security of the national category. Certainly, the English often conceive of Britain in terms of an "enviable stability", unrocked by occupation, defeat in war or internal revolution (Anderson, 1992; Nairn, 1988). In contrast, Scotland, Wales and, in particular, Northern Ireland still have folk memories of English invasion which render their own national identities less secure. This assumption of English/British stability and historical continuity is reflected, albeit in an oblique form, in popular constructions of England as "traditional", "conservative" and the often anachronistic stereotypes of English folk and ways of life. It would, however, be unwise to regard national "stability" as a prior historical fact which precluded the English from ever conceiving of cognitive alternatives to the *status quo*. The English British have also experienced potential crises such as war and class conflict (Anderson, 1992), and Nairn (1977) suggests that the British state was regarded as precarious even in the heyday of Empire. Moreover, there have clearly been historical moments in which English/British national identity has not been "thought-lessly" taken for granted (in particular in periods during, and in the aftermath of, war—see Chambers, 1989). As Colls (1986) argued: "The obverse of a nation which is insisted upon as solid is a nation feared as fragile" (p. 29). Rather than assuming English/British stability "is an historical given one might instead enquire how this image of national security has been socially accomplished. There is some evidence of political attempts to construct a notion of English British "stability" through reference to historical continuity (Chambers, 1989; Samuel, 1989b). Moreover, historical work suggests that the "fact" that England appears to encapsulate qualities of permanence and stability may be due to the ability of the category to be rendered strategically invisible at times of potential crisis. This ability to "vanish into thin air" (Tajfel, 1982) has meant that potential "national" threats such as immigration and European integration have been generally constructed as threatening to the integrity of "Britain" rather than of "England" (Crick, 1991; Donald, 1990).

One of the major findings of the stereotyping studies was that respondents constructed highly heterogenous images of the English. Although it is common to regard images of group heterogeneity as the consequence of automatic psychological processes, it is possible to argue that the construct of English heterogeneity may be regarded as an ideological accomplishment. Historically, the British Empire was constructed in terms of a valued ethnic diversity, and the English constructed histories which represented themselves as an (originally) ethnically diverse people, a "glorious amalgam" (see Strathern, 1992). A construct which has, perhaps, proved to have more historical vitality (and is apparent in the responses to my studies) is the notion of the English as fundamentally diversified in terms of social class (Nairn, 1977; Anderson, 1992). It is possible that the widespread perception of the British/English as diversified in terms of class and "race" may have precluded the development of a sense of "horizontal community" (Anderson, 1983) which some theorists have regarded as the basis of the construct of nation. Historians have also noted the ways in which the English have, at various times, come to regard themselves as a heterogeneous "nation of individualists". Samuel (1989a), for example, traces "English" values of individualism to the Puritan revolution which encouraged sectarianism and religious tolerance. He suggests that, as a consequence, English people may have been encouraged to define themselves as individuals against the national polity.

Although the perception of internal heterogeneity may mitigate the conceiva-bility of the English British as a national unity, the situation may, in fact, be more complex. It is, of course, common for social identity theorists to regard a perception of self and others in terms of "individual differences" as functionally distinct from a conception of self or others in terms of category (e.g. national) membership (Tajfel, 1978; Turner, 1987). However, the possibility that a category (in this case the English) may regard individualism as distinctive, normative, *group* behaviour suggests that there may be problems in this distinction. Let us consider, for example, the following extract from a public address by Stanley Baldwin in 1924:

> in no nation more than the English is there a diversified individuality. We are a people of character . . . let us see to it that we never allow our individuality as Englishmen to be steam-rollered. The preservation of the individuality of the Englishman is essential to the preservation of the type of the race, and if our differences are smoothed out and we lose that great gift, we shall lose at the same time our power. Uniformity of type is a bad thing.

> (p. 5)

Baldwin, like many others of his time, regards heterogeneity (the existence of "a diversified individuality") as a positive, *distinctively English* attribute. It is not clear that respondents in my studies, conducted in the early 1990s, shared this sort of self-conscious construction of English superiority-in-diversity, nevertheless it may be that their behaviour in presenting the English in terms of a diverse array of types, traits and habits reflects this cultural legacy. The fact that internal heterogeneity may (even if in the past) have been regarded as a *distinctively* English attribute raises some interesting issues for social identity theorists. Many theorists, following Turner (1987), suggest that social identification leads to self-stereotyping which, in turn, leads to *identical* behaviour on the part of individual group members (see Condor, 1990). However, if a group regards itself as characterised by internal heterogeneity, then it follows that a consequence of social identification might be the adoption of a range of diverse ("eccentric") behaviours on the part of individual group members. The consequence may be that, paradoxically, the existence of the group, and of group-typical behaviour, may thus become functionally invisible.

Perhaps the most commonly-cited reason why the English British might take their national identity for granted, is the fact that they constitute a "dominant" national group, both in terms of (past) Imperial and world dominance and in terms of (current) economic and cultural dominance of the UK. Social psychologists often assume that group membership may be less salient to members of dominant social groups. The behaviour of respondents in my studies on national identity certainly appears to parallel that of "dominant" group members in so far as they chose to represent themselves as individuals rather than in terms of group membership (Deschamps, 1982).

It is often suggested that such a lack of group-awareness on the part of members of dominant social groups may be a consequence (intended or otherwise) of ideological hegemony. There are clearly contexts in which the English construct cultural images which present themselves as "normal" and unexceptional, and other nationalities, including the Scottish, Welsh and Irish, as "different" (one only has to think of those jokes which begin, "An Englishman, a Scotsman and an Irishman walk into a bar . . ."). It is possible that some of the features of subjects' responses in my studies may reflect such a tendency to assume Englishness as unexceptional. It was notable that, in attempting to characterise England, respondents very often referred to images of the nation as it appeared to, or was represented by, "foreigners". Their stereotypes of the English also appeared to rely on "second-hand" images (anachronistic Hollywood clichés, literary figures) rather than personal experience or belief. Although the apparent blindness of the English to their own national identity may be partly attributable to cultural dominance, we should not overlook the complexities of this process. The English do not wield hegemonic control over some closed cultural system. In their everyday lives, the English are themselves confronted with images which present other nations (particularly the USA) as the norm.

It is also possible to regard the non-salience of English national identity as an ideological achievement by the English as a dominant social group. Historical analysis suggests that, in order to achieve political stability, the governing class of the British Empire adopted a tactic of "toleration" which often involved the stimulation of cultural identities of the various sub-ordinated constituent nations, and a corresponding tendency to down-play the distinctiveness of the English (Nairn, 1977). For example, during Victorian times there developed a picturesque notion of Scottish culture which enabled a celebration of Scottish identity without at the same time posing any threat to the State. The construction of such images need not necessarily be seen as conspiratorial (Pittock, 1991), but they did create positive national distinctive-ness for subordinate groups which may ultimately have worked in the political interests of the English (cf. van Knippenberg, 1978). Similar official tendencies to down-play the existence of distinctive English interests or cultural forms have also been apparent more recently. Nairn (1988), for example, notes that the Investiture of the Prince of Wales,

> took the form of a non-ethnic parade in which "England" was entirely and mysteriously absent, while Welshness was patted on the head.
>
> (p. 227)

and Strathern (1992) notes that when the 1987 Macdonald enquiry (which was set up to look at racial violence in Manchester schools) set about suggesting positive images of various ethnic groups, they found it virtually impossible to identify a constructive image of "the English". Although there is no necessary one-to-one correspondence between "culture" as crafted by intellectuals and politicians, and "culture" as lived by ordinary individuals, nevertheless the provision of vehicles for, and barriers to, the expression of national identities is likely to affect popular culture and experience. It is likely that the current dearth of symbols of Englishness constrains the everyday expression and, possibly the conceptualisation, of a distinctive English national identity.

Reference to English "dominance" does not, however, provide a simple solution to the problem of the (reported) non-salience of English national identity in my studies. Rather, it raises a complex set of questions concerning the bases upon which the English can, in fact, be said to constitute a "dominant" national group. One important issue concerns who is to be granted authority to decide on whether a group is "dominant" or "sub-ordinate". Is this decided on the basis of objective (social scientific) criteria? Or (as social identity theorists would apparently suggest) on the basis of the subjective representations of the social actors themselves? This presents an analytic problem in so far as that members of dominant or subordinate social groups do not necessarily recognise the objective status of their groups, and different group members may hold divergent perceptions of the power and status of their group (Condor, 1989). In the case of the present studies, it was not clear that the respondents did regard England as a "dominant" group— one prevalent representation of the nation focused on weakness and decline (which was possibly attributable to the fact that respondents tended sponta-neously to describe "England" in comparison to nations outside the UK). In many respects, respondents' behaviour (the group derogation, the resistance to self-categorisation or identification) could be interpreted as typical of mem-bers of *low*-status social groups.

Another possibility is that respondents *did* regard England as a high-status group in the international arena, but regarded this status as illegitimate. Certainly, respondents often expressed a sense of guilt and shame with respect to the *idea* of English/British superiority. Moreover, respondents commonly expressed values of human equality and of individualism which were seen to be antithetical to the value of nationalism. Although social identity theory does allow for the possibility that, through a conflict of values, people who regard themselves as members of high status groups may regard their social position as illegitimate (e.g. Turner and Brown, 1978), this is rarely followed through in the course of research. Rather, it is commonly assumed that intergroup behaviour may be reduced to a simple quest for status (cf. Hogg and Abrams, 1990), and that members of "dominant" or "high status" groups will contentedly bask in reflected glory.[9]

The issue of status also forces us to confront the possibility that group images (stereotypes, social representations and so forth) need not be seen simply as reports of subjective processes. They may also constitute aspects of strategic rhetoric designed to maintain or enhance the relative standing of one's group (Condor, 1990; van Knippenberg, 1978). This raises a third possibility: that the respondents in my studies did regard their nation as "high status" or "dominant", and that their construction of England as a sad little country in tragic decline populated by vulgar or derisible people, was designed to preclude challenges to the status quo.

Pride and Prejudice: the Social Functions of the English Autostereotype

In this final section of the chapter I shall focus on two aspects of the English autostereotype: the "grotesque" characteristic of "patriotism", and the "normative" characteristic of "good manners". I shall explore the possibility that the functional invisibility of English national identity—the general failure of my respondents to demonstrate national identification or pride might, paradoxically, reflect the respondents' self-application of norms of "correct" English behaviour.

Patriotism

It will be recalled that respondents in my studies regarded "patriotism" and "nationalism" as particularly characteristic of "the English" (and of "the British"). However, this was not a "normative" image in the sense that it constituted a template for English behaviour. Rather, it was discussed as a shameful possibility. A commonly cited character was the monstrous "lager lout": the football hooligan or package tourist, toting Union Jack boxer shorts and proclaiming English ethnic superiority. Respondents also expressed a more general abhorrence of nationalism and patriotism which they associated with that great anathema of the modern West, "prejudice" (Billig *et al.*, 1988).

Manners and Politeness

If "patriotism" is regarded as a monstrous possibility, "manners" and "politeness" are regarded as positive (although possibly archaic and slightly humorous) aspects of English National Character. "Manners" are, of course, associated with norms of social performance and, in particular, may be seen to legitimate forms of inauthenticity.[10] It may be that one of the reasons why nationalism and patriotism are regarded as shameful is that the *open demonstration* of national pride, is seen to violate the (specifically English) norm of polite conduct. In this respect it is worth noting the extent to which respondents in my studies tended to display a sense of "public" national self-awareness, focusing on the *appearance* of England and of English folk to outsiders. The grotesque Little Englander was typically discussed in terms of his *visible* actions (most particularly the public display of the Union Jack) which were seen to constitute an affront to others.

If the public display of national pride is seen as unmannerly, it follows that a performance of the normative English stereotype may involve the demonstration of *non*-patriotic behaviour. The fact that a group that espouses norms of mannerly conduct may, as a paradoxical consequence, enact a social identification by apparently failing to enact a social identification poses serious questions for the methods typically used by social identity theorists which assume that the performance of social identities necessarily takes transparent forms (Abrams, 1990).

Symbolic Patriotism

A number of commentators have described how, in an attempt to avoid the stigma of "prejudice", people may voice racist sentiments in subtle ways (Barker, 1981; McConahay, 1986). Rather than openly expressing attitudes which demean other people, racist sentiments may be expressed in terms of general cultural values. Thus, for example, racial segregation or repatriation may be advocated on the basis that the action or "demands" of Black people violate general liberal norms of equality.

A parallel form of this process may be identified in the nationalist discourse of the English. We have already noted that, possibly as a consequence of the English norm of "manners", English people may deny feelings of national identity and pride. They may even, on occasions, demonstrate their lack of nationalistic "prejudice" by expressing derogatory attitudes towards their own nation. It is, nevertheless, possible to identify more subtle ways in which, under such circumstances, English people may express notions of national superiority. There is a subtle and (in my experience) pervasive argument which goes as follows:

1. National identity is largely irrelevant to me.
2. I am not ethnocentric: the English have many negative traits
3. However, although they are often "better than us" in many respects "other people" demonstrate a deplorable nationalism and ethnocentrism.
4. Therefore, it follows, that "we" are better than "them" in so far as we are not as ethnocentric as "them".

As an example of this process in operation, let us consider the following conversation with a middle-aged couple whom I interviewed at Manchester Airport. The interview was ostensibly about the Channel Tunnel:

Ken: Well, I think that [. . .] in general, I think that it's a good thing to have more contact with Europe. It might stop us thinking we're the best.

Hannah: Yes, I agree. But then, those countries [. . .] well, a United Europe seems to have made things worse in some places, don't you think? When you go to other countries, there seems to be an awful lot of nationalism rammed down your throat.

Ken: Yes, I wouldn't like it if it meant that the English got more nationalistic, like the French, say, are now. Or other European [inaudible], for that matter. I wouldn't like it for England to get like that.

Hannah: Yea. It's not like, well it's not like there's any excuse. Some countries, like in Eastern Europe, well, you can understand it. Wales, too. I can understand the Welsh wanting some national pride. But not places like France and Germany. I wouldn't like to see England getting like that. A nation of lager louts.

Ken: But thinking of Europe, even they're not as bad as America.

Hannah: No and it would be awful if England got like that. It wouldn't be nice at all.

This conversation illustrates the subtle nature that expressions of English national pride can take. It is never openly suggested that England is "better than" other countries. Rather, it is implied that, through their open demonstration of nationalistic sentiment, the advanced industrial nations of Europe and the United States are contravening a universal value (it is "not nice"). England, by contrast, is "not like that". An interesting feature of this conversation is the suggestion that what is important is not the *feeling* of national pride, so much as the *expression* of that sentiment, especially in the presence of "outsiders (Hannah speaks of nationalism being "rammed down your throat").

The importance of the performative aspect of nationalism is expressed more clearly in my second illustrative example. This is taken from a (relatively naturally-occurring) conversation taped in one of my undergraduate seminar groups. In this part of the conversation two English students who had been on an exchange scheme to the USA are describing their experiences:

Carole: The thing is, they keep going on about how they are great, and all that. How they are the best.

Marie: Yea.

Carole: In front of us, you know. Telling us that they're the best country in the world and all that.

Marie: Yea. All the time.

Carole: Here, in England, you don't . . . well, when they come here we might secretly think we're great, but we wouldn't say it.

Marie: No, we don't say it. And we don't say to JYAs [students from the USA], you know, England, it's so great, it's better than America.

Carole: That doesn't mean that we don't secretly think that it is.

Marie: No, but, you know, students here they wouldn't go about boasting like that. They wouldn't say it.

In this case it is clear that the basis for negative social comparison between the USA and "England" (which might, in this conversation also stand for "Britain" or "we at Lancaster University") is the *performance*, the public expression, of nationalist sentiments. The difference between "us" and "America" is that (although "we" might secretly think "ourselves" better) "we" do not engage in public displays of national pride ("boasting"). Once again, the implicit argument seems to be that, as a nation, "we" are better than "them", on the ground that "we" are not as (overtly) nationalistic as "them".

Notes

1. The construct of an "indigenous English" is, of course, highly problematic. For the purposes of this chapter, I shall be focusing my attention on those individuals whose "identity" (objectively-defined) as English is relatively unambiguous. That is to say, individuals who belong to the white majority, who were born in England of English parents, and who have not lived outside England for any extended length of time.

2. Other authors have suggested that, of the national groups of the UK, the English may be the most reluctant to accept the term "British" as self-descriptive (Crick, 1991).

3. Even the British "national anthem" is, in fact, a hymn to monarchy rather than to nation.

4. It is common for relatively sophisticated commentators to overlook the potential for contextual variation in the expression of national identity and sentiment. For example, researchers often suggest that observations of the expression of particular forms of national sentiment in the context of football spectatorship, or as evidenced in newspaper reporting, can inform us about English/British identity tout court (e.g. Kellas, 1991).

5. Britain has no "national" sports team, except the "British Lions", which include Southern Ireland.

6. There was no evidence that respondents in any of the studies I report in this chapter distinguished between "patriotism" and "nationalism" (cf. de Roose, 1992).

7. For example, in the methods section of their paper, Eagly and Kite (1987) claim to have studied stereotypes of a number of "nationalities" including "Great Britain" but in the results section, there is mention only of subjects' responses to the category "English".

8. The following analysis assumes that the phenomena observed in these studies are likely to be peculiar to English respondents. In the absence of comparative data from other national groups, this assumption is, of course, provisional.

9. It may be that the failure of social scientists to research and write on English national identity reflects similar assumptions, based both on commonsense and on a knowledge of the rhetorical uses to which notions of Englishness have been put by political thinkers such as Enoch Powell (see Nairn, 1977). It may be that there is an underlying assumption on the part of liberal social scientists that any serious intellectual consideration of Englishness would constitute an affront to minorities.

10. As an aside, it might be noted that inauthenticity appears to constitute an important feature of the performance of an English Character in other respects as well. For example, the Norm of Humour enables positive group images to be presented as-if-ironically (e.g. to be associated with an apparently humorous stock character, or to be presented as laughably anachronistic) thus avoiding the appearance of ethnocentrism.

References

Abrams, D. (1990). How do group members regulate their behaviour? In D. Abrams and M. Hogg (eds), *Social Identity Theory: Constructive and Critical Advances*. Brighton: Harvester-Wheatsheaf.

Anderson, B. (1983). *Imagined Communities: Reflections on the Origin and Spread of Nationalism*. London: Verso.

Anderson, P. (1992). *English Questions*. London: Verso.

Baldwin, S. (1924/1926). "England" Address presented at the annual dinner of the Royal Society of St.George, at the Hotel Cecil. Reprinted in: *On England and Other Addresses*. London: Phillip Allan & Co.

Barker, M. (1981). *The New Racism*. London: Junction Books.

Best, G. (1982). *Honour among Men and Nations: Transformations of an Idea*. Toronto University of Toronto Press.

Billig, M., Condor, S., Edwards, D., Gane, M., Middleton, D. and Radley, A. (1988). *Ideological Dilemmas: A Social Psychology of Everyday Thinking*. London: Sage.

Billig, M. *Nationalism as an international ideology: Imagining the nation, others and the world of nations*.

Blake, R. (ed.)(1982). *The English World: History, Character and People*. London: Thames & Hudson.

Bommes, M. and Wright, P. (1982). "Charms of residence": the public and the past. In Centre for Contemporary Cultural Studies, *Making Histories: Studies in History-writing and Politics*. London: Hutchinson.

Bourdieu, P. (1984). *Distinction: A Social Critique of the Judgement of Taste*. London: Routledge.

Brennan, T. (1990). The national longing for form. In H. Bhabha (ed.), *Nation and narration*. London: Routledge.

Buchanan, W. (1951). Stereotypes and tensions as revealed by the UNESCO international poll. *International Social Science Bulletin*, **3**, 515–28.

Buchanan, W. and Cantril, H. (1953). *How Nations See Each Other*. Urbana: University of Illinois Press.

Chambers, T. (1989). Narratives of nationalism: being "British". *New Formations*, **7**, 83–103.

Clifton, A., McGrath, D., and Wick, B. (1976). Stereotypes of woman: a single category? *Sex Roles*, **2**, 135–48.

Coetzee, F. (1992). English nationalism and the first world war. *History of European Ideas*, **15**, 363–8.

Colley, L. (1992). *Britons: Forging the Nation 1707–1837*. New Haven CT: Yale University Press.

Colls, R. (1986). Englishness and political culture. In R. Colls and P. Dodd (eds), *Englishness: Politics and culture 1880–1920*. London: Croom Helm.

Colls, R. and Dodd, P. (1986). *Englishness: Politics and Culture 1880–1920*. London: Croom Helm.

Condor, S. (1989). "Biting into the future": social change and the social identity of women. In S. Skevington and D. Baker (eds), *The Social Identity of Women*. London: Sage.

Condor, S. (1990). Social stereotypes and social identity. In D. Abrams and M. Hogg (eds), *Social Identity Theory: Constructive and Critical Advances*. Brighton: Harvester Wheatsheaf.

Condor, S. (forthcoming (a)). Democracy and the British national character. To appear in C. Barfoot (ed.), *National and Ethnic Stereotypes*.

Condor, S. (forthcoming (b)). "And So Say All of Us"?: Some thoughts on "experiential democratization" as an aim for critical social psychologists. To appear in T. Ibanez and L. Ineguez (eds), *Critical Social Psychology*. London: Sage.

Crick, B. (1991). The English and the British. In B. Crick (ed.), *National Identities: The Constitution of the United Kingdom*. London: Blackwell.

Deaux, K., Winton, W., Crowley, M. and Lewis, L. (1985). Level of categorization and content of gender stereotypes. *Social Cognition*, **3**, 145–67.

De Roose, F. (1992). The politics of patriotism. *History of European Ideas*, **15**, 55–9.

Deschamps, J-C. (1982). Social identity and relations of power between groups. In H. Tajfel (ed.), *Social Identity and Intergroup Relations*. Cambridge: Cambridge University Press.

Diehl, M. and Jonas, K. (1991). Measures of national stereotypes as predictors of the latencies of inductive versus deductive judgements. *European Journal of Social Psychology*, **21**, 317–30.

Donald, J. (1990). How English is it?: popular literature and national culture. *New Formations*, **12**, 31–47.

Eagly, A. and Kite, M. (1987). Are stereotypes of nationalities applied to both women and men? *Journal of Personality and Social Psychology*, **53**, 451–62.

Feldman, D. (1989). Jews in London, 1880–1914. In R. Samuel (ed.), *Patriotism: The Making and Unmaking of British National Identity (Vol II: Minorities and Outsiders)*. London: Routledge.

Gellner, E. (1983). *Nations and Nationalism*. Oxford: Blackwell.

Giddens, A. (1985). *The Nation-state and Violence*. Cambridge: Polity Press.

Gilroy, P. (1987). *The Ain't no Black in the Union*. London: Hutchinson.

Hall, S. (1992). The question of cultural identity. In S. Hall, D. Held and T. McGrew (eds), *Modernity and Its Futures*. Cambridge: Polity.

Hobsbawm, E. and Ringer, T. (eds)(1983). *Invention of Tradition*. Cambridge: Cambridge University Press.

Hogg, M. and Abrams, D. (1990). Social motivation, self-esteem and social identity. In D. Abrams and M. Hogg (eds), *Social Identity Theory: Constructive and Critical Advances*. Brighton: Harvester Wheatsheaf.

Hopkins, N. and Reicher, S. The construction of social categories and processes of social change: arguing about national identities.

Howkins, (1986). The discovery of rural England. In R. Colls and P. Dodd (eds), *Englishness: Politics and Culture 1880–1920*. London: Croom Helm.

James, W. (1989). The making of black identities. In R. Samuel (ed.), *Patriotism: The Making and Unmaking of British National Identity (Vol II: Minorities and Outsiders)*. London: Routledge.

Katz, D. and Braly, K. (1933). Racial stereotypes of one hundred college students. *Journal of Abnormal and Social Psychology*, **28**, 280–90.

Kearney, H. (1991). Four nations or one? In B. Crick (ed.), *National Identities: The Constitution of the United Kingdom*. London: Blackwell.

Kellas, J. (1991). *The Politics of Nationalism and Ethnicity*. London: Macmillan.

Kelly, A. (1989). Ethnic identification, association and redefinition: Muslim Pakistanis and Greek Cypriots in Britain. In K. Liebkind (ed.), *New Identities in Europe: Immigrant Ancestry and the Ethnic Identity of Youth*. London: Gower.

Kohn, H. (1940). The genesis and character of English nationalism. *Journal of the History of Ideas*, **1**, 69–94.

Langford (1989). A polite and commercial People: England 1727–1783. Oxford: Clarendon Press.

MacIntyre, A. (1981). *After Virtue*. Notre Dame: University of Notre Dame Press.

Mackay, J. and Thane, P. (1986). The Englishwoman. In R. Colls and P. Dodd (eds), *Englishness: Politics and Culture 1880–1920*. London: Macfarlaine, A. (1978). *The Origins of English Individualism*.

Marquand, D. (1991). Nations, regions and Europe. In B. Crick (ed.), *National Identity: The Constitution of the United Kingdom*. London: Blackwell.

Marques, J. (1990). The black-sheep effect: out-group homogeneity in social comparison settings. In D. Abrams and M. Hogg (eds), *Social Identity Theory: Constructive and Critical Advances*. Brighton: Harvester Wheatsheaf.

McConahay, J. and Hough, J. (1976). Symbolic racism. *Journal of Social Issues*, **32**, 23–45.

Nairn, T. (1977). *The Break-up of Britain: Crisis and Neo-nationalism*. London: New Left Books.

Nairn, T. (1988). *The Enchanted Glass: Britain and its Monarchy*. London: Century Hutchinson.

Newman, G. (1987). *Rise of English Nationalism: A Cultural History 1740–1830*. London: Weidenfeld & Nicolson.

Pittock, M. (1991). *The Invention of Scotland: The Stuart Myth and the Scottish Identity 1638 to the Present*. London: Routledge.

Plamenatz, J. (1973). Two types of nationalism. In E. Kamenka (ed.), *Nationalism, the Nature and Evolution of an Idea*. London:

Porter, R. (ed.)(1992). *Myths of the English*. Cambridge: Polity Press.

Potter, J. and Wetherell, M. (1987). *Discourse and Social Psychology: Beyond Attitudes and Behaviour*. London: Sage.

Reicher, S. (1991). Mad dogs and Englishmen? telling tales from the Gulf. Paper presented to the British Association, "Science 91" meeting, Plymouth, August.

Samuel, R. (1989a). Introduction: exciting to be English. In R. Samuel (ed.), *Patriotism: The Making and Unmaking of British National Identity (Volume 1: History and Politics)* London: Routledge.

Samuel, R. (1989b). Continuous national history. In R. Samuel (ed.), *Patriotism: The Making and Unmaking of British National Identity (Volume 1: History and Politics)*. London: Routledge.

Stallybrass, P. and White, A. (1986). *The Politics and Poetic of Transgression*. London: Methuen.

Strathern, M. (1992). *After Nature: English Kinship in the Late Twentieth Century*. Cambridge: Cambridge University Press.

Stone, L. and Stone, J. (1984). *An Open Elite? England 1540–1880*. Oxford: Clarendon Press.

Tajfel, H. (ed.) (1978). *Differentiation between Social Groups*. London: Academic Press.

Tajfel, H. (1981). *Human Groups and Social Categories: Studies in Social Psychology*. Cambridge: Cambridge University Press.

Tajfel, H. (1982). Instrumentality, identity and social comparisons. In H. Tajfel (ed.), *Social Identity and Intergroup Relations*. Cambridge: Cambridge University Press.

Turner, J. (1987). *Rediscovering the Social Group: A Self-categorization Theory*. Oxford: Blackwell.

Turner, J. and Brown, F. (1978). Social status, cognitive alternatives and intergroup relations. In H. Tajfel (ed.), *Differentiation between Social Groups*. London: Academic Press.

van Knippenberg, A. (1978). Status differences, comparative relevance and intergroup differentiation. In H. Tajfel (ed.), *Differentiation between Social Groups*. London: Academic Press.

Wiener, M. (1985). *English Culture and the Decline of the Industrial Spirit 1850–1980*. Harmondsworth: Penguin.

Williams, J. and Best, D. (1982). *Measuring Sex Stereotypes*. Beverley Hills: Sage.

Acknowledgement

I should like to thank Scott Lash, Steve Reicher and John Urry for their helpful comments on earlier versions of this chapter.

5

The Construction of Social Categories and Processes of Social Change: Arguing about National Identities

NICK HOPKINS and STEVE REICHER

Dundee University, Scotland and University of St Andrews, Scotland

Although stability is always temporary and more apparent than real, the last few years have seen quite dramatic transformations in Europe. In particular, the social and political maps of the "east" have been redrawn as several higher-order categories—e.g., the Soviet Union and Czechoslovakia—have collapsed. Meanwhile, in the "west", currently existing states face internal challenges from regionalist and nationalist movements while at the same time having to redefine themselves and their relations with each other as the European Community (EC) continues to develop.

Inextricably linked with these developments are transformations in people's representations of who they are and their relationship with others; categories and identities that were once routinely used in self-definition are in the process of being replaced by others which have very different meanings. For example, following the "Peaceful Divorce" in Czechoslovakia, self-categorisations as Czechoslovakian, with all that this entails for one's understanding of the social world, are no longer so relevant. Nor indeed can their meaning remain the same as in the relatively recent past. Put simply, the social context in which such a categorisation derives its meaning has changed; the adoption of a categorisation as Czechoslovakian when others define themselves as Slovak or Czech must now necessarily entail a definition of self in relation to these "newer" categories. Similarly the meaning of the categories Slovak or Czech cannot remain the same for the processes of nation-building require these to be redefined in contrast from each other (and indeed from the older Czechoslovakian order). But of course, it is not simply the case that such changes in self-definition occur in response to, or somehow "after the event" (e.g., after the "divorce"). Instead, changes in the way in which we construe ourselves and our relations with others are a crucial step in the very process of change itself; without such changes in representation, action which transforms the world cannot be pursued.

Although not quite so dramatic as the changes in eastern Europe, people in western Europe are also in the process of redefining themselves and their relations to others. In many respects these developments throughout the continent are inextricably linked. For example, as those others against whom we in the West compare and contrast ourselves are changed, so too it follows that we in the West may change in the ways in which we may conceive of ourselves. A rather different sort of linkage may also be identified. While Western European audiences watching television scenes of flag-waving crowds and demonstrations may not be able to experience directly the transformations in self-definition that participation in collective social protest may bring (Reicher, 1987), they can at the very least share in the realisation that change is possible. Indeed, the mere fact that change can be seen to occur, exposes social arrangements as contingent rather than as "natural" and may have the consequence of encouraging such audiences to view their own situation in a different light. As one leading Scottish nationalist observed, the previously unthinkable collapse of the Berlin Wall may mean that the "Berlin Walls" in the Scottish imagination are also rocked and alternative visions entertained.

The other significant development affecting the ways in which those in the West represent themselves and their relations with others is of course the EC. Perhaps more than ever before, the category "Europe" refers to a social/political category as well as a geographical area, and as the nature of the category and who is to count as belonging is transformed, people's understandings of how they can and should act are similarly changed. Lest anyone doubt the social significance of such category definitions one need only refer to the ways in which definitions of "Europe" which contrast the "West" from the "Rest" support racist acts (Balibar, 1991; Nederveen Pieterse, 1991; Webber, 1991). But of course the development of "Europe" has other consequences which are of particular relevance for this chapter's focus—the process of social change whereby social relations within current states are redefined. The idea of a "Europe of the regions" is a relatively recent construction which offers a very different vision of the nature of the categories that constitute Europe and the power relations between them (Harvie, 1994). The potential impact of such visions upon how people view themselves and their relationship with the current power structure are enormous, and it is interesting to note the high profile of "Europe" in many nationalist movements (see Lindsay, 1991, for an analysis of the "European" dimension in the Scottish National Party's thinking).

This chapter takes as its focus these processes of social change by exploring the case of a nationalist challenge to a current Western European state. Before considering the specifics of this nationalist project we consider social psychological analyses of self-categorisation and social change, identify some drawbacks in particular formulations, and suggest an alternative which we then illustrate.

Social Change and Social Identity

The concept of social identity is central to current social psychological theory. Initially developed in the guise of Social Identity Theory (SIT) as a means to explore intergroup relations and processes of social change (Tajfel, 1978, 1982; Tajfel and Turner, 1979) it made the point that people may define themselves as category members as well as in terms of their individuality and demonstrated that intergroup behaviour cannot be reduced to interpersonal behaviour (Hogg and Abrams, 1988; Tajfel, 1982; Turner, 1975). Recent work conducted by Turner and his co-workers (Turner, 1985; Turner et al., 1987; Turner et al., 1993) has addressed the wider question of what makes group behaviour, per se, possible and has focused on the social psychological nature and consequences of social categorisation. According to Self-Categorisation Theory (SCT) the psychological basis for group behaviour is the categorisation of self with others and a depersonalisation in perception with common-category members perceiving themselves to be equivalent/interchangeable and as different from equivalent/ interchangeable outgroup members. As a corollary, depersonalised perception determines collective behaviour with those defining themselves as category members self-stereotyping themselves in accordance with their representation of the category (Turner, 1985).

Although SIT and SCT are distinct theories addressing different questions both, quite rightly, view people's action as dependent upon their understandings of how they relate to others. This is quite explicit in SIT's approach to social change. According to the theory a subordinated group's action is contingent upon their perception of what is possible and legitimate in their relations with those constituting the established order. Particular attention is paid to the subordinated group's beliefs concerning the legitimacy and stability of the hierarchy, the permeability of the inter-category boundaries, the cognitive availability of alternative constructions of the groups' social relations, and the nature of their beliefs concerning social change (Tajfel and Turner, 1979). While having the undoubted merit of explaining the adoption of particular strategies of social change in terms of this matrix of possibilities, a key question remains to be addressed. Put simply, while strategies of social change are contingent upon beliefs about what is possible and legitimate we are still faced with explaining how such beliefs arise, i.e. how do people come to hold a particular representation of their place in the social world and their social relations with others rather than any number of others?

One possible way of addressing this question is to approach it as a question about how people come to adopt particular social categories as meaningful for their self-definition. As defining the self implies defining oneself in relation to others it follows that the adoption of a particular category necessarily involves a commitment to a particular model of social relations and, as a corollary, that we can approach the issue of the perception of social relations through exploring how people come to adopt particular categories (Reicher, 1993). By way of example, consider the categories of nation and class. On the one hand to define oneself in terms of a national category inevitably implies a matrix of social relations structured in terms of international relations and the pursuit of "the national interest". On the other hand, to define oneself in terms of a class categorisation implies a model of social relations bound up with class interests. If it is accepted that these categories imply particular definitions of how the world is structured and hence the forms of action that are possible given those social relations, then the issue of which category is adopted will have fundamental consequences for what actions are deemed possible. For example, if one defines oneself and others in terms of national categories, the strategies of action associated with a class categorisation (e.g. the labour movement's internationalist solidarity with overseas workers) are fundamentally irrelevant and redundant (Reicher, 1993). How then can we explain how particular categories come to be adopted?

The Salience and Definition of Social Categories

Turner *et al.* (1993) explain variations in self-categorisation as being a function of "accessibility" and "fit". "Accessibility" refers to the individual's readiness to use a particular category according to their goals, motives and past experiences. "Fit" takes two forms. The first, or "comparative fit", refers to the relationship between categories and the distribution of the stimuli that are to be categorised. It is explained through the concept of "meta-contrast" which states that stimuli are more likely to be categorised as an entity to the degree that the average differences between them are less than the average differences between them and the remaining stimuli that comprise the frame of reference. The second, or "normative fit", implies that if a particular categorisation is to be accepted as appropriate, there must be a congruency between the category's social meaning and the nature of the stimuli. As an illustration of these forms of fit consider the conditions in which gender categories would be used to represent a discussion between men and women; such categories would be meaningful if all the males said one thing and all the females another (comparative fit) and the males and females took positions consonant with gender stereotypes (normative fit).

This formulation of self-categorisation has many advantages. Firstly, the theory rejects the view that the perception of self and others in terms of social categories is a form of distorted self-perception occasioned by information-processing capacity limitations (Oakes and Turner, 1990). Indeed, precisely because the theory recognises that people do act in terms of group memberships, it recognises that there are real patterned differences in behaviour that may meaningfully be represented in terms of social categories. Secondly, it implies that the self is not a fixed mental structure but the expression of a dynamic process of judgement in which the categorisation of self derives from the relationship of the perceiver to social reality. In other words, all self-categorisations are comparative and variable, dependent upon the nature of the frame of reference within which the self is to be defined. For example, as the extent of the comparative context is enlarged to include others that are more different from self, the individual's self-categorisation will become more inclusive to include those previously categorised as dissimilar (and vice versa). Thirdly, because the meta-contrast ratio is comparative it implies that both the selection of categories and their definition is dependent upon the context. Simply put, the category prototype (the position which best represents the intra-category similarities and inter-category differences) is dependent upon the frame of reference. This has been empirically demonstrated in recent studies; Australians' definition of what it means to be Australian depends upon whether they are judged in isolation or whether Americans are judged at the same time (Turner *et al.*, 1993). Similarly, Australian's perceptions of Americans depend upon whether Iraq or the Soviet Union is included in the frame of reference (Haslam *et al.*, 1992).

While this formulation has the great merit of recognising that the definition of self and others in terms of social categories is appropriate because of real patterned differences in behaviour, it is open to potential readings which imply that the social categories that are used to define the world may be automatically "read off" the social context by an isolated individual engaged in an internal cognitive act of computation. The problems of this reading may be illustrated by considering the example of the Gulf war. Reicher (Reicher, 1991, 1993; Reicher and Hopkins, 1993a, 1983b) argues that in order to make sense of this war one must identify the nature of the conflict and who was involved, and that these issues were far from clear. Was it a conflict between two adjacent dictatorships? Was it a conflict between a dictator and the rest of the world? Was it a conflict between the West and the Islamic world? The point here is that who was to be viewed as part of the context and indeed how their actions were to be construed is not a given but rather a site of argument. Firstly, there could be arguments about the range of the context, i.e. which actors and what actions should be included as constituting the context. Secondly, regardless of the degree of agreement over the range of actors and actions to be included there is the issue of the basis on which positions are to be judged to be similar or different. As Billig (1987) observes it is always possible to argue over which pieces of information should be selected for attention; the selection of one dimension as a basis for judging the similarity or difference between stimuli cannot be taken as "given" but is instead a site of argument. Put more concretely, when considering the reaction of Arab states, should we pay attention to their leaders' pronouncements or to those of spiritual leaders, or to the number and size of the pro- and anti-war demonstrations? (Reicher, 1991, 1993; Reicher and Hopkins,

1993a and 1993b). Thirdly, because we can deliberate over the meaning of any category and debate the nature of the dimensions that define any category, we can do much more with our categories than simply apply them to the stimulus world (Billig, 1987). Instead we can argue about a category's meaning and hence dispute its contextual relevance.

The overall logic of these observations is that analyses of category salience which tie categorisation to reality can be vulnerable to overly mechanical readings unless they explicitly treat the definition of that reality as other than as a non-problematic "given". To some degree SCT's vulnerability to such a mechanistic reading arises because the concept of "accessibility" (which does imply processes of choice and selection and which could highlight the role of human agency in construing the world) remains relatively undeveloped. A more general factor concerns the adoption of particular research methodologies. As Reicher (1993) observes, a methodology which pre-defines the nature of the social context and the dimensions along which people are to be judged necessarily positions the individual as a passive observer and renders them powerless to advance alternative constructions. In other words there is a danger that a methodology which constrains people's opportunity to argue may support an image of the social actor in which the ability to reconstruct and reinterpret the world is omitted. The problem of course is that without this ability to reconstruct the world and one's relations with others, actions that change that world are impossible, with the result that it becomes increasingly difficult to see how current theorising allows the conceptual space for the psychological processes needed for change. Recognising the role of argument is a first small step in restoring to people the agency that so many models of action neglect.

As we propose to illustrate this approach through material which makes considerable reference to categories of "nation" we now turn to the analysis of this category.

The Category "Nation" and the Meanings of National Identities

Anderson's (1983) analysis of the "nation" as an "imagined community" makes the point that the concept refers to a collective identity extending beyond the immediate context to include others that can never be known. In so doing he draws our attention to the social and material developments that have made such "imagined communities" possible. Historically, one of the most important was the emergence of a technological means of communicating and disseminating the concept and Anderson pays particular attention to the role played by developments in print media, e.g., the development of "national" newspapers. A second historical development was the emergence of a concept of time which allowed the different constituents of the community to be imagined as acting simultaneously. Again, Anderson observes that this only emerged in the relatively recent past. Thirdly, he explores how the correspondence between the boundaries of opportunity (e.g.

the limits to one's geographical and social mobility) and the boundaries of the imagined community was an important determinant of national consciousness. The observation that the "nation" does not only exist in the imagination but also in practice once again emphasises the intimate relationship between representation and action; just as particular self-categorisations define what action is possible so one's experience of what is possible may support and sustain the development and maintenance of particular self-categorisations.

"Nations" are not then as Walter Bagehot thought "as old as history" (1872, 1872; cited in Connor) but much more modern social constructions (Anderson, 1983, Gellner, 1983; Nairn, 1977). However, awareness of this modernity should not lead us to dismiss such categories as meaningless. Indeed, the concept "nation" has distinctive meanings which make it distinctively powerful. One of the most important is the idea of an horizontal comradeship in which all the members of a community are bound together despite material inequality. Another is the idea that the nation came before "us" and continues to live on endlessly after "us". Indeed Anderson draws parallels between the national imagination and the religious imagination; although one is sacred and the other secular, both serve to mitigate death and suffering by "transforming fatality into continuity and by linking the dead with the yet to be born" (1983, 18). In similar vein Kitching (1985) highlights the category's distinctive meanings through contrasting nationalism with other political ideologies. Here he observes that while we have "national" Tombs of the Unknown Soldier (often complete with "eternal flames"), we do not have (and nor do we find it easy to imagine) a "Tomb of the Unknown Marxist" or a "Cenotaph for Fallen Liberals". As Kitching explains, the difference arises because neither Marxism nor Liberalism is much concerned with death and immortality, whereas the category "nation" most certainly is. That the category is bound up with notions of past, present and future, allows us to make some sense of the paradox of "the objective modernity of nations" on the one hand, and "their subjective antiquity in the eyes of nationalists" on the other (Anderson, 1983, 14). It also helps explain the "passionate" forms of action that action in accordance with this category can engender (Kitching, 1985).

Because nations are not "natural" or "given" but are instead social constructions (Jackson and Penrose, 1993), produced and reproduced through a series of social practices, it follows that we cannot accept that "national" identity exists "apart from" or "beneath" its social representation, or outside the conditions of its making (Macdonald, 1993). With these observations in mind historians and social anthropologists have paid particular attention to the processes whereby public life and culture are "nationalised" (Lofgren, 1989). One aspect of this project has been the study of how cultural flows are organised and transformed within national borders. Another is the study of how these cultural elements are turned into symbols of the "nation" (Alonso, 1988; Brow, 1990; Foster, 1991; Lofgren, 1989) and "national" traditions "invented" (Hobsbawm and Ranger, 1983). These analyses have not only explored the processes whereby particular constructions of who is to count as belonging and what it means to belong are given concrete expression (e.g. in museums or public rituals) but have also explored how these definitions are bound up with attempts to mobilise "the people" for or against particular political projects.

From a social-psychological perspective contests over the breadth and meaning of national categories can never be finished for, as Billig (1987) observes, categories are always invoked and defined in particular ways in the context of controversy and when there are alternatives. Indeed, even those ideas that are so thoroughly "nationalised" as to have the status of "national" myths (Samuel and Thompson 1990; and Tudor, 1972) remain sites of argument and interpretation to be used by one protagonist against another. Nor should this surprise us. Precisely because such myths are viewed as expressions of the nation's essence, the definition of such myths as congruent with particular political projects is a key step in gaining these projects' wider acceptance. By way of example consider the many uses to which the "myth" of Scottish "egalitarianism" may be put (this is exemplified by the mythology surrounding the "lad o'pairts"—a talented son of a crofter who has the opportunity to develop his talents and "progress" in society). It may be used by conservatives to imply that societal status is based upon merit (and that change is unnecessary); by nationalists to imply that class division is "alien" to Scottish society (and that all Scots should stand together avoiding the "siren calls" of class politics); or by socialists seeking to identify "radical" or "democratic" roots for their class politics in the Scottish psyche. As McCrone observes, "the flexibility of the myth derives from its neutrality; it is radical or conservative depending on its framing assumptions" (1992, 115). Similar observations have been made about the flexibility and ambivalence surrounding the Englishman's supposed freedom-loving, "anti-statism"; just as it may be argumentatively defined to support a popular mobilisation against fascism (as in the 1930s "Popular Front" strategy developed by the British Communist Party), so too it may be defined in ways that are supportive of a right-wing populism (e.g. Thatcherism). Or as Schwartz pithily observes "'the free-born Englishman defending his home' is abstract until we know who he is defending it from—Nazi invasion and fascism or Asians who have moved next door" (1982, 88).

In the remainder of this chapter we will explore how the relevance and nature of various social categories is a site of contestation. In general terms we have sought to achieve three things. Firstly, to demonstrate how different constructions of the social context may be advanced in order to support one form of categorisation over another. Secondly, to illustrate how the contents or meaning of these various categories is a site of debate. Thirdly, to explore the consequences of these various constructions for one's understanding of the social relations that constitute the social world and hence the appropriateness and legitimacy of particular courses of action.

Scotland, Britain and Europe

The material discussed below is taken from interviews and speeches given by activists, candidates and MPs before and after the 1992 General Election in Scotland. Throughout this time Scotland's relationship with the UK was high on the political agenda. With the exception of the (governing) Conservative Party, all of the major electoral parties in Scotland advocated constitutional change (ranging from the establishment of a Scottish Parliament within the framework of the UK, to the establishment of a totally separate state). The existing constitutional position dates from 1707 when Scotland joined with England and Wales in the United Kingdom under a treaty of Union. This guaranteed the continuation of Scotland's national institutions (e.g. the legal system) and made provision for Scottish representation in the Westminster Parliament.

Our analysis focuses on the constructions advanced by those seeking to maintain the status quo (the Conservative Party) and those advocating independent statehood (the Scottish National Party: SNP). Given these parties' political programmes we could expect different constructions of the context and the relevant social categories for action. More specifically we could expect the SNP to offer constructions which support self-categorisations in terms of the category Scotland while undermining those based upon Britain. With regard to the Conservatives we could expect constructions which undermine attempts to mobilise around "Scottishness" in the pursuit of social change and advance the category Britain as the basis for self-definition. Secondly, we could expect these spokespeople to offer different definitions of the meaning of these various categories. With the Conservatives seeking to maintain the Union we could expect constructions which define Scottishness and Britishness so as to be entirely compatible, thereby construing action in defence of the Union (the status quo) as both legitimate and appropriate. With the SNP's project of independence we could expect SNP spokespeople to define the categories in ways which identify incongruencies between Scotland and Britain, thereby legitimating particular strategies of social change. Further, given the importance of membership of the European Community in the SNP's policy ("Independence in Europe" was their campaign slogan), we could also expect arguments that define congruencies between being Scottish and European. Thirdly, we could expect arguments about the strategy of mobilising people around the category "nation". Here we will not only explore the constructions advanced by the SNP and the Conservatives but one advanced by a party advocating a very different form of social change (a non-electoralist party of the Left).

In order to explore these arguments about the relevance and meaning of national categories we have divided our analysis into two sections. In the first we will concentrate on how the proponents of change (the SNP) and the defenders of the status quo (the Conservatives) construe what national categories are relevant (i.e. Scotland versus Britain) and how these relate to each other and to Europe. In the second section we will consider how these parties and a non-electoralist party of the Left debate whether it is proper and acceptable to use national categories as the basis for political mobilisation.

Analysis

What National Categories?

In this section we explore how the SNP sought to make the people's Scottishness relevant for political self-definition and action while making Britishness irrelevant and how the Conservatives sought to make Britishness relevant while undermining the political relevance of Scottishness. In the light of our argument that the adoption of a particular categorisation rather than another is dependent upon processes of argumentation we pay particular attention to the way in which the meaning of the social context and the various categories is defined and the consequences of these definitions for the legitimacy of particular forms of action.

The SNP

1   Scotland as relevant

One way in which the category Scotland was advanced as a relevant basis for action was through locating the forthcoming election within an historical context of Scottish/English conflict. According to one SNP MP speaking at a pre-election public meeting this

> is an historic election and every one of us individually and collectively is on the spot in 1992. Just as in 1314 the political/military circumstances at that time put the nation on the spot at Bannockburn, this is the modern Bannockburn. We're not talking about crossing swords, we're talking about crossing a ballot paper. But the essential issues are exactly the same. There was no way off the Bannockburn field in 1314, you either stood or you ran away. It's exactly the same in 1992. We either stand up and face our responsibilities or we bow the knee to power south of the border.
>
> (Jim Sillars, speech, 26.3.92)

The construction of a parallel between the present and the past battle of Bannockburn (a key Scottish victory over the English army of Edward 1) construes the meaning of the election as being one of "national struggle" in which the category Scotland is relevant. Further, the structure to this construction implies that there is a continuity in the nature of the Scottish nation's struggle, thereby developing a sense of common-category membership which unites the present population of Scotland with those that fought against the English at Bannockburn. This is reinforced by his observations about the burden carried by "this generation" of Scots:

> now whether we are blessed or cursed, this generation, I don't know. I believe we should be blessed, that we are going to have on our shoulders, this generation alone ... the sole responsibility for deciding what is the future of Scotland. We are going to decide.

Here then is an example of how the distinctive meanings of the category "nation" allow a particular construction of the present. Because the concept "nation" implies the existence of a community of people flowing through time in pursuit of an historical project, it allows a construction of the present in which it is possible to talk of a generation having a responsibility to past and future generations of Scots. This not only illustrates some of the distinctive meanings of the category but also highlights the intimate relationship between definitions of the meaning of the context and the meanings associated with particular categories; just as arguments may define the context in such a way as to support particular categories, so too the meanings associated with particular categories may contribute towards the definition of the meaning of the context.

2   Britain as irrelevant

Another way in which the meaningfulness of the category Scotland was advanced was by undermining the meaningfulness of the superordinate category—Britain.

2a   Britishness as non-existent or as meaning Englishness

One strategy was to deny that the category could legitimately refer to a community of people; "there is a British state but there is not a British Nation. I think the Scots try to make it into one nation, they worked harder at it than the English. The English, the English never worked seriously at it at all" (SNP activist, interview). Another was to redefine the category British as referring to the English; "I'm a Scot and a European. 'British' I really see as being English" (SNP activist, interview) or "the United Kingdom is a fiction. It is in fact England with Scottish and Welsh appendages. It's the state of England" (SNP MP, interview). In similar vein another SNP MP argued that Britishness was essentially Englishness and that the Scots were subjected to "a massive propaganda effort" to make them think otherwise. These latter constructions not only deny the existence of a genuinely superordinate UK/British identity (rendering it meaningless as a basis for mobilisation) but also have the effect of construing Britishness as English domination and hence as constituting an anti-Scottishness.

2b   Englishness and Scottishness as incompatible

The incongruency between Scottishness and Britishness made possible by the above was developed as the categories of Scottishness and Englishness were defined as being fundamentally different. Consider this SNP MP's construction of a contrast between the Scottish and English psyches:

> The trouble with the Scots is that without their own government they therefore don't have a political system which actually reflects the true nature of the Scottish psyche. What I mean by that is that now we have policies in education, in law which are based on alien English ideas which are being imposed. For example, the Poll Tax, which is a very good example and privatisation of water are two issues being imposed upon Scotland by a minority Tory government on a basically English philosophy . . . the Scottish attitude to our institutions is fundamentally different from that in England. We still have a sense of community in Scotland.

(SNP MP, interview)

Of particular interest is the way in which the policies of the Conservative (or "Tory") government (e.g. the introduction of the "Poll tax"—a flat rate tax levied without regard for individuals' incomes) is construed as expressive of a "basically English philosophy" rather than (say) in terms of the government's class politics. With Englishness defined in these terms and Scottishness as its opposite ("a sense of community"), the incongruity between the national categories is clear. So too is the need for political autonomy; the absence of a "political system which actually reflects the true nature of the Scottish psyche" means that the essence of Scottishness is under attack from "English alien ideas". Again this construction not only constitutes an argument against the relevance of a self-definition in terms of Britishness but also advances a construction which supports the meaningfulness of the category Scotland. Indeed, all Scots are called to defend distinctively Scottish values against an alien ideology.

3   Scotland, Britain and Europe

Another construction of the incompatibility between Scottishness and Britishness was achieved in the context of discussions about Europe. Sometimes Europe was introduced in order to develop a contrast between Englishness and Scottishness (e.g. "so much of what is Scottish is much more firmly based in a European context" (SNP candidate, interview). Elsewhere, Europe was spoken about in the context of the SNP's policy of "Independence in Europe". Consider for example this SNP MEP's construction of Scotland's "European" status:

> In the community the view of the UK is that they are half-hearted. De Gaulle said years after UK entry; "England has not yet joined the community". For once I don't mind the misuse of the term "England". Scotland on the other hand is a European nation in spirit and history. Bruce's first act was to join the Hanseatic League. Our students went regularly to Leiden, Paris, Bologna, Valladolid. We have a Euro system of law. We had an Alliance with France for 800 years, with joint citizenship—a forerunner of the EC itself. In 1707 we got England and lost Europe. It was not a good bargain.
>
> (Ewing, speech, 25.9.93)

The overall consequence of this is to construe the relations between Scotland, Britain and Europe as problematic and in need of change. Indeed, this construction develops a congruency between Scotland and Europe at the same time as it develops an incongruency between Scottishness and Britishness. As a consequence it construes the social relations of the status quo as incongruent with Scotland's natural orientation and defines the SNP's strategy of social change as a return to a state which is more in keeping with the category's nature.

The Conservatives

1   Britain as relevant

While the SNP advanced constructions which served to fracture Britain into England and Scotland, Conservative spokespeople advanced constructions which cemented these categories together. One strategy was to define the social context in such as way as to foreground the commonalities of the United Kingdom. Take for example the constructions advanced by the Prime Minister:

> People across the world now look to Britain. We are giving a lead to others in crises and difficulties in every part of the globe ... The Union is I believe the rock on which this Kingdom's authority rests. Standing together we have moulded the history of much of the world. Separating or separated we would be tossed on its tides.
>
> (John Major, speech, 25.3.92)

> Our admirers and our rivals across the world ..think that we are mad. . . Can you, dare you, conceive of it? Consider the outcome. The walls of this island fortress that appear so strong, undermined from within; the United Kingdom untied; the bonds that generations of our enemies have fought and failed to break, loosened by ourselves.
>
> (John Major, speech, 5.4.92)

This construction widens the frame of reference that constitutes the context to include other national categories and so allows the Prime Minister to identify and foreground commonalities that unite the elements of the UK in contrast from others. Further, the Prime Minister's construction of the common category of the UK in terms of its solidity and the international context in terms of its turbulence, has the effect of making the category especially meaningful and worthy of defence. Indeed he continues to appeal to all inhabitants of the UK as Britons: "Wake up, my fellow countrymen. Wake up now, before it is too late" (5.4.92). The Union "is quite literally the national issue" (30.3.92) which "grips our very being as the British people" . . . "there is no division in the British flag between red and blue. In it and under it we are one people" (5.4.92). (This latter is a reference to the "Union Jack" which contains the blue of the Scottish flag and the red of the English flag.)

2   Scotland as irrelevant

2a   Scotland as non-existent

One way of undermining the SNP's construction of the election as being about deciding Scotland's future (and hence undermining the contextual relevance of the categories of England and Scotland) was to challenge the idea that it was actually possible to mobilise people as Scots. One MP argued:

> If the British constitution is to be changed it is the British people who must decide . . . The Scots, the English, . . . the mixed Scots and English and Irish all mixed up in marriages. I mean I'm a twelfth English! We must all have the right, not just because we happen to be resident above a certain parallel like the 48th parallel in Korea. See, before the Union the Scots lived north, you know the milk chocolate lived one side and the plain chocolate lived the other. Now it's liquorice allsorts in the whole jar. You can't just draw a line in the jar and say the liquorice allsorts above it are Scots liquorice allsorts and the ones below it are English liquorice allsorts. They're not.
>
> (Conservative MP, interview)

With Scottish and English no longer existing as discrete peoples associated with a geographic territory (a key association in "national" discourse), and no rationale for differentiating between those above and below an arbitrary border, any sense of the election being about Scots and English is undermined. Indeed, this construction implies that attempts to mobilise people in Scotland on the basis of their "Scottishness" is quite meaningless; whatever the election in Scotland is to be about it cannot be about the Scottish people declaring independence for the people in Scotland (and England) are so intermingled that they can only be meaningfully described as British.

2b Scottishness and Britishness as compatible

Another way of undermining the political relevance of Scottishness is to present it as entirely congruent with Britishness. One formulation of this congruency was to define Scottishness as a basic "lower-order" identity that all Scots have as a "natural" part of their make-up. One put it like this:

> Yes I'm Scottish, we're all Scottish. I'm as Scottish as any one else but I stand for the party of Union ... [independence] is not going to make me more Scottish, it's not going to make anybody more Scottish ... It's like Dundee is part of Scotland, Scotland is part of the UK, the UK is part of Europe and Europe is part of the international structure and I think that the nearer you come down to the bottom, you're just coming to what's sort of inbred and inherent and this sense of belonging. And I think everyone in Europe would have that but it doesn't mean to say they're any less European.

> (Conservative candidate, interview)

Here any contradiction between Scottishness and Britishness is denied through a construction of the former as an "inbred and inherent" "sense of belonging" that has a natural existence regardless of personal politics and the superstructure of the state. Interestingly, whereas the SNP used "Europe" in order to construct a contrast between Scotland and England, this construction uses Europe in order to advance the argument that different levels of identification are entirely possible. Indeed, the fact that the category "Europe" is a category associated with "the future" allows those using this construction to advance the status quo (Scotland's membership of the UK) as in keeping with the flow of history; "it's interesting in all the talk about Europe, we've been practising it for 300 years! We can tell them all about it." (Conservative MP, interview)

Other speakers sought to construct a Scottish/British congruency through arguing that membership of the UK allowed Scottishness to flourish. For example, one Government Minister argued:

> We are Scotland's oldest political party, we have been serving Scotland for nearly 300 years— long before the Labour or SNP parties were a gleam in their founders' eyes. Our party has an honourable and legitimate Scottish view point to put to the electorate ... Advocates of change have in the past been inclined to claim the emotional high-ground about the future of Scotland. They parade their Scottishness as unique to their cause. I yield to no-one in my Scottishness and believe that I do have some understanding of the needs and aspirations of the people of Scotland. I therefore yield the high-ground to none. It is not anti-Scottish to be for the Union, rather it is anti-Scottish to put the future of Scotland at risk ... For all of us who love Scotland, let us ensure her continuing place as a full partner within the United Kingdom.

> (Lord Makay, 6.3.92)

This quite explicitly wrests "Scottishness" back from the nationalists, emphasises the Scottishness of the Unionist viewpoint and contrasts this with the anti-Scottishness of those that put "the future of Scotland at risk".

In order to advance the congruity between Scottishness and Britishness some spokespeople identified a genuinely superordinate Britishness which was irreducible to Englishness. For example, one Conservative MP argued:

> I yield to no-one in my support for Scotland and things Scottish and equally I yield to no one in my support for things British. I can get just as emotional about my Britishness as I can about my Scottishness. They are not in opposition they are in fact complimentary . . . believe that Britishness represents our values, our institutions and our tolerance. I think that's what Britishness is. I believe that the British are the most tolerant race on this planet. That's probably more exemplified anywhere in the world than in England. Only the English would have accepted the mass immigration that they have had over the last 30 or 40 years.. So that's part of what makes us British, the 83% who live in England. And that kind of tolerance married to the drive and impetus that we get from the Scots is reflected in all our institutions . . .
>
> (Conservative MP, interview)

In this construction Britishness draws upon the best of the constituent elements (Scottishness and Englishness). Consequently, although fundamentally informed by Englishness, it is not synonymous with it, nor does it contradict Scottishness. This congruency gains particular force through the elision of the categories "Scottish" and "British" made possible by the racialisation of the category "British"; the use of the term "race" clearly implies that it is possible to talk of a British "people" and "nation", and identifies qualities that Scots and English have in common by virtue of their common "race". The argument that this "Britishness" is reflected in "all our institutions" is developed as the same speaker continues:

> the British are not law-abiding in the sense that the Teutonic races are. The Germans are law-abiding, you lay down the rules, they will do exactly what the rules tell them. We will question the rules, that's the first thing we will do. The second thing is, if everyone does it, it doesn't matter whether or not it's legal, as long as everyone does it. In other words, you must consider what your peers are saying, and that's part of being this grouping and getting into little institutionalised organisations

Overall, the contrast between the British and the "Teutonic" "races" advances a common categorisation of Scots and English and defines the key dimensions of this category in terms of a particular relationship to social institutions. The importance of this is that it has the effect of construing the institutions of British society as the concrete expressions of this British psyche so constructing a fundamental congruency between all Britons and "their" institutions. Interestingly, one of the institutions offered by way of example, is the Westminster Parliament (the object of attack by Scottish Nationalists who often characterise it as an essentially English institution). Another is the British military. Indeed, for this MP, the high number of Scots in the military is taken as confirmation of the Scots' Britishness; the Scots "like what goes with the military and the organisation, the dressing up and the wearing of the uniform, the allegiance to something that we understand; this Britishness and the Monarch". (See Wood, 1987, for a discussion of the place of the Scottish solider in (re)producing Scotland's Britishness.)

3   Scotland, Britain and Europe

The argument that Scottishness was guaranteed rather than threatened by Britishness was also advanced in the context of arguments about Europe. For example one Conservative candidate argued that while Britishness was "more descriptive than personal to the individual" the UK provided the network of social relations in which Scottishness could flourish..

> We use a pneumatic drill to break the ground and we allocate the gravel if you like to the individual parts where it is needed. And I think it would be very difficult for us on our own to yield the pneumatic drill . . . it is the bigger crunch of the UK which takes us forward but allows us as integral parts to derive undoubted benefit from that . . . So I think as part of the UK we enjoy the benefits of that influential presence and that is what in turn helps us to preserve what it is that matters to us and what is important to us and what is discernibly Scottish.
>
> (Conservative candidate, interview)

A similar construction was advanced by another who sought to argue that an independent Scotland would have less influence in Europe than possible through membership of Britain.

> Well, you know you are moving Scotland out of a great institution which has benefited beyond comprehension . . . in marriage to an extent in which individuals Miss Scotland and Mr. England would never have done before they became Mr. and Mrs. Britain and you are going to just turn it into a tiny commonwealth republic . . . I mean Austria is not an important place and it has three times the population of Scotland and it's at the crossroads of Europe . . . Scotland finds Westminster which speaks the same language and has a homogenous population in Britain difficult to accept. On what possible basis is it going to accept orders from Mr. Delors who's never been to Scotland, will never come to Scotland, from Brussels, who don't speak the same language?

Not only does this construction identify the benefits brought by Britain but it also advances the argument that an independent Scotland would be particularly vulnerable to the imposition of alien ideas/values by those that know nothing of her. In other words, while the SNP sought to create a sense of incompatibility between Scotland and Britain and compatibility with Europe, this does the opposite; the compatibility is between Scotland and Britain and the incompatibility between Scotland and Europe. Obviously this not only has implications for the relevance of particular categories but also defines the nature of the social relations between these categories and hence the course of action that is appropriate.

Conclusion

Reviewing the material presented in this first section highlights an interesting reverse symmetry in the two constructions. Both sets of spokespeople seek to foreground one category as relevant while undermining the other. Firstly they define the context in different ways so as to identify different categories for self-definition (compare for example the SNP spokesperson's use of Bannockburn in order to foreground a self-categorisation as Scottish and the Prime Minister's construction of an international context in order to foreground a self-categorisation as British). Secondly, they define the nature of the categories in such a way as to buttress the political meaningfulness of the preferred category: according to the SNP Scotland is incompatible with Britain and Britain is therefore irrelevant to "us" while according to the Conservatives, Britain is compatible with Scotland and therefore Scotland is irrelevant to "us".

Obviously these constructions of (in)compatibility do not simply serve to advance particular categories as the basis for self-definition but they also define particular courses of action as appropriate. According to the one construction, Britishness constitutes an attack on Scottishness to be met by action which undermines the Union. According to the other, Britishness is compatible with and indeed provides a defence of Scottishness with the result that attacks upon the Union are to be resisted. In similar vein these categories' relationship with Europe is constructed in such a way as to reveal differing forms of (in)compatibility and hence advance particular models of social relations and social action.

Whither National Categories?

Thus far we have explored the arguments advanced for and against particular national categories as the appropriate bases for self-definition (and action). There may of course be other bases for self-definition and here we explore several arguments about the appropriateness of using categories based upon the concept of "nation". This material comes from two rather different debates. The one may be termed the "radical" debate and refers to arguments which advance a very different form of social change. More specifically it comes from a non-electoralist party of the Left and allows us to explore how others may attempt to mobilise people on the basis of class rather than national categories. The other may be termed the "mainstream" debate and concerns the arguments between the Conservatives and the SNP over the political and moral appropriateness of mobilising people on the basis of national categories. This debate is interesting because it makes the point that while the category "nation" is one of the most universally accepted (Anderson, 1983), people's action in terms of it can be construed in different ways with some forms of action being defined as morally and politically unacceptable. As the maxim "I am a patriot, he is a nationalist and they are tribalists" (cited by Gellner, 1983; 87) indicates, action in terms of one's own national category may be construed in terms of high principle while the similar behaviour of others is construed more negatively. Indeed, the real significance of this quote is that it makes the point that some categories are so well established that their status (and the practices which reproduce them) are normal and beyond questioning while the status and practices of less established categories are problematised and rendered "deviant". Given the consequences of such constructions for people's perceptions of the social, moral and political appropriateness of acting in terms of these different categories such arguments are clearly worthy of attention and it is to these that we now turn.

The Mainstream Debate; Britishness and the Nature of Nationalism

As an example of the attempted delegitimation of action in terms of national categories consider this Conservative MP's construction:

> they tell me that nationalism is on the march—that all over the world suppressed instincts are striving to burst forth. They imply that it's a virtue; extremism in France, riots on the streets of Marseilles, Fascism on the rise in Germany . . . We put all that behind us hundreds of years ago. Let no one pretend that we've never been through it. The Kingdoms of England fought each other to obliteration . . . still strike a nerve in Yorkshire and Lancashire . . . Nationalism nearly destroyed it (Britain)—German nationalism— Scotland couldn't have stopped Hitler alone. But nor could England. Or Wales. Or Ireland. None of us. Together we did. This Union of ours did.
>
> (Heseltine MP, speech, 7.4.92)

Two aspects of this construction are especially striking. The first is the characterisation of nationalism as the bursting forth of thoroughly evil instincts. The second is the construction of Britain as a category that has risen above these outdated instincts and which indeed has triumphed over them. This construction therefore creates a contrast between the political project of those arguing for and against the break-up of Britain. The former are the "nationalists" who imply that these evils are a virtue. The latter are those who oppose these evils and wish to maintain a category that triumphed over them. This construction therefore manages to condemn action in terms of the category "nation" because the one category (Britain), and the strategies of "big-state" nationalism that maintain it, are so naturalised as to appear "given" and "normal" leaving the term nationalism as a term of abuse to be directed against the opposition. As a consequence the relations of the status quo are naturalised and rendered non-problematic while the political strategy of the opposition are foregrounded as "deviant" and illegitimate.

In the face of such constructions, the proponents of change must offer alternative constructions which problematise that which their opponents seek to naturalise. In the examples below this is achieved through redefining Britain and the projects of nationalism.

In our first example the speaker anticipates the argument that action in terms of the category Scotland is insular and morally unacceptable through advancing a construction of Britain which highlights its English nationalism. He argues that the Scots were "being put in a situation where you've got this bogus internationalism which is Britishness . . . You're being asked to go along with a con" . . . the Scots "are not being asked to surrender Scottish awareness that we may be better world citizens. If you surrender your Scottish awareness you will simply become the assimilated Englishman" (SNP activist, interview). Whereas the Conservative speaker had constructed Britain as triumphing over nationalism, this speaker construes Britain as anything but non-nationalist. Indeed, the argument against Scots' action in terms of the category Scotland is presented as a deceitful trick—a "con"—which offers not internationalism but "the assimilated Englishman" (sic). In other words, the Scots' action in terms of Scotland is entirely appropriate because their opponents (i.e. those that advocate the maintenance of the Union) are in effect acting in terms of their national category—England and Englishness.

In our second example a prominent SNP campaigner advances a particular construction of nationalism which was prompted by an opponent's jibe that "nationalism had died with Hitler". The speaker describes his response in these terms:

> sorry Hitler was on your side not mine; he wasn't in favour of freedom for small nations . . . the problem is not Nationalism . . ., the problem is Imperialism. Imperial people want to tell other people how they should live, where they should live. As Nationalists as we use the word we are not wanting anything for ourselves that we don't want for everybody else.

(SNP Candidate)

Redefining the meaning of nationalism through developing a contrast between it and imperialism allows the speaker to reclaim nationalism as a force for positive change (rather than nasty aggression). Indeed there is a sense in which it is almost as if the maxim cited above has been rephrased along the lines of "I'm a nationalist (positive) you are Imperialists (negative)". Certainly this formulation foregrounds the ideology and practices of "big" states (e.g. Britain). Further not only are these rendered non-natural but they are also presented as oppressive thereby legitimating the subordinated's action in terms of their national categories. Consequently, far from action in terms of national categories being defined as morally inappropriate, it is entirely legitimate and but a simple assertion of a wider, generally applicable principle.

A striking feature of these contrasting constructions is the argumentation around Hitler. On the one hand we have a construction which defines him as the prototypical exemplar of nationalism, while on the other we have a construction which defines him as the prototypical exemplar of its antithesis. The interesting point here therefore is that both sets of protagonists make Hitler prototypical of the opposition. Obviously, the fact that the same figure can be used to define different sides is entirely consonant with our general argument that the dimensions that define a category and its contrast with others are open to argument. Further, it is clear that these different constructions imply very different models of the social world and the acceptability of action in terms of national categories.

The Radical Debate: Arguing for the Categories of Class

Here we explore how others active in the 1992 General Election argued for the adoption of a very different set of categories—those based upon class. The Socialist Workers Party (SWP) is a non-electoralist revolutionary party of the Left, which, although highly critical of the Labour party, traditionally campaigns for a Labour vote. In a speech given at a pre-election public meeting calling for just such a Labour vote, the invited speaker argued against voting SNP. His immediate target was an argument that such a vote was appropriate because Scotland is more collectivist and that a Left politics was more achievable than in

England. His overall construction identified class division as running the length and breadth of Britain—indeed he argued that "Britain is the most class-ridden society in the world." He then continued how "within the British state I think Scotland is actually one of the places with the most naked open class divisions. You know people go on about the South East of England. I think a walk through Edinburgh teaches what naked class division is". Turning his attention to England he focused on the area that is frequently advanced as exemplifying the reactionary nature of the English—the South East (especially the inhabitants of the English county of Essex). His construction described this area as marked by "massive obvious class divisions" with London "a seething bloody cesspit of class divisions". He then explicitly addressed the construction of those living in Essex:

> people go on about Essex-man and Essex-woman . . . it makes me bloody annoyed. Essex is the county of Dagenham, Tilbury—the docks—it is the county that saw the Colchester ("riots") the upheavals in Colchester about the Poll Tax. The people that make these jokes about—what are they about?—it is the ruling class making jokes about the people they call Sharon, you know the high heels, the typists and all the rest of it that come in from Essex into the city of London to do shit low-paid work, low wages, as alienating as Timex. It is anti-working class. Essex is populated by those people.

This construction singles out the industrial centres of Dagenham and Tilbury and the mass protests against the Poll Tax and so defines the context as one in terms of class struggle. Given his construction of Scotland as similarly divided along class lines he then points to the common experiences of those in Essex and those in Timex (a well-known local factory in Dundee, Scotland). Of particular interest is his engagement with the popular construction of "Essex-man" and "Essex-woman" as crudely materialistic. By identifying the source of this categorisation as the "ruling-class" and characterising it as anti-working-class, he conveys a construction which identifies Essex as being populated by people who suffer ruling-class condescension. This weakens the acceptability of the dominant categorisation and, through highlighting the class antagonism that lies behind it, reemphasises the relevance of class categories.

The speaker also constructed a contrast between the categories of class and the SNP's advocated strategy of "Independence in Europe". Here, he argued that although the rhetoric surrounding Europe was attractive ("'Scotland in Europe' sounds very nice! You know, baguettes in Dundee. Wine bars. Sunny. You know it sounds lovely!") "we" knew what the reality was; heightened international competition with Scotland forced to compete as a low-waged economy with countries such as Portugal and Greece. Having singled out this dimension and constructed a definition of Europe around it, he then defined the social relations that such a category would sustain. For example, he described how the European strategy would mean that Scottish workers would be faced with the "national" argument that "we're all Scots together, we've got to pull together" and how in this context the strategies of change implied by an analysis in terms of class (e.g. industrial militancy) would be undermined. In other words, the class construction offered by this speaker was associated with quite explicit arguments about the consequences of particular self-definitions for particular strategies of social change. Indeed he argued against viewing the category "Europe" as relevant not because "Europe" is incompatible with national categories (as is sometimes argued), but for precisely the opposite reason: "Europe" will render the nation increasingly salient and so will act as an impediment to "real" social change.

Discussion

As the concept of the "nation" has come under scrutiny from historians and anthropologists it is now a commonplace to make the point that there is nothing natural or given about the "nation"; "nationalism is not the awakening of nations to self-consciousness; it invents nations where they do not exist" (Gellner, 1983, 168). This is not of course to say that the category "nation" is a masquerade or that it is fabricated under false pretences. Rather it is to say that it is imagined and cannot be analysed as if it existed independently of the beliefs and actions of those that define themselves as constituting the category (McCrone, 1992; Anderson, 1983). The implication that national identities cannot be analysed outside their making (Macdonald, 1993) has been manifested in the attention paid by historians and social anthropologists to the place of "national" events (e.g. royal ceremonies; Cannadine, 1983) and "national" objects (e.g. national portraiture; Bruce and Yearly, 1989) etc. in the (re)production of particular definitions of the national community (Alonso, 1988; Lofgren, 1989).

Although clearly congruent with an approach which explores the social practices through which national identities are (re)produced our analysis has more explicitly taken as its focus the issue of argumentation and so has developed the point that the (re)production of particular categories cannot be assumed to be non-problematic. Indeed, following Billig's (1987) observation that categories are only invoked and defined in particular ways where there are alternatives, our analysis makes the point that any construction which implies a particular category and its definition is open to contestation and indeed constitutes an argument against alternative ways of viewing things. The implications of this are several.

For example, consider the analysis of categorisation. As we hope to have demonstrated the issue of which categories are to be used as a basis for action cannot be read off from the social context for this context is itself in need of definition and constitutes a site of contestation with different protagonists arguing over the significance and meaning of the social world. Nor can the definition of context be separated from the definition of categories and their contents; while defining the context may support the usage of particular categories rather than others, so too the meaning of these categories (and hence their contextual relevance) is a matter for argument. For example, the contrasting definitions of the category Britain advanced by our protagonists demonstrate that the meaning of the category is a site of contest and that as different meanings are advanced so our understanding of the context changes (e.g. from one in which

Scottishness is under threat to one in which Scottishness is protected). An even more striking example of the fundamentally contestable nature of category prototypes and their implications for our understandings of the nature of the conflict is provided by the mainstream parties' contrasting uses of Hitler. Here the same figure is used by different protagonists to advance very different constructions of themselves and their opponents with enormous consequences for our understandings of the context and hence the nature and acceptability of particular courses of action.

Of course, to argue that people's constructions of the social world are based upon the adoption of particular categories and that the selection and definition of these categories are key sites of struggle is only the first step in the direction of an analysis of social change. While it is possible to demonstrate the range of constructions and how these support and legitimate particular actions, this in itself tells us little about how particular constructions come to "win out" over their rivals. Indeed, it could be argued that although attention to argumentation has the advantage of recognising a key component of our ability to act upon and transform the world, it is on its own deeply problematic; in the absence of any discussion of the constraints which determine which constructions are accepted or rejected it offers an image of the world in which social change is simply dependent upon unconstrained choice.

The reality of course is that choices are constrained. Just as categories define the possibilities for action in the world, so too the practices that are possible bear upon the relevance of the categories. That the adoption of categories is dependent upon the possibility of particular practices is a point highlighted by those researching the use of racialised categories to represent migrant workers (Miles, 1984, 1989; Miles and Phizacklea, 1984; Reicher, 1986, 1993). While complex, it seems that the use of racialised categories rather than class categories can be partly explained by the absence of practices that could support the latter; the absence of campaigns for more and better housing, educational provision and so on meant that there were few opportunities to develop categorisations which were inclusionary rather than exclusionary and left the field open to alternative categorisations which explained housing and education problems in terms of "their" presence.

But if our approach to social change is incomplete and requires an exploration of the relationship between the possibilities for particular forms of practice and category acceptance, our demonstration of the range of categories and definitions that may be adopted does have some more immediate methodological implications.

Firstly, the observation that category definitions are always produced within a context of controversy and are organised against alternatives suggests that an analysis of social change which focuses upon one group and neglects the actions of the other(s) is inadequate. Simply put, unless we appreciate the arguments of both we will not be able to explain how and why the one advances the category definitions that it does, nor how this may in turn prompt a counter-definition from the other and so on. In other words precisely because the analysis of argumentation requires that we examine the nature of the constructions against which a particular construction is advanced (Billig, 1987), we are inevitably drawn away from a narrow focus upon the experiences of those that are subordinated and towards a more properly inter-group analysis of the dynamics of social change.

Secondly, our analysis implies that when researching people's perceptions of their social world any methodology which assumes particular categories necessarily forces our participants to respond in terms that may not be their own. For example, a questionnaire examining views about the EC in terms of its benefits for "Britain" would necessarily only speak to those for whom such a construction was relevant. The options facing the others are either to refuse to respond or to accept the relevance of the category and the implicit "nationalisation" of the issue. Either way our research "findings" could have the effect of reproducing the view that the adoption of this category is non-problematic and even inevitable. Nor is this simply a problem of research design for a third and final observation flows as a corollary. Anything that encourages the view that particular categories are inevitable may be regarded as contributing to their reification and naturalisation. Where these are the very categories that others are seeking to undermine and challenge we are faced with the prospect of a social psychology which, while acknowledging social change, actually has the unintended consequence of reproducing the status quo. If one considers the distinctive meanings and power of the concept "nation", the dangers of such a consequence are especially apparent. Precisely because this category is bound up with notions of place and belonging and has the potential to articulate with the category "race" (Miles, 1989), the category "nation" has a particular power to define who is to count as belonging and who is classed as Other. If change is to be possible and alternative constructions of the world entertained, academics must be sensitive to their own role in the reproduction of such a potent category (see Jackson and Penrose, 1993) and ensure that their theories, and the practices upon which they are based, facilitate rather than inhibit change.

References

Alonso, A. M. (1988). The effects of truth: re-presentations of the past and the imagining of community. *Journal of Historical Sociology*, **1**.

Anderson, B. (1983). *Imagined Communities: Reflections on the Origin and Spread of Nationalism.* London: Verso.

Balibar, E. (1991). Es gibt keinen staat in Europa: Racism and politics in Europe today. *New Left Review*, **186**, 5–9.

Billig, M. (1987). *Arguing and Thinking: A Rhetorical Approach to Social Psychology.* Cambridge: Cambridge University Press.

Brow, J. (1990). Notes on community, hegemony, and the uses of the past. *Anthropological Quarterly*, **63**, 1–5.

Bruce, S. and Yearly, S. (1989). The social construction of tradition: the restoration portraits and the Kings of Scotland. In D. McCrone, S. Kendrick and P. Straw (eds), *The Making of Scotland: Nation, Culture and Social Change.* Edinburgh: Edinburgh University Press.

Cannadine, D. (1983). The context, performance and meaning of ritual: the British monarchy and the "invention of tradition". In E. Hobsbawm and T. Ranger (eds), *The Invention of Tradition*. Cambridge: Cambridge University Press.

Connor, W. (1978). A nation is a nation, is a state, is an ethnic group, is . . . *Ethnic and Racial Studies*, **1**, 377–400.

Foster, R. J. (1991). Making national cultures in the global ecumene. *Annual Review of Anthropology*, **20**, 235–60.

Gellner, E. (1983). *Nations and Nationalism*. Oxford: Basil Blackwell.

Harvie, C. (1994). *The Rise of Regional Europe*. London: Routledge.

Haslam, S. A., Turner, J. C., Oakes, P. J., McGarty, C. and Hayes, B. K. (1992). Context dependent variation in social stereotyping 1: the effects of intergroup relations as mediated by social change and frame of reference. *European Journal of Social Psychology*, **22**, 3–20

Hobsbawm, E. and Ranger. T. (eds)(1983). *The Invention of Tradition*. Cambridge: Cambridge University Press.

Hogg, M. A. and Abrams, D. (1988). *Social Identifications: A Social Psychology of Intergroup Relations and Group Processes*. London: Routledge.

Jackson, P. and Penrose, J. (1993). *Constructions of Race, Place and Nation*. London: University College London Press.

Kitching, G. (1985). Nationalism; the instrumental passion. *Capital and Class*, **25**, 98–116.

Lindsay, I. (1991). The SNP and the lure of Europe. In T. Gallagher (ed.), *Nationalism in the Nineties*. Edinburgh: Polygon.

Lofgren, O. (1989). The nationalisation of culture. *Ethnologia Europaea*, **19**, 5–23.

McCrone, D. (1992). *Understanding Scotland: The Sociology of a Stateless Nation*. London: Routledge.

Macdonald, S. (1993). Identity complexes in Western Europe: social anthropological perspectives. In S. Macdonald, *Inside European Identities*. Providence/Oxford: Berg.

Miles, R. (1984). The riots of 1958: Notes on the ideological construction of "race relations" as a political issue in Britain. *Immigrants and Minorities*, **3**, 252–75.

Miles, R. (1989). *Racism*. London: Routledge.

Miles, R. and Phizacklea, A. (1984). *White Man's Country*. London: Pluto.

Nairn, T. (1977). *The Break-up of Britain*. London: New Left Books

Nederveen Pieterse, J. (1991). Fictions of Europe. *Race and Class*, **32**(3), 3–10.

Oakes, P. J. and Turner, J. C. (1990). Is limited information processing capacity the cause of social stereotyping? In W. Stroebe and M. Hewstone (eds), *European Review of Social Psychology*, Vol. 1. Chichester: Wiley.

Reicher, S. D. (1986). Contact, action and racialisation: some British evidence. In R. Brown and M. Hewstone (eds), *Contact, Conflict and Intergroup Encounters*. Oxford: Blackwell.

Reicher, S. D. (1987). Crowd behaviour as social action. In J. C. Turner, M. Hogg, P. J. Oakes, S. D. Reicher and M. Wetherell (eds), *Rediscovering the Social Group*. Oxford: Blackwell.

Reicher, S. D. (1991). Mad dogs and Englishmen: telling tales from the Gulf. Paper presented to the British Association *Science '91* meeting. Plymouth, August.

Reicher, S. D. (1993). On the social construction of social categories: from collective action to rhetoric and back again. Conference paper.

Reicher, S. D. and Hopkins, N. (1993a). Social categorisation and social influence: an analysis of category arguments in anti-abortionist rhetoric. Paper submitted for publication.

Reicher, S. D. and Hopkins, N. (1993b). Constructing categories and mobilising masses: an analysis of Thatcher's and Kinnock's speeches on the British miner's strike. Paper submitted for publication.

Samuel, R. and Thompson, P. (1990). *The Myths We Live By*. London and New York: Routledge.

Schwartz, B. (1982). "The people" in history: the Communist Party Historian's Group, 1946–56. In Centre for Contemporary Cultural Studies, *Making Histories: Studies in History-Writing and Politics*.

Tajfel, H. (ed.) (1978). *Differentiation between Social Groups: Studies in the Social Psychology of Intergroup Relations*. London: Academic Press.

Tajfel, H. (1982). *Social Identity and Intergroup Relations*. Cambridge University Press.

Tajfel, H. and Turner, J. C. (1979). An integrative theory of intergroup conflict. In W. G. Austin and S. Worchel (eds), *The Social Psychology of Intergroup Relations*. Monterey, Calif.: Brooks-Cole.

Tudor, H. (1972). *Political Myth*. London: Pall Mall Press.

Turner, J. C. (1975). Social comparison and social identity: some prospects for intergroup behaviour. *European Journal of Social Psychology*, **5**, 5–34

Turner, J. C. (1985) Social categorisation and the self-concept: a social cognitive theory of group behaviour. In E. J. Lawler (ed.), *Advances in Group Processes: Theory and Research*, Vol. 2. Greenwich, Conn.:JAI Press.

Turner, J. C., Oakes, P. J., Haslam. A. and McGarty, C. (1993). Self and collective: cognition and social context. *Personality and Social Psychology Bulletin*.

Webber, F. (1991). From ethnocentrism to Euro-racism. *Race and Class*, **32**(3), 11–17.

Wood, S. (1987). *The Scottish Soldier*. London: Archive Publications.

6

Ascribed Identities and the Social Identity Space: An Ego/Ecological Analysis

MARISA ZAVALLONI

Université de Montréal, Canada

> I think it immensely difficult to study mental phenomena and the only guide for methodology is the universal one-use any tool or weapon that comes to hand, and stick with any tool or weapon that works.
>
> (Searle, 1992)

The subject of this book challenges us "to rethink the psychological analysis of the processes that are influencing changes in identities at individual, subgroup and national levels across Europe". This is tantamount to raising the old question of how psychology can best work together with the neighbouring sciences of sociology, history or anthropology to analyse nationalism. The result of these efforts in the past has not been a success story, yet the need to fill the psychological space in sociological or historical analyses always resurfaces. For instance, in her remarkable essay on "Nationalism", Greenfield (1992) argues that a student of society cannot be oblivious to psychological processes because they perform in social processes "the role of necessary conductors, mediating between social structures and cultural formations at different stages in social transformation. The final outcome at any stage is affected by the nature of the psychological processes involved. Every social phenomenon is, therefore, psychological and nationalism is no exception" (p. 496).

Greenfield uses Mannheim's (1953) concept of "style of thought" to define nationalism, a term that "subsumes the related phenomena of national identity and consciousness". In interacting with sociology, and with the political and cultural sciences, psychology could offer an explanation of how consciousness experiences national, ethnic or gender identities.

95

Greenfield (1992) who adopted a Weberian view of social reality, considers that the study of meaningful orientations and of the motivation of social actors is the "central subject" of sociology. However, the psychological processes that underlie these meaningful orientations and the motivation that leads to the creation of social reality remain obscure. Greenfield chooses to treat the psychological dimension of nationalism as given. What emerges from this analysis is the importance of a psychological state: re-sentiment and of some defence mechanisms that neutralise feelings of inferiority derived from a situation of anomie.

I will argue here that re-sentiment and the psychological states that Greenfield associates to defense mechanisms, are the result of wider identity processes that are involved in the creation of subjective states and of social consciousness. But, as Searle (1992) contends in his recent work *The Re-discovery of the Mind*, it is precisely the erasing of consciousness that has characterised psychology in the last fifty years, including today in cognitive science, and some branches of philosophy. As a result, according to him, these fields have produced views that are implausible or clearly false, such as the claim that we do not have subjective mental states. He then goes on to argue that "there is no way to study the phenomena of the mind without implicitly or explicitly studying consciousness". I would add that, in its present form, even social constructionism does not escape this criticism. Its early promise to be an alternative to positivism and to behaviourism fades as its proponents consistently address the question of how the mind constructs the social. For example, Gergen (1992) introduces sociorationalism as a "metatheory that places the locus of knowledge not in the mind of a single individual but in the collectivity . . . it is in the process of social interchange that rationality is generated" (p. 207). It is extraordinary to propose that there are no minds at work doing the social interchange. Initiated by Foucault's (1966) rhetorical description of the individual as a "rift in the order of things", the implausible claims about the death of Man, the death of the author (Barthes), the death of the subject (Le Man) and death of the Self (Gergen, 1991) have swept academia in several disciplines. In psychology, this rhetorical stance may have had an appeal for behaviourist-trained psychologists, by offering a new way of avoiding the need to confront the reality of consciousness and subjectivity.

When Searle (1992) argues that there is no way to study the phenomenon of the mind without implicitly or explicitly studying consciousness and subjectivity he strikes for me a comforting chord. If words, such as *mind* and *cognition* are popular, the word *consciousness* has all but disappeared from psychological discourse. For instance, I found surprising that Gustav Jahoda (1966) in his review of our book *Identité sociale et conscience: an Introduction to Ego-ecology* (Zavalloni and Louis-Guerin, 1984) found it difficult to translate conscience (consciousness) into psychological English and settled for representation. It should be clear by now, how lonely and fraught with misunderstanding, it has been to study for many years the relations between ascribed identities and social consciousness in an intellectual climate so unresponsive to the issue.

At first, my co-researchers and I did not set out to study social consciousness as such. We wanted to understand how each identity subset (nation, gender, social class and so on) would interplay at the representational level with all the other subsets and this question is still hotly debated. In order to examine these processes, we have developed an intensive interview methodology, involving repeated in-depth explorations of individual respondents. In brief, the focus of our analysis is the words the respondent uses about herself and the linkages between words and themes. The technique combines discourse, narrative and word association methods. Appendix A gives an example of how the interview method works and the type of analysis possible. The theoretical approach informing this research we have called ego/ecological psychology. As the respondents in our research began to talk freely, the concepts of psychology that were at our disposal such as traits, stereotypes, needs, or social identity theory were shown to be irrelevant to account for what we were finding. Psychoanalysis was not helpful either. The words that were produced hinted at identity or subjectivity, as a particular organisation of consciousness. Identity was emerging as a transactional entity, which is to say, as that part of consciousness which in a continuous transaction with the world produces words, actions, representations, and feelings about Self, Alter and society. Social consciousness was embedded in this transactional entity.

The nature of this transaction began to surface when we observed a peculiar heterogeneity between the foreground discourse and the representations that were elicited as background thinking when this discourse was produced.

For example, suppose a respondent described *we* the English as charming, poetical, interesting and he might reactivate as background thinking words that accompany these words at the periphery of consciousness, for instance representation of himself and of the members of the Conservative Party Oxford Student Club to which he had belonged (see Appendix A). We have found that every respondent producing words describing social groups, at the same time, automatically and unconsciously summons up personal memories and private desires in the background. Vice versa, identity content at its most private and

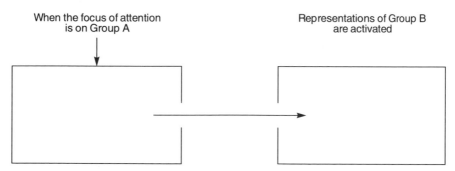

FIGURE 6.1   The group recoding process in the creation of social consciousness

subjective when focal words activate, as background, thinking about the social world.

At the time, we called this phenomenon a group recoding (Zavalloni, 1971; and Zavalloni and Louis-Guerin, 1984). It was a descriptive term; now, the theoretical implications of this recoding in understanding the creation of social consciousness as well as personal identity have become more clear. This recoding suggests that there are some words that, by reappearing in many different spheres of our inner world, connect each of these to the others. A basic mechanism of consciousness seems to have emerged by which some words reactivate, ceaselessly, automatically, images and representations that were *making connections* between the social and the personal world. This finding will require us to think differently about memory and natural thinking in the area of the Self and of social identities.

Identity Words as Cells of the Mind: Observing Consciousness at Work

We think of memory as a storehouse of propositions and images ... But we should think of memory rather as a mechanism for generating current performance, including conscious thoughts and actions, based on past experiences.

(Searle, 1992, 187)

Searle (1992) has introduced the hypothesis of the "background" as an unconscious state that is the prerequisite for the work of consciousness, a feature of our representation of reality. Searle's general background hypothesis fits the description of the particular background that was emerging from our research, what we called background thinking (*pensée de fond*). As we began to explore the associations to what, for lack of a better term, we have called *identity words*, the crucial importance of background thinking began to surface. Identity words are words produced spontaneously to describe social groups. As such they could have been described as *stereotypes*.

As soon as we began to display the associative network of *identity words*, the respondents' values, desires, projects began to surface. That is to say, these words would reappear as descriptors of a person, motivation, attitudes, values, interests, aspirations, social consciousness, and so on. Identity words become "psychological cells", to borrow Vigotsky's expression.

If a person produces spontaneously a word that describes a WE (the in-group) and the Self (this is the case 75% of the time), this word will *necessarily* be associated to each of the following elements:

Feelings	*Natural thinking*	*Psychological domains*
e.g.	e.g.	e.g.
Self-esteem	What I am	Self-concept
Destiny	What we are	Stereotypes
Admiration	What people I like are	Identification, reference
Passion	What interests me	Motivation

| Liking | What is valuable | Values |
| Attraction | What I like in people | Attitudes |

Words that express the binary opposition of these qualities will be activated as descriptors of some out-groups, as the embodiments of counter-values and negative feelings.

	What I don't want to be
DESPISE	What we are not
DISLIKE	What is not interesting
HATRED	What is not valuable

This conglomerate can be seen as an *identity complex*. Background thinking represents that part of consciousness that while not summoned up or activated at a given moment, will give meaning to the focal subject of consciousness.

A *background thinking hypothesis* could be advanced. Whenever an element of this complex enters consciousness, or is encountered in the outside world, all the other elements that comprise it will be automatically, unconsciously re-activated (the resonance effect). This reactivation, or resonance, provides a continuous and automatic *rehearsal* of the content of emotional memory. This hypothesis explains the experience of continuity in relation to our identity (Zavalloni, 1989).

These results suggest a reversal of present day research strategy in psychology. What is considered a distinct psychological domain becomes an integral part of a coherent system. In this system, words spontaneously produced, replace the hypothetical construct. They play a central integrative role, in a ceaseless, automatic oscillation between distinct representational spheres. As *transdimensional* entities they remain unchanged, while acquiring meanings specific to each dimension through associated images, referents, and experiential memories (Zavalloni and Louis-Guerin, 1988). The traditional search for generalities and mechanisms that characterise the nomothetic tradition will be redirected towards the rational thinking processes.

The Identity Triangle

Let us go back to the example of *group recoding* provided by our respondent. Answering why he described the English as *interesting, poetical, charming* he said that: *they are the centuries old product of great universities such as Oxford and Cambridge* (see Appendix A). As indicated before, the group and the Self prototype was the Oxford Students Conservative Club.

This triad: group, identity prototype, Self could be represented as a triangle whose elements are dynamically related.

Figure 6.2 aims to represent the continuous transaction between the person and her socio-cultural environment. This model of natural thinking postulates the

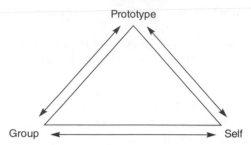

IDENTITY TRIANGLE

FIGURE 6.2   Representation of the transaction between the person and sociocultural environment

existence of a specific identity-related energy which links the various components of the identity triangle. As I stated elsewhere: "Identity related energy is invested in a representation of alter and re-activates this mental content in association to the self. This activation is experienced subjectively as affect and reflects a durable association between a desirable characteristic of alter and the Self. Simultaneously it creates a condition that will generate interest and passion (motivation), for those aspects of the world that are compatible with this initial association" (Zavalloni, 1986, 340).

The Creation of a Collective Identity: The Case of Germany

Stemming from protocol analysis, this model can be applied to interpret literary and ideological discourse. Much cultural and political activity is spent in promoting and sometimes creating new national or ethnic identities in an atmosphere of collective and personal exaltation. Cultural agents create ideologies, as Debray would say, through the action of rendering public private conviction. The identity triangle permits us to interpret the source and the argumentative power of a particular ideology. The development of the extraordinary German Nationalism in the early nineteenth century offers an appropriate material to illustrate my argument. Germany was described by the ideologues, visionaries, theorists of the time, as "the only true, ideal, nation in the world" (Greenfield, 1992, 364). Germany was a "universal man to whom God has given the whole earth as a home" (Fichte).

The historians credit a religious movement, pietism, and a cultural movement, romanticism, as the origin of German nationalism. Pietism was a variant of religious mysticism that became widespread at the end of the seventeenth century. Its central assumption was the emotional experience of unity with Christ and the Passion became the focal element. Blood, wounds and physical suffering added value to everything: they were associated with war, being a soldier, death. Whether experienced or inflicted on others, wounds were sanctified. They

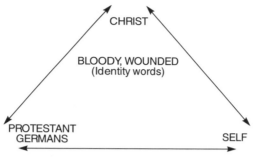

FIGURE 6.3   The German national identity triangle

became the sublime signs of spiritual purity and strength and of moral righteousness, and paved the road to glory. Klopstock, a famous religious-pietist poet, wrote patriotic poetry in which blood is associated with beauty: The crucifixion is a precious splendid, bloody day, "Christian martyrs are covered with sublime wounds, and Germanic youth with beautiful wounds" (cited by Greenfield (1992), 332). (See Figure 6.3.)

This discourse demonstrates how a bloody, wounded image oscillates from Christ (identity prototype), the Self (the writer) and the Germans. The constant reading of the Bible, that characterised a pietist household, favoured the connection between Christ (identity prototype) and the Self. This connection is then extended to the Nation (identity triad). A pre-existent (to be documented) concern with war, at the time, would resonate with the theme of the Passion.

Greenfield asserts that pietism provided the language as well as the legitimisation of the new German identity and she uses two psychological concepts, re-sentiment and defence mechanisms, to interpret these beliefs, whereas an ego-ecological reading of these discourses enables us to see the identity triangle subterraneously at work. Re-sentiment appears a plausible motive, but within a context of identity processes. The romantic vision created a new version of the identity triad God, Self and the Nation by appropriating a more secular link between these elements: genius.

The Romantics developed the idea of genius "that denoted original, and thus ultimate creativity, that turned its possessor into a God on a smaller scale and put him above ordinary mortals, making feeling both the source and the signs of creative power" (Greenfield, 1992, 334). Self, God and Nation are connected by a shared ontological characteristic: genius. "Every good human being is always progressively becoming God. To become God, to be human, to cultivate oneself are all expressions that mean the same thing" (Schlegel, quoted in Greenfield, 1992, 331).

It should be stressed that this God-like humanity did not include women. Women were "creatures of nature in the midst of human society" as Goethe

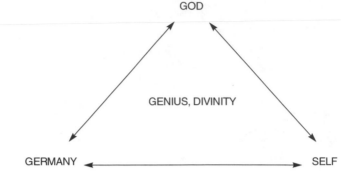

GOD

GENIUS, DIVINITY

GERMANY   SELF

FIGURE 6.4

would put it. While the culture was becoming indifferent to religion, the Self and the nation was deified. The pietist identity triangle (Germany, Self and God), is now kept together by identity words that speak of genius, as a divine attribute of Self and of the Nation. According to Fichte the German nation was a "totality which lives and represents a particular law of the development of the divine . . . The Divine has deemed this people to be made its vesture and its means of directly influencing the world." Addressing the Germans, he stated: "you are of all modern people the one in whom the seeds of human perfection most unmistakably lies".

Accounting for the extraordinary popularity of these views, Greenfield describes their proponents as: "the voice of the people, they spoke to every German who could read through their novels, poems and periodicals, and by this means they furnished the terms in which they readers thought" (Greenfield, 1992, 359). An ego/ecological analysis would stress that by adopting these views, the Germans created an environment in which the extraordinary claims of cultural agents could appear plausible. The readers, as Germans, would partake in this exalted position, while the ideologues as geniuses would become identity prototypes. From the ideologues' standpoint the society's response was making (small) Gods out of them. New versions of similar identity triangles were to be provided later by the Nazis as well as by extreme right movements. An ego/ecological reading of the romantic movement would emphasise the power of the word *genius*, which resonated in its transdimensionality as the expression of deep-seated desires. In 1786 Moser wrote: "Germany is suffering from an epidemic . . . this is the mania for genius." This hankering after a state of genius spread to other nations and may account for the impact of the romantics on Western thought. For instance Woolf in *Moments of Being* relates her father's youthful obsession with the desire of becoming a genius. Leslie Stephen was given to temper tantrums, a behaviour that was considered at the time as a proof of genius.

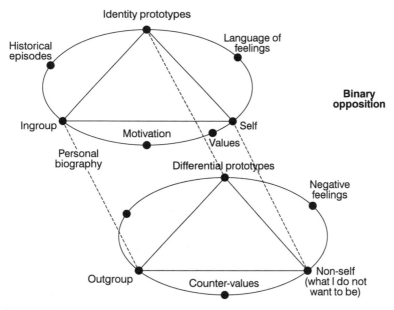

FIGURE 6.5

The ego/ecological analysis has shown the complex life of identity prototypes in the mind of respondents (Zavalloni, 1988) as targets of love, admiration, that is to say to their rationality.

Identity prototypes can be described as structural forms of Alterity whose image is reactivated whenever the focus of attention is on some attribute, actualised or desired, of the Self or of a relevant in-group.

The identity triangle suggests a particular organisation of the mind and, simultaneously, a mechanism of identity and of cultural production in which Alter as identity prototype plays an important role. Alter, as prototypes of differentiation, are also of great importance in social life. They are associated with attributes or categories opposite to those representing the Self and the in group. Alter as the binary opposition of identity prototypes, are dehumanised and become the targets of hatred. For example, the ideologues of German romanticism saw the West, the French and the Jews in particular, as the incarnation of evil: "I hate all Frenchmen without distinction in the name of God and of my people, I teach this hatred to my son . . . the odious French notion. . ." (Arndt) "An impure shameless, undisciplined race. I wish they all would go to the devil." Anti-semitism also escalated. "Blended with the romantic Weltanschauung, ressentiment focused its passionate but diffuse bitterness and hatred of the world", comments Greenfield, who ascribes these views "to re-sentiment fuelled by the fact that Germany was seen as inferior in terms of reason, individual liberty, and political equality". This explanation

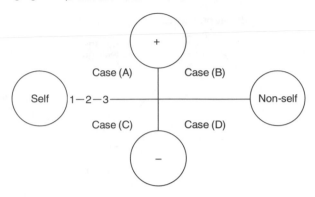

Case A: describes qualities that a person shares with in-groups
Case B: display the ideal, or the desirable
Case C: display negative aspects of the Self or victimisation, or received threat
Case D: anti-values, dehumanisation (binary opposition of what is in case A)

FIGURE 6.6   The elemental social identity space

is somewhat difficult to verify since it represents a judgement of a scholar who interprets these statements from her standpoint. It would, certainly, not be corroborated by their producers. I would argue that the emergence of these views is related to general identity processes and that the experience of Alter in mental life can be clarified by the display of the *elemental identity space* (Zavalloni and Louis-Guerin, 1984). The *elemental identity space* is a model that results from the intersection of two axes that characterise *identity words*: self-applicability and affectivity. This intersection produces four sub-spaces: case A, B, C, D. (See Figure 6.6.)

A *focused introspection method* permits determinination of the self-applicability and the value (or affect) of each category produced to describe a group membership (*identity word*). The respondent indicates if the category is applicable or not to the self (mostly (SI), somewhat (S2), little (S3), not all (S4)). He then classifies each word in terms of its affective connotation: positive, negative or neutral. The representational contextualisation method was applied to each of these words. Detailed information on a person's values, motives, social behaviour, life story is obtained using as a starting point background thinking we activated by the original free-responses. Up to twelve hours of interviewing spread over several sessions have not been uncommon. The aim of the procedure is to break the linear sequence of discourse which goes from word to word. By "suspending" foreground discourse it permits the emergence of *background thinking* that silently accompanies each word.

Fundamental differences in the apprehension of Alter (as group or individual) are functions of its position in the elementary identity space. These positions could be described according to two principal modes: the identity/ differentiation mode and the relationality mode. The relationality mode refers to the feelings (attraction–rejection, love, hate etc.) activated by the Alter. These feelings are a function of the position of Alter in the elemental identity space as the implicit referent of groups descriptions. The identity triangle illustrates the position mode of Alter in Case A. Alter that occupies Cases B and D are in positions of differentiation. Case D which includes all the qualities/attributes/states that a person considers as negative and foreign to the Self will strike a compatible Alter with this negative material. We may locate the source of this negative content in the binary opposition of what is produced in case A. To pursue the example of German romanticism, case D includes the French and the Jews. To go a step further: the feeling of common destiny, rather than being the initial motor, results from the automatic, subconscious activation of what we value, hope, desire and admire as background thinking of words produced to describe some groups.

Alter's position of identity/differentiation will determine, in part, the type of relationality with which he will be experienced. Love, admiration, feeling of common destiny will invest Alter in Case A, hatred, readiness to destroy will invest Alter in the position of negative differentiation (Case D). In the identity mode, Alter (as individual or group) inhabits Case A or B of the elemental social identity space and is a member of an identity triad. As such it acquires the complex meaning that accompanies, as background thinking, each group's description. The relationality mode will produce a feeling of common destiny towards Alter as group, (e.g. Germans) and a feeling of love and admiration for the prototypes (cultural heroes). These feelings become pride when the Self is the referent of a group's description. The person's transaction with the world leads to an accumulation of meanings, memories and emotions that resonate in their totality whenever a part of this complex is activated. Each case activates some identity elements.

Greenfield's interpretation of the discourse of German nationalism can be summarised as follows:

DISCOURSE GERMANS as divine (case A)	{ REALITY (according to Greenfield)} WEST: more freedom, more reason (case B)
(PSYLOGICAL CAUSE) re-sentiment dangerous races (case C)	DISCOURSE FRENCH JEWS as inferior (case D)

Greenfield fills two cases (B and C) of the elemental identity space with hypothetical elements, whereas the present model emphasises identity processes that are structurally universal. What the identity model suggests, is that the response to re-sentiment cannot be understood without a firm understanding of identity processes that shape the counteraction. For example Case D rather than being a particular occurrence, is a universal component of the identity system. What changes is the target of dehumanisation. For example, for many of us, Hitler and Nazism fit completely in case D. An analysis of the Sartre/de Beauvoir interviews shows that case D in the former included a wide array of Sorbonne professors, of professionals and of bourgeoisie (Zavalloni, 1986). Sartre's violent statements, in his famous preface to Fanon's book, where he champions cutting the throat of Frenchmen (*les colons*) in Algeria, is another example of the dehumanising power of case D. As this example shows, the usual distinction between in-groups and out-groups is too narrow when exploring the meaning and the roots of groups representations. In the majority of the protocols obtained, a change in the qualifier of groups membership from WE to THEY, activates prototypes of differentiations and non-self applicable categories (case D). For instance in protocol X, THEY THE ENGLISH are described as: *conceited, arrogant, eat badly, dress badly* and the prototypes activated in relation to these categories are the: *local politicians, city councillors and similar types* (differentiation prototypes)(see Appendix A).

The elemental identity space can be used to understand the representations of gender in patriarchal culture. As Gerda Lerner (1993), an historian, summarises it: "in the course of the establishment of patriarchy and constantly reinforced as the result of it, the major ideas systems which explain and order Western civilisation, incorporated a set of unstated assumptions about gender, which powerfully affected the development of history and of human thought" (p. 3). These include the idea that men are "naturally" superior, and women "weaker", and inferior in intellect and rational capabilities. Men are engaged in "transcendent" activities and women in "immanent" activities. The dynamic that underlies the various cases of the elemental identity space easily explains the dehumanisation of women.

To conclude, the data analyzed in terms of the elemental identity space suggest a structural propensity for dehumanisation and hatred as part of the experience of Alterity and require a more complex analysis of the relations between social groups, including what underlies ideological arguments. Also, groups differ in terms of power and privileges, as a result there are a variety of standpoints from which threats, alliances and confrontations can be articulated. For instance an issue that is currently being debated in the US has to do with Blacks' "racism" towards Whites. Some Black academicians argue that no one can be called "racist" unless he has the power to implement his belief. Therefore a Black cannot be considered a racist when expressing anti-Whites views. We need to know more about the conditions for the exacerbation of the content of case D. A situation of this occurrence as we witness today in many parts of the world will require an understanding of how the various parts of the elemental identity space interconnect.

I would propose that ego/ecological psychology provides a framework for analysing the potential for and limits to change national identities. In many respects it shows how the options for change are restricted. Background thinking and memory resonance constrain the possibilities for substantial change either individually or culturally.

Appendix A: Protocol Analysis

The respondent (Rt): English, 50 years old, banker and ex-diplomat. Oxford educated. Has held important posts in the Conservative Party.

NATIONALITY:

WE the English are . . . **capable of great things in conditions of extremity, interesting, poetical, charming. (S+)**

Q.   When you describe the English as capable etc . . . what do you mean?

A.   *During the war the English were capable of extraordinary things. Now that the conditions are less dangerous they are doing poorly. Economically the Germans and the French are better off. I was thinking of the pilots of the RAF during the war and who had two months of life expectancy.*

A wealth of biographic information was then provided. X an RAF pilot, after being hit he fell into the hand of the Germans, was held captive, succeeded in a dangerous escape, etc.

Q.   When you describe the English as interesting, etc .. what do you mean?

A.   *They are the centuries old product of great universities such as Oxford and Cambridge.*

Q.   WHOM DO YOU SEE?

A.   *The members of the Oxford's Conservative Party Students Club.*

(Rt belonged to it during his students days and some of its other members have become lifelong colleagues and friends: **Experiential Group**.)

*In addition to excelling in their profession as journalists, government ministers, diplomats, museum curators they cultivate a wide range of interests, write poetry (***identity prototypes***). Each one of them is a very unique person.*

Rt indicates that he shares these interests and activity (actions, motivations, values). For example, Rt has submitted recently a poetry manuscript to an editor, his friends call him the "expert in charm" and his wife a "club's man".

Reconstructing the identity triangle

Step 1   Group ----> poetical, charming, interesting
Step 2   Self
Step 3   Experiential Group

The number of experiential groups which operate in the recoding of social groups vary according to the respondents. In the present protocol the image of the Oxford students' Conservative Party Club, was activated as the implicit referent of several groups. In addition to nation (WE/THEY English) these include: **social class** (defined as upper middle), occupation (defined as ex diplomat and banker), **political affiliation** (defined as conservative). The attributes generated to describe these groups would vary accordingly. To cite just a few, social class would generate **brain power** (it is required to get there) political affiliation **concerned with the public good, wanting to preserve what is valuable**, the profession would generate **intelligent** (a prerequisite to be a banker or a diplomat). In each case these characteristics were judged by Rt to be egomorphic and reflect his actions, motivations, and values. There were no differences in the responses obtained in the THEY conditions.

The creation of Alter: contrast and assimilation.

The qualities and the outlook in life that are the result of an Oxford education and the ideology of the conservative party are also apparent in the counter values or contrasts (Kelly, 1955) through which outgroups are evaluated.

When the qualifier THEY replaces WE in association to the nation (THEY the English are . . .) Rt produces as free-descriptions: **conceited, badly dressed, eat badly. (NON-SELF negative)**. The image of local politicians (town councillors) with a provincial outlook was activated as background thinking. This image contrasts with the national politicians, the implicit referents of WE the English.

Rt describes the proletariat (opposite social class) as **boring, uninteresting, all the same**, these characteristics representing the binary opposition of *interesting, charming, are all very unique persons.*

The Germans are described as **vulgar and badly mannered** (implicit referent: industrialists and bankers). Africans are described as **lacking intellectual distinction, due to their exposure to poor education in missionary schools** (implicit referent: diplomats).

The contrast effect play also at the level of political ideology. The members of the Conservative Party are seen as *concerned with the common good*, whereas those who belong to the Labour Party are seen as *selfish* and *self-seeking*.

The assimilation effect occurs when describing the French as *very similar to the English, contrary to common assumptions* (implicit referent: French diplomats and journalists educated at elite schools "Grandes Ecoles").

The data indicate that the Oxford setting into which Rt entered three decades before has become the centre of his social and personal identity. Its image is activated automatically, almost unconsciously when perceiving the world and when acting in everyday life.

References

de Beauvoir, S. (1983). *La cérémonie des adieux*. Paris: Gallimard.

Foucault, M. (1966). *Les mots et les choses*. Paris: Gallimard.

Gergen, M. (1966). The social constructionist movement in modern psychology. *American Psychologist*, 266–75.

Gergen, M. (1991). *The Saturated Self*. New York: Basic Books.

Greenfield, L. (1992). *Nationalism*. Cambridge, Mass: Harvard University Press.

Jahoda, G. (1987). A novel approach. *New Ideas in Psychology*, **5**.

Mannheim, K. (1983). *Essays on Sociology and Social Psychology*. New York: Oxford Press.

Sartre, J.P. (1961). Introduction. In F. Fanon (ed.), *Les damnés de la terre*. Paris: Maspero.

Searle, J. (1992). *The Rediscovery of the Mind*. Cambridge, Mass.: MIT Press.

Vigotsky, L. (1986). *Thought and Language*. Cambridge, Mass.: MIT Press.

Wetherell, M. and Potter, J. (1993). *Racism*. New York: Harvester Press.

Woolf, V. (1976). *Moments of Being*. New York: Harcourt and Brace.

Zavalloni, M. (1971). Cognitive processes and social identity through focused introspection. *European Journal of Experimental Social Psychology*, **1**, 235–60.

Zavalloni, M. (1986). The affective representational circuit in the creation of identity. *New Ideas in Psychology*, **4**, 333–49.

Zavalloni, M. and Louis-Guerin, C. (1984). *Identité sociale et conscience: Introduction l'égo-écologie*. Montréal: Presses de l'Université de Montréal.

Zavalloni, M. and Louis-Guerin, C. (1988). *Revue Internationale de Psychologie Sociale*, **1**(2), 173–87.

7

Spanish International Orientations: Between Europe and Iberoamerica

JOSÉ R. TORREGROSA

Universidad Complutense de Madrid, España

Introduction

Spanish foreign policy has had traditionally two main orientations (leaving aside USA which may be the most important from the point of view of realpolitik): Europe, because of historical coexistence, and America, because of the "discovery, conquest, and colonisation", and the complex relationships which they brought about. Both are central ingredients of Spanish identity, either as a nation or as a Nation State. Given the simultaneous belongingness to these two worlds, one can think of a possible conflict of identifications and interests, if an exclusive commitment to any of these had to be made.

In the context of increasing "Europeanisation", the position of the Latin-Americans as a referent group for Spanish people becomes worthy of investigation. Is there any specifically differentiated feeling of attachment, or community, with the Latin-Americans among the Spaniards? Is there still a belief or a feeling that there exists a cultural and/or psychological affinity with, or belongingness to, a symbolic community beyond Spain itself? Are there any psychological bases for the so called "Iberoamerican Community of Nations"?

This chapter draws on survey data to explore the extent to which this dual orientation is reflected in Spanish public opinion and to discuss its character-istics. I shall consider data from three different surveys within a briefly sketched sociohistorical context. Two of the surveys involve a representative sample of 1200 Spanish people aged 18 and above and they took place in January 1991 and January 1992. The sample of the third survey comprised 100 people from each of seven professional groups: writers, University professors, clergymen, managers, journalists, liberal professions (medical doctors, lawyers and engineers) and politicians. The sample was drawn from respective groups in Madrid (243), Barcelona (224), Seville (80), Valencia (76), Bilbao (76) and La Coruna (56). This survey was conducted in the autumn of 1992.

Europe as an Aspiration

By the turn of the twentieth century Spanish society was living through a period of a deep social crisis, starting with the Napoleonic invasion, the traumatic war with the United States and the loss of its last colonies in 1898. This year was called the year of "National Disaster".

In this context of generalised pessimism a current of thought known as *regeneracionismo*, a main proponent of which is Joaquin Costa, defended the idea that Spain should look to Europe and assimilate its values and patterns of social organisation in order to come out of its decadence. It should stop searching for its "national essences" in an idealised past and look towards its current European environment.

This point was taken over by Jose Ortega y Gasset who may be considered as the central figure of twentieth century Spanish thought. Mirroring that collective mood, in 1911 Ortega said:

> To be Spanish is certainly a painful destiny . . . Spain does not exist as a nation . . . Regeneration is inseparable of Europeanization; that's why immediately after the reconstructive emotion was felt that Europeanization idea came to mind. Regeneration is the wish, Europeanization is the means to satisfy it. It was truly seen from the beginning that Spain was the problem and Europe the solution.
>
> (Ortega, 1989, 19)

And a little before in the same text:

> To feel the distressing Spanish reality implies the comparative perception of the splendid European possibility . . . To grieve for Spain is the will to become Europe.
>
> (Ortega, 1989, 18)

A literal interpretation of this text would certainly be misleading. It is not the mimetic spirit, but that of emulation, stimulation. It is not a question of abandoning a historical identity in order to copy another one. Rather it is to recognise the open character of it and, in spite of its serious situation, to undertake creatively its reconstruction in view of the values represented by Europe, that is those of Modernity. According to Ortega, above all Europe is science.

It might be interesting to recall that Ortega was an early theoretician of the European supranationality. He pointed out how the political reality in the form of national independent states did not respond any more to the sociocultural and economic reality of Europe. Underlying this national plurality and as a result of multiple relationships, a common psychological layer has been developing which was to give rise to the formation of the European nation and the European state.

Europe is not and will not be the inter-nation because that means in the view of the historical record a hollow, a vacuum and no more. Europe will be the supranation.

(Ortega, 1976, 238)

Certainly, there were other currents of thought proposing similar ideas to those of Ortega in the beginning of the century in Spain. I have focused on Ortega's position because the scope and pervasiveness of his influence have been incomparable since early 1920s until today (even though he died in 1956). His influence was not limited to academic or political circles. It reached the public at large. Even today's modernising rhetoric which the socialists are using in the electoral campaigns could be traced to the views held by Ortega y Gasset. If we come down from the plane of ideas, or ideologies, to that of social processes, it might be appropriate to recollect that from the late 1950s until the early 1970s, millions of Spaniards were emigrating to European countries looking for work. Similarly, a few years later, millions of Europeans travelled as tourists to Spain. In both cases the Spaniards could experiment with the *comparative perception of the splendid European possibility.*

In the late 1960s and early 1970s, for social movements, labour, students and the political opposition to the Franco regime, Europe meant freedom (*la libertad*), the referent which should be involved against the authoritarian Regime. Even the Regime itself asked to be admitted to the Common Market at a date as early as 1962, taking into account its political and economic dependence.

On the other hand, given the sociohistorical conditions so briefly portrayed, the formation of a strong unitary Spanish nationalism was impossible. The weakness of the Spanish Nation State manifested as we have seen in the year of 1898, and later on in the Civil War of 1936–39, had as a consequence the formation of a diversified and plural Spanish national identity, in which some "peripheric" nationalisms (mainly Catalan and Basque) will not only appear as alternatives but as a negation of the Spanish national identity itself. In this context, Europe meant, on the one hand, the solution by dissolution of all internal problems, and on the other hand, the membership which could increase the so much needed collective self-esteem. It is not surprising then that under these conditions resistance to the entry into the European Community was so scarce, in spite of the restriction that it supposed for the agrarian sector, or the tariff disarmament in the industrial one. The signing of the Treaty was presented, and probably experienced symbolically by the great majority of the population, as a *confirmation* of an historical aspiration to "Europeity".

Therefore, either from the perspective of the history of ideas and social movements, of economics, or from the point of view of the mirror glass game of collective identities, the experience of Europe as an aspiration had to be strong among the Spaniards. The survey data considered in this chapter shows this.

TABLE 7.1   Mean ratings of favourable sentiments towards world areas or countries*

European Community	3.18	3.80	6.09
Iberoamerica	3.00	3.52	5.81
Eastern Europe	2.87	3.42	5.25
Japan	2.75	3.24	4.74
Countries of Black Africa	2.73	3.20	4.80
India	2.72	3.15	4.59
North America (USA and Canada)	2.62	3.13	4.79
Arab countries of North Africa (Morocco, Algeria, Egypt)	2.53	3.02	4.71

N1 = 1200   N2 = 1200   N3 = 744

* In N1 scores range from 4 (very favourable) to (very unfavourable) with no neutral point.
  In N2 scores range from 5 (very favourable) to 1 (very unfavourable) with 3 as neutral point.
  In N3 scores range from 7 (very favourable) to 1 (very unfavourable) with 4 as neutral point.

Table 7.1 which includes the responses to the question "what are your sentiments towards each of these countries or block of countries: very favourable, fairly favourable, fairly unfavourable or very unfavourable?" shows that the most favourable sentiment seems to be for the European Community in all cases. Also, when the question is put in a hypothetical way, asking "who would you like to be the winner in a football match in which the European and Latin-American selections will face each other?", the great majority seems to identify with Europe; 48% and 55% of the first and second sample respectively preferred Europe to win while 23% of the first sample and 21% of the second sample preferred Latin-America to win.

Now, if the confrontation instead of being global between continents is between countries, some of which belong to Europe and some to Latin-America, the preferred country to win in the first place is a Latin-American one (Argentina) (see Table 7.2).

TABLE 7.2   Preferred winner in football match between the European and Latin-American selections

	First Place	Second Place		First Place	Second Place
Japan	10.5	8.2	Ecuador	10.3	11.3
Hungary	2.8	4.5	Austria	8.3	8.6
Nigeria	4.4	4.7	Hungary	4.3	6.1
Holland	8.3	16.6	Honduras	5.9	8.9
Algeria	2.7	5.4	Holland	10.0	17.8
Great Britain	9.7	11.0	Argentina	32.5	15.7
Argentina	28.5	13.0	None	8.2	8.7
None	5.2	6.5	D.L/N.A.	20.5	23.5
D.K./N.A.	27.3	29.2			

N1 = 1200 N2 = 1200

TABLE 7.3   Mean ratings of liking for different peoples

Italians	6.37	5.95	6.88
Mexicans	6.37	—	6.66
Argentinians	6.31	6.25	6.69
Japanese	5.98	5.71	5.94
Germans	5.61	5.45	6.09
Russians	5.56	5.42	6.41
Chinese	5.54	—	5.47
Portuguese	5.47	5.45	6.58
French	5.37	5.23	5.76
North Americans	5.18	5.08	5.48
Polish	5.14	—	6.18
Africans	5.14	—	5.86
English	4.89	4.96	5.59
Gypsies	4.14	—	5.66
Moroccans	4.12	4.10	5.20
	N1 = 1200	N2 = 1200	N3 = 744

To identify with Europe as a whole seems to be different from identifying with specific countries which are part of Europe. This observation finds further support in another type of question shown in Table 7.3 "who do you like . . . the following peoples". The responses ranged from 0 (not at all) to 10 (very much). First, the similarity in rank orderings mainly in the first two samples which are representative of the adult Spanish population is notable. Table 7.3 shows that a Latin group of peoples (Italian, Argentinian, Mexican) is the most liked by the Spanish, while the Moroccans, Gypsies, English and North Americans are the least liked. The fact that this structure of preferences happens to emerge in a sample of well-qualified and educated persons suggests that this is a structure of international attitudes quite generalised among the Spanish. The post positive attitudes towards the Latin, with the exception of Portuguese, in the two general population samples seem to respond to a sentiment of sympathy and perceived similarity between the Spanish and these peoples. The origins of these perceptions can be found in history. Historical factors may also account for the relatively little liking for the English and North American and, to a lesser extent, for the French. It is obvious that European national identities have been constructed to a great extent through wars with each other; one only has to go for a walk in the squares, schools, museums or palaces in European countries to be reminded of this. Victory halls, triumphal arches, statues of generals and admirals, heroes of "la Résistance", all appear before us as symbols in which national identities have been forged and kept in the collective memory of European peoples. It is many years since Spaniards have had any war, with the exception of the Civil War. However, they seem to keep memory of those which they had in the past, as it seems to appear in their international attitudes. Otherwise, it is difficult to understand how peoples so admired in other respects are comparatively so little liked.

The Orientations towards Iberoamerica: On the Iberoamerican Community of Nations

The idea of achieving a certain form of continental unity in Latin-America goes back to the same beginnings of its independence. Bolivar envisioned such unity in the form of a confederation of peoples sharing the same language, religion, customs and traditions.

This imagined community by *"el libertador"* did not go very far in reality however. The newly liberated peoples had to lay a new institutional base and a new legitimacy and reorganise their economies. The immediate and urgent problems left little time to the new leaders for unitary undertakings (Safford, 1987). On the other hand, the United States of the North actively opposed any such project for a united states in the south, according to sound *realpolitik* logic.

The rapprochement sentiment started to arise anew once the old colonial power, Spain, ceased to be a threat and hegemonic North America was perceived as a new one. So a process of rapprochement started again among the Latin-American peoples and their old "mother country". The North American interventions in the area, specially when Mexico lost half of its territory in 1847, had created resentment towards the United States in the Peninsula as a consequence of the humiliation due to the war of 1898.

Sectors of the Spanish intelligentsia which did not share the Europeanism of Ortega but who fostered a re-encounter of archetypes in Spanish history as opposed to the modernity represented by Europe, will find in the idea of America and its potential development a way in which to reaffirm their collective identity. It was rediscovery which soothed wounded national sentiment; but it allowed also to look to the future.

Such a mood accompanied the intensification of relations which went on until the end of the Republic and the beginning of the Civil War.

After the war thousands of professionals, scientists, professors, who were on the republican side, went in exile to different Latin-American countries, mainly to Mexico and Argentina. This was a different emigration from that which went to America before and comprised mainly peasants and workers. The exile experience of these republicans forced them, from a situation of direct personal involvement, to think about the relationship between Spain and Iberoamerica, and to a widening of their identifications and national loyalties. From the beginning they could feel that they were not simply exiled or *"desterrados"* but *"transterrados"* (moved from one country to another). This is a notion put forward by the philosopher Jose Gaos; to express that although not in their country of origin, the one to which they now arrived was not alien or foreign to them. Because of the intellectual prestige of many of these exiles it is difficult to overestimate the importance this "pilgrim Spain" has had in increasing the awareness and interest of the Spaniards for America (Abellan and Monclus, 1989).

In Spain itself, intellectuals and politicians of Franco's regime did not forget the theme of Hispanoamerica. On the contrary they used it as a central element of the Spanish national identity designed by the authoritarian ideology. With a fascist and nostalgically imperialist rhetoric in a first period, and later emphasising the traditional and Catholic values of "eternal Spain", "Mother country" and "Hispanicity" (Hispanidad) were spoken about as a space of cultural and spiritual integration constituted by a set of values which was opposed equally to socio-liberal materialism of the west and to Marxist ideology.

This idealistic and authoritarian discourse was well tuned with the conservative and Populist Latin-American sectors, providing the regime with an international support that it so badly needed. However during this period the Institute of Hispanic Culture was created, designed and conceived as a state organisation for promoting and facilitating educational and cultural exchanges. Working groups of specialists in Latin-American themes were formed and some periodicals and publications started (Rubio Cordon, 1989). With the transition to democracy this Institute was renamed as the Institute for Iberoamerican Cooperation.

So the two ideological Spains had, at least, one thing in common: their links to Latin-America.

With the commemoration of the V Centenary of 1492, America was very present in Spanish public opinion. Many encounters, meetings and all sorts of events have taken place over several years. This commemoration has been criticised on many grounds. Starting with the words "discover", "commemoration", "celebration", indigenous writers and leaders have pointed out that it may be inappropriate to celebrate a date which implies the violent conquest and destruction of their culture and ancestors. The eurocentrism implied by the term discovery has also been pointed out, and other terms like "encounter of cultures", "civilisations shock", "concealment" have been proposed.

The commemoration of events of this nature, which imply a retrospective look, can be considered as part of a process of maintaining and/or changing collective identities, particularly national identities. The past may be invoked to reinforce communication and understanding or even for a collective mea culpa and expiation. All of that may have happened to different degrees during the commemoration of the V Centenary by Spanish society.

One of the possible meanings of this commemoration may lie in the concept of the Iberoamerican Community of Nations. This is the meaning given by the Mexican philosopher Leopoldo Zea:

"The point of departure of a Motherland of motherlands which would embrace all our peoples on both sides of the Atlantic dreamed of by the great leaders of the Hispanoamerican independence" (Zea, 1989, 204).

Defined in this manner the concept of this Iberoamerican Community expresses the wish of a project, more or less utopian, of convergence and integration of the Iberoamerican countries in some form of supranational organisation. Psychologically it would imply an emerging sentiment of cultural and/or political belongingness wider than that of the national states integrated in it.

In recent years the concept has had more visibility and organisational concreteness for public opinion as a result of the institutionalisation of the conference of Heads of State and Government of those countries. In this context, in which intellectuals and politicians speak of the reality of a project and the project of a reality, it may be asked to what extent it is possible to use survey data to examine the existence of orientations, attitudes, opinions, beliefs and sentiments which may be interpreted as evidence of the presence of this project in public opinion and ultimately in Spanish identity.

Concerning the stated interest of the Spanish population towards different areas of the world, it is Europe for which they show the highest interest and, with much difference in the second place, Iberoamerica. We have also seen that in terms of favourable or unfavourable sentiments the samples show a similar pattern, although in this case the differences are smaller (see Table 7.1). It is difficult to know the meaning of responses to questions of this type, referring to abstract attitudinal objects such as areas of the world or countries. But it does not seem an overstatement to think that higher scores reflect a certain positive predisposition towards these countries. It is possible that this trend does not imply an underlying attitude but an orientation created by the perceived desirability of the response in the interview situation, or other normative expectations. But even in this case the problem of having to account for why certain areas or countries—some of which have a clear historical meaning for the Spanish—give rise to more or less favourable sentiments still remains.

On the other hand if the stated preferences for specific winners in sport competitions or matches may be interpreted as a form of identification, the higher identification with Europe seems clear in the data. This result is obvious, particularly if we take into account the fact that the question assumed that Spain was part of the European selection. However, what is worth emphasising is that even under these conditions more than 20% of the sample seems to prefer the Latin-American selection as winner. Besides, if the question is not presented in terms of a dilemma implying an option between two continental selections but in terms of specific countries the preferences are clearly in favour of the Latin-American ones (Table 7.2).

These survey data seem to point to a generalised sentiment of affinity or identification with Iberoamerica (or at least with a very significant country such as Argentina). Here it will suffice to remind ourselves of what happened with Spanish public opinion, and in Iberoamerica in general, during the war in the Falklands, in spite of the negative image in which the military Argentinian government had previously been perceived.

TABLE 7.4   Percentage of sample agreeing with the idea "Nowadays there is much talk about the possibility of organizing an Iberoamerican Community of Nations, which would integrate the Spanish and Portuguese speaking countries"

Agree very much	18.2	16.0
Agree much	22.1	23.0
Agree	26.5	29.0
Do not agree at all	10.3	10.2
D.K./N.A.	22.9	21.8
	N1 = 1200	N2 = 1200

Another body of evidence which is consistent with what I am trying to point out is the survey data about Spanish attitudes to the so-called economic immigration. In the last decade Spain has changed from being a country of emigration to one of immigration. There does exist justified concern about increasing signs of xenophobia and ethnic discrimination, sometimes with open expressions of violence. Three surveys about the attitude of the Spaniards towards immigrants show a consistent *positive discrimination* towards Latin-Americans (CIRES, 1991, 1992, 1993) in comparison with the attitudes towards other ethnic or national groups. This is specially true among the most educated strata of the population. These differential attitudes would be hard to understand but for the fact that it can be assumed that a sentiment of belongingness or of inclusion in the same linguistic or historical and cultural community exists, transcending the dividing political and geographical lines.

Responses to the direct question about the agreement with the idea of the Iberoamerican Community of nations appears in Table 7.4. Put in such a way, it seems difficult to disagree with. The same categories in which responses are codified are not symmetrical; having three steps of agreement and one of disagreement. Even if the respondents do not understand the question being posed to them it is consequently easy to be in agreement. The high percentages of N.R. makes one suspect such a bias. These considerations seem less relevant if they are extended to the third sample (N3) in which the university level of education and the social position of respondents suggest a good understanding of the question. In this case an analogy between the British Commonwealth and the Iberoamerican Community was established and they were questioned about the "desirability" and the "possibility" of such a community in the Spanish-speaking peoples. Scores could range between 0 (not at all) and 10 (yes, wholly). The mean "desirability" for all the sample was 7.1 which fairly coincides with general samples, and the mean for "possibility" was 4.3 which indicates that expectations about the implementation or realisation of such a community are not very optimistic.

If the attempt is made to oppose the perception of Spain's membership to Europe or Latin-America, as it happens with the first two items in Table 7.5 we

TABLE 7.5 Percentage of agreement and disagreement with the notion that Spain should align itself with Latin-America

	Agree	Disagree	Agree	Disagree	Agree	Disagree
The Iberoamerican Community of Nations is no doubt a great idea but Spain is Europe and its roles are essentially in Europe	55.6	25.4	66.8	18.6	52.2	31.3
Spain is geographically in Europe, but because of its language, history and traditions should mainly relate itself to Latin-America	49.6	39.4	53.0	37.7	40.5	37.8
Spain is the mother country of Latin-America and this role should prevail above all other considerations, even economic interests	26.7	54.1	32.2	49.7	8.1	81.0
	N1 = 1200		N2 = 1200		N3 = 744	

can see again a general trend of a preferred orientation towards Europe. However, the statement that "Spain in spite of being in Europe, must relate itself mainly to Iberoamerica", also has considerable support. The intended problematic character of these two items in Table 7.5 seems to have been perceived, given the high overlapping in both responses. The contradiction implied in these two options does not seem to be experienced by the population; although in the third sample it holds to some extent (about 15% of the sample). Finding themselves in the dilemma of having to decide between Europe and Iberoamerica they again will go for Europe (in fact they have already done so).

Nevertheless, it is also evident that the idea of a strong link with Iberoamerica has been, and it seems that it will be, a central reference for Spanish international orientations, although they do not have the perception that this aspect of their identity is contradictory with the other one.

Finally it seems that those links should lose their idealistic overtones implied in the concept of "Mother country" (Table 7.5) and establish the links in a more pragmatic way.

Concluding Remarks

From survey data about international opinions and attitudes of Spaniards it is possible to observe differential response patterns that we believe do not only express a transient collective mood but a more stable structure of evaluations, preferences, opinions and so on, which are related to significant aspects of their collective memory and of their future aspirations, that is their collective identity as a nation which, although in a different way, is involved in two ongoing processes of supranationality, Europe and Iberoamerican Community of Nations. The European aspirations do not seem to exclude negative recollections about its relationships with other European nations as the rankings on the liking of different peoples seem to indicate. The lower liking of the British and North American could be interpreted as an expression of an "historical resentment" towards the Anglo Saxon world.

The acceptance of the idea of the Iberoamerican Community of Nations may be said to have a collective psychological foundation in: (a) a sentiment of affinity and belonging to a cultural and historical community, shown in the differential responses towards countries and peoples as well as a positive discrimination towards Latin-American immigrants and (b) an historical resentment to which I have just referred.

The sociohistorical and psychosociological perspectives of these international orientations help us to understand the idea of an Iberoamerican Community as a project of supranationality, however Utopian it may be, in which the Spanish identity feels involved.

References

Abellan, J. L. and Monclus, A. (eds)(1989). *El pensamiento español contemporaneo y la idea de América*, Vol. II. Madrid: Editorial Anthropos.

CIRES, Centro de Investigaciones de la Realidad Social, C/ Orense, 35, 28029 Madrid.

Ortega y Gasset, J. (1989). *Ensayos sobre la generación del 98*. Madrid: Alianza Editorial.

Rubio Cordon, J. L. (1989). El oficialismo institucional: El instituto de cultura Hispánica. In J. L. Abellan and A. Monclus (eds), *El pensamiento español contemporaneo y la idea de América*, Vol. II. Madrid: Editorial Antropos.

Safford, F. (1987). Politics, ideology and society. In L. Bethell (ed.), *Spanish America after Independence c. 1820–1870*. Cambridge: Cambridge University Press.

Zea, L. (1989). 12 de octubre de 1492: Descubrimiento o encubrimiento? In L. Zea (ed.), *El descubrimiento de América y su sentido actual*. Mexico: Fondo de Cultura Económica.

8

Dimensions of Social Identity in Northern Ireland

KAREN TREW AND DENNY E. BENSON

Queen's University of Belfast, Northern Ireland and Kent State University, United States

Academic and official commentaries generally use the terms "Protestants" and "Catholics" to refer to the two communities in Northern Ireland. However, Whyte (1990) noted that the practice of using religious labels for these communities is quite recent and twenty years ago it was not unusual to describe the dichotomy in terms of unionist and nationalist or the Ulster British and the Ulster Irish. Whyte argued that the main advantage for researchers of using the Protestant/Catholic labels is that they seem to correspond to the fundamental reference groups for people living in Northern Ireland. Furthermore, it is usually assumed that although these labels are denominational they also reflect contrasting national identities and political allegiances as the division between Catholics and Protestants is not tempered by an overarching shared national identity or competing sources of group identification (Horowitz, 1990; Moxon-Browne, 1991).

The Northern Ireland problem is often conceptualised in terms of a clash of religious identities, but as research has demonstrated group identities are dynamic and subject to situational influences and changes across time. For example, a series of attitude surveys summarised by Trew (in press) clearly show how, between 1968 and 1992, more Protestants saw themselves as British and less saw themselves as Irish while more Catholics saw themselves as Irish and less saw themselves as British. These surveys also found that in the 1980s the label "Northern Irish" gained popularity as a badge of identity for both Catholics and Protestants.

Similarly, when Waddell and Cairns (1986) studied the effects of situations on ethnopolitical identity in Northern Ireland by instructing subjects to

123

indicate their position on a scale ranging from "very British" to "very Irish", as expected Protestants showed a preference for British identity and Catholics tended to choose the Irish identity. However, whereas the Catholic respondents only felt either more or less Irish, the Protestant group revealed a more complicated pattern of identification. They felt most British when there was a possible threat to their identity (e.g. IRA violence) and they felt Irish on occasions which were related to Irish culture and residence in the island of Ireland.

Gallagher (1989) added to our understanding of the complexities of sociopolitical identity in Northern Ireland by using experimental methods and qualitative techniques to explore the impact of religious, national or political group labels on intergroup behaviour. His results suggested that firstly, these identities were not necessarily interchangeable for Protestants although there was an essential unity between the religious and political identities for Catholics. Secondly, the meaning of the group labels varied for ingroup members according to their political party preference. As Gallagher (1989) concluded "a label . . . may identify or represent an identity, but it says nothing about the significance or meaning attached to that identity nor does it appear to include the possibility of differential significance of meaning".

This chapter presents findings from the first large-scale study which has used traditional survey methodology in an effort to assess empirically the relationships among the various identities available to Catholics and Protestants in Northern Ireland and the meanings and attachments associated with these identities.

Theoretical developments in sociology and psychology have increasingly been concerned with the nature and role of the self, self-concept and identity. Researchers from many perspectives have been exploring identity and the self-concept. Within social psychology, there has been little cross-referencing between those (mainly European, but increasingly including Americans) whose interest in this area derived from the social identity theory of intergroup relations (e.g. Hogg and Abrams, 1990) and those whose interest derived from other perspectives (e.g. Breakwell, 1992; Deaux, 1991, 1992; Oyserman and Markus, 1993). It is therefore not surprising that few psychological social psychologists seem to have developed any links with sociological social psychologists who are working from perspective of identity theory associated with the symbolic interactionists as developed in the 1980s by people like Stryker, Serpe, Callero, Burke and others.

Any attempt to draw on several different perspectives on the self must take account of the potential problems associated with different methods as well as meanings. As Breakwell (1992) noted "achieving definitional consensus in this area is virtually impossible", but it is possible that there is considerable overlap between apparently different dimensions of the self or alternatively that diverse perspectives can be integrated to provide a more global understanding of the nature of social identity. The measures, which were employed in the survey of social identity in Northern Ireland, were designed to assess dimensions of the self which are seen to be central from the perspectives of structural symbolic interaction theory and social identity theory respectively.

Structural Symbolic Interaction Theory

Emanating most directly from the work of G. H. Mead (1934), symbolic interaction theory posits that the "meaning" of an object, a person, or a behaviour is learned from other human beings by learning what symbols are attached to those objects, persons, or behaviours. For symbolic interaction theory one's definition of self, with attendant emotional, behavioural, and cognitive consequences, occurs as a result of the processing and interplay of symbols as they are affected and constrained by roles and role partners. Symbolic interaction theory is nowadays seen as being divided into two "schools"; the "Iowa" and the "Chicago". While these differences are too involved to discuss here, proponents of the former hold that it is possible to investigate the various concepts and processes of the theory using quantitative techniques and survey methods. Proponents of the latter believe this does violence to these concepts and processes, preferring the use of qualitative data gathering techniques and case study methods. Anchored in the "Iowa" school of symbolic interaction theory, Stryker (1980) and others (e.g. Rosenberg, 1979) have focused on the manner in which elements of social structure, such as the social role, help to shape and define a person's sense of self. Hence, this particular "version" of symbolic interaction theory is termed "structural symbolic interaction theory" and the aspect concerned with the development of self is called "Identity theory". The major concepts of Identity theory are: society (social structure), social role, self-concept or "self", role identity, and the related concepts of identity salience and identity commitment (cognitive and affective).

For Identity theory, the concept of society refers to all large-scale patterns of social activity created by human beings (e.g. the social institution of family and religion) that persist over long periods of time. A social role is a particular pattern of behaviour located within an institution that is performed by a person (e.g. the behavioural configuration that a person called a "Protestant" performs in the institution of religion). Self-concept or "Self" refers to all the characteristics a person believes they possess, the meaning of these characteristics, and the way they are organised. Thus a woman might define herself in order of importance to herself, as Irish, an architect, a wife and intelligent. The concept of "role identity" refers to internalised and organised symbolic aspects of these role designations, with accompanying meanings and behavioural expectations, associated with playing a particular social role. The more that a person's social networks revolve around that identity, the more rewards the person receives for having that identity (cognitive commitment), the more interaction they will have based on that identity (affective commitment—extensive), and the more affectively involved they will be with the identity (affective commitment—intensive). Identity theory argues that increasing levels of commitment to a particular identity lead to increased salience for that identity and its impact on what the person thinks, feels and does.

These processes spawn self-concepts which are both idiosyncratic and at the same time shared in common with other people in a particular society. Therefore, modifications in how people are connected to the social structure produce changes in commitment to social roles that, in turn, produce changes in identities, producing changes in self. Consequently, as identities alter in presence, meaning, commitment or salience, changes are produced in how the person processes information about an identity, how they feel about that identity, and the behavioural choices people make that are pertinent to that identity (e.g. Callero, 1985; Stryker, 1991).

Identity Theory and Authenticity

A number of writers (e.g. Erickson, 1993; Gecas, 1986 and 1991; Turner, 1987; Turner and Billings, 1991) have discussed the relationship between having a particular role identity and the extent to which the person believes that identity reflects who they "really are." That is, to what extent are the characteristics of the role isomorphic with the person's perception of their own idiosyncratic characteristics and systems of self-meaning? In the context of the present study, the question is whether the respondents believe that the role identity they have chosen as the "best" description of "who they are", reflects the "kind" of person they think they are. If so, that identity can be said to be an "authentic" one; if not the identity is "inauthentic", "false", and contradictory to their own self-values.

Discussing the motivational aspects of "authenticity", Gecas (1991) argues that people will try to avoid or escape role identities perceived to be "inauthentic" because being in this position leads to feelings of self- estrangement, anomie and depression. Thus, if presented with choices, Identity theory would predict that a person would not incorporate such a role identity into their self-structure. The construct of authenticity has not been extensively used in empirical research (cf. Keto and Benson, 1993; Reid, Epstein and Benson 1994, in press; Zurcher and Snow, 1981). Using this construct should help more fully explore the dimensions of the various identities displayed by the people of Northern Ireland.

Social Identity and Psychological Research in Northern Ireland

Social identity theory (SIT) has provided the starting point for most psychological research on intergroup conflict in Northern Ireland (Cairns, 1982; Trew, 1992). Social identity was defined by Tajfel (1981) as "that part of an individual's self-concept which derives from his[her] knowledge of his[her] membership of a social group (or groups) together with the value and emotional significance attached to that membership" (1981, 255). Tajfel argued that the relative status of societal groups and value-laden comparisons between such groups may become an important aspect of an individual's self image.

Accordingly, membership of a minority group may potentially confer negative social identity, especially in a social system which is perceived to be both stable and legitimate.

Among the unresolved issues which were raised by research on social identity in Northern Ireland is the question of whether Protestants and Catholics see themselves as minority or majority groups. According to the "Double Minority" model (Jackson, 1971), as Protestants are the minority in the island of Ireland and Catholics are the minority in Northern Ireland both groups should identify themselves as threatened minorities and therefore those who identify with these groups are potentially faced with negative social identities. However, Cairns (1982), who reviewed the available evidence, concluded that Catholics and Protestants in Northern Ireland appear to possess relatively positive social identities. He proposed that these findings could be understood within a Double Majority model.

Until recently, researchers had to use indirect and often very ingenious methods (e.g. Stringer and Cairns, 1983) in order to examine empirically how individuals evaluated their own groups. According to Cairns (1987), these studies suggest that "Protestants possess a definite positive identity while Catholics also evaluate their social identity positively but in a less clear-cut way." The recent development of a collective self-esteem scale (Crocker and Luhtanen, 1990) provides the first opportunity directly to measure how individuals evaluate the ingroup with which they identify. Although this scale was developed to assess satisfaction with and positive evaluation of belonging to unspecified groups, it can be linked to particular groups (Ethier and Deaux, 1990; Luhtanen and Crocker, 1991).

The use of this scale provided not only a basis for assessing how individuals in Northern Ireland evaluate their own groups but it also enabled us to compare directly dimensions of the self which are embedded in Social Identity theory with those which are associated with Structural Symbolic Interaction theory.

Methodology

The Sample

The subjects for this study were first-year psychology undergraduates at Queen's University of Belfast who were attending the initial laboratory classes. They were asked to complete the questionnaire at the end of their classes by the class demonstrators. All agreed to participate in the study but thirty questionnaires had to be discarded because they were incomplete or spoiled.

Measures

All instrument items, response categories, factor loadings and Cronbach's Alpha scores can be found in the Appendix to this chapter.

Identity Preference

Identity preference was measured by presenting the respondent with nine very common and well-known political and religious "identity labels" in Northern Ireland and asking them to choose which one of these terms "best describes" them. Later in the instrument, the respondent was asked to look again at the nine labels and choose the one that was the "**second** best description of them". The "identity labels" are: a Protestant, a Loyalist, a Catholic, a Unionist, a Nationalist, Ulster, Irish, Northern Irish, and British.

Identity Salience

The salience of the identity chosen as the "best description" and the one chosen as the "**second**-best description" was measured by a modification of the Callero (1985) "Identity Salience Scale". This scale consists of five items with a Likert response format of four choices. Principal components factor analysis with varimax rotation shows these items load on a single dimension. The Cronbach's Alpha score for this scale for this sample is .82.

Identity Commitment

This variable was measured by combining separate scales measuring cognitive commitment and affective commitment—both (2)intensive and (3)extensive. All three scales were adapted from the work of Burke and Reitzes (1991). The five items assessing the concept of cognitive commitment measure the degree to which a person feels rewarded for holding a particular identity. The items assessing affective commitment (both the four items for intensive and the three for extensive), tap the extent to which a particular identity involves and embeds the person in a network of others for whom that identity is important. Principal components factor analysis with varimax rotation, shows these twelve items do load only on their respective dimensions. Correlational analysis (not shown) demonstrates that the scales assessing the three types of identity commitment are significantly correlated ($p < .001$). The Cronbach's Alpha score for this scale for this sample is .81.

Sense of Authenticity

This construct was measured by a three-item scale developed for this research. In accordance with the theoretical properties of the construct (see above) and scored in a Likert format, the three statements are: "Being (*this description*) is consistent with my important values", "Deep down, I often feel that being (*this description*) is not really 'me'", and "Most of the time I like thinking of myself as (*this description*)". Principal components factor analysis with varimax rotation, indicates that these three items load on a single factor. The Cronbach's Alpha score for this scale for this sample is .71.

To obtain a measure of discriminant validity, the three items in this "authenticity" scale were combined with the five items measuring a cognate construct—identity salience. This scale was chosen because it is well known in the literature and has good scale properties. When subjected to principal components factor analysis (using varimax rotation), the eight items cleanly loaded on two separate dimensions. The zero-order correlation between these two scales is a modest and not significant .14. These procedures suggest that the three items comprising the measure of authenticity have good discriminate validity. While the reliability of the scale is only "respectable" (DeVellis, 1991), it should be observed that, *ceteris paribus*, it is more difficult to achieve higher alpha scores with relatively few scale items (Carmines and Zeller, 1980).

Collective Self-esteem

The collective self-esteem scale used in this study was a modified version of the sixteen-item scale developed by Crocker and her colleagues (Crocker and Luhtanen, 1990). It is based on the combined scores from four four-item subscales. These are: membership-esteem (how good or worthy a member they are of their social group); private collective self-esteem (how good they judge their social group); public collective self-esteem (how other people evaluate their social group), and identity importance (the importance of group membership to their self-concept). Principal components factor analysis with varimax rotation, shows that the items of each of the four subscales, load cleanly and exclusively on their respective dimensions. The average inter-item correlation for the 16 items is .32 ($p < .001$) and the entire scale has a Cronbach's alpha for this sample of .84. These calculations indicate that, while each four item question set is assessing a different aspect, the entire scale is tapping the common dimension of collective self-esteem, and is a reliable measure of this construct.

The above information confirms that the measures used in this study have very acceptable psychometric properties and, thus, should allow good assessment of the respective constructs (DeVellis, 1991).

Results

The following information is intended as a "demographic" profile of the 370 respondents in this study. Sixty-eight per cent of the sample were women, 32% were men. The mean age was 19.9. Seventy-three per cent of the sample were either eighteen or nineteen years old. Fifty-two per cent of sample described themselves as "Catholic", 34% described themselves as "Protestant", with 8% describing themselves as "other" (6% did not answer the question). Twenty- eight per cent lived in a "city", 39% lived in a "rural area" and 34% lived in an "urban area". Twenty-six per cent of the sample lived in Belfast, 16% lived in County Antrim (Belfast is located in this county), and another 23% lived in County Down which is adjacent to County Antrim. Eight per cent of the sample was from the Republic of Ireland. Twenty-six per cent reported their political party preference as Social Democratic and Labour, 20% the Alliance party, 16% reported "other", and 16% had a preference for either the Democratic Unionist Party or the Official Unionist Party. Almost 6% reported their political party preference as Sinn Fein.

Identity Preferences

Table 8.1 contains the information concerning the identities chosen from the list of nine identities by the respondents as being most important, and the second most important, description of themselves.

As can be seen from Table 8.1, the identity of "Irish" and that of "Northern Irish" were chosen most often with almost 30% of the respondents choosing one or the other as their most important identity of the list of nine identities. The third and fourth most important identities for the respondents were "British" (15.7%) and "Catholic" (13.0%). None of the respondents chose the identities of "Loyalist" or "Unionist" as their most important identity. The identity of "Nationalist" was chosen by almost 2% while the identity of "Ulster" was chosen by 1.5%.

The most important second identity was that of "Catholic" (24.9%) with "Northern Irish" a close second (22.4%). The third, fourth and fifth choices for the second most important identity were closely grouped at "Irish" (14.3%), "Protestant" (13.8%), and "British" (12.7%). "Loyalist" was not chosen by anyone and the identities of "Unionist", "Nationalist" and "Ulster" were chosen by only a handful of respondents.

Summarising these results it can be observed that the three most important identities for these respondents ("Irish", "Northern Irish", and "British") are all

TABLE 8.1   Numbers and percentages for the identity chosen as best describing the respondent and the second best description (N = 370)

	'I would best describe myself as:'		*'The second best description of me is:'*	
	N	%	N	%
A Protestant	33	08.9	51	13.8
A Loyalist	00	00.0	00	00.0
A Catholic	48	13.0	92	24.9
A Unionist	00	00.0	05	01.4
A Nationalist	07	01.9	17	04.6
Ulster	05	01.4	20	05.4
Irish	109	29.5	53	14.3
Northern Irish	109	29.5	83	22.4
British	58	15.7	47	12.7

national as opposed to explicitly religious or political identities. The "religious" identities ("Catholic" and "Protestant") were more likely to be chosen as a second rather than a most important identity. Combining the two identity choices indicates that the identity of "Northern Irish" is the one chosen most often; 51.9% ($N = 192$) choose it as either their most important or their second most important, with the second overall choice being "Irish" (41.8%; $N = 162$).

Identity Combinations

As Thoits (1992) and Benson (1993) have noted, investigating different identity configurations may have more explanatory potential for a wide variety of questions than exploring the effects of a single identity. Because we asked the respondents about their two most important identities, it is possible to go beyond the analysis of a single identity and to *begin* to analyse identity configurations. The cross-classification of respondents' first and second identity choices can be found in Table 8.2.

The identities listed on the rows in Table 8.2 are the first choice of the respondents; those in the columns are the second. As can be seen in that table, the identity combination chosen most often is that of "Irish-Catholic" ($N = 58$). The second most common choice is a tie between "Catholic-Irish" and "Northern Irish-British", followed closely by "Northern Irish-Catholic" and "Irish-Northern Irish". Further inspection of the data in Table 8.2 reveals that for the first choices of "Protestant" "Catholic" and "British", the choice of a second most important identity falls, essentially, to one of two identities. The dispersion of the second choice is much greater for the "Irish" and "Northern Irish" identities.

The second identity choice for the group of 109 who initially chose the "Northern Irish" identity reveals that two identity configurations that would not usually be found together—"Protestant-British", and "Irish-Catholic"—do combine here and, in roughly equal numbers. Fifty-two "Protestant-British"

TABLE 8.2   Cross-classification of Most Important Identity (Row) with Second Most Important Identity (Column) (N = 370)

	Prot.	Loyal.	Cath.	Union.	Nation.	Ulster.	Irish.	Nr. Ir.	Brit.	Tot.
Protestant	2	0	0	2	0	5	0	13	11	33
Loyalist	0	0	0	0	0	0	0	0	0	0
Catholic	0	0	2	0	1	0	30	14	1	48
Unionist	0	0	0	0	0	0	0	0	0	0
Nationalist	0	0	3	0	0	0	4	0	0	7
Ulster	0	0	0	0	0	0	1	3	1	5
Irish	5	0	58	0	16	2	0	27	1	109
N. Irish	22	0	29	0	0	10	17	1	30	109
British	22	0	0	3	0	3	1	25	2	58
Totals	51	0	92	5	17	20	53	83	47	370

make the identity of "Northern Irish" their first choice as well as forty-six "Irish-Catholics". This remarkable finding may signal the occurrence of "identity searching." Of all the nine "identity labels", the identity of "Northern Irish" is the one with the least amount of symbolic connections to the historic conflict in Northern Ireland. It may be that these young university students are attempting to create psychological distance between the provinces' conflicts and cleavages and important markers of self. As such, this identity ("Northern Irish") would be a relatively "new" identity. Thus, the cultural and linguistic meanings for this identity have not yet been carefully developed, articulated, honed and anchored to the symbolically important events associated with the provinces' "troubles."

Given the less than distinct meanings for the "Northern Irish" identity, it would follow that if one chose this identity as a self descriptor, s(he) would be somewhat uncertain about the exact dimensions of that choice. At the same time, the "identity labels" traditionally associated with the cleavages of the province, e.g. "Catholic," or "Protestant" have meaning structures firmly embedded in, and carefully explicated by, the cultural and symbolic life of Northern Ireland. Consequently, it would be expected that the level of salience and authenticity for the identity of "Northern Irish" would be lower than for the "traditional" identities of "Irish," or "British".

Dimensions of Identity

Salience

Based on the above discussion, Structural Symbolic Interaction theory (Callero 1985; Serpe 1987; Stryker, 1968, 1980, and 1991), would predict that mean levels of salience for the identity of "Northern Irish" would be lower than for the "traditional" identities of "Catholic", "Protestant", or "Irish." On the basis of the argument that for Protestants in Northern Ireland, the identity of "British" is held with ambivalence and without strong structural or symbolic support from the mainland British (e.g. Bruce, 1986; Whyte, 1990) it would also be predicted that the salience level for the identity of "British" would not be as high as the "traditional" identities.

The data in Table 8.3, which contains the information regarding salience levels for the five most important identities chosen by the respondents in this study, confirm these predictions.

Mean identity salience scores are lower for the identities of "Northern Irish" and "British" than for "Protestant", "Catholic", or "Irish". T tests (not shown) confirm that the difference between the means for the identities of "Northern Irish" and "British" is not significant; the difference between the highest mean score ("Catholic") and the lowest ("British") is significant at $p < .001$. These data indicate that if one's most important identity (of the nine listed) is either "Catholic" or "Irish", it is more important to the person than if the "most important" identity is either "Northern Irish" or "British".

TABLE 8.3   Means and standard deviations for the degree of salience, commitment, sense of authenticity and collective self-esteem for the identity chosen as 'describes me best'.

	Protestant (n = 33)	Catholic (n = 48)	Irish (n = 109)	N. Irish (n = 109)	British (n = 58)
Identity salience					
Mean	11.33	13.43	13.14	10.51	10.31
s.d.	3.26	2.64	3.03	2.26	2.63
Identity commitment					
Mean	26.91	25.04	24.36	21.14	21.85
s.d.	6.78	3.98	5.24	3.68	4.76
Sense of authenticity					
Mean	8.06	8.65	8.81	7.52	7.81
s.d.	1.y77	1.30	1.47	1.23	1.78
Collective self-esteem					
Mean	41.97	45.04	45.71	40.75	41.87
s.d.	5.49	4.25	5.79	4.45	5.54

With respect to identity combinations, it should be noted that the mean salience score for the "Irish-Catholic" combination is 13.80 and that for the "British-Protestant" combination is 10.36. A t test (not shown) confirms that this is a statistically significant difference ($p < .001$).

As noted above, the maximum possible range of scores for the identity salience scale is 0 (not at all salient) to 20 (maximum salience). The means for levels of identity salience for all five identities (and the two identity combinations) range between 10.31 to 13.80, which suggests that while there are significant differences in the level of salience for these identities, none of them is *highly* salient for these respondents.

Commitment

Table 8.3 also contains data for the levels of identity commitment for the five major identities in this study. Inspecting mean scores for identity commitment reveals that those holding a "Protestant" identity show the highest level of commitment with the levels of commitment for the identities of "Northern Irish" and "British" being the lowest. The standard deviation for the identity of "Protestant" is also the highest of the five identities (6.78). This indicates that there is more variation in commitment levels for this identity than any of the others, i.e. respondents who said this was the best description of who they are display both more *and* less commitment to the identity. One possible explanation for this finding is that greater variation exists in what it "means" to be a "Protestant" (Whyte, 1990). Another possibility is that these Protestant respondents may see themselves as "besieged" by a strong, organised Catholic minority and, consequently, "over-commit" to the identity. As with levels of salience, *t* tests (not shown) confirm that the difference between the means for the highest identity commitment level ("Protestant"), is significantly ($p < .05$) different from the next highest ("Irish") and from the lowest ("Northern Irish", $p < .001$). Additionally, there are statistically significant differences ($p < .001$) between the levels of commitment for the identity of "Irish-Catholic" (25.86) and for "British-Protestant" (22.19).

As noted earlier, the maximum possible range of scores for the identity commitment scale is 0 (no commitment) to 57 (maximum commitment). Given that the means for levels of identity commitment for all five identities fall below the scale mean of 28.5 suggests that the respondents are not *highly* committed to these identities.

Sense of Authenticity

Table 8.3 also contains data on the degree to which respondents feel that their most important identity reflects core aspects of their sense of self. As shown in the data, those respondents selecting the identity of "Irish" and "Catholic" display the highest sense of authenticity (mean = 8.81 and 8.65, respectively) with the identity of "Northern Irish" eliciting the lowest level of authenticity (mean = 7.52); a significant difference from both of the two former identities (t tests not shown). Again, there is a difference between the identity configurations of "Irish-Catholic" and "British-Protestant" with the former having a mean authenticity score of 9.00 and the latter, 7.72. A *t* test (not shown) confirms that this is a significant difference ($p < .001$).

A possible explanation for the findings on the dispersion of scores for the level of commitment to the identity of "Protestant" (discussed above) resides in the possibility of lower feelings of authenticity for this identity emanating from differences in how that identity is perceived by others. Thus, while the respondents who selected this identity feel that it is the best description of "who they are", they are ambivalent about having strong commitments to this identity. This may be because of the public perception of contradictory (positive and negative) dimensions of this identity and, consequently, the choice of the Protestant identity is accompanied by a lower sense of authenticity for the identity. This explanation for the greater standard deviation in commitment scores for the "Protestant" identity, however, does not seem to be supported. While authenticity scores for those selecting the "Protestant" identity are not as high as those for "Catholic" and "Irish", they are higher than those for the identities of "Northern Irish" and "British". Research by O'Donnell (1977), Stringer and Cairns (1983), and Weinreich (1982, as cited in Cairns, 1987), has found evidence that Catholics in Northern Ireland were more ambivalent than Protestants about the evaluation of their social identity. If it can be assumed that greater identity ambivalence will produce lower feelings of authenticity, then the data reported here must be seen as contrary to that reported in those studies and may reflect change in the actual and perceived status of Catholics in Northern Ireland over the last decade (O'Connor, 1993).

As noted above, the maximum possible range of scores for the sense of authenticity scale is 0 (no sense of authenticity) to 12 (highest sense of authenticity). The means for levels of identity salience for all five identities range between 7.52 and 8.81, which suggests that the respondents regard these identities as reflecting many of the characteristics they believe they possess.

Collective Self-esteem

From the perspective of Social Identity theory, the collective self-esteem scale developed by Crocker and Luhtanen (1990) provides the first scale which assesses how individuals evaluate their membership in a social group. Table 8.3 contains mean collective self-esteem scores for each of the identities. Respondents selecting the "Irish" and "Catholic" identities had the highest collective self-esteem. These means were significantly different from the mean collective self-esteem scores for respondents selecting the "Protestant", "British" and "Northern Irish" identities (*t* test not shown). Those selecting the "Northern Irish" identity had the lowest mean collective self-esteem score.

The maximum possible score on the collective self-esteem scale is 64 and the minimum 16. As the group means, which ranged from 40.75 to 45.71, were all above the mean for this scale this suggests that in general respondents had obtained a positive social identity from their group membership as suggested by Cairns (1982, 1987). However, it seems that the "Irish" and "Catholic" identities were more positively evaluated than the "British", "Protestant" or "Northern Irish" identities, which was not predictable from previous research.

Relationships between Dimensions

The bivariate relationships among the measures of identity salience, collective self-esteem, identity authenticity and identity commitment shown in Table 8.4 are all significant ($p < .001$) as predicted by social identity theory and structural symbolic interaction theory. Similar patterns of association emerged from the intercorrelations (not shown) of these dimensions computed for each

TABLE 8.4   Zero-order correlations for the variables of salience, authenticity, commitment and collective self-esteem for the first identity

	Commitment	*Authenticity*	*Collective self-esteem*
Authenticity	0.559**		
Collective self-esteem	0.554**	0.673**	
Salience	0.598**	0.680**	0.717**

$**p < 0.001$

identity separately. The evidence from these data indicates that when identities are seen as salient, the person also reports commitment to that identity, evaluates the group positively and feels that the identity is an authentic reflection of the kind of person they think they are. Further research is required to assess the dynamics of these relationships but it seems that the associations are not dependent on the ascribed status of group.

Summary of Results from Measures

The data in Table 8.3 indicate that, with one exception, respondents who believe that the identity of "Irish" or "Catholic" or the combination of "Irish-Catholic" are the best descriptions of themselves, display higher collective self-esteem, more commitment to that identity, feel that identity is more salient and more authentic than the respondents selecting other identities or identity combinations. The one exception is that those who chose the identity of "Protestant" display greater commitment to this identity than those selecting other identities. Those choosing the identities of "Northern Irish" and "British", or the combination of "British-Protestant" display the lowest levels of collective self-esteem, identity salience, commitment, and authenticity. The relationships among the dimensions are strong, positive and significant.

Discussion

Using Social Identity Theory (Tajfel, 1981) and Identity Theory as developed from Structural Symbolic Interaction Theory (e.g. Stryker, 1980), this research has pursued several questions using a sample of university students from Northern Ireland. One, is it possible to develop psychometrically adequate measures of some of the important constructs from each theory? Two, if this is possible, can patterns of results for these constructs be found in this population? Three, do those identifying themselves as Protestants and Catholics differ on various dimensions of social identity? Four, to what extent can dimensions of Social Identity theory be combined with those from Structural Symbolic Interaction theory? Liebkind (1992) argues that such interdisciplinary activity is "imperative".

As Phinney notes, all too many studies on ethnic identity have used scales having questionable reliability and validity and, therefore, "the most serious need in ethnic research is to devise reliable and valid measures of ethnic identity" (1990, 510). The scales used in this research do have good psychometric properties and, hence, we have confidence in the results flowing from their use. Unlike many previous studies (Phinney, 1990) these scales were used on young adults as opposed to children. We assume that questionnaires which are completed anonymously provide a relatively neutral non-threatening context with which to sample ethnic identity. In such a context, it is possible that the durable salience of socio-political identities may be underestimated but the evidence of any coherent pattern of response should be a useful indicator of enduring relationships and stable associations. Therefore, we encourage the use of these scales by other researchers studying aspects of ethnic identity.

Using these measures, we have found very clear patterns for the constructs in our sample, both between and within groups. Overall, those saying that the best description of themselves is the identity of "Irish" or "Catholic" display more commitment to that identity and feel it is more authentic than the counterpart identities of "British" or "Protestant". At the same time, most of the respondents do not regard these identities as highly salient for themselves. These findings are consistent with work by Mugny (1982), Moscovici (1985)and Phinney (1990) in psychology, and Blau (1977) in sociology, that strong, vocal minorities in conditions of stable interaction, display more identification with their group than do members of the "majority" group.

We have also shown that aspects of Social Identity theory can be combined with aspects of Structural Symbolic Interaction theory. As other research has shown (e.g. Callero, 1985; Reid, Epstein and Benson, 1994, in press; Serpe, 1987), the public identities assessed in this research were not viewed as terribly salient by the respondents who described themselves as having the identities. This is consistent with the view that "private" identities, such as those connected with family and occupation, are most salient for most people most of the time. As both Social Identity theory and Structural Symbolic Interaction theory would maintain, the less salient the identity, the more likely it will be influenced by the context of the interaction involving the identity (Liebkind, 1992).

Although Northern Ireland is a highly dichotomised society and most of the students in this study had grown up with the political violence as a background, the immediate environment in which they completed their questionnaires was relatively neutral. Ethier and Deaux (1990) have argued that in America, identity questions become paramount for minority students during the transition period from school to a predominantly white university. In Northern Ireland, however, this transition involves Catholic students moving to a university with a Catholic majority. Previous research (Trew, 1983b), in which the socio-political identities of first-year students were sampled at a time of considerable political tension in Northern Ireland, indicated that religious denomination was not a salient dimension in their self descriptions. The present study confirms these findings but suggests that traditional socio-political identities are still moderately salient for the respondents and most of them accept and value these identities to some extent. There is, therefore, a reservoir of identity commitment available among these students which can readily become mobilised whenever the social context elicits these identities. As Darby (1986) argued, "ethnic identities like seeds could be inert for decades and still retain their fertility".

For this sample, who were a young and educated group of young people, there were also some signs that suggest that thirty years of conflict and violence in Northern Ireland may have contributed to the creation of shared common identity associated with the regional identity "Northern Irish". The survey evidence reviewed by Trew (in press) indicates that a growing minority of both Protestants and Catholics in the population identified themselves as "Northern Irish" when given the choice of national identities. Waddell and Cairns (1991) also found support for the acceptability of the Northern Irish identity to both Protestants and Catholics when they asked students to make six paired comparisons between four identities, British, Irish, Ulster and Northern Irish. Catholic students rejected the British and Ulster identities but accepted the Irish or Northern Irish identification whereas the British, Northern Irish and Ulster identities were almost equally acceptable to Protestants so that it seemed that these terms might be interchangeable depending on the situation.

One reason for the emergence of the Northern Irish identity in recent years has been suggested by Moxon-Browne (1991) who argued that the ambiguity of the Northern Irish label serves to make it less divisive than other possible national labels available to Protestants and Catholics. For Catholics it does not legitimise political boundaries or compromise their aspirations as the term can refer geographically to the northern part of the island of Ireland. Similarly, the Northern Irish identity does not compromise the British identity of Protestants as the term can be seen as derived from "Northern Ireland", an officially designated region of the United Kingdom. It is, therefore possible that in the light of the continuing violence in Northern Ireland both Protestants and Catholics may find that they can acknowledge their common heritage without threatening their strong group allegiances. This process may have began as Mairaid Corrigan-Maguire, one of the founders of the peace movement in Northern Ireland in the 1970s, noted:

> This is an exciting and questioning time when people are searching for a new way to express their identity . . . What you'll find is that more and more people now are talking in terms of a "Northern Ireland" identity rather than the old stale "unionist" or "nationalist".
>
> (Ms Mairaid Corrigan-Maguire: Peace People spokeswomen quoted in the *Belfast Telegraph*, 25 January 1994)

References

Abrams, D. and Hogg, M. A. (eds) (1990). *Social Identity Theory: Constructive and Critical Advances.* London: Harvester Wheatsheaf.

Benson, D. E. (1992). Religious orthodoxy in Northern Ireland: the validation of identities. *Sociological Analysis*, **53**, 219–28.

Benson, D. E. (1993). Toward an explanation of "Just World" beliefs and processes. Paper delivered at the meetings of the American Sociological Association, Miami, Florida.

Benson, D. E. and Sites, P. (1992). Religious orthodoxy in Northern Ireland: the validation of identities. *Sociological Analysis*, **53**, 219–28.

Benson, D. E. and Trew, K. (in press) Facets of self in Northern Ireland: explorations and further questions. In A. Wicklund and Oosterwegel (eds).

Blau, P. (1977). *Inequality and Heterogeneity: A Primitive Theory of Social Structure.* New York: The Free Press.

Breakwell, G. M. (1992). Processes of self-evaluation: efficacy and estrangement. In G. M. Breakwell (ed.), *Social Psychology of Identity and the Self Concept.* London: Surrey University Press.

Bruce, S. (1986). *God save Ulster! The Religion and Politics of Paisleyism.* Oxford: Clarendon Press.

Burke, P. and Reitzes, D. (1991). An identity theory approach to commitment. *Social Psychology Quarterly*, **54**, 239–51.

Cairns, E. (1982). Intergroup conflict in Northern Ireland. In H. Tajfel (ed.), *Social Identity and Intergroup Relations*. Cambridge: Cambridge University Press.

Cairns, E. (1987). *Caught in Crossfire: Children and the Northern Ireland Conflict*. Syracuse: Syracuse University Press.

Callero, P. (1985). Role-identity salience. *Social Psychology Quarterly*, **48**, 203–15.

Carmines, E. G. and Zeller, A. (1980). *Reliability and Validity Assessment*. Beverly Hills: Sage.

Crocker, J. and Luhtanen, R. (1990). Collective self-esteem and ingroup bias. *Journal of Personality and Social Psychology*, **58**, 60–7.

Darby, J. (1986). *Intimidation and the Control of Conflict in Northern Ireland*. Dublin: Gill & Macmillan.

Deaux, K. (1991). Social identities: thoughts on structure and change. In R. C. Curtis (ed.), *The Relational Self: Theoretical Convergence in Psychoanalysis and Social Psychology*. London: The Guilford Press.

Deaux, K. (1992). Personalizing identity and socializing self. In G. M. Breakwell (ed.), *Social Psychology of Identity and the Self Concept*. London: Surrey University Press.

DeVellis, R. F. (1991). *Scale Development: Theory and Applications*. Beverly Hills: Sage.

Erickson, R. (1993). Beyond an identity theory approach to commitment: self-meanings, self-values, and the biographic self. Unpublished manuscript.

Ethier, K. and Deaux, K. (1990). Hispanics in ivy: assessing identity and perceived threat. *Sex Roles*, **7/8**, 427–40.

Gallagher, A. M. (1989). Social identity and the Northern Ireland conflict. *Human Relations*, **42**, 917–35.

Gecas, V. (1986). The motivational significance of self-concept for socialization theory. In E. Lawler (ed.), *Advances in Group Process*. Greenwich, CT: JAI Press.

Gecas, V. (1991). The self-concept as a basis for a theory of motivation. In J. Howard and P. Callero (eds), *The Self-society Dynamic: Cognition, Emotion, and Action*. Cambridge: Cambridge University Press.

Hogg, M. A. and Abrams, D. (1990). Social motivation, self-esteem and social identity. In D. Abrams and M. A. Hogg (eds), *Social Identity Theory: Constructive and Critical Advances*. London: Harvester Wheatsheaf.

Horowitz, D. L. (1990). *Community Conflict: Policy and Possibilities*. Occasional Paper No 1. Centre for the Study of Conflict. University of Ulster: Coleraine.

Keto, S. and Benson, D. E. (1993). Zoological Parks and the role identity of the zoo volunteer, Unpublished paper.

Liebkind, K. (1992). Ethnic identity—Challenging the boundaries of social psychology. In G. M. Breakwell (ed.), *Social Psychology of Identity and the Self concept*. London: Surrey University Press.

Luhtanen, R. and Crocker, J. (1991). Self-esteem and intergroup comparisons: towards a theory of collective self-esteem. In J. Suls and T. A. Wills (eds), *Social Comparison, Contemporary Theory and Research*. Hillsdale: Lawrence Erlbaum.

Mead, G. H. (1934). *Mind, Self and Society: From the Standpoint of a Social Behaviorist*. Edited and with an introduction by Charles W. Morris. Chicago: University of Chicago Press.

Moscovici, S. (1985). Innovation and minority Influence. In S. Moscovici, G. Mugny and A. E. von Avermaet (eds), *Perspectives on Minority Influences*. London: Academic Press.

Moxon-Browne, E. (1991). National identity in Northern Ireland. In P. Stringer and G. Robinson (eds), *Social Attitudes in Northern Ireland*. Belfast: Blackstaff Press.

Mugny, G. (1982) *The Power of Minorities*. London: Academic Press.

O'Connor, F. (1993). *In Search of a State: Catholics in Northern Ireland*. Belfast: The Blackstaff Press.

O'Donnell, E. E. (1977). *Northern Irish Stereotypes*. Dublin: College of Industrial Relations.

Oyserman, D. and Markus, H. R. (1993). The sociocultural self. In J. Suls (ed.), *Psychological Perspectives on the Self* (Vol. 4). Hillsdale NJ: Erlbaum.

Phinney, J. S. (1990). Ethnic identity in adolescents and adults: review of research. *Psychological Bulletin*, **108**, 499–514.

Reid, S. A., Epstein, J. S. and Benson, D. E. (forthcoming). Role identity in a disvalued occupation: the case of female exotic dancers. *Sociological Focus*.

Rosenberg, M. (1979). *Conceiving the Self*. New York: Basic Books.

Serpe, R. T. (1987). Stability and change in self: a structural symbolic interactionist explanation. *Social Psychology Quarterly*, **50**, 44–55.

Stringer, M. and Cairns, E. (1983). Catholic and Protestant young people's ratings of stereotyped Protestant and Catholic faces. *British Journal of Social Psychology*, **22**, 241–6.

Stryker, S. (1968). Identity salience and role performance: the relevance of symbolic interaction theory for family research. *Journal of Marriage and the Family*, **30**, 558–64.

Stryker, S. (1980). *Symbolic interactionism: a social structural version*. Palo Alto: B Cummings.

Stryker, S. (1987). Identity theory: Developments and extensions. In K. Yardley and T. Honess (eds), *Self and Identity: Psychosocial Perspectives*. New York: Wiley.

Stryker, S. (1991). Exploring the relevance of social cognition for the relationship of self and society: linking the cognitive perspective and identity theory. In J. Howard and P. Callero (eds), *The Self-society Dynamic: Cognition, Emotion, and Action*. Cambridge: Cambridge University Press.

Tajfel, H. (1981). *Human Groups and Social Categories*. Cambridge: Cambridge University Press.

Thoits, P.A. (1992). Identity structures and psychological well-being: Gender and marital status comparisons. *Social Psychology Quarterly*, **55**, 236–56.

Trew, K. (1983). Group identification in a divided society. In J. Harbison (ed.), *Children of the Troubles: Children in Northern Ireland*. Belfast: Stranmillis College.

Trew, K. (1983a). A sense of national identity: fact or artefact? *The Irish Journal of Psychology*, **6**, 28–36.

Trew, K. (1992). Social psychological research on the conflict. *The Psychologist*, **5**, 342–44.

Trew, K. (in press). What it means to be Irish seen from a northern perspective. *The Irish Journal of Psychology*.

Turner, R. (1987). Toward a sociological theory of motivation. *American Sociological Review*, **52**, 15–27.

Turner, R. and Billings, V. (1991). The social contexts of self-feelings. In J. Howard and P. Callero (eds), *The Self-society Dynamic: Cognition, Emotion, and Action*. Cambridge: Cambridge University Press.

Waddell, N. and Cairns, E. (1986). Situational perspectives on social identity in Northern Ireland. *British Journal of Social Psychology*, **25**, 25–31.

Whyte, J. (1990). *Interpreting Northern Ireland*. Oxford University Press.

Zurcher, L. R. and Snow, D. A. (1981). Collective behaviour: social movements. In M. Rosenberg and R. H. Turner (eds), *Social Psychology: Sociological Perspectives*. New York: Basic Books.

Appendix

MEASURE OF MOST IMPORTANT IDENTITY

Please choose from the list below the term that you feel best describes how you feel

| A Protestant | A Unionist | Irish | A Loyalist | |
| A Nationalist | Northern Irish | A Catholic | Ulster | British |

I would best describe myself as _____

MEASURE OF SECOND MOST IMPORTANT IDENTITY

Now study the descriptions again and choose the one which you feel is the second best description of how you see yourself

| A Protestant | A Unionist | Irish | A Loyalist | |
| A Nationalist | Northern Irish | A Catholic | Ulster | British |

The **second** best description of me is _____

MEASURE OF IDENTITY SALIENCE

Thinking *only* of this choice, read the following statements and decide the extent to which you agree or disagree with the statement. (Responses are on a four point scale from strongly agree to strongly disagree. Factor loadings are in parentheses after each item.)

Being (*this description*) is something I rarely even think about. (.7760)

For others to know me as I really am, it is important for them to know that I am (*this description*). (.6373)

I really don't have clear feelings about being (*this description*). (.7492)

For me, being (*this description*) is an important part of who I am. (.8490)

For me, being (*this description*) means more to me than just being a citizen in this society. (.8071)

Per cent of Total Variance Explained = 58.8% Cronbach's Alpha = .82

IDENTITY COMMITMENT

(Combination of Cognitive and Affective—Intensive and Extensive)

Cognitive commitment

I get a great deal of satisfaction and fulfillment from being (*this description*). (.7663)

Being (*this description*) is very beneficial and rewarding in terms of my future. (.6945)

People say I am right to think being (*this description*) is important. (.7532)

I get praised for being (*this description*). (.7219)

Others will be disappointed in me if I fail as a (*this description*). (.6156)

Affective commitment—intensive

If I could no longer be (*this description*), my significant other (spouse, fiancee, lover) would be unhappy. (.8334)

If I stopped being (*this description*) my best friends would be unhappy. (.8214)

If someone said something bad about (*this description*) people I would feel as if they had said something bad about me. (4656)

My parents would be very unhappy if I was not married to someone who was also (*this description*). (.5713)

Affective commitment—extensive

(Responses are on a 7-point scale from "All" to "None")

How many of your friends would stop being your friend if you no longer thought of yourself as (*this description*)? (.8368)

How many people that you know would be unhappy if you no longer thought of yourself as (*this description*)? (.8553)

How many people that you know would you not see any longer if you no longer thought of yourself as (*this description*)? (.8358)

Per cent of Total Variance Explained = 58.2% Cronbach's Alpha = .81

SENSE OF AUTHENTICITY

(Responses are on a 4-point scale from "Strongly Agree" to "Strongly Disagree")

Being (*this description*) is consistent with my important values. (.7948)

Deep down, I often feel that (*this description*) is not really "me." (.6508)

Most of the time I like thinking of myself as (*this description*. (.8302)

Per cent of Total Variance Explained = 63.4% Cronbach's Alpha = .71

COLLECTIVE SELF-ESTEEM SCALE

(Responses are on a 4-point scale from "Strongly Agree" to "Strongly Disagree")

Private collective self-esteem

I often regret that I belong to this group. (.6664)

In general, I'm glad to be a member of this group. (.8158)

Overall, I often feel that this group is not worthwhile. (.7656)

I feel good about this group. (.7865)

Per cent of Total Variance Explained =57.9% Cronbach's Alpha = .75

Public collective self-esteem

Overall, this group is considered good by others. (.7381)

Most people consider this group, on the average, to be more ineffective than other social groups. (.5387)

In general, others respect this group. (.7824)

In general, others think that this group is unworthy. (.7638)

Per cent of Total Variance Explained =50.8% Cronbach's Alpha = .67

Importance of identity

Overall, my membership in this group has very little to do with how I feel about myself. (.8205)

This group is an important reflection of who I am. (.8975)

This group is unimportant to my sense of what kind of a person I am. (.8093)

In general, this group is an important part of my self-image. (.7277)

Per cent of Total Variance Explained =72.7% Cronbach's Alpha = .87

Membership self-esteem
  I feel I am a worthy member of this group. (.7529)
  I don't feel I have much to offer this group. (.7659)
  I am a cooperative participant in this group. (.7245)
  I often feel I am a useless member of this group. (.7277)
  Per cent of Total Variance Explained =55.2% Cronbach's Alpha = .72

COLLECTIVE SELF-ESTEEM SCALE COMPRISES SCORES FROM:
  Private Collective Self Esteem
  Public Collective Self Esteem
  Importance to identity
  Membership Self-esteem
  Average inter-item correlation is .322($p < .001$)
  Per cent of Total Variance Explained = 61.6% Cronbach's Alpha = .84

9

Cultural-Political Differences in Perception of Ethnic Concepts in Central-Eastern and Western Europe

VIERA BACOVA AND PATRICIA ELLIS

Slovak Academy of Sciences, Slovakia and University of Luton, England

Introduction

The current restructuring of Europe particularly in Central and Eastern Europe as well as the opening of the political boundaries offer exciting challenges and opportunities for academic contribution to the current debates. However it also highlights potentially significant differences in understandings, approaches and context that need to be acknowledged and addressed.

Much of the research in the social sciences to date has been confined within national boundaries. Major factors have been political particularly with regard to Central-Eastern Europe, but the diversity of language within Western Europe has played an important role, too. This has constrained the extent of cross-European research activity and the access for academics to new theoretical approaches being developed within individual European countries.

The expansion of the membership of the European Economic Community (now the European Union) and the democratic rebirth of the Central and Eastern European countries have supported and encouraged greater interchange and travel within the newly emerging European academic community. At the same time there has been a general acceptance of English as the *lingua franca* of the academic community. But apparent commonality of language can mask potentially significant differences in understandings and approaches. These reflect different traditions within academic disciplines as well as diverse historical developments of the national communities within which they are situated.

The political and economic revolutions that have swept Central-Eastern Europe since the late 1980s have thrown such considerations into particularly sharp relief. Western Europeans could be perceived within the twentieth century as sharing a relatively comparable political development within a capitalist framework which has been different from that of Central-Eastern Europe. Since 1945 the countries of Central-Eastern and Western Europe have adopted approaches to their political, economic and social organisation which have significantly differentiated their societies at very fundamental levels. The present adoption of forms of "western capitalism" in Central-Eastern Europe does not necessarily mean that the values, understandings and priorities of the citizens have become the same as those in Western Europe.

Terminological Issues

Not only social scientists but politicians, writers, journalists and ordinary people face mounting ambiguity in the use of ethnic concepts. Many of these terms are indeterminate and vague carrying different meaning in the context of diverse discourse communities. The names of many ethnic categories are overlapping, arbitrary and fuzzy. They reflect the historical heritage, current events, needs of people, habits, and language of the groups of people who use them and refer to the kind of reality that implies that whatever the denotation it can be arbitrary and confusing. Perhaps Stern (1992) in his essay "What is German?" aptly summed up the situation when he said

> national identity, folk-soul, national community (*Volksgemeinschaft*) or whatever more or less neutral or awkward words we choose—all these expressions are part of various cultural vocabularies, they denote the arrangements of a cultural consensus and derive their meanings from it. Such expressions do not lend themselves to the setting up of the kind of definitions that Aristotle bequeathed to western philosophies: like labels on boxes, his "categorical" definitions denote fixed entities, whereas cultural expressions refer to fluid, variable states of affairs and overlapping functions, to values which are relative to their time and place.

In general there are three kinds of knowledge and comprehension of the ethnic concepts at our disposition today. In spite of their interconnection these three sources create a great deal of confusion. These are:

1. political rhetoric;
2. social science approaches;
3. everyday knowledge and usage of the concepts.

Politicisation of Ethnic Concepts

Ethnic issues are one of the current focuses of politics. The views of politicians and state representatives are instrumental in forming opinions about the character of ethnicity and at the same time are used to justify political acts. The explanation of ethnic phenomena presented by politicians and political parties are often dictated by power interests and by the possibility of use (or misuse) of "ethnicity" for political aims. The mass media are saturated with the views of politicians. Individual pieces of information conveyed through the mass media can support or criticise the approaches of particular political parties or representatives. In summary politicians have a significant impact on public opinion. Many of the ethnic concepts have been assigned special meanings by social scientists but these meanings have, subsequently, been popularised and exploited for political purposes. Consequently they have also in turn acquired different meanings in the vocabulary of scholars.

The politicisation of keywords creates an additional difficulty for scholarly writers. Riggs (1991a) believes, that even if academics have a clear idea in mind when using a word, it is difficult to use it precisely because its emotional and political connotations so readily come to mind.

Social scientists experience this situation as frustrating and uncomfortable. As a consequence they try to develop methods for removing the ambiguity (for example Riggs, 1991a, 1991b, to introduce at least one attempt). But as Bacal recorded, "the conceptualization of ethnicity remains today as elusive as it is notorious as a public topic" (Bacal, 1990, 2).

Social Theories Related to Ethnicity

The social scientific theories of ethnicity—and these are criticised by many academics—suffer from a lack of coherency, consistency and are often in tow to politicians motivated to justify their acts. However, there are many serious attempts to discover the nature and sources of ethnicity in human society. The contemporary theories differ according to a preference for either a primordial or a situational approach to ethnicity, i. e. ethnicity is conceived as a phenomenon deeply rooted in human substance or as implanted from the outside under the pressure of circumstances or the situation in which the ethnic group is found. The other criteria for classifying theories of ethnicity may be the universalistic vs substantialistic approach or formalistic vs essentialistic definitions of ethnicity.

Everyday "Ethnic" Knowledge and Its Determinants

In everyday interaction individuals also take into consideration the social categories in which the person they communicate with belongs. If the individual lives in an ethnically heterogeneous environment one of the categories is the ethnic membership of the person. The degree to which an individual considers this category as an important factor in their general evaluation depends on the historical period and predominant social ideology but also on the particular situation and circumstances. The last but not the least determinant in the evaluation of ethnicity is the beliefs of an individual about what ethnicity actually is; what its role in human life is; its intrinsic value or worth and so on. This complex matrix of beliefs can be called implicit theory of ethnicity (Bacova, 1993) and can be defined as the individual's mental conceptions, schemas, constructions and so on used to describe, explain and anticipate human "ethnic behaviour" and understand ethnic phenomena as such. The motivation for the creation of ethnic theories derives from the continual confrontations within the multiethnic societies of the modern world. But this concerns the core of individual personality as the person needs to make clear his/her own identity including the ethnic component.

Ethnic implicit theories are "naïve" in their very sense and as a consequence the use of the term "theory" is only figurative. It would be more exact to speak about constructions. Compared with physics, biology, chemistry but also history, literature or the other arts, the majority of the population receive no systematic education around ethnic issues except the sporadic ideologically motivated efforts to stimulate patriotic feelings or pride in one's own nation. That is the reason why the individuals produce the "natural", in some sense immature and experience-based explanations of observable ethnic phenomena. These naïve explanations face the corresponding social scientific theories. The naïve "theories" are uncritical, immature, implicit, unreflective and self-affirmative. There is the absence of doubt and control. Many of these characteristics can be found in some of the studies on ethnicity. Some of the studies are tainted by "the ethnic worldview" of the authors. The field of ethnicity is still beset by difficulties in determining which of the opinions or bits of information are exact, systematic, precise and free of confusing ambiguities. Unfortunately in this arena social scientific theories are not able to serve as a standard for comparison and assessment of the implicit theories of ethnicity.

Implicit theories of ethnicity are shared and used by individuals and groups of people living in the same social environment. These "theories" as with social representations function as one of the sources of ethnic ideology and they mobilise the people in all ethnic and nationalistic movements. It should be stressed that ethnicity as a complex phenomenon also contains other features beyond the cognitive components. The power of the idea of ethnicity lies in its ability to influence the emotional disposition of each individual. Not only in mass movements but also on the individual (micro) level the emotional component is often more important and has a greater impact on individual behaviour than the cognitive components.

It can be assumed that both individuals and groups differ in their implicit ethnic theories due to their different positions in society. At the same time a group of people share the same opinions because of their common experiences, similar historical "fate" and perspectives on common life.

Historical Development and Resulting Ethnic Ideologies

In the history of European countries at least two main conceptions of ethnicity and nationalism in the form of creation of the nation/state can be demonstrated. In the main in West European countries the category of the nation emerged as a consequence of the preceding economic, social, cultural and political developments. Consolidation of administrative, legal and cultural institutions became the base of "national unity". In the characterisation of a nation of this type it is possible to talk about a community with its own state. The emerging ideology consequently was less compelled to seek justification by recourse to an ethnocentric heritage and it could afford to legitimise the existing power relationships in concepts of modern political ideology stressing the values of property, liberty and equality.

In the other type of national development in Europe (traditionally Central-Eastern European countries) national unity was formulated as a desire, lacking adequate economic, social, political and cultural foundations. Here the concept of "the nation" came before the establishment of the proper national-state institutions. This type of national ideology demonstrated an overwhelming concern for fictions and symbols. The imagined realm of the nation was created by the language of historical writing, literature, by painting, sculpture and by the work of devoted groups of national revivalists. Ethnocentric cultural heritage played an important role in nation-formation. This type of national ideology can be classified as focused upon the idea of the nation defined in concepts of culture by contrast with the previous type which is centred upon the idea of the nation defined in the concept of a state.

Smith (1986) in his exploration of the origins of nations, delineated two major categories: the "territorial" nation and the "ethnic" nation. The first type takes its name from "a sense of territory and from the effects of interaction within clear cut geographical boundaries." This was very much a Western European model with the features of citizenship and common culture. Clear examples of this type of nation would be the UK and France. The second type is the "ethnic" nation within which Smith would define most Central-Eastern European states. This model traces its history from "home-based polyethnic empires made up of a host of separate ethnic communities and cultures subordinated to a core ethnie exercising political domination . . . and placing dynastic allegiance before other loyalties". Often the pressures from the central governments to exert their cultural homogenisation programmes upon the outer reaches of their empires had the opposite effect and generated a new consciousness of ethnic separateness such as in Slovakia. For Smith it is this dualism at the heart of the concept of the "nation" that has "inevitably resulted in a profound ambiguity in the present-day relations between ethnie and the states in which they are so often incorporated".

From that different historical background the various ethnic ideologies arose which influence the approaches to ethnic issues today.

Reflections on Ethnicity and the Majority-Minority Position

As treated in the social sciences ethnicity and related terms have a different connotation ("flavour") compared with the term nation-state and this may be appropriate in Western Europe. Nation-state is associated predominantly with the majority in the current states (native or mainstream people) while ethnicity relates to the minorities in the state. It is unusual to refer to and therefore to study the ethnicity of the majority (for example ethnicity of the English, French etc.), but it is usual to talk about and to study the ethnicity of particular groups who are usually "immigrant" groups in these societies (for example Pakistanis) as the minorities in the state. As a consequence the concept of minorities includes quite different categories of people in Western and Central-Eastern European states. In Central-Eastern European states the minorities are former citizens of other— often neighbouring states—who became the minority not because of immigration, but as a consequence of shifting the boundaries and they may have lived in the same territory for centuries.

Glazer and Moynihan (1975) sum up the term "ethnicity" as referring to a social group which consciously shares some aspects of a common culture and is defined primarily by descent which will usually involve mother tongue and race. In turn race has been seen as a biological or genetic construct in which humans share genetically similar features. However it is also often used as a synonym for ethnicity as in the case of the Irish or the Jews. A third usage is in the idea of the "social race", an intergroup or intercultural relations distributing distinctive social status to perceived physical differences.

In the UK, ethnicity is associated in popular discourse with immigration. As a former colonial power with a particular relationship with areas distributed across the world, the post-war period has seen a major settlement of immigrants from the former empire. These groups with their descendants form a growing and noticeable part of the population of major cities but they do however form a small minority of the overall population. This structure is in contrast to the experience of countries and communities of Central-Eastern Europe. Here ethnicity and ethnic groups are associated with shifting political boundaries rather than movements of people. The significant numbers of Hungarians in present day Slovakia can trace their history back hundreds of years and inhabit territory that has over time formed part of several different nations including Hungary.

Glazer and Moynihan (1963, 1975) in their sociological research in the USA questioned the concept of assimilation of immigrants or ethnic minority groups into American society. They found that while language and culture are very quickly lost in first and second generations, ethnic minority groups maintained an identity albeit changed characteristics of identity. They described this in terms of adoption of a strategy of self-categorisation. The society under consideration, the USA, is a country of "immigrants" in which the majority of the population are not and could not describe themselves as indigenous. Indeed the actual indigenous population is very small and occupies a low-status position within the society. Transferring this experience of transitions in identity and language to the UK with its different structures is questionable and it would certainly not appear from the evidence to be applicable to the long-established ethnic minority groups situated in various Central-Eastern European countries.

It is not only sociology that has not furnished sufficient cross-continent explanations. Hutnik (1991) as a social psychologist exploring ethnic identity is critical of the extent to which psychology has contributed adequately to the explanation of the relationship between ethnic minority and majority groups and the associated areas of identity.

The social setting usually assumed for ethnic studies in that of a sovereign state and "a society" is conventionally equated with the population of such a state. Certainly, within the boundaries of any state's population, it is possible (and useful) to distinguish between ethnic communities whose members form a numerical minority and others who form a majority. Notwithstanding the extreme opinion that every member of a minority group is the subject of discrimination, being a member of minority has many consequences based on diversity from the mainstream. Minority membership often compels the need for adjustment and flexibility which is not required from members of majority groups.

Aims of the Study

The authors of this chapter were concerned to initiate a research programme which would contribute to the debates about cross-European research and the examination of national/ethnic identity. They had come together through their membership of an interest group convened by Weinreich (1992) to look at different ethnic identities in Europe. At the very beginning of their discussions they found it difficult to easily understand each other as they used ethnic terms in a manner that derived from their own ethnic/national backgrounds. Consequently the idea arose to investigate the comparative perception of ethnic concepts between their countries.

The initial hypothesis was that the concepts of nation and ethnicity would be viewed in significantly different ways in their two countries. This would also be true but probably to a lesser extent for other concepts that the authors believe lie in the same sphere of perceptual operation as nation and ethnicity. This set of concepts was seen as being positioned in the political and cultural areas of response for citizens. Given the different political and cultural histories of the UK and Slovakia, it was assumed that these would influence the perceptions of the inhabitants of these two countries and would appear as differences.

In general the aims of the research work presented in this study was:

1. to explore the nature of responses to the concepts of nation and ethnicity and other political, cultural and minority related concepts;
2. to explore the links between the concepts;
3. to initiate mapping of the terrain of these political and cultural concepts;
4. to start a cross-European collaborative research programme and to identify potentially significant directions for further work.

Hypotheses

The following hypotheses were tested:

1(a)   There would be differences in the perception of a range of ethnic concepts between the samples of inhabitants of the Slovak Republic, the Central European state that in history has followed the idea of the ethnic nation and the samples of inhabitants of the UK where the idea of citizenship and the nation-state has dominated.

1(b)   There would be differences in the perception of a range of ethnic concepts between the members of the ethnic majority and the ethnic minority within the Slovak and British samples assuming that the ethnic majority-minority position in society mediates perceptions and interpretations of ethnic concepts.

2   The links between the ethnic concepts would be differently patterned within each of the samples. Main differences in patterns would be found within the groups of political concepts (state, nation, nationality), cultural concepts (culture, mother tongue, race) and minority related concepts (ethnic minority, ethnicity, minority rights, minority language).

3   With the semantic differential scales there would be differences between the evaluative, understanding, potency and activity scales. All samples would be expected to use all these scales. It was assumed that the Slovak samples would differ from the British samples in usage of the scales for the rating of the political group of concepts due to different history, political culture, terminology and recent developments. It was also assumed that the minority samples within the Slovak and British samples would use the evaluative scales more for minority related concepts than the majority samples.

Method

Subjects and Procedure

The Slovak samples

The Slovak sample was made up of 155 students altogether drawn from the final year of schooling and the first two years of University in Kosice. Kosice in Eastern Slovakia is an industrial town with a population of approximately 250,000 inhabitants. There were ninety-five men and sixty women in the total Slovak sample with a mean age of 18.4 years (SD = 1.55). They were all inhabitants and state citizens of the Slovak Republic. Those students who perceived themselves as of Slovak nationality formed the "Slovak Majority" (*n* = 90) sample and those who perceived themselves as of Hungarian nationality (representing the largest ethnic minority in the Slovakia) formed the "Slovak Hungarian Minority" sample (*n* = 65). The respondents in the Slovak Hungarian sample were all students in a secondary school which operates in the Hungarian language. They could choose from the Slovak or Hungarian version of the questionnaire. There was little difference between the two Slovak samples in age.

The British samples

The British sample of sixty-seven students was drawn solely from the first-year modular degree scheme at the University of Luton. Luton, in the south-east of England, is also an industrial town and has a population of approximately 180,000. The British students were asked to give their ethnic origin and on the basis of this information they were divided into a "British Majority" ($n = 42$) and a "British Minority" ($n = 25$) sample.

The characteristics of the total sample are given in Table 9.1.

Students were chosen as the subjects in this initial project as it was assumed that by virtue of the activity of studying, they were considering a range of ideas and issues and therefore likely to have given some thought to the concepts under examination. The further idea was to ensure some real comparability between two countries by using subjects with a similar position in their own societies. However, it turned out that in several characteristics the intake into the two student groups differed between the two societies reflecting different policies in education. The British samples while more homogenous in the focus of their studies than the Slovak samples were more disparate in age and ethnicity as well as in gender balance.

Measures

A questionnaire was used as the means of collecting data. Apart from one sheet asking for personal and demographic information and an introductory explanation, the questionnaire consisted of a set of semantic differential sheets covering

TABLE 9.1   The age and gender characteristics of the four samples

	Sample				
	Slovak majority	*Slovak Hungarian minority*	*British majority*	*British minority*	*Total*
Age					
n	90	65	42	25	222
min	17	17	18	18	17
max	30	20	46	62	62
mean	18.73	17.83	22.12	25.76	19.9
std deviation	1.9	0.54	6.89	10.6	
Gender					
Male	46	49	13	6	114
Female	44	16	29	19	108

ten concepts for the British sample and an additional three concepts for the Slovak Majority and Slovak Hungarian Minority samples to reflect known differences in the use of terminology in that society.

In comparative research involving samples operating in different languages scaling techniques are advantageous in that they minimise the potential difficulties involved in the translation of ideas both in devising the instrument and in categorising the responses. Given that the aim of the study was to explore the meanings attached to a set of concepts in the area of nationality and ethnicity, the semantic differential technique was considered the most appropriate approach to employ.

Ten core concepts were identified after extensive discussion between the authors. These were: state, nation, nationality, ethnicity, ethnic minority group, mother tongue, culture, ethnic minority rights, race, ethnic minority language. In addition for the Slovak Majority and Slovak Hungarian Minority samples, the three extra concepts "state belonging", "national belonging" and "national minority" were inserted into the instrument following the concept nationality. These were deemed to be important terms in Slovak society which do not have exact parallels in British society. In this study the results provided are only concerned with concepts used by all four samples.

Fourteen bipolar dimensions were compiled using a seven point scale. The first five together formed the "evaluative" factor, these were: good–bad, fair–unfair, worthless–valuable, friendly–unfriendly, confident–insecure. The "potency" factor was made up of the following scales: strong–weak, changeable–unchangeable, responsive–unresponsive. A single scale represented the "activity" factor: active–passive. The final five scales formed the "understanding" factor: modern–traditional, understandable–unintelligible, simple–complicated, predictable–unpredictable, promising–unpromising. To the extent that it was possible to identify potential "positive" and "negative" ends to the scales, these were mixed in their direction of polarity to overcome response set.

The personal and demographic questions were made up of a common core with variations to reflect the different terminology and situations in the two societies. Common to both samples were questions on: age, gender, mother tongue. For the Slovaks and Hungarians living in Slovakia they were also asked for: state membership, nationality as recorded on their identity card, nationality as they perceived it. The parallel questions for the British were: nationality as recorded on a passport, nationality as they would define it, ethnic origin as they would define it.

Data Analyses

A data file was constructed with four basic sample characteristic variables and 140 concept/scale variables. A correspondence analysis of the ten ethnic concepts across the fourteen semantic differential scales was used to investigate differences and similarities in concept profiles. Correspondence analysis permits simultaneous analysis of both concepts and semantic differential scales. The graphical outcomes of the correspondence analysis demonstrate which concepts have similar distributions over scales and which scales have similar distributions over concepts, as well as which concepts and which scales deviate markedly from their "global" distributions.

The analysis of the data was carried out on the four samples. These were: Slovak Majority, Slovak Hungarian Minority, British Majority, British Minority. In the text, the two Slovak samples will be usually referred to as the "Slovak sample" and the "Hungarian sample".

Correspondence Analysis Outcomes

Correspondence analysis allows an examination of the relationship between the two groups of variables in a multidimensional space. The analysis is based on contingency or "correspondence" tables and produces plots using the row and column scores which can be used for analysing the relationship between the row and column variables. In the analysis of semantic differential data, the important advantage of correspondence analysis over other multivariate statistical methods is that the plot gives the possibility of simultaneous investigation and comparison of the patterns of concepts and scales rather than a separation of concepts and scales. The correspondence analysis plot therefore provides a complete overview of the similarities and differences of the concepts and between the distribution of the scales simultaneously. Concepts and scales with similar patterns lie together in the same part of the plot and concepts and scales with diverse patterns lie at opposite points from the origin.

Figures 9.1 to 9.4 show the correspondence analysis plots for the four samples: Slovak, Hungarian, British Majority, and British Minority. The first dimension (X-axis) produced by the analysis has singular values of 0.10724, 0.08644, 0.04156, and 0.07382 respectively for each sample (percentage explained: 69%, 79%, 46% and 73% respectively). The second dimension (Y-axis) has singular values of 0.05413, 0.02682, 0.02597 and 0.02575 respectively for each sample (percentage explained: 18%, 8%, 18% and 9% respectively). Although the inertia for the second dimension (Y-axis) appears to be relatively small for each sample, there is a justification for keeping both dimensions. The decisive factor appears to be that the correspondence tables used in this research are $m \times n$ matrices. They contain as the rows the ethnic concepts and as the columns the semantic differential rating scales. The prime interest has been in the examination of the relationship between the concepts and scales simultaneously. This was also the reason for the canonical normalisation option as this type of normalisation treats the rows (ethnic concepts) and columns (rating scales) symmetrically.

The graphical representation of the particular concepts and scales in the form of plots for each sample show the similarities and differences in the perception of the respondents. The analysis and interpretation of the plots focuses on the three groupings outlined in the hypotheses: cultural, political and minority related.

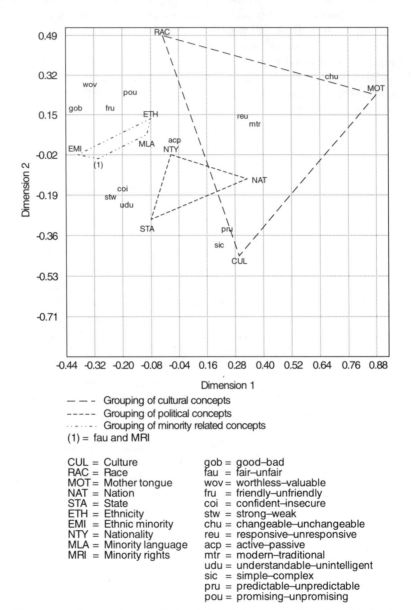

FIGURE 9.1 Correspondence analysis solution of the concepts-by-scales table for the Slovak majority sample

— — — Grouping of cultural concepts
----- Grouping of political concepts
·····-·- Grouping of minority related concepts
(1) = fau and MRI

CUL = Culture
RAC = Race
MOT = Mother tongue
NAT = Nation
STA = State
ETH = Ethnicity
EMI = Ethnic minority
NTY = Nationality
MLA = Minority language
MRI = Minority rights

gob = good–bad
fau = fair–unfair
wov = worthless–valuable
fru = friendly–unfriendly
coi = confident–insecure
stw = strong–weak
chu = changeable–unchangeable
reu = responsive–unresponsive
acp = active–passive
mtr = modern–traditional
udu = understandable–unintelligent
sic = simple–complex
pru = predictable–unpredictable
pou = promising–unpromising

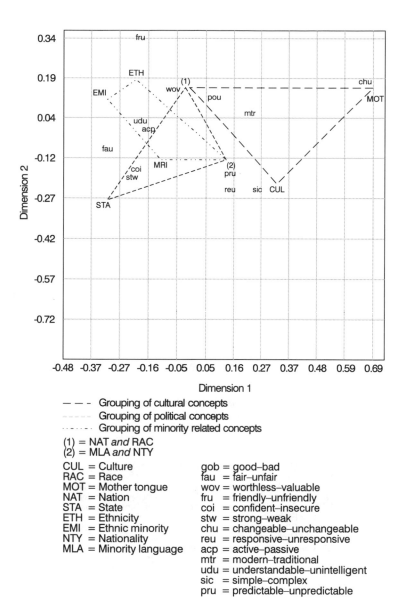

FIGURE 9.2   Correspondence analysis solution of the concepts-by-scales table for the Slovak Hungarian minority sample

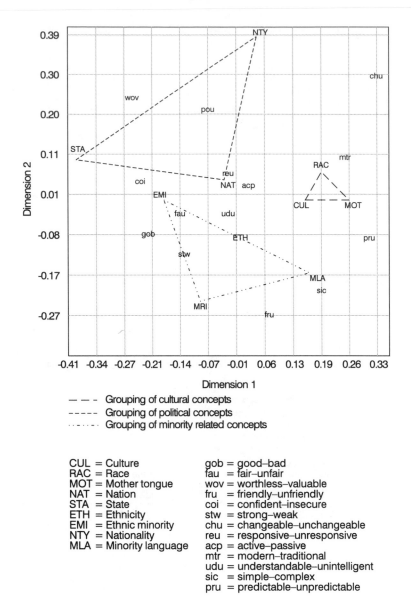

FIGURE 9.3   Correspondence analysis solution of the concepts-by-scales table for the British majority sample

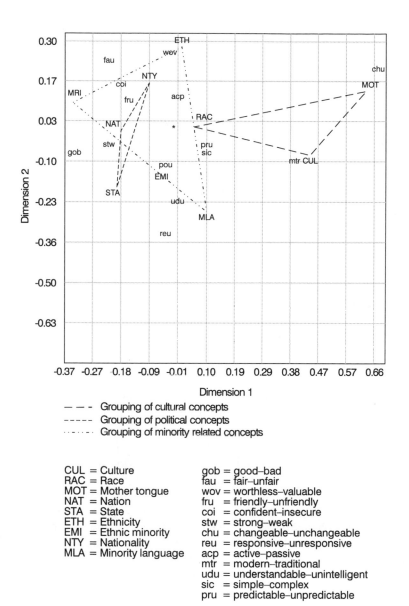

FIGURE 9.4   Correspondence analysis solution of the concepts-by-scales table for the British minority sample

Cultural Concepts: Culture, Mother Tongue and Race

All "cultural" concepts are represented on the right and at the top of the plots for each of the samples. The concept of culture is represented on the right from the origin on each plot. In the main it is not far from the origin. In the Slovak sample this concept is judged with the scales "simple–complicated" and "predictable–unpredictable". The mean value of the scales is closer to the poles "simple" and "predictable" for the concept of culture. In the Hungarian sample this concept is linked to the scale "predictable–unpredictable" (closer to the pole of "predictable"), in the British Minority sample it is the scale "modern–traditional" (closer to the pole of "traditional"). No scale is particularly used with this concept in the case of the British Majority sample.

There is a surprisingly salient similarity in the perception of the concept "mother tongue" in each of the samples. It is represented always on the right and in each sample with the greatest distance from the origin. It means this concept attracted relatively more discriminatory evaluation compared to the other concepts. The nearest scale, i.e. the scale particularly used for the concept of mother tongue, is the same for three of the samples: it is the scale "changeable–unchangeable". The Slovak sample is closer to the pole of "changeable", the Hungarian sample is in the middle of the scale and the British Minority sample is closer to the pole of "unchangeable". However for the British Majority sample it is the scales "modern–traditional" and "predictable–unpredictable" which are represented close to the concept of Mother Tongue and in both cases in the middle of the scales.

The concept of race is found on the right for the British Majority sample. It moves closer to the origin for the British Minority sample but still on the right. For the Hungarian sample it moves to the top of the plot. It is represented at great distance from the origin at the top for the Slovak sample. Thus the concept is relatively far from the origin for both of the Majority samples (Slovak and British) and near to the origin for the Minority samples (Hungarian and British). The concept of race is almost identical with the concept of nation for the Hungarian sample and it is connected with the scale "worthless–valuable" for that sample (closer to the pole of valuable). For the British Majority sample the concept is close to the scale "modern–traditional" (middle of the scale). For the British Minority sample the scales which are very close to the concept of race are "predictable-unpredictable" (closer to the pole of unpredictable) and "simple–complicated" (closer to the pole of complicated). No scale is used predominantly with the concept of race for the Slovak Majority sample.

Political Concepts: State, Nation and Nationality

The political concepts are mostly found on the left of the plots. It is concerned mainly with the concept of state. State is considered along the scales "confident–insecure" (as confident), "strong–weak" (as strong) and "understandable–

unintelligible" (as understandable) for the Slovak sample. For the Hungarian sample the concept of state is connected with the same two scales, however, this sample perceived the concept of state on the opposite pole: insecure and unintelligible. There are no particular scales used with the concept of state for either of the British samples.

The representation of the concept of nation is the most controversial. For the Slovak sample this concept is represented more on the left without any connection with a particular scale. It is moving more to the origin for the Hungarian sample (becoming almost identical with the concept of race). The scale "worthless–valuable" is the nearest scale (closer to the pole valuable). This concept appears to be quite neutral (near to the origin) for the British Majority sample and it is linked to the scales "responsive–unresponsive" and "active–passive" (close to the end of responsive and active). For the British Minority sample the nearest scales are "strong–weak" and "friendly–unfriendly" (closer to the ends of strong and unfriendly).

The representation of the concept of nationality is placed at the origin for both the Majority samples (Slovak and British) and is more on the right for the Hungarian sample. For the Slovak Majority sample the concept of nationality is right at the origin and it is considered by the scale "active–passive" (as active). The concept is represented at the top of the plot for the British Majority sample without any scale connection. The concept of nationality is almost identical with the concept of minority language in the Hungarian sample and is linked to the scale "predictable–unpredictable" and "responsive–unresponsive" (as predictable and responsive). The concept of nationality appears to be near the origin in the British Minority sample with a loose connection with the scale "friendly–unfriendly".

Minority Related Concepts: Ethnicity, Ethnic Minority, Minority Language, Minority Rights

The special separate grouping of the minority related concepts is found in both the Majority samples. In the Slovak sample this grouping is represented completely on the left; in the British Majority at the bottom of the plot. Here the grouping of the minority related concepts do not overlap with the other concepts. Different patterns can be found for the two Minority samples. In the Hungarian sample the concept of minority language is almost identically represented with the concept of nationality and the concept of minority rights goes nearer to the concept of state. In the British Minority sample all the minority related concepts overlap mainly with the political concepts.

For the Slovak sample the concept of minority rights had a strong connection with the scale "fair–unfair" (as fair). For the Hungarian sample the concept of minority language (identical with nationality) was considered on the scale "predictable–unpredictable" (as predictable). The British Majority sample considered the concept of ethnic minority on the scale "fair–unfair" (as unfair) and the concept of minority language on the scale "simple–complicated" (as complicated). For the British Minority sample the concept of ethnicity was connected with the scale "worthless–valuable" (as valuable), the concept of ethnic minority with the scale "promising–unpromising" (as promising) and the concept of minority language with the scale "understandable–unintelligible" (as understandable).

The Effects of Slovak and British Citizenship and Ethnic Majority–Minority Membership on the Perception of Ethnic Concepts

Hypotheses 1(a) and 1(b) predicted that there would be differences in the perception of the particular ethnic concepts between the samples of inhabitants of the Slovak Republic which is a Central European state and the samples of inhabitants of the UK which is a Western European state. Also it was predicted that there would be differences in the perception of the concepts between the members of the ethnic majority and ethnic minorities within the Slovak and British samples. The first notable feature of the plots (Figures 9.2 to 9.4) is that they show different patterns for the concepts as well as the scales between the samples. This supports the predictions of hypotheses 1a and 1b. Further examination of the particular plots indicates different links between the patterns of ethnic concepts as was predicted in hypothesis 2. The main differences in the patterns were found within the groupings of cultural concepts (culture, mother tongue, race), political concepts (state, nation. nationality) and minority related concepts (ethnic minority, ethnicity, minority rights, minority language).

The Slovak Majority sample perceived the cultural concepts as quite distinctive, discriminating between them very sharply. For the Slovak sample the concepts of culture, mother tongue and race meant very different entities. At the same time the Slovak Majority sample considered the concept of nation and the concept of culture as very similar. It can be promulgated that the perception of the concept of nation by the Slovak Majority sample was not as a political concept but as belonging to the cultural area. On the other hand, the respondents in the Slovak Majority sample did not discriminate between the minority related concepts (ethnic minority, ethnicity, minority language, minority rights) as these concepts are represented very close to each other. The concept of nationality is represented right at the origin of the plot. This demonstrates the obviousness of that concept for the Slovaks. Political concepts (state, nationality and nation) are represented relatively close to each other. Except for the concept of nation the three groupings of concepts (political, cultural and minority related) do not overlap for the Slovak Majority sample. Cultural concepts lie opposite to the minority related concepts. The distance between the concept "mother tongue" and the concept "ethnic minority" (which lie on opposite sides of the origin) is the largest of any other distances between the concepts. The concept considered with the most scales is the concept "state" (three scales), then "culture" (two scales), minority rights (one scale) and mother tongue (one scale).

The Slovak Hungarian Minority sample plot show different patterns. Again there is relatively a great discrimination within the grouping of the cultural concepts. The discrimination within the groupings of the political and cultural concepts is greater than for the Slovak Majority sample but in contrast with the Slovak Majority sample, the three groupings completely overlap. The minority related concepts are interwoven with the political ones as well as with the cultural ones. For the Hungarian respondents living in Slovakia the concept of nation was identical with the concept of race and they perceived the concept of nationality in the same way as the concept of minority language. This corresponds with the constant efforts of members of the Hungarian minority group to keep their language as the main cultural sign of their different national identity. The distance between the concept of mother tongue and the concept of state (which lie on the opposite side of the origin) is the largest of any distances between concepts for the Slovak Hungarian sample.

The concept considered with the most scales was the concept of state and minority rights (two scales), then minority language and nationality (two scales), culture (one scale), mother tongue (one scale) and nation and race (one scale).

The graphical representation of the correspondence analysis solution for the British Majority sample is reminiscent in certain ways of that of the Slovak Majority sample in that the three groupings of cultural, political and minority related concepts are completely separated from each other. The greatest discrimination is to be found within the political concept and with the concept of nation near to the origin. Relatively great distinction is found within the minority related concepts group. The smallest discrimination can be found within the cultural concepts group which are represented very close to each other. The concept of nationality lies opposite the minority related concepts and the concept of state lies opposite the cultural concepts. The concept of nation appears to be neutral (obvious) as it lies near the origin. The marginal concepts in the plot which have a great distance between each other are mother tongue vs state (opposite of each other) and nationality vs minority language and minority rights (opposite of each other). This sample used the most scales with the concept of ethnic minority (two scales), minority language (one scale), race (one scale).

In the British Minority sample the grouping of the cultural concepts lies opposite the political and minority related concepts. The latter two are interwoven with the concepts of minority rights and ethnic minority appearing to be close to the political concepts. The concept of race appeared to be neutral (obvious) within the British minority sample as it lies near the origin. The distance between the concept of mother tongue and the concept of minority rights and state (which lie on the opposite side of the origin) is the largest of the distances between the concepts. It appears that the British minority sample used the scales effectively, more scales were used and attached to the concepts compared to the other samples.

With the semantic differential scales it was assumed (in hypothesis 3) that there would be differences in use of the evaluative, understanding, potency and activity scales. All samples were expected to use all these scales, but the Slovak samples were expected to differ from the British samples in usage of the scales for the rating of the political group of concepts. It was assumed that the minority samples within the Slovak and British samples would use the evaluative scales more for minority related concepts.

The results are not clear enough to confirm these hypotheses. This is partially because in the plots it is relatively difficult to find unambiguous criteria for distance comparison between the concepts and scales. Nevertheless, scale groupings which are traditionally assumed with the semantic differential scales such as the evaluative, understanding, potency and activity factors were not found. The scales which were attached to the concepts most frequently were: confident–insecure, strong–weak, simple–complicated and changeable–unchangeable. The samples differed in attaching the scale close to the concepts: the British Minority sample uses the most scales, the British Majority sample uses the least scales.

Discussion

The overall hypothesis informing this research was that the concepts under discussion would be different between the two societies examined and between the majority and minority members as this would reflect the nature of the different histories, different current affairs and with this different official terminology. It was assumed as well that differences would be found between respondents in terms of their majority vs minority position in society. The results overall would appear to support the hypothesis in general.

Before proceeding with this section, it is important to consider the implications of the sample characteristics for this subsequent discussion. The sample by definition, i.e. young people in education, cannot be considered representative of the population as a whole. However they constitute a reasonable basis for first work in this area because of the reasons stated in the methods section of the chapter. Therefore it is understood throughout the discussion that all results must be interpreted within this constraint. As can be seen from the samples' characteristics, they include ethnic diversity for the British samples but ethnic homogeneity for the Slovak samples. The level of diversity in the British samples was a reflection of a particular intake to a psychology degree rather than a sample design which reflected the nature of British society as a whole. However, in spite of these constraints within the sample, the authors believe that the results obtained with this sample are statistically significant at a level that indicates that these differences would probably be also found in the wider population.

The questionnaires were answered in late February/early March 1993. On 1 January 1993 the new state of Slovakia came into existence with the concept of the enduring nation of Slovaks being stressed as a major *raison d'être* for the creation of Slovakia. The earlier "velvet revolution" with the overthrow of communism had brought about not only the independent state of Czechoslovakia but the potential reassertion of the Slovak nation and its recognition in the world. The British sample's experience has been basically of stability of the state and nation which in terms of the world order can trace its independent status over hundreds of years. For the British apart from the ethnic minority groups and the Irish, it is also basically a history of a position of dominance not subservience.

Talking to young people of Slovak nationality in Slovakia at that time, the evidence was that "nation" and "membership of a nation" were a subject of frequent and lively discussion and the impression is of a passionate commitment to the idea of being part of a Slovak nation though not necessarily a commitment to the formation of the new state. However, it was not the same with the young people of Hungarian nationality in Slovakia. The relationship of Slovakia with Hungary contains several traditionally sensitive issues. These include Slovak worries over possible Hungarian attempts to seek revisions in the borders fixed by the 1919 Trianon Treaty, the dispute over the Gabcikovo dam on the Danube River and a very special problem is presented by the status of the Slovak minorities in Hungary and the more numerous Hungarian minority in Slovakia. The latter group is worried about the general hardening of the political climate and several specific measures taken by the Slovak authorities. The Hungarian minority in Slovakia accepted the new state with feelings of insecurity, fear and worries about further developments of ethnic minority politics (Butor and Butorova, 1993).

In contrast, several of the British sample commented that this was the first time they had really considered the ideas in the questionnaire. The Maastricht Treaty has been perhaps the first major event for many years to pose a challenge to ideas of national identity in Britain. Within this context, the images generated by the responses on the questionnaire to the concept of nation can be seen as the Slovaks being romantic and enthusiastic about the idea but being younger and politically inexperienced compared to the less committed, more cynical approach of an older and more politically experienced British sample.

On many concepts (nation, state, culture, mother tongue, and race mainly) the Slovak samples were more willing to use the breadth of the scales than the British samples who tended to remain in the middle. The minimum and maximum mean positions for the Slovak samples on the seven point scales were 1.4 and 6.4 while the British samples overall only operated between 2.2 and 5.5. Four potential factors may have influenced the responses: differences in cultural ideas on self expression; differences in level of feeling invoked by the concepts; differences in the appropriateness of the dimensions for the samples; differences in the mode of introduction to the questionnaire.

The Slovaks were consistently more positive about some concepts than the British samples and the sample of Slovak Hungarian Minority. They viewed the nation particularly positively in terms of being good, valuable, friendly, confident, strong, responsive, understandable and promising. For the British sample their responses were overall relatively non-committal keeping to the middle band on the scales. This pattern of responses fits well with the experiences of the samples as national groups.

Overall the Slovak sample were slightly less "positive" about the state than the nation. On the other hand the state as a concept elicited a very significantly different response between the Slovak Majority and Slovak Hungarian Minority samples. But overall the differences between Central-Eastern and Western country are very visible in this concept. The concept of state also invoked a broader band of responses from the British sample than nation. The British samples had a somewhat negative view of the state although the British Minority sample differed in a positive direction from the Majority sample. Most of the British students have spent all their adolescence and adult life in a society where the government has stressed as a major aspect of its ideology and its policy implementation the diminution of the role of the state. The emphasis has been on individual responsibility and a move away from the "nanny state". However for members of ethnic minorities, the state has had a role to play in not only protecting but promoting their wellbeing. The British responses to the concept of the state would appear to be consistent with this political context.

British and Slovak samples differed significantly in responding to the concept of culture. Again the Slovak Majority sample was "positive" towards the concept using a broader band of the dimension scales than the British, particularly the British Majority sample. The Slovak Hungarian Minority sample differed from the Slovaks on four dimensions, but still they were positive about the concept of culture. However, there were ten significant differences between Slovak and British samples. The British Majority in sample are more insecure, less confident about culture and see it as weaker than the other samples. Within Britain, there has been an undercurrent of feeling concerned with the perceived diminution of the dominant culture as the ethnic minority groups increase as a proportion of the population. The British Minority sample also see culture as less changeable than the other three samples which may reflect their experience of the apparent enduring nature of minority cultures within British society. The Slovak sample saw culture as more responsive, active, modern, understandable and simple than the British samples together. This may well reflect their experience of living in a society with a smaller range of and differences between cultures. For the British, their society is more complex on a cultural dimension with greater differences between cultures across a broad spectrum of facets which include language, dress, food, music, religion, family organisation.

The pattern of the concept of mother tongue was more complex than for previously discussed concepts. The British samples differed significantly on the "evaluative" dimensions from the Slovak samples with the East–West difference presenting the more positive responses from Slovakia and the British Minority the least positive. In comparison with the British as a whole, the Slovak samples saw mother tongue as more valuable, confident, active and understandable. The makeup of the samples may well have contributed to these complex patterns in the responses. In the Slovak samples, all gave the Slovak or Hungarian language as their mother tongue whereas there was not the same level of homogeneity within the British sample. In addition, Slovak society has basically only one major mother tongue language other than Slovak which is widely recognised and this is Hungarian. This is not the case with Britain which has over 100 mother tongue languages. In addition, Slovak society offers the opportunity for the Hungarians to retain their language by supporting Hungarian schools, although there are frequent queries about the usage of the Hungarian language in the public arena. There is an ongoing debate in Britain about the responsibility of the state through education to maintain any mother tongue apart from English and Welsh in Wales.

A major aim of the study was to explore the interrelationships between concepts. Groupings of political, cultural and minority related concepts demonstrate quite different patterns in all of the four samples.

The Slovak Majority sample discriminated most strongly within the cultural concepts, less on political concepts and relatively do not discriminate within the minority related concepts. All the three groupings were separated with the one exception: nation is drawn out to the sphere of the cultural concepts.

In the Slovak Hungarian Minority sample the three groupings were interwoven—mainly the minority related and political concepts and they were all internally discriminated relatively to the same degree.

For the British Majority sample the most discrimination can be found within the political concepts. The least differences were among the cultural concepts which are perceived as very close. Again the separated patterns of the three groupings can be found.

For the British Minority sample the political and minority related concepts were interwoven. They discriminated most in the minority related concepts with the concept of race "pulled" to the minority related concepts.

Conclusion

Within the framework of this research, factors associated with culture, political development and position proved to be dominant in the perception of basic ethnic concepts. This may be explained by the strong social-political-historical impact of these issues. The past and present of a country and its interethnic relations are the subject of collective views and social representations at the group and society level. The extent to which an individual accepts these is dependent more on his/her social position (given by the place in the social system) than individual-psychological characteristics and influences. This was true for the respondents from Slovakia and the UK as they differed very strongly in their perception of almost all of the presented concepts. Perhaps even more importantly they clustered the concepts into different categories and varied in their perception of the distance between concepts.

The consistent usage or preference for particular scales was found with the evaluative scales used for the concepts of nation, culture, mother tongue in the

Slovak Majority sample. It can be assumed that this was influenced by the recent political developments in their country. The Slovak Hungarian Minority sample reflected not only its Central-Eastern European historical developmental "heritage" but also their position in the society in their perception of the particular ethnic concepts. The British samples in turn reflected their positions in the UK with its significant colonial history and subsequent demographic trends.

From the results it seems to be characteristic for the ethnic majority members that they are not predisposed to recognise and acknowledge differences within minority matters (denoted in Slovakia as "minority related" and in the UK as "cultural"). At the same time the ethnic minority members characteristically draw links between the minority related concepts and the political ones.

Whatever else the authors have achieved in the paper, the complexity of cross-European research is evident. However complexity should be a challenge to further action. Hopefully the 1990s will be the decade in which the development of many more programmes of collaborative work between social psychologists and other social scientists from Central-Eastern and Western Europe will flourish.

References

Bacal, A. (1991). *Ethnicity in the Social Sciences*. Centre for Research in Ethnic Relations, University of Warwick, Coventry.

Bacova, V. (1993). The implicit theories of ethnicity: do they exist and what are they? Paper presented at the Vth International Conference on Ethnographic Nationality Research, 7–9 October 1993, Bekescsaba, Hungary.

Butor, M. and Butorova, Z. (1993). Slovakia after the split. *Journal of Democracy*, **4**, 71–83.

Glazer, N. and Moynihan, D. P. (1963). *Beyond the Melting Pot*. Cambridge, Mass.: Harvard University Press.

Glazer, N. and Moynihan, D. P. (eds) (1975). *Ethnicity: Theory and Experience*. Cambridge, Mass: Harvard University Press.

Hutnik, N. (1991). *Ethnic Minority Identity: A Social Psychological Perspective*. Oxford: Oxford Science Publications.

Riggs, F. W. (1991a). Ethnicity, Nationalism, Race, Minority: a semantic/onomantic exercise (Part 1). *International Sociology*, **6**, 281–305.

Riggs, F. W. (1991b). Ethnicity, nationalism, race, minority: a semantic/onomantic exercise (Part 2). *International Sociology*, **6**, 443–63.

Smith, A. D. (1986). *The Ethnic Origins of Nations*, Oxford: Blackwell.

Stern, J. P. (1992). *The Heart of Europe*, Oxford: Blackwell.

Weinreich, P. *et al.* (1992). Comparative Research on National/Ethnic Identities, Unpublished Research Projects, University of Ulster, Jordanstown.

10

Changing Social Identities of the Bulgarians

VELINA TOPALOVA

Institute of Sociology, Bulgarian Academy of Sciences, Bulgaria

The changing social identities at individual and social group levels are a significant consequence and, at the same time, an important factor in the transformations taking place in Bulgarian society along the road to its democratisation. The processes of self-identification and identification with a particular social group or category occur within the overall context of perceived changes, such as changes in social differentiation and social inequality, in the social divisions often determined by the categories of the "we–they" dichotomy. Important aspects of the social group identification are the intragroup identity and the intragroup solidarity, the intergroup perception and the perception of intergroup distances and conflicts.

For the purposes of the following analysis data have been used from three Bulgarian surveys, representative for the country with respect to the main sociodemographic characteristics (Topalova, 1992a, 1992b, 1993a). The first of them was carried out within the framework of a joint Bulgarian-Polish project (Koralewicz and Ziolkowski, 1990; Ziolkowski, 1991). The Polish survey on the sociopolitical and economic views of the Poles used a national representative sample of 1900 subjects and was carried out in 1988, in the period preceding the first free parliamentary elections, which marked the beginning of the process of radical social transformations in Poland. After making the necessary adaptations a large part of the Polish questionnaire was used in the Bulgarian survey conducted on a national representative sample of nearly 3000 subjects, in a similar period from the point of view of the ongoing processes of social change and democratisation of the social system, in May 1990, just before the first free parliamentary elections in Bulgaria. This fact makes possible a sensible comparison of data from the two surveys, despite the two-year interval between them.

In October 1991, the Bulgarian study was replicated within the framework of a broader national research programme for a longitudinal study of the social group differences and the changes in values, social representations and social identity during the period of transition. A national representative sample of nearly 1200 subjects was used. Part of the instruments were used for the third time in a national representative survey carried out in July 1993 on a sample of nearly 2000 subjects. The comparative analysis of data from the Bulgarian surveys carried out in 1990, 1991, and 1993 makes it possible to outline some of the directions of change in the sociopolitical cognitions and values as well as of changes in social identity over this key period of social transformation.

Data have been used from a very simple method, employed in our three successive surveys, studying the social identification and the representation of social distances, based upon the perception of the "we-they" opposition. In this, respondents were instructed to sort a set of 30 cards containing the names of social characteristics, social positions and roles, occupations, as well as the names of particular persons in two groups: "we"—where they would place themselves, and "they". Those cards which were considered unsuitable for either of these two groups were placed in the group of "the rest-others".

The categories written out on the cards have been selected in such a way that they could describe the most important dimensions of the perception of social self-identification and social differentiation of our contemporary society. They could be classified into four basic classes: (1) primary groups—in addition to the category of "I myself" these involve definitions of family members, relatives, friends, colleagues, neighbours who have rather the function of outlining the pole of "we"; (2) categories reflecting some basic institutional dimensions of the social division: political (political parties and movements, opposition), religious (church representatives and institutions), organisations and institutions related to power (administrative, parliamentary, military, media); (3) pairs of opposite characteristics related to the basic dimensions of social differentiation: economic, political, religious; (4) names of basic, representative socio-occupational characteristics (worker, agricultural worker, clerk, engineer, research worker, self-employed).

In the following comparative analysis we have used a general indicator of locating each of the 30 categories on the "we-they" continuum. It has been calculated as a difference between the percentage of assignments of the respective category to "we" and the percentage of its assignments to "they", assuming that the percentage of assignments to "the rest" is zero. For example, in 1990 55.8 per cent of the respondents assigned the category "poor" to "we", and 19.7 per cent—to "they". "Rich" is assigned to "we" by 5.6 per cent, and to "they" by 60.5 per cent. The differences between the percentages of assignment to "we" and "they" are +36.1 for "poor" and -54.9 respectively for "rich", representing the localisation indicators of these two categories on the "we–they" continuum. As a result a dimension from +100 to -100 was obtained, which served as a basis for measuring the degree of social self-identification and social distance with respect to a particular social group, or to its individual representative. A score of +100 would mean that all the respondents have assigned the given category to the group of "we", that of -100—that all the respondents have assigned it to the group of "they", and 0—that the percentages of assignment to "we" and "they" are equal.

Data analysis results will be presented further in three directions: (1) the specificity of social identity and the perception of social distances in Poland and Bulgaria at the general level of the studied population; (2) comparative analysis of the social identification of the objectively existing basic social groups (classes) constituting society and the perception of actual distances between them; (3) Finally, an attempt will be made to outline the tendencies of change in social identity and the representations of intergroup distances in Bulgaria in the period of social transition (1990–93).

Social Identity and Perception of Social Distances in Bulgaria and Poland

Some modifications of the techniques used were made in the follow-up surveys such as the substitution and adding of new categories, to achieve a more adequate coverage of the latest social and political realities. Table 10.1 presents the global indicators for each of the 30 categories (with the exception of "myself") used in the 1990, 1991 and 1993 surveys.

The general ranking of categories, based on the overall indicators of the Bulgarian population is indicative of both the respondents' social identification and the intergroup perceptions and distances.

The arrangement of the categories offered for sorting on the studied dimension is distinctly asymmetrical. The social groups and categories in relation to which closeness is declared are less in number than the ones to which distance is shown. Data obtained from the three studies testify to some gradual narrowing of the "gap" between the categories assigned to "we" and those assigned to "they". This can be regarded as certain moderation of polarisation of the general perception of Bulgarian society in the categories of the dichotomy "we"–"they" in the years of transition.

Mainly members of the primary groups were assigned to the group of "we": friends and relatives, work-mates, neighbours; these have, at the same time, the function of a reference point in determining the "we" pole.

The remaining categories assigned to "we" include the socio-occupational, political, economic, and religious dimensions of the social structure. They also give the basic profile of the Bulgarian population's self-identification: workers and agricultural workers, nonparty members, poor, nonreligious.

The negative section of the dimension "they", a larger one, comprises the remaining categories, to which a different degree of social distance has been demonstrated. The strongest tendency is the one of outlining a social distance from the rich, as well as from the representatives of the different structures of power: director, military man, TV journalist (editor of TV news), member of Parliament.

TABLE 10.1   Ranking of the categories according to their position on the "we–they" continuum in Bulgaria

	1990	1991	1993
My closest friend	+92.7	+85.1	+84.3
My closest relative	+89.7	+78.8	+83.4
Colleague	+77.6	+70.9	+75.0
Neighbour	+70.1	+63.4	+64.7
Worker	+63.0	+44.7	+54.0
Fellow villager	+55.2	+47.0	+59.0
Nonparty member	+48.7	+356.3	+49.4
Agricultural worker	+47.2	+26.4	+24.1
Poor	+36.1	+45.7	+36.1
Nonreligious	+20.7	+16.4	+17.7
Religious	-2.3	-6.5	+1.7
Member of the Bulgarian Socialist Party	-5.3	-22.8	-21.5
Engineer	-12.0	-3.9	-7.2
Priest	-15.0	-20.6	—
Militant of the Bulgarian Socialist Party	-16.7	—	—
Clerk	-18.6	-11.4	-11.4
Patriarch Maxim	-19.0	—	—
Member of the Bulgarian Agrarian Union	-19.3	-17.4	-21.5
Alexander Lilov	-19.4	-38.6	-13.1
Research worker	-21.7	-17.4	-18.7
Self-employed	-22.4	-14.0	-12.3
Chief Mufti	-23.4	—	—
Member of the Union of Democratic Forces	-24.2	-4.8	-4.3
TV journalist	-27.4	-21.5	-23.4
Zhelyu Zhelev/Philip Dimitrov	-28.5	-23.5	-17.3
Militant of the Union of Democratic Forces	-29.1	—	—
Military man	-30.0	-23.6	-18.1
Director (Boss)	-42.5	-39.1	-0.8
Rich	-54.9	-54.0	-43.3
Member of Parliament	—	-51.3	-39.3
Ahmed Dogan	—	-51.2	-45.9
President Zhelyu Zhelev	—	-5.0	+5.0
Simeon Koburgotski	—	-30.2	-28.1
Member of MRF	—	—	-43.3

In many aspects the results approach those from the general ranking of categories based on the Polish data (Ziolkowski, 1991) as well as those obtained from a similar study carried out in Slovakia. The high coefficient of correlation ($r = 0.94$) between Bulgarian and Slovak data, concerning the general ranking of categories (Plichtova, 1993), also show a significant similarity in the way the general social structure is perceived in the former socialist societies.

There are, however, significant differences, more salient when analyzing the categories along the four classes. The Bulgarian population, compared to the Polish one, manifests a greater tendency to identify with the primary groups. This may be due to a stronger traditionality and patriarchality of the social life of the Bulgarians.

TABLE 10.2   Position of the different groups of categories on the "we–they" continuum in Poland and Bulgaria

	Bulgaria, 1990		Poland 1988
Nonreligious	+ 20.7		– 30.2
Religious	– 2.3		+ 53.9
Priest	– 15.0		+ 31.6
Patriarch Maxim	– 19.0		—
Chief Mufti	– 23.4		—
Cardinal Glemp	—	+ 33.3	
Pope John Paul II	—		+ 56.2
Poor	+ 36.1		+ 39.5
Rich	– 54.9		– 35.3
Director	– 42.5		– 16.7
Military man	– 30.0		-20.0
TV journalist	– 27.4		– 28.9
Self-employed	– 22.4		– 12.4
Research worker	– 21.7		– 1.2
Clerk	– 18.6		– 19.9
Engineer	– 12.0		– 1.4
Agrarian worker	+ 47.2		+ 41.3
Worker	+ 63.0		+ 48.9
Member of the Bulgarian		Member of the Polish	
Socialist Party	– 5.3	United Workers Party	– 42.3
Socialist Party	– 5.3	United Workers Party	– 42.3
Militant of BSP	– 16.7	Party secretary	– 45.4
		Member or CC of PUWP	– 57.3
Alexander Lilov	– 19.4	W. Jaruselski	– 43.4
Nonparty member	+ 48.7	Nonparty member	+ 29.5
Member of Union of			
Democratic Forces	– 24.2		
Militant of UDF	– 29.1	Militant of Solidarity	– 27.4
Zhelyu Zhelev	– 28.5	Lech Walesa	– 12.3

The largest gap between the two populations, however, is to be found in their attitude to religion.

The Poles show greatest identification with the religious community and the representatives of the church, and outline the largest distance from the nonreligious, while for the Bulgarians the direction of the answers distribution is the opposite. The religious dimension is, in general, less differentiating for the Bulgarian society than for the Polish one, and the church representatives and institutions are to a greater extent the object of an indifferent attitude. Many culturological speculations have been made with respect to the low level of religiosity of the Bulgarians which relate both to the peculiarities of the national historical process, and, particularly, the late autonomy of the Bulgarian church and its role in social life, as well as to some specific differences between the Orthodox religion and Catholicism.

As far as the economic dimension of social differentiation is concerned, the self-identification with the poor is almost the same in the two populations. The

Bulgarians, however, outline a larger distance from the rich than the Poles. Historically, the Bulgarian society is economically less differentiated and with strongly developed egalitarian frame of mind.

There are significant differences also in the perception of the social class differentiation, based on the occupational characteristics. Both the Bulgarians and the Poles report positive identification only with the social groups of workers and peasants, and show, to a different degree, a distance from the remaining occupational groups—a medium distance, with respect to the intellectuals, and a large one, with respect to occupational groups connected with the structures of power. However, the perception of the socio-occupational differentiation in Bulgaria is more salient as compared with Poland. The range of "we-they" choices within which the socio-occupational groups are situated is significantly larger for the Bulgarian population. Furthermore, there is an impressive difference in the attitude to some socio-occupational groups. The Poles manifest a comparatively smaller distance from the occupations of intellectual work— engineers and, particularly, scientific workers, as well as from some representatives of the structures of power (directors, military men).

Special consideration of the established differences concerning the political dimension of social differentiation is deserved, since it is crucial for the development of the political processes of democratisation. Both the Bulgarians and the Poles show a distance from the representatives of the political parties and movements but to a different degree. While the attitudes of both populations to the representatives of the local opposition (at that time Solidarity in Poland and the Union of Democratic Forces in Bulgaria) are similar, with the exception of the attitudes to their leaders, their attitudes to the representatives of the communist party are quite different. The Poles manifested a great distance from the representatives of the communist party hierarchy at all levels, while the distance outlined by the Bulgarians is considerably smaller, especially concerning the rank and file in the party, the attitudes to these people is very close to the self-identification line. These results account very well for the different outcomes of the parliamentary elections held in Poland in 1988, and in Bulgaria in 1990. It seems that the different election results are due to the extent of distance from and rejection of the communist party, rather than to the large-scale identification with the opposition.

Thus, the most significant differences in social identification in Poland and Bulgaria established concerned: (1) religion, (2) the political parties, and especially, the communist party, (3) the rich and (4) some socio-occupational groups.

Social Group Identification and Perception of Intergroup Distances

In the background of the general population characteristics significant differences come to the fore in the social identification and the perception of the social distances between the existing groups in society objectively determined on

TABLE 10.3 Position of the socio-occupational categories on the "we–they" continuum according to the scores given by the particular socio-occupational groups Bulgaria 1990

	Managers	Intellectuals	Admin. workers	Workers in trade and services	Skilled manual workers	Unskilled manual workers	Agricultural workers	Self-employed	
Worker	+25	+31	+60	+80	+81	+70	+65	+77	+488
Agricultural worker	+28	+21	+35	+55	+53	+52	+79	+47	+370
Engineer	+31	+37	-37	-12	-25	-32	-38	0	-42
Clerk	+20	-4	-7	+26	-26	-38	-37	-46	-104
Self-employed	-30	15	-23	-21	-24	-22	-34	-28	-194
Research worker	-10	+15	+35	-20	-29	-27	-29	-34	-100
Military man	-5	-32	-33	-25	-19	-37	-29	-26	-206
TV journalist	-10	-19	-42	-35	-26	-25	-23	-30	-210
	+28	-18	-33	-27	-26	-41	-33	-39	-189
Director	+59	+53	+64	+82	+10	-33	-23	-10	

the basis of socioeconomic and demographic indicators such as gender, age, education, type of settlement, social class and occupational status, etc.

We shall report here only some findings on the most significant differences in the social identity and representations of intergroup distances between the basic socioprofessional groups determined by their objective social status. In both the Polish and the Bulgarian surveys of 1990 the following general classification of social groups has been used: managers and administrators; intellectuals; administrative workers, white-collar workers; skilled manual workers; unskilled manual workers; agricultural workers; self-employed. In the Bulgarian surveys of 1991 and 1993 we used a modified version of the same classification.

Table 10.3 presents the values of the global indicator (calculated as the difference between the percentages of assigning a given socio-occupational category to "us" and to "they") for each of the basic, objectively defined in the sample socio-occupational groups. The indicated sums in the last column of the table show the way in which each of the suggested socio-occupational categories has been chosen by respondents with different objective social positions (i.e. who chose whom).

The last line of the table gives the sums of scores of defining the socio-occupational categories. These sums show the way in which people characterised by a definite objective social position have dealt with the notions of "we" and "they" (i.e. who chose how).

According to the global indicators in the last column of Table 10.3 the socio-occupational categories studied are divided into three distinct groups: (1) predominantly workers and agricultural workers are assigned to the "we" group; (2) there is a definite social distance to the category of engineers, research workers and clerks; and (3) there is a great distance to the socio-occupational categories related to the structures of power (director, TV journalist and military officer) as well as to the category of "self-employed". A significant differentiation is observed in the scores given by the representatives of the various socio-occupational groups in the sample.

The strongest and most salient self-identification is that of agricultural and industrial workers with their own socio-occupational category, while the social group self-identification of the others takes a more vague and fuzzy form. What deserves mentioning is the distance shown in 1990 to their own social group on the part of the self-employed (-28) and the change in the direction of their self-identification: in 1991 (+40) and in 1993 (+53).

As far as the proportion is concerned between the positive and the negative indicators of the choices made by the different socio-occupational groups presented in the last line of Table 10.3: the workers and agricultural workers tend to identification with their own group (inner-group solidarity) and reciprocity among one another, but also to reticence and self-isolation, showing distance in relation to all other social groups. This applies to a great extent to the group of self-employed as well, which identifies itself mainly with the workers and agricultural workers. The rest of the groups reveal a weaker inner-group coherence and a stronger tendency to broaden the boundaries of "we"—the range becoming broader with the less reciprocity and solidarity they enjoy on the part of the others, thus blurring the social differences. A stronger intragroup cohesion and emotional distance to the others are observed for those social groups which occupy the lower levels, economically and politically, in the social hierarchy.

The comparison made with Polish study data shows similar tendencies in the social group identification, obviously characteristic of the former socialist societies (Ziolkowski 1991), due, to a large extent, to the ideology of egalitarianism and to the tendency of opposing the manual to the mental labour groups, as well as due to the critical attitude to the authorities.

Change in Social Identity and Representations of Intergroup Distances in the Period of Social Transition

What are the tendencies of change in the social identification and the perception of social distances, outlined as a result of the comparative analysis of data from the three Bulgarian surveys, carried out in 1990, 1991 and 1993?

Most significant is the change in the perception of the political segment of our social life.

A considerable increase is observed in the perceived social distance from the representatives of the Bulgarian Socialist Party and a decrease in the distance from the representatives of the Union of Democratic Forces to the point of identification though slight with the group of its followers, more salient in 1991. This radical shift on the "we–they" dimension is an expression of change in social consciousness, which has made the winning of the parliamentary elections by the political opposition in 1991 possible.

Data for 1993 show that at the level of the total population studied the greatest social distance is revealed towards the adherents of the Movement for Rights and Freedoms (-43.3), followed by those of the Bulgarian Socialist Party (-21.5), and a relatively smaller distance (-4.3) to the adherents of the Union of Democratic Forces: it is noteworthy that the distance towards the leaders of the corresponding political parties is, as a rule, greater than towards their rank-and-file members and adherents.

As far as the economic dimension is concerned—the great social distance from the rich in 1993 has decreased and the identification with the poor has been the strongest in 1991.

Contradictory attitudes and even a greater distance from religion and the church are very common in 1993. A slight tendency is observed of decrease in social identification with the nonreligious and of cutting the anyway short distance to the religious people, however, the opposite is valid with the official representatives of the church—the priests.

Some latent dimensions became also more active in 1991 and 1993 and some new dimensions emerged as factors in the perception of social differentiation: differences between the adherents of the republic or the monarchy (President

Table 10.4 Position of the different groups of categories on the "we–they" continuum in Bulgaria 1990, 1991, 1993

	Bulgaria		
	1990	*1991*	*1993*
Alexander Lilov	−19.4	−38.6	−13.1
Militant of BSP	−16.7	—	—
Member of BSP	−5.3	−22.8	−21.5
Zh. Zhelev/Ph. Dimitrov	−28.5	−23.5	−17.3
Militant of UDF	−29.1	—	—
Member of UDF	−24.2	+4.8	−43.3
Rich	−54.9	−54.0	−43.3
Poor	+36.1	+45.7	+36.1
Nonreligious	+20.7	+16.4	+17.7
Religious	−2.3	−6.5	−1.7
Priest	−15.0	−20.6	—
Patriach Maxim	−19.0	—	—
Chief Mufti	−23.4	—	—
Ahmed Dogan	—	−51.2	−45.9
President Zh. Zhelev	—	−5.0	+5.0
Simeon Koburgotski	—	−30.2	−28.1
Deputy in the Parliament	—	−50.3	−39.3
Director	−42.5	−39.1	−0.8
Military man	−30.0	−23.6	−18.1
TV journalist	−27.4	−21.5	−23.4
Self-employed	−22.4	−14.0	−12.3
Research worker	−27.7	−17.4	−18.7
Clerk	−18.6	−11.4	−11.4
Engineer	−12.0	−3.9	−7.2
Agrarian worker	+47.2	+26.4	+24.1
Worker	+63.0	+44.7	+54.0

Zhelev and the Bulgarian tzar in exile Simeon Koburgotski), ethnical differences which, along with a political and religious intolerance, find expression in the most salient form in the distance from Ahmed Dogan—leader of the third political force in the country—The Movement for Rights and Freedoms.

The only dimension within the framework of "we–they" differences which decreases is the socio-occupational differentiation. Although the dichotomous division of social groups (workers and peasants vs others), as well as the comparatively greater distance from the occupational groups, connected with the structures of power, have been preserved, the narrowing of the intergroup gaps in the Bulgarian society, presumed to be the result of the current economic and ideological transformations, is evident.

The data on the sum total of the choices made for each of the representatives of the different social groups testify to: (1) the gradual decrease in identification with the workers and agricultural workers, and (2) simultaneous decrease in the social distance towards power-related socio-occupational groups (director, military officer, TV journalist, deputy); as well as in general towards the representatives of some categories of mental labour (engineers, research workers, clerks), and also towards the category of the self-employed.

The established tendencies in the study of social identity and the perceived social distances lead to some more general conclusions.

Apparently, in spite of the national specificities, there exist a lot of common characteristics of the social identity and the perceived social distances in the former socialist societies, in the initial stage of their transformation, especially. The similarities are to be found both on the level of the total population, and on the level of the social groups, differentiated on the basis of objective criteria.

The comparative analysis of data from the three successive Bulgarian studies outlines a twofold tendency: in the process of social transformation the differentiation of social identity as an indicator of the formation of a more heterogeneous society increases and at the same time the contrast in the general perception of the dichotomous social division in the category of "we–they" decreases.

The comparison of data concerning the objective development of the sociopolitical and economic processes and the transformation of the structure of Bulgarian society in the period under study with the data we obtained on the changes in social identity and the perceived social distances shows that the anthropocentric approach is applicable and diagnostic enough in the attempt to characterise, through the changes in social consciousness, the dimensions of the objective state and the tendencies of change in the society undergoing transition.

References

Koralewicz J. and Ziolkowski, M. (1990). *Mentalnosc spoleczno-polityczna Polakow w koncu lat '80tych*. Poznan: Nacom.

Plichtova, J. (1993). Relation between Marxism and social representations of individuals and social groups in Czecho-Slovakia. Paper presented at the International Conference "Changing European Identities: Social-Psychological Analysis of Social Change", Farnham Castle, Surrey, May 1993.

Topalova V. (1993). Changes in the perception of social structure in Bulgaria and Poland. In J. Plichtova (ed.), *Cultural Construction of Democracy*. Department of Social and Biological Communication. Slovak Academy of Sciences, Bratislava.

Ziolkowski M. (1991) MY-ONI. Pszyczynek do badania percepcji spolecznych i politycznych podzialow w Polsce w koncu lat osiemdziesiatych (maszynopis).

11

Nationalism as an International Ideology: Imagining the Nation, Others and the World of Nations

MICHAEL BILLIG

University of Loughborough, England

Isaiah Berlin has written that "no century has seen so much remorseless slaughter as our own" (1990, 175). Even as the century moves through its final decade, the tally of death keeps mounting. In 1991 the world's most powerful nation led an alliance of twenty-six other nations. The exact number of Iraqis killed in this brief but intense conflict will probably be never known, but combined civilian and military deaths were probably around a quarter of a million. During the war the US president's popularity soared to unprecedented peaks, only to fall dramatically two years later as the war slid from popular consciousness.

The Gulf War dramatically illustrates what, in the late twentieth century, is thought to be worth killing and dying for. The popular cause behind the alliance's war can be understood negatively. This was not a religious war—a modern crusade by Christian nations against Islam. The West had previously been supporting Iraq against the Islamic Republic of Iran; Muslim and Christian armies fought alongside each other, as the attacks against Iraq were mounted from the nation of Mecca. The war was not fought in the name of a particular political creed, for the alliance comprised an assortment of democratic republics, constitutional monarchies, dictatorships and absolute monarchies. An alliance, which included President Assad's Syria and which sought to restore the ruling house of Kuwait, could hardly be fighting for the democratic principle. Nor was the alliance mobilised against a philosophy. Ba'athism had not disturbed US foreign policy before the Gulf crisis; nor, indeed, had Saddam Hussein's crimes against the Iraqi people.

The gassing of Kurdish women and children failed to provoke the sort of global reaction, which followed the annexation of Kuwait, an established nation with UN membership and its own postage stamps. Over fifty years earlier, another alliance had reacted similarly. The Second World War had not been prompted by the German government's mistreatment of its own citizens. No foreign government had committed its soldiery to rescue German Jewry. But once the German government started making national flags, rather than individual citizens, disappear, then war became inevitable.

In this, one can see the force of nationalism within political thinking of the twentieth century. The assumptions of this nationalism are not revealed by the actions of governments which have territorial ambitions over neighbouring nations: after all, such actions harken back to an earlier era before the rise of nation-states (Hinsley, 1986). The nationalist assumptions are demonstrated in the actions of nations which will readily fight to prevent, or reverse, such annexations. Such actions suggest that notions of national integrity are firmly embedded within contemporary ideology. In other ages, populations may have been mobilised to kill for gods. In our age, lives are to be sacrificed for the "nation"—not even "our" nation—as if an aura attends the very idea of nationhood.

World of Nations

Although nationalism needs to be considered in a wide context, social scientists have sometimes tended to take a restricted view of the issue. For instance, nationalism is often treated as the ideology of two sorts of social movement. Extreme right-wing political movements, which advocate a politics based tightly around loyalty to the nation, are described as nationalist. So too are movements which aim to establish new independent nation-states, often seeking liberation from colonial empires (for examples of social scientists linking nationalism to social movements, see, for example, Melucci, 1989; Schlesinger, 1991; Coakley, 1992). Such approaches tend not to view nationalism as an endemic property of nation-states. Instead, they see nationalism as a force which threatens the stability of established nations. In consequence, nationalism appears as a "surplus phenomenon", which wells up intermittently in the form of social movements. By contrast, the present approach views nationalism as a major constituent feature of the contemporary world, for it is the ideology by which nation-states are reproduced as nations.

To begin with, the global success of nationalism as an ideology must be emphasised: the contemporary world is a world of nations. Other political ideologies seem restricted by comparison. The doctrines of liberalism are confined to particular parts of the world—Marxist ideas are even more restricted territorially. However, the idea of "nationhood" is general. As Birch (1989) has pointed out, the globe's entire land surface, with the exception of Antarctica, is "now divided between nations", making nationalism "the most successful political ideology in human history" (p. 3). If the globe is covered by nation-states, then so will it be filled with discourses, representations and habits of thought which reproduce the nation-state as the accepted, and generally desired, form of community today.

In this sense, nationalism is not an ideology which is linked to specific nation-states: it is more generally an international ideology. Nationalism not only permits different peoples to think of themselves as uniquely different "nations", deserving their own independent state (Anderson, 1983); but it allows these communities to be imagined in a uniform, globally distributed way. Nationalism provides the general concept of "nation", which fuels the political imagination of aspiring national social movements, right-wing dictatorships and established nation-states. If ideologies make the contingent social world appear "natural" (Billig, 1991; McLellan, 1986; Eagleton, 1991; Ricoeur, 1986), then nationalism can refer to those beliefs and assumptions by which it appears "natural" for the world to be divided into separate nation-states, and, thus, for the world of nations to be reproduced as today's "natural" social environment.

Characteristics of Nationalism

Some broad characteristics of the world of nation-states can be briefly stated. Three features will be mentioned: (a) the nature of the nation-state; (b) its historical recency; and (c) the socio-psychological creation of national citizenry.

(a) Giddens (1985, 1987) has described nation-states as "territorially bounded . . . administrative units", which act as political "power-containers" (1985, 3). In the modern world, one nation-state does not imperceptibly merge into an other, in the way that some linguistic and tribal communities do. Instead, nations mark out their boundaries with precision, materially and symbolically emphasising the limits of their extent. The boundaries are crucial, for each nation-state claims a sovereign monopoly of the right to violence within its territory. Part of being a nation-state is to claim the right to use violence against those who violate the boundaries or who challenge the state's internal monopoly of violence (Giddens, 1990). These "rights" are internationally recognised, being enshrined, for instance, in the charter of the United Nations (Hinsley, 1986). Saddam Hussein's brutal persecution of Iraqi Kurds did not violate the principle of the state's right to violence within national boundaries. However, the invasion of Kuwait violated borders. Indeed it aimed to dissolve the boundaries themselves, threatening, thereby, the symbolic force attached to all national boundaries.

(b) The world of nations is of comparatively recent origin, for the nation-state, as a distinct, bounded power-container, belongs to the modern era. There are differing accounts to explain why the nation-state emerged. Gellner (1983 and 1986) has pointed to the importance of industrialisation and the need for centrally controlled systems of education; Anderson (1983) argues for the importance of printing and the spread of discursive literacy; Mann (1992) also stresses the spread of discursive literacy, but adds that the growth of commercial capitalism should not be forgotten; Kennedy (1988) emphasises the military advantage of the centrally organised nation-state; Smith (1986) underlines the importance of pre-existing ethnicities. Such authors may dispute the underlying factors, but they do not dispute the comparative modernity of the nation-state.

If, as Giddens (1987) claims, "we live in a world nation-state system that has no precedent in history" (p. 166), this recency is often denied within nationalist ideology itself. As a way of "naturalising" the world of nations, nationalist theorists have claimed that nations have always existed. To give an example: Walter Bagehot, the Victorian journalist and author of the classic *English Constitution*, posed the question in his *Physics and Politics*, "What are nations?" He answered by asserting that nations are "as old as history" (1873, 83). Thus, the modern nation-state was claiming itself to be a "natural", rather than historically created, form of sovereignty, which was bringing ancient national destinies to their fruition. To achieve this sense of antiquity, the nations of Europe, during their period of formation in the eighteenth and nineteenth centuries, regularly invented traditions (Hobsbawm and Ranger, 1983). In this way, the new political units, publicly and symbolically proclaimed their antiquity and their "naturalness".

The conventional and transnational symbols of national particularity, such as the border-post, the passport and the nation anthem are all modern creations. Mediaeval Europe, with its complex segmented patterns of loyalty, was not divided into bounded, centrally administered political units (Mann, 1988). Nor was there any expectation that its patterns of governance would be reproduced across the world (Anderson, 1983; Hobsbawm, 1992). In fact, for mediaeval Europeans there was no conception of the world as a whole in the modern sense, for the world disappeared into unknown edges of darkness. This is very different from the conception, or representation, of the world today. Not only is the world represented as a physical totality, but also as a political and moral entity. In this respect, the national order, as a morally constituted order, has filled the dry spaces of the total globe.

(c) In consequence, the world of nations is not merely a political form, but it is also psychological or ideological form. Giddens (1985) has asserted as much in his definition of nationalism: "By 'nationalism' I mean a phenomenon that is primarily psychological—the affiliation of individuals to a set of symbols and beliefs emphasizing communality among the members of a political order" (p. 116). Giddens, however tends to associate the psychological conditions of nationalism with particular, intermittent moments (see also Giddens, 1987). However, the socio-psychological dimensions of nationalism can also be seen to be constant and banal, permitting the reproduction of the established nation as a nation. If nationalism belongs to the modern age, and if it is primarily psychological, then it is creating new socio-psychological forms, both in its intermittent and constant forms.

Above all, one might say that nationalism provides new forms of identity, or, to adapt the terminology of Althusser (1971), it provides new ways of "hailing" the subject as a national citizen. As Harris states, the conditions for attachment have changed from previous times: "Under mediaeval serfdom, each serf was tied to a piece of land and to a particular lord; now every inhabitant is expected to be tied to one national soil and one government, or to be an outcaste" (1992, 258). In the world of nations, everyone is expected to possess a national identity, which links them to one, and usually only one, national entity (Smith, 1986). These expectations of national identification are not confined to particular forms of nation-state, but they are endemic within the world of nation-states itself. As Gellner (1983) suggests, to the modern person "a man [sic] must have a nationality as he must have a nose and two ears". Gellner adds that "having a nation is not an inherent attribute of humanity, but it has come to appear as such" (p. 6).

To define nationalism in terms of social movements, which seek to alter existing arrangements of nation-states, is to take a restricted view of something which is more general. Nationalism, far from being a "surplus" phenomenon, is a general ideological condition of the contemporary world. It is an international ideology in two senses: not only is it spread across nations, but also it represents and "naturalises" the world of nations itself. In this way, nationalism encompasses the ideological forms and socio-psychological attachments by which nationhood, and thereby the international world of nation-states, can be reproduced.

Familiar Signs of Nationalism

If nationalism is an international ideology in the contemporary world, then it is important to study its mundane aspects, in order to understand how the notion of nationhood is embedded in contemporary consciousness. This means avoiding the temptation to seek the nature of nationalism in its extreme manifestations, such as the re-emerging fascist movements of Europe or the actions of Serbian ethnic cleansers. The danger of concentrating upon the extreme instances is that the daily, non-extreme signs of nationalism, which are part of today's "natural" environment, would slip by unnoticed. Instead, one should expect that nationalism informs the thinking, indeed the imagination, of ordinary members of the "imagined communities" which are modern nation-states.

Anderson's notion of "imagined communities" points to the importance of the socio-psychological dimensions of nationalism. For there to be an "imagined community" there must be acts of collective imagination, which "invent" the national society (see also Moscovici, 1993). As Anderson states, "the nation is always conceived as a deep horizontal comradeship" (1983, 16). Nevertheless, Anderson does not specify the socio-psychological dimensions involved in accomplishing the collective conception of this horizontal bond. In particular, one can ask how the collective imagination operates and also what themes, or representations, are to be imagined. Giddens, in claiming the importance of the socio-psychological dimensions of nationality, offers a clue about the nature of this psychology. He mentions the "deeply layered ideological implications" of nationalism and comments allusively that "it is around the intersection between discursive consciousness and 'lived experience' that the ideological consequences of nationalism will cluster" (1985, 220). If Giddens is correct, then ordinary ways of speaking and experiencing the world—or the habitus, to use Bourdieu's term—will be suffused with nationalist meanings, creating an environment in which it seems "natural" to possess national identities. This means that analysts should pay particular attention to the way that the sociopsychological aspects of nationhood are constituted within familiar discourses.

One can inquire what nationalist elements are embedded in the discursive consciousness. At this point, the importance of viewing nationalism as an international ideology can be stressed. If one has a restricted view of nationalism and takes extreme social movements as exemplars, then one might be drawn to the limited conclusion that the essential characteristics of nationalism lie in stereotypes which glorify the ingroup and which posit outgroups as despised enemies. However, nationalism, as an international and banal ideology, involves more than the imagining of ingroups and outgroups: "we" and "them" have to be imagined as nations, and, thus, nationhood itself has to be imagined (Breuilly, 1985). Just as Balibar (1991) claims that there can be no racism without theories, so nationalism involves theories, or representations, rather than discrete stereotypes. These theories will not necessarily be recognised as theories, for they take the form of common-sense assumptions about the naturalness of nations in a world of nations. Thus, nationhood and the "world of nations" have to be imagined, for these enable "us", not just to imagine "ourselves" as a group, but, most importantly, to imagine "ourselves" as a national "us".

(a) **Imagining the Ingroup** The imagining of "our" nation is the most obvious aspect of nationalism. The nationalist imagination is constructed around the first person plural, for it is an imagining of who "we" are (Billig, 1993). This includes an imagining of the self, and the linking of the self with a category, as is described in some social psychological theories of social identity (Turner *et al*, 1987; Abrams and Hogg, 1990). In addition, the category itself has meaning, for a nation is not imagined to be any ingroup. The national group is a particular sort of group, for the idea of nationhood involves an imagining of the community as possessing a unique spatial-temporal identity and claiming entitlement to its own political independence. As Smith (1990) has written, to create sense of national identity, a population "must be taught who they are, where they come from and whither they are going" (p. 184).

Social historians have documented how the growth of nationalism has been accompanied by the creation of traditions, myths, collective memories and so on (Hobsbawm, 1983; Samuel, 1989; Samuel and Thompson, 1990; Schwartz, Zerubavel and Barnett, 1986; Schwartz, 1990). The collective remembering (and collective forgetting) will be accomplished through the production of shared histories, which depict the nation as a distinct community, and thereby make sense of the present, as the past is created.

In this way, the nation is imagined as a unique community, with its own historical destiny and homeland. A sense of particularity is to be constructed, for "our" nation is to be conceived as different from other nations. In that particularity lies "our" sense of being "us". In England, for example, the Royal Family is frequently used to construct this sense of national particularity (Nairn, 1988; Billig, 1990). Billig (1992) describes how English families claimed that there would be no nation without the Royal Family. They declared themselves to be reluctant to imagine the nation without a monarchy. If the monarchy is imagined as a sign of national particularity, then to imagine the nation without monarchy is to imagine "our" nation to be like other nations—it is to de-imagine the particularity of the nation. Moreover, it is to de-imagine the self as a member of the nation. Even those respondents, who would openly criticise members of the Royal Family, would resist de-imagining their own national selves.

In western democracies, the sense of nationhood is daily reinforced by newspapers and television, which report the words of politicians. National politicians—the important politicians of the present age—continually "hail" the nation, claiming to represent its best interests. As Harris (1992) comments, "nationalism today provides the framework and language for almost all political discussion" (p. 269). It could hardly be otherwise, so long as nations are political units (Giddens, 1990). Grand mythic themes are not necessary for the familiar evocation of nationhood, for national politicians, discursively evoke the national community in familiar, clichéd ways. A simple, ambiguous word, such as "we", can accomplish much in this regard. Political speakers typically use a "syntax of hegemony", which permits the particular interest to be posited as the general interest. Politicians evoke an ambiguous "we" which constantly and unremarkably elides distinctions between self, party, nation and "the universal audience" (Billig, 1991, 1993; Maitland and Wilson, 1987; Seidel, 1975; Wilson, 1990; and see Perelman and Olbrechts-Tyteca (1971) for a discussion of the rhetoric of the universal audience). In doing this, politicians habitually represent the general interest in terms of the imagined national interest of "we the nation'.

So familiar are the evocations of nationhood in political discourse that they have hardly been studied as such—either in terms of their extent or their ideological depth. A typical, and unremarkable, instance can be given. American presidential campaigns are filled with displays of patriotic colours and flags; the rival candidates claim to speak for the "true America". This is not merely cynical vote-grabbing, but it is part of the business of seeking to represent the imagined community of the nation. Immediately after the result of the 1992 election had been declared, the candidates gave short addresses "to the nation". President-elect Clinton began by hailing "my fellow Americans". He spoke about the "clarion call for our country" and ended by accepting with a full heart the responsibility of being "the leader of this, the greatest country in human history". Outgoing President Bush used a similar rhetoric, addressing "all Americans", who "shared the same purpose, to make this, the world's greatest nation, more safe and more secure and to guarantee every American a shot at the American dream" (reported in *Guardian*, 5.11.1992).

Such remarks are so banal that they scarcely register in the consciousness of the television-viewer or newspaper-reader. If it is easy to overlook their ideological content, then that is precisely the point. The concept of "nationalism" should include the easy speaking of, and the easy hearing of, such discourses, which fill the political discursive consciousness the world over.

(b) **Imagining the Outgroup** Social psychologists, studying the cognitive basis of social categorisation, have stressed that an ingroup identity involves the imagining of an outgroup (Tajfel, 1981; Eiser, 1986). A social category divides the social world into ingroup members and non-members (or outgroup members). Some social psychological theories of identity assume that the linking of the self with the ingroup category is the fundamental feature in the process of group identification. Self-categorisation theory suggests that the motivation to construct a positive ingroup self-identity is psychologically prior to the differentiation from outgroups: the motivation leads to the acceptance of an ingroup category and, hence, to the differentiation from the corresponding outgroup (Turner *et al.*, 1987; Haslam and Turner, 1992). However, such approaches tend not to examine the use of language, and especially the use of group categories, in actual discursive settings (Edwards, 1991). To use a social categorisation in discourse and to apply it to oneself implies a distinction between ingroup and outgroup. This can be observed in actual discursive utterances about "our" nations: the use of "we", to indicate a nation, implies a contrasting "them", and *vice versa* (Potter and Wetherell, 1987; Wetherell and Potter, 1982; and see also Hall, 1991). In these instances, there is no reason for supposing that the "we" is prior to the "them", for the two discursively coincide.

Historically, myths about the nation tend to be developed as the nation is being created in contradistinction to other nations. Nations imitate the national forms of other nations, but do so in ways which proclaim their own national uniqueness. This is apparent as a nation liberates itself from a colonial power. As it fights for its freedom, so it creates its own history. During the American War of Independence, George Washington was transformed from a man of ordinary talents into a mythic hero, as he became a symbol of plain, non-British virtues (Schwartz, 1987). During the eighteenth century, Britain developed many of its modern symbols of nationhood, especially those relating to the monarchy. Frequently these were developed in conscious contradistinction from French styles of nation-making (Cannadine, 1983; Colley, 1992). The first recorded cartoon, which depicts John Bull as an "Englishman", also shows a Frenchman; Bull is as fat and generous as the Frenchman appears thin and meagre (Surel, 1989). Thus, the iconographic stereotype of "our" national character (a model offered as a type for identification) was created in contrastive differentiation from the stereotype of "them". In this sense, there is an implied argumentative dimension within the stereotype (Billig, 1987). An identification *with* the ingroup caricature is also an identification *against* the rival Other. Bhabha (1990), adapting a more general rhetorical point made by Kristeva (1986), claims that national affirmation is achieved through negation. There is no need to imagine one's particularity, unless it is a separation from "others", who are imagined as fundamentally different.

Accordingly, the discourses about the national ingroup—its history, its culture, its interests – are not innocent. They are both an affirmation and also a negation, for, in imagining "us", they also imagine Otherness (Wetherell and Potter, 1992). Billig (1992) found that British families, talking about the monarchy, did not merely repeat myths of nationhood. Continually there was a contrastive dimension: "our" history is longer than the history of others; "our" monarchy is the "real" monarchy; no other country has this tradition; the Americans envy "us". In saying all this, other countries (Americans, foreigners, "them") have to be imagined. If there is no "they", then "we" have no special destiny. Even the discourses of apparently supra-national identities can share this characteristic. A newspaper article quoted young people talking of a European identity. A transatlantic gaze was apparent: "The Americans are so arrogant. Europe needs its own identity" said a typical adolescent (*Independent on Sunday*, 22 November 1992).

The extracts from the presidential candidates illustrate the point. Both Bush and Clinton, in constructing their image of America and in addressing their "fellow Americans", used similar phrases: "the greatest country in human history"; "the world's greatest nation". The world and its history had other nations. Speakers and audience could assume that for "us" to be the greatest, there must be other, lesser nations in a background environment of "them". By this evocation of the great ingroup, a shadowy world of outgroup stereotypes is indicated.

The soothing power of "we"—evoking the unity of a people—also separates "us" from "them". Such a discursive matrix provides the possibility for discursive projection. The Other can be invoked as the representation of the characteristics which "we" deny that "we" possess. As Kristeva (1988) indicates, the Other is a continual feature of contemporary consciousness—indeed, it is part of "ourselves". In Western democratic nations, "we", and especially "our" political leaders, continually claim "ourselves" to be tolerant, reasonable. This self-imagining conveys the image Others who are unreasonable by comparison (Billig, 1991). The discourses of "our" tolerance are often used to argue for immigration restrictions to keep "them" from "our" country. "They" are to be blamed for threatening "our" tolerance, stretching it to the limit; thus, in the name of "our" tolerance and "their" intolerance, "we" propose harsher measures to keep "them" from "us" (van Dijk, 1987, 1991, 1992; Barker, 1981; Billig, 1991; Wetherell and Potter, 1992).

Such discourses about immigrant Others are not confined to extreme right-wing politicians (Hainsworth, 1992); they have more deeply mainstream roots in the very conditions of contemporary national politics. The imagining of the national community is also an imagining of boundaries, and, thus, an imagining of Others beyond the boundaries. The control of immigration and the proclamation of criteria for citizenship are one of the main powers of national governments, as economic markets become increasingly globalised (Harris, 1992; Castles, 1992). When governments invoke these powers, so their discourses inevitably evoke "us" and "our" boundaries, and, thereby, they suggest the image of a diffuse, threatening, "them". In such discourses, more is at stake than stereotypes, for stereotypes, in this context, are the means to depict Otherness, not a discursive end in themselves. In this way, nationalism depicts the constant sense of difference, lurking beyond the national boundaries, and threatening to seep across those boundaries to dilute "our" sense of "ourselves".

(c) **Imagining the World of Nations** Nationalism not only includes within-group affiliations and sentiments; not only does it construct a constant and politically mobilizable sense of Otherness. It also places "us" and "them" within a world of nations—an international world. Linguistically, the concept of "international" was formulated along with the formation of nation-states. In fact, the word "international" was quickly incorporated into the vocabulary of national languages, having been introduced by Bentham in his *Introduction to the Principles of Morals and Legislation* (see Bentham, 1982, especially, 297n).

The Bush and Clinton comments illustrate the imagining of an international world. Phrases such as "the greatest country in human history" and "the world's greatest nation" evoke a world filled with nations, now and in the past. The comments affirm the naturalness of such a world: this is the world—the natural habitat—in which "we" (humans, Americans, "you" and "I") live, as well as "them" (the others). Moreover, the comments suggest that "history" and "the world" can be imagined as totalities, and their components ranked in terms of some moral order of greatness.

Such imagining involves a sense of the universal. To imagine ingroups and outgroups is to imagine nations in their particularity. However, the world of nations is not the sum total of particularities, for this is a world in which particularism is universalised (Robertson, 1990, 1991). There are universal, and mimetic, symbols of particularity. New nations do not invent nationhood afresh, but each newly independent nation, in proclaiming its uniqueness and in seeking to gain the recognition of established nations, copies the universal pattern for expressing difference. Flags, anthems and military uniforms follow a general, conventional pattern, which itself symbolises particularity. In symbolising this mimetic particularity, the new flag indicates universality: the new nation (whatever its geographical or economic position) has become a "proper" nation, joining the "world community" of nations.

Recently, there has been much comment about globalisation and the decline of the nation-state, as if the new postmodern era of politics will be a post-national one (e.g. Bauman, 1993; Held, 1989, 1992; Hall and Held, 1989; Hobsbawm,

1990; Friedman, 1988; Camilleri, 1990; but see Smith, 1990, for an excellent critique of the assumptions of the globalisation hypothesis). Sometimes it is assumed that the growth of transnational and supranational agencies is evidence for the decline of national sovereignty. However, one needs to be careful. Although governments may have limited room for manoeuvre in terms of economic policies, nationalism retains its potent ideological force. Transnational economic organisations may not be ideologically visible, but, in the more visible world of politics, international organisations do not necessarily symbolically undermine the ideology of nationhood (Giddens, 1990; Smith, 1990). Most notably, the United Nations, far from representing the end of nationhood, represents the world of nations as a moral order, or a "community of nations".

Social scientists, investigating nationalism, have paid a great deal of attention to stereotypes of particular national outgroups, with "otherness" being depicted in terms of particular outgroup characteristics. The imagining of the world as a moral "community of nations" has been comparatively neglected, and, with it, there has been a neglect of the internationalisation of Otherness. The "Other" here is not imagined merely in terms of a difference from "us". Indeed, the world of nations, imagined as a "community of nations", is depicted as being filled with different "others". Instead, there is a deeper, more menacing imagining of Otherness. In this case, the Other not only threatens "us", but it threatens the "community of nations" as a moral order, on whose behalf "we" claim to speak.

If there is a "new world order", following the collapse of the Soviet Union as a super-power, then this is not likely to be a de-nationalised, global order, in which the concept of nationhood will have disappeared. Already, the USA is bidding to construct an international hegemony, through which the "world's greatest nation" seeks to effect a global *pax americana*. Such a hegemony not only constructs the "world community" (the world of nations), but it also depicts ideological Others, who threaten the imagined world order. The figure of the international terrorist is such an Other, to be depicted as an enemy of moral order and reasonableness itself (Reich, 1990). Nation-states may commit far more violence than terrorists, but each terrorist act threatens more than individual lives. It challenges the monopoly to violence, which is claimed by nation-states: it challenges "our" international right to "our" national violence—a right which is to be asserted by further violence to suppress the Other.

The construction of a nationally-led, international hegemony involves the claim to represent the world of nations. This claim can be expressed philosophically as well as politically (Billig, 1993). It includes imagining how nations should and should not behave. Particular nation-states, and their rulers, can be depicted as Other, outside the imagined moral community of "proper" nations. In pursuing its strategic interests in the Gulf, the US government not only appealed successfully to the patriotism of its own citizens, who put the American flag in their windows and who bought sufficient copies of the national anthem to make it the number one hit record of the war weeks. The US government also invoked the image of the "national community". It claimed to speak for an imagined world in a state of moral outrage: the "world" could not stand by, the "world" had to rescue Kuwait, and the "world" had to bomb the citizenry of Baghdad.

As such, contemporary nationalism involves more than the imagining of particular nations in some sort of balance-sheet of good and bad stereotypes. It is an imagining of the world as a moral order of nations, which is embedded deeply and internationally in contemporary consciousness. Forthcoming battles for global hegemony will be ideologically fought over the right to speak for the world and to lead the imagined world of nations. The danger is that the more such higher moral purposes are affirmed, the more that Others will have to be negated. Also, a prediction can be made: the strange morality of our century will persist in the foreseeable future, so that the imagined life of nations will continue to be valued above the lives of living humans.

References

Abrams, D. and Hogg, M. A. (1990). *Social Identity Theory.* New York: Springer.
Althusser, L. (1971). *Lenin and Philosophy and Other Essays.* London: New Left Books.
Anderson, B. (1983). *Imagined Communities.* London: Verso.
Bagehot, W. (1873). *Physics and Politics.* London: Henry S. King.
Balibar, E. (1991). Is there a neo-racism? In E. Balibar and I. Wallerstein (eds), *Race, Nation, Class.* London: Verso.
Barker, M. (1981). *The New Racism.* London: Junction Books.
Bauman, Z. (1993). *Postmodern Ethics.* Oxford: Blackwell.
Bentham, J. (1982). *An Introduction to the Principles of Morals and Legislation.* London: Methuen.
Berlin, I. (1990). *The Crooked Timber of Humanity.* New York: Alfred A. Knopf.
Bhabha, H. K. (1990). DissemiNation: time, narrative and the margins of the modern nation. In H. K. Bhabha (ed.), *Nation and Narration.* London: Routledge.
Billig, M. (1987). *Arguing and Thinking: A Rhetorical Approach to Social Psychology.* Cambridge: Cambridge University Press.
Billig, M. (1990). Collective memory, ideology and the British Royal Family. In D. Middleton and D. Edwards (eds), *Collective Remembering.* London: Sage Press.
Billig, M. (1991). *Ideology and Opinions: Studies in Rhetorical Psychology.* London: Sage Press.
Billig, M. (1992). *Talking of the Royal Family.* London: Routledge.
Billig, M. (1993). Nationalism and Richard Rorty: the text as a flag for the *pax Americana. New Left Review,* **202**, 69–83.
Birch, A. H. (1989). *Nationalism and National Integration.* London: Unwin Hyman.
Breuilly, J. (1985). Reflections on nationalism. *Philosophy of the Social Sciences,* **15**, 65–75.
Camilleri, J. A. (1990). Rethinking sovereignty in a shrinking, fragmented world. In R. B. J. Walker and S. H. Mendlovitz (eds), *Contending Sovereignties.* Boulder: Lynne Rienner.
Cannadine, D. (1983). The context, performance and meaning of ritual: the British monarchy and the "invention of tradition". In E. Hobsbawm and T. Ranger (eds), *The Invention of Tradition.* Cambridge: Cambridge University Press.
Castles, S. (1992). Migrants and minorities in post-Keynsian capitalism: the German case. In M. Cross (ed.), *Ethnic Minorities and Industrial Change in Europe and North America.* Cambridge: Cambridge University Press.
Coakley, J. (ed.) (1992). *The Social Origins of Nationalist Movements.* London: Sage.
Colley, L. (1992). *Britons.* New Haven: Yale University Press.
Eagleton, T. (1991). *Ideology: an Introduction.* London: Verso.
Edwards, D. (1991). Categories are for talking. *Theory and Psychology,* **1**, 515–42.
Eiser, J. R. (1986). *Social Psychology.* Cambridge: Cambridge University Press.

Friedman, J. (1988). Cultural logics of the global system: a sketch. *Theory, Culture and Society*, **5**, 447–60.

Gellner, E. (1983). *Nations and Nationalism*. Oxford: Blackwell.

Gellner, E. (1987). *Culture, Identity and Politics*. Cambridge: Cambridge University Press.

Giddens, A. (1985). *The Nation-state and Violence*. Cambridge: Polity.

Giddens, A. (1987). *Social Theory and Modern Sociology*. Cambridge: Polity.

Giddens, A. (1990). *The Consequences of Modernity*. Polity: Cambridge.

Hainsworth, P. (ed.) (1992). *The Extreme Right in Europe and the USA*. London: Frances Pinter.

Hall, S. (1991). The local and the global: globalization and ethnicity. In A. D. King (ed.), *Culture, Globalization and the World-system*. Basingstoke: Macmillan.

Hall, S. and Held, D. (1989). Citizens and citizenship. In S. Hall and M. Jacques (eds), *New Times*. London: Lawrence & Wishart.

Harris, N. (1992). *National Liberation*. London: I.B. Taurus.

Haslam, S. A. and Turner, J. C. (1992). Context-dependent variation in social stereotyping 2: the relationship between frame of reference, self-categorization and accentuation. *European Journal of Social Psychology*, **22**, 251–77.

Held, D. (1989). The decline of the nation state. In S. Hall and M. Jacques (eds), *New Times*. London: Lawrence & Wishart.

Held, D. (1992). The development of the modern state. In S. Hall and B. Gieben (eds), *Formations of Modernity*. Cambridge: Polity Press.

Hinsley, F. H. (1986). *Sovereignty*. Cambridge: Cambridge University Press.

Hobsbawm, E. J. (1983). The invention of tradition. In E. Hobsbawm and T. Ranger (eds), *The Invention of Tradition*. Cambridge: Cambridge University Press.

Hobsbawm, E. J. (1990). *Nations and Nationalism since 1780*. Cambridge: Cambridge University Press.

Hobsbawm, E. J. and Ranger, T. (eds) (1983). *The Invention of Tradition*. Cambridge: Cambridge University Press.

Kennedy, P. (1988). *The Rise and Fall of the Great Powers*. London: Unwin Hyman.

Kristeva, J. (1986). Word, dialogue and novel. In T. Moi (ed.), *The Kristeva Reader*. Oxford: Blackwell.

Kristeva, J. (1988) *Etrangers à nous-mêmes*. Paris: Fayard.

Maitland, K. and Wilson, J. (1987). Pronominal selection and ideological conflict. *Journal of Pragmatics*, **11**, 495—512.

Mann, M. (1992). The emergence of modern European nationalism. In J. A. Hall and I. C. Jarvie (eds), *Transition of Modernity*. Cambridge: Cambridge University Press.

Mann, M. (1988). European development: approaching a historical explanation. In J. Baechler (ed.), *Europe and the Rise of Capitalism*. Blackwell: Oxford.

McLellan, D. (1986) *Ideology*. Milton Keynes: Open University.

Melucci, A. (1989). *Nomads of the Present*. London: Hutchinson Radius.

Moscovici, S. (1993). *Inventing Society*. Cambridge: Polity Press.

Nairn, T. (1988) *The Enchanted Glass*. London: Radius.

Perelman, C. and Olbrechts-Tyteca, L. (1971). *The New Rhetoric*. Notre Dame, Ind: University of Notre Dame Press.

Potter, J. and Wetherell, M. (1987). *Discourse and Social Psychology*. London: Sage.

Reich, W. (1990). Understanding terrorist behavior: the limits and opportunities of psychological inquiry. In W. Reich (ed.), *Origins of Terrorism*. Cambridge: Cambridge University Press.

Ricoeur, P. (1986). *Lectures on Ideology and Utopia*. New York: Columbia University Press.

Robertson, R. (1990). After nostalgia? Wilful nostalgia and the phases of globalization. In B. S. Turner (ed.), *Theories of Modernity and Postmodernity*. London: Sage.

Robertson, R. (1991). *Globalization*. London: Sage.

Samuel, R. (ed.) (1989). *Patriotism, Volume III: National Fictions*. London: Routledge.

Samuel, R. and Thompson, P. (eds) (1990). *The Myths We Live By*. London: Routledge.

Schlesinger, P. (1991). *Media, State and Nation*. London: Sage.

Schwartz, B. (1987). *George Washington: The Making of an American Symbol*. New York: Free Press.

Schwartz, B. (1990). The reconstruction of Abraham Lincoln. In D. Middleton and D. Edwards (eds), *Collective Remembering*. London: Sage.

Schwartz, B., Zerubavel, Y., and Barnett, B. M. (1986). The recovery of Masada: a study in collective memory. *Sociological Quarterly*, **27**, 147–64.

Seidel, G. (1975) Ambiguity in political discourse. In M. Bloch (ed.), *Political Language and Oratory in Traditional Society*. London: Academic Press.

Smith, A. D. (1986). *The Ethnic Origins of Nations*. Oxford: Blackwell.

Smith, A. D. (1990). Towards a global culture? *Theory, Culture and Society*, **7**, 171–91.

Surel, J. (1989). John Bull. In R. Samuel (ed.), *Patriotism, Volume III: National Fictions*. London: Routledge.

Tajfel, H. (1981). *Human Groups and Social Categories*. Cambridge: Cambridge University Press.

Turner, J., Hogg, M. A., Oakes, P. J., Reicher, S. D. and Wetherell, M. (1987). *Rediscovering the Social Group*. Oxford: Blackwell.

van Dijk, T. A. (1987). *Communicating Racism*. Newbury Park: Sage.

van Dijk, T. A. (1991). *Racism and the press*. London: Routledge.

van Dijk, T. A. (1992). Discourse and the denial of racism. *Discourse and Society*, **3**, 87–118.

Wetherell, M. and Potter, J. (1992). *Mapping the Language of Racism*. Hemel Hempstead: Harvester/Wheatsheaf.

Wilson, J. (1990). *Politically Speaking*. Oxford: Blackwell.

12

Regional Identity Formation and Community Integration in the Lega Lombarda

CARLO E. RUZZA

University of Surrey, England

The Lega Lombarda has emerged in Italy as a powerful political party and a formidable social movement precisely at the time when the old political system collapsed under corruption scandals. The moral and organisational crisis of the Italian state emerged, in all its gravity. As scores of politicians and local administrators are arrested for embezzlement, bribery and even for favouring the Mafia, the Lega Lombarda has grown, in less than a decade, from 0 to 20 per cent of the vote of Lombardy, the wealthiest region in Italy.

The success of the Lega is rooted in several organisational and politically contingent factors such as the emergence of a charismatic leader, and the impact of the end of the cold war on Italian politics. But above all, this success relied on new ideological elements which emerged in conjunction with a territorially based regional identity. Lombards began to attach a specific meaning to their territorial background.

In this chapter I will examine how the Lega Lombarda as a social movement emerged as a visible actor in the life of supporting communities. First, some references to the history of the Lega's emergence will provide a necessary background. The Lega Lombarda was founded in 1982 by Umberto Bossi, who was inspired by the leader of a small and established Northern Italian independence movement: the Union Valdotaine. It acquired some visibility in 1985, when it first competed in the electoral arena. Initially, it participated in a few local elections and obtained 2.5 per cent of the valid votes in the province of Varese. In 1987 it participated in the Lombardy regional election and was chosen by 2.7 per cent of registered voters. This figure grew to 6.5 per cent in the European election of 1989, to 16.4 per cent in the regional election of 1990

(Mannheimer and Biorcio, 1991) and, most recently, to 20.5 per cent in the national election for the Senate of 1992.

From 1987 to 1992 there has been an increase in support of 17.8 per cent and in recent years the Lega has maintained its substantial electoral strength. The Lega Lombarda owes this success to a winning combination of sensitivity to the grievances of its electorate, and the zeal of its activists. It was not directly helped by the media, and certainly not by alliances with established political forces. Undeniably, its visibility in the media increased over time, but media attitudes towards it remained negative.[1]

Similar to other ethnic movements that have recently appeared in several European countries, the Lega Lombarda advocates cultural, economic and political self-determination, even if the extent and nature of each of these goals has shifted over time. However, the Lega Lombarda does not exhibit some of the characteristics typical of traditional regional or "ethnoterritorial"[2] movements.

These movements tend to enjoy a legitimacy in the local population due to a long lasting fight against domination from outside, i.e. a feeling of protest against foreign rule passed from one generation to the other. The struggle for self-determination in these regions is heavily dependent on crucial social or cultural patterns which give the movement an indispensable unifying and legitimising force. During its formative period the Lega did not have such regional historical patterns of identification at its disposal. Nor did it have any of the elements that preclude the formation of such movements, such as a distinctive language or religion.

Until recently, most people who grew up in Lombardy were not too concerned with being Lombards or even aware of it. For instance, one might have felt Milanese, since a strong localist tradition has been present there for a long time, which is sustained, as in other nearby cities, by a distinctive dialect and an indigenous literature. But Lombardy is not a concept that traditional localist subcultures even named. At most there was a distinction between unspecified "northerners" and "southerners". In this chapter I will argue that Lombardy, as a repository of territorial identities, was the ingenious creation of the Lega Lombarda. Through it the Lega was able to overcome the narrow boundaries of localism, and present itself as the herald of a shared heritage and the interpreter of a broader social movement.

The Lega argued that the "natural" or indigenous values of the Lombard and northern Italian culture in general are conducive to morally healthy, productive, prosperous and efficient communities. They argued that a destruction of these values had occurred through the negative influence of other cultures, particularly southern Italian influences. As a result of this, a problem of unsatisfactory public services and political corruption had emerged in Lombardy and all over Italy.

As a solution the Lega advocated a new awareness of Lombards' regional identity, and through the Lega their acquisition of a directive role in Italian politics. This would bring about a regeneration of Italian politics through a renewal of the political class, and the indictment of all corrupted politicians.

Northern Italian enthusiastic acceptance of the Lega's message has puzzled the traditional political forces, some of whom had insisted, without success on similar themes, such as the moralisation of political life. The relevant distinctive element seems to be simply the creation of a Lombard identity, and the consequent mobilisation of large constituencies.

This chapter examines how such a result was achieved. That is, which processes stimulated the emergence of a new regional identity, and to what extent they were intentionally stimulated by the Lega.

Methodology

In order to examine the formation of a Lombard identity various methods have been employed. A set of in-depth interviews with Lega activists were conducted in 1992. A study of Lega activist materials was conducted for the period 1985–91. A study of national media coverage of the Lega was conducted on the two main Italian newspapers, the *Corriere* and the *Repubblica* for the same period. A 1990 survey analysis of a representative sample of 1146 young (18–22 years old) northern Italians was considered (included youth living in Tuscany and Emilia Romagna). This is the age group and the locality of residence of the great majority of voters and activists.

Discussion

I have identified a number of elements that are crucial in the process of identity construction, and are congruent with similar processes discussed in the literature. These are the constitution of an enemy, the role of language and the role of the media in influencing discourse. A demographic analysis based on the 1990 survey shows that young Lega voters are more often males, relatively uneducated and employed. Politically they situate themselves at the centre of the political spectrum. Culturally they are conservative. More so than other youth, they despise drug addicts, thieves and drunkards.

The Enemy: Identities Against

The Lega merges in a coherent ideological package several threatening aspects of contemporary Italian society. These include a generalised dislike for politicians, southerners and immigrants. The Lega activist literature points to the predominantly southern Italian representation in the ranks of the politicians and in the inefficient state bureaucracy. The dislike for politicians is evident among young Lega voters and is much higher than among non Lega voters (38% versus 59%).

This dislike is even extended globally towards politics in general. They are particularly "disgusted" by politics. But specifically, the Lega Lombarda blamed the southerners, whose particularistic culture and absence of a work ethic is said to have colonised the Italian state and its political parties. Many Lombards, on the contrary, believe they express radically different values; they feel part of a European culture. They are proud of their economic success and feel exploited by the south of Italy.

More recently, recruitment politics has suggested a partial redefinition of the threat, which is now also found in non-white immigrants. In a society that in the last few decades has undergone the impact of heavy internal migrations, and more recently of external ones. Anti-immigrant feeling in Italy (immigrants are largely non-white) is evident among young Lega voters. While 33.7 percent of them are "very much bothered" by immigrants, among the non-voters a smaller 11.2 percent are "equally bothered". A Chi-Square test showed a statistically significant association between voting and anti-immigrant feeling ($p \sim o$).

The Lega Lombarda has thus manufactured a successful ideological package which mixes a variety of widespread complaints. This package at the same time brings support to the Lega and helps constitute a previously very weak regional Lombard identity. This process is shown by the higher percentage of Lega voters who primarily identify their sense of belonging regionally. 31.3 per cent of Lega voters identify with their region as their first choice of territorial identification, compared to 12.1 per cent of non Lega voters who tend to identify more strongly with Italy (36.2% compared to 23.9% of Lega voters—Chi-Square test showed that the association between voting for Lega and identification with region was statistically significant ($p \sim o$).

The Language of the Lega

In its early years the Lega utilised the local dialect extensively. Properly re-defined as "the language of the Lombard Nation", the dialect had the characteristic of being a clear boundary-spanning device. At night activists re-wrote street signs in dialect, sometimes creating problems for the non-natives. It was also a fast and effective way of gaining exposure without having to be committed to specific political programs. Since the Lombard dialects generally drop the last vowel from standard Italian, it was sufficient to efface with spray paint a single letter from street signs to make a political statement.

However, over-reliance on dialect proved counter-productive. Many educated young people do not master it, and dialects vary significantly in small areas. There was a risk of creating barriers within the movement instead of enhancing solidarity. In addition, using the dialect had an alienating effect on those potential members who had at least one southern parent, but were born in the north. This problem acquired even wider dimensions after the Lega decided to propose an alliance with other northern leagues, and create a larger political unit called the Lega Nord.

Furthermore, the emphasis on dialect appeared too parochial and lent itself to ridicule. For instance, in city hall meetings a working class communist mayor could tease a young Lega city councillor about an imperfect understanding of the dialect. Thus, recently, the reliance on the dialect appears to be significantly reduced.

A new linguistic invention—a language code taken directly from the street and imported into the political arena has increasingly replaced the dialect. The public speeches of the Lega rely heavily on metaphors, catchphrases, common-places taken from everyday language and re-interpreted in political terms. For instance, a Lega's billboard poster states that "The Lega cleans the engine (of politics)". It is a simple message, taken directly from advertising and expressed in ordinary language.

To appreciate the extent of this innovation one has to consider that over the years Italian politicians have developed an extremely convoluted and baroque political jargon. It sounds obscure to most Italians. It assumes an insider's knowledge of political affairs, and the ability to "read between the lines." Presenting themselves as an anti-system movement, the Lega has chosen a language that—as an activist says—seeks to bring politics "down to the level of common people". It appears as a de-sacralisation of politics.

This becomes evident if we consider that one of the most common slogans is a simple affirmation of masculine sexual prowess, in crude language. It is a sentence used as a disingenuous reaction to complicated questions or comments by political opponents. It does not make sense, but it creates disconcertion,[3] embarrassment and anger in political circles. It provokes hilarity and elation among activists, and conveys the anti-system component of the Lega. Vulgarity is raised to the status of a virtue because it possesses a simplicity and directness that is felt to be lacking elsewhere.

Not surprisingly, with so much "machismo" the rate of females among activists is very low. However, to a part of the Italian public this emphasis on simplicity appears refreshing, and is understood. It seems to convey the views and the anger of working people. It seems more difficult to lie, cheat and embezzle in such simple language, than in the Byzantine speeches of professional politicians. A similar device was adopted by new social movements in the early 1980s. To complicated and unconvincing speeches of political opponents groups of activists would react by chanting *scemo, scemo* (stupid, stupid) in a tone children use to tease each other.

The choice of a vulgar speech code goes together with the utilisation of simple and at times clearly incorrect syntactic structures which appear as a literal translation from the dialect. It is meant as a statement about the personal background of Lega voters, an electorate of wealthy artisans, small businessmen and shopkeepers. Thus it has almost the same identity-forming result as using dialect, without the previously discussed shortcomings. In addition it has allowed a simplification of complicated problems, and offers an opportunity for activists with little education to be active.

Enhancing Feelings of Common Belonging

The Lega recruits entire circles, or people who know one another superficially, such as people already affiliated to recreational clubs. The Lega proselytise in soccer clubs. Activists go to stadiums on Sundays and set up discussion tables. Thus, for many people the Lega becomes something visible, a presence to be considered. The Lega assumes the role of a socialising agent for peer groups. To those who do not meet in schools or factories, the Lega offers a cultural referent: a sense of group identity based on territorial belonging. To understand the need for a socialising agent one needs to consider the crisis of large industries and of the village as a social system.

Unlike other states, for instance France or Britain, in Italy the population lives prevalently in small villages and towns. The village as a social system was traditionally centred on a set of age and gender-specific meeting places. These included the parish and food stores for adult women, the tavern for adult men, and Catholic clubs and sport activities for adolescents. In Leftist areas the "Casa del Popolo" (People's House) also provided a socialising venue. Work in factories also came to provide an additional meeting opportunity.

In recent decades, cultural, political and economic forces have altered the situation and produced a decline of meeting opportunities. The decline of the Communist party and the secularisation process meant that the many Communist and Catholic meeting places were no longer available, nor was the ideology which motivated the engagement in common activities. Similar changes occurred in the workplace (Offe, 1983; Melucci, 1988).

In northern Italy, from the 1970s onward, many factories were closed down, replaced by a network of cottage industries and family-sized workshops. This process was made possible by technological innovation, and emerged as a reaction to victorious unionisation in factories, raising labour costs, and a taxation system which draws an unfair proportion of resources from medium- and large-sized productive units (Pizzorno, 1978).

A new system of spread-out workplaces emerged as a successful economic innovation, but it threatened the sense of community which was typical of the small towns. It also threatened the workers' identity that had emerged in larger work units. The process of secularisation reduced the socialising role played by Catholic workers associations.

Changing lifestyles connected to the decline of the extended family also contributed to the disruption of local communities (Zavalloni and Louis-Guerin, 1985). Massive migrations from the south were also felt as a menace in village communities traditionally characterised by cultural and social stability. However, there is no direct causal link between immigration and support for the Lega. Highly supportive communities are not those with the highest immigration rate, but those that because of their isolation feel more threatened.[4]

Communities with a high immigrant presence are already modern in that they are multi-cultural and socially mobile. In these places support for the Lega comes late and on a lower level. For example the case of Milan. In regard to the crisis of the village as a social system, the Lega has provided a solution. It offers a unifying element at the ideological level and a socialising activity in the practice of activism as well as in the multifarious recreational activities connected with the Lega.

Ideological Vacuum, Loss of Identity and the Lega

Culturally, the Lega project was only feasible because the Lega filled an ideological vacuum left behind by those political forces which up to the 1980s dominated the political scene in Italy: Communism and Catholicism (Tarrow, 1989). People are no longer "naturally" socialised into one of these political-cultural groups, nor could they expect from them a viable political project in this period of ideological crisis.

In this situation previously culturally marginalised groups of the village are able to attribute a new dignity to their political views. Communism is no longer a viable political alternative to the existing system, and likewise the Catholic Church can no longer take for granted unreflecting participation in the Catholic *weltanschauung*. Furthermore, the main national parties are ever less able to integrate people into political and social life, since they are considered part of an irresponsive and corrupt system. With its striving for a region-oriented politics the Lega Lombarda offers a new reference.

Ideology and Identity: On Being a Lombard

As it has been shown, activists of the Lega Lombarda share a faith in a distinctive ideological package.[5] This is centred on a Lombard identity grounded in the value of honest hard work as a moral duty and as a prized inclination. It extends to a reiterated appreciation for "facts rather than words" and from this there descends a distrust for career politicians, their convoluted language and corrupted morals. The singular elements of this ideological package have been present in Italian public discourse for some time, and have been abundantly reflected by the media. However, its fulcrum—the Lombard identity—is a new one.

Ethnic identities have the property of appearing to be timeless, even if they were minted yesterday (Anderson, 1983). The Lega Lombarda profited from this fact.[6] But why was the Lega successful in convincing people that there was such a thing as being a Lombard? And was it indeed the league which did this? An answer must be sought in two different domains. Sociologically, in its effective use of symbolism, and in the social background and associative needs of its activists. Philosophically in the crisis of competing visions of community.

Symbols and Theatrical Action Forms

The Lega has mobilised people who live in small villages and have never engaged in protest politics before. This result has been achieved through an extensive use of symbolism. The symbolic production of the Lega has effectively re-utilised in new protest contexts old symbolic codes, such as the traditional symbolism of nation states. To express the right to independence of northern Italy, the Lega has invented a flag, an anthem, a passport and has minted symbolic northern Italian money. Lega's demonstrations always include the protracted display of large flags and the reiterated collective singing of anthems. Less obtrusive symbols such as Lega ties, tie pins and wrist watches are frequently sported. In personal interviews, activists expressly acknowledge the importance of these objects and actions for the creation of "a sense of community". In addition, symbols are necessary to remind activists of the Lega's claimed characteristics, such as its nobility conveyed through effigies of a medieval warrior in armour and brandishing a sword; they are representations of a medieval Lombard hero.

To an important extent, integration in political movements consists also in the symbolic staging of a meaning that individuals and groups can use to define themselves (Edelman, 1971; Melucci, 1980; Gamson, 1992). For instance the leader of the Lega, Bossi, has stated that the Lega is "oiling its Kalashnikovs" (Soviet-made machine guns) or that if judges attempt to involve the Lega in corruption scandals to undermine its credibility, their lives would be worth the price of a bullet. These statements are then immediately dismissed by Bossi himself as irony, and nobody doubts that they are indeed only figures of speech, but they remind people that the Lega is something different. Theatrical politics is in this sense crucial for the Lega's appeal and to support activism. To preserve the image of passion for radical change is evidently still more important than defending claims of citizenship in the Italian institutional framework. Similarly, to wear a tie-pin representation of the Lombard medieval warrior expresses values of courage and military solidarity that support activism.

Symbolic actions constitute a common space for the different peer groups which would otherwise be limited in their activities. People belonging to different groups engage in communal symbolic action. This does not necessarily mean that this action happens in places which are not dissimilar to those of other political organisations (such as bars, sport facilities, or public squares); rather it is essential to see that the Lega gives new communal (political) meaning to these places.

The availability of selective incentives is limited by the social heterogeneity of activists (Tilly, 1978). Shared symbols focus activism and homogenise groups' values. They are media for selective recruitment, indoctrination, identity formation and motivation maintenance, which are important elements in the chances of success for the movement.

Symbolic actions are unstructured activities which are compatible with somewhat differing definitions of the situation. They leave enough ambiguity to cushion dissent so that they can soften or pre-empt conflict. Furthermore, symbolism permits highly visible action even with a very limited number of actors (Eder, 1985).

Theatrical protest emphasises individual contributions over mere testimonials of organisational loyalty. It provides individuals with a more finely grained repertoire through which they can express but also form identities (Cohan, 1985). More conventional forms of collective action such as marches assert organisational power through the members' physical presence. The focus is on the organisation's official line rather than on members utilising the organisation as a vehicle for their political statements. This difference in collective action is important because it relates to the structure of the production and distribution of legitimacy and authority within a movement.

These findings can explain why apparently "irrational" actions are important to the Lega's success even when they do not reach a large public or raise funds. They show how psychological changes, such as the creation of a sense of community, have a known instrumental value to the movement.

The Decline of the Nation State and the Call for Community

Besides the social developments mentioned above, which have created this political and ideological vacuum, there is one further decisive recent trend in western societies to which the rise of the Lega Lombarda owes much of its success: the gradual decline of the nation-state. The decrease in the importance of the nation-state is first of all the result of the increasing internationalisation of politics and of the economy.

Transnational political and economic organisations are taking over more and more of those functions originally performed and controlled by the nation-state. The process of unification of the European Union is only the most important and visible milestone in a process which is draining the nation-state of its classical functions: the guarantee of security against foreign enemies, the establishment of a national economic unit, and the security of the national economy.

On two levels the Lega creates this community: firstly through its widespread network of personal relations and activities, integrating individuals beyond the actual political work (Vimercati, 1990; Balbo and Manconi, 1990). Secondly, the ideological programme of the Lega, through symbolic action, constantly referring to a community defined by regional or ethnic criteria. At the level of the creation of an "imagined community" in which a face-to-face relation with all potential members of the group is not possible, the Lega presents itself as the defender of an identity that is threatened by the disintegrative force of modern society, immigration, political corruption and bad administration (Cappelli and Maranzano, 1991).

Conclusions

My original aim was to explain the emergence and success of the ideology of the Lega Lombarda. I have done so by proposing the emergence of a new regional identity that emerges as an answer to multi-causal processes which threaten previous identities.

The constitution of a new identity, that of Lombards which partially replaces previous ones has illustrated processes of identity formation in social movements. The "we" feeling that supports a movement (Calhoun, 1989; Diani, 1992) has been achieved in the case of the Lega Lombarda through a set of concurrent dynamics. These included in the early stages of this movement the use of a distinctive language, and its cultural glorification, and the creation of an external enemy: southerners and immigrants, and with an implied similarity, corrupted politicians. Also, the role of symbols and theatrical action forms contributed to the creation of a "we" feeling. Subsequently, a more developed ideological package based on populist elements and territorial separatism or "strong federalism" promoted a sense of diversity which also constituted an element of pride. On that basis the concept of a new community, that of the Lombards, acquired value and a new sense of sacrality which supported political participation.

The Lega meets the demands of people whose desire for political participation was previously hindered by their subcultural standing. In addition, the Lega's call for a regional identity promises the protection or the reconstruction of an authentic and integrated social community. Its political project is successfully related to the widespread feeling of uneasiness towards the gradual disintegration of the traditional lifeworld (especially the world of the village). The Lega's organisational networks as well as its ideological programme are convincingly responsive to the needs for common belonging.

In its emphasis on Lombard identity the Lega itself became a driving force in a social process through which the attachment to a community is shaped. The Lega utilised this attachment politically for mobilisation purposes, and profited from the consequences of that mobilisation. The results were remarkable in an Italian political system used to very modest changes.

The issues the Lega raise have an extremely high coverage because they address those problems that the Italian public is presently mostly concerned about: the corruption in the political system, the "partitocrazia", the inefficiency of public services, and the alienation between citizens and state agencies. What the Lega claims to stand for, in other words, is the protest of civil society against an anonymous, non-responsive and wasteful state.

These topics are omnipresent in the public arena and they express a growing rejection in Italian society of the way politics is traditionally carried out. The inadequacies of the Italian nation state and of the politics performed in Rome are no longer described as national problems; conversely, the Lega is assertively interpreting these grievances as being due to the lack of (Northern) regional self-determination. It is not only that the issues raised by the Lega are to a large extent consonant with those high on the public agenda, but the Lega claims to offer realistic solutions to them, namely by proposing a strong federal order.

Hence, the Lega owes its success, firstly, to the fact that the diagnosis of problematic aspects of social life was done convincingly as the need for political change has become pervasive. Secondly, the description of the untenable social conditions was presented, together with a concrete proposal of how this change has to be brought about. Furthermore, one should consider that in order to motivate people it is necessary that the proposed frames meet the lifeworld experiences of those who are intended to be mobilised (Gordon and Gergen, 1968; Rosenberg and Turner, 1981). It is not very likely that people change their scheme of interpreting social events and start to act politically according to the goals of the movement, if the discrepancy between the individual belief system and the movement's ideology is too wide (Schlesinger, 1991).

The Lega, however, was able to achieve this result. It spoke in a language and with concepts familiar to its audience. The fight against an anonymous and abstract entity called "the state" is often replaced by a campaign against concrete enemies: the Roman politician, *i partiti* (in its denunciatory meaning), the "lazy" southerner, or the "parasitic" immigrant.[7] The stigmatisation of those who are by definition excluded from the community defined as Lombardian or "north" is thus an integral part of the attempt to "create" regional identity. Finally, the Lega Lombarda's success is due to the new awareness of regional and minority rights in Europe as well as to the increased public's interest on issues essential to the Lega's political programme.

This interest was not promoted by the Lega alone, but it spurred a subtle interplay between the development of public opinion and the Lega's activities. It is a mutual process in which neither the development of public opinion nor the engagement of the Lega in media discourse can be seen as the *only* explanation for the success of this new political actor. Public discourse is a form of societal communication which is beyond the direct control of the collective agents. Nevertheless it is the crucial mediator between the movement's claims and their success (Calhoun, 1989).

Although a high degree of this regional movement's success is evidently due to the skills of an effective political entrepreneur, Umberto Bossi, he merely channelled pre-existing social processes. He became the charismatic leader of this movement, providing a sense of direction to the other Leagues, and forming with the Lega Lombarda a powerful organisation, but he would not have emerged as a leading figure if specific identity processes had not occurred. And this process could only have occurred as a consequence of larger processes of collapse of traditional identities.

References

Anderson, B. (1983). *Imagined Communities*. London: Verso.
Balbo, L. and Manconi, L. (1990). *I razzismi possibili*. Milano: Feltrinelli.
Cappelli, S. and Maranzano, D. (1991). *La gente e la Lega*. Milano: Greco and Greco.

Calhoun, C. R. J. (1989). The problem of identity in collective action. In J. O. Huber (ed.) *The Macro–micro Divide*. Beverly Hills: Sage.

Cohen, J. E. L. (1985). Strategy of identity: new theoretical paradigms and contemporary social movements. *Social Research*, **52–4**, 663–716.

Cross, J. P. (1990–91). The Lega Lombarda: A Spring protest or the seeds of federalism? *Italian Politics and Society*, **32**, 20–31.

Diani, M. (1992). The concept of social movement. *The Sociological Review*, **40**, 1–25.

Edelman, M. (1971). *Politics as Symbolic Action*. Chicago, IL: Markham.

Eder, K. (1985). The new social movements: moral crusades, political pressure groups, or social movements. *Social Research*, **52**, 869–90.

Erikson, E. (1968). *Identity, Youth and Crisis*. New York: Norton.

Eyerman, R. and Jamison, A. (1991). *Social Movements. A Cognitive Approach*. Cambridge: Polity Press.

Gamson, W. A. (1988). Political discourse and collective action. In B. Klandermans, H. Kriesi and S. Tarrow (eds), *From Structure to Action: Comparing Social Movement Research across Cultures (Vol. 1, International Social Movement Research)*. Greenwich, CT: JAI Press.

Gamson, W. A. (1992) The social psychology of collective action. In A. D. Morris and C. McClurgh Mueller (eds), *Frontiers in Social Movement Theory*. New Haven: Yale University Press.

Gordon, C. and Gergen K. (1968). *The Self in Social Interaction*. New York: J. Wiley.

Goffman, E. (1974). *Frame Analysis: An essay on the Organization of Experience*. New York: Harper & Row.

Hobsbawm, E. J. (1992). *Nazioni e nazionalismi dal 1780*. Torino: Einaudi.

Liebkind, K. (ed.) (1989). *New identities in Europe*. Aldershot, UK: Gower.

Klandermans, B. (1988). The formation and mobilization of consensus. *International Social Movement Research*, **1**, 173–96.

Mannheimer, R. and Biorcio, R. (eds) (1991). *La Lega Lombarda*. Milano: Feltrinelli.

McAdam, D. (1985). *Political Process and the Development of Black Insurgency*. Chicago: University Press.

Melucci, A. (1980). The new social movements: A theoretical approach. *Social Science Information*, **19**, 199–226.

Melucci, A. l. (1985). The symbolic challenge of contemporary movements. *Social Research,* **52**, 789–816.

Melucci, A. l. (1988). Getting involved: identity and mobilization in social movements. *International Social Movement Research*, **1**, 329–48.

Offe, C. (1983). "New social movements: challenging the boundaries of institutional politics", unpublished manuscript, Bielefeld, p. 16.

Pizzorno, A. (1978). Political exchange and collective identity in industrial conflict. In C. Crouch and A. Pizzorno (eds), *The Resurgence of Class Conflict in Western Europe since 1968*. London: Macmillan.

Rosenberg M. and Turner R. (1981). *Social Psychology: Sociological Perspectives*. New York: Basic Books.

Ruzza, C. and Schmidtke, O. (1993). Roots of success in the Lega Lombarda: Mobilization dynamics and the media in West European politics. *West European Politics*, **2**, 1–23.

Schlesinger, P. H. (1991). On national identity (2): Collective identity in social theory. In P. H. Schlesinger (ed.), *Media, State and Nation: Political Violence and Collective Identities*. London: Sage.

Suls J. (ed.) (1982). *Psychological Perspectives on the Self*. London: Lawrence Erlbaum.

Tarrow, S. (1989). *Democracy and Disorder*. Oxford: Oxford University Press.

Tilly, C. (1978). *From Mobilization to Revolution*. Reading: Addison–Wesley.

Vimercati, D. (1990). *I Lombardi alla nuova Crociata*. Milano: Mursia.

Zavalloni M. and Louis-Guerin, C. (1985). *La socio-écologie des identités sociales*. Paris.

Notes

1. See Schmidtke and Ruzza, 1993.
2. Joseph R. Rudolph, Jr. Thompson and J. Robert, "Ethnoterritorial Movements and the Policy Process", *Comparative Politics*, **17**, April 1985, p. 291–311.

3. The actual slogan—unfortunately untranslatable—is "La Lega ce l'ha duro."
4. See Renato Mannheimer and R. Biorcio (eds), *La Lega Lombarda*, Feltrinelli, Milano, 1991.
5. For the concept of ideological package see: William A. Gamson (1988), Political discourse and political action, *International Social Movement Research*, Vol. 1, Jai Press, 219–44. On the role of ideology in social movements see: Carlo Ruzza (1990), Strategies in the Italian peace movement, *Research in Social Movements, Conflicts and Change*, **12**.
6. A sizable portion of Lombard voters state that they strongly identify with their regional background. However many more Lega voters retain their localist identity as their primary identification. Be that as it may, it is clear that there has been a rise in regional identification.
7. As Gamson and Modigliani put it, "ideological packages"—in this case of a radically federal order and of regional self-determination—"are usually displayed through signature elements that imply the core frame and involve the whole with handy condensing symbols" (Gamson and Modigliani (1987), The changing culture of affirmative action, *Research in Political Sociology*, Vol. 3, Jai Press, 137–77). They furthermore state in this context: "Every policy issue is contested in a symbolic arena ... Their (the movement's advocates"/O.S.) weapons are metaphors, catchphrases, and other condensing symbols that frame the issue in a particular issue" (p. 143).

13

A Safe European Home? Global Environmental Change and European National Identities

JONATHAN CHASE

Social Psychology European Research Institute, University of Surrey, England

Introduction

Social psychologists have recently shown interest in various identities that derive from political structures. Of these identities perhaps national identity has received the most attention. This chapter will consider how various environmental change processes might affect the emergence of a supra-national identity (that of being European).

The increasing impact of human action on the natural environment raises a number of issues. In this chapter I will discuss some of the social psychological processes involved in Global Environmental Change (GEC) phenomena. In addition, I also want to look at the reverse relation—that is the impact of GEC phenomena on these social psychological processes. In particular, I will look at the relationship between GEC phenomena and identity processes, especially national identities. In the first instance I will argue that identity processes have implications for the social construction of GEC phenomena as well as for the potential solutions to the problems they pose. In the second instance, I will argue that global environmental change processes will increase the likelihood of inter-nation conflict. However, research to date has tended to ignore the relevance of identity and (social) representational processes for these issues. These points are especially pertinent in the European context but are also relevant more generally.

The chapter will start with a discussion of political change before considering the nature of GEC with particular emphasis on the distribution of costs and benefits of the causes and consequences of GEC. Social identity and social representational approaches to national identity will then be considered. Research on the

209

determinants of environmental behaviour will then be reviewed. It is argued that social processes are central to environmental behaviour but have been neglected. This will be illustrated by a discussion of the role of representation in providing an environmental frame for some issues but not for others. The potential for environmental change to provide threats to various dimensions of identity will then be discussed. Finally, some conclusions will be made.

Social Change

Changing Identities in Europe

Social psychologists have been concerned with the way in which people perceive and react to changes in known phenomena and the emergence of novel phenomena. This approach may be termed an assimilationist one; the focus is on how new phenomena are assimilated according to already present processes. Social psychologists are also concerned with the way in which these new phenomena may alter social and psychological processes and structures. This approach may be termed an accomodationist one; new phenomena elicit novel processes.

One reason for research on social change to focus on national identity is readily apparent. The present period shows considerably greater change in political structures than has been the case since the end of the Second World War (Tilly, 1992). While these changes are centred in Europe and ex-Soviet Asia they obviously have implications and effects on the global system. Recent events such as the collapse of the USSR and the expansion and development of the EU have raised the salience of national identity (Miszlivetz, 1991). In the first case, suppressed national identities were found to be only dormant. In the second case, the emergence of a supra-national level of political organisation is perceived to present a threat to already extant national identities. In the UK, for instance, political debate and media discourses are full of references to British or English identity. The perceived threat to national identities has even been likened to a "moral panic" (Husbands, 1994).

The interest in national identity also reflects social psychologists' concern with issues of social change (e.g. Elder, 1994). The condition of modernity is typified by increasingly intense and rapid change in technology and social structures. Rapid social change in both technology and material structures and in social structure and practices is characteristic of modern societies. Public perceptions of these changes are important phenomena at both social and individual levels. At the social level it affects governmental policy, at the individual level it may affect the self-concept.

The Structure of Global Environmental Change

The effects of human action on the environment are now being recognised to be widespread. While there is still considerable uncertainty about these effects it is clear that change is occurring and will continue to do so.

In order to understand people's behaviour in regard to environmental issues it is first necessary to provide a clear characterisation of the nature (both physical and social) of these environmental change processes.

I will briefly discuss some of the features of some global environmental change processes. This will focus on the distribution of costs and benefits across individuals and social groups. However, it should be noted that this distribution is by no means clear-cut. For instance, there is a good deal of uncertainty about the expected costs and benefits.

The impact of human behaviour upon the environment ranges from the local to the global, from the short- to the long-term, and from the reversible to the irreversible. The immediate costs and benefits of various activities which impact on the environment are rarely evenly or equitably spread (McMichael, 1993). For instance, the benefits of burning coal in power stations go to the owners (and possibly the consumers) of those power stations while the costs of acid rain are typically exported to another state. This would be reversed in regard to the costs of cleaning up such coal-burning power stations. These cost-benefit distributions often map onto objectively defined social groups, such as classes, ethnic groups, and, especially, nations.

The longer-term outcomes associated with actions which impact on the environment are often very uncertain. Will global warming give Siberia a temperate climate? How does acid rain affect trees? Will a technological "solution" be developed within a given time-span? Does increased CO_2 mean larger harvests?

In general, environmental problems have the characteristics of social dilemmas (Dawes, 1980; Chase, 1992). In the simplest form of social dilemma, where the individual faces a binary choice, one choice gives the individual a better outcome than the other choice, however, if everyone chooses the dominant choice then all are worse off than if everyone had made the other, dominated, choice. In other words, one choice is rational for the individual as an individual while the other choice is rational for the individual as a member of the collective or group. This conflict of interest is often described as being between the individual and the group but is better described as a conflict between the individual as an individual and the individual as a member of the group.

Social dilemmas include conflict between the interests of individual actors (at various levels—nation-state, commercial organisation, age cohort, geographical area, individual) as individuals and as members of collectivities (UN, EC, nation-state, commercial union, family, etc.). This conflict may also exist within an individual actor (e.g. between present and future self).

The fact that many environmental problems have the structure of a social dilemma may explain the apparent discrepancy between the high levels of self-reported environmental concern (e.g. Krause (1993) found that about 75 per cent of the respondents in a survey described themselves as environmentalists) and the low levels of pro-environmental behaviour. This is exactly what one would

TABLE 13.1   Some causes and effects of different GEC processes

	Causes	*Effects*
Acid rain	Both human and natural causes	Moderately well-understood. The distribution is uneven and local
Global warming	Complex, some causal pathways well-understood, others less so. Many industries, groups and individuals involved	Poorly understood and complex. The distribution is uneven across the world
Ozone depletion	Well-understood. Largely due to human activity. Relatively few industries involved	Well-understood. The distribution of outcomes is relatively even across the world

expect if environmental action is social dilemmatic. Even though each person desires a common outcome the individually rational action is to do nothing to provide for that outcome.

An example may show this more clearly. If I am concerned about global warming I could buy a catalytic converter for my car to cut down the discharge of exhaust gases which contribute (fractionally) to global warming. However, the benefit I gain from this is minute and equal to the benefit every other individual also gains from my action while the cost is solely to myself. Additionally, my contribution is so slight that unless many (millions) of other people also act global warming will still occur. Finally, if everyone else does act so as to reduce global warming but I do not then I will benefit but not incur the costs.

It is important to note here that the structure and processes of specific GEC events actively construct social groups through the creation of common fate for a set of (potential) individuals. So, for instance, the threat to Oxley's Wood in South East London from the planned South East London River Crossing has led to the formation of protest groups the members of which are quite disparate (e.g. pagans, bird watchers, parents, Friends of the Earth, etc.). This is as well as individual's membership of social groups determining their positioning within the dilemma structure, i.e. their particular set of costs and benefits.

National Identities

Social Identity and National Identity

While identity is a central factor in this analysis it is by no means clear how it should be theorised. Social identity theory is most commonly used (by social psychologists but not necessarily by researchers in other disciplines) when membership of social groups is the research focus. However, a problem with SIT is its lack of concern regarding historical and content factors of identity. Instead, relatively abstract and universal processes are prioritised.

Thus, membership of political groups is explained by the capacity of that group to provide positive distinctiveness as a function of group size. Abrams (1994) argues that SDP members showed greater commitment to their group than did Conservative or Labour members due to the greater distinctiveness of the SDP consequent on its smaller size. It could be argued that the SDP has less chance of political power due to its lower level of support and therefore only the more committed bother to join it.

More importantly, the argument based on the potential of the group to provide distinctiveness ignores the meaning of that group to the person or persons. One does not join a group or adopt an identity merely because of its size. The SIT analysis would not be able to predict which of various equal-sized groups a person would affiliate to. This point emphasises the need to consider other possible identities and group memberships that are available to the person and which could satisfy distinctiveness (and other) needs. This argument does not imply that political party affiliation does not serve a function of maintaining or increasing distinctiveness. Rather, it suggests that may not be the main, or even a, reason for the party (or other group) affiliation.

In order to explain why one group rather than another is affiliated to one needs to consider the content of that group identity, the identity as a representation. Thus, the approach adopted here will be loosely based upon both identity theory and social representational theory.

A number of researchers have suggested that a synthesis of social identity theory and social representations theory (SRT) would provide greater explanatory power than either one alone (e.g. Breakwell, 1992; Elejabarrieta, 1994). Such an integration has the potential to provide a better understanding of the relationships between social power structures and individual representations and constructions of reality. For instance, the association of a new phenomenon with a specific known concept may serve a function for members of a social group (e.g. AIDS/HIV as divine retribution makes vulnerability more controllable).

Social representations theory is also appropriate for the study of social change because it explicitly focuses on the way in which new phenomena become associated with already established representations. SRT states that SRs are dynamic, being constructed and re-constructed through social interaction. Thus, they vary across both time and context. SRs function to make the new and unfamiliar familiar through processes of anchoring and concretisation. As novelty necessarily implies change this theory is highly relevant to the study of social change.

Representing National Identities

A concern with the representational aspect of identity allows their temporally contingent nature to be explored. National identities are produced through collective experience across time. A recognition of this fact focuses attention on the way in which the national identity or identities are presented and re-presented through individual and collective action (Connerton, 1989). The recent commemoration of D-Day is an example of how present public events re-enact and interpret the past. Barrett's chapter shows how children's representations of various non-UK European nationalities incorporate elements derived from representations of events in World War Two.

Geography and the physical environment also appear to be important elements in national identities. As Penrose (1993) says most people find it hard to think of a nation that has no coherent territory. This perceived link between people and place supports the perception that nations are "natural" rather than socially constructed. The boundaries of nation states are defended on the grounds of features of the natural environment. It was argued, for instance, at the beginning of the nineteenth century that the natural boundaries for France were the Rhine, the Pyrenees, the Mediterranean and the Atlantic and Channel coasts. Perhaps the reliance on arguments to natural features regarding the naturalness of nationality is most clear concerning the UK. Its status as an island provides apparently indisputable integrity to the nation. The recent completion of the Channel tunnel has undermined this isolation. It is worth noting that SRT argues that one characteristic of a social representation is that it is not perceived as a representation but as reality. On this criterion national identities are clearly social representations.

Aside from these roles geography may contribute in other ways to the representation of national characteristics. This will be briefly discussed now and in more detail below. SRT proposes that social representations include central iconic elements. The physical environment may provide such concrete images around which other elements of the representation can associate. The assumption of a link between place and character has a considerable history (Schama, 1991). For instance, the forests of Northern Europe are gloomy and wet and Northern Europeans are perceived to be more serious than are Southern Europeans (Linssen and Hagendoorn, 1994).

Research on the Determinants of Environmental Behaviour

Attitudes, Knowledge and Environmental Behaviour

The main approaches to explaining environmental behaviours and actions have focused upon knowledge, attitude and/or personality factors. That is attempts are made to explain pro-environmental behaviour in terms of a person's attitudes towards, and/or knowledge about, a specific environmental target or in terms of the presence of a specific "green" personality (e.g. Christianson and Arcury, 1992; Lansana, 1992; Herrera, 1992). The attitudinal and knowledge approach has led to the suggestion that there is an identifiable constellation of attitudes and knowledge typifying those people who engage in "pro-environmental action". An example of this is the "New Environmental Paradigm" (Dunlap and Van Liere, 1978; DeHaven-Smith, 1988).

For instance, a large amount of research has been done on the effects of the Chernobyl incident on public opinion using an attitudinal approach (e.g. Midden and Verplanken, 1990; Peters *et al.*, 1990). Even when data was gathered in more than one country (e.g. Eiser *et al.*, 1990) attitudes are simply compared between nations, with no analysis (nor indeed relevant data collected) of how identification processes, in this case national identities, might affect the representation of environmental issues, the attribution of responsibility for their causes and remedies, the costs and benefits, etc.

A meta-analysis of research on responsible environmental behaviour found that knowledge of issues, knowledge of action strategies, locus of control, attitudes, verbal commitment and an individual's sense of responsibility were associated with such behaviour (Hines *et al.*, 1986). While this supports the importance of these variables it also demonstrates the relatively narrow approach of much "proenvironmental" research. The meta-analysis is constrained by the studies upon which it is based—i.e. identification and other social processes have not been examined in this context.

Another commonly used approach, though perhaps more popular among economists than psychologists, is the Contingent Valuation Method (CVM). CVM involves asking people to place a (usually) monetary value upon some environmental good (e.g. clean water, Harris (1984); a river, Green and Tunstall (1990); and straw-burning, Hanley (1988)). These methods include strongly individualistic assumptions similar to those implicit in the attitudinal and personality research already discussed.

Some research does hint at more social processes. West Germans were found to consider the probability of a Chernobyl type accident to be much less in West Germany than in the USSR (Peters *et al.*, *op. cit.*). Given that most accidents are the product of human error the superiority of West German technology does not explain this result. While perceived differences in regulatory practices might also explain this result group processes may be present. It suggests that risk from reactor accidents is seen as coming from an outgroup rather than from the ingroup.

However, in general, research has concentrated on intra-individual variables which are conceptualised with little or no reference to social dimensions. Demographic data (e.g. sex, age, SES) are used merely to define comparison groups.

A PSYCLIT search on environmental research (1992–95) gave 183 references. A crude classification of these found that about 100 studies were surveys, about 30 were theoretical, about 20 were experimental, 3 were quasi-experimental surveys, 3 were meta-analytic and the remainder were unclassifiable. While it is not suggested that this is a representative sample of the literature nor that the analysis is more than crude it does suggest a predominance of survey and, by implication, questionnaire methods.

I am not saying that survey research is necessarily more or less valid than any other research method. It does, however, tend to require certain assumptions, such as a stable set of factors "inside" a respondent's head (e.g. attitudes, personality, etc.). The CVM (and associated methods) is based upon similar assumptions (i.e. a stable, endogenous utility function). As a consequence of focusing on the individual the situational or contextual (proximal and distal, representational and physical) determinants of, and influences on, behaviour are neglected. (A minor example of the context dependency of behaviour in regard to environmental targets, which may include research instruments, is Armstrong and Impara's (1990) finding that changing the order of presentation between knowledge and attitude items significantly affected the responses to the attitude items.) Thus, the dynamic, constructive and processual nature of the determinants of human behaviour are doubly denied. Firstly, stable structures are assumed; secondly, the context with which the person interacts is ignored.

This emphasis on the individual can be illustrated by the way that even a variable as apparently social as "social responsibility" is operationalised only at an individual level. For instance, Keen's (1991) measure is *"Every person must work to solve pollution problems."* This characterises interaction as being interpersonal and ignores the group level of analysis.

While an intra-individual approach is valid and does provide valuable information about and understanding of some of the psychological processes relevant to pro-environmental action, it is incomplete. There are a number of reasons why this approach is limited in its ability to explain and predict environmental behaviour.

In part, this may simply be the result of research being located at the national and not the international level. (This is being remedied by, for instance, the current EC SEER initiative.) But the limitations may also occur because of the nature of environmental issues.

Research to date does provide some useful information about the determinants of environmental behaviour. However, I would suggest that a broader analysis of representational (i.e. including social as well as cognitive representational processes) and identification processes would significantly improve explanatory and predictive power.

Identity, Behaviour in Social Dilemmas and Environmental Action

As environmental issues are instances of collective action, it is appropriate now to discuss research on the causes of behaviour in a social dilemma. While many factors have been found to affect behaviour in social dilemmas (e.g. trust, group size, motives; see Dawes, 1980, for a review) only the effects of social identities and group membership will be discussed here.

In terms of identity interaction in a social dilemma may occur in three different ways. Firstly, people may interact as individuals with salient personal identities. In this case no social identity providing commonality is present other than the most basic one of "person" and, therefore, the interaction is an interpersonal one. Secondly, people may interact as members of a common social identity, a

TABLE 13.2   Cooperation in a social dilemma

Identity	Relative cooperation
Inter-person	Medium
Inter-group	Low
Intra-group	High

superordinate group identity. In this case, the interaction is an intra-group one. Thirdly, people may interact as members of one or another of two or more salient group identities. In this case, the interaction is an inter-group one. To recap, interaction in a social dilemma may be interpersonal, intra-group, or inter-group.

Brewer and Kramer (1986) and Kramer and Brewer (1984) found that the introduction of group identities changes the level of cooperation in a social dilemma from that found when the interaction is at the inter-personal level. When a superordinate group identity is present and the interaction is at the intra-group level then cooperation increases from that found when the interaction is at the inter-personal level. When different group identities are present and the interaction is at the inter-group level then cooperation decreases from that found when the interaction is at the inter-personal level (see Table 13.2).

Research using naturally occurring and important social groups also shows that identity processes affect behaviour in a social dilemma. Tyson et al. (1988) found that both black and white South African students were more cooperative with a black other than with a white other. This finding (and a similar but reversed one by Kremer et al. (1988) where both Catholic and Protestant subjects were less cooperative with a Catholic than a Protestant other in Northern Ireland) shows that group processes do affect behaviour in a social dilemma but neither necessarily in a simple manner nor necessarily in favour of the ingroup.

It is apparent, then, that group level interaction in social dilemmas offers both hope and danger. However, identity may also affect behaviour in social dilemmas through attributions about the cause of resource depletion. Rutte et al. (1987) manipulated the amount of resource present (scarce and abundant) and the cause of the resource level (ingroup cause or natural cause) in a social dilemma. They found that subjects' behaviour varied as a function of the cause of scarcity. The difference in harvest size (the dependent variable) between abundance and scarcity conditions was greater in the natural than in the ingroup condition. This implies that there is greater restraint when the cause of scarcity is perceived to be one's own group. Unfortunately, an outgroup cause condition was not present in this study. One suspects that less restraint would have been found in such a condition if it had been run.

Given that the effects of environmental change consequent upon the actions of (some) humans often involve the differential distribution of costs and benefits across social groups the potential for increasingly competitive interaction between groups must be considered to be present. This can be seen at present in the case of Slovakian plans to divert the Danube which are causing concern in Hungary and conflict between the two countries. It would seem likely that Hungarians might attribute the cause of their water scarcity to the Slovakian outgroup, thus, increasing the likelihood of conflict. At an individual level of analysis, the judged benefits and perceived voluntariness of exposure to a risk/s have been found to be related to both risk estimates and risk tolerance (Baird, 1986). In the case just discussed, these factors would map onto national identities.

Group membership has been also been found to affect behaviour regarding environmental issues when survey rather than experimental designs were used. Some recent research does show that measures of identity can contribute significantly to the explanation of environmental behaviour even when attitudinal measures are also elicited. Sparks and Shepherd (1992) included measures of identification with "Green consumerism" as well as standard attitudinal and past behaviour measures. The identification measures had a significant relationship with intended behaviour that was independent of the other variables. Similarly, Ashford (1994) found that affiliation to an environmental group, in the sense of some form of psychological identification with that group, was an independent predictor of intention to perform pro-environmental action. This is an interesting advance. However, it explains neither the process by which identification occurs nor how people perceive and respond to environmental change.

So two points emerge from this social psychological analysis of environmental change.

1. Many (if not all) environmental change phenomena show the characteristics of a social dilemma even though the particular structure of any one process may vary.
2. Social identifications, especially national identity, will affect individuals' responses to these changes. Increased conflict between social groups, again, especially nations, may be a consequence.

Representations of Environmental Problems

A discussion of how environmental issues are represented raises the question what is "environmental behaviour"? Is it any behaviour that affects the environment? Or only those behaviours that are intended to bring about specific effects on the environment? While one might sidestep this question and hope that an answer will emerge empirically through a consensus one might hope in vain. I would argue that the distinction between the outcome of behaviour and the intention that, perhaps, produces it is crucial. On the one hand, all behaviour affects the environment. On the other hand, only some (very few) behaviours are intentionally environmental. For instance, in the seventeenth century hats made from beaver fur were first sold in France, then recycled into hats sold in Spain before being again recycled and sold to the African market. Was this driven by environmental concerns or by economic ones? Given the slaughter of beaver and other fur-bearing animals in North America, I would suggest that the economic motive dominated. (It should be noted that the latter, more limited definition allows environmental behaviour to be treated as peripheral rather than central. However, this argument does not mean that one or other definition is right so much as that the definition guiding any particular study should be explicitly stated.)

In order to distinguish between these two definitions one needs a scientific analysis of the consequences of human action on the global (and local) ecosystem/s as well as an analysis of the social construction of environmental action. For the former, biologists, chemists and physicists are more central but for the latter social scientists are required.

Environmental issues are constructed and given meaning at a social level, especially, by media and special interest group actions. An analysis at the individual level fails to investigate the construction of environmental issues, a process which is prior to environmental behaviour and may contribute to the type (if any) of behaviour required on the part of the individual. Thus, a purely individualistic approach is inadequate in regard to environmental issues.

The way in which environmental issues are represented may affect the way in which people respond to them. Rochford and Blocher (1991) found that the interpretive frame was an important determinant of action by people coping with flooding. The representation of the flooding as being a "natural" or an "unnatural" disaster was directly related to intended action in regard to the threat. Olekalns (1994) also found that different frames (Gain/loss, fixed/variable payoffs, cooperative/competitive strategies) affected the outcome of negotiations in a bargaining situation.

Perhaps I can illustrate this point with an example drawn from an analysis of the media (TV and newspapers) being carried out by Chase, Hammond and Panagopoulos as part of an EC SEER initiative funded research project. This research on the social and psychological determinants of environmental behaviour is being carried out by teams in the UK, France, Italy, Germany and Portugal.

TV programs and newspapers were collected across the second and fourth weeks in February and references to environmental issues were noted. A range of environmental issues were given coverage in an environmental context, e.g. global warming, ozone depletion, pollution, conservation of (mainly exotic) species. However, some other equally environmental issues were not presented as such but were instead framed in terms of conflict between social groups. In particular, the issue of depletion of fish stocks was framed in terms of national sovereignty with no reference being made to the environmental dimensions. I would suggest that this shows how the framing of the specific issue determines the way in which it is responded to. And, how the nature of environmental change—its transnationality will tend to elicit framing in terms of nationality.

This instance is particularly interesting when compared against the recent coverage of whaling. The coverage of whaling has had a strong environmental frame applied to it as well as focusing on conflict at the international level. In the UK TV media Norway and Japan are cast as nations of whale killers.

In the instance of the depletion of fish stocks the conflict is about territoriality and national rights while in the whaling instance it has been framed as a conflict between Norway and Japan and the whales with other countries in the international community acting as proxies for the whales— the action is on the whales' behalf. No one has adopted such a role for the cod, herring, sprat, etc.

The presence of a particular identity may determine whether the costs or benefits of an action are salient. For instance, for Norwegians the immediate costs of stopping whaling may be more salient than the benefits while the reverse could be true of members of non-whaling nations. Even when an "environmental identity" is present (e.g. membership of Greenpeace) it may be fragile and easily overwhelmed by national identity once a conflict between nations frame is present. For instance, worker members of international socialist groups before the First World War responded to the conflict at a national rather than international level of identification.

What this suggests is that representational processes are important in the framing of the situation as one where environmental considerations are relevant and that identities, in particular national ones, are important factors in the framing of situations. Vining (1987) found that people's environmental decisions were sensitive to different decision contexts and to different writing styles.

Psychological Effects of Global Environmental Change

Effects on Identity

Thus far, I have focused upon how social identification processes and social identities, in particular national identities, can affect people's behaviour in regard to environmental change. I will now turn to look at the implications of environmental change for identity.

Firstly, I would argue that environmental change may present a threat to identity (Breakwell, 1986). Identity process theory suggests that there are four identity principles:

1. the self-esteem principle;
2. the continuity principle;
3. the distinctiveness principle;
4. the efficacy principle.

Here, although I will concentrate upon the implications of GEC processes for the continuity principle I will comment upon their possible effects upon other of the identity principles. This states that people try to maintain "persistent sameness with oneself" (Erikson, 1980). This does not mean complete consistency is required but rather that inconsistencies between past and present selves can be explained according to some continuous development or narrative. Memory processes may be especially significant in regard to the continuity principle.

Environmental change, by its nature, affects the physical environment in which we live. Research on place identity (e.g. Proshansky *et al.*, 1983) and on social and individual memory (Fentress and Wickham, 1992) shows how one's physical surroundings contribute to one's sense of identity. Changes in the physical environment may also affect the self concept. (This may be especially true of "natural" environments. Sebba (1991) found that almost all adult subjects identified the most important place in their childhood with the outdoors.) Unstable environments will retain fewer cues to past cognitive, affective and behavioural states. The effects of global environmental change may radically alter the local climate, the ecology and even the geography as patterns of erosion and deposition shift. Thus, environmental changes may lead to changes in the self concept and as continuity in the physical environment decreases, so too may continuity in the self identity decrease.

The potential impact of environmental change on national identity can be seen in Melman's (1991) analysis of historical novels and conventional histories in regard to the development of an "English identity". Of the three factors he identified one was the construction of a national geography defining England. This was not just the identification of geographical boundaries but also the construction of a particular representation—"an emerald set in a silver sea". The representation of the English climate as temperate resonates with that of the English character as tolerant. (Perhaps both of these representations have taken a battering in recent years.) Thus, representations of national character or identity may be intimately bound up with representations and experience of the physical environment. The experience, and representation, of the physical environment may act as a figurative nucleus in the formation of a social representation of a national identity. (Incidentally, this also shows the importance of analyzing the specific content of an identity representation as well as the general process of identification.)

GEC processes may also affect people's perceptions of their distinctiveness, especially in regard to group level categorisations. A quote from a letter to the *Independent* illustrates this point:

> Orwell was right and knew perfectly well that the pre-eminent verdancy of English fields and gardens is no jingoistic illusion but something that arises quite naturally from our equally distinctive climate.
>
> (*Independent Magazine*, p. 7, 08/05/1993)

This shows how the physical environment may be explicitly linked to national identity. In this case both climatological and vegetational aspects are mentioned and, thus, contribute to distinctiveness.

GEC processes may also impact upon individuals' perceived efficacy. If GEC processes occur then the climate and associated ecologies will become more and more unpredictable. This may result in people perceiving greater uncertainty in the environment and, therefore, less control over their outcomes.

So, two points emerge from this discussion:

1. Global environmental change will result in a perception of threat to one's identity. This will be particularly acute in regard to maintaining a sense of continuity to one's identity.
2. In that the threat to identity may be perceived as originating from groups with which one does not identify a source of conflict additional to the resource conflict already mentioned may occur.

Other Implications

The impact of global environmental change may have further ramifications for our sense of self. The natural world has provided both the environment or context in which humanity evolves and exists and an other against which it defines itself. Linssen and Hagendoorn (1994) suggest that one explanation for the different perceptions of Southern and Northern Europeans sociability may be due to the warmer and drier climate in the South allowing public interaction more freedom. The adoption of a "café society" in the UK, for instance, has been suggested as one possible positive consequence of global warming. More seriously, however, this provides another way in which GEC may affect identity and the self concept. Changes in the climate and the environment may alter the ease or difficulty of interaction between individuals and groups.

The stability and constancy of that environment are now moot. Uncertainty about the taken for granted structure of everyday life, e.g. the seasons, may increase. The relationship between people and environment is fundamentally altered. A pure "natural world" that shows no trace of human action is increasingly distant. In fact, it no longer exists on the surface of the Earth being relegated to the interior of the planet and to deep space.

The differentiation between the natural and the artificial will continue to break down as the natural world becomes more and more a product of human action (even if unintentionally so). The "natural" is becoming evermore interpellated by the artificial. The inorganic mimics the organic and sentient in the shape of computers, genetic engineering creates new organisms, the world warms and the weather changes. This may result in an additional perceived threat to identity as distinctiveness in regard to a fundamental dichotomy—"human" versus "natural"—decreases.

GEC presents a challenge to all the nations of the world. As such it may be taken to provide superordinate group goals. In other words, responding to these challenges successfully requires action from at least many, if not all, national groupings. Sherif *et al.* (1961) suggest that the successful achievement of such goals may help produce a superordinate group identity. Certainly, common experience may contribute to common identity even when other social identities are present. Combat troops at the front in both, but especially the First, World Wars expressed some solidarity with their opponents. Therefore, a concerted EU program of action to address GEC might positively affect the development of a common European identity. However, Sherif *et al.* also point out that the failure to achieve the superordinate goal may intensify intergroup conflict. Thus, such a program might be advised to start with the more achievable and limited goals of controlling acid rain rather than global warming. The former goal, as has been shown, is more local and discrete than the latter.

Conclusion

There are a number of possible responses to the issues raised here. These include:

1. Exploring the role of geography and the physical environment in regard to identity. This needs to go beyond that of place identity which tends to maintain a distinction between place identity and other social identities.
2. Theorising the relationship between identity and representational processes and behaviour in regard to the environment. In particular, how do identity processes affect the perception of the costs and benefits associated with various consumer and/or industrial activities?
3. Including measures of identity as well as standard attitudinal measures in questionnaires. This is necessary in order to test hypotheses derived from (2).
4. Explicitly manipulating the context along theoretically relevant dimensions. So, for instance, the environmental items in a questionnaire could be embedded in different contexts designed to elicit different identities.

Global environmental changes are occurring, will continue to occur, and will increase in intensity and effect. The probability of people exerting restraint varies depending, in part, upon the structural properties of particular processes which cause these changes.

Social psychology can help encourage pro-environmental behaviour in order to reduce some environmental impacts and also aid in the development of new ways of relating to the environment. In order to do this social psychology must be more pro-active.

The development of a superordinate European identity could contribute to more cooperation on environmental issues. However, the extent to which environmental issues are framed in terms of conflict between nations may decrease the likelihood of a superordinate identity emerging (the environment being framed in differentiating rather than integrating terms) and, thus, further decrease the likelihood of cooperation.

References

Abrams, D. (1994). Political distinctiveness: an identity optimising approach. *European Journal of Social Psychology*, **24**, 357–65.

Ashford, P. (1994). Social psychological dimensions in environmental response. PhD thesis, University of Surrey.

Armstrong, J. B. and Impara, J. C. (1990). The effects of order of test administration on environmental attitudes. *Journal of Environmental Education*, **21**(3), 37–9.

Baird, B. N. (1986). Tolerance for environmental health risks: the influence of knowledge, benefits, voluntariness, and environmental attitudes. *Risk Analysis*, **6**(4), 425–35.

Breakwell, G. M. (1986). *Coping with Threatened Identities*. London: Methuen.

Breakwell, G. M. (1992). Identity, social representations and actions: sex and politics. Paper presented at the British Psychological Society Social Psychology Section Conference, 20–22 Sept., University of Surrey, UK.

Brewer, M. B. and Kramer, R. M. (1986). Choice behaviour in social dilemmas: effects of social identity, group size, and decision framing. *Journal of Personality and Social Psychology*, **50**, 543–9.

Chase, J. (1992). The self and collective action: dilemmatic identities? In G. M. Breakwell (ed.), *The Social Psychology of Identity and the Self Concept*. London: Academic Press.

Christianson, E. H. and Arcury, T. A. (1992). Regional diversity in environmental attitudes, knowledge, and policy: The Kentucky River Authority. *Human Organization*, **51**(2), 99–108.

Connerton, P. (1989). *How Societies Remember*. Cambridge: Cambridge University Press.

Dawes, R. M. (1980). Social dilemmas. *Annual Review of Psychology*, **31**, 169–93.

DeHaven-Smith, L. (1988). Environmental belief systems: public opinion on land use regulation in Florida. *Environment and Behaviour*, **20**(3), 276–99.

Dunlap, R. E. and Van Liere, K. (1978). The new environmental paradigm: A proposed measuring instrument and preliminary results. *Journal of Environmental Education*, **9**, 10–19.

Eiser, J. R., Hannover, B., Mann, L., Morin, M. and van der Pligt, J. (1990). Nuclear attitudes after Chernobyl: a cross-national study. *Journal of Environmental Psychology*, **10**, 101–10.

Elder (Jr.), G. H. (1994). Time, human agency, and social change: perspectives on the life course. *Social Psychology Quarterly*, **57**, 4–15.

Elejabarrieta, F. (1994). Social positioning: a way to link social identity and social representations. *Social Science Information*, **33**, 241–53.

Erikson, E. H. (1980). *Identity and the Life Cycle*. New York: Norton.

Fentress, J. and Wickham, C. (1992). *Social Memory*. Oxford: Blackwell.

Green, C. H. and Tunstall, S. M. (1990). *The Amenity and Environmental Value of River Corridors*. Flood Hazard Research Centre, Enfield.

Hanley, N. (1988). Using contingent valuation to value environmental improvements. *Applied Economics*, **20**, 541–49.

Harris, B. S. (1984). Contingent valuation of water pollution. *Journal of Environmental Management*, **19**, 199–208.

Herrera, M. (1992). Environmentalism and political participation: toward a new system of social beliefs and values? *Journal of Applied Social Psychology*, **22**, 657–76.

Hines, J. M., Hungerford, H. R. and Tomera, A. N. (1986). Analysis and synthesis of research on responsible environmental behaviour: a meta-analysis. *Journal of Environmental Education*, **18**(2), 1–8.

Husbands, C. T. (1994). Crises of national identity as the "new moral panics": political agenda setting about definitions of nationhood. *New Community*, **20**, 191–206.

Keen, M. (1991). The effect of the Sunship Earth program on knowledge and attitude development. *Journal of Environmental Education*, **22**(3), 28–32.

Kramer, R. M. and Brewer, M. (1984). Effects of group identity on resource use in a simulated commons dilemma. *Journal of Personality and Social Psychology*, **46**, 1044–57.

Krause, D. (1993). Environmental consciousness: an empirical study. *Environment and Behavior*, **25**, 126–42.

Kremer, J., Gallagher, A., Somerville, P. and Traylen, G. (1988). Social categorization and behaviour in mixed-motive games: a Northern Ireland study. *Social Behaviour*, **3**(3), 229–36.

Lansana, F. M. (1992). Distinguishing potential recyclers from nonrecyclers: a basis for developing recycling strategies. *Journal of Environmental Education*, **23**, 16–23.

Linssen, H. and Hagendoorn, L. (1994). Social and geographical factors in the explanation of the content of European nationality stereotypes. *British Journal of Social Psychology*, **33**, 165–82.

McMichael, A. J. (1993). *Planetary Overload: Global Environmental Change and the Health of the Human Species*. Cambridge: Cambridge University Press.

Melman, B. (1991). Claiming the Nation's past: The invention of an Anglo-Saxon tradition. *Journal of Contemporary History*, **26**, 575–95.

Midden, C. J. H. and Verplanken, B. (1990). The stability of nuclear attitudes after Chernobyl. *Journal of Environmental Psychology*, **10**, 111–19.

Miszlivetz, F. (1991). The unfinished revolutions of 1989: the decline of the nation-state? *Social Research*, **58**, 781–804.

Olekalns, M. (1994). Context, issues and frames as determinants of negotiated outcomes. *British Journal of Social Psychology*, **33**, 197–210.

Penrose, J. (1993). Reification in the name of change: the impact of nationalism on social constructions of nation, people and place in Scotland and the United Kingdom. In P. Jackson and J. Penrose (eds), *Constructions of Race, Place and Nation*. London: UCL Press, 27–49.

Peters, H. P., Albrecht, G., Herren, L. and Stegelmann, H. U. (1990). "Chernobyl" and the nuclear power issue in West German public opinion. *Journal of Environmental Psychology*, **10**, 121–34.

Proshansky, H. M., Fabian, A. K., and Kaminoff, R. (1983). Place-identity: physical world socialization of the self. *Journal of Environmental Psychology*, **3**, 57–83.

Rochford, E. B. and Blocher, T. J. (1991). Coping with "natural" hazardous stressors: the predictors of activism in a flood disaster. *Environment and Behaviour*, **23**(2), 171–94.

Rutte, C. G., Wilke, H. A. and Messick, D. M. (1987). Scarcity or abundance caused by people or the environment as determinants of behaviour in the resource dilemma. *Journal of Experimental Social Psychology*, **23**, 208–16.

Schama, S. (1991). Homelands. *Social Research*, **58**, 11–30.

Sebba, R. (1991). The landscapes of childhood: the reflection of childhood's environment in adult memories and in children's attitudes. *Environment and Behaviour*, **23**, 395–422.

Sherif, M., Harvey, O. J., White, B. J., Hood, W. R., and Sherif, C. W. (1961). *Intergroup Conflict and Cooperation: The Robbers' Cave Experiment*. Norman: University of Oklahoma Press.

Sparks, P. and Shepherd, R. (1992). Self-identity and the theory of planned behaviour: assessing the role of identification with "Green Consumerism". *Social Psychology Quarterly*, **55**, 388–99.

Tilly, C. (1992). Futures of European states. *Social Research*, **59**, 705–17.

Tyson, G. A., Schlachter, A. and Cooper, S. (1988). Game playing strategy as an indicator of racial prejudice among South African students. *Journal of Social Psychology*, **128**, 473–85.

Vining, J. (1987). Environmental decisions: the interaction of emotions, information, and decision context. *Journal of Environmental Psychology*, **7**, 13–30.

14

Vietnamese Refugees in Finland—Changing Cultural Identity

KARMELA LIEBKIND

University of Helsinki, Finland

Ethnic/Cultural Identity and Acculturation Attitudes

The principal aim of this study is to investigate the various components and changes of ethnic/cultural identity among young Vietnamese refugees in Finland and their parents or care-givers. The question of the relationship between ethnic/cultural identity and global identity is also addressed.

Changing identification patterns within and across ethnic boundaries modify the self-constructs and/or the value systems of individuals. For different ethnic groups, different features of their culture may contribute to their sense of ethnic identity (Liebkind, 1989a, 1992; Weinreich, 1989; Phinney, 1990; Sue and Sue, 1990; Rosenthal and Feldman, 1992). In this study, culture is conceptualised as shared patterns of belief and feeling towards issues like child-rearing habits, family systems and ethical values or attitudes (Fernando, 1991).

The broad area of research that has dealt with groups in contact is the acculturation literature (Phinney, 1990). Psychological acculturation refers to the changes in identity, values, behaviour and attitudes that occur through contact with another culture. In principle, both cultural groups could influence each other equally, but in practice one tends to dominate the other (Berry *et al.*, 1987; Berry, 1990). Acculturation is a multilinear process, a set of alternatives rather than a single dimension ending in assimilation or absorption in a dominant culture (Liebkind, 1984, 1989a; Berry, 1990). The ways in which the ethnic/cultural minority wishes to relate to the dominant group have been termed acculturation attitudes (Berry *et al.*, 1987). The two basic issues members of ethnic/cultural minorities have to address are (a) whether or not they consider it to be of value

227

to maintain their cultural identity and characteristics, and (b) whether or not they consider it to be of value to maintain relationships and contact with the dominant group (Berry *et al.*, 1987).

From a more psychological point of view, Sue and Sue (1990) formulate a five-stage model of individual ethnic identity development, where the crucial issues to be addressed concern attitudes towards (a) the self (i.e. self-esteem), (b) others of the same minority (i.e. one's own cultural group), (c) others of other minority groups (not very relevant in relatively monocultural societies), and (c) majority individuals (Sue and Sue, 1990). With different attitudes towards these issues individuals may go through stages of conformity, dissonance, resistance/immersion, introspection and integrative awareness (Sue and Sue, 1990).

If the answers to questions (a) and (b) posed by Berry *et al.* (1987; Berry, 1990) are dichotomised for simplicity, four varieties of acculturation attitudes can be derived. Alienation/marginalisation occurs if one rejects one's own culture but does not adopt the majority culture. One is caught between two worlds and accepted by neither. Assimilation means rejection of one's own culture and adoption of the majority culture. This is the counterpart of the conformity stage of Sue and Sue (1990). Especially adolescents who, in their attempts to become "mainstream", reject skills necessary to interact with their own culture, are at particular risk for maladjustment. Separation occurs when individuals emphasise their own culture and withdraw from contact with the dominant culture. This is the counterpart of the rejection/immersion stage of Sue and Sue (1990). It provides temporary protection but involves risks of maladjustment if it implies failure to learn how to interact in the mainstream context (Phinney *et al.*, 1990).

There is an argument and some empirical evidence that the last option, maintaining both one's own ethnic traditions and contacts with the majority culture (the integrative awareness stage of Sue and Sue), affords the best psychological outcomes (Berry *et al.*, 1987; Rumbaut, 1991; Phinney *et al.*, 1990; Sue and Sue, 1990). Berry (1990) emphasises, however, that acculturation may be "uneven" across domains of behaviour and social life; for example, one may seek economic assimilation (in work), linguistic integration (by way of bilingualism) and marital separation (by endogamy)(Berry, 1990, 217). Sue and Sue (1990) imply the same in saying that members of cultural minorities "may evidence conformity characteristics in some situations, but resistance and immersion characteristics in others" (Sue and Sue, 1990, 116).

The Ethnic/Cultural Identity of Vietnamese Refugee Youth

Studies of generational differences in ethnic identity tend to show an erosion of ethnic identity in later generations of immigrants (Rosenthal and Feldman, 1992, Rick and Forward, 1992; and Liebkind, 1993). Rick and Forward (1992) found that overall acculturation level was a significant predictor of the degree of intergenerational differences and conflicts perceived by Hmong refugee youth.

Intergenerational conflicts within refugee families, in turn, are linked to both school problems and mental health status of adolescent refugees (Lin *et al.*, 1984; Nguyen and Williams, 1989).

This is not difficult to understand if one considers the traditional Vietnamese family values and compares them to their Western counterparts. As has been pointed out by several authors (e.g. Chang, 1982; Rosenthal and Feldman, 1992; White and Marsella, 1989; Ho, 1987; Nidorf, 1985), the concept of self in the Eastern world is quite different from that in the Western world. For traditional Southeast Asians, self and the family are integral, not separable concepts (Nguyen and Williams, 1989). The notion of family and filial piety is the single most important construct binding and organising Southeast Asian psychological experience and social reality (Nidorf, 1985). The Southeast Asian family is often multigenerational and characterised by tight boundaries. Family members are expected to be loyal to each other and to distrust outsiders. Hierarchical authority applies both to age and to gender. Regardless of what parents do, children are obligated to give respect and obedience, sibling rivalry and aggression are discouraged, and wives are expected to be the nurturant caretakers of both husband and children. The energy and creativity of mothers are channelled primarily into taking care of their children, with whom they form strong emotional bonds (Ho, 1987).

To such families, cultural transition is a severe blow. When relatives and close friends are no longer available for emotional support, the traditional hierarchical structure and rigidity of family roles make the expression and resolution of conflicts within the nuclear family very difficult, if not nearly impossible, leaving members with a high degree of vulnerability. Discrepancies in acculturation between husband and wife and between parents and children can have negative effects for the whole family. If the children adopt Western ways of assertiveness and freedom of choice and speech, the parents may feel threatened and demand even more respect and deference (Ho, 1987; Phinney, 1990). Considering the prevailing gender roles in the Nordic countries, the cultural gap experienced by the Vietnamese in Finland is of considerable magnitude.

The Study of Identity Change and Its Consequences

One of the most obvious and frequently reported consequences of acculturation is social disintegration accompanied by personal crisis. However, these problems are not inevitable and depend on a variety of different factors (for reviews, see Canadian Task Force, 1988; Berry, 1990). Cultural isolation appears to be a major stressor, as does separation from family members. Several authors stress the supportive and protecting function of "ethnic enclaves", communities of co-nationals (Beiser, 1988, 1991; Westermeyer, 1987; Furnham and Bochner, 1990).

Psychological studies of acculturation are particularly relevant in present-day Europe, where migration and refugee upheavals continue to abound. Of all kinds of acculturating groups, refugees are the most vulnerable (Berry *et al.*, 1987; Berry,

1990). Refugees experience high levels of unpredictability, stress and power-lessness, leading to higher incidences of depression, anxiety and psycho-somatic complaints (Furnham and Bochner, 1990). For refugees, the contrast between past, present and future poses exceptionally great problems of continuity (Knudsen, 1990). Recent literature has repeatedly reported that refugees in general and the Indochinese in particular have experienced greater psychological distress and dysfunction than other immigrant or native-born groups (Liebkind, 1993; Rumbaut, 1991; Beiser, 1991; Canadian Task Force, 1988; Westermeyer, 1987).

Within social psychology, studies in the change of ethnic identity have been mostly elaborated in the field of ethnolinguistic identity (e.g. Clément and Noels, 1992; Sachdev and Bourhis, 1990a), while studies in the change of social identity are moving from a descriptive approach on the one hand (e.g. Garza and Herringer, 1987) and a mainly experimental approach on the other (e.g. Tajfel, 1978) towards a greater acknowledgement of the multidimensionality, con-textuality and affectivity of social identity (e.g. Hinkle and Brown, 1990; Johnston and Hewstone, 1990; Hogg and Abrams, 1990; Sachdev and Bourhis, 1990b). However, social identity theorists have traditionally tended to ignore both the larger literature on ethnicity and acculturation and the larger literature on self-esteem (Liebkind, 1992). As a consequence of the latter omission, personal (or global) identity and social (or ethnic) identity are often confused. Empirically, measures of collective self-esteem and personal self-esteem are only moderately correlated (Crocker and Major, 1989). Self-esteem is multiply influenced and members of low-status groups do not necessarily have low self-esteem (Hogg and Abrams, 1990).

The Social Context of Vietnamese Refugees in Finland

The Vietnamese refugees in Finland form an ethnically heterogeneous (North, South and Chinese Vietnamese) but socially rather homogeneous (predominantly lower class) group. They have arrived in Finland from 1979 onwards for other reasons than their own choice, and have, since 1987, been dispersed in small groups throughout the country in more than 100 municipalities (Matinheikki-Kokko, 1991; Liebkind, 1993).

The first group of quota refugees from Indochina in 1979 consisted of 100 persons. Before that, Finland had received only 182 refugees from Chile in 1973. Still the total number of refugees is only around 10,000, the largest single group still being the Southeast Asians (N = ca. 2500). Internationally, therefore, Finland is far behind other Western countries in the scope of its refugee policy. The proportion of immigrants and refugees in Finland is the lowest in Europe, ca. 1 per cent. Finland has resettled refugees only on so called humanitarian grounds, meaning that they have not been eligible for other third countries. Five ministries, the local municipalities and the Red Cross are all responsible for some part of the resettlement process, which means overlapping and unclear division of labour. Although lip-service is given to the principle of multi-culturalism, in practice the term "adaptation" still stands for total assimilation (Laitinen and Oksanen, 1986; Matinheikki-Kokko, 1991, 1992).

The relationship between the concrete acculturation experience of individuals and the resulting acculturative stress depends on a variety of moderating factors, including the nature of the host society. Argument and some evidence exist that mental health problems may be less among immigrants and refugees in countries with multicultural ideologies (with attendant tolerance for cultural diversity) than assimilationist ones (with pressures to conform to a single cultural standard) (Berry *et al.*, 1987). Especially the policy of refugee dispersal has proved to be a serious mistake in several countries (Westermeyer, 1987; Liebkind, 1990; Dalglish, 1989). There is a significant inverse relationship between the density of any ethnic migrant group and the rate of mental illness in that group (Furnham and Bochner, 1990). Viewed in this perspective, the possibilities of the Vietnamese refugees in Finland to receive social and emotional support in their acculturation process are not the best possible.

Problems of Sampling in Studying Vietnamese Refugees

Ethnic/cultural identity changes in the acculturation process. In empirical studies of this process, cross-sectional research, employing a time-related variable such as length of residence or generational status, is a common alternative to longitudinal research (Berry, 1990). In this study, both length of residence and generation were used to assess the acculturation process. The sample includes 159 young refugees born between 1969 and 1976 who arrived in Finland 1979–89, and their parents and care-givers (total $N = 280$). The mean age of the youth group was 17.5 years. In the adult sample, 22 per cent were care-givers and the rest were parents. The ratio of males to females was equivalent in the two generations (adults = 49% males, youth = 53% males), as was the ratio of residents in the capital area to residents in (16 municipalities of) the rest of the country (adults = 40%, youth = 45%). Fifty-nine per cent of the male and 52 per cent of the female parents/care-givers participated in the work-force. In presenting the results, the total numbers vary somewhat according to the number of missing answers to specific questions.

Yu and Liu (1986) describe a multitude of practical and methodological problems encountered in an empirical study of Vietnamese refugees in California, USA. Accuracy of basic sociodemographic data was below the general standard in the host country, interactional problems and the establishment of trust between researchers and refugees took several months, and especially sampling difficulties were tremendous (Yu and Liu, 1986). A special stumbling block was to obtain a roster of names with correct addresses. Most available information turned out to be old or inaccurate, and the most reliable service agencies initially ignored the researcher's requests for cooperation. Later, when cooperation was reached through personal contacts with key personnel, many agencies turned out to lack address lists because of lack of manpower or other reasons. Having finally established a sample through other sources, 60 per cent of the Vietnamese the researchers tried to contact had already moved elsewhere, especially the numerous unattached individuals (Yu and Liu, 1986). The final per cent of the population fitting the sample criteria interviewed in this study (62.4%, $N = 280$), must, therefore, be considered satisfactory. A multitude of sources, including the refugees themselves (and a Vietnamese research assistant working for seven months in the preparatory stage of the project), were used in order to establish the sample. Four (occasionally five) members of the Vietnamese refugee community acted as co-workers in the study, and the project was from the very start planned together with them and other members of the community.

Methodological Problems and Some Solutions in Studying Ethnic/Cultural Identity

Within the social sciences, theoretical writing on ethnic identity far outweighs empirical research. Most of the empirical work on ethnic identity has concentrated on young children, with a focus on minority children's racial misidentification or preference for White stimulus objects (e.g. Aboud, 1988). Far less work has been done on ethnic identity beyond childhood (Phinney, 1990). In the studies done, there is no widely agreed-on definition of ethnic identity (Liebkind, 1992). Ethnic identity has empirically been treated as the ethnic component of social identity, as mere self-identification, as feelings of belongingness and commitment, as the sense of shared values and attitudes or as attitudes towards one's group. Some studies have concentrated on the cultural aspects of ethnic identity, e.g. language, behaviour and values (for an extensive review, see Phinney, 1990).

Subjective self-identification as a member of an ethnic group (also called self-definition) is important because it locates the individual within a particular cultural framework. Although self-identification is clearly an essential starting point in examining ethnic identity, it was not specifically assessed in about half of the studies reviewed by Phinney in 1990. Recently, however, self-identification has been used as the single or major indication of ethnic identity (e.g. Clément and Noels 1992; Lalonde *et al.*, 1992; Rosenthal and Feldman 1992; Liebkind, 1993).

Ethnic/cultural self-identification tells us something about the extent of an individual's culturally endorsed behaviour and attitudes, but fails to tell us the whole story (Rosenthal and Feldman, 1992). People may use an ethnic label and yet have no strong feeling of concern for their culture or even have negative attitudes towards their own group. Consequently, it is important to assess general positive or negative attitudes towards maintenance of one's own culture (Phinney, 1990). Even this is not enough, however. One may have a positive attitude towards maintenance of one's own culture without necessarily endorsing that culture oneself. In empirical research, a wide variety of ethnic involvement, cultural activities and attitudes have been assessed (see e.g. Phinney, 1990). Most often the assessment implies direct questions ("how often/much do you . . ."), but only rarely have subjects been asked to rate themselves on attitudes or values characteristic of their specific culture (Phinney, 1990). However, there are a few exceptions to this rule (e.g. Ting-Toomey, 1981; McDermott *et al.*, 1983; Nguyen and Williams 1989).

In this study, ethnic self-identification was assessed by asking the respondents to indicate whether they feel (1) totally Vietnamese/Chinese-Vietnamese to (5) totally Finnish (Liebkind, 1993). The mid-option, (3) equally much Vietnamese/ Chinese-Vietnamese and Finnish, allowed for a balanced bicultural self-identification. The acculturation attitudes of the respondents were assessed through the extent to which they agreed or disagreed with a number of arguments related to the two issues regarded by Berry *et al.* (1987) to be most central for acculturation (cf. section 1 of this chapter). Nine of the arguments indicated an attitude towards the dominant culture, five towards the respondents' own culture. An example of the former is "The Vietnamese should associate more with Finns" and of the latter "It is a shame if refugee children do not know their mother tongue". The Cronbach Alpha of the first scale is .77 and of the second .68.

In order to assess the actual degree of acculturation of the respondents, a twenty-nine-item questionnaire of traditional Vietnamese family values, developed and translated to Vietnamese by Nguyen and Williams (1989), was used. Some of the items also cover Western family values towards adolescent individuality and independence. Examples of the items are "When a girl reaches the age of 16, it is all right for her to decide whom to date and when", "Parents always know what is best", and "A family should do something together regularly". The statements can be conceived of as a sample of the shared beliefs (and their opposites) of child-rearing and family values endorsed within the Vietnamese culture. The scale was used both as one single measure of adherence to traditional family values (alpha = .76) and as three factors extracted from a maximum likelihood factor analysis (all general reliability coefficients >.70). The first factor indicated the degree of tightness of family bonds and solidarity, the second the extent of acceptance of childrens' autonomy and freedom of choice, and the third the adherence to traditional hierarchical family structures based on age and gender.

Finally, global self-esteem was assessed by the self-evaluation (i.e. degree of positive evaluation of self) index of the IDEX programme, developed by Weinreich for the purpose of identity structure analysis (Weinreich, 1980, 1989; Liebkind, 1982, 1984, 1989b). The identity instrument used for elicitation of these indices was an applied form of the Role Construct Repertory Grid (RCRG) developed by Kelly (1955; Fransella and Bannister, 1977; Liebkind, 1984, 1989c). The RCRG used in this study included twelve entities (persons to be assessed, including the self) and twelve bipolar constructs (dimensions on which the persons are assessed). The constructs were elicited from thirteen key informants from the refugee group in the preparatory stage of the project and then supplied to the respondents in the study.

Results

The Vietnamese refugees studied clearly identify themselves as Vietnamese rather than Finnish, but the youth considers itself to be more Finnish than the adults, and for them this change in ethnic self-identification is correlated with length of residence in Finland (Liebkind, 1993). The ethnic self-identification of the adults, however, is not affected by length of residence. As a consequence, the gap between the ethnic self-definitions of the two generations seems to increase with time (Liebkind, 1993).

The acculturation attitudes of this sample are dependent on both gender and generation (Berry, 1990). The younger generation is less orientated towards their own culture than are their parents (generation effect of gender by generation analysis of variance $F(1,276) = 13.8$, $p < .001$). However, the generations do not differ in their orientation towards the dominant culture. Instead, there is a gender difference; the males are more strongly orientated towards the dominant culture than the females, especially the adult females (gender effect of gender by generation analysis of variance $F(1,276) = 7.4$, $p < .01$).

It seems obvious that there are very few in this sample of Vietnamese refugees who would wish to abandon their own culture and thus assimilate or become marginal (Berry et al., 1987, Berry, 1990; Sue and Sue 1990). If this is also true of the total population of Vietnamese refugees in Finland cannot be concluded with any certainty. It is possible that the proportion of marginals and assimilationists is higher among those who did not participate in the study. The separation option, however, seems to be frequently preferred by the adult women of this sample. This group is also the least acculturated, i.e. adheres most to traditional family values, especially regarding the degree of children's autonomy and freedom of choice (cf. Table 14.1).

TABLE 14.1 Support for children's autonomy and freedom of choice (Factor 2 of the Nguyen & Williams Scale, 1989) according to gender and generation

	Men	Women	Boys	Girls	Total
M:	0.04	−0.80	0.27	0.32	−0.00
DL	0.86	0.99	0.69	0.67	0.91
N:	59	61	84	74	278

Two-way analysis of variance; F (3, 274) = 27.85, p < 0.001
Source under the null hypotheses:

	F	df	p
Generation × Gender	21.28	1,274	<0.001
Generation	49.28	1,274	<0.001
Gender	16.59	1,274	<0.001

In order to assess the relationship between level of acculturation (i.e. adherence to traditional family values) and acculturation attitudes, a mid-point split was effected on the attitude scale measuring orientation towards the dominant culture. This allowed a classification of each individual as falling either above or below the mid-point of orientation towards the dominant group (mid-point = 9). Among the adults, those having a weak orientation towards the dominant culture adherred clearly more to traditional cultural values (generation effect in orientation by generation analysis of variance $F(1,274) = 50.6$, $p < .001$). This was true also for the youth with regard to support for children's autonomy and freedom of choice (orientation effect in orientation by generation analysis of variance $F(1,274) = 11.1$, $p < 001$). Surprisingly, however, those boys who were strongly orientated towards the dominant group actually adhered *more* to traditional hierarchical family roles based on age and gender than did the boys who had a weak orientation towards the dominant group ($t = 3.03$, $df = 72$, $p < .01$). This was not true for the girls or the adults.

Turning to the measure of global self-esteem, the females of this sample have lower global self-esteem than the males (gender effect of generation by gender analysis of variance $F(1,272) = 6.3$, $p < .05$), and the youth have a lower self-esteem than the adults (generation effect of generation by gender analysis of variance $F(1,272)$ $p < .05$). The degree of orientation towards the dominant culture is associated with global self-esteem among the adults only. Those with a stronger orientation towards the dominant culture have higher self-esteem ($t = 2.2$, $df = 117$, $p < .05$). Among the youth, no such effect of acculturation attitude is discernible. However, the picture changes completely when we turn to the prevailing degree of acculturation, to the adherence to traditional Vietnamese family values. Both in the youth sample and among all females there is a significant inverse association between acculturation and self-esteem, although acculturation contributes alone very little to the total variance of the self-esteem measure ($R^2 = .04$, $p < .05$).

Clearly, it is the roles of the females and the youth within the family which differ most in the Vietnamese and Finnish cultures. Adoption of Finnish cultural beliefs in these matters seems to decrease, rather than increase, the global self-esteem of females and youth. Together the length of stay in Finland, the acculturation attitudes towards both dominant culture and own culture, and the prevailing degree of acculturation (adherence to traditional family values) explain significantly the global self-esteem of the females (girls and women), especially the adult women (cf. Table 14.2).

In the total sample, a combination of adherence to one's own cultural values and a clear orientation towards the dominant culture is associated with higher self-esteem. This reflects the integration option of Berry (1990), which thus proves to afford the best psychological outcome. The beneficial effect of a clear orientation towards the dominant culture is especially evident among the adult women. Among all the females, especially the girls, it is the adherence to one's own cultural values which is associated with higher self-esteem.

TABLE 14.2 The effects of length of stay, acculturation attitudes and degree of acculturation on the self-esteem of Vietnamese refugees in Finland* (regression analysis)

	p of total model:	R2	Variable:	beta	p of beta:
Total sample	<0.01	0.05	Time:	−0.10	
			OriDC:	0.17	<0.01
			OriOC:	−0.01	
			Trad:	0.13	<0.05
Adults	<0.05	0.11	Time:	−0.17	<0.10
			OriDC:	0.26	<0.01
			OriOC:	−0.05	
			Trad:	0.01	
Children	n.s.	0.04	Time:	0.00	
			OriDC:	0.08	
			OriOC:	−0.01	
			Trad:	0.18	<0.05
Males	n.s.	0.04	Time:	−0.02	
			OriDC:	0.19	<0.05
			OriOC:	0.01	
			Trad:	0.07	
Females	<0.05	0.09	Time:	−0.16	<0.10
			OriDC:	0.15	
			OriOC:	−0.04	
			Trad:	0.22	<0.05
Men	n.s.	0.06	Time:	−0.08	
			OriDC:	0.14	
			OriOC:	−0.09	
			Trad:	−0.10	
Women	<0.05	0.19	Time:	−0.24	<0.10
			OriDC:	0.40	<0.01
			OriOC:	−0.01	
			Trad:	0.17	
Boys	n.s.	0.07	Time:	0.10	
			OriDC:	0.20	<0.10
			OriOC:	0.03	
			Trad:	0.20	<0.10
Girls	n.s.	0.05	Time:	−0.12	
			OriDC:	−0.05	
			OriOC:	−0.07	
			Trad:	0.15	

Time = length of stay in Finland
OriDC + strength of orientation towards dominant culture
OriOC = strength of orientation towards own culture
Trad = degree of adherence to traditional family values

Summary and Conclusions

Regardless of generation or gender, the Vietnamese refugees studied clearly identify themselves as Vietnamese rather than Finnish, are rather unanimous in their wish to maintain their own culture, and adhere to more than they reject traditional Vietnamese family values. There are, however, also important generational and gender differences. The females are more often weakly orientated towards the dominant culture than the males. Particularly the adult women who adhere more to the traditional family values, i.e. they are less acculturated. Especially, they are opposed to the Western type of autonomy and freedom of choice for children in the family. Considering that the youth in this sample is much in favour of such Western values, and that the traditional role of the women is to devote their time and energy to bringing up their children properly, the resulting intergenerational conflicts are likely to impinge on the women's identity.

Although the self-esteem of females is higher if they adhere to traditional family values than if they do not, the self-esteem of females and the youth is in general lower than that of the males and the adults respectively. Acculturation attitudes have an opposite effect to the acculturation level on the self-esteem of adults. Those adults, mostly women, who are only weakly orientated towards the dominant society, have lower self-esteem than those who are strongly orientated towards the host society. Consequently, only integrative acculturation attitudes (adherence to one's own cultural values combined with a clear orientation towards the host society) are shown to have an unequivoqually beneficial effect on global self-esteem.

In general, however, the acculturation variables explain only a small part of the total variance of the self-esteem measure. The generally weak association between collective and global (personal) self-esteem seems, therefore, to be reflected also in the small variance of global self-esteem explained by cultural identity (level of acculturation) (Crocker and Major, 1989, cf. section 3). The direction of the associations found, however, supports the notions of the psychological importance of integrative acculturation attitudes. It is possible, however, that the impact of acculturation variables on self-esteem is an indirect one. If the females adhere to traditional Vietnamese family values, this may create a family context with less internal conflict than is the case if the females are more acculturated. Consequently, it could be this family context, rather than a more Vietnamese cultural identity per se, which is beneficial for the self-esteem of the females.

Although it is difficult to find, in this sample, marginal or outright assimilationist acculturation attitudes, many of the adult females seem to be at risk for maladjustment because of separation from or rejection of the dominant culture. As time goes by, their self-esteem is decreasing, evidently being negatively affected by their separatist attitude. The only protection seems to be a strict adherence to traditional values, but this protection may be more illusory than real, as lack of skills to interact with the dominant culture threaten to heighten the intergenerational conflicts. These identity patterns seem to be reflected in earlier results from this study, according to which females from both generations report more anxiety and depression symptoms than males, on both Western and culture-specific symptom scales (Liebkind, 1993). The most distressed group is the adult women. As many as 34% of them have anxiety scores above the cut-off point for high emotional distress (Liebkind, 1993). In studies on acculturative stress, females have frequently been noted to experience more stress. (Berry *et al.*, 1987; Berry, 1990). Whether this pattern really indicates greater female stress or, for example, a greater tendency to subscribe to symptom statements, is not always easy to judge. However, the patterns of ethnic/cultural and global identity found among the adult women in this study support the findings of increased acculturative stress in this group.

Some of the boys in this sample seem to feel a need to fall back on traditional gender roles when strongly confronted with the dominant culture. As for the males in general, no dramatic results were found in this study. However, their way of reacting to acculturative stress may be beyond the scope of this study. Only anecdotal evidence is available on divorce, homicide, suicide and attempted suicide among the Vietnamese refugees in Finland, as no authority has found reason enough to keep such statistics. The refugees themselves are, however, very concerned about the increasing rates, mainly due to male reactions.

In this study of the changes in ethnic/cultural identity of Vietnamese refugees we are only beginning to reveal the complexity and multidimensionality of the subjective experience of exile and acculturation. These experiences seem to depend, to a considerable degree, on age and gender, and they cannot be understood without close scrutiny of the particular cultural values clashing in the acculturation process. The results from this study indicate that a relatively low level of acculturation and yet a willingness to participate in the host society affords the best psychological outcome for most minority members.

References

Aboud, F. (1988). *Children and Prejudice*. New York: Basil Blackwell.
Beiser, M. (1988). Influence of time, ethnicity and attachment on depression in Southeast Asian refugees. *American Journal of Psychiatry*, **145**, 46–51.
Beiser, M. (1991). The mental health of refugees in resettlement countries. In H. Adelman (ed.), *Refugee Policy: Canada and the United States*. Centre for Refugee Studies, York University and Center for Migration Studies of New York, Inc., Toronto: York Lanes Press Ltd.
Berry, J. W. (1990). Psychology of acculturation. In J. J. Berman (eds), *Cross-cultural Perspectives*. Nebraska Symposium on Motivation 1989, vol. 37, Lincoln, University of Nebraska.
Berry, J. W., Kim, U., Minde, T. and Mok, D. (1987). Comparative studies of acculturative stress. *International Migration Review*, **21**, 491–511.
Canadian Task Force (1988) *Review of the Literature on Migrant Mental Health*. Canadian Task Force on Mental Health Issues Affecting Immigrants and Refugees. Health and Welfare, Ministry of Supply and Services in Canada.
Chang, S. C. (1982). The self: a nodal issue in culture and psyche—an Eastern perspective. *American Journal of Psychotherapy*, **36**, 67–81.
Clément, R. and Noels, K. A. (1992). Towards a situated approach to ethnolinguistic identity: the effects of status on individuals and groups. *Journal of Language and Social Psychology*, **11**, 203–32.
Crocker, J. and Major, B. (1989). Social stigma and self-esteem: the self-protective properties of stigma. *Psychological Review*, **96**, 608–30.
Dalglish, C. (1989). *Refugees from Vietnam*. London: Macmillan.
Fernando, S. (1991). *Mental Health, Race and Culture*. Hampshire: Macmillan in association with Mind Publications.

Fransella, F. and Bannister, D. (1977). *A Manual for Repertory Grid Technique*. London: Academic Press.

Furnham, A. and Bochner, S. (1990). *Culture Shock: Psychological Reactions to Unfamiliar Environments*. London: Routledge (1st printing 1986).

Garza, R. T. and Herringer, L. G. (1987). Social identity: a multidimensional approach. *Journal of Social Psychology*, **127**(3), 299–308.

Hinkle, S. and Brown, R. (1990). Intergroup comparisons and identity: some links and lacunae. In D. Abrams and M. A. Hogg (eds), *Social Identity Theory: Constructive and Critical Advances*. New York: Harvester Wheatsheaf.

Ho, M. K. (1987). Family therapy with Asian/Pacific Americans. In M. K. Ho (ed.), *Therapy with Ethnic Minorities*. Newbury Park: Sage Publications.

Hogg, M. A. and Abrams, D. (1990). Social motivation, self-esteem and social identity. In D. Abrams and M. A. Hogg (eds), *Social Identity Theory: Constructive and Critical Advances*, New York: Harvester Wheatsheaf.

Johnston, L. and Hewstone, M. (1990). Intergroup contact: social identity and social cognition. In D. Abrams and M. A. Hogg (eds), *Social Identity Theory: Constructive and Critical Advances*, New York: Harvester Wheatsheaf.

Kelly, G. A. (1955). *The Psychology of Personal Constructs*, Vols I and II, New York, Methuen.

Knusden, J. C. (1990). Cognitive models in the life histories. *Anthropological Quarterly*, **63**, 122–33.

Laotonen, I. and Oksanen, L. (1986). *Pakolaisena suomessa* [Refugee in Finland]. Selvitys vuonna 1983 Suomeen saapuneiden Indokiinan pakoliasten sijoittumisesta yhteiskuntaan opakolais-keskuksesta muuton jälkeen [Report on the resettlement in the Finnish society of Indochinese refugees arrived in Finland 1983 after leaving the reception centre], Helsinki, Sosiaalihallituksen raportti nro 11 [The National Board of Social Welfare, report no. 11].

Lalonde, R. N., Taylor, D. M. and Moghaddam, F. M. (1992). The process of social identification for visible immigrant women in a multicultural context. *Journal of Cross-Cultural Psychology*, **23**, 25–9.

Liebkind, K. (1982). The Swedish-speaking Finns: a case study in ethnolinguistic identity. In M. Tajfel (ed.), *Social Identity and Intergroup Relations: European Studies in Social Psychology*. Cambridge: Cambridge University Press.

Liebkind, K. (1984). *Minority Identity and Identification Processes: A Social Psychological Study. Maintenance and Reconstruction of Ethnolinguistic Identity in Multiple Group Allegiance*. Helsinki, Commentationes Scientiarum Socialium 22.

Liebkind, K. (1989a). Conceptual approaches to ethnic identity. In K. Liebkind (ed.), *New Identities in Europe: Immigrant Ancestry and the Ethnic Identity of Youth*. Aldershot: Gower Press.

Liebkind, K. (ed.)(1989b). *New Identities in Europe: Immigrant Ancestry and the Ethnic Identity of youth*. Aldershot: Gower Press.

Liebkind, K. (1989c). Patterns of ethnic identification among Finns in Sweden. In K. Liebkind (ed.), *New Identities in Europe: Immigrant Ancestry and the Ethnic Identity of Youth*. Aldershot: Gower Press.

Liebkind, K. (1990). Pakolaisten mielenterveys ja identiteetti [Mental Health and Identity of Refugees]. *Suomen Lääkärilehti* [Medical Journal of Finland], **45**(35), December, 3211–16.

Liebkind, K. (1992). Ethnic identity—challenging the boundaries of social psychology. In G. M. Breakwell (ed.), *Social Psychology of Identity and the Self Concept*. London: Surrey University Press/Academic Press.

Liebkind, K. (1993). Self-reported ethnic identity, depression and anxiety among young Vietnamese refugees and their parents. *Journal of Refugee Studies*, **6**, 26–39.

Lin, K. M., Masuda, M. and Tazuma, L. (1984). Problems of eastern refugees and immigrants: adaptational problems of Vietnamese refugees. Part IV. *The Psychiatric Journal of the University of Ottawa*, **9**, 79–84.

Matinheikki-Kokko, K. (1991). *Pakolaisten vastaanotto ja hyvinvoinnin turvaaminen Suomessa* [The Resettlement and Social Welfare of Refugees in Finland], Sosiaali-ja terveyshallituksen raportti noro. 40 [The National Board of Health and Social Welfare, report no. 40]. Helsinki: VAPK-kustannus.

Matinheikki-Kokko, K. (1992). *Pakolaiset kunnassa: kenen ehdoilla?* [Refugees in the Municipality: On Whose Conditions?] Sosiaali-ja terveyshallituksen raportti noro. 69 [The National Board of Health and Social Welfare, report no. 69]. Helsinki: VAPK-kustannus.

McDermott, J. F., Robillard, A. B., Char, W. F. A., Hsu, J., Tseng, W.-S. and Ashton, G. C. (1983). Re-examining the concept of adolescence: differences between adolescent boys and girls in the context of their families. *American Journal of Psychiatry*, **140**, 1318–22.

Nguyen, A. N. and Williams, H. L. (1989). Transition from East to West: Vietnamese adolescents and their parents. *Journal of the American Academy of Child and Adolescent Psychiatry*, **28**, 505–15.

Nidorf, J. F. (1985). Mental health and refugee youths: a model for diagnostic training. In T. C. Owan (ed.), Southeast Asian mental health: treatment, prevention, services, training and research. US Department of Health and Human Services. Rockville: National Institute of Mental Health in collaboration with Office of Refugee Resettlement.

Phinney, J. S. (1990). Ethnic identity in adolescents and adults: review of research. *Psychological Bulletin*, **38**, 499–514.

Phinney, J. S., Lochner, B. T. and Murphy, R. (1990). Ethnic identity development and psychological adjustment in adolescence. In A. R. Stiffman and L. E. Davis (eds), *Ethnic Issues in Adolescent Mental Health*. London, New Delhi, and Newbury Park: Sage.

Rick, K. and Forward, J. (1992). Acculturation and perceived intergenerational differences among Hmong youth. *Journal of Cross-Cultural Psychology*, **23**, 85–94.

Rosenthal, D. A. and Feldman, S. S. (1992). The nature and stability of ethnic identity in Chinese youth. *Journal of Cross-Cultural Psychology*, **23**, 214–27.

Rumbaut, G. (1991). Migration, adaptation and mental health. In H. Adelman (ed.), *Refugee Policy: Canada and the United States*. Centre for Refugee Studies, York University and Center for Migration Studies of New York, Inc. Toronto: York Lanes Press Ltd.

Sachdev, I. and Bourhis, R. Y. (1990a). Language and social identification. In D. Abrams and M. A. Hogg (eds), *Social Identity Theory: Constructive and Critical Advances*. New York: Harvester Wheatsheaf.

Sachdev, I. and Bourhis, R. Y. (1990b). Bilinguality and multilinguality. In H. Giles and W. P. Robinson (eds), *Handbook of Language and Social Psychology*. Chichester: John Wiley & Sons.

Sue, D. W. and Sue, D. (1990). *Counselling the Culturally Different: Theory and Practice*. New York: John Wiley & Sons.

Tajfel, H. (ed.) (1978). *Differentiation between Social Groups: Studies in the Social Psychology of Intergroup Relations*. European Monographs in Social Psychology, no. 14, London: Academic Press.

Ting-Toomey, S. (1981). Ethnic identity and close friendship in Chinese-American College students. *International Journal of Intercultural Relations*, **5**, 383–406.

Weinreich, P. (1980). *Manual for Identity Exploration Using Personal Constructs*. SSRC Research Unit on Ethnic Relations, University of Aston, Birmingham, England.

Weinreich, P. (1989). Variations in ethnic identity: identity structure analysis. In K. Liebkind (ed.), *New Identities in Europe: Immigrant Ancestry and the Ethnic Identity of Youth*. Aldershot: Gower Press.

Westermeyer, J. (1987). Prevention of mental disorder among Hmong refugees in the U.S.: lessons from the period 1976–1986. *Social Science and Medicine*, **25**, 941–47.

White, G. M. and Marsella, A. J. (1989). Introduction: cultural conceptions of mental health research and practice. In A. J. Marsella and G. M. White (eds), *Cultural Conceptions of Mental Health and Therapy*. Dordrecht: D.Reidel Publishing Company.

Yu, E. S. H. and Liu, W. T. (1986). Methodological problems and policy implications in Vietnamese refugee research. *International Migration Review*, **20**, 483–501.

15

Migrant Identities in Conflict: Acculturation Attitudes and Perceived Acculturation Ideologies[1]

GABRIEL HORENCZYK

Hebrew University, Israel

Introduction

Maines (1978) has provided us with the important distinction between two different processes involved in inter- and intracultural migration, namely, the migration of "bodies" and the migration of "selves". Societies dealing with massive influxes of immigrants naturally tend to concentrate their main efforts on coping with the great demands posed by the migration of "bodies", which exert the most urgent pressure on the host institutions. Thus, issues connected with the meeting of migrants' material needs, such as housing and employment, are foremost on the absorption agenda.

But "identities migrate every bit as much as bodies" (Maines, 1978, p. 242); and we would like to argue that issues related to the complex migration of "selves" must not be left unresolved, even at the earliest phases of the migration process. Failure to deal with problems concerning the inevitable changes in social and personal identities may lead to detrimental consequences, which, though perhaps less noticeable, may be no less harmful in the long range.

Our study may be viewed as part of our efforts to better understand the socio-psychological aspects of migration and acculturation processes. The impact of cultural transition appears to affect all facets of the self; such a major relocation is likely to lead to significant reconstructions of both personal and social identities. In other words, the extreme shift in the social ecology of the self (Hormuth, 1990) entailed by transcultural migration will demand radical changes in self-perception and behaviour until ecology and self are again stabilised.

The Interplay between "Old" and "New" Identities

The investigation of these changes in migrants' identities may turn out to be a difficult and often frustrating research endeavour. Within the framework of refugee research, the term "delayed psychological arrival" (Liebkind, 1993a) points to the accumulating evidence showing that psychological problems related to migration tend to appear at later stages of the migration process, when physical and material needs have been met to a certain extent. It seems to us, moreover, that "selves" tend to migrate not only "more slowly" but also in a more complex trajectory, than their containing "bodies." Unlike physical transition, changes in ethnic and cultural identity are usually not abrupt. During all phases of the intercultural migration process, newcomers have to continuously reorganise the delicate structure of their various subidentities—those related to their membership in the new host society and those involving their attachment to the values of their former culture.

Various models have been suggested for describing distinct patterns of such interplay between the social and cultural identity of the host society and the former identity still prevailing, with different degrees of intensity, within the migrant ethnic community. Bochner (1982), for example, classified expatriates and sojourners into four broad categories: "passing" types reject their culture of origin, embracing the second culture; "chauvinistics", on the other hand, reject the second culture while exaggerating the first one; individuals of the "marginal" type vacillate between the two cultures; and "mediating" migrants try to synthesise both cultures.

A similar conceptualisation was developed by the cross-cultural psychologist Berry (1990), as part of his interest in the psychological aspects of the acculturation process. According to Berry (1990), minority members of plural societies (such as immigrants) must confront two important issues—the extent to which they wish to maintain their minority cultural identity, and the desired degree of intercultural contact with majority members. For the sake of conceptual simplicity, the model assumes dichotomous decisions on each of the issues ("yes" or "no" to the maintenance of minority identity, and "yes" or "no" to intercultural contact). By posing the two issues simultaneously, a conceptual framework is generated that defines four types of acculturation attitudes: integration, assimilation, separation, and marginalisation. Table 15.1 displays the four varieties of acculturation attitudes as possible combinations of dichotomised attitudes towards the "old" (minority) identity and the "new" host identity (this terminology is different from Berry's conceptualisation, but it will serve our purposes of recognising identity conflicts involved in the migration process). Separate scales for each of these modes of acculturation have been developed by Berry and his colleagues for use with various acculturating groups. The four

TABLE 15.1   Berry's Model of Accumulation Attitudes (modified)

	Attitudes towards "new identity"	
Attitudes towards "old identity"	Positive	Negative
Positive	Integration	Separation
Negative	Assimilation	Marginalization

attitudes are operationalised in culturally specific ways, with the statements dealing with topics which were found relevant to acculturation in each of the investigated groups. (For a description of the scale construction technique, and a review of the reliability, validity, and correlates of the scales, see Berry *et al.*, 1989).

Identity reconstruction during cultural transition, however, seems to us to be a more complex process involving intricate communicational transactions, in which immigrants calibrate their identities trying to make sense of what they expect and what is expected from them in the new setting. We believe, therefore, that a more complete picture of cultural identity redefinition can be achieved by taking into account not only the migrants' own attitudes towards acculturation, but also their views regarding the expectations held by the receiving society with regard to their social and cultural integration. These perceptions about the host cultures's "acculturation ideologies" may be a major factor affecting the route and speed of the migration of selves.

The conceptual framework proposed above could be used for mapping not only the migrant's own acculturation attitudes, but also their views regarding the perceived acculturation ideologies of the host culture. We would then predict a discrepancy between the "actual" acculturation attitudes held by the immigrants and their perceptions of the "expected" attitudes. This disparity would reflect, to a great extent, the migrant's position as a minority individual vis-à-vis the resource-rich majority. In this situation, the newcomer sees the host society as demanding the submission of minority values and identities to the larger national mainstream culture. On the other hand, selves migrate slowly, and the migrant finds it difficult to abandon his primordial sentiments and attachments and become totally absorbed within the host society. Thus, it is reasonable to expect immigrants to perceive the host culture's expectations from them in regard to assimilation as much stronger than their own willingness to assimilate.

The Study

As part of our efforts to understand various aspects of the process of identity reconstruction among Russian immigrants to Israel, we developed a research instrument designed to measure both migrants' own acculturation attitudes and their perceptions of the host society's acculturation ideologies or expectations.

Based on previously collected informal data, several areas of identity-related
behaviour relevant to the Russians' acculturation were identified and, for each
area, four 7-point Likert-type items corresponding to the four types of
acculturation attitudes were included in the questionnaire. Following are a few
examples of these items:

> We live in Israel and we have to relinquish our Russian culture and our old habits; we have to
> adopt the Israeli way of life—to think and act like Israelis.
>
> (culture—assimilation)
>
> I prefer to speak mainly Russian, and to use Hebrew only when necessary.
>
> (language—separation)
>
> I would like to celebrate the Jewish holidays without abandoning the holidays we used to
> celebrate in the Soviet Union.
>
> (religion—integration)
>
> I cannot share my thoughts and feelings either with Russian immigrants or with Israelis.
>
> (friendship—marginalisation)

The questionnaire was administered to 100 adolescent newcomers from
Russia who had been living in Israel between twelve and thirty months,
studying in regular high-school classes together with Israeli students. Both
sexes were almost equally represented. The respondents were presented with
the items dealing with acculturation attitudes twice: The first part of the
questionnaire asked for their own opinions regarding each of the statements,
while the second time they were requested to relate to the same items as a
typical Israeli classmate would want them to respond in order to be
considered "good immigrants".

We also decided to investigate, in this study, the acculturation ideologies of the
migrants' Israeli peers. One of the typical aspects of "culture shock" is confusion
in roles, role expectations, values, feelings, and identity (Oberg, 1960, cited in
Furnham, 1990). Misperceptions regarding aspects of ethnic and cultural identity
and identification need not be an exception to this state of uncertainty
characterising the immigrant's social judgments during the early phases of his or
her adjustment to the new society.

As a first attempt to assess the degree of accuracy of the migrants' perceptions
of the acculturation ideology held by the host society, we administered the
acculturation-attitude questionnaire to 100 Israeli classmates of our Russian
immigrant subjects, again with both sexes almost equally represented. The
questionnaire included the same items that were presented to the migrant
respondents, and they also appeared twice in the questionnaire. The first time the
Israeli subjects were asked "How do you think a typical Russian immigrant
classmate of yours would answer these questions?", and later they were
requested to indicate how they would want a classmate to respond to the items
in order to be a "good immigrant".

Preliminary analyses revealed considerable variability in the migrants' own
acculturation attitudes across the various areas of identity-related behaviours.

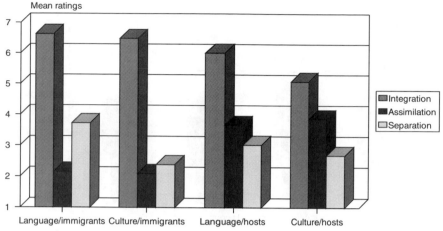

FIGURE 15.1   Actual acculturation attitudes

This finding is consistent with claims raised in the migration literature (e.g. Scott and Scott, 1989) propounding a contextualisation of acculturation and acculturation attitudes. Individuals tend to adopt different options of acculturation in different situations. It has been suggested (Sodowsky *et al.*, 1991) that the acculturation of a minority individual is best described by a composite profile rather than by a single score. We were therefore prevented from creating combined scales for the various modes of acculturation, and will present the results for the different spheres of cultural and social engagement separately.

The Rhetoric of Integration

Although comparisons of responses based on single-item measures should be treated with caution, we would like to mention a salient finding which exhibits a considerable degree of consistency across the groups and perspectives included in the study: The integration mode is generally regarded as the preferred acculturation attitude by both immigrants and hosts. Figures 15.1 and 15.2 display the mean scores of three modes of acculturation (the attitude of marginalisation has been excluded because of its extremely low level of endorsement) for two central identity-related areas—language and culture; the results obtained for the other areas show highly similar patterns.

The findings obtained for the expected acculturation attitudes among our host respondents, if generalisable, have considerable sociological value. Within the context of Jewish immigration to Israel in recent history, it may indicate a remarkable change in the Israeli society's "acculturation and absorption

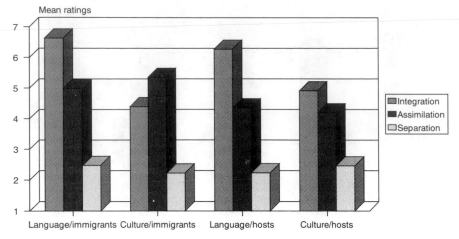

Mean ratings

Integration
Assimilation
Separation

Language/immigrants   Culture/immigrants   Language/hosts   Culture/hosts

FIGURE 15.2   Expected acculturation attitudes

ideology", a tendency towards growing multiculturalism and pluralism. This stands in contrast with policies explicitly or implicitly adopted during the large waves of immigration from Arab countries during the 1950s, which aimed at replacing important aspects of the migrants' ethnic and religious identity with features of the developing Israeli identity. It would seem that the ongoing public discourse about the negative short- and long-term effects of those public attitudes (reflected, for example, in the disregard of the newcomers' family patterns and religious customs) on the migrants' personal and social integration (Smooha, 1978) has brought about a marked shift in the general attitude of Israeli society towards acculturation. It is reasonable to assume that this new orientation, expressed at least at the rhetorical level, has been also influenced in some extent by the growing call for multicultural sensitivity and the application of pluralistic policies voiced in Western societies around the world (Smith and Bond, 1993; Takaki, 1993).

The widespread endorsement of the integration attitude by the migrants themselves may—again, if generalisable—challenge claims about the general unwillingness of Russian immigrants to adopt central cultural and societal components of Israeli identity and become full members of Israeli society. One of the conclusions included in a recent report published by the Behavioural Sciences Department of the Israel Defence Forces, for example, stated that "it seems that the immigrants would prefer to live in Israel within a framework of 'cultural autonomy' . . . with their [migrant] friends, and on the basis of their original culture, distancing themselves from the Israelis". Our findings, however, indicate a noteworthy acceptance of the integration attitude, to a similar one to what is expected from the immigrants by their Israeli counterparts.

Conflicting Attitudes towards Assimilation

It seems that, in the collective discourse about acculturation, the rhetoric of integration has been widely adopted, by both the hosts and the immigrants. Moreover, the migrants not only choose the integration attitude, but also tend to perceive Israeli society as expecting them to endorse it to a quite similar extent. These expectations are also quite accurate, judging by our Israeli subjects' expectations about the acculturation of immigrants. All this seems to suggest that the immigrants' immersion in their new society is free of conflicts, and that the intergroup perceptions and expectations are fully consonant.

A closer look at our findings, however, reveals a less idyllic picture. It appears that the rhetoric of integration does not have the same meaning for the majority and the minority groups participating in the acculturation process. Before elaborating on this claim, let us briefly refer to the way Bochner and Berry conceptualise the "mediation" and "integration" attitudes. Bochner (1982) views the "mediating" type as an individual who manages to reach a synthesis between the culture of origin and the new host culture, keeping the norms of both cultures salient since they are perceived as capable of being integrated. The effects of this attitude on the individual, according to Bochner, are personal growth and cultural preservation, while in the society it tends to promote inter-group harmony. Similarly, Berry (1990) states that when the integration option is preferred "there is some degree of cultural integrity maintained, while moving to participate as an integral part of the larger social network" (p. 244). Research evidence suggests that individuals favouring the integration mode tend to experience lower acculturative stress and show higher levels of subjective adaptation and self-esteem (see, for example, Liebkind, 1993b; Zheng and Berry, 1991).

Our findings, complemented by informal impressions and by responses to semi-structured interviews recently conducted with migrants at different stages in the transition process (Ta'ir, 1993), suggest, however, that the integration attitude is not always the neat result of a successful synthesis between the two cultures. We claim that quite often this mode of acculturation involves a delicate balancing between the two identities, a calibration process that may require a considerable degree of uneasy compromise and frustration. While all the parties to the tacit immigration contract (Kloss, 1971) may agree on the integration formula, less agreement should be expected if the terms of integration were to be specified in detail. Given that integration involves both the maintenance and the relinquishment of the culture of origin, hosts and migrants may disagree on the preferred degree of weakening of the newcomer's previous identity.

Table 15.2 shows the results obtained for the assimilation attitudes in two major domains of identity-related activity: language and culture. Mixed analyses of variance for each of the areas of activity separately reveal significant group X perspective interactions (language: $F(1,199) = 38.92, p < 0.01$; culture: $F(1,195) = 79.60, p < 0.01$). Multiple comparisons between means from the interaction tables were performed using paired t-tests with Bonferroni corrections on the p-values.

TABLE 15.2   Mean ratings (and standard deviations) of assimilation attitudes in two areas of activity, by group and perspective

Area	Immigrants (N = 100)		Hosts (N = 100)	
	Actual	Perceived	Actual	Perceived
Language	2.16 (1.60)	4.98 (2.07)	3.66 (1.81)	4.35 (2.09)
Culture	2.10 (1.55)	5.35 (2.00)	3.86 (1.92)	4.20 (2.15)

As predicted, migrants tend to express less willingness to assimilate as compared with their perceptions regarding the hosts' expectations from them (language: $t = -11.12$, $df = 99$, $p < 0.01$; culture: $t = -13.29$, $df = 99$, $p < 0.01$).

This finding can contribute to our understanding of emotional problems among migrant individuals. According to self-discrepancy theory (Higgins, 1989), psychological discomfort is induced by conditions where the person's self-concept does not match his or her self-guides; more specifically, discrepancies between the "actual" self and the "ought/other" self (the individual's representations of the attributes that significant others believe he or she ought to possess) are likely to lead to vulnerability to agitation-related emotions. Adolescent immigrants are likely to see the acculturation expectations of their host peers as indicative of the criteria for successful adaptation to their new society. However, as our results suggest, migrants may not be willing to fully comply to these demands, and this conflict between their own attitudes and their perceptions about the expectations of their peers may play a role in the development of anxiety-related disturbances.

Israeli respondents, while also exhibiting relatively high levels of expectations from the migrants to assimilate, show markedly weaker discrepancies between these attitudes and the assimilation attitudes attributed to their migrant counterparts (language: $t = -3.06$, $df = 99$, $p < 0.05$; culture: $t = -1.68$, $df = 99$, n.s.). Let us interpret this finding speculatively in terms of majority-minority relations: we would suggest that members of the host majority would prefer not to see their high expectations that migrants should assimilate as a "coercive" ideology standing in sharp contrast with the migrant's own reluctance to relinquish older attachments in favour of the new identity. Thus, according to our interpretation, majority members tend to attribute to the newcomers relatively high levels of motivation to assimilate, giving their "acculturation ideology" a more liberal flavour.

Conclusions

The findings from our study demonstrate the complex and multifaceted nature of identity reconstruction following transcultural migration. When acculturation ideologies—those held by the host society and those perceived by the migrants—are taken into account, a conflicted picture of acculturation emerges from beneath the rhetorically accepted surface attitude of integration. The consensual endorsement of this integration attitude seems not to unambiguously resolve the tensions experienced by migrants between two frequently opposing forces: adherence to their minority identity and adoption of the majority social and cultural identity. It has been suggested that individuals strive to achieve a balance between the demands posed by their various identities (Horenczyk and Nisan, 1993); the relative positions of the identities in the hierarchical self-structure often regulate the somewhat automatic decision-making process at times of identity conflict, but there are many situations in which other principles need to be called into action in order to grant expression to the various components of the self. Some circumstances, however, do not allow for such a compartmentalisation of identities and identity actualisation (Horenczyk, 1994), and individuals have to struggle with inner identity conflicts which may lead to anxiety feelings and other types of psychological discomfort.

Migrant individuals may adopt different cognitive and behavioural strategies for dealing with acculturation conflicts. Strategies are also likely to vary across different areas of social and cultural engagement and upon contextual circumstances. As indicated by Mendoza (1984), a minority person might adopt, for instance, separation attitudes with respect to marriage partner preferences, assimilation attitudes in terms of dress customs, and integration attitudes concerning food or celebration of major holidays. Situational factors, such as economic pressures or crisis situations, may also affect, at least temporarily, acculturation attitudes and behaviours: many new immigrants to Israel, for example, reported a strong sense of "togetherness" and "common fate" with their host Israelis under the missile attacks during the Gulf war. Moreover, as indicated earlier, the migration of selves tends to follow a complex trajectory. Findings from an exploratory study (Ta'ir, 1993) suggest that the balance between the various ethnic/national subidentities changes during different phases of the migration process. Our study explored acculturation attitudes and conflicts among a specific group of migrants—Israeli adolescent newcomers from the former Soviet Union, and more research is needed in order to substantiate and expand the conclusions derived from our investigation. A fuller understanding of identity changes during migration will have to address individual differences and contextual influences, among various age groups and migrant populations.

References

Berry, J. W. (1990). Psychology of acculturation: understanding individuals moving between cultures. In R. W. Brislin (eds), *Applied Cross-cultural Psychology*. Newbury Park, CA.: Sage.

Berry, J. W., Kim, U., Power, S., Young, M. and Bujaki, M. (1989). Acculturation attitudes in plural societies. *Applied Psychology: An International Review*, **38**(2), 185–206.

Bochner, S. (1982). The social psychology of cross-cultural relations. In S. Bochner (eds), *Cultures in Contact: Studies in Cross-cultural Interaction*. Oxford: Pergamon.

Higgins, E. T. (1989). Self-discrepancy theory: what patterns of self-beliefs cause people to suffer? In L. Berkowitz (eds), *Advances in Experimental Social Psychology*. New York: Academic Press.

Horenczyk, G. (1994). Hyphenated identities in conflict. Manuscript submitted for publication.

Horenczyk, G. and Nisan, M. (1993). The actualization balance of ethnic identity. Manuscript submitted for publication.

Hormuth, S. E. (1990). *The Ecology of the Self: Relocation and Self-concept Change*. Cambridge: Cambridge University Press.

Kloss, H. (1971). Language rights of immigrant groups. *International Migration Review*, **5**, 250–68.

Liebkind, K. (1993a). Self-reported ethnic identity, depression and anxiety among young Vietnamese refugees and their parents. *Journal of Refugee Studies*, **6**(1), 26–39.

Liebkind, K. (1993b). Vietnamese refugees in Finland: changing cultural identity. Paper Presented at the Conference *On Changing European Identities: Social-Psychological Analyses of Social Change*. Farnham Castle, Surrey.

Maines, D. R. (1978). Bodies and selves: notes on a fundamental dilemma in demography. *Studies in Symbolic Interaction*, **1**, 241–65.

Mendoza, R. H. (1984). Acculturation and sociocultural variability. In J. L. Martinez and R. H. Mendoza (eds), *Chicano Psychology*. Orlando: Academic Press.

Scott, W. A. and Scott, R. (1989). *Adaptation of Immigrants*. Oxford: Pergamon Press.

Smith, P. B. and Bond, M. H. (1993). *Social Psychology across Cultures*. London: Harvester Wheatsheaf.

Smooha, S. (1978). *Israel: Pluralism and Conflict*. Berkeley: University of California Press.

Sodowsky, G. R., Lai, E. W. M. and Plake, B. S. (1991). Moderating effects of sociocultural variables on acculturation attitudes of Hispanics and Asian Americans. *Journal of Counseling and Development*, **70**, 194–204.

Ta'ir, U. (1993) *Patterns of ethnic and national identity among Soviet immigrants at different phases of the migration process*. Master Thesis, The Hebrew University (in Hebrew).

Takaki, R. (1993). *A Different Mirror: A History of Multicultural America*. Boston: Little, Brown and Co.

Zheng, X., and Berry, J. W. (1991). Psychological adaptation of Chinese sojourners in Canada. *International Journal of Psychology*, **26**, 451–70.

Note

1. This research was supported by a grant from the NCJW Research Institute for Innovation in Education. I would like to thank the staff of the Melitz Center for Jewish and Zionist Education for their assistance with the data collection. I am especially grateful to Zvi Bekerman for his intensive and creative help and to Karmela Liebkind for her insightful comments to an earlier version of the paper.

Part Three

Constructing a European Identity

16

A Social Identity Perspective on European Integration

MARCO CINNIRELLA

Royal Holloway and Bedford New College, University of London, England

Introduction

In this chapter, European integration is used as an empirical vehicle for exploring limitations and weaknesses in what will be referred to as the social identity paradigm. This paradigm comprises both Tajfel's social identity theory (Tajfel, 1974; Tajfel and Turner, 1986) and Turner's self-categorisation theory (Turner, 1987). Although there are important differences between these theoretical perspectives, at the same time they share a common core of key assumptions which has meant that the distinction between the two is often blurred.

Henri Tajfel's social identity theory owes something to both Festinger's notion of social comparison (Festinger, 1954), and Bruner's "new look" perspective (e.g. Bruner, 1957), illustrating that the social identity paradigm, even from its conception, was influenced by both cognitive and social psychology. Social identity theory was an attempt to provide a social psychological perspective on intergroup conflict and prejudice, to make horrors such as genocide and war more understandable to the social scientist. At the heart of social identity theory is the notion that an individual's membership of social categories and social groups often constitutes an important aspect of that individual's self-concept. Tajfel argued that individuals usually desire a sense of positive self-worth, of positive self-esteem, and that this need is extended to the groups with which we identify, since they are also aspects of the self. In order to maintain a positive self-esteem when we think of our group memberships, Tajfel argued that we engage in intergroup comparisons, attempting to construe our own in-groups as both different from, and superior to, out-groups of which we are not members. This underlying drive to be different and superior was termed the need for *positive distinctiveness*, and it lies at the heart of social identity maintenance in Tajfel's theory. Since the mid-1970s, social identity theory has spawned a wide range of empirical and theoretical research, and the theory is undoubtedly one of the most important perspectives on intergroup relations available to social psychologists.

In *Rediscovering the Social Group* (Turner *et al.*, 1987), Turner and his associates developed self-categorisation theory, a bold attempt to build on social identity theory in order to explain both inter and now, *intra*-group processes. Whereas Tajfel's social identity theory had focused on intergroup relations, Turner argued that self-categorisation—the act of categorising oneself as a member of a social category—lies at the heart of *all* group processes. This led to self-categorisation models of conformity, group polarisation, and stereotyping, and marked a point where the social identity perspective took on more of the properties of a theoretical paradigm. Taken as a whole, social identity and self-categorisation theories could arguably be considered to offer a complete treatment of group processes.

Despite many successful applications of the social identity paradigm to ecologically valid instances of intergroup conflict, there remain some underlying weaknesses in the paradigm, and it is some of these which are addressed by the research shortly to be discussed.

In many ways the most crucial issue focused on here refers to the scale of social identities. Both Tajfel and Turner's theories claim a broad level of general-isability—in terms of both social identification and self-categorisation, all groups are taken as essentially equivalent. It is our contention, however, that large-scale social categories and groups—for example racial categories—have properties which make them rather different to smaller, more concrete groups such as families. In the following discussion it is suggested that the social identity paradigm, in its present form, presents an inadequate treatment of large-scale social categories. In essence, it is suggested that social conformity pressures, stereotyping and salience mechanisms, may all operate somewhat differently in large-scale categories (LSCs). The creation and diffusion of group belief structures are much more complex in large-scale, diffuse entities, with the mass media often having considerable influence over the definition of in-group norms, as well as the general salience of large-scale categories like national identity. Large-scale social categories are also often associated with a marked heterogeneity of norms, prototypes, and stereotypes, and can exhibit a powerful degree of influence over other social identities individuals might choose to adopt. This is an especially important weakness in the sense that large-scale categories such as gender, nationality and race, represent precisely the kind of category memberships the social identity perspective was formulated in order to explain.

A further area of potential weakness in the social identity paradigm is associated with its treatment of individual differences and the self. Tajfel frequently suggested that social identity theory need not include a sophisticated model of self, since it was specifically focused on intergroup relations and occasions when individuals acted in unison. However, with the advent of self-categorisation theory and its associated turn towards intra as well as inter-group processes, this argument seems much less persuasive, and there is little evidence to suggest that self-categorisation theory deals with these issues any more adequately than social identity theory. Today, theorists are questioning the impoverished treatment of motivation within the social identity paradigm, its simplistic model of the self, and its neglect of individual differences. Some of these weaknesses will be explored shortly, and suggestions made as to how they might be overcome.

Rather than explore the weaknesses in the social identity paradigm highlighted above in a purely theoretical manner, they are instead discussed in relation to an empirical study of European integration and its effects upon national and European social identities. The process of European integration is a particularly challenging topic for the social identity paradigm, not least because national and European identities are abstract, diffuse, and highly complex social categories, properties which make them particularly troublesome to a paradigm often enamoured of laboratory experimentation with what some have called "nonsense groups" (Fraser and Foster, 1984). It should, at the same time, be emphasised that at present, there is very little empirical or theoretical research which is able to shed light on the implications of European integration for national and European *identities*—the current research also, therefore, plugs something of an empirical gap in the literature on European integration.

Despite some useful attitudinal studies of European integration (e.g. the *Eurobarometer* surveys; Hewstone, 1986), there remains little or no existing research that can shed light on the issue of whether Europeans are actually coming to internalise a sense of European *identity*, to think of themselves as "Europeans", and to attach importance to such a self-categorisation. It is important to appreciate that attitudes and social identities are not inter-changeable, equivalent concepts. Although attitudes are often shared by members of social groups, and can come to serve identity functions (cf. Katz, 1960; Abelson and Prentice, 1989), social identification is a far richer concept, encompassing a good deal more than the notion of an attitude towards a social category or group. While an attitude towards European integration is a relatively finite evaluative belief, or alternatively, discursive strategy (cf. Potter and Wetherell, 1987), a social identification/self-categorisation with Europe implies the engagement of self and motivation with the notion of a European social collective. This means that the adoption of a European identity will have consequences for the self-concept, and self-esteem, which are likely to be more profound than those associated with the adoption of attitudinal beliefs or discourses. From Turner's self-categorisation theory (Turner, 1987), one may go further and suggest that self-categorisation as a European may be accompanied by self-stereotyping, which involves the internalisation of perceived European norms and stereotypes, and the perception of oneself as a typical European on key attributes.

In this sense then, adopting a European social identity, and self-categorising oneself as a European, is potentially much more significant than simply adopting or espousing pro-European attitudes. In fact, there is evidence to suggest that attitudes may vary as a result of fluctuations in the salience of social identities: this was a phenomenon demonstrated even before social identity theory was formulated, by theorists working within the reference group tradition (see Hyman and Singer, 1968, for a review).

In this chapter, the social identity paradigm is combined with Moscovici's theory of social representations, in a broadly integrated perspective on European integration. It is important to recognise that, in taking a social identity perspective, one inevitably also raises questions concerning social representations—shared constructions of reality generated in the course of social interaction (cf. Moscovici, 1984; 1988), since social identities are inevitably associated with systems of shared beliefs, such as stereotypes and norms (cf. Breakwell, 1991; Duveen and Lloyd, 1986; Lyons and Sotirakopoulou, 1991). There is an increasing need to appreciate the context for identity construction afforded by social representations, and to recognise therefore that changes in the construction of social identities are almost always associated with changes in the content, or the endorsement of, social representations. This being the case, it is suggested that questions of social identification and social representation are often inseparable.

The Empirical Basis of the Current Discussion

The empirical foundations upon which the current discussion is based, derive from three separate studies conducted over the period 1991–93, all of which explored aspects of national and European identity construction in the context of moves towards European integration (Cinnirella, 1993). The first study employed a cross-national questionnaire, focusing on identity and attitudinal issues pertaining to national and European identities, and containing both fixed-response and open-ended questions. This questionnaire was administered to university students in the United Kingdom and Italy, early in 1991. In the second phase of research, the British data were supplemented by a small-scale in-depth interview study focusing at a more qualitative level on British and European identity construction. In the third and final stage of research, a fixed-response format questionnaire was administered to British students, and focused on some specific issues pertaining to social identity theory and its application in studies of large-scale social category membership.

Respondents in all studies were Higher Education students who had volunteered to take part in a study of "opinions about your own country and European integration". In the United Kingdom, data were collected from 107 respondents (63 female, 44 male) as part of the cross-national study, most of whom were studying at the various colleges of the University of London. Italian respondents, who numbered 137 (99 female, 38 male), were approached at the

University of Bologna. Respondents for the United Kingdom interview study, were 25 University of London students (13 female, 12 male) who had volunteered to take part in the study, and had not completed the previous questionnaire. Respondents for the third phase, questionnaire study, which was also only conducted in the UK, numbered 121 (74 female, 42 male, 5 missing responses), all being volunteers. In both the United Kingdom and Italy, respondents in all studies were required to hold a British or Italian passport respectively.

In this chapter, some of the wider implications of this empirical research for social identity construction are examined. More detailed discussions of the empirical data in relation to European integration and its manifestations in Britain and Italy, can be found elsewhere (Cinnirella, 1993).

European Integration as the Study of Multiple Identities in Interaction

It is likely that certain key social categories, such as political party affiliation, nationality, and race, may well have implications for the other social identities adopted by individuals. For example, adoption of a particular political stance and internalisation of its related ideology might entail the acceptance of social representations of other social categories and groups. This is the phenomenon I have previously referred to as *mediation* (Cinnirella, 1991), a process which essentially involves the social representations of one social category or group having consequences for other social groupings. This use of the term mediation is somewhat different to Zavalloni's (Zavalloni, 1971, 1973), in that I make no assumptions about mediating categories or groups necessarily being smaller than the mediated social entity.

It therefore becomes imperative to take into account the *networking* or interconnections between various social categories and groups, if one is to gain an insight into social identity processes. Recent theorising on the salience of social identities (cf. Oakes, 1987), has led to the implicit assumption that, most of the time, in any given situation a single social identity—that which is highest in salience—will have the most consequence for individuals. This has had the unfortunate consequence of leading most social identity and self-categorisation research to ignore the interactions between multiple group memberships which might well be simultaneously salient, albeit to different degrees (cf. Breakwell, 1991; Deaux, 1992; Nesdale, 1989). In fact, as Scheibe (1983) argued, the significance of any single social identity for an individual depends largely on the *other* social identities contained in that person's identity repertoire. McCall (1987) has gone as far as to suggest that the management of one's set of identities is one of the most significant problems facing individuals today.

It must be stressed that investigations of mediation, networking, and similar phenomena should make use of multi-level perspectives (Lorenzi-Cioldi and Doise, 1990; Himmelweit, 1990). Networks of social identities and social representations might be constructed at the individual, group, and societal levels, and the interaction between these levels is likely to be complex. In addition, to the extent that the networking of identities forms a possible topic of conversation, and might be implicitly carried in mass media social representations, it should be clear that the creation of social identity networks is likely to be a negotiative process.

The current research seeks to demonstrate how national and European identities have become intertwined through the process of European integration, and to this extent, how a focus on either identity in isolation would be somewhat naïve. At one important level of analysis therefore, the interactions between national and European identities can be examined in terms of *multiple group memberships, or multiple social identities in interaction.* Here, one of the most important issues is how such identities are interconnected—we might, for example, ask whether national and European identities are consonant, dissonant, or indifferent (Hofman, 1988; see also Allen *et al.*, 1983).

It appears that one of the most important ways in which British and Italian orientations towards Europe may differ, is precisely in terms of the perceived relationship between national and European identities. British national identity proved to be significantly stronger than European identity across two separate questionnaire studies conducted as part of the current research (MANOVA analysis on 1991 data gave multivariate $F(7,100) = 14.503$, $p < .001$; MANOVA on 1993 data gave $F(7,108) = 17.650$, $p < .001$). These differences emerged on fixed-response measures of social identity which have enjoyed widespread use among followers of the Tajfel-Turner tradition (cf. Tajfel, 1974; Turner, 1987).

Evidence that the European identities manifested by British respondents were relatively weak when compared to their national identities, was also forthcoming from the interview study. Here, it was apparent that British respondents found it quite difficult to think of *anything* which made them feel proud to be European, but had far fewer problems when discussing objects of *national* pride. In fact, not only did the British respondents express significantly lower levels of European than national identity, but they often construed these two social identities as *mutually incompatible*, or what Hofman (*op. cit.*) might have called dissonant.

Given the congruence of qualitative and quantitative data across all three phases of the current research, it seems that there is good evidence that British national identity is stronger, more salient, and more positive, than its European counterpart. When considered in the context of previous research (e.g. Hewstone, 1986; Furnham and Gunter, 1989; Sotirakopoulou, 1991), and the extensive *Eurobaromètre* surveys, there seems little reason to suggest that the current results will be limited to the student subject groups on which they were based. A strong British national identity, and a weak, poorly defined European equivalent, seems compatible with the existing body of, albeit largely attitudinal, data. For example, when the question "Do you ever think of yourself as a citizen of Europe? Often, sometimes or never?" was posed in *Eurobaromètre* polls 17 and 19, large groups of respondents (especially in the UK) "never" thought of themselves as citizens of Europe. A further question of interest asked whether respondents felt the EC should go further than a single Common market. It is interesting when considering the possibility of a European identity being embraced by the British, to note how some 57 per cent of British respondents in 1988 suggested that the EC should NOT go further than a common market, with only 24 per cent being in favour of going further. This contrasts sharply with the responses of the Italians in the 1988 poll, which indicated that some 71 per cent were in favour of going beyond a common market, with only 12 per cent being against such moves (cf. *Eurobarometre 29*).

In marked contrast to the British, Italian respondents in the cross-national questionnaire study manifested a European identity which was significantly stronger, in terms of salience and affective dimensions, than their Italian national identity (Multivariate $F(7,123) = 7.893$, $p < .001$). A further MANOVA analysis indicated that the Italian respondents expressed a significantly stronger overall level of European identity than the British respondents (Multivariate $F(7,229) = 4.465$, $p < .001$). Significant univariate differences emerged between the British and Italian respondents on three quantitative measures of European identity, two of which may be considered to tap both the fit and accessibility elements of salience (cf. Oakes, 1987) respectively, and one of which relates to perceptions of interdependence.

It is our contention that one of the primary reasons for the Italians appearing to manifest both more positive attitudinal orientations, and a stronger European identity, than the British, is precisely because many Italians construe the networking between their national and European identities as compatible, and even mutually reinforcing. One of the more important bases for such a construal, appears to be the hope that closer ties with the European Community might bring some order to an Italian nation plagued by corruption, organised crime, and inefficiency (cf. Barzini, 1983; Cinnirella, 1993). In some ways therefore, Italian pro-Europeanism may in part be associated with attempts to bolster an otherwise faltering sense of Italian *civic identity*—i.e. that part of national identity specifically associated with the state and its institutions.

One further element of networking, concerns the frequent interconnections forged between political affiliations and European sentiments. These interactions between political and European identities in Britain are often rather more complex than seems to be the case in other European nations, such as Italy. While in Europe, there is an overall trend for left-wing parties and their supporters to be more pro-European than their right-wing counterparts (cf. recent *Eurobarometre* surveys), in Britain it is often much more difficult to perceive clear-cut party differences. Here, the key in many ways appears to be the desire to simply take the opposite stance to that adopted by one's political opponents. This fluctuating relationship between political and European identities was apparent in the current research. In the first phase questionnaire, Conservative respondents expressed a significantly weaker, and more negative European identity than Labour voters (Multivariate $F(7,49) = 2.897$, $p = <.025$; cf. Cinnirella, 1993). However, in the third phase questionnaire, there were found to be no significant

Table 16.1 MANOVA comparing perceived importance of goals for European integration across political orientation (British respondents)

Overall multivariate effect (Pillais Test):
Value = 0.268 F (10,70) = 2.565   Sig. of F = 0.011   (n = 81)

Significant univariate effects:
Ensuring the economic prosperity of Britain
Left-wing mean = 6.773; Right-wing mean = 8.000 p < 0.033
Preventing the loss of separate national identities
Left-wing mean = 5.432; Right-wing mean = 8.081 p < 0.001
(Importance ratings ranged from 1 (not important) to 10 (extremely important))
(Significance levels derive from F-tests, and are 2-tailed)

---

differences on European identity measures between left-wing and right-wing respondents, in keeping with the unstable relationship between politics and European issues in Britain.

Nevertheless, orientations to Britain and Europe have their *qualitative* as well as quantitative aspects, and this being the case, a MANOVA was conducted on third-phase data, in order to investigate whether left and right-wingers differed in the importance they attached to various goals for European integration (Table 16.1). It can be seen from an examination of Table 16.1, that there is evidence for a multivariate difference in importance ratings (Multivariate $F(10,70) = 2.565$, $p < .011$). Significant univariate differences occur on two questions, with right-wingers in both cases rating the goal as more important than left-wingers. The first goal pertains to the economic prosperity of Britain, with the second suggesting that the preservation of separate national identities is important. Given the fact that right-wingers often appear to manifest a stronger level of British identity (Cinnirella, 1991), it is not surprising that they should stress these two dimensions, both of which have dominated the mass media coverage of European issues (cf. Sotirakopoulou, 1991), as well as being prominent themes in open-ended responses throughout the various phases of the current research. What is perhaps most pertinent about these two goals, is that they both tend to have the interests of Britain at their heart, as indeed, many right-wing respondents appeared to have.

Social Representations as a Context for Social Identity Construction

European and national identities are in a state of flux at present, with the fate of one being tightly bound-up with that of the other. Moves towards further European integration demand that citizens re-think the meaning and nature of nationhood. At the same time, one should note that existing social representations of nations and Europe constitute a context and background within which new social representations may be negotiated. These new representations may therefore derive in part from a re-working of existing social beliefs, with new and potentially challenging social representations being *anchored* into more comfortable, existing systems of beliefs (Moscovici, 1984). The major vehicle for the dissemination of these social representations is the mass media—especially newspapers and television (Schlesinger, 1991). When citizens come to construe their national, European, and other social identities, they do so only after taking stock of the pertinent social representations available to them.

It is, therefore, almost impossible to ask questions about national and European identities without also raising the issue of relevant social representations on which such identities are based. Since representations of European nations, and even of European integration, have been circulating in society for a good few centuries now, the study of European integration is certainly not just the study of *new* social representations—it is the study of how new representations are networked and anchored into existing ones, and, furthermore, how such networks of representations lay the foundations for the construction and re-formulation of social identities.

Respondents across all three phases of the current research reported that they seldom discussed matters concerning European integration, either with their immediate peers, or with other people in general. This being the case, the mass media subsume an especially critical role as purveyors of information about European integration.

The Role of the Mass Media in the Construction of Large-scale Social Categories

One of the reasons why the mass media are so crucial in the analysis of European integration, is that both national and European identities are based upon membership of *large-scale social categories (LSCs)*. While social identity theorists have assumed their theories are broadly applicable to all manner of social categories and groups (see, for example, Turner, 1984), large-scale, diffuse entities such as nations, raise some serious problems, especially for the Self-Categorisation Theory (SCT) of Turner and associates (Turner, 1987). One case in point concerns the nature of social influence processes in LSCs. Turner's referent informational influence model (Turner, 1991; Turner and Oakes, 1989) is largely based upon laboratory experiments where the process of social influence is reduced to brief, decision-making encounters where group norms and beliefs are conveniently reduced to positions on fixed-response scales, with potentially disastrous consequences for external validity. Unfortunately, outside the environment of the psychological laboratory, conflicting norms, stereotypes, and social representations clamour for the attention of in-groupers, who are typically not armed with a battery of questionnaires for their fellow in-groupers to complete and thus aid them in discerning the group's beliefs. The referent informational influence model leaves the possibility of group beliefs becoming enshrined in relatively stable social representations unexplored. Furthermore, the treatment of group leadership and status structures, which might conceivably have cross-situational stability, is simplistic. Leadership, for example, involves much more than simply being perceived as prototypical of the category, despite what Turner and his associates would have us believe (see, for example, Turner and Oakes, 1989).

Social influence processes are particularly complex in large-scale social categories, where in-groupers will typically only ever interact with a sub-group of the wider category. This being the case, in-groupers might court the approval of particular sub-groups, but not be overly concerned with the norms and beliefs associated with other sub-groups of the wider category. In a similar manner, self-presentation and audience effects may be specifically associated with particular sub-groups—after all, it is only those with access to the mass media who can manipulate their self-presentation at a nation-wide level. Since the task of discerning the key beliefs and norms of large-scale categories and groups is potentially problematic, the mass media play a crucial role, since it may be only via newspapers, television, and film, that large numbers of category members can be reached.

The media also serve to increase the *salience* of LSCs at certain times. It seems to be the case that identities based on potentially diffuse social category memberships often lie dormant and below everyday consciousness thresholds, somewhat reminiscent of what Ralph Turner has termed a "subterranean level of consciousness" (R. H. Turner, 1987). This, however, should not disguise the inherent *potency* (Hofman, 1988) such identifications have *when aroused*, and it is the media who often play a large part in encouraging their re-emergence. Future research might endeavour to investigate what we might call *critical situations*—these are events, situations, perhaps just locations, which are especially likely to make particular social identities salient. It is already fairly obvious that war, for example, almost always represents a critical situation for national identity. The charting of such critical situations might enable a better understanding of when large-scale social categories and groups may come to influence behaviour and social perception. In part, such recommendations are reminiscent of Walter Mischel's call for a social psychology of situations (Mischel, 1977; see also R. H. Turner, 1987).

Since the mass media play such a crucial role in defining representations and manipulating the salience of large-scale categories, there is an urgent need for further analysis of the mechanisms by which the media achieve such effects. It certainly cannot be assumed that mass media representations filter down unproblematically to readers and viewers (Sotirakopoulou, 1991), and the whole field of mass media effects remains replete with conflicting perspectives and ambiguous empirical findings (cf. Roberts and Bachen, 1981; Roberts and Maccoby, 1985). Clearly, further social psychological investigation of this field would benefit both the social representations and social identity paradigms.

The British Mass Media and European Integration: Cod Wars, Delors, and Yorkshire Puddings

Those few researchers who have published work which includes content analysis of the media treatment of European integration, have tended to conclude that the British mass media have been particularly negative and suspicious about the whole issue, at least over the last decade or so. Hewstone (1986) for example, pointed to the frequent use of negative metaphors in the British media treatment of European issues, such that much time was spent discussing the unfortunate existence of butter mountains, wine lakes, and cod wars between British and French fishermen. If, as Hewstone (op. cit.) suggests, the British tend to have a traditional dislike for the French, then the mass media appear to be adept at ensuring such ill-feeling continues—we cannot forget in a hurry one of the headlines which adorned the *Sun*, Britain's most widely read daily newspaper, on 1 November 1991—it simply read: "Up yours Delors!" An additional tendency, especially in the British tabloid press, has been a persistent focus on some of the more bizarre and at times apparently senseless ramifications of EC legislation. Thus there has been much debate over the future of the traditional British sausage, whether Yorkshire puddings will have to be manufactured in Yorkshire to warrant their name, and so on. The effect of such stories is to trivialise the whole process of European integration, and to suggest that in some sense, elements of British tradition and culture are under threat from the European project.

Despite the fact that researchers know relatively little about the mechanisms behind mass media effects, there nevertheless remains an interesting parallel between the comments of British respondents in empirical research, and trends apparent in media content. Sotirakopoulou (1991) for example, found that both the *Guardian* and *The Times* adopted similar orientations to European integration, in both cases voicing concern over encroachments upon national sovereignty, and the threat posed to national identity. Of crucial importance here is that these very same issues were at the heart of respondents' comments and answers in Sotirakopoulou's interview and questionnaire research.

Similar concerns appeared to underlie the relatively unenthusiastic orientations many British respondents adopted towards European integration in the current research. Open-ended responses from both the questionnaire and interview data indicated that British respondents tended to feel their national identity to be threatened by the loss of sovereignty and ultimate control over national matters they perceived to be associated with European integration. In the third phase questionnaire, when respondents came to rate the importance of a variety of goals for European integration, "preventing the loss of separate national identities" was rated as significantly more important than "encouraging a sense of common European identity" ($p < .001$, 2-tailed). Many British respondents felt European integration might entail a loss of national identity, as if a European identity could not be embraced without having some detrimental effect upon national sentiment.

The Italian Media: European Integration? The Sooner the Better ...

In contrast, the mass media in Italy have tended to adopt a rather positive orientation towards European integration and the EC. There has certainly been much less concern about the EC encroaching upon national sovereignty than that voiced in Britain. This favourable mass media attitude appears to be mirrored in that of the Italian people, at least, as far as opinion poll data is considered. Thus, in *Eurobaromètre* polls, the Italians are almost always the most ardent supporters of both the EC and the process of integration in general (see also, Hewstone, 1986). In an opposite manner to the British, many Italian respondents in the current research appeared to actually want the EC to have *more* power over Italian affairs than it currently has, presumably because they feel EC governing bodies are more efficient than their Italian counterparts (see also *Eurobaromètre* 29 for congruent patterns in attitudinal data).

Whatever Happened to the Individual in Social Identity Theory?

There is a sense in which both Tajfel's social identity theory, and Turner's self-categorisation paradigm, chose to ignore any detailed questions about the nature of self, and, more generally, issues associated with individual differences (cf. Schiffman and Wicklund, 1992).

Motivation—Is Self-esteem Maintenance Enough?

Recently, it has been suggested, or sometimes implied, that the social identity paradigm cannot be conveniently divorced from such issues any longer (see for example, Abrams, 1992; Breakwell, 1986, 1991; Deaux, 1992). One aspect of this neglect of self and individual differences pertains to the adequacy of motivational constructs contained within the social identity paradigm. It is in some ways quite bizarre that self-esteem maintenance *via positive distinctiveness* has often been the *only* motivation directly addressed by social identity theorists. This is bizarre in as much as theorists not directly associated with the theory have often postulated a variety of other probable motivations associated with social identity (see, for example, Deaux, 1992; Doob, 1964; Stagner, 1967). Deaux has made the interesting suggestion that attachment to ascribed social identities is more related to "fundamental questions of meaning and self-knowledge" than self-esteem motivations (Deaux, 1992, 26). In a similar vein, Mitchell (1981) has proposed that being a member of a large-scale social group such as a nation provides the individual with a sense of psychological comfort and security. Abrams, himself generally sympathetic to the social identity paradigm, has proposed that consistency, control, material wealth, meaning, power, self-efficacy, and self-knowledge all be added to the list of potential motivating factors behind social identity construction (Abrams, 1990, 1992).

In many ways, the social identity paradigm has dwelt exclusively on self-esteem maintenance via positive distinctiveness since this is so often at the heart of intergroup conflicts, the phenomena which have, to a large extent, driven social psychologists in this area. However, groups do not always engage in intergroup conflict, and it is just as important to explain everyday social identity construction in relatively pacific groups. In addition, recent theorising in the social identity paradigm suggests the possibility of groups which do not rely on frequent intergroup comparisons (cf. Brown *et al.*, 1992). In such *autonomous groups* (Brown *et al.*, *op. cit.*), positive distinctiveness often seems to take second place to motivations such as psychological security, stability, and so forth. If the social identity paradigm is truly the complete theory of group processes Turner (1987) claims it is, then the motivations behind autonomous groups must be examined, and urgently.

Over the three empirical phases of the current study, evidence emerged which seemed to demonstrate how motivations of power and control appear to play an important part in the construction of both national and European identities, especially in Britain. British respondents appeared to demonstrate in open-ended responses a marked concern for matters of sovereignty, and a desire to exert control over world affairs, both of which seem suggestive of the importance of control and power motivations in the current context. In the third phase of research, British respondents were asked to indicate the extent to which they either agreed or disagreed with a variety of motives which might potentially be associated with British and European identities. It can be seen from Table 16.2, that control, autonomy, and distinctiveness were perhaps the most strongly endorsed motivations associated with British identity.

What is particularly interesting, is that the self-esteem measure was endorsed significantly less than the top three motives. While the importance of distinctiveness as a motive is certainly supportive of social identity theory, the relatively low level of support for the self-esteem motive is also rather problematic for Tajfel's variant of the social identity paradigm. It seems quite likely, given the saliency of the national sovereignty issue for the British, that the motives for autonomy and control might be especially linked to British identity *when this identity is considered in the context of European integration.* One interesting avenue for further research on motivation and identity to explore, is to attempt to map out and perhaps predict what kinds of situations and identities are associated with various motivations, and whether fluctuations in these associations are at all systematic.

It can be seen from Table 16.3 that the pattern of motives typically endorsed by respondents when they thought about European identity, is rather similar to that associated with British identity. In particular, one may note the primacy of control as a motivation, which was in fact, endorsed significantly more than all other motives in the analysis. Once again, it is also important to observe how self-esteem appears to be among the *least* important motivations included, being endorsed significantly less than control, power, autonomy, distinctiveness, and stability.

Table 16.2 Mean endorsement of British Identity motives

Motive	Abbreviation	Mean response
Control	CON	4.252
Autonomy	AUT	4.241
Distinctiveness	DIS	4.198
Power	POW	3.826
Stability	STA	3.776
Self-esteem	S-E	3.713
Self-preservation	S-P	3.661

(Response scale: 1 (Disagree with motive) – 7 (Agree with motive))
ANOVA (repeated measures): F (6, 106) = 4.162, p = 0.001
"Protected" t-tests comparing mean ratings – Significance of differences (2-tailed):

	S-E	AUT	STA	CON	POW	DIS
AUT	0.007					
STA	n.s.	0.006				
CON	0.003	n.s.	0.016			
POW	n.s.	0.042	n.s	0.008		
DIS	0.002	n.s.	0.011	n.s.	0.028	
S-P	n.s.	0.002	n.s.	0.003	n.s.	0.004

Table 16.3 Mean endorsement of British Identity motives

Motive	Abbreviation	Mean response
Control	CON	4.283
Autonomy	AUT	3.973
Distinctiveness	DIS	3.774
Power	POW	3.614
Stability	STA	3.605
Self-esteem	S-E	3.211
Self-preservation	S-P	3.070

(Response scale: 1 (Disagree with motive) – 7 (Agree with motive))
ANOVA (repeated measures): F (6, 106) = 7.963, p = 0.001
"Protected" t-tests comparing mean ratings – Significance of differences (2-tailed):

	S-E	AUT	STA	CON	POW	DIS
AUT	0.003					
STA	0.029	n.s.				
CON	<0.001	0.012	<0.001			
POW	0.001	n.s.	0.017	0.045		
DIS	0.050	n.s.	n.s.	<0.001	0.032	
S-P	n.s.	<0.001	0.003	<0.001	<0.001	0.002

It does seem likely that some motives may not be tapped by self-report measures of the type utilised in the third-phase questionnaire. In many ways therefore, the aspect of motivation addressed herein is probably best described as part of the *self-concept*, i.e. that part of the self readily accessible to the respondents.

Orientation towards National and European Identities

A further means by which individuals might come to *customise* their social identities, much in the same way that Breakwell (1991) has suggested they customise social representations, is in terms of the *orientation or type of attachment* individuals adopt towards the identity. Kelman (1969), for example, himself specifically interested in national identity, proposed that some individuals develop *sentimental* attachments to the nation, which are based on emotional ties to national culture and symbols. National identity based upon sentimental attachments is likely to be particularly robust and affect-laden, and is usually accompanied by the internalisation of a nationalistic ideology. Those individuals who reject such ideologies might still develop an attachment to the nation, but one which is based on *instrumental* dimensions, such as gains versus losses type analyses of the benefits associated with citizenship, satisfaction with political organisations and public services, etc. While the distinction between sentimental and instrumental attachments may sometimes appear blurred, Kelman has nonetheless provided a useful conceptual tool for examining the different manifestations of national identity, and, it is suggested here, such a distinction can also be usefully applied to the subject of *European* identity. Among other things, a knowledge of the kind of orientation adopted towards European identity might offer clues as to its stability, its potency (Hofman, 1988), and its salience (cf. Oakes, 1987). Despite the limitations of such potentially simplistic heuristic devices, it is, nevertheless, interesting to note how the sentimental-instrumental distinction is highly congruent with similar notions suggested by Hewstone (1986), Inglehart and Reif (1991), and others. In as much as different orientations might in turn be reflected in differences at the level of motivations associated with identities, then such constructs might aid the further investigation of the motivational bases of social identification. There would be much utility in future research which attempted to investigate the situations, social representations, and so forth, which influence the orientation adopted towards a social identity.

In the current study, open-ended questionnaire and interview responses suggested a multi-dimensional British identity, encompassing instrumental orientations based largely upon satisfaction with democratic and other state institutions, but also strong sentimental orientations to Britain, deriving from a powerful attachment to national culture and heritage. When it came to thinking about being European, something which British respondents found rather difficult, instrumental orientations predominated, with the pros and cons of integration being carefully weighed-up, and no sense of common cultural ties within Europe, which might have allowed for a sentimental/symbolic attachment (cf. Cinnirella, 1993). In contrast the Italians often felt their cultural and historical heritage to be intimately bound-up with that of Europe. The allegiance to Europe and further integration many Italian respondents demonstrated was, rather like their Italian national identity, both instrumental *and* symbolic in nature—the Italians did think about what they might get out of integration, but they also were aware of symbolic ties with their European neighbours. These differences serve to demonstrate that British and Italian manifestations of European identity differ in both quantitative *and* qualitative terms, and both dimensions should be given equal import.

Possible Selves and the Temporal Dimensions of the Self

One of the more subtle factors able to differentiate between those who are broadly pro-European and those who feel wary of European integration, is the nature of the temporal perspective adopted. Here, the notion of *possible selves* (Markus and Nurius, 1984, 1986, 1987) is useful. These essentially represent individuals' beliefs about what they were in the past, what they are at present, and what they might become in the future. I would like to suggest an extension of the possible selves concept to encompass both individual and *group-located* possible selves. Such shared possible selves might be similar to the notion of perceptions of *cognitive alternatives* to the intergroup situation (Tajfel and Turner, 1979, 1986) which may come to be shared between in-groupers. In as much as possible selves appear to be in both culture (e.g. the media) and cognition (e.g. self-schemas—cf. Markus and Nurius, 1987), their study offers interesting possibilities for collaboration between researchers working within the fields of social identity, social cognition, and social representations.

In terms of possible selves and their relevance for the current discussion, it is useful to consider the impact of the British empire and its aftermath. As Hewstone (1986), Crick (1991), and other theorists have suggested, social representations of the empire are likely to enjoy considerable longevity, and there is a sense in which the British continue to believe that Britain remains the most powerful nation on the face of the earth. In open-ended responses to the questionnaire and interview questions, there certainly was evidence for such beliefs, which essentially involve a focus on the Britain of the past—what we might here call a *past-oriented* possible self. When considering European integration, many British respondents felt such a possible self was under threat—losing sovereignty somehow involved not just a loss of *current* power and control, but was also perceived as being incompatible with Britain's imperial *past*. Those few Britons who *were* eager to embrace a European identity tended to adopt a *future-oriented* perspective, dwelling on what *might* be achieved, and making use of positive future possible selves. In a similar manner, the Italian respondents were much more concerned with the future, typically feeling that European integration was an endeavour with great potential. Such opinions are congruent with *Eurobaromètre* data which indicate that the Italians do not necessarily feel they have gained a great deal *yet* from EC membership—the crucial point is that they feel they may do so *in the future*. In essence, therefore, there are indications that a European identity is more likely when a positive, future European possible self is perceived, and, crucially, *desired*.

In phase three of the current research, this association between European identity and possible selves was further examined, this time at a more quantitative level, and using only British respondents. The sample was split into two groups, based on whether respondents felt that being European will become more ($n = 66$) or less ($n = 23$) important by the year 2000. A between-subjects MANOVA was then conducted, with the European identity measures as dependent variables. Despite unequal cell-sizes, homogeneity of variance assumptions were met, and the MANOVA indicated a significant multivariate difference between groups (Multivariate F (7,81) = 3.09, p <.006). Inspection of the univariate statistics indicated that, on all European identity measures, those respondents who felt being European would become more important, reported significantly higher levels of European identity than respondents who felt being European would become less important. This provides at least suggestive, quantitative evidence of an association between European identity and possible selves. In particular, it seems that a more positive orientation towards a European future is often associated with at least an embryonic sense of European identity. Such results should be considered in the light of the congruent observations arising from the open-ended questionnaire and interview responses from the previous phases of the current research.

Forging a Stronger European Identity: Some Suggestions

The integrative approach which begins to emerge from the perspective forwarded in the current discussion has certain implications for the future of European integration. If integration is to be readily embraced then it requires both favourable social representations and, to an extent, the acceptance of some form of European identity. It is possible to sketch out in a general way some of the factors which might facilitate a more favourable climate towards integration and the EC in Britain. These might include:

1. Encouraging perceptions of an *outgroup* with which to compare Europe. There is certainly nothing quite like an outgroup, in terms of power to encourage in-group homogeneity and solidarity. From the current research, it emerged that the USA and Japan are already used by some British and Italian respondents as out-groups for Europe (see also Billig, 1992a, 1992b, regarding the USA as an outgroup). However, given that recent research in the social identity paradigm has pointed towards the possibility of groups which make few intergroup comparisons (Brown *et al.*, 1992), one should perhaps

ask the question: should a comparative European identity be encouraged when it might lead to potentially conflictual intergroup relations?

2. Make European identity and orientations towards integration more *multi-dimensional* in Britain. If the Italian example is informative, then it might be wise to encourage a greater awareness of the *cultural* possibilities inherent in European integration, and to stress that these do not in any way threaten national culture, but rather complement it. Such a development largely depends on changes in the identity orientation adopted by British citizens, which in turn relies on social representations of integration being broadened to include cultural dimensions. The key point here is that European integration can be perceived as more than just the EC and economic integration, and if perceptions are broadened, then they might be more resilient when EC membership sometimes appears detrimental to Britain in economic terms.

3. *Networking* national and European identities so that they are perceived as *mutually compatible*, rather than conflcitual. Alternatively, national and European identities might be construed as *unrelated*. Italy, the USA, and other nations, serve to demonstrate the viability of both regional and national identities which can co-exist in a relatively harmonious manner. There is no reason to suppose that a homologous construction of national and European identities might not also be possible. If European identity is posited as a truly *continental-level identity*, then it could co-exist with national identities. The crucial point here is to remove the destructive perception of European integration and Euro-identity as a *threat* to national identity in Britain.

4. *Balancing mass media representations of integration and the EC.* As the primary source of social representations concerning European issues, the mass media could be encouraged to adopt a more balanced approach to such matters, and to avoid where possible the kind of trivialisation so tempting to the tabloids. It is only by means of a change in the social representations circulating in society, that the changes in social identity construction recommended in points 1–3 above might be possible.

5. *A European socialisation and education.* Attitudes and general emotional orientations to nations are forged rather early in childhood, before children are even able to fully comprehend what nations and continents actually are (Tajfel and Jahoda, 1966). Furthermore, education often instils a particularly nationalistic perspective on world history, such that the similarities, cultural and historical ties between European nations, tend not to be presented (see also Robinson, 1991). It seems, therefore, that a European identity would be most robust if also instilled during this critical period, when socialisation in the family and via education has such power to instil favoured social representations and identities. There are already encouraging indications from the *Eurobaromètre* opinion polls that, across Europe, the young are perhaps the most enthusiastic about integration. This suggests, perhaps, that social representations and social identities might be more malleable at an early age.

These suggestions are tentative in nature, and by no means meant to exhaust the list of possible strategies by which a European identity might be instilled. In as much as social psychologists often have little power to influence the mass media, educational practices, and so on, then the realisation of these strategies might be over-optimistic. Of course, by no means everyone desires a European identity or the general process of European integration to develop. I do not feel the need to detail possible strategies which might be employed by those who would wish to *prevent* or *stifle* a sense of European identity—such people, it would appear, are realising their aims quite successfully in Britain at present, without any need for advice from social psychologists. It is worth noting, however, that the antithesis of many of the strategies outlined in points 1–5 could also be employed by those who wished to *prevent* the emergence of a European identity and pro-European orientation. For example, such individuals might choose to downplay the possibility of any European outgroup(s); attempt to maintain a unidimensional and instrumental orientation to Europe; suggest that national and European identities are incompatible; continue to distance European issues from the general public; diffuse negative social representations of integration via the mass media; and ensure a strongly nationalist and anti-European environment in early socialisation and education.

Conclusions

The study of European integration holds much promise for the development of new, integrative methodological and theoretical approaches in social psychology. The perspective suggested in the current discussion is one which is based on the assumption that questions of social identity and social representation are often inseparable. This is particularly the case in terms of European integration, where the different perspectives adopted by citizens in Britain and Italy, for example, may well be traceable to different identity constructions, which, ultimately, derive from rather different social representations.

Paradoxically, the fact that European integration raises problems for the social identity paradigm is, in a way, more a reflection of the paradigm's promise than of its limitations. It is suggested that the social identity paradigm could have much more to say about large-scale social categories and individual differences, if some of its current assumptions are periodically challenged and developed. Despite outlining a number of weaknesses in the social identity paradigm, this is a theoretical perspective worth developing and persisting with, as Roger Brown (1986) noted, there is something about social identity theory in particular which just intuitively seems right. Given the tenacity of intergroup conflicts throughout the world, now, more than ever, social psychology requires an adequate theory of social identification and its role in group processes.

References

Abelson, R. P., and Prentice, D. A. (1989). Beliefs as possessions: a functional perspective. In A. R. Pratkanis, S. J. Breckler and A. G. Greenwald (eds), *Attitude Structure and Function*. Hillsdale, N.J: Lawrence Erlbaum Associates.

Abrams, D. (1990). How do group members regulate their behaviour? An integration of social identity and self-awareness theories. In D. Abrams and M. A. Hogg (eds), *Social Identity Theory—Constructive and Critical Advances*. Hemel Hempstead: Harvester Wheatsheaf.

Abrams, D. (1992). Processes of social identification. In G.M. Breakwell (ed.), *Social Psychology of Identity and the Self Concept*. London: Surrey University Press/Academic Press.

Allen, V., Wilder, A. and Atkinson, M. (1983). Multiple group membership and social identity. In T. Sarbin and K. Scheibe (eds), *Studies in Social Identity*. New York: Praeger.

Barzini, L. (1983). *The Impossible Europeans*. London: Weidenfeld and Nicolson.

Billig, M. (1992a). *Talking of the Royal Family*. London: Routledge.

Billig, M. (1992b). Monarchy, nationalism and equality. Paper presented at research seminar, Department of Social Psychology, London School of Economics and Political Science, 10 March.

Breakwell, G. M. (1986). *Coping with Threatened Identities*. London: Methuen.

Breakwell, G. M. (1991). Identity, social representations and action: sex and politics. Presented at the British Psychological Society Annual Conference (social psychology section). University of Surrey, Guildford, 20–22 September.

Brown, R. (1986). *Social Psychology*, 2nd edn. New York: Free Press.

Brown, R. J., Hinkle, S., Ely, P. G., Fox-Cardamone, L., Maras, P. and Taylor, L. A. (1992). Recognizing group diversity: individualist-collectivist and autonomous-relational social orientations and their implications for intergroup processes. *British Journal of Social Psychology*, **31**, 327–42.

Bruner, J. S. (1957). On perceptual readiness. *Psychological Review*, **64**, 123–51.

Cinnirella, M. (1991). Social identity theory and European integration: a study of national and European identity in the U.K. and Italy. Presented at the British Psychological Society Annual Conference (social psychology section), University of Surrey, Guildford, U.K., 20–22 September.

Cinnirella, M. (1993). Social identity perspectives on European integration: a comparative study of national and European identity construction in Britain and Italy. Ph.D. thesis, London School of Economics and Political Science (University of London).

Crick, B. (1991). The English and the British. In B. Crick (ed.), *National Identities: the Constitution of the United Kingdom*. Oxford: Basil Blackwell.

Deaux, K. (1992). Personalizing identity and socializing self. In G.M. Breakwell (ed.), *Social Psychology of Identity and the Self Concept*. London: Surrey University Press/Academic Press.

Doob, L. (1964). *Patriotism and Nationalism: Their Psychological Foundations*. New Haven: Yale University Press.

Duveen, G. and Lloyd, B. (1986). The significance of social identities. *British Journal of Social Psychology*, **25**, 219–30.

Euro-Baromètres, (1974–). Brussels: Commission of the European Communities (English language edition).

Festinger, L. (1954). A theory of social comparison processes. *Human Relations*, **7**, 117–40.

Fraser, C. and Foster, D. (1984). Social groups, nonsense groups and group polarization. In H. Tajfel (ed.), *The Social Dimension: European Developments in Social Psychology*, vol. 2. Cambridge/ Paris: Cambridge University Press, Maison des Sciences de l'Homme.

Furnham, A. and Gunter, B. (1989). *The Anatomy of Adolescence: Young Peoples' Social Attitudes in Britain*. London: Routledge.

Hewstone, M. (1986). *Understanding Attitudes to the European Community: A Social-psychological Study in Four Member States*. Cambridge: Cambridge University Press.

Himmelweit, H. T. (1990). Societal psychology: implications and scope. In H. T. Himmelweit and G. Gaskell (eds), *Societal Psychology*. London: Sage.

Hofman, J. E. (1988). Social identity and intergroup conflict: an Israeli view. In W. Stroebe, A. W. Kruglanski, D. Bar-Tal and M. Hewstone (eds), *The Social Psychology of Intergroup Conflict*. New York: Springer Verlag.

Hyman, H. H. and Singer, E. (eds) (1968). *Readings in Reference Group Theory and Research*. New York: The Free Press.

Inglehart, R. and Reif, K. (1991). Analyzing trends in West European opinion: the role of the Eurobarometre surveys. In K. Reif and R. Inglehart (eds), *EUROBAROMETER: The Dynamics of European Public Opinion*. London: Macmillan.

Katz, D. (1960). The functional approach to the study of attitudes. *Public Opinion Quarterly*, **24**, 163–204.

Kelman, H. C. (1969). Patterns of personal involvement in the national system: a social psychological analysis of political legitimacy. In J. M. Rosenau (ed.), *International Politics and Foreign Policy—A Reader in Research and Theory*. New York: The Free Press.

Lorenzi-Cioldi, F. and Doise, W. (1990). Levels of analysis and social identity. In D. Abrams and M. A. Hogg (eds), *Social Identity Theory—Constructive and Critical Advances*. Hemel Hempstead: Harvester Wheatsheaf.

Lyons, E. and Sotirakopoulou, K. (1991). Images of European countries. Presented at the British Psychological Society Annual Conference (social psychology section), University of Surrey, Guildford, 20–22 September.

Markus, H. and Nurius, P. (1984). Possible selves. Presented at British Psychological Society Self and Identity Conference, University College, Cardiff, Wales, July.

Markus, H. and Nurius, P. (1986). Possible selves. *American Psychologist*, **41**(9), 954–69.

Markus, H. and Nurius, P. (1987). Possible selves: the interface between motivation and self-concept. In K. Yardley and T. Honess (eds), *Self and Identity: Psychosocial Perspectives*. Chichester: John Wiley & Sons.

McCall, G. J. (1987). The structure, content, and dynamics of self: continuities in the study of role-identities. In K. Yardley and T. Honess (eds), *Self and Identity: Psychosocial Perspectives*. Chichester: John Wiley & Sons.

Mischel, W. (1977). The interaction of person and situation. In D. Magnusson and N. S. Endler (eds), *Personality at the Crossroads: Current Issues in Interactional Psychology*. Hillsdale, NJ: Erlbaum.

Mitchell, C. R. (1981). *The Structure of International Conflict*. London: Macmillan.

Moscovici, S. (1984). The phenomenon of social representations. In R. M. Farr and S. Moscovici (eds), *Social Representations*. Cambridge/Paris: Cambridge University Press, Maison des Sciences de l'Homme.

Moscovici, S. (1988). Notes towards a description of social representations. *European Journal of Social Psychology*, **18**(3), 211–50.

Nesdale, A. R. (1989). Category salience: distinctiveness or functionalism? In J. P. Forgas and J. M. Innes (eds), *Recent Advances in Social Psychology: An International Perspective*. Amsterdam: North-Holland.

Oakes, P. J. (1987). The salience of social categories. In J. C. Turner, M. A. Hogg, P. J. Oakes, S. D. Reicher and M. S. Wetherell (eds), *Rediscovering the Social Group: A Self-categorization Theory*. Oxford: Basil Blackwell.

Potter, J. and Wetherell, M. (1987). *Discourse and Social Psychology: Beyond Attitudes and Behaviour*. Sage: London.

Roberts, D. F. and Bachen, C. M. (1981). Mass communication effects. *Annual Review of Psychology*, **32**, 307–56.

Roberts, D. F. and Maccoby, N. (1985). Effects of mass communication. In G. Lindzey and E. Aronson (eds), *The Handbook of Social Psychology*, 3rd edn. New York: Random House.

Robinson, P. (1991). Human beings and barbarians in the states of Europe. Presented at the British Psychological Society (Social Psychology section) annual conference. University of Surrey, Guildford, 20–22 September.

Scheibe, K. E. (1983). The psychology of national identity. In T. R. Sarbin and K. E. Scheibe (eds), *Studies in Social Identity*. New York: Praeger.

Schiffman, R. and Wicklund, R. A. (1992). The minimal group paradigm and its minimal psychology. *Theory and Psychology*, **2**(1), 29–50.

Schlesinger, P. (1991). *Media, State and Nation: Political Violence and Collective Identities*. London: Sage.

Sotirakopoulou, P. K. (1991). Processes of social representation: a multi-methodological and longitudinal approach. PhD thesis, University of Surrey.

Stagner, R. (1967). *Psychological aspects of international conflict*. Belmont, Ca.: Brooks-Cole.

Tajfel, H. (1974). Social identity and intergroup behaviour. *Social Science Information*, **13**(2), 65–93.

Tajfel, H. and Jahoda, G. (1966). Development in children of concepts and attitudes about their own and other nations: a cross-national study. *Proceedings of the XVIIIth International Congress of Psychology*, Symposium 36, 17–33, Moscow.

Tajfel, H. and Turner, J. C. (1979). An integrative theory of intergroup conflict. In W. G. Austin and S. Worchel (eds), *The Social Psychology of Intergroup Relations*. Monterey, Calif.: Brooks/Cole.

Tajfel, H., and Turner, J. C. (1986). The social identity theory of intergroup behaviour. In S. Worchel and W. G. Austin (eds), *Psychology of Intergroup Relations*. Chicago, Ill.: Nelson-Hall.

Turner, J. C. (1984). Social identification and psychological group formation. In H. Tajfel (ed.), *The Social Dimension: European Developments in Social Psychology*, vol. 2. Cambridge: Cambridge University Press.

Turner, J. C (1987). A self-categorization theory. In J. C. Turner, M. A. Hogg, P. J. Oakes, S. D. Reicher and M. S. Wetherell (eds), *Rediscovering the Social Group: A Self-categorization Theory*. Oxford: Basil Blackwell.

Turner, J. C. (1991). *Social Influence*. Milton Keynes: Open University Press.

Turner, J. C. and Oakes, P. J. (1986). The significance of the social identity concept for social psychology with reference to individualism, interactionism and social influence. *British Journal of Social Psychology*, **25**, 237–52.

Turner, J. C., Hogg, M. A., Oakes P. J., Reicher S. D. and Wetherell, M. S. (eds) (1987). *Rediscovering the Social Group: A Self-categorization Theory*. Oxford: Basil Blackwell.

Turner, R. H. (1987). Articulating self and social structure. In K. Yardley and T. Honess (eds), *Self and Identity: Psychosocial Perspectives*. Chichester: John Wiley & Sons.

Zavalloni, M. (1971). Cognitive processes and social identity through focused introspection. *European Journal of Social Psychology*, 235–60.

Zavalloni, M. (1973). Social identity: perspectives and prospects. *Social Science Information*, **12**, 65–92.

Acknowledgements

This research was funded by ESRC research award R00429024719.

17

Social Representations of History and Attitudes to European Unification in Britain, France and Germany

DENIS J. HILTON, HANS-PETER ERB, MARK DERMOT AND DAVID J.
MOLIAN

*Ecole Supérieure des Sciences Economiques et Commerciales,
Cergy-Pontoise, France, University of Mannheim, Germany, University of
East London, England and Imperial College School of Management,
England*

One of the uses of myth is that it explains why the world is the way it is. Take the example of the Gonja tribe of Northern Ghana given by Goody and Watt (1963). When the tribe was first studied at the beginning of this century, their land was divided into seven territories. When asked to explain their history, they explained that they were descended from a great ancestor, Ndewura Jakpa, who had seven sons, and that when he came down from the Niger Bend to conquer and settle the land he gave a piece of land to each of his sons, thus creating the seven territories. Subsequently, the land was reorganised into five territories, because one had supported an invader, and the British introduced boundary changes. Some fifty years later, when asked about their history, the Gonja gave the same answer as before, but with a slight modification. The great ancestor Ndewura Jakpa, they said, had five sons.

Goody and Watt (1963) use this example to illustrate Malinowski's claim that a myth may serve as a "charter" which justifies why the world is the way it is, by explaining how it came to be that way. Our aim in this paper is to explore how European histories may also function as "charters" for the peoples of Europe, which shape not only their sense of themselves, but also their view of the world around them and their attitudes to it. In particular, we shall consider how different representations of recent European history in Britain, France and Germany may be related to their attitudes to European integration, as expressed by the 1991 Maastricht Treaty. We conclude by discussing the importance of representations of history in the formation of national identity, and strategies for its management.

Social Representations of History and National Identification in Europe

Europe is closely identified with history in the popular imagination. One speaks of the "Old World", and tourists flock to Europe to experience the heritage enshrined in old and beautiful cities such as Oxford, Cambridge, Paris, Heidelberg, Vienna, Venice and Prague, rather than to bathe in the sun or admire natural wonders. It is thus surprising that social psychologists have paid little detailed attention to the role of perceptions of history in forging European identities. Thus Bloom (1992), in a thorough review of the relationship between personal identity, national identity and international relations, does not discuss how representations of history may play a part in forming national identity. Likewise, Hobsbawm (1992) refers to a common past as one of the building blocks of nationalism, along with a common ethnicity, language and culture, without exploring its function in detail. Hewstone (1986) briefly considers the role of history in shaping attitudes to the European community, but in terms of the historic reasons which led countries to join (or not to join), rather than in terms of the mental representations of history currently held by inhabitants of member countries.

Writers such as Bloom, Hewstone and Hobsbawm have paid more attention to factors such as shared language, ethnicity or political and economic objectives in the formation of national identity. It may be tempting to regard collective consciousness of a shared past as epiphenomenal, while other factors, such as perceived economic costs and benefits, will determine attitudes to issues such as membership of the European community (Hewstone, 1986). In this view, socially shared representations of European history may be regarded as a kind of cognitive anachronism, a sort of mental residue laid down through schooling, media and tale-telling that has no real influence on current political attitudes. However, we will argue that such representations can have an important influence on political attitudes. Moreover, this influence may be quite independent of utilitarian and other considerations.

Structure, Function and Salience of Social Representations of History

Social representations of history are important to forging national conscious-ness just as an individual's biography is crucial to the formation of personal identity (Greenwald, 1980). A group's history defines its achievements and uniqueness in much the same way that an individual's history does for the person.

However, there are important differences between national history and personal biography.

Firstly, collective representations of history are the subject of intensive media discussion in the press, and on radio and television (Moscovici, 1984). Secondly, they are implicit "causal theories" which explain and justify attitudes (Moscovici, 1984). Thirdly, they are shared representations that explain group similarity and cohesion rather than individual differences in attitudes or personality (Jaspars and Fraser, 1984). And finally, they are representations that are disputed by different groups in a pluralistic society (Moscovici, 1989). This may be seen at an international level, as in the "Bomber Harris" controversy over wartime bombing between Britain and Germany in late 1992, or in the *Historikerstreit* ("Battle over history") between German historians in the late 1980s. Consequently, unlike personal biographies, national histories are social representations which underpin socio-political attitudes.

These differences between national history and personal biography may help explain why attempts to generalise theories of social identity to national groups have tended to overlook the role of history in the construction of national identity. In the first place, theories of social identity tend to privilege the role of group membership rather than individuating characteristics such as personality or biography in the formation of personal identity (Tajfel and Turner, 1979). Furthermore, many of the kinds of groups customarily studied (social class, sex, occupation) tend not to define themselves in terms of history. While an individual might find pride in his own personal biography in becoming rich after poor beginnings, rare indeed is the justification of one's pride in being middle class by reference to the great achievements of the bourgeoisie in history.

Nevertheless, representations of history may be manipulated to serve the functions of bolstering self-esteem through valorisation of one's group. This is a basic postulate of social identity theory, as when, for example, economically disadvantaged blacks in America and Britain privilege success in sports, music and "cool", dimensions on which they score relatively well compared to more prosperous whites (Tajfel and Turner, 1979). Thus, economically disadvantaged Britain may privilege the concept of a "just war", which accords her moral superiority over her wartime opponent, Germany, as well as warranting her status as a world power, represented by such symbols as her place on the UN Security Council. Morally disadvantaged Germany may, on the other hand, may dispute the moral superiority of the British in the Second World War (as in the dispute over the ethics of bombing civil populations at the end of 1992), and privilege the importance of economic motivations in explaining international action. Such differing strategies for obtaining nationally mediated self-esteem may well explain the quite differing ways that Britain and Germany reacted to the Gulf war crisis in 1990, with Britain emphasising military solutions and Germany economic ones (Hilton, 1993).

As well as serving important social identity functions, social representations of history also have structural properties that argue for their importance. History has the form as well as the function of myth; that is to say, as well as explaining how the world came to be the way it is, history makes for great stories. What British schoolboy has not thrilled to the story told of the Battle of Britain, when a few latter-day knights in their Spitfires and Hurricanes stood between Hitler's Nazi hordes and the destruction of Christian civilisation? What French schoolchild has not admired the courage of resistants from Joan of Arc to Jean Moulin and Charles de Gaulle, or the genius and ambition of Napoleon? Consequently, history has properties that make it a "strong" representation in the sense of Sperber (1984). That is, historical stories are likely to establish themselves widely and durably in society, due to the propensity of the human mind to retain narrative structures in memory (Bower, 1976; Mandler and Johnson, 1977; Thorndyke, 1977).

Incidental evidence suggests that such social representations of history may indeed influence a national group's behaviour. One line of evidence comes from McClelland's (1961) analysis of the relationship between childhood folktales and national economic performance. McClelland showed that the achievement imagery content of folktales told to schoolchildren in twenty-five different countries was not related to the contemporary economic output of those countries, but predicted economic output in those countries twenty-five years later. This prediction is consistent with McClelland's view that cultural "symbol systems" (e.g. folktales) influence thought and behaviour, not the other way round. History, of course, would seem to be just such a cultural "symbol system".

More closely related to our current concerns is the finding of Schuman and Rieger (1992) that Americans' favourability to the Gulf War was predicted by their preferred historical analogy. Thus Americans who considered the comparison between the Gulf War and the Second World War to be most apt, comparing Hussein to Hitler and emphasising the justice of the war, were more likely to favour intervention in the Gulf than Americans who favoured the Vietnam analogy, which stresses the probability of losing a war that few Americans today consider to have been a just one. Schuman and Rieger (1992) observed strong generational effects in the distribution of these representations at the outset of the Gulf crisis, in that older Americans preferred the analogy with the Second World War, whereas younger Americans preferred the analogy with Vietnam. Clearly, generational experience predisposed acceptance of different representations. Interestingly, however, as the outbreak of war neared, the Second World War analogy began to dominate in both groups.

In conclusion, there seem to be good reasons on both functional and structural grounds to expect that social representations of history are related to political attitudes. In particular, we expect that social representations of recent European history will be related to attitudes to European unification. As we will recount below, allusions to history came to figure prominently in public debate about the Maastricht Treaty.

Historical Allusions in the Public Debate over the Maastricht Treaty

Shortly after the successful re-unification of Germany in 1990, the twelve member states of the European Community signed the Maastricht Treaty in December 1991. The Maastricht Treaty pledged major steps forward to the long-heralded steps of European unification. In particular, the Twelve agreed to the institution of a single European currency, common social and immigration policies, and an integrated foreign and defence policy, with the exception of Britain which held a single currency as an option, and was exempted from the social chapter.

The Maastricht Treaty stimulated an international debate over the pros and cons of European unification. Referendums were held in Denmark, Ireland and France during the summer of 1992. The Danes rejected the treaty narrowly, the Irish were largely in favour, and the French accepted it by a slender majority. The degree of public scepticism about Maastricht surprised both the politicians who had signed the treaty, and the markets, whose loss of confidence in the ideal of economic unification contributed to the forced exits of the British pound and Italian lire from the European Monetary System. These events fostered the perception that the enthusiasm of the political and economic elites for European unification had got ahead of general public opinion.

This *decalage* between the opinions of Euro-enthusiasts and others was perhaps most clear in France, traditionally well-disposed to the European community (Hewstone, 1986). Until a few months before the referendum in September 1992, there was a clear majority of 65–70 per cent in favour of the treaty. However, in the last weeks, a strong cross-party coalition of extreme right, centre-right and left-wing anti-Europeans threatened to overturn this majority. After strong counter-attacks from pro-European centre-right and centre-right politicians, the Maastricht Treaty was supported by 51 to 49 per cent.

Of more particular interest for the present analysis than opinion poll swings is the way in which the political debate developed in France during this period. For example, as debate heated up in the weeks before the referendum, more and more frequent explicit reference was made to the Germans, to such an extent that *Liberation* carried an article on how Germans were becoming wearied and even "scandalised by their caricature". Whereas debate had initially focused on economic and political advantages stemming from European unification, later appeals on both sides explicitly referred to the nature of French and German identity, the march of history and so on. For example, in a televised interview, Jack Lang, the No. 3 of the French Government, argued for European unification on the grounds that if it had not been taking place, Western Europe would risk tearing itself apart in the same manner as the ex-Yugoslav states were currently doing. Moreover, he argued for accepting currency unification on the grounds that the Germans would not always be willing to sacrifice their Deutschmark.

By the end of the French referendum campaign, then, the public debates had moved on from economic and political issues of monetary union, social rights and foreign policy to wider issues having to do with national identity and the lessons of history. The question therefore arises as to what extent attitudes to European unification are determined by "utilitarian" issues, by which we mean the traditional "pocketbook politics" concern with policies which affect a voter's material well-being and wealth, such as employment, income, job and personal security, as opposed to other factors, such as emotional reactions, social identifications, social perceptions and social representations of history. However, even this very general question remains to be investigated empirically. Below, we report an exploratory three-nation study which addresses this relationship in the context of other factors that may be expected to predict attitudes to European unification.

Utility, Social Identity, Social Perception and Social Representations of History in Formation of Attitudes to European Unification

Our aims in investigating the relationship between social representations of history and attitudes to European unification were twofold. Firstly, we wanted to establish whether there was indeed a relation between social representations of history and attitudes to European unification. And secondly, we wanted to establish whether any relationship between social representations of history and attitudes to European unification exists independently of other cognitive structures such as the utilitarian consequences of European unification, social identifications, attitudes to foreigners, emotional reactions to European unification, and perceptions of national heritage.

The first set of factors we studied we term *utilitarian* issues, following Hewstone (1986). These issues have to do with the perceived costs and benefits of the Maastricht Treaty. We predicted that the more that respondents agreed that European unification would lead to positive rather than negative consequences, the more they would have positive attitudes to European unification. Such a relationship would be consistent with the theory of reasoned action proposed by Fishbein and Ajzen (1975), which has been used to explain a wide range of behaviours, including voting (Ajzen and Fishbein, 1980). We considered these utilitarian issues to define a "rational baseline" model of preference.

The second kind of factor that we considered was social identification, either with one's country or with Europe. We considered that those who identified strongly with their own country would be against European integration, particularly if subjects perceived an opposition between their national identification and European identification. We suspected that this might be the case with the British (cf. Cinnirella, 1993). Subjects who identified themselves as European would, we expected, be in favour of European unification. This last prediction would be in keeping with previous research which showed that German subjects who felt themselves to be German and were proud of being German were more in favour of German re-unification (Hilton *et al.*, 1992). This study showed that both the attitudes to German re-unification of both the students and non-students studied were relatively weakly associated with beliefs about the "utilitarian" consequences of re-unification (effects on employment, income, national security etc.) but strongly associated by "social identification" factors, such as self-identification as and pride in being German and feelings of connectedness with East Germans.

The Hilton *et al.* (1992) study also found that attitudes to re-unification in West Germany were more strongly correlated with emotional reactions to re-unification rather than "cold cognitions" involving pragmatic analyses of the costs and benefits of re-unification (cf. Abelson *et al.*, 1982). We therefore included measures of respondents' emotional reactions to European unification to see to what extent they were related to such "hot cognitions".

Another set of factors that we expected might influence attitudes to European unification was attitudes to foreigners. We predicted that xenophiles would be in favour of European unification whereas xenophobes would be against. For all three national groups we measured attitudes to salient national groups that were both part of and not part of the European community.

We also expected that the perceived importance of one's national heritage might influence attitudes to unification. One might expect that Britons who value the British Commonwealth might be against European unification for fear of losing this heritage, whereas Germans who value their technical skills might be in favour, due to the improved access to export markets.

Finally, we assessed respondents' representations of history by presenting them with certain key events in recent European history and asking them to explain them. For example, we predicted that British and French respondents who endorsed internal attributions which blamed Germans for Hitler's rise to power in 1933 rather than external explanations which deculpabilised them would be against European unification, since they would not want to share a "common space" with Germans. On the other hand, Germans who showed this pattern of attribution might be predicted to favour European unification as a means of counterbalancing dangerous tendencies in the German people.

Using this framework, we conducted a study of attitudes to European unification in three countries in the summer and autumn of 1992: Britain (November 1992), France (September, 1992) and Germany (June 1992). Our aim was not to conduct opinion polls in these three countries, but to study comparable populations of social science and business students in each country in order to assess different structures of opinion in the three countries. We were interested to assess the relative contribution of utilitarian, social identification, social perception and historical social representation factors on attitudes to European unification. To summarise, we predicted that British, French and German subjects would all be favourable to European unification to the extent that: a) from a utilitarian point of view, the benefits of European unification were perceived to outweigh its costs for one's country; b) one had a strong European but a weak national identification; c) one had a favourable attitude to national groups in the European community; and d) European unification was associated with positive rather than negative emotional reactions. In addition, we had a number of more specific predictions about the relationship between perceptions of national heritage and social representations of history and attitudes to European unification which we shall describe when we present the target events used.

Subjects

Subjects were thirty-five British psychology and business students drawn from the University of East London and Imperial College Management School, London; forty French business school students from the Ecole Supérieure des Sciences Economiques et Commerciales (ESSEC), Cergy-Pontoise; and 50 German social science and business students from the University of Mannheim.

Method

In all three countries, the same overall design was used for the study, which was administered in the form of a questionnaire which took approximately twenty-five minutes to complete. However, the exact questions used and their wording varied slightly from country to country.

Firstly, respondents were asked a series of questions about "utilitarian" issues related to European unification, such as whether they were in favour of a single European currency, tightening or loosening immigration controls, allowing foreigners to vote in elections, of their own country playing a leading role in Europe. They were also asked to assess their agreement on seven-point scales for assertions about the likely consequences of European unification on such things as their own country's language and culture, their own country's job market, their own country's farmers and environmental protection. British and French but not German subjects were also asked whether they agreed that European unification would enable other European countries to counterbalance the power of a unified Germany and whether it would allow European countries to develop a properly effective foreign policy.

Secondly, respondents were asked a series of questions about their social identifications. Thus they were asked to mark on seven-point scales the extent to which they were proud of their nationality, felt themselves to be British/French/German, and felt themselves to be European.

Thirdly, respondents were asked a series of questions about their emotional reactions to Europe. They were thus asked to mark on seven-point scales how they felt when they thought about a completely unified Europe, whether it made them feel: happy; European; disappointed; enriched; content; worried; patriotic; or disadvantaged.

Fourthly, they were asked about their perceptions of other social groups. Thus they were asked to mark on eleven-point scales (ranging from -5 to +5) how much they liked various peoples. The target nationalities used for each group are given in Table 17.1.

TABLE 17.1   Mean scores for selected items

	Britain	France	Germany
Attitudes to			
European unification	4.69	5.17	3.22
Beliefs related to European unification			
For single currency	3.78	2.83	2.96
For welcoming immigrants	3.51	3.06	3.71
For vote for foreigners	4.58	2.83	4.72
For principal role of one's own country in Europe	5.96	4.98	3.26
Fear bad cultural effects on one's own country	2.87	2.45	2.16
EU will improve job market	4.53	4.15	3.48
EU will worsen situation of farmers in won country	4.40	3.72	4.26
EU will increase environmental efforts	5.89	5.79	3.52
EU will enable unified and effective foreign policy	4.36	4.66	///
EU will enable other countries to counterbalance Germany	4.38	4.94	///
Social identifications			
Proud of one's own nationality	4.67	5.41	3.12
Extent to which I feel British/French/German	4.34	5.72	3.90
Extent to which I feel European	4.07	5.24	4.68
Emotions evoked by European unification			
Happy	4.36	5.00	3.80
European	4.24	5.24	4.42
Disappointed	2.32	1.89	2.32
Enriched	3.73	4.47	4.66
Content	4.11	5.00	4.06
Afraid	3.89	2.42	3.60
Patriotic	3.38	3.91	1.92
Disadvantaged	2.53	2.23	2.48
Liking for other nationalities			
Americans	7.41	7.98	6.92
Arabs	///	6.35	///
English	///	6.91	7.38
French	6.80	///	7.84
Germans	6.40	7.06	///
Indians	7.59	///	///
Italians	8.00	8.74	///
Pakistanis	7.24	///	///
Poles	7.05	7.62	6.14
Portuguese	///	///	7.10
Russians	7.10	7.57	7.28
Spanish	///	8.36	///
Turks	///	///	6.54
West Indians	8.95	///	///

N.B. This scale was measured on an 11-point bipolar scale ranging from very negative to very positive.

Attributions for Hitler's rise to power			
Versailles treaty	4.57	4.41	4.61
Hitler's personality	5.62	5.45	5.08
Fear of Bolshevism	4.27	4.34	3.61
Economic conditions	5.64	5.83	6.20
Lack of democratic tradition	4.53	3.67	4.72
German mentality	4.76	3.25	4.74
Instability of Weimar	4.69	5.20	5.56
Mass unemployment	5.27	5.33	6.14

Fifthly, subjects in all groups were asked to judge how important a series of features were to describing their country (in the case of the British and French), or their nationality (in the case of the Germans). No specific hypotheses were made, and we will report these results selectively, primarily to aid interpretation of other findings.

Finally, social representations of history were assessed. Respondents were asked to evaluate their agreements with attributions for several important events in recent European history on seven-point scales. These events were changed from country to country in accordance with our intuitions about which events had most impinged on the historical consciousness of each country.

Thus all respondents were asked to explain post-war prosperity. In the German case, respondents were asked to evaluate attributions for the post-war German "economic miracle" which laid emphasis on factors either internal or external to the German people:

1. German will to succeed;
2. the advantages afforded by a new beginning after "Zero Hour" (Stunde Null);
3. the support of the Marshall plan;
4. the help of the European community;
5. the technical ability of the Germans.

We predicted that Germans who attributed the German economic miracle to factors internal to the German people would be less favourable to European unification than those who attributed it to external factors.

In the British and French cases, respondents were asked to evaluate attributions of the peace and prosperity of Europe after the Second World War to:

1. the Franco-German entente;
2. the construction of the European community;
3. American involvement in Europe (NATO, etc.); and
4. general conditions of technology, etc.

We predicted that British and French respondents who attributed post-war prosperity to factors internal to Europe would be more in favour of European unification than those who attributed it to external factors.

British and French respondents were also asked to evaluate attributions of the liberation of France to:

1. the over-extension of Germany;
2. the efforts of the French resistance;
3. the efforts of the Free French under de Gaulle;
4. the efforts of the Americans;

5. the efforts of the British;
6. the efforts of the Russians.

We expected that British subjects who attributed the liberation of France most to the efforts of the Americans, British and Russians would be "Atlanticists" who would be against European unification. We suspected that French subjects might reason differently; that if France had been liberated by her own efforts (de Gaulle and the Resistance), then they would be against European unification because a strong France did not need it.

British respondents alone were asked to evaluate attributions for the British victory in 1945 to

1. the will and determination of the British people;
2. British technical skill (radar, sonar, intelligence, etc.);
3. the importance of the cause for which the war was fought;
4. the contribution of the Russians;
5. the contribution of the Americans;
6. the contribution of the British Empire (now Commonwealth);
7. the leadership of Winston Churchill;
8. the natural defence provided by being an island; and
9. mistakes made by the Germans.

Our prediction was that those who attributed British success to internal factors would be against European unification because a strong Britain would not need it.

Finally, British, French and German respondents all had to evaluate attributions of Hitler's assumption of power in 1933 to

1. the consequences of the Treaty of Versailles (peace agreement after the First World War);
2. Hitler's personality,
3. fear of the Bolshevik revolution;
4. economic conditions at that time in Germany;
5. the lack of a democratic tradition in Germany;
6. German mentality (xenophobia, etc.);
7. political disorder in the Weimar republic; and
8. mass unemployment.

We predicted that German subjects who attributed Hitler's rise to power to features internal rather than external to the Germans would be in favour of European unification as a way of counterbalancing dangerous tendencies in the German national character. We predicted the opposite pattern for the British and French; subjects who attributed Hitler's rise to power to factors internal rather than external to the German people would be against European unification, because they would not wish to share a common political space with a people with such negative characteristics.

Each group was administered a measure of their attitude to European unification. For the British and French respondents this variable was phrased as: "To what extent are you for or against ratification of the Maastricht Treaty", whereas German respondents were asked whether they believed that their own national sovereignty should be strengthened or shared out in a European framework. The German phrasing of the dependent variable was different to that used in the British and French samples because, at the time that data were collected (June 1992), we suspected that the Maastricht Treaty as such was not yet salient enough a concept in the mind of German public opinion to form a clear attitude object. In addition subjects were asked whether their attitude towards European re-unification was determined more by emotional considerations or by rational consideration of the pros and cons. Finally, respondents were asked to rate on seven-point scales whether they were left- or right-wing, and to what extent they considered themselves to be religious.

In addition, British and French respondents had to evaluate how well a selected list of features characterised their own country, and German subjects answered a number of questions about which countries they considered to be Germany's most important allies, what they considered to be the personality characteristics of Germans, about the origin of various inventions, and were asked to evaluate a series of historical figures. These questions do not form part of the present study and the results are therefore not reported here, except where they aid interpretation of central issues in the study.

Results

The mean scores for each sample's response to the questions are reported in Table 17.2. We correlated attitudes to the Maastricht Treaty with responses to all other items on the questionnaire. Some of these zero-order correlations are reproduced in Table 17.2. They enable similarities and differences to be established between the three samples in terms of which factors are strongly associated with attitudes to European unification.

Utilitarian Factors and Attitudes to European Unification

The results support the hypothesis that perceptions of the utilitarian costs and benefits of European unification will predict attitudes to it. There are reasonably strong correlations between beliefs about the utilitarian aspects of re-unification and attitudes to European unification in all three samples. This indicates that attitudes to European unification can be generally predicted to be more positive if one favours major commitments of the Maastricht Treaty (single currency, vote for foreigners) or believes that the treaty will have positive effects in some domains (job market, foreign policy, balancing of German power) and will not

TABLE 17.2   Zero-order correlations of selected items with attitudes to European unification

	Britain	France	Germany
Beliefs related to European unification			
For single currency	−0.05	0.64**	0.36**
For welcoming immigrants	0.10	0.32*	0.26*
For vote for foreigners	0.42**	0.35*	0.32*
For principal role of one's own country in Europe	0.07	−0.03	−0.33**
Fear bad cultural effects on one's own country	−0.19	−0.51**	−0.09
EU will improve job market	−0.43*	0.36*	0.24*
EU will worsen situation of farmers in won country	−0.33*	−0.29*	0.17
EU will increase environmental efforts	0.07	0.25	0.11
EU will enable unified and effective foreign policy	−0.00	0.42*	///
EU will enable other countries to counterbalance Germany	0.34*	0.23	///
Social identifications			
Proud of one's own nationality	−0.01	0.03	−0.19
Extent to which I feel British/French/German	−0.00	0.10	−0.01
Extent to which I feel European	0.26	0.11	0.01
Emotions evoked by European unification			
Happy	−0.05	0.31*	0.10
European	0.32*	0.30*	0.04
Disappointed	−0.06	−0.19	−0.28*
Enriched	0.26	0.37*	0.27*
Content	0.15	0.46**	0.27*
Afraid	−0.15	−0.28*	−0.25*
Patriotic	−0.14	−0.02	−0.32*
Disadvantaged	−0.08	−0.16	−0.11
Correlations with liking for other nationalities			
Americans	−0.08	0.09	−0.26*
Arabs	///	0.39**	///
English	///	0.19	0.05
French	−0.01	///	−0.19
Germans	−0.06	0.04	///
Indians	0.13	///	///
Italians	0.04	0.40**	///
Pakistanis	0.16	///	///
Poles	0.16	−0.12*	0.16
Portuguese	///	///	0.17
Russians	0.32*	0.11	−0.14
Spanish	///	0.25	///
Turks	///	///	0.02
West Indians	0.03	///	///
Attributions for Hitler's rise to power			
Versailles treaty	0.53**	0.21	−0.04
Hitler's personality	−0.23	0.48**	−0.08
Fear of Bolshevism	−0.04	0.30**	−0.09
Economic conditions	−0.05	−0.02	−0.12
Lack of democratic tradition	−0.46**	−0.00	0.01
German mentality	−0.24	0.09	0.07
Instability of Weimar	−0.07	0.30*	−0.27
Mass unemployment	0.14	−0.02	−0.15

have negative effects in other domains (cultural effects on one's own country, effects on farmers). On the whole, the results support the view that a utilitarian analysis of the economic and political costs and benefits of Maastricht affects attitudes to the treaty in all three samples.

However, there are considerable differences between the samples as to which variables are strongly related to attitudes to Maastricht. Thus, favouring a single European currency is strongly associated with favourable attitudes in the French and German samples, but not the British one, perhaps reflecting the fact that France and Germany are obliged by the treaty to accept a single European currency, whereas Britain is not. Conversely, opposition to the treaty is associated with fears of negative cultural effects on one's own culture in the British and French samples, but not the German one, perhaps reflecting a greater pride in the unique nature of their own national traditions in Britain and France but not Germany.

Social Identifications and Attitudes to European Unification

There was none of the predicted relationships between attitudes to European unification and pride in one's own nationality, the extent to which one feels British/French/German, or to which one feels European. This null result is surprising if one assumes that identification with one's national group or the idea of Europe should affect attitudes to European integration (e.g. Cinnirella, 1993). The same questions had been good predictors of West Germans' attitudes to German re-unification (Hilton et al., 1992). However, this null result throws into relief the significance of the correlations with attitudes to European unification obtained with other measures. We will return to this null result in the discussion.

Emotional Reactions and Attitudes to European Unification

Attitudes to European unification are weakly associated with degrees of emotional reactions in all three countries. In no case did we observe the strength of correlations that we observed between emotional reactions and attitudes to German re-unification in West German samples in 1990 (Hilton et al., 1992). Our conclusion is that European unification does not seem to be a central attitude topic (Krosnick and Abelson, 1992), strongly associated with emotional reactions.

Perception of Other National Groups

Liking for some peoples from other countries correlated significantly with attitudes to the Maastricht Treaty in all three samples. As would be expected, positive attitudes to the Maastricht Treaty correlated with positive attitudes to other national groups, except in the German case where favourability to European unification correlated with negative attitudes to Americans. However, these results were intermittent and moderate in strength, indicating that these factors have only a weak impact on attitudes to the Maastricht Treaty. We thus move directly on to the results concerning the relationships between attributions for historical events and attitudes to European unification.

Social Representations of History and Attitudes to European Unification

None of the German sample's attributions for the German economic miracle correlated with attitudes to European unification. In the British sample, none of the attributions for post-war prosperity correlated with attitudes to European unification. However, as predicted in the French sample, attitudes to European unification correlated positively with attributions of post-war prosperity to the Franco-German entente ($r = .36, p < .01$) and to the construction of the European community ($r = .27, p < .05$). No other significant correlations were observed for this event.

In the British sample, positive attitudes to European unification correlated negatively with attributions of France's liberation in 1994 to the efforts of the French resistance (-.30) and the Russians (-.31), and attribution of Britain's victory in 1945 to the will and determination of the British people (-.29). No significant correlations were observed in the French sample for the Liberation in 1944. Finally, we come to an event that was presented to all three samples, namely Hitler's rise to power in 1933. The results show that attributions for this event correlate significantly with attitudes to European unification in all three countries. The British and French results are strong (all $ps < .01$) and seem relatively easy to explain. Endorsements of internal attributions which imply that the Nazi period is due to something about the nature of the Germans (e.g. their lack of democratic tradition) were correlated with negative attitudes to European unification, whereas attributions which implied that the Nazi period was due to external, transient factors (e.g. Versailles peace treaty, Hitler's magnetic personality, fear of Bolshevism) were correlated with positive attitudes to European unification. These patterns seem consistent with the view that the British and French are going to feel more comfortable about inhabiting a common European "space" with the Germans if they endorse attributions which lessen their implied responsibility for the Nazi period and predict that it is unlikely to re-occur.

From the German point of view, however, the line of reasoning may be expected to be different. We interpret the correlation of attributions of Hitler's rise to power to the instability of the Weimar Republic with negative attitudes to European unification in the following way: Germans who believe that Nazism was due to the instability of the Weimar Republic fear a repetition of this scenario due to the sacrifice of the Deutschmark, which has guaranteed them economic stability since the Second World War.

In sum, attitudes to European unification seemed to be correlated with utilitarian beliefs, emotional reactions to unification, attitudes to foreigners and representations of certain key events in recent European history but not to social identification. We return to this last point later. Below, we consider the question as to whether social representations of history contribute independent variance in predicting attitudes to European unification.

Multiple Regression Analyses of Factors Predicting Attitudes to European Unification

We performed some follow-up regression analyses to assess whether social representations of history explain unique variance in attitudes to European unification. In all three national groups, we entered three of the strongest "utilitarian" variables in first, and then examined whether other types of variables could be entered which would improve the predictive power of the regression equation.

In the British sample ($n = 35$) the regression equation created by entering the belief that the vote should be given to foreigners, the belief that European unification will improve the home job market and the belief that European unification will enable other countries to counterbalance Germany explained 33% of the variance in attitudes ($r^2 = .58$, $p < .01$). We found that the regression equation would be improved by entering attributions of Hitler's rise to power to a lack of democratic tradition ($t = -3.24$, $p < .005$) or to the Versailles treaty ($t = 3.18$, $p < .005$), by the belief that the Liberation of France in 1944 was due to the efforts of the French Resistance ($t = -2.83$, $p < .01$) and marginally by the belief that the British Commonwealth is an important feature of Britain ($t = -1.98$, $p < .06$). The other variables selected, attitudes to the Russians, belief that the French liberation was due to the contribution of the Russians, and belief that the British victory in 1945 was due to the will of the British people, did not add any significant explanatory power.

A similar analysis was performed on the French sample ($n = 40$). We began by entering utilitarian beliefs that there should be a single European currency, that European unification would lead to an improvement in the home job market and belief that European unification would have negative effects on French culture, resulting in an equation that explained 54% of the variance ($r = .73$, $df = 3,33$, $p < .0001$). Three of the selected variables excluded from this equation would add explanatory power if entered: attributions of Hitler's rise to power in 1933 to his personality ($t = 2.19$, $p < .05$) and to the instability of the Weimar Republic ($t = 2.05$, $p < .05$), and the importance of culture in the concept of France ($t = 2.19$, $p < .05$). No additional explanatory power was gained by entering any of the other selected variables into the equation: feeling of happiness in response to European unification; feeling enriched in response to European unification; attitude towards Italians; attitude to Arabs; and attributions of post-war prosperity to European construction.

In the German sample we began by entering the utilitarian beliefs that Germany should adopt a single European currency, that Germany should play the leading role in Europe, and that foreigners should have the vote, thus producing a regression equation that explained 25% of the variance in attitudes to European unification (multiple $R = .50$, $df = 3,47$, $p < .005$). Of the selected variables that we examined, only the judgment that Britain was an important ally ($t = -2.31$, $p < .05$) and feeling patriotic in response to European unification ($t = -2.07$, $p < .05$) would have added explanatory power to the regression equation. The others that failed to do so were the feeling of being disappointed in response to European unification, attitudes to Americans, to East Germans, attribution of Hitler's rise to power to political disorder in the Weimar Republic, considering the Poles to be important allies, and attribution of the failure of the East German state to socialism.

The results for the British and French samples clearly suggest that even when the utilitarian variables are controlled for, the history variables add explanatory power in predicting attitudes to European unification, an important testament of their importance. In the German sample, the finding that beliefs that Germany should retain her own currency and play the leading role in Europe, together with feelings of patriotism evoked by European currency predicted negative attitudes to European unification, suggest that German attitudes to re-unification may well be conditioned by what Habermas (1992) calls "DM-Nationalism", the feeling that Germany has the most powerful economy in Europe and should hold onto the Deutschmark, which gives Germans their high standard of living.

Social Identifications and Attitudes to European Unification

As noted above, the failure to find a statistically significant relationship between measures of national and European identification and attitudes to European unification was surprising. One possible explanation for our failure to find a relationship may have been that we had not properly operationalised these variables. However, inspection of the data did not support this conjecture. To begin with, with our measures of national pride ("How proud are you to be x") and self-categorisation ("How x do you feel yourself to be") were convergent in all three samples. Thus these measures correlated .58, .57 and .58 (all $ps < .05$) in the British, German and French samples respectively. These two measures correlated with our European self-categorisation measure ("How European do you feel yourself to be?") respectively .29 and .16 in the British sample (both n.s.), .15 and .23 in the French sample (both n.s.), and .08 (n.s.) and -.25 ($p < .05$) in the German sample. Consequently, the measures appeared to have some internal coherence. Furthermore, our social identification measures appeared to behave quite as would be expected in other ways.

Thus, our measures of national identity seemed to predict quite a number of judgments in all three samples. Strong national identification tended to be associated with hostility to admitting foreigners or giving them the vote, attributions for history which valorise the ingroup, and valorisation of the positive aspects and devalorisation of the negative aspects of one's national heritage. If an outgroup is valorised, either through attributions or favourable perceptions, it tends to be the Americans or the Russians rather than a European neighbour. Our conclusion is that our measures of national identification are generally valid, even if they do not predict attitudes to European unification.

What of our measure of "feeling European"? Inspection of the data shows that this measure correlates with many of the measures of emotional responses to European unification, but with relatively few others. However, these feelings (of being European, enriched, patriotic) were not the classic simple emotions (happiness, fear) that were strongly evoked by German unification in German subjects (Hilton *et al.*, 1992). Although we also measured these emotions here, their relatively low correlation with feelings of being European and attitudes to European unification suggest that this social identification and this issue were less involving for our subjects than national identification and German re-unification were for German subjects. Nevertheless, the fact that "feeling European" does correlate with a number of variables does suggest that this social identification does have at least some importance in predicting opinions and attitude positions.

The finding that national and European identifications did correlate with social representations of history and perceptions of national heritage suggests that the concepts are related in some network of "national self-concept" beliefs. However, the association may not be perfect, and certain types of beliefs may be more relevant in some contexts than others. For example, at the cognitive level, representations of history may serve as political "scripts" (cf. Abelson, 1973) which are cued by certain contexts, such as foreign policy decisions. It is for this reason that they, rather than other cognitive structures such as self-categorisation or perceptions of involved foreigners, may "drive" political choices about European unification. Schuman and Rieger's finding of a strong association between Americans' preferred "scripts" for the Gulf War (in terms of analogies with World War II or Vietnam) and policy preferences provides support for such a view.

If this is so, we may have to expand our notion of a "national self concept" to include a complex of weakly-linked cognitive structures such as degree of national identification, but also possession of culturally shared beliefs about the nation's history and heritage. Principles of cognitive consistency predict that there should be coherence between these sets of beliefs, but this need not always be the case. For example, as Hewstone (1986) notes, Italians appear to have a very high opinion of themselves but a very low opinion of Italy, whereas the reverse appears to be have been true of West Germans. Such dissociations point to the need to differentiate separate components of a "national self-concept".

Conclusions

The study has investigated the correlates of attitudes to European unification in Britain, France and Germany. In all three cases, "utilitarian" factors predict support for European unification, broadly confirming the findings of Hewstone (1986), although the particular factors given the most weight vary from country to country. However, in Britain and France, attributions for Hitler's rise to power in 1933 also predict support for European unification, quite independently of utilitarian factors. In the German sample, attributions for Hitler's rise to power correlate significantly with attitudes to German re-unification, although they did not add independent predictive power to a regression equation including utilitarian factors. The finding that attributions about the past do not predict attitudes to European unification independently does not of course imply that they have no effect on these attitudes; it is quite possible that their effect is mediated through other variables. It is possible, for example, that the French and the Germans are in favour of a common currency (the strongest predictor of attitudes to European unification in these samples) because of historical factors. In this context, it is worth noting that French support for a single currency is predicted by attributions of Hitler's rise to power to the Versailles treaty (.35), and that German support for a single European currency is predicted by beliefs that the post-war German economic miracle was due to the Marshall Plan (.31) and the European Community (.29).

The study thus suggests that representations of history may play an important role in understanding attitudes to European unification. In particular, the legacy of Hitler still seems to cast a long shadow over Europe. Arguments about recent European history are therefore not futile squabbles over a past long since dead, rather they are arguments whose results may determine how we deal with our present problems. Social psychologists should therefore recognise the importance of these representations in the construction of a European identity.

Whereas positive social identity is usually thought of as being created through a favourable comparison with others (Tajfel and Turner, 1979), the existence of a troubled history may enable Europeans to construct a positive and coherent self-image, through a comparison of Europe's present unity with her conflict-ridden past. Such a strategy for creating a European identity has the advantage of not creating outgroups, unlike the proposal that Europeans should gain consciousness of their identity through contrasting themselves to the USA and Japan (Cinnirella, 1993). Research on social comparison processes has indeed shown that contrasting the performance of the self to that of oneself at other times, as well as to that of others, is a meaningful source of positive self-evaluation (Smith *et al.*, 1989).

Future research has a number of questions to answer. For example, the study suggests that young educated elites will view the same issue through the prism of world-views conditioned by different "histories". This finding runs counter to the expectation that an "international middle class" will be relatively immune to the appeals of nationalism (Bloom, 1992). The historically informed "prejudice" formed in this way is indeed not the "gutter nationalism" of disfavoured and less educated social groups. However, the "collective wisdom" of such august institutions as *Die Welt* or *Der Spiegel* or the Foreign Office or the Royal Air Force may be all the more pernicious for not being recognised as historically informed prejudice. Although these institutions may contain many individuals who are highly skilled in the utilitarian analysis of pros and cons, due to culturally determined perceptions the premises they start from may be very different indeed. It is for this reason that studies of international differences in attitudes to matters of common European interest may profit from studies of socially shared representations of history.

References

Abelson, R. P. (1973). Structural analysis of belief systems. In R. C. Schank and K. M. Colby (eds). *Computer Models of Thought and Language*. San Francisco: W.H. Freeman.

Abelson, R. P., Kinder, D. R., Peters, M. D. and Fiske, S. T. (1982). Affective and semantic components in political person perception. *Journal of Personality and Social Psychology*, **42**, 619–30.

Ajzen, I. and Fishbein, M. (1980). *Understanding Attitudes and Predicting Social Behavior*. Englewood Cliffs, N.J.: Prentice Hall.

Barzini, L. (1983). *The Europeans*. London: Penguin Books.

Bloom, W. (1992). *Personal Identity, National Identity and International Relations*. Cambridge: Cambridge University Press.

Bower, G. H. (1976). Experiments in story understanding and recall. *Quarterly Journal of Experimental Psychology*, **28**, 511–34.

Cinnirella, M. (1993). A social identity perspective on European integration. Paper presented at the Conference on *Changing European Identities: A Social Psychological Analysis of Social Change*, Farnham, England.

Fishbein, M. and Ajzen, I. (1975). *Belief, Attitude, Intention and Behavior*. Reading, Mass.: Addison-Wesley.

Goody, J. and Watt, I. (1963). The consequences of literacy. *Comparative Studies in Society and History*, **5**, 304–26.

Greenwald, A. G. (1980). The totalitarian ego: Fabrication and revision of personal history. *American Psychologist*, **35**, 603–18.

Habermas, J. (1992). Yet again: German nationalism—A unified nation of angry DM-Burghers? In H. James and M. Stone (eds), *When the Wall Came Down: Reactions to German Re-unification*. London: Routledge & Kegan Paul.

Hewstone, M. (1986). *Understanding Attitudes to the European Community: A Social Psychological Study in Four Member States*. Cambridge: Cambridge University Press.

Hilton, D. J. (1993). The struggle for German history. Unpublished manuscript, ESSEC.

Hilton, D. J., Erb, H.-P. and Strack, F. (1992). Attitudes to German re-unification: Cognitive, emotional and social identification factors. Paper presented at the East-West Meeting of the European Association for Experimental Social Psychology, Munster, Germany.

Hobsbawm, E. (1992). *Nations et nationalisme depuis 1780: Programme, mythe, réalité*. Paris, Editions Gallimard (French translation of *Nations and Nationalism since 1780: Programme, Myth and Reality*, Cambridge University Press, 1990).

Jaspars, J. M. F. and Fraser, C. (1984). Attitudes and social representations. In R. M. Farr and S. Moscovici (eds). *Social representations*. Cambridge: Cambridge University Press.

Joseph, G. (1991). *Une si douce occupation. . . Simone de Beauvoir et Jean-Paul Sartre 1940–1944*. Paris: Albin Michel.

Krosnick, J. A. and Abelson, R. P. (1992). The case for measuring attitude strength in surveys. In J. Tanur (ed.). *Questions about Questions: Inquiries into the Cognitive Bases of Surveys*. New York: Russell Sage Foundation.

McClelland, D. (1961). *The Achieving Society*. Princeton, N.J.: Van Nostrand.

Mandler, J. and Johnson, N. S. (1977). Remembrance of things parsed: Story structure and recall. *Cognitive Psychology*, **9**, 111–51.

Moscovici, S. (1984). The phenomenon of social representations. In R.M. Farr and S. Moscovici (eds), *Social Representations*. Cambridge: Cambridge University Press.

Moscovici, S. (1988). Notes toward a description of social representations. *European Journal of Psychology*, **18**, 211–50.

Schuman, H. and Rieger, C. (1992). Historical analogies, generational effects, and attitudes toward war. *American Sociological Review*, **57**, 315–26.

Smith, R. H., Diener, E. and Wedell, D. H. (1989). Intrapersonal and social comparison determinants of happiness: a range-frequency analysis. *Journal of Personality and Social Psychology*, **56**, 317–25.

Sperber, D. (1984). Anthropology and psychology: towards an epidemiology of representations. *Man*, **20**, 73–89.

Tajfel, H. and Turner, J.C. (1979). An integrative theory of intergroup conflict. In W. G. Austin and S. Worchel (eds), *The Social Psychology of Intergroup Relations*. Monterey, Ca: Brooks Cole.

Thorndyke, P. W. (1977). Cognitive structures in comprehension and memory of narrative discourse. *Cognitive Psychology*, **9**, 77–110.

Acknowledgments

We would like to thank Michelle Bergadaa for her help in obtaining the French subjects in this study, and Ed Fink for helpful comments on a previous version.

18

How Group Membership is Formed: Self Categorisation or Group Beliefs? The Construction of a European Identity in France and Greece

XENIA CHRYSSOCHOOU

Université Paris V René Descartes, France

The coincidence of several fundamental disturbances has once again forced Europe into a critical phase in its history. The reunification process under way in certain countries and the important changes in the Eastern half of the continent, as well as the upsurge of nationalism and its tragic results, witnessed in the ex-Yugoslavia, form the heavy burden of almost existential questions which Europe asks itself today.

We find ourselves before a social field which beckons us to test the conceptual instruments available within social psychology. It provides us with the opportunity to use social psychological theories previously tested in the "artificial" context of the laboratory, to explain why people are killing each other in ex-Yugoslavia, why after the euphoria which accompanied the fall of the Berlin wall, the East Germans still find themselves estranged from their Western "brothers", and moreover why is European unification not readily supported by the public in several European countries.

But are problems such as these within the sphere of competence of social psychology? The response must be "yes". If our theoretical instruments seem to hesitate before the complexity of these problems, this is in no way proof of their incompetence. What is at stake for social psychologists is of major importance. On the one hand at last researchers can test social psychological concepts in a real situation, but perhaps even more importantly, the current social reality obliges researchers to rethink these concepts, widen and change their perspectives.

Our concern is focused in particular on the construction of a European Identity which could emerge along with "belonging" to the EU. Being a citizen of one of the State-Members of the European Union confers both privileges and duties as it automatically generates members of a community, a supra-national category—that of the European.

Do these citizens perceive themselves to be members of a European community and which criteria are involved in this implication?

We are faced with a case where the category exists without constituting a psychological group, as those who are the "elements" of the group do not necessarily consider themselves as such. But at what point, can we affirm precisely that a group (according to the larger sense of the term-category) exists?

This question is not merely posited on an intellectual level. Students of intergroup relations have not lost sight of the fact that belonging to a group can also invite such phenomena as ethnocentrism. Moreover, Europe gives us the possibility to study the growth of a psychological group from its roots. What then are the responses which social psychology can offer and what are the theoretical and empirical directions which we should explore?

Social Psychology and Theories of Identity

The most recent theory of social identity, as it was expressed by Tajfel and his collaborators, marks the return of the individual and seeks to explain phenomena such as intergroup behaviour on an intra-individual level. Thus, for example the personal motivation of each person, as part of the group, to acquire and maintain a positive social identity is at the origin of ethnocentrism. The literature includes abundant experimental research which shows that categorisation, the perception of the world in terms of categories, constitutes the necessary and sufficient conditions for these behaviours to take place.

Turner (1981a and 1981b) enlarged this conception, speaking about self-categorisation (the perception of oneself as being a member of a group) as being a necessary condition for group behaviour. Identification, the "old" concept used by Erikson, becomes a crucial element, not only for group behaviours, but also as a condition of their formation.

A group, in its wider sense category, exists because certain individuals identify or are identified as being a part of the particular group. The forming of categories is a subject which preoccupies cognitive psychology. Here once again is an element which invites us to reflect upon European Unification and the probable birth of a new category of identity, the European, in terms of reference groups and belonging. How do social categories form? In other words how, by which processes and upon what basis, do individuals identify with one category or another, and how do they proceed, when invited to do so, to form new categories?

Turner's theory does not offer a response to this question. Although he sees the processes of self-categorisation and identification as cognitive mechanisms that make group behaviour possible, he is not precise about how these mechanisms work. At the end of his 1981 article, in the *Cahiers de Psychologie Cognitive*, he admits to the limits of his theories but he says that we must not consider these as merely limits or setbacks but rather as indicators of future directions for further research because empirical research does not permit us to understand (1) how the processes of social categorisation are formed and internalised, (2) the conditions under which these identifications become a salient basis for cognitions and behaviour, and (3) the implications of the social identification model for the theoretical and empirical distinction between interpersonal and group behaviour.

These remarks are even more important as they implicitly contain a critique of this model made by Di Giacomo and Leyens (1981) who examined the predictive level of the model, that is to say when and why individuals will define themselves as belonging to a certain category. They conclude that the idea that there is a basis for prediction when the category becomes salient is a tautology, and therefore an unsatisfactory response.

Two logical questions follow, remaining to be elucidated: (a) How does the sentiment of belonging become salient, that is to say how does one pass from a level of belonging to a level of identification? (b) How does a new category of identity come into existence?

Concerning the first question, the argument which consists of saying that the individual, constantly in quest of a positive social identity, will only identify with the categories which can offer him/her a positive feeling of self-esteem, is hardly more convincing than the first hypothesis. Often individuals identify with groups or categories which are associated with negative qualifications and in spite of which these individuals are proud of belonging to such a group.

On the other hand it does not seem sufficient to say that an identity group is created from the moment when individuals are categorised or categorise themselves as members. The simple acknowledgement of one's belonging is not enough for individuals to feel a part of this group. In order for this to happen they must be deeply conscious of this belonging, thus permitting them to identify with the group. We are thus faced with the situation whereby we admit that a psychological group does not exist as the individuals do not identify with it, without asking the question of how they will identify with this entity which hardly exists. The second question, we have raised, thus remains unanswered.

At this stage, it seems important to insert a sort of parenthetical remark. Even though categories such as sex and nationality exist, to which one may belong "de facto", nothing can lead us to suppose that these constitute important reference-identity groups which can be salient for an individual.

This justifies establishing a distinction between "belonging" and "identification". Identification process includes three aspects: (a) knowledge of being part of this group ; what are group beliefs and characteristics; (b) affects towards the group and emotional reactions; (c) commitment. Furthermore, one can, for example, belong to a group without identifying with it: it suffices to consider the example of transsexuals who even though they belong to the category of their original sex, they do not identify with this category. Also, one can very well identify with a group without belonging to it. These processes have been very much discussed concerning reference groups. Simply belonging to a group does not necessarily lead to certain actions, whereas identification can incite the actions which correspond with the group.

Thus a certain psychological continuum may be observed between on one extreme: belonging and non-identifying, and on the other belonging and identifying. Between these two poles, different degrees of identification can be observed, permanent or temporary, activated each time by situational elements. In this way we can explain the individual behaviours in the condition corresponding with Tajfel's minimal paradigm. The experimental situation renders salient, the identification with the only group-belonging possible and available in a given context and thus the individuals have reacted as a consequence of this identification.

However, one should not belittle the importance of identification for the formation of the psychological group. Also, since much empirical data has brought to light the evidence of links between social identity and group behaviour, it is important at present to expand the theory, by taking into account Turner's suggestions concerning the role of (1) variables such as similarity, common fate, proximity, shared threat and other unit-forming factors which function as cognitive criteria for the segmentation of the social world into discontinuous social categories, (2) social influence processes whereby individuals are persuaded by significant others to define themselves in terms of specific social categorisations and (3) other processes whereby social categories are internalised as aspects of the self concept.

Evidently, Turner remains vague on this subject and does not define these processes. It is therefore necessary to elaborate and develop the theory of self-categorisation in order to understand the identity processes in the context of the European Unification.

Having responded to the question of knowing why individuals identify with certain social categories, we must now respond to the question of how. Once these two questions have been elucidated we will perhaps be able to better understand the functioning of reference groups and belonging as we will no longer be obliged to call for explanations on an individual level in order to explain group behaviour.

Belonging to Categories, Identification and Group Formation

In analysing identity, Zavalloni and Louis-Guerin (1984) propose that we consider the individual and his relation to the world, as being objectively situated in a social matrix. The elements of this matrix are the different groups to which people belong "de facto" or by affiliation, such as membership of a given society or culture. This approach contextualises identity which can permit us to understand the elements which become meaningful in reference to what happens in a given social context.

According to this point of view, the group, as a social category, does not exist concretely but rather it constitutes an abstract entity and in this sense, it can only be a reconstruction from the contents of memory. The group cannot have meaning except by its "incarnation" in real or imaginary people or personages and situations, its meaning is only an imprint. It is these people, whether real or symbolic and these situations which found and selectively orient the way each of us apprehends the social world and others. These "image-prototypes" are not only specific personages or situations, but reflect an entire imaginary schema. We can thus conclude that the construction of a group is founded and coexists with "image-prototypes" which can be either real or imaginary.

The content as well as the formation of these "image-prototypes", must then be studied. Obviously the imaginary schema is particular to each individual. Nevertheless it should not seem strange to say that there exists a common shared basis for at least the larger categories in which one has been socialised.

This common basis observable in the representations of social categories should be investigated in order to understand the impact of identity on the behaviour and actions of groups. Studying the content of "image-prototypes" as they are portrayed by the individual members can help clarify the manner by which these members perceive and experience their belonging, and also the degree to which they identify with this category, and at the same time it can reveal to us the elements which compose the common basis shared by the individual members.

This level of analysis justifies our turning towards Bar-Tal's approach (1990) which introduces the concept of group belief. According to this conception, the members of the group share beliefs, and in particular certain ones which can be said to constitute the "groupness" or principle of cohesion holding the group together.

These beliefs are the origin of the formation of groups. The group entity is constructed based upon a certain number of group-beliefs that the individual members are conscious of sharing. The individuals identify as belonging to a certain group as they consider that the group constitutes an entity of which they are a part. These beliefs do not constitute a super-existential entity of the group but rather it is the individuals who hold these beliefs. The fundamental element of psychological group formation must then be group beliefs, convictions that the members of the group are conscious of sharing and which they consider as defining their "groupness" within the social field.

This argument has the advantage of reinstating the group at the heart of this debate. This permits us to pass over the explanation of group behaviour by intra-individual factors and thus, to provide explanations on the intra-group level, or even on an ideological level. It is in our interest, we believe, to return to the study of the social group as an entity, to posit it as an object of research if we wish to understand the identity processes at the social level as well as inter-group relations.

With this proposition it is not a question of denying the importance of the process of self-categorisation or identification as they were described by Turner. Bar-Tal himself said that the approach goes beyond self-categorisation, without however abandoning this approach. According to this conception the emphasis is put on the fundamental group belief "we are a group" for the formation of groups. At the same time, in order for a category of individuals to become a psychological group it is necessary to have other group beliefs which can define the unity and essence of the group so that it can develop coordinated and interdependent activity.

It therefore seems reasonable to hypothesise that the group beliefs render salient the already existing aspect of *de facto* belonging, and secondly that they constitute the cognitive basis upon which individuals can choose to identify with one category or another. These salient categories would then be considered important for individual's definitions of self-concept. From the moment when individuals consider that certain group beliefs are shared and define an entity, one can claim that a new psychological group has been created. Following this, on the basis of group beliefs, the individuals will perceive themselves as being part of this group. However, someone could argue that individuals do not always choose the groups to belong to, as it seems to have been suggested. In these cases, the individuals, even though they are categorised as belonging to certain categories, may not be concerned with them at the level of identity. These groups or categories are not a part of their self-concept and thus do not constitute a reference group for their identity.

In this way, even if the individuals are seen as acting as a group and are categorised as such by other individuals or groups, this does not necessarily imply the real existence of the group as such. For this to be so, it is still necessary that the members perceive themselves as such and that the group exists on a phenomenological level. In the same way, it can be the case that individuals see themselves as being members of a group even if others do not conceive of them as being so. As we have explained, there is not necessarily a coincidence between objective social identity, as in "de facto" belonging, and on the other hand, identification with these groups (which Zavalloni calls "subjective identity" or consciousness of belonging to a group).

Thus, we believe that group beliefs are the necessary and prior condition for identification, and that the latter remains the necessary condition for the construction of social identity, for the formation of the psychological group, and for group behaviour. In this way, the identification with a group ceases to be a strictly cognitive process but it is closely linked with the content which has activated these processes.

This approach permits us to respond to Turner's first proposition concerning the unifying factors and cognitive criteria which segment the world in terms of social categories. Variables such as proximity, similitude, common fate, and pregnance, proposed by Campbell (1958) can constitute or instruct group beliefs. The group beliefs may have any kind of content, as groups differ according to their composition, their experiences, their objectives, their structures and the context in which these groups behave. Obviously groups have beliefs concerning their norms, values, objectives and their ideology but all of these beliefs do not necessarily constitute group beliefs, because for this to be the case they would have to be shared by the individual members who conscious of this fact, consider these beliefs to be necessary for their unity. The shared beliefs which will become group beliefs are those which are functional, distinct, or those proposed by significant authorities as being important.

It remains then, to elucidate the genesis of these group beliefs. The formation of the fundamental group belief is based upon social, perceptual and cognitive processes on the basis of which individuals become aware of their commonality and perceive themselves as being part of a given community. The group beliefs satisfy several needs of the individual members and this is the basis upon which they decide to identify with the group. Moreover, the group beliefs permit the differentiation between the group and the out-groups, and construct the orientation of the group by way of the knowledge they procure.

In conclusion, one could claim that group beliefs constitute a fundamental element of group existence. They are the basis upon which the members constitute their social reality, the basis of the structure of the group. Moreover group beliefs can be instruments of influence, determining attitudes and behaviours towards the out-groups and thus constituting determinants for group behaviours. This is why group beliefs constitute both a cognitive and social perspective concerning the study of groups.

Within this conceptual framework the two questions we raised earlier on, as to how belonging becomes salient and how psychological groups are formed, can be answered. The problem is to know how a group belief is generated.

At this stage the similarity between group beliefs and social representations comes into play as the latter are defined as "a form of knowledge, socially elaborated and shared, having a practical goal and converging towards the construction of a reality shared by a certain social ensemble" (Jodelet, 1989, 36). This definition can be just as well applied to the concept of group belief. Also, Jodelet (1989) explains that social representations intervene in processes such as the definition of personal and social identities, group expression and social transformations. They constitute the definitions shared by members of a group and construct a consensual vision of reality for this group and of its relations with the other groups.

Effectively, the theoretical similarities between these two concepts can be seen at multiple levels, and we will not be able to address all of these points in the context of the present discussion. On the other hand, one may put forward the hypothesis that group beliefs are a part of and have their origin in the social representations, and that they are forms of socially elaborated and shared knowledge. However, group beliefs differ from social representations in that the individual members are conscious of sharing them and, even more importantly, they consider these beliefs as being the foundation of an entity of which they are a part.

We must underline the fact that if we wish to know the basis upon which identification with a group is founded, it is in our interests to work with both of these concepts. Just as Turner suggests and Zavalloni and Bar-Tal's approaches propose.

To conclude, it is claimed that if social identity is the cognitive mechanism by which group behaviour is made possible and that social identification is the cognitive mechanism by which group formation is possible, then group beliefs are the necessary conditions by which social identification takes place, and that group beliefs derive their content from social representations specific to each group.

The Construction of National and European Identity of French and Greeks

In the following sections some of the results of an exploratory study designed to examine group beliefs and affective aspects of identification will be discussed. The study involved conducting forty-eight semi-directive interviews with forty-eight men and women in France and Greece.

As this is an exploratory research, and our purpose has not been to build up a quantitatively representative sample of the population of the two countries; interviewees were drawn from a variety of occupational groups (e.g. liberal professions, artistic and intermediaries). The subjects were between thirty and forty-five years old. This age group was chosen based on the assumption that individuals in this age range would have already concluded the often transitory period which precedes professional stability. Furthermore they did not experience the Second World War.

The interviewees had not been alerted to the subjects to be discussed in the interviews. They were first asked to respond to a questionnaire which included ten affirmations to be completed beginning with "I am . . .". Actually, our objective was, among others, to have information on the definitions individuals gave of "the European", but we chose this procedure in order to avoid the kind of bias entailed by the following type of question, "What is a European for you?", as this question presupposes the existence of this category. Once the individuals described themselves by completing these affirmations we asked them why (or why not) they felt (or didn't feel) the need to describe themselves as Greek or French, or European, and to explain what this choice signified for them. It is important to take note of the fact that none of the subjects described themselves as being European.

During the interviews the following six themes were discussed:

1. What does it mean for you to be Greek/French?
2. What is your opinion about Europe?
3. What are the positions of the countries which are members of the EEC?
4. What is Greece's place in particular?
5. What is France's place in particular?
6. What does it signify for you to be European?

A thematic and structural content analysis of the interviews was done (Bardin, 1992). This chapter is concerned with only one part of the thematic analysis. It is mainly based on the answers given in the areas covered by the interviews described above. This analysis focuses on the investigation of the identification process; that is on group beliefs, affects related to the two groups, as well as the intergroup relations and status of the two countries involved.

The opinions given by the individuals about Europe allow us to understand better their implication in the construction of the social category of European, as well as the role of this construction in enhancing the salience of national identity.

The following discussion of our data uses some examples to show the extent to which empirical evidence supports the theoretical position described in the previous sections. Indeed, the purpose of this discussion is to debate the necessity to conceptualise the identification process in terms of the three aspects already mentioned (group beliefs, affects, commitment), as well as the intergroup relations upon which the latter are based.

Below we will focus first on the identification to the Nation and to Europe, then on the salience of the national identity and finally to the intergroup relations and participation.

Identification to Nation and to Europe

Concerning the sentiment of belonging to a national group we observe that the individuals in both groups, attribute much importance to this aspect even if it is not spontaneously introduced in the interview (only two Greeks and two French people presented themselves with mention of the national identity in the "Who am I" part of the study). Two significant examples clearly illustrate this point . . . "being Greek that means everything to me"; "Being French, that represents a cultural identity . . . that . . . I'm proud enough to be French".

The Greeks derive a lot of their pride from the importance of the ancient Greek civilisation and consider that this is what offers them a place in Europe. This civilisation is considered as their own and permits them to compare their in-group in the past with the out-groups either present or past in order to affirm positive elements of identity; "the basis, the origin of language of all University studies, started with Greek history, and Greece today does not have the place it deserves. If there weren't the ancient Greeks, what we call Europe today wouldn't be Europe but a region of barbarian in-fighting." "The Greek has a weighty inheritance, this civilization weighs heavily . . . I myself, I was a sailor and when I used to travel around I thought that I was better than all the others because we have a weighty history, we made poems, we made history, we had great wise men and philosophers, I don't think anything else can compare with that, no? A civilisation like the German one that manufactures cars that can't compare with a philosopher like Plato or Aristotle. So, I've got the right to believe that I'm better."

What constitutes national identity for the Greeks is history, tradition, religion, language, the mentality and the territory. French identity is felt to be more culturally oriented showing through a certain open-mindedness, humanitarian sensitivity, the respect for human rights, the ideals of the Revolution of 1789, but also a certain taste for art and the quality of life. "As I live in a country which has always been ahead of the times in terms of humanitarianism, and an openness towards the world, I find that it suits me, I mean it's exactly that, my kind of mind-set. It's a country of art and culture . . . we have a sensitivity to this which is recognized as being national". Also another interviewee stated that "We were the models, for the development of many a country, I believe . . . and we still are . . . we are very attached to the universal declaration of human rights and the citizen, of which, in any case it was we ourselves who inspired this".

The language constitutes an important element, and is mentioned spontaneously, "the language in spite of everything, follows the evolution of a people, even if this isn't direct, it has influence on a larger vision of the world, the structures of a country, the notion of discourse, and finally the way in which we argue". However, language has an ambivalent place with regards to national identity because it does not suffice in defining a French person. "Speaking French . . . does that suffice for . . . for recognizing a French person? No, I don't think that either. There are lots of foreigners who speak French."

These elements uphold the idea that there exists an "ensemble" of group beliefs concerning the nation and justifying its existence which allows individuals to recognise themselves as members of this nationality. One would have the tendency to say that for the Greeks, the bornes of the national group are less flexible than that of the French. Greek national belonging is defined by non-permeable elements such as the territory, the language and the religion. It seems however that French nationality, is more open because it suffices to accept and to sign the Republican contract in order to be a part. These examples permit us to illustrate our theoretical ideas in showing group beliefs concerning national belonging which facilitate identification with the group. Even if in truth, the individuals have not chosen to belong to the national group (of which they are a part by belonging *de facto*) they seem however to have constructed an entire group of shared beliefs which lead them to "accept" this belonging, assimilating it to a choice. Also, Hobsbawm (1990) after having studied different criteria for defining a nation since the birth of the modern nation states there do not exist any objective criteria for designing communities which are susceptible to become nations. A community considers itself as a nation based on a group of shared beliefs, according to which, people recognise (or do not recognise) in a subjective way, as being a part of this group. Hobsbawm cites Renner (1899, p. 213) who compared individual belonging to a nation and the belonging to a religious group, that is to say a status which "the individual who has reached the age of majority chooses freely himself, de jura".

Otherwise, even if there exists a common representational sphere concerning Europe, the elements of this field do not constitute group beliefs. Thus, even though the individuals all consider that Europe constructs itself on an economic basis, this shared belief is not an element of the foundation of unity. "Europe is a group of financial and agricultural/industrial concerns and nothing else. I think its interest remains mediocre for the most part of people who don't have those kinds of interests, monetary exchanges and money . . .". European union does not constitute an entity for the people who compose it, and thus consequently, they do not perceive of themselves as members. "For me . . . Europe is abstract." "The European countries are obliged to regroup but this should not be the principal justification, or if it has to be, this should not be in a capitalistic perspective but in a perspective of the defense of the interests of the whole planet." The absence of group beliefs concerning Europe, can be an explanation for the lack of identification of individuals to this category. Otherwise the fact of being European, for the French, expresses itself in terms of opposition to the Americans. Moreover, this comparison remains vague, and is based on "culture". As a differentiating element, culture (we Europeans have a culture as opposed to the Americans who do not) is a distinguishing principal of Europe but not a unifying one. It seems also that the French do not pose the problem of identifying themselves as Europeans because they construct this identity with relation to their national identity as though the former is modeled after the latter. "I don't think there is much of a difference between French people and 'Europeans' let's say especially Northern Europeans, or . . . well . . . Europeans". Also, the definition of the European is strongly linked to the idea of unification and the European is likewise someone who is interested or involved in this unification process. "I also feel European because I am completely open to this construction." For the Greeks, the European is described as someone who thinks about the economic interests of Europe, the mentality of the union, living beyond Greek frontiers, living in Occidental Europe, or living in Northern Europe . . . an inhabitant of Europe. We can note here the absence of adjectives designating attributes of the European, which leaves us to conclude that we are not yet in the presence of a stereotypical content, and that the Greeks do not really feel included in this category. "When we speak of a European, we admire him, because we have admired the Europeans for a long time now, we never refer to 'Mediterraneans', we refer ourselves to northern Europeans."

Another important element is that European identification is always conceived of with reference to national identity. Thus individuals consider themselves as

Europeans because they are citizens of countries which are part of the EU. In this way, European belonging is positively experienced, if it is seen as being beneficial for the belonging country of reference. For example: "First, as French person, I am a citizen of the world, thus I am a citizen of Europe, a citizen of the world. Oh yes of course I am European because I am part of a country which is a part of Europe, when one says Europe, it is understood the group of countries which has formed European Community."

The Greeks, on the other hand, when comparing themselves to the model of the European, citizen of Western Europe, they tend to not see themselves as being part of this group, but they believe that thanks to their ancient civilisation they have the right to a place in the European Community, thus as a national group they hope to benefit from credits in order to ameliorate their own economy and desire also that their national interests be supported by the community. The conflicts with Turkey are mentioned in almost all the interviews. On this point, they seem not to be very trusting, going as far as to say that they are ready to make the effort to "be more European" if "they" the Europeans, are ready to prove that they will support the Greeks in the future. "The Greek person wants to become European but he also wants certain assurances ... I often see European countries, for example France, behaving in a more friendly manner towards Turkey than towards Greece, why is that? I myself being European, being part of the European community ... isn't it more important that Europe sustain me more than the others who are not part of the EEC. I am afraid as a Greek that they may abandon me ... that I might find myself on the edge of catastrophe, and right away ... they back away and leave you alone to fend for yourself. The proof? When it came to Cyprus they didn't do a thing."

According to this vision, Europe has no chance of constructing itself in terms of an entity in which the members act in an interdependent manner. For the moment, the unifying elements proposed by the political actors do not seem to function in a way that they can be considered as group beliefs.

Salience of National Identity

The project of European Unification does not only fail to unite the individuals involved but also has the effect of bringing out the importance of national identity. The following remarks illustrate this fact: "That did not come to me spontaneously (to present myself in terms of being Greek) but if for example, the subject of discussion were to be the EEC or the Balkans maybe that would have come up right away." Another remark is also quite significant: "I present myself in terms of being Greek to a European, because he must know of Greece, whereas elsewhere they may not know Greece." Or "maybe if one questioned me in an English waiting room, maybe I would have said that I am French". Thus it seems that national identity is "activated" in certain circumstances and in reference with certain pertinent groups including among others the European Community. This reaction should certainly not astonish us, as we know that no group can exist in a social void and that it must take its place in relation to other groups. What interests us here is that if Europe brings out national belonging, in doing so it provokes a certain closing up and the return of the nation. The individuals express a strong desire to keep their cultural identity and way of life. The fear of being "homogenised" is shared by both Greek and French subjects. "Personally I'm a bit afraid . . . all the countries must make an effort in order not to lose our socio-cultural identities. Work is upheld to be the chief virtue. In France we are able to put things into their proper place. I am not so sure that Europe will allow us to stay this way. I'm afraid Europe will threaten our good-natured side, we will have to give things up." "The Greek would say: I am Greek from Europe, and I work for the economic good of Europe, but beyond that, it doesn't interest me, I take off during the European holidays but I also celebrate the 25th March and October 28th (Greek holidays) . . .". "We would be a country of retired people because of the climate, all those who retire in Europe will come to Greece, and if lots of foreigners arrive, they will transform the people, there won't be any more Greece."

Two complementary remarks seem important concerning the construction of the European identity and the influence of national belonging on this construction.

Intergroup Relations

It seems then, that it is national intergroup relations which control the manner by which European unification is constructed. Thus, the economic dimension, rendered salient by the EEC, confers a certain status on to each country and thus a certain degree of "Europeanness". Thus the French consider that France will "get the upper hand" and that France is a "light-house nation". The Greeks on the other hand express a certain sentiment of inferiority fearing that the others do not have a very good image of them . . . "already, just to know of Greece is something positive even if the image one has is negative". "What they think of Greece is unimportant, as long as they at least know of it." "Greece is seen as a past glory, and now we see it as a third world country not a European one." "The Greeks have to make a lot of efforts to live up to the average of the European." "The Greeks would feel more European if they could consider them as an equal . . . we can not succeed in this union if there are some in first class and others in second." This inferiority is due, according to the respondents, to the contrast between ancient and modern Greece and to this country's modest economy.

Belonging to Europe and Participation

The last remark about these interviews, concerns the participation of individuals in the European Community. Once again the individuals speak of the lack of participation and concerted efforts on behalf of the citizens; Europe seems to be very remote, and they feel as though they have no control over its actions and decisions. "All the decisions are made on a political level which eludes the grasp of the citizen." Or "I can't say either that I am against Europe ... anyway we have no means to pressure or change whatever it is we don't like, in the sense of what is currently given ... all of a sudden I feel a bit indifferent towards the effort being made now because it is not that effort which should be being made ... but I'm not really against it ... that's not really an option either." This remark is essential on the identity level when we think about the importance of participation for the construction, and behaviour of a group, and also in the formation of a consensus. Moscovici and Doise (1992) consider participation to be a fundamental need and think that "responding to this need, the group no longer appears as a given, or an association exterior to the individuals who hold it together and constraining them to fill a prescribed role, to occupy a certain space. It is their work, it brings them closer together and makes them feel that everything undertaken together has been done by choice." (p. 74) It is thus evident, that the lack of participation of the citizens in European construction represents a serious set-back to the formation of group identity. Given the objective of this first analysis of the interviews, we believe we have illustrated our theoretical claims and shown the need to direct the research towards other theoretical directions for analysing the identity processes. It is high time to seek out the processes of internalisation of identity categories situating them in the social context and in terms of intergroup relations. The concepts of group beliefs and social representations can be useful to us, if the problem of their genesis is resolved.

Discussion

In this chapter, the question of how the feeling of belonging to a group is created was addressed. European identification, which offers the possibility of becoming a new identity category, gives us the occasion to consider a plurality of aspects of this debate, finally leading us to the necessity of exploring the notion of the social group.

At the centre of our preoccupations we find identification and formation of the psychological group as constituting a group of "belonging" and a reference group.

Starting from Turner's theory (1981 and 1987), we have tried to show the limits of such an approach, limits which Turner himself points out as being exemplary, as indicators of new directions which should be explored in this field. We have first clarified the distinction between belonging and identification, followed by an analysis of the mechanisms by which the identification process takes place.

The complexity of the construction of social realities obliges social psychologists to go beyond declarative conclusions as it no longer suffices to simply state that self-categorisation is a necessary and sufficient element for the constitution of a psychological group. We must now examine how this categorisation process takes place.

Responding to these questions requires that we turn to the concept of group belief (Bar Tal, 1990). This concept can constitute the necessary condition by which a group can be produced. It remains to be understood precisely under which conditions a belief becomes a group belief. The response to this question can be gleaned from the theoretical field of social representations. We believe to have illustrated these elements in our interviews, having thus shown that the absence of group beliefs can be a cause for the non-identification of individuals with Europe. Of course, our analysis is not sufficient in itself in confirming this hypothesis on the important role of group beliefs in the formation of an identity group. This idea, however, merits further development. Our intention was to demonstrate the insufficiencies of the theory of self-categorisation and thus to open up the debate. The concept of the social group must be resituated at the heart of our theoretical and empirical preoccupations. This is the only means of getting over the theoretical obstacles erected by the construction of identity. As this construction does not exist in a social void, we must take into account its content, which can shed light on the processes in question.

Over the course of our interviews we were able to bring up other important points. For example we have shown that intergroup relations form the sphere of consensus in which group beliefs and social representations concerning Europe are generated. On the other hand, the fact that Europe seems to challenge national belonging, leads us to believe that there will be a reconstruction of national identity which will have to leave room for the European one. It is also possible that the image and status of the national groups change under the influence of Europe. There will then be a movement in two directions: national belonging and intergroup relations will condition the representation of Europe and at the same time Europe will condition individuals' perceptions of their national groups.

In this perspective, the notion of participation becomes essential. On the one hand it can constitute a factor of polarisation of attitudes or even a factor in the formation of new values. Its relevance to our concerns lies in the fact that participation can constitute a unifying factor and thus a factor inducing the formation of groups. Moscovici and Doise remark that "that which institutes consensus and makes it convincing is not the accord/agreement involved but rather the participation of those who have so concluded. Thus it does not constrain them, and has no legitimacy except by the participation of each of the individuals concerned." (p. 9) The European consensus, a first step towards identification with Europe, requires the participation of its citizens. But as we observe in our interviews the respondents often complained about their lack of participation in the construction of Europe. The parallel between identification and participation and their role in the formation of groups is a subject which merits further reflection.

European identity is far from having been constructed, and we have shown several ways in which appropriate theoretical directions can be explored.

Research has been undertaken along the lines of the social representation of Europe (Echebarria *et al.*, 1992; Sotirakopoulou *et al.*, 1990) or attitudes towards unification (Hewstone, 1986).

We have taken an alternative approach. As the social representation of Europe does not yet exist, we suggest that instead of studying the social representation of Europe (as an object), to study Europe as a new element to be integrated in the representations of Nations (which can be considered legitimately as objects at the present time). The processes of anchoring and objectification seem the most useful for us in achieving this goal.

Our purpose in this chapter was mainly to put forth questions, that we consider to be important for researchers in social psychology as well as relevant to the construction of Europe.

References

Apostolidis, T. (1992). A propos de la contribution de Sotirakopoulou and Breakwell. *Ongoing Production on Social Representations*, **1**, 39–43.

Abrams, D. and Hogg, M. A. (1990). Social identification, self-categorization and social influence. In W. Stroebe and M. Hewstone (eds), *European Review of Social Psychology*. Chichester: J. Wiley & Sons.

Allen, V. L. and Wilder, D. A. (1975). Categorization, belief similarity and intergroup discrimination. *Journal of Personality and Social Psychology*, **32**, 971–73.

Bardin, L. (1989). *L'analyse de contenu*, 5th edn. Paris: Presses Universitaires de France.

Bar Tal, D. (1990). *Group Beliefs: A Conception for Analysing Group Structure, Processes and Behaviour*. New York: Springer-Verlag.

Bloom, W. (1990). *Personal Identity, National Identity and International Relations*. Cambridge: Cambridge University Press.

Campbell, D. T. (1958). Common fate, similarity, and other indices of status of aggregates of persons as social entities. *Behavioural Science*, **3**, 14–25.

Di Giacomo, J. P., and Leyens, J. P. (1981). Quelques remarques à propos du modèle d'identification sociale et de son niveau d'explication théorique. *Cahiers de Psychologie Cognitive*, **1**, 119–21.

Doise, W., and Lorenzi-Cioldi, F. (1991). L'identité sociale comme représentation. In V. Aebisher, J. P. Deconchy and E. M. Lipiansky (eds), *Idéologies et représentations sociales*. Cousset: Delval.

Echebarria, A., Elejabarieta, F., Valencia, J. and Villarreal, M. (1992). Representations sociales de l'Europe et identités sociales. *Bulletin de Psychologie*, **45**, 280–88.

Flick, U. (1992). Combing methods–lack of methodology: discussion of Sotirakopoulou and Breakwell. *Ongoing Production on Social Representations*, **1**(1), 43–8.

Hewstone, M. (1986). *Understanding Attitudes to the European Community: A Social-psychological Study in Four Member States*. Cambridge: Cambridge University Press and Paris: Editions de la Maison des Sciences de L'Homme.

Hobsbawm, E. (1992). *Nations et nationalisme depuis 1780. Programme, mythe, réalité*. Paris: Gallimard.

Horwitz, M. and Rabbie, J. M. (1982). Individuality and membership in the intergroup system. In H. Tajfel (ed.), *Social Identity and Intergroup Relations*. Cambridge: Cambridge University Press and Paris: Editions de la Maison des Sciences de L'Homme.

Jaspars, J. M. F. (1981). On rediscovering Sociology. *Cahiers de Psychologie Cognitive*, **1**, 122–3.

Jodelet, D. (ed.) (1991). *Représentations sociales*, 2nd edn, Paris: Presses Universitaires de France.

Lipiansky, E. M. (1986) L'identité nationale comme représentation. In P. Tap (ed.), *Identités sociales et changement sociaux*. Toulouse: Privat.

Morin, E. (1987). *Penser l'Europe*. Paris: Gallimard, Au vif du sujet.

Moscovici, S. and Paicheler, G. (1978). Social comparison and social recognition: two complementary processes of identification. In H. Tajfel (ed.), *Differentiation between Social Groups: Studies in Social Psychology of Intergroup Relations*. London: Academic Press.

Moscovici, S. and Doise, W. (1992). *Dissensions et consensus*. Paris: Presses Universitaires de France.

Mugny, G. (1981). Identification sociale et influence sociale. *Cahiers de Psychologie Cognitive*, **1**, 124–6.

Paicheler, G. (1981). La face cachée des groupes sociaux. *Cahiers de Psychologie Cognitive*, **1**, 127–8.

Rouquette M-L. (1981). Le groupe: présence d'une notion et absence d'un concept. *Cahiers de Psychologie Cognitive*, **1**, 129–30.

Sotirakopoulou, P. K., Lyons, E. and Breakwell, G. M. (1990). Representations of 1992. Communication to the Annual Conference of the Social Psychology Section of BPS. Leeds, 15 September 1990.

Sotirakopoulou, P. K. and Breakwell, G. M. (1992). The use of different methodological approaches in the study of social representations. *Ongoing Production on Social Representations*, **1**, 29–38.

Tajfel, H. (1973). La categorisation sociale. In S. Moscovici (ed.), *Introduction à la Psychologie sociale*, vol.1. Paris: Larousse.

Tajfel, H. (1978). Social comparison, similarity and ingroup favoritism. In H. Tajfel (ed.), *Differentiation between Social Groups: Studies in Social Psychology of Intergroup Relations*. London: Academic Press.

Tajfel, H. (1982). Social psychology of intergroup relations. *Annual Review of Psychology*, **33**, 1–39.

Turner, J. C. (1978). Social comparison, similarity and ingroup favoritism. In H. Tajfel (ed.), *Differentiation between Social Groups: Studies in Social Psychology of Intergroup Relations*. London: Academic Press.

Turner, J. C. (1981a). Towards a cognitive redefinition of the social group. *Cahiers de Psychologie Cognitive*, **1**, 93–118.

Turner, J. C. (1981b). Redefining the social group: a reply to commentaries. *Cahiers de Psychologie Cognitive*, **1**, 131–8.

Turner, J. C. (1982). Towards a cognitive redefinition of the social group. In H. Tajfel (ed.), *Social Identity and Intergroup Relations*. Cambridge: Cambridge University Press and Paris: Editions de la Maison des Sciences de l'Homme.

Turner, J. C., Hogg, M. A., Oakes, P. J., Reicher, S. D. and Wetherell, M. S. (1987). *Rediscovering the Social Group: A Self Categorization Theory*. Oxford: Basil Blackwell.

Zander, A., Stotland, E. and Wolfe, D. (1960). Unity of group, identification with group, and self esteem of members. *Journal of Personality*, **28**, 463–78.

Zavalloni, M. and Louis-Guerrin, C. (1984). *Identité sociale et conscience*. Toulouse: Privat and Montréal: Presses Universitaires de Montréal.

19

Components of Social Identity or the Achilles Heel of the Field in the Case of European Integration?

ELISABETH S. SOUSA

ISPA, Portugal

The European ideal of the deep cooperation and coordination of nation-states as well as the concern for peace and human rights born after the Second World War (cf. e.g. Schuman's statement of 9 May 1950) is well documented in the literature (e.g. Faber, 1982; Louis, 1989; Pescatore, 1974; Stein and Waelbroeke, 1976). The result was a new European legal order, a supra-national power, expressed in terms of: (a) the primacy of the European Law over National Laws; and (b) the self-executing effect (cf. e.g. the VanGend en Loos determination of 5 February 1963, and the Costa/ENEL determination of 15 July 1964 by the European Court of Justice). Still, from the very beginning things have not been easy.

Unlike earlier times, the revolution which took place in Europe after the Second World War was not led by public opinion, and relegated political elites to second place. The European Court of Justice has bypassed the absence of a consensus of European political elites (trapped by interest conflicts), and has lost no time in formalising new values and norms which affect the sovereignty of nation-states (cf. e.g. Lauwaars, 1973; Lecourt, 1976; Tizzano, 1967). Public opinion was assigned a passive role at least until the Maastricht Treaty ratification which led to a referendum in some countries. In other words, change was brought about without participation from the citizens. However, in the best interest of EC citizens, mechanisms were created so that they could have an active voice and apply to the European Court whenever their interests were not fairly served by national institutions.

Also, with time, ethics turned out to be a neglected issue in a Europe now successfully employing economics as the centre of cooperation between nations, despite the fact that, under the umbrella of the art. 235 of the Treaty of Rome, some common decisions were taken beyond economic cooperation. The Single European Act expressed a step further on integration. Political elites and governance acknowledged that: (a) economic integration implies political integration, (b) consensus may run against liberalism. Indeed, the rule of unanimity may inhibit changes.

Nevertheless, one had to wait for the Maastricht meeting and the signing of a new Treaty to have politicians committed to proceed accordingly. This was a move backwards given that the Schuman plan proposed a federal model. At the same time, it showed that political elites became involved and interested in discussing their views.

In formal terms, the spectrum of common action was enlarged and specified by those who agreed to cooperate more deeply. Still, a consensus was not achieved by political elites as to the form this deeper European integration should take. Given that federalism had been the preferred form of integration in the 1950s, the recent decisions are another move backwards (cf. Micklinghoff, 1980; Munch, 1962; Ophuls, 1965; Pescatore, 1975; Reuter, 1952).

Thus, the Maastricht Treaty creates new objective realities. The supranational nature of EC decisions was recognised by elites. Its action spread, reducing the sovereignty of nation-states. The new Treaty covers almost all sectors of social life (cf. articles 3, 3-A and 3-B). This will affect individual citizens in the EC, the nation-states involved, and the world. The idea of (a) a European citizenship with new civic rights and free circulation of citizens within EC, the constraints imposed on third countries (cf. Chengen's agreement), (b) of making one's European identity felt in the transnational space (art. B, art. J1), a clear statement of its higher inclusive nature with obligations for the nation-states and (c) the evolution towards a single currency to be achieved at the third moment, among other features, challenge the status quo.

From a psycho-social perspective this state of affairs is interesting. It is true that identities are changing in a formal manner but, what do citizens think about it and how do they feel about it? How do they conceive diversity in Europe? How do they react to trends towards homogeneity within Europe? Inclusive or competitive communities (cf. Tonnies, 1947)? Do social identifications to national spaces and/or to the European matrix moderate the way citizens see integration in Europe?

Social Identifications

Several authors have suggested that group membership is mainly the cognitive operation of social categorisation (e.g. Doise and Sinclair, 1973; Messick and Mackie, 1987; Simon, 1993) by which the individual locates himself or herself within a value-laden system of categories (e.g. Hogg and Abrams,

1988; Tajfel and Turner, 1979). In this vein, Turner (1981 and 1987) has assumed that the first question determining group membership is how we perceive and define ourselves and not how we feel about others. This was taken for granted by most researchers. A unidimensional view of identification to social groups came to be emphasised. Also, membership of social categories has not been distinguished from membership of social groups for the purpose of social identification mechanisms (cf. Doise, 1988; Rabbie and Horwitz, 1988; Tajfel, 1982; Turner, 1988). Identification has been conceived as leading individuals to adopt interpersonal strategies that enhance the distinctiveness between groups and social categories in ways that favour own group (Hogg and Abrams, 1988; Tajfel and Turner, 1979).

In the 1970s Tajfel (1972, 1978, 1982) had defined social identity as that part of individuals' self-concept which derives from knowledge of membership of a social group together with the value and emotional significance of that membership. Social identification, a central variable, was conceived as a multicomponent process. Given the development of cognitivism in social psychology, the fact is that the affective-emotional significance of membership of social groups turned out to be a neglected issue. The assumption became: Individuals would not only acknowledge membership of a social group but also redefine their social identity in terms of the group when interacting with others.

It is not surprising then, that few researchers address the possibility of a multicomponent nature of social identifications. Even if some include affects in their measures (e.g. Bourhis and Sachdev, 1987), they do not subscribe to this perspective. One of the rare exceptions, Hinkle (1988b, 1989) empirically showed its multidimensional nature and suggested that the affective component may be more important than was previously thought. Also, Sousa (1989 and 1993) related the affective component of identifications to attributional processes. This researcher has shown that, when faced with a negative event pertaining to the ingroup, affectively dis-identified subjects tend to attribute it to internal factors whereas subjects affectively identified attribute it to external factors. Indeed, if one accepts that individuals attempt to gain self-positivity from their membership of social groups, then there is no strong reason to assume subjects identify with an imposed social group or category when it cannot prompt self-superiority. Intergroup differentiation which favours one category or group is related to an increase in individual's self-esteem (Hogg *et al.*, 1986; Lemyre and Smith, 1985; Oakes and Turner, 1980) whereas differentiation which does not, implies dissatisfaction if not loss of self-esteem (cf. e.g. Brown and Lohr, 1987; Wagner *et al.*, 1988). It has been suggested that even though individuals behave in group terms sometimes their behaviour may be aimed at generating differentiation from the features recognised as characterising the group in specific contexts when it cannot prompt positive distinctiveness. Rijsman (1983) reported that in a category comparison setting, subjects assigned to inferior categories tend to dissociate from their category, decreasing performance levels, whereas subjects belonging to a superior group increase the quality of their performances as a means of justifying their inclusion in the superior category (cf. also Ng, 1986; Snyder *et al.*, 1986; Turner *et al.*, 1983; Waddell and Cairns, 1986). Individuals' appraisals of a group may lead to unexpected patterns of group behaviour.

When both the cognitive and the affective components are harmonious, individuals hold a strong positive identification. They do not only acknowledge membership of the category or group but they are also affectively attached to the membership. The result is ingroup favouritism. This is what we shall call hot or high identification. In some other cases, components of identification are disharmonious. Individuals acknowledge membership of a category or group to which they would prefer not to belong. Membership of the category or group is perceived as externally determined but impossible to alter. Thus, structural pressures lead to acceptance of the category label, but at the same time affects become powerful. As a result differentiation processes may have different meanings. This is what we shall refer to as cold identification or low identification. It is reasonable to think that national identities may vary with respect to the identification processes they trigger.

Competing and Inclusive Identities

Following Turner's self-categorisation theory one might expect EC citizens to redefine their identities, and create new opposing categories in the transnational space. Category assimilation would pervade, citizens exhibiting a supranational level of identification. Nevertheless, recent EC developments, namely the outcome of the referendum on the Maastricht Treaty, and nationalist trends in Europe suggest a more complex picture. Further, social and economic cohesion which is still being pursued within the EC, the requests from the EC poorer countries, the move backwards as to the type of integration that will be preferred, cast some doubts over and even challenge some of the predictions of the cognitivist theories of group relations. Moreover, the Portuguese case is paradigmatic given the fact that there was not a referendum, and in order to evoke constitutional restrictions it would have been useful to have brought the case before the Constitutional Court which did not happen.

From an historical perspective, Portuguese national identity is very old, dating from the twelfth century. Its contribution to Europe was recognised by other nation-states. Still, for centuries, Portugal nurtured the idea of an empire in the transnational space, and to some extent relegated Europe to second place. Unlike other European nation-states, the geography of the country, its borders, have remained unchanged. Portugal did not enter the Second World War. More recently, with the 1974 democratisation process, and the end of its empire, this nation-state missed on its European role.

This led us to consider configurations of affective membership to two social categories (national and European), disregarding their formal inclusive level. The reasons for ignoring the formal inclusive level at this step are the specific characteristics of Portugal, and the fact that EC citizens were left aside from the process of European Unification.

Hypothesis one was formulated as follows: high identified individuals will express more positive attitudes and thoughts towards the social categories at issue than individuals cognitively identified but affectively dis-identified (low identified individuals). Despite the formal inclusive level of memberships, hypothesis two states that subjects will privilege national over European identities.

Thus, the attraction to the national category (high vs low) and to the European category (high vs low) given a clear and objective high external pressure on the social categorisation as Portuguese and EC citizens was expressed in a 2 × 2 design.

Also, representational complexity on the issues was studied. As a matter of fact, several authors have suggested that less complex representations give rise to more extreme positions given the reduced number of dimensions to be taken into account (e.g. Linville, 1982 and 1985; Judd and Park, 1982; Simon, 1993).

Method

One hundred and eighty Portuguese individuals (90 males and 90 females) volunteered to participate. Sixty subjects did not complete all the questionnaire. Thus, they were only included in the analysis of the semantic contents.

The investigation took place in Lisbon at the beginning of 1993. Subjects were seen individually. Subjects filled in a booklet consisting of four parts: (1) semantic contents associated to the ideas of Portugal, EC (Portugal/EC makes me think about ...) (free-contents); (2) their identification with the categories of "Portuguese" and "EC citizen". This measure was obtained by asking subjects on a free-format "To what extent do you feel ... (name of the social category)", "what does it mean to you being ... (name of the social category)"; (3) EC representational complexity which included eight items (being involved with EC issues (yes/no format); number of people known who work at the EC; number of people known who are involved with EC issues; their description (on a free-format), number of countries visited; reasons for visiting other EC countries (free-format), readings on EC and type of reading (technical books, newspapers, magazines) (multiple responses) (4) attitudes towards the Maastricht Treaty and the EC each composed of four items on five-point response scales. Five point scales ranged from entirely disagree (= 1) to entirely agree (= 5). After completion of the booklet, the experimenter checked for the relevance of these categories.

Results

Classification of Subjects According to Type of Identification

Subjects were divided into High vs Low identification groups for each of the two social categories on the basis of the "Yes" or "No" spontaneous answers. Other type of lexical units (meanings odd identifications and more fine-grained distinctions in the verbal protocols were neglected given the very small numbers).

Classification of Subjects According to the Complexity of their Representations

Subjects were classified in one of the three levels of complexity considered: low, medium and high. These levels resulted from the analysis of the answers to the set of questions on the topic. Low complexity was operationalised in the following terms: not being involved with EC issues, did not know people working at the EC or being involved with EC issues, had not travelled abroad, did not read things on EC issues (either newspapers or professional readings). Medium knowledge implied knowing one or more persons either working at EC or involved with EC issues while describing them (him/her) in a similar manner, having read things about EC (newspapers or magazines), having travelled abroad (despite the motives), being involved or not with EC issues. High complexity implied knowing two or more persons either working or involved with EC issues, differently characterised, being personally involved with EC issues, having read things about EC (in books or in specialised magazines), having travelled abroad.

Semantic Contents Evoked by the Stimuli

A Factor Correspondence Analysis (Benzécri, 1973; Greenacre, 1984; Lebart and Morineau, 1984) was performed on a simple binary matrix of free contents associated by four groups to the two stimuli (Portugal and EC). The groups were constituted on the basis of two affective identification levels (High vs Low) × two social categories (National and European) which led to: high identification to both the National and the European categories (HNHE), high identification to the National category and low identification to the European category (HNLE), low identification to the National category and high identification with the European category (LNHE), low identification to both the National and the European categories (LNLE).

Factor Correspondence Analysis is a principal components method which, unlike other methods, simultaneously accounts for both the variables' and the subjects' distributions by using an inertia principle which

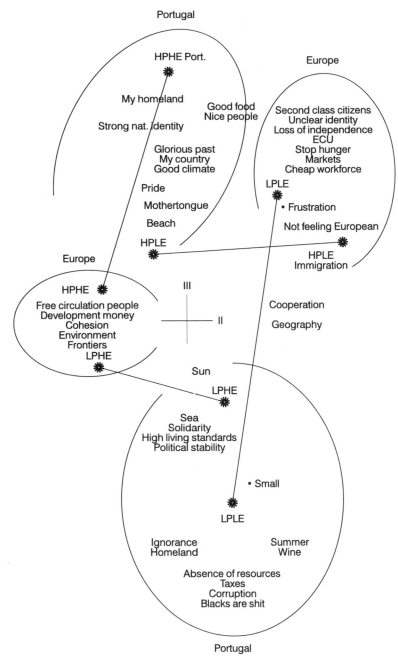

FIGURE 19.1   Distances between Portugal and Europe as a function of social identifications

is derived from a chi-squared rather than an Euclidean metric. In our case, lexical proximities express common discourse whereas lexical distances reflect content opposition. Further, the discourse is assigned to subjects. Thus, the interpretation of the space configuration allows one to identify the subjects who said "x" and "y" by opposition to subjects who said "z". From the seven factors extracted, the first three which were associated to 66 per cent of the variance of the matrix were the only ones to reach significance. It is important to note that the first factor (Lambda1 = .86; T = 34%) is a scale factor. It expresses a sharp distinction between the number of lexical units associated to the two stimuli. The second and third factors are to be analyzed simultaneously given similar Lambda values and similar associated variances (Lambda2 = .41, $T2$ = 16%; and Lambda3 = .41, $T3$ = 16%).

The main opposition concerns the lexical discourse evoked by the two stimuli: Europe and Portugal. Few different lexical units contribute to the stimulus PORTUGAL whereas many define EUROPE, in the first axis. Contents about Portugal are stereotyped, and homogeneous. Groups come close (cf. right side of Figure 19.1). In contrast, contents about Europe suggest diversity. An opposition of perspectives about Europe, between those who feel European and those who don't (cf. FII), clarifies Factor I.

Results of Factor I and II of the Factor Correspondence Analysis

The main consensual idea among subjects was to remain Portuguese ("want to be Portuguese"). Those who were highly identified with Portugal expressed concern for the national identity perceiving it in danger. In their words "negative for identity", "loss of identity", "loss of national culture", "loss of sovereignty", "second-class citizens". Those who identified with Europe seemed to be concerned ("dissatisfaction") with "stat(ing) (their) national identity" given "immigration legislation" in the EC and "cohesion" problems. These subjects considered themselves as members of "(. . .) a great club", missing on "economic progress", "development".

The analysis of Factor II and III revealed other features. When framing the discourse on the nation-state, those who were low identified with both Europe and Portugal (LPLE) focused on "blacks shit", "ignorance", "homeland", "absence of resources" (in the national space), "small (country)", "taxes", "corruption", "high living standards" among other ideas. Subjects low identified with Portugal but highly identified with Europe (LPHE) were still close to this perspective given they had common negative ideas about their nation-state. When focusing on the European context—Europe—LPHE subjects stated their "frustration". Given "loss of independence", they become "second class citizens", "cheap work force", "have an unclear identity", "not feeling European". In addition, they stated "cooperation" in close relation to "geography" (cf. Figure 19.2).

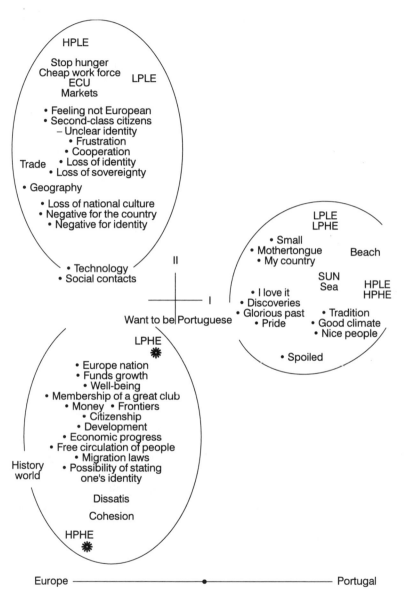

FIGURE 19.2 Distances between Portugal and Europe as a function of social identifications

Results of Factor II and III of the Factor Correspondence Analysis

When focusing on the national context, subjects highly identified with it but low-identified with Europe (HPLE) enhanced their national identities: "strong national identity", "pride", "glorious past", "good food", "nice people", "mother tongue", "my country", "my homeland" etc. When focusing on Europe they clearly stated their dissatisfaction with this membership. In doing this they came close to those who did not feel either Portuguese or European (LPLE).

Those subjects highly identified to both Portugal and Europe (HPHE) stated a "strong national identity", their "pride", a "glorious past" of the country ("my country") focusing on the "mother tongue", the "homeland". Europe emerged as a source of "development", "money", a geographic place for "free circulation of people".

The relative distances between group dictionaries to the two stimuli suggest a strong distance between Europe and Portugal for those low identified with both social categories, a very close link for those highly identified with Europe and low-identified with Portugal (LPHE), and the central role of the national membership for those highly identified to both social categories (HPHE) and those highly identified to their nation-state but low-identified with Europe (HPLE).

Type of Identification and Attitudes towards the Maastricht Treaty and the EC

The next step aimed at testing whether these patterns of identification to the national social category expressed different attitudes. Also, it aimed at analysing the effect of the complexity of the representations on the issue.

We did not have subjects who did not feel Portuguese and at the same time were very well informed. Thus, we computed a one-way analysis on complexity. However, representational complexity on EC did not frame attitudes towards the Maastricht Treaty (Global $M = 3.1$). A two-way analysis of variance (ANOVA), identification to the Portuguese category (cold vs hot) $\times$ gender (males vs females) was computed on the average scores of the attitudinal items concerning the Maastricht Treaty. Neither gender ($F(1,114) = 2.04$, $p < .10$) nor type of identification ($F(1,114) = 2.81, p < .10$) attained significance. Still, low identified subjects were slightly unfavourable to the Treaty.

A two-way analysis of variance (ANOVA), identification to the Portuguese category (cold vs hot) $\times$ gender (males vs females) was computed on the average scores of the attitudinal items concerning the EC. A main effect emerged for identification, $F(1,117) = 8.29$, $p < .005$ (significant explained variance of the model at the level of $p < .05$). High identified subjects showed a more positive attitude towards the EC ($M = 3.8$) than low identified subjects ($M = 3.1$). Gender did not frame different attitudes.

Concluding Remarks

Our results highlight the multidimensional nature of social identification and emphasise the importance of the affective component of social identifications. They are consistent with data reported by Hinkle (1989) and Sousa (1993). Thus, they are inconsistent with cognitive conceptualisations of groups which would not predict differences as a function of the affective component of social identification (e.g. Hogg and Abrams, 1988; Linville, 1985; Simon, 1993; Turner, 1987). Moreover, our results cast doubts on the general discrete character of ingroup representations as developed by Simon (1993; Simon and Pettigrew, 1990). Only in some cases, subjects seem to construct social categories as mere aggregates of separate entities. This was the case for those affectively dis-identified with both categories. Apparently, from the spontaneous discourse, when positive affects are at stake, individuals hold a strong positive social identity. When they are not, individuals construct the ingroup in a rather dispersed way, and personal identities become salient. Indeed, further studies should be conducted.

Also, our data on EC integration are not consistent with the self-categorisation theory which would predict assimilation rather than contrast. Subjects high identified to their national category and low identified with the European category privileged competitive identities. Similarly, subjects high identified to both social categories displayed ethnocentrism. This was not the case when subjects were not highly identified to both categories: subjects focused negative contents of the national category and displayed a rather individualistic, if not racist discourse. In this case, distances between categories were sharpened. Subjects who were not highly identified to their nation-state while being highly identified to Europe might be seen to display an inclusive perspective.

At a different level, there are reasons to believe that supra-ordinate power relations may not be easily accepted by citizens, if not divide citizens. This may lead to unexpected perverse processes in the European space. Most of our subjects preferred a horizontal perspective of power. Moreover, the ethical dimension of the development of the EC has not emerged from the spontaneous discourse. One may speculate about a possible increase of differentiation trends, given a strong formal pressure to homogeneity. It is true that an explicit reference to the need of preserving cultures, and the subsidiary principle, registered in a formal manner, might balance and smooth reactions. Still, it is not clear whether citizens are aware of it. In addition, it is not clear whether what political elites conceive as national culture matches that of civil societies. Finally, the lack of consensus on the model of EC integration (cf. Etzioni, 1965), and on the possibility of new EC members, complicate the picture.

References

Benzecri, J.-P. (1973). *L'analyse des données*, Vol 2. Paris: Dunod.
Brown, R., Condor, S., Mathews, A., Wade, G. and Williams, J. (1986). Explaining intergroup differentiation in an industrial organisation. *Journal of Occupational Psychology*, **59**, 273–86.

Brown, B. B. and Lohr, M. J. (1987). Peer group affiliation and adolescent self-esteem: an integration of ego identity and symbolic-interaction theories. *Journal of Personality and Social Psychology*, **52**, 47–55.

Brown, R. and Ross, G. F. (1982). The battle for acceptance: an exploration into the dynamics of intergroup behaviour. In H. Tajfel (ed.), *Social Identity and Intergroup Relations*. London: Cambridge University Press.

Doise, W. (1988). Individual and social identities in intergroup relations. *European Journal of Social Psychology*, **18**, 99–112.

Doise, W. and Sinclair, A. (1973). The categorization process in intergroup relations. *European Journal of Social Psychology*, **3**, 145–53.

Etzioni, A. (1965). *Political Unification: A Comparative Study of Leaders and Forces*. New York: Holt, Rinehart and Winston.

Faber, G. (1982). *The European Community and Development Cooperation*. The Netherlands: Von Gorcun.

Greenacre, M. J. (1984). *Theory and Applications of Correspondence Analysis*. London: Academic Press.

Hinkle, S., Fox-Cardamone, D. L., Taylor, L. A. and Crook, K. (1989a). Studies in social identity theory: owngroup identification and dimensions of intergroup comparison, Paper presented at the East/West Meeting EAESP, Jablonna.

Hinkle, S., Taylor, L. A. and Fox-Cardamone, D. L. (1989b). Intragroup identification and intergroup differentiation: a multicomponent approach. *British Journal of Social Psychology*, **28**, 305–17.

Hogg, M. and Abrams, D. (1988). *Social Identifications*. London: Routledge.

Hogg, M., Turner, J., Nascimento-Schulze, C. and Spriggs, D. (1986). Social categorization, intergroup behaviour and self-esteem: two experiments. *Revista de Psicologia Social*, **1**, 23–37.

Inglehart, R. (1977). *The Silent Revolution*. Princeton: Princeton University Press.

Judd, C. and Park, B. (1988). Outgroup homogeneity: judgments of variability at the individual and the group levels. *Journal of Personality and Social Psychology*, **54**, 778–88.

Lauwaars, R. (1973). Lawfulness and legal force of community decisions. Geneva: Leyde.

Lebart, L. and Morineau, A. (1985). *Système portable pour l'analyse des données (SPAD)*, Paris: CESIA.

Lecourt, R. (1976). *L'Europe des juges*. Brussels: Bruylant.

Lemyre, L. and Smith, P. (1985). Intergroup discrimination and self-esteem in the minimal group paradigm. *Journal of Personality and Social Psychology*, **49**, 660–70.

Linville, P. (1982). The complexity-extremity effect and age-based stereotyping. *Journal of Personality and Social Psychology*, **42**, 193–211.

Linville, P. (1985). Self–complexity and affective extremity: don't put all of your eggs in one cognitive basket. *Social Cognition*, **3**, 94–120.

Louis, J.-V. (1989). *L'ordre juridique communautaire*. Luxembourg: Commission des Communautés Européennes.

Messick, D. and Mackie, D. (1987). Intergroup relations. *Annual Review of Psychology*, **40**, 45–81.

Micklinghoff, F. (1980). L'intégration de l'Europe et le fédéralisme. *Mezzogiorno d'Europa*, **2**.

Munch, F. (1962). Föderalismus, Völkerrecht und Gemeinschaften. *Die Öffentliche Verwaltung*, 649–50.

Ng, S. H. (1986). Equity, intergroup bias and interpersonal bias in reward allocation. *European Journal of Social Psychology*, **11**, 439–43.

Oakes, P. and Turner, J. (1980). Social categorization and intergroup behaviour: does minimal intergroup discrimination make social identity more positive? *European Journal of Social Psychology*, **10**, 295–301.

Ophuls, C. F. (1965). Die europäischen verträge als planungsverfassugen. In J. Kaiser (ed.), *Planung*. I, Baden-Baden.

Pescatore, P. (1974). *The Law of Integration*. Geneva: Leyde.

Pescatore, P. (1975). L'intégration européenne: perspective nouvelle pour le pouvoir judiciaire. *Journal des Tribunaux*, 237–41.

Rabbie, J. M. and Horwitz, M. (1988). Categories versus groups as explanatory concepts in intergroup relations. *European Journal of Social Psychology*, **18**, 117–23.

Reuter, P. (1952). Le plan Schuman. Recueil des Cours de l'Académie Internationale de Droit, II.

Rijsman, J. (1983). The dynamics of social competition in personal and categorical comparison situations. In W. Doise and S. Moscovici (eds), *Current Issues in European Social Psychology*, Vol I, Cambridge: Cambridge University Press.

Sachdev, I. and Bourhis, R. Y. (1987). Social categorization and power differentials in group relations. *European Journal of Social Psychology*, **15**, 415–34.

Simon, B. (1983). On the asymmetry in the cognitive construal of ingroup and outgroup: a model of egocentric social categorization. *European Journal of Social Psychology*, **23**, 131–48.

Simon, B. and Pettigrew, T. F. (1990). Social identity and perceived group homogeneity: evidence for the ingroup homogeneity effect. *European Journal of Social Psychology*, **20**, 269–86.

Snyder, C. R., Lassegard, M. A., and Ford, C. E. (1986). Distancing after group success and failure: basking in reflected glory and cutting after failure. *Journal of Personality and Social Psychology*, **51**, 382–88.

Sousa, E. (1989). Social identification patterns and ingroup derogation. Paper presented at the East-West Meeting of the EAESP, Jablonna.

Sousa, E. (1993). Social identification and attribution patterns. In M-F. Pichevin, M-C. Hurtig and M. Piolat (eds), *Studies on the Self and Social Cognition*. Singapore: Scientific World.

Stein, E., Hay, P. and Waelbroeck, M. (1976). *European Community Law and Institutions in Perspective: Text Cases and Readings*. Indianapolis.

Tajfel, H. (1972). La catégorisation sociale. In S. Moscovici (ed.), *Introduction à la Psychologie Sociale*, vol I, Paris: Larousse.

Tajfel, H. (1978). *Differentiation between Social Groups*. CA: Academic Press.

Tajfel, H. (1982). *Social Identity and Intergroup Relations*. Cambridge: Cambridge University Press.

Tajfel, H. and Turner, J. (1979). An integrative theory of intergroup conflict. In W. G. Austin, and S. Worchel (eds), *The Social Psychology of Intergroup Relations*. Monterey, CA, Brooks/Cole.

Tizzano, A. (1967). *La Corte di Giustizia delle Comunità Europee*, Naples.

Tonnies, F. (1947). *Comunidad y sociedad*. Buenos Aires (Spanish translation).

Turner, J. C. (1981). Towards a cognitive definition of the social group. In J. C. Turner and H. Giles (eds), *Intergroup Behaviour*. Oxford: Blackwell.

Turner, J. C. (1987). *Rediscovering the Social Group: A Self-categorization Theory*. Oxford: Basil Blackwell.

Turner, J. (1988). Comments on Doise's individual and social identities in intergroup relations. *European Journal of Social Psychology*, **18**, 113–16.

Turner, J. C., Sachdev, I., and Hogg, M. A. (1983). Social categorization, interpersonal attraction and group formation. *British Journal of Social Psychology*, **22**, 227–39.

Waddell, N. and Cairns, E. (1986). Situational perspectives on social identity in Northern Ireland. *British Journal of Social Psychology*, **25**, 25–32.

Wagner, U., Lampen, L. and Syllwasschy, J. (1988). In-group inferiority, social identity and out-group devaluation in a modified minimal group study. *British Journal of Social Psychology*, **25**, 15–23.

20

Intergroup Attitudes, Levels of Identification and Social Change

MARGARITA SANCHEZ-MAZAS

University of Geneva, Switzerland

For quite a long time social psychology has addressed the issue of social identity in the context of intergroup relations. Since the early 1970s, a theoretical framework has been developed, based on the general idea that tension and hostility between groups has deeper psychological roots than those involved in an objective conflict of interests, as proposed by the "realistic conflict theory" (Sherif, 1966). This line of research, referred to as Social Identity Theory (Tajfel, 1978, 1981, 1982; Turner, 1975; Tajfel and Turner, 1979, 1986), addresses intergroup relations in the light of the general process of social categorisation by which individuals structure and simplify their social environment by grouping people into meaningful categories. This process provides a distinction between "we" and "they", leading people to think of themselves and others in terms of category memberships. People's social identity is derived from the knowledge that they belong to a certain category and from the subjective meaning associated with this awareness. When, according to some aspects of social reality, people define themselves primarily as group members (rather than as individuals), they are motivated to differentiate their own group (ingroup) from the others (outgroups) in order to achieve a positive social identity. On the basis of the hypothesis that people strive to maintain or to seek a positive social identity through the distinctiveness of the ingroup, the theory explains the pervasiveness of discrimination in intergroup relations, even though actual conflict of interest is not at stake (cf. Brewer, 1979).

With the development of Europe, however, the concern is no longer identity management from an intergroup approach alone. We should also address the transition from a certain level of identification, such as the national one, to a higher or "supranational" level of identification. That is, the way people will conceive themselves in the case of category assimilation rather than category differentiation needs to be accounted for. An appropriate framework for dealing with this issue is self-categorisation theory (Turner, 1985; Turner *et al.*, 1987), which posits that people categorise themselves at different levels of abstraction and generalisation. Self-categorisation denotes people's behaviour in terms of personal or social self, according to whether the situation evokes individual or shared identity. Turner and his colleagues indeed showed the self to be flexible in that individuals appear capable of ensuring their self-concept by categorising themselves into more or less inclusive ingroups. If assimilation of outgroups into new larger ingroups does not threaten one's positive social identity, the development of a European identity transcending former national ones indeed would be possible.

With the restructuring of Europe and the availability of a new and broader identification schema, however, we observe the concomitant development of specific infra-national or regional groupings and, in some countries like Switzerland, majority-based reservations about engaging in Europe. This chapter's goal is to outline possible constraints people might have in redefining their social self in broader terms, as well as ways to overcome these possible constraints.

Fundamental to the issue of Europe are the social-psychological processes underlying the emergence of a higher-order identity. This emergence, of course, is not independent of the world-wide context wherein this takes place. In terms of the self-categorisation theory, just as the creation of any ingroup presupposes the existence of an outgroup, the constitution of a higher-order ingroup proceeds from the widening of the frame of reference and the designation of higher-order outgroups. Although not always recognised, of utmost importance also are the processes involved in the transition from one ingroup to another possible, more inclusive, ingroup. And this new group can be considered or refused as a membership group. Put otherwise, the process towards a European identity might be problematic as long as potential European citizens continue to view other nation's citizens as outgroupers. Moreover, for some people, compatriots' involvement with these outgroupers may be a source of de-identification with the ingroup.

Hence, it may well be that initial attitudes towards the outgroups need to be taken into account. This chapter's major argument will be that increasing the salience of a category comprising both in- and outgroup may either enhance or undermine a collective identity, depending on the particular view people hold of a relevant outgroup. Specifically, I discuss the results of several experiments conducted with individuals holding moderately or strongly negative attitudes towards the outgroup and who appeared to be particularly resistant to contextual transformations such as variations in the intergroup comparison modes or induced categorical representations.

Ingroup Identity: Besides or Against the Outgroup

Change in the form that positive identity preservation can take when an intergroup comparison has been made salient was examined by Mummendey and Schreiber (1983). According to these authors, individuals may secure their positive self-concept either by discriminating against or by simply differentiating themselves from outgroups. What orientation will be taken depends on the conditions under which both groups are assessed. The results of their study indicate that when subjects had to evaluate the ingroup and the outgroup on a single dimension (negatively interdependent allocation mode) they tended to give preference to their own group more than when the evaluation was made on two separate dimensions (independent allocation mode). A negatively interdependent allocation mode ("what the other group gains, my group loses") favours outgroup discrimination. By contrast, an independent allocation mode (in which both groups are evaluated separately) appears to dissipate the prevalent tendency to favour one's group over the outgroup and encourages intergroup differentiation (van Knippenberg and Ellemers, 1990).

Following this research, we propose the hypothesis that depending on their initial view of outsiders, individuals would secure their positive identity mainly by discriminating against the outgroup or by simply differentiating it from the ingroup. That is, a negatively interdependent way of thinking the relations between one's fellow countrymen and foreigners might be the typical mode of reasoning in xenophobia. More tolerant attitudes towards foreigners should instead be characterised by independent assessments meaning favourable judgements of one's own as well as the outgroup.

Study 1 was designed to test these ideas. It was set up as an allocation task involving 118 Swiss nationals from different socio-economic and cultural backgrounds (Mugny et al., 1991, exp. 1). The subjects were divided according to their initial attitude towards foreign residents in Switzerland. This was done by means of a pretest asking subjects to express on a scale from 8 to 22 per cent what percentage of foreigners they considered to be desirable in their country. The subjects who put the limit below 15 per cent (given as the current percentage of foreign population) were considered as "xenophobes", those favouring the status quo as "intermediates" and those who put the limit above 15 per cent were considered as "xenophiles". The experimental manipulation consisted of the induction of a negatively interdependent versus an independent allocation mode. Subjects had to attribute points to express to what extent they approved of five claims (related to improvement in education, in social assistance, in job opportunities, in training facilities and political rights), the beneficiaries being on the one hand Swiss nationals (i.e. the ingroup) and foreign residents (i.e. the outgroup) on the other hand. In the negatively interdependent condition, subjects distributed a total of 100 points "neither more or less" to be divided between Swiss and foreigners. In this way the points allotted to one group were necessarily subtracted from those accorded to the other. In the independent

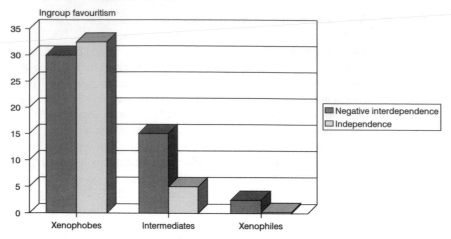

FIGURE 20.1   Ingroup favouritism as a function of allocation mode and subject classification

condition, subjects attributed to the ingroup and, independently, to the outgroup a number of points that could be as high as 100 for each group. Thus the points allotted to one group were not necessarily dependent on those accorded to the other.

The allocations over the five claims were summed up into one index. The results showed xenophobes to express a strong ingroup favouritism, regardless of the allocation mode condition (see Figure 20.1). Xenophiles expressed virtually no ingroup favouritism, again irrespective of experimental conditions. Intermediates, however, showed ingroup favouritism under a negatively interdependent allocation mode, but no favouritism at all under an independent allocation mode. In terms of identity management, these results suggest that under independence intermediates obtain a positive social identity by means of intergroup differentiation without outgroup discrimination. In both conditions xenophilic subjects treat outgroup members as ingroup ones and probably include Swiss and foreigners in the same membership category. Xenophobes continued to discriminate even when allowed to make allocations that run contrary to the use of ingroup favouritism as a means of preserving ingroup distinctiveness. This indicates that their positive social identity is associated with a tendency to persistently seek an advantage for the ingroup over the outgroup. Xenophobes thus obtain and maintain a positive social identity by intergroup differentiation and outgroup discrimination.

Study 1 verified the general hypothesis that attitudes towards an outgroup are related to the way an individual represents intergroup relationships and manages his/her social identity within an intergroup context. The more hostile an individual is to an outgroup, the more s/he will invest in maintaining a discrepancy between his/her own group and "the others". It was further hypothesised that this need for intergroup differentiation, through outgroup discrimination, would in turn affect the recategorisation processes and the construction of an identity at a higher level of generalisation. This was the question addressed in a second experiment, which involved only subjects from similar social and cultural origins. Because in study 1 outgroup attitudes were, at least partially, related to the social status of individuals (those from working class backgrounds had a lower mean in the pretest than the middle class and upper middle class subjects; see Roux *et al.*, 1993), the following studies, involving individuals of equal social status, were intended to address ideological and attitudinal differences more directly.

Changing Identity: Assimilation of Outgroups or Dissimilation from Ingroups

Some researchers have specifically focused on the effects of an induced one-group categorisation (including ingroup and outgroup members) upon the preferential treatment for one's own group, that is upon ingroup bias (Gaertner *et al.*, 1989). Attenuation of this bias would result from the blurring of intergroup boundaries brought about by the process of social categorisation that accentuates intra-category similarities and inter-category differences (Tajfel and Wilkes, 1963; Tajfel *et al.*, 1974). By this process, outgroup members presented together with ingroup members are recategorised as members of a more inclusive ingroup, since the cognitive salience of intergroup boundaries has been reduced. Consequently, outgroup members are brought closer to the self and evaluated more positively (Gaertner *et al.*, 1990). However, one can also imagine that enhanced salience of a one-group category, instead of decreasing the social distance with outgroup members, increases the social distance with ingroup members. That is, a one-group representation may lead people to recategorise ingroup members as outgroup ones.

The purpose of study 2 was to test the proposition that if the salience of an one-group categorisation may homogenise ingroup and outgroup members, individuals would not necessarily conceive themselves as members of the new aggregate. Either they will include outgroup members in a broader ingroup, or reject former ingroup members towards the outgroup. With the first orientation ingroup benefits will be extended to the one-group entity whereas with the second, allocations to the one-group will be closer to those normally allotted to the outgroup. Again, initial attitudes with respect to the outgroup could be used to predict these categorisation orientations. The particular need for xenophobes to maintain a social distance with the foreigners was expected to prevent identification with a category implying a categorical fusion (Doise, 1978) with this particularly relevant outgroup.

Indeed, several authors demonstrated that a context assimilating in- and outgroup may provoke aversive reactions when individuals are strongly interested in retaining ingroup distinctiveness (Deschamps and Brown, 1983; Brown and Wade, 1987). Accordingly, people with initially favourable attitudes towards the outgroup may be likely to consider membership of a new, broader group and hence be able to categorise themselves at a higher level. In contrast, people strongly opposing the outgroup would dissimilate themselves from the one-group category and categorise themselves at a subordinate or even individual level. To test this prediction, the procedure of study 1 was repeated with the addition of a third assessment mode involving a unique allocation for both groups, as a means of making the one-group categorisation salient. In the latter condition, the gains of one group are also the gains of the other, the interests of "Swiss and foreigners together" being positively and perfectly interrelated.

In this study (Sanchez-Mazas *et al.*, in press), 141 Swiss apprentices participated. A pretest, similar to the one used in study 1, was used to classify subjects as xenophobes and xenophiles (this time the latter subgroup included both intermediates and xenophiles). The negatively interdependent and independent allocation modes were the same as in study 1. The one-group categorisation was induced by means of a "positively interdependent" allocation mode, in which subjects had at their disposal an amount of 100 points to be allocated to "the Swiss and foreigners together" as collective beneficiary. Thus, they used a single percentage to give their approval for each of the five claims. As previously, a single index was computed for ingroup, outgroup and one-group allocations.

The results for the xenophobes showed a clear ingroup favouritism both under the negatively interdependent and the independent condition. For the xenophiles, the favouritism was somewhat more marked under the negatively interdependent allocation mode but was still marginally present under independence. Thus, the category of foreigners appeared indeed as a relevant outgroup. Concerning the allocations to the one-group, the results showed that the one-group was given more points by xenophiles than by xenophobes, thus already indicating different adjustments to the one-group entity, depending on initial positions. However, to answer the main question addressed here (whether people categorise the one-group as an ingroup or as an outgroup) the one-group allocations under positive interdependence were first compared with the ingroup allocations under independence. As can be seen in Figure 20.2, it appeared that xenophiles allocated the one-group the same amount under positive interdependence as the ingroup under independence. Thus, xenophiles would extend the ingroup benefits to the one-group category. In contrast, xenophobes allotted significantly less resources to the one-group under positive interdependence than to the ingroup under independence. Furthermore, for xenophobes, the difference between the one-group allocations under positive interdependence and the ingroup allocations under independence was larger than the difference between these one-group allocations and the outgroup allocations under independence. Put otherwise, xenophobes appeared to treat the one-group category as an outgroup rather than as an ingroup.

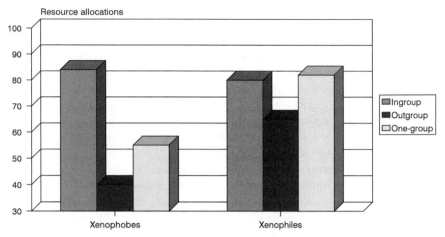

FIGURE 20.2   Allocations to the ingroup, the outgroup and the one-group by xenophobes and xenophiles

With study 2 we were able to show that categorising ingroup and outgroup into a single but broader entity proceeds alternatively from an ingroup or an outgroup reference point. Being openminded towards the outgroup leads individuals to maintain membership in a collective entity, thus suggesting a self-categorisation at a superordinate level. Negative attitudes with respect to the outgroup, in contrast, inhibit this higher level categorisation. In this case, group membership is likely to be defined predominantly within an intergroup framework. The salience of a one-group categorisation, instead of reducing the social distance between groups, seems to evoke a de-categorisation from the ingroup.

Taken together, these experiments support the idea that the individual's intergroup attitudes determine particular managements of and levels of social identity. First, the results highlight the beneficial effects of the variations in the way in- and outgroup are assessed on behaviour and categorisation processes. These effects, however, appear to be limited to individuals holding moderate intergroup attitudes; more biased individuals remain insensitive to the variations in intergroup assessments. Second, the experiments suggest that attitudes firmly entrenched in intergroup differentiation may not only hinder identification with a one-group category, but sometimes even undermine former ingroup memberships.

Tackling Intergroup Attitudes Through Social Influence

Because attitudes towards the outgroup appear to be crucial to the effectiveness of both the intergroup comparison modes and the induction of a one-group category, social influence and persuasion may be a relevant way of altering these attitudes in the first place. For more biased individuals, attitudes may be more easily accessible to change than their definition of their social identity. And it may be likely that attitude changes affect in turn the flexibility of the self and the self-categorisation processes. Hence, we examined whether influence attempts could lead xenophobic individuals to adopt a complementary rather than a competitive way of assessing both groups and whether these influence attempts contribute to redirect the self-categorisation processes towards higher levels of generalisation.

In our research we focused on minority sources for two reasons. First, a position that overtly puts forward equal rights for nationals and foreigners is still normatively minoritarian in most, if not all, European countries. Second, tolerant attitudes and open-mindedness towards foreigners imply a minority influence on a majority point of view and way of thinking, given the social reality in which our experiments were conducted. In the Swiss socio-political context of the two last decades, several initiatives of solidarity with immigrant workers only attracted a minority of votes. Nowadays, more radical popular initiatives promoting political rights for foreign residents are on their way and several minoritarian groups are campaigning in their defence. Such interventions endow different characteristics, according to the status or the ideological stance of the particular minority. Differences can be found in the conflictiveness of their argument as well as in the type of relationship between nationals and foreigners they advocate (Mugny and Pérez, 1985; Pérez et al., 1989). The effectiveness of minority influence would, ultimately, depend on particular features of their persuasive attempts.

Study 3 focused on xenophobic subjects, who did not exploit the opportunity offered by the independent allocation mode to counteract their usual thinking in negatively interdependent terms. It was assumed that if the independent allocation mode per se was not effective, it would nevertheless favour attitude change to a greater extent than the negatively interdependent mode, when induced in combination with minority influence. Because negative interdependence was found to be typical of the xenophobic way of assessing in and outgroup, it may reinforce rather than attenuate the discriminatory logic of xenophobes. We therefore examined the combined effects of these intergroup allocation modes (negatively interdependent versus independent) and a minority appeal arguing directly in favour of the rights of foreign residents.

From the research on minority influence (Moscovici, 1976; Mugny, 1982; Moscovici et al., 1985; Mugny and Pérez, 1991; Paicheler, 1988), we derived the hypothesis that the effectiveness of a minority source relates to the conflict it evokes, rather than to the approval it receives. We also know that this type of influence often takes the form of conversion (Moscovici, 1980; Moscovici and Mugny, 1987) and manifests itself into an indirect rather than direct impact. Hence, a minority source may be initially rejected but eventually elicit positions more in line with its argument, despite, or perhaps because of, the conflict it engenders (Pérez and Mugny, 1990a). Therefore we expected a minority influence at an indirect level, in the form of more favourable intergroup attitudes, in conditions involving independent rather than negatively interdependent allocation mode, especially when the minority used a conflictual tone. In study 3 (Mugny *et al.*, 1991, exp. 2), 109 Swiss apprentices were retained for analysis on the basis of their hostile pretest-attitude to the presence of foreigners in their country. Before distributing resources between Swiss and foreigners in either a negatively interdependent or independent way, they were presented with a xenophile appeal attributed to a minority group. It argued for foreigners' rights in an imperative versus an optative style, that is in a more versus less conflictual tone. In the imperative condition, the proposals in favour of foreigners (dealing with various social rights) were all introduced by the formulation "it is absolutely essential that. . .", whereas in the optative condition this introduction said "it would be desirable if. . .". The main dependent variables were ingroup favouritism and attitudes towards the foreigners.

Results showed first of all that the subjects strongly disagreed with the content of the minority statement, whatever tone of argument was used. The results for allocations showed that, consistent with the xenophobes' responses found in study 1, ingroup favouritism did not vary across conditions, neither as a function of negatively interdependent versus independent allocation mode, nor as a function of optative versus imperative style of argument. The negatively interdependent allocation mode therefore appeared unmodified, despite the opportunity offered by independent allocations to orient the behaviour in the direction of intergroup complementarity. Concerning attitudes, two different indexes wcrc computed, one based on five statements present in the minority appeal (direct influence), the other one based on five claims not explicitly alluded to in the appeal (indirect influence). No difference was found between conditions on direct influence. At the indirect level, however, more favourable attitudes towards foreigners were found under independent rather than interdependent assessment. Furthermore, as predicted, this contrast was stronger in the imperative rather than in the optative condition. Thus, independent allocations favoured indirect influence, suggesting that minoritarian campaigns have some interest, when challenging "hard" attitudes, in thwarting discrimination while preserving some intergroup distinctiveness.

The optative versus imperative style of arguing of course is not the only minoritarian strategy that could be considered. Of particular interest for our purpose are those strategies that instead of appealing for more tolerance towards the outgroup, thus maintaining the intergroup differentiation, enhance common interests, similarities between groups, the importance of uniting or, put more generally, that are based on superordinate concerns. This type of minority influence may be seen as a normative context that would back up the induction of a one-group categorisation. As such, would it help a self-categorisation at a higher level to arise from an induced one-group representation? This was the question addressed in the following study.

Human Rights and Social Change

Most issues, within the current *Zeitgeist*, are addressed in terms of humanitarian norms. Human rights are not only alluded to by large social groups, such as in massive popular reactions following the perpetration of racist crimes. They are used by certain minoritarian groups in their antiracist or antixenophobic fight as well. One particular feature of these influence endeavours is their focus on superordinate rather than intergroup arguments. An interesting question was therefore to assess the impact of a minoritarian appeal dealing with human rights and equalitarian norms together with the induction of a one-group or an in/outgroup categorisation. In order to give as much ecological validity as possible to our experimental situation, we employed as influence message a text that had actually been circulated in the social context and that was originated from a real antiracist and antixenophobic group. This message was headed "Chart for Equal Rights" and advanced a series of claims relating to education, social and political rights, housing, social protection, all presented as fundamental rights for every human being. As such, the outgroup, foreigners living in Switzerland, was not mentioned at all. A control condition without message was introduced to assess the impact of the influence attempt.

In this study, the independent allocation mode was contrasted with a positively interdependent allocation mode. The proposed message, dealing with super-ordinate concerns, was compatible with a one-group categorisation, more so than with an intergroup differentiation. It was therefore expected to reinforce the effects of the induced one-group categorisation (positive interdependence) both upon the attitudes towards foreigners and the self-categorisation processes towards a higher level of generalisation. Following our past research, however, this was more likely to occur for moderate and low rather than high xenophobic individuals. It was plausible that the most xenophobic individuals would support a humanitarian message while refusing the categorical assimilation implied by the positively interdependent allocations. Research on prejudice provides suggestive evidence that biased people may support equalitarian concerns while simultaneously maintaining discriminatory beliefs (Katz and Hass, 1988; Billig *et al.*, 1988). It was predictable therefore for xenophobes to be influenced in their attitudes by a humanitarian message, though more so when in- and outgroup were assessed separately rather than together. This would further suggest that in the case of strongly hostile intergroup attitudes, influences on attitudes benefit from an independent allocation mode not only with respect to a negatively interdependent one (Mummendey and Schreiber, 1983; Mugny *et al.*, 1991) but also with respect to a positively interdependent one.

In study 4 (Sanchez-Mazas, in preparation), the design was a $2 \times 2 \times 2$ factorial, involving Allocation Mode (independent versus positively interdependent), Social Influence (message versus no message) and Initial Attitude (xenophobe versus xenophile). The dependent variables were the allocations to ingroup, outgroup and one-group and the attitudes towards the outgroup. The pretest and the manipulation of the allocation mode were identical as in the preceding experiments. After giving their opinion about the desirable percentage of foreigners in their country, half the subjects read the "Chart for Human Rights" attributed to a minority source and were asked to indicate to what extent they approved of its content. After the reading or immediately following the pretest, the manipulation of allocation mode was introduced. In one condition, the subjects had to allocate resources to Swiss and foreigners separately (independent condition), in the other condition they assessed Swiss and foreigners together (positively interdependent condition). Finally, they filled out an attitude questionnaire containing seven statements in favour of foreigners (e.g. right to low cost accommodation, to dual nationality for immigrant children, political rights, reuniting of families, etc.). These attitude statements were of an indirect nature, since they assessed attitudes towards foreigners, not alluded to in the message.

On the basis of the pretest, the 120 Swiss apprentices participating in this experiment were classified as xenophobes or xenophiles. The source was seen as clearly minoritarian by xenophobes and xenophiles. Although both categories did agree with the content of the message, this support was more marked for xenophiles than for xenophobes. The results for attitudes (the ratings were summed together into one index) indicated that xenophobes had less favourable attitudes than xenophiles. This effect was qualified by an interaction between Influence, Allocation Mode and Initial Position, showing that xenophobes expressed less favourable attitudes under positively interdependent than independent allocation mode, while xenophiles expressed more favourable attitudes under positively interdependent than independent mode, albeit only in the Influence condition. Thus, consistent with the results of study 3, the effects of the induced allocation modes upon indirect attitudes did appear in case of an influence attempt, for both xenophobes and xenophiles.

To know whether the one-group allocation mode contributed to redirect the categorisation processes towards a higher level, the ratings were analysed in the same way as in the second experiment reported above (see Sanchez-Mazas et al., in press). The one-group ratings under positive interdependence were first compared to the ingroup ratings under independence (see Figure 20.3). Results showed that xenophobes clearly favoured the ingroup under independence over the one-group under positive interdependence whereas no difference appeared between ingroup and one-group allocations for xenophiles. An interaction between the three variables (Influence, Allocation Mode and Initial Position) further specified that the above effects hold for the control condition, whereas in the influence condition xenophiles rated higher the one-group than the ingroup. Thus, xenophiles gave identical allocations to the one-group and to the ingroup in the control condition whereas in the influence condition they increased the one-group allocations with respect to the ingroup ones. This suggests that for xenophiles, the salience of a normative context induced by influence processes not only favours positive attitude change but can help developing a superordinate identification.

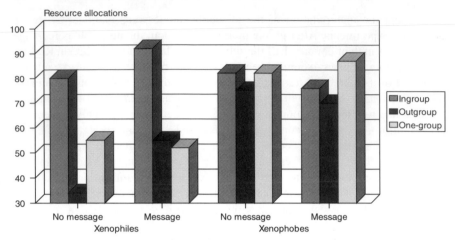

FIGURE 20.3   Allocations to the ingroup, the outgroup and the one-group as a function of allocation mode, subject classification and social influence

Also, the one-group ratings under positive interdependence were compared to the outgroup ratings under independence. This analysis showed that xenophiles, as expected, rated higher the one-group than the outgroup. For xenophobes, the results indicated that they allocated more resources to the outgroup in the influence condition than in the control condition while the means for one-group allocations did not change according to whether influence was induced or not. However, as shown in Figure 20.3, these subjects also increased the ingroup allocations in the influence condition with respect to the control condition. As a result, the amount of ingroup favouritism remained the same, whatever the context (message vs no message). This reflects that the message dealing with human rights exerted influence specifically on the in- and outgroup separate allocations. It led the xenophobes to bring the outgroup allocations up to the level of those of the one-group category where the ingroup was included. However, this increase was "compensated" by a corresponding increase of ingroup allocations. Finally, since the one-group allocations were not affected by the induced influence attempts, we can conclude that social influence did not help xenophobes to categorise the one-group entity as ingroup.

Discussion and Conclusions

The major goal of this chapter was, as mentioned, to stress the importance of considering changes in managements and levels of social identity from the point of view of attitudes. With the first experiment we began extending our knowledge about the meanings associated with different intergroup allocation modes and their correspondence with intergroup attitudes and ideological positions. The results showed that these allocation modes were particularly resistant to change when well defined attitudes were involved. Whatever mode was induced, negatively interdependent or independent, outgroup discrimination ensued for xenophobes and intergroup equality for xenophiles. It was also seen that individuals who were intermediate between an anti- and a pro-foreigners position were sensitive to the variation of the induced allocation modes. The opportunity to make independent allocations counteracted these individuals' inclination towards outgroup discrimination and led them to treat the outgroup as favourably as the ingroup.

With study 1 we could propose the notion that the behaviour performed in these intergroup settings did correspond to particular ways individuals manage their social identity and seek a positive self-concept. For xenophobes, outgroup discrimination seems necessary to maintain a positive social identity, as shown in study 3 as well. Xenophiles' behaviour, in contrast, shows that their positive self-concept does not depend on intergroup discrimination. However, their equal treatment for both groups whatever allocation mode was induced (even under negative interdependence) may be due to the fact that foreigners as such were not a relevant comparison group. More interestingly, the results for the intermediates indicate that under different circumstances, the individuals' self-concept may be secured either by discriminating against the outgroup or by simply differentiating it from the ingroup.

These results support the idea that leading people to perceive the intergroup relationship as noncompetitive encourages them to resort to more desirable strategies than ingroup favouritism, such as fairness, in order to secure one's own positive identity (Mummendey and Schreiber, 1983; Branthwaite et al., 1979; Billig, 1973). Still, the results for xenophobes indicate that the induction of different intergroup assessments do not deflect them from ingroup favouritism as a norm of conduct.

Study 2 focused more specifically on behaviour performed under different levels of categorisation. Because xenophobes' social identity preservation was found in study 1 to be related to intergroup discrepancy, we expected more aversive reactions towards the intergroup assimilation induced by the positively interdependent allocation mode, than for less xenophobic subjects, whose openness to intergroup equality should predispose to joint assessments. Although foreigners turned out to be a relevant outgroup for xenophobes and xenophiles (as demonstrated by the ingroup favouritism in the separate assessments), the former allotted significantly less resources than the latter to the one-group which included this outgroup. As such, this result might suggest that depending on their attitudes, people are more or less ready to sacrifice ingroup resources when these are interrelated with outgroup resources. However, examination of one-group allocations relative to ingroup independent allocations on the one hand and outgroup independent allocations on the other hand discards this interpretation. These comparisons provided support for the hypothesis that a superordinate entity including former ingroup and outgroup is categorised either as ingroup or as outgroup depending on people's initial positions towards the outgroup. The results showed indeed that the xenophobes' allocations to the one-group category were closer to the outgroup allocations than to the ingroup allocations. Conversely, the xenophiles' allocations to the one-group were not different from ingroup allocations. These results indicate that the behaviour performed under the positively interdependent condition has to be regarded as ingroup behaviour in the case of xenophiles and behaviour towards an outgroup in the case of xenophobes.

In terms of social identification, the results of study 2 suggest that the salience of a one-group category is likely either to elicit a removal of intergroup boundaries and a possible identification with a broader ingroup or a shift of intergroup boundaries and the subsequent definition of the social identity outside the former ingroup. By implication, the induction of a one-group category would result in further subdivisions of the former ingroup. Additional research is needed however to assess the effects of this de-categorisation process which could lead individuals either to categorise themselves at an individual level or to seek alternative subgroups to identify with. Replaced in the European context, these findings could help to understand the processes underlying dissimilation from the European Community and even with former relevant national categories and motivating the expression of national concerns in more extreme forms.

One theoretical implication of these findings is concerned with the factors accounting for a decreased intensity of affiliation with the ingroup. In the framework of the Social Identity Theory, individuals attempt to leave their ingroup when its evaluation with reference to other specific groups is unsatisfactory. The antecedent conditions for alienation from the ingroup are primarily conceptualised in relation to unequal status between different social groups (Tajfel, 1975; Ellemers *et al.*, 1988). The emergence of intergroup uniting with the construction of Europe leads us to rethink these antecedent conditions in the circumstances where an ingroup assimilates former relevant outgroups. As the data suggest, a process of this kind is likely to weaken the subjective attachment to the ingroup among at least part of its members. Further research might in particular assess whether this dissociation from the ingroup is accounted for by the aversion for the outgroup and the need to maintain the social distance or by the perceived ingroup failure to further fulfil the aspirations of some of its members.

Another question that must be addressed in relation to the construction of a European identity is the meaning of the one-group categorisation. Categorisation is assumed to be intrinsically comparative, contextual and relative to a frame of reference (Turner *et al.*, 1987). The greater the frame of reference, i.e. the more people are included within the comparative context, the more inclusive the level of self-categorisation. People will conceive themselves more in terms of their social category if other groups are taken for comparison in the frame of reference. Hence, European members may define their outgroups outside Europe and engage in intergroup relationships based on the processes of intergroup comparison, on the need for distinctiveness, if not of superiority, of their membership group. It would be useful to know for example whether the construction of the European identity is related to increased intergroup comparison with extra-European communities. Given that members of these extra-European groups are present within Europe, namely as immigrants or asylum-seekers, the emergence of the European identity together with increased differentiation from non-Europeans would not necessarily result in more harmonious intergroup relations.

Both study 1 and study 2 pointed to the importance of addressing attitude transformation for strongly biased individuals, as a first step for more outgroup acceptance, that in turn may weaken the rigid link between positive social identity and intergroup differentiation. In experiments 3 and 4 we assessed the combined effects of induced influence processes and intergroup allocation modes upon attitudes towards the outgroup. Study 3 showed that even when backed up by a minority appeal, independent allocations did not deflect xenophobes from their discriminatory functioning, thus supporting the idea that negatively interdependent assessments of ingroup and outgroup correspond to the xenophobic way of managing the social identity. A conflictual stance was not even likely to reduce the magnitude of favouritism in independence with respect to interdependence.

However, despite the resistance that emerged repeatedly at the direct level of influence (disagreement with the source, ingroup favouritism, negative attitudes expressed on the propositions raised by the minority), independent allocations did allow a latent influence typical of the conversion effect. This evokes the conditions under which the validation process (Moscovici, 1980) that is the recognition of the minority viewpoint as having an alternative value, has been supposed to operate. Indirect minority influence through validation supposes the targets' descentration from their point of view and a socio-cognitive functioning mode characterised by divergent thinking (Nemeth, 1986). It suggests complex cognitive activity on the part of the target (Maass *et al.*, 1987) and specifically a process of social constructivism (Mugny and Pérez, 1988) based on decentring. This implies in particular that comparison processes do not monopolise all the targets' attention and their concern to defend a threatened social identity (Pérez and Mugny, 1990b). Similarly, we can assume that in the realm of social influence dealing with intergroup relations, the targets' cognitive activity must be freed from certain social comparisons that can be assumed to be particularly compelling in negative interdependence, where they foster competition. In this sense, because it is not felt too compelling for identity management strategies, independence may be specifically beneficial when minority influence is involved, supposing initial resistance but at the same time an impossibility to neglect a conflictual point of view.

The results of study 4 first showed that an influence attempt specifically designed to enhance a self-categorisation at a higher-level did not lead xenophobic individuals to assess the one-group entity as an ingroup. The same processes as in study 2, that is categorisation of the one-group as outgroup rather than ingroup and individuals' de-categorisation from the ingroup, are supposed to operate, even in a context of social influence. In this sense, the results directly address influence strategies that resort to superordinate categorisations in order to promote intergroup solidarity or to develop a collective identity in the perspective of a unified Europe. In this last study, we have also seen that independence facilitated an indirect influence. This effect may as in study 3 be explained by the fact that the allocation mode, in this case positive interdependence, can be regarded as an intergroup comparison context inhibiting the validation process. Indeed, positive interdependence may absorb the target's attention because it constrains dissimilation, contrary to independent assessments.

An alternative explanation could be that within an influence context that makes salient an equalitarian norm, the discriminatory behaviour under independence appears to be contradictory with this egalitarian norm. A message emphasising human rights and equalitarian norms was incompatible with the actual discriminatory behaviour of xenophobic individuals. Hence, biased individuals would change their attitudes at the indirect level because of the normative conflict introduced by the source. This interpretation found support in the results for the xenophobic subjects in experiment 4, showing under independence at the same time an agreement with the egalitarian statement and nevertheless strong outgroup discrimination. As far as xenophobes were concerned, we can assume the presence of two contradictory elements, discrimination and egalitarism, leading to a value conflict, as conceptualised by Tetlock (1986). Value conflict refers to "differentiation", that is the recognition of diverse dimensions of an issue and "integration", that is the development of conceptual connections among them. Following Tetlock's idea that people are likely to think about an issue in integratively complex ways when it entails two conflicting values and Moscovici's contention that attitude change emerges from an intense socio-cognitive conflict (Moscovici, 1980), the effects for indirect attitudes found in the last study could be regarded from an approach explaining social influence from a conflict elaboration perspective (Pérez and Mugny, 1993).

There is indeed some first evidence for the idea that a normative conflict lies at the heart of attitude change (Sanchez-Mazas et al., 1993). This is the case when the egalitarian norm is made salient and relevant for the recipients by its anchoring into a reference group, but directly conflicts with the targets' discriminatory behaviour. Paradoxically then, if a negatively interdependent allocation mode can be seen from an intergroup approach as confining individuals to their competitive behaviour, it can be used, even more efficiently than an independent mode, to elicit a normative conflict inducing changes in attitudes and norms of behaviour. Moreover, in the realm of race-related attitudes as well, the perspective of inducing conflicts between some manifest negative behaviour or evaluation of the outgroup and an antidiscriminatory norm interiorised in the individual's value system, provides stimulating insights about the means likely to reach and to modify latent racism (Pérez *et al.*, 1993).

Taken together, the research program discussed here suggests that the social categorisation approach may have some limitations in dealing with intergroup behaviour. Induced variations of the categorisation processes through different rating methods may lead to the elimination of outgroup discrimination or to recategorisation of the outgroup as ingroup, as far as strongly prejudiced attitudes are not involved. These inductions in the studies reported here proved to be efficient for individuals who had to some degree already broken with xenophobia. This suggests that intergroup attitudes are to be considered when predictions are to be made about the beneficial effects of changing the categorical representations in order to bring groups together or to enhance superordinate identifications. When a rigid discriminatory intergroup system appears to be rooted in ideological positions, the perspective of inducing normative conflicts which address primarily prejudiced beliefs and ambivalent attitudes offers new possible paths for addressing social changes aimed at developing a sense of collective identity.

References

Billig, M. (1973). Normative communication in a minimal intergroup situation. *European Journal of Social Psychology*, **3**, 339–44.

Billig, M., Condor, S., Edwards, D., Gane, M., Middleton, D. and Radley, A. (1988). *Ideological Dilemmas: A Social Psychology of Everyday Thinking*. London: Sage Publications.

Branthwaite, A., Doyle, S. and Lightbown, N. (1979). The balance between fairness and discrimination. *European Journal of Social Psychology*, **9**, 149–63.

Brewer, M. B. (1979). In-group bias in the minimal intergroup situation: a cognitive-motivational analysis. *Psychological Bulletin*, **86**, 307–24.

Brown, R. and Wade, G. (1987). Superordinate goals and intergroup behaviour: the effect of role ambiguity and status on intergroup attitudes and task performance. *European Journal of Social Psychology*, **17**, 131–42.

Deschamps, J. C. and Brown, R. (1983). Superordinate goals and intergroup conflict. *British Journal of Social Psychology*, **22**, 189–95.

Doise, W. (1978). *Groups and Individuals*. Cambridge: Cambridge University Press.

Ellemers, N., Van Knippenberg, A., De Vries, N. and Wilke, H. (1988). Social identification and permeability of group boundaries. *European Journal of Social Psychology*, **18**, 497–513.

Gaertner, S. L., Mann, J. A., Murrell, A. J. and Dovidio, J. F. (1989). Reducing intergroup bias: the benefits of recategorization. *Journal of Personality and Social Psychology*, **57**, 239–49.

Gaertner, S. L., Mann, J. A., Dovidio J. F., Murrell, A. J. and Pomare, M. (1990). How does cooperation reduce intergroup bias? *Journal of Personality and Social Psychology*, **59**, 692–704.

Katz, I. and Hass, R. G. (1988). Racial ambivalence and American value conflict: correlational and priming studies of dual cognitive structures. *Journal of Personality and Social Psychology*, **55**, 893–905.

Maass, A., West, S. G., and Cialdini, R. B. (1987). Minority influence and conversion. In C. Hendrick (ed.), *Group Processes*. Newbury Park, NJ: Sage.

Moscovici, S. (1976). *Social Influence and Social Change*. London: Academic Press.

Moscovici, S. (1980). Toward a theory of conversion behaviour. In L. Berkowitz (ed.), *Advances in Experimental Social Psychology*, Vol. 13. New York: Academic Press.

Moscovici, S. and Mugny, G. (eds) (1987). *Psychologie de la conversion*. Cousset: Delval.

Moscovici, S., Mugny, G. and Van Avermaet, E. (eds) (1985). *Perspectives on Minority Influence*. Cambridge, Paris: Cambridge University Press, Editions de la Maison des Sciences de l'Homme.

Mugny, G. (1982). *The Power of Minorities*. London: Academic Press.

Mugny, G. and Pérez, J. A. (1985). Influence sociale, conflit et identification: étude experimentale autour d'une persuasion "manquée" lors d'une votation. *Cahiers de Psychologie Sociale*, **26**, 1–20.

Mugny, G. and Pérez, J. A. (1988). Minority influence and constructivism in social psychology. *British Psychological Society Social Psychology Section Newsletter*, **19**, 56–77.

Mugny, G. and Pérez, J. A. (1991). *The Social Psychology of Minority Influence*. Cambridge: Cambridge University Press.

Mugny, G., Sanchez-Mazas, M., Roux, P. and Pérez, J. A. (1991). Independence and interdependence of group judgments: xenophobia and minority influence. *European Journal of Social Psychology*, **21**, 213–23.

Mummendey, A. and Schreiber, H. J. (1983). Better or just different? Positive social identity by discrimination against, or by differentiation from outgroups. *European Journal of Social Psychology*, **13**, 389–97.

Nemeth, C. (1986). Differential contributions of majority and minority influence. *Psychological Review*, **93**, 23–32.

Paicheler, G. (1988). *The Psychology of Social Influence*. Cambridge: Cambridge University Press.

Pérez, J. A. and Mugny, G. (1990a). Minority influence, manifest discrimination and latent influence. In D. Abrams and M. Hogg (eds), *Social Identity Theory: Constructive and Critical Advances*. Hertfordshire: Harvester-Wheatsheaf.

Pérez, J. A. and Mugny, G. (1990b). Changement d'attitude, crédibilité et influence minoritaire: interdependance et independance de la comparaison sociale. *Revue Suisse de Psychologie*, **49**, 150–8.

Pérez, J. A. and Mugny, G. (eds) (1993). *Influences sociales: La théorie de l'élaboration du conflit*. Neuchâtel-Paris: Delachaux and Niestle.

Pérez, J. A., Mugny, G., Llavata, E. and Fierres, R. (1993). Paradoxe de la discrimination et conflit culturel: études sur le racisme. In J. A. Pérez and G. Mugny (eds), *Influences Sociales: La Théorie de l'élaboration du conflit*. Neuchâtel-Paris: Delachaux and Niestle.

Pérez, J. A., Mugny, G. and Roux, P. (1989). Evitement de la confrontation idéologique: quelques déterminants psychosociaux des stratégies persuasives. *Revue Internationale de Psychologie Sociale*, **2**, 151–63.

Roux, P., Sanchez-Mazas, M., Mugny, G. and Pérez, J. A. (1993). Minority influence and the psycho-social mechanisms of discrimination. In K. S. Larsen (ed.), *Conflict and Social Psychology*. London: Sage Publications.

Sanchez-Mazas, M., Roux, P. and Mugny, G. (in press). When the outgroup becomes ingroup and when the ingroup becomes outgroup: xenophobia and social categorization in a resource allocation task. *European Journal of Social Psychology*.

Sanchez-Mazas, M., Pérez, J. A., Navarro, E., Mugny, G. and Jovanovic, J. (1993). De la paralysie intragroupe au conflit normatif: études sur l'avortement, la contraception et la xénophobie. In J. A. Pérez and G. Mugny (eds), *Influences sociales: La théorie de l'élaboration du conflit*. Neuchâtel-Paris: Delachaux and Niestle.

Sherif, M. (1966). *In Common Predicament: Social Psychology of Intergroup Conflict and Cooperation*. Boston: Houghton Mifflin.

Tajfel, H. (1975). The exit of social mobility and the voice of social change. *Social Science Information*, **14**, 101–18.

Tajfel, H. (ed.)(1978). *Differentiation between Social Groups: Studies in the Social Psychology of Intergroup Relations*. London: Academic Press.

Tajfel, H. (1981). *Human Groups and Social Categories: Studies in Social Psychology*. Cambridge: Cambridge University Press.

Tajfel, H. (1982). *Social Identity and Intergroup Relations*. Cambridge: Cambridge University Press.

Tajfel, H., Sheikh, A. A. and Gardner, R. C. (1964). Content of stereotypes and the inference of similarity between members of stereotyped groups. *Acta Psychologica*, **22**, 191–201.

Tajfel, H. and Turner, J. C. (1979). An integrative theory of social conflict. In W. G. Austin and S.

Worchel (eds), *The Social Psychology of Intergroup Relations*. Monterey, CA: Brooks/Cole.

Tajfel, H. and Turner, J. C. (1986). The social identity theory of intergroup behaviour. In S. Worchel and W.G. Austin (eds), *Psychology of Intergroup Relations*, Chicago: Nelson-Hall.

Tajfel, H. and Wilkes, A. L. (1963). Classification and quantitative judgement. *British Journal of Social Psychology*, **54**, 101–14.

Tetlock, P. E. (1986). A value pluralism model of ideological reasoning. *Journal of Personality and Social Psychology*, **50**, 819–27.

Turner, J. C. (1975). Social comparison and social identity: some prospects for intergroup behaviour. *European Journal of Social Psychology*, **5**, 5–34,

Turner, J. C. (1985). Social categorization and the self-concept: a social cognitive theory of group behaviour. In E. J. Lawler (ed.), *Advances in Group Processes*, Vol. 2, Greenwich, CT: JAI Press.

Turner, J. C., Hogg, M., Oakes, P. J., Reicher, S. D. and Wetherell, M. S. (1987). *Rediscovering the Social Group: A Self-categorization Theory*. Oxford: Basil Blackwell.

Van Knippenberg, A. and Ellemers, N. (1990). Social identity and intergroup differentiation processes. In M. Hewstone and W. Stroebe (eds), *European Review of Social Psychology*, Vol. 1. Chichester: Wiley.

Note

These studies were carried out with the support of the Fonds National Suisse de la Recherche Scientifique.

21

English Children's Acquisition of a European Identity

MARTYN BARRETT

Social Psychology European Research Institute, University of Surrey, England

Introduction

This chapter reports the results of an exploratory study which was conducted to collect some initial data concerning the development of European identity in English children. There do not appear to have been any previous empirical studies which have investigated the development of children's supranational identity. Consequently, the aim of this initial study was to collect some preliminary data which could be used to guide the design of a more intensive and systematic investigation of children's development in this area.

The theoretical framework which was used to structure this study was based upon an integration of some of the principal insights provided by social representation theory (Moscovici, 1988; Farr and Moscovici, 1984; Breakwell and Canter, 1993) and social identity and self-categorisation theory (Tajfel, 1981; Turner, 1987; Hogg and Abrams, Oakes *et al.*, 1994). This framework was as follows.

Children are *de facto* members of various social groups, including regional, national and supranational groups. "Regional" and "supranational" groups can be defined by reference to the intermediate-level term "national" group. A national group is a named category of people who, objectively, share common legal rights and constraints, a common economy, and a common geographical territory (often a single nation-state) within which mobility may take place; more contentiously, the members of a national group also share common historical representations and myths of origin, and a common language and a common public culture (see Deutsch, 1966; Connor, 1978; Smith, 1991, 1992). A regional group may then be defined as a named subset of a given national group, whose members are born in

349

and live in a particular geographical region which forms just one part of the larger national territory; and a supranational group may be defined as a larger named group which includes not only all of the members of a particular national group, but also members of other national groups as well. Thus, an English child who has been born in and lives in London is *de facto* a Londoner (a regional group membership), a Southerner (a second regional group membership), an English person (a national group membership) and a European (a supranational group membership).

In infancy and early childhood, before any concepts of either Londoners, Southerners, English people or Europeans have been acquired, the child's membership of such groups does not yet have any direct impact upon the child's own subjective self-categorisations. However, even at this early stage, other people's behaviour towards the child may be influenced by the child's group memberships. Thus, the child's behaviour may begin to be patterned according to these memberships at a very early age, even though that child may not yet have acquired any explicit knowledge of these social groups.

However, the child will eventually begin to acquire an explicit knowledge of at least some of the social groups to which he or she belongs. It is possible that the child will first acquire a knowledge of those groups which are the most socially marked (i.e. those groups which are made most salient by other people when interacting with the child). Initially, the child might only acquire the name of the group, and have very little other explicit knowledge of what that name actually denotes. Furthermore, the child's knowledge of geographically-based social groups may or may not be tied to the child's developing knowledge of the geographical territories which are involved (i.e. the child's knowledge base may be either integrated or fragmented at this early stage of development). However, once children have acquired at least a partial knowledge of some of these concepts, they can then begin to identify with, and subjectively categorise themselves as members of, some of these groups; this enables them to begin to locate themselves in their own social system relative to the members of other social groups.

In addition to this subjective act of self-categorisation, the acquisition of a regional, national or supranational identity usually entails at least the partial acquisition and internalisation of beliefs, attitudes and values which are shared with other people who also identify with that group. These shared representations are likely to contain not only beliefs concerning the ingroup itself, but also beliefs and evaluations of perceived outgroups. The representations may assign a high value to membership of the ingroup, and a lower value to membership of outgroups; as a consequence, the social identity acquired by the child may serve to produce high positive self-esteem. However, this may not always be the case; there may be some outgroups which are regarded with as much positive affect as (or possibly with more positive affect than) the ingroup. The social representations which are internalised by the child (and which thus come to form a part of the child's own cognitive representations) may subsequently mediate and reify the child's perceptions and interpretations of the world; as a consequence, these representations may also mediate the child's subsequent acquisition of further information about the world. For example, if the child encounters members of outgroups during holidays in other countries, the information which is potentially available to the child might be selectively attended to, and hence selectively assimilated, as a direct consequence of the channelling effects of the child's existing cognitive representations.

There is no *a priori* reason to suppose that the specific contents of the cognitive representations which are acquired by the child, and which serve to define ingroups and outgroups for that child, are derived from any one single source. Instead, such contents may be derived from a variety of different sources: from the social representations which prevail in the child's community (which are accessed through the child's communicative interchanges with other people, and through media presentations of ingroups and outgroups and of their category members); from direct personal experience of category members gained through travel experience (which, as noted above, may only lead to the selective assimilation of information); and from more formal pedagogical sources such as teachers and educational materials. It is also possible that the child's own cognitive processes of generalisation and abstraction from specific category exemplars influence the cognitive contents of the categorical representations. For example, it may be the case that the child's cognitive processes accentuate certain perceptible contrasts and differences which exist between the exemplars of different social categories, in order to achieve an optimal cognitive differ-entiation between the various categories; these same cognitive processes might also lead the child to de-emphasise or to underestimate the shared features which are common to the members of different categories.

During the course of development, the child will acquire a multiplicity of self-categorisations, social identities, and beliefs, feelings and values concerning both ingroups and outgroups. A particular self-categorisation, social identity, and set of associated beliefs, feelings and values will be mobilised or deployed when the child's membership of a particular category becomes salient due to social or psychological contextual factors. In other words, the level of self-categorisation employed by the child (whether as a Londoner, a Southerner, an English person or a European) will vary depending upon the specific comparative context in which the child's categories and representations are being activated. Thus, if this context requires a comparison to be made between the self and a group of Northerners, then the child's identity as a Southerner may be activated; on the other hand, if the context requires the child to make a comparison between the self and the inhabitants of Africa, then the child's identity as a European may be activated instead.

The above theoretical framework is necessarily extremely speculative at this stage when little developmental evidence is available either to substantiate or to refute many of its specific proposals in relationship to the development of either regional or supranational identities. However, this framework is at least compatible with existing evidence on the development of national identity in children (see below). Furthermore, this framework is useful at this early stage of enquiry, in that it facilitates the identification of some of the variables which need to be explored empirically in order to achieve an effective understanding of the development of regional, national and supranational identities in children. Thus, in order to investigate the acquisition and development of European identity in English children, it would seem necessary to measure, among other variables: the children's knowledge of the geographical territory which defines the continent of Europe, and their knowledge of their *de facto* membership of the category of European people; whether or not the children subjectively categorise themselves as Europeans; the affective value which they place upon membership of this category; the beliefs and feelings of the children concerning members of the category of European people; and the sources of information from which the children have obtained their knowledge of Europe and European people.

Consequently, in designing the present study, an attempt was made to measure these variables. In addition, the design of the study was informed by a close reading of the existing literature on the development of children's national identity. As noted above, although there have not been any previous studies which have explored the development of supranational identity in children, there have been several studies which have examined issues and topics which have a bearing upon the development of children's national identity: see, for example, Piaget and Weil (1951), Jahoda (1962, 1963a, 1963b, 1964), Lambert and Klineberg (1967), Tajfel *et al.* (1970), Middleton *et al.* (1970), Johnson *et al.* (1970), Tajfel *et al.* (1972), Moodie (1980), Barrett and Short (1992), Gimenez de la Peña and Barrett (1992), Barrett and Farroni (1993) and Barrett and Wilson (1994). Two of these studies have also looked at children's understanding of the relationship between regional identity and national identity: Piaget and Weil (1951) examined four- to fifteen-year-old Genevan children's understanding of the relationship between being Genevese and Swiss, while Jahoda (1963a, and 1964) looked at six- to eleven-year-old Glaswegian children's understanding of the relationship between being Glaswegian, Scottish and British.

These studies have revealed the following picture concerning the development of children's knowledge and beliefs about their own country and national group. Before about five to six years of age, children seem to have very little knowledge of their own nationality or country, and they are often unable even to give the name of their own country (Piaget and Weil, 1951) or, if they are able to give this name, their understanding of what this name refers to is extremely vague and nebulous (Jahoda, 1963a). From about six years of age, some children only describe members of their own national group using third person pronouns in ways that suggest that they do not yet consider themselves to be members of this group (e.g. "they are like us", "they dress like we do"; Lambert and Klineberg 1967). In addition, up until the age of about seven, children do not seem to have a systematic preference for their own country or for members of their own national group, and this preference only begins to develop between seven and nine years of age (Piaget and Weil, 1951; Middleton *et al.*, 1970).

Children's knowledge of other countries and members of other national groups also begins to develop during middle childhood (Barrett and Short, 1992; Gimenez de la Peña and Barrett, 1992; Barrett and Farroni, 1993). Children's ability to name other countries tends to be very poor before about seven years of age; thus, many five and six year olds have difficulty in understanding the concept of a foreign country, and in naming foreign countries (Jahoda, 1962). However, after seven years of age, children's knowledge of the geography of other countries begins to expand, with boys' geographical knowledge of other countries often being more accurate than that of girls (Barrett and Farroni, 1993). This growth of geographical knowledge is accompanied by the acquisition and elaboration of concepts of the people who live in other countries (Lambert and Klineberg, 1967; Barrett and Short, 1992; Gimenez de la Peña and Barrett, 1992). Interestingly, children sometimes acquire very strong affective responses to particular groups of foreign nationals (i.e. strong likes and dislikes) before they have acquired any concrete knowledge about those groups (Johnson *et al.*, 1970; Barrett and Short, 1992; and Gimenez de la Peña and Barrett, 1992). And, as noted above, from about seven years of age onwards, children come to acquire a systematic preference for their own country and nationality over other countries and nationalities (Piaget and Weil, 1951; Middleton *et al.*, 1970), although they may still feel very positively indeed about certain other countries and national groups as well (Barrett and Short, 1992; Gimenez de la Peña and Barrett, 1992).

As far as children's understanding of the relationship between their regional identity and their national identity is concerned, the studies by Piaget and Weil (1951) and Jahoda (1963a, 1964) indicate that, before about nine or ten years of age, children can have difficulty in understanding that one can simultaneously have two geographically-based identities. For example, Piaget and Weil found that children younger than seven to eight years of age did not understand the part–whole relationship between the city and the country in which they lived; instead, they seemed to conceptualise the city and the country as being spatially juxtaposed side-by-side. These children also denied that they were simultaneously both Genevese and Swiss. Children aged between 7–8 and 10–11 understood the spatial relationship between city and country, but not the relationship between being Genevese and Swiss; whereas only children who were older than ten to eleven understood that they were simultaneously both Genevese and Swiss. Jahoda's (1963a, 1964) study, however, revealed that this developmental sequence postulated by Piaget is very oversimplistic, and that children do not always master the spatial relationship (between city and country) before they master the conceptual one (between regional and national identity). Nevertheless, Jahoda also found that many (although not all) six-to-nine-year-old children denied that they were simultaneously both Scottish and British.

These lines of evidence from previous studies were used to inform the design of the present study in several ways. Firstly, they suggest that, if English children do acquire a European identity during the course of their development, they are unlikely to do so before six years of age. English children are also unlikely to have any knowledge of the category of "European people" before that age. These findings also suggest that children below the age of ten may have particular difficulties in acknowledging that they simultaneously have both a national identity and a supranational identity. Of course, these ages might just be lower bounds; it is quite possible that the acquisition of a European identity, and the acquisition of beliefs and feelings about the category of "European people", do not occur until much later in the course of children's development (if, indeed, they occur at all). Thus, it was decided, for the purposes of this initial study, to test children at three different age points: at six years of age, at ten years of age, and at fourteen years of age. In addition, because sex differences have been found in the development of geographic knowledge of other countries, it was also decided to compare the development of boys and girls in this domain.

The Study

The study involved interviewing 120 children using a semi-structured interview schedule. The children who were interviewed fell into three age groups. The six-year-old age group contained 20 boys and 20 girls aged between 6 years 1 month and 7 years 0 months (mean age 6.5 years); the ten-year-old age group contained 20 boys and 20 girls aged between 10 years 0 months and 11 years 3 months (mean age 10.6 years); and the fourteen-year-old age group contained 20 boys and 20 girls aged between 14 years 2 months and 15 years 2 months (mean age 14.7 years). All of the children were born in England, held British nationality, and lived in either Middlesex, Surrey, or South West London. The schools from which the children were recruited for the study had mixed catchment areas in terms of the social and economic backgrounds of the children who attended them, but precise socio-economic data on each individual child who was interviewed was not collected.

Each child was interviewed individually in their school. During interviewing, the children were allowed to talk about side issues if they wanted to, explanations and rephrasings of the questions were given if these were needed, and "don't know" responses were accepted. The questions making up the interview schedule fell into five main categories: (1) Questions which were designed to assess the child's basic factual knowledge of the geographical territory which defines the continent of Europe, and the child's knowledge of the fact that England is a part of Europe. (2) Questions which asked the child about whether he/she categorised himself/herself as a European. (3) Questions which asked about the child's affective responses to being English and to being European. (4) Questions which were designed to assess the beliefs and feelings of the child concerning the members of the category of European people. (5) Questions asking the child about his/her sources of information about Europe and European people. The specific questions making up the interview schedule are shown in Table 21.1.

TABLE 21.1   The questions contained in the interview schedule

1. Can you tell me what country we live in?
2. Are you glad you are English/British or not? [choice of adjective dependent upon answer to first question]
3. Can you tell me if England/Britain is bigger or smaller than Europe? [order of mention of "bigger" and "smaller" randomly varied]
4. Can you tell me what countries make up Europe?
5. [If England/Britain has not been mentioned in answer to question 4] Is England/Britain a part of Europe?
6. Which European countries have you been on holiday to?
7. Are you a European person?
8. Why/why not?
9. [If yes to question 7] Are you glad to be a European person or not [if no to question 7] Would you like to be a European person or not?
10. Why/why not?
11. What do you think European people are like, can you tell me anything about them?
12. What do you think is good about being a European person?
13. What do you think is bad about being a European person?
14. In what ways do you think European people are different from Americans?
15. In what ways do you think European people are different from Chinese people?
16. In what ways do you think European people are different from Africans?
17. Would you rather be European, American, Chinese or African? [order of mention randomly varied]
18. Why would you rather be . . .?
19. Do you think European people are friendly or not friendly or what?
20. Do you think European people are happy or unhappy or what?
21. Do you think European people are nice or not nice or what?
22. Do you think European people are dirty or clean or what?
23. Do you think European people are aggressive or peaceful or what?
24. Do you think European people are good or bad or what?
25. Do you think European people are clever or not clever or what?
26. Do you think European people are hardworking or lazy or what?
[In questions 19 to 26: order of mention of the two adjectives in each question randomly varied]
27. Would you like to have friends that come from lots of different parts of Europe?
28. Why/why not?
29. Where do you think you learnt all this information about Europe and European people? [child questioned about each individual source, as follows]
    holidays in one or more European countries
    relatives in one or more European countries
    friends in one or more European countries
    books
    comics
    newspapers
    television
    radio
    teachers
    friends at school
    parents
    siblings
    grandparents

The children's responses to the questions were assigned to categories which were designed as far as possible to reflect the diversity of answers while still enabling statistical tests to be applied. The reliability of the categorisation was checked by using a second coder who independently coded a random sample of 10% of the total. The percentage agreement between the first and second coders was 93%, indicating a reasonably high level of reliability in the categorisation of the data.

The Findings

The Children's Basic Geographic Knowledge of Europe

The first few questions in the interview schedule were primarily designed to assess the children's basic geographic knowledge of Europe. First of all, it transpired that nearly all of the six-year-olds (83%) and all of the ten- and fourteen-year-olds knew the name of their own country: the vast majority of these children referred to their own country as "England", although a handful at each age (2 six-year-olds, 4 ten-year-olds, and 7 fourteen-year-olds) referred to it as "Britain". This slight ambiguity concerning the name of one's own country is, of course, also a characteristic of English adults (Condor, 1993). The majority of the children at each age also knew that England/Britain is smaller than Europe (73%, 83% and 95%, respectively; from this point onwards, whenever three percentage figures are cited, these always refer to the responses of the six-year-olds, the ten-year-olds and the fourteen-year-olds in that particular order).

However, when it came to the children's knowledge of the countries which make up Europe, there were substantial differences between the answers of the six-year-olds and the answers of the two older groups of children. When they were asked this question, the six-year-olds were only able to name 0.3 countries on average, whereas the ten- and fourteen-year-olds were able to name 4.6 and 6.4 countries on average, respectively. The difference between the six- and the ten-year-olds was statistically significant, but that between the ten- and the fourteen-year-olds was not. The ten countries that were most frequently mentioned by each age group, listed in order of frequency, are shown in Table 21.2. As can be seen from this Table, a very high proportion of the six-year-olds' responses were incorrect answers, whereas relatively few of the ten- and fourteen-year-olds gave incorrect answers. In addition, when the children were asked whether England/Britain is a part of Europe, only a small minority of the six-year-olds gave an affirmative answer, whereas the majority of the ten- and fourteen-year-olds did so (20%, 85% and 93%, respectively). Once again, the difference between the six- and the ten-year-olds was statistically significant, but that between the ten- and the fourteen-year-olds was not.

In addition to these differences in the children's geographic knowledge which were associated with age, there were also differences which were associated with sex. Specifically, the six-year-old boys provided significantly more correct

TABLE 21.2   The ten countries mentioned most frequently by the children in each age group, when asked what countries make up Europe, listed in order of frequency; asterisks indicate incorrect responses

Six-year-olds	Ten-year-olds	Fourteen-year-olds
England	England	France
Germany	France	Spain
Africa*	Spain	Germany
France	Germany	England
Ireland	Ireland	Italy
India*	Italy	Ireland
America*	Scotland	Portugal
Australia*	Wales	Scotland
California*	Russia	Wales
Iraq*	Holland	Belgium

answers than the six-year-old girls in response to the question asking for the name of their own country, and the boys provided significantly more correct answers than the girls overall in response to the question about whether England/Britain is bigger or smaller than Europe. In addition, in response to the question asking for the names of the countries that make up Europe, the boys were able to name significantly more European countries than the girls. These findings are consistent with those of Barrett and Farroni (1993) concerning the existence of sex differences in children's geographic knowledge of Europe.

The children were asked about the European countries which they had visited for their holidays, in order to see whether this type of travel experience bore any systematic relationship to the children's knowledge of Europe. Various analyses were conducted in order to try and identify any consistent relationships between travel experience and geographic knowledge of Europe as measured by the first five questions in the interview. However, no such relationships were found.

The Children's Self-categorisations, and their Feelings about Being English and European

When the children were asked the question "Are you a European person?", 3%, 70% and 68% of the children at each age replied in the affirmative. The difference between the responses of the six- and the ten-year-olds was statistically significant, but that between the responses of the ten- and the fourteen-year-olds was not. The children were asked to justify their responses. The majority of the six-year-olds were unable to provide any justification of their answers (only 32% could do so), whereas the majority of ten- and fourteen-year-olds could offer some explanation of their response to the preceding question (57% and 70%, respectively). Once again, the difference between the six- and the ten-year-olds was significant, whereas that between the two older age groups was not. The only type of explanation which occurred with any substantial frequency at any age was the geographical explanation (i.e. that the child was European because England/Britain was geographically a part of Europe, or the child was not European because England/Britain was geographically not a part of Europe). Geographical explanations were produced by 18% of the six-year-olds, by 43% of the ten-year-olds and also by 43% of the sixteen-year-olds; the difference between the youngest group and the two older groups was statistically significant. It is possible, of course, that the children's answers here were a consequence of the geographical context which had been created by the initial set of questions in the interview; too much reliance should not therefore be placed upon this particular finding.

The children's answers to this question about whether they classified themselves as European people were cross-analyzed against their answers to the earlier question about whether or not England/Britain is included within Europe. It was found that the majority of six-year-olds (78%) denied that England/Britain was a part of Europe and denied that they were European; while the majority of ten- and sixteen-year-olds affirmed both that England/Britain was a part of Europe and that they themselves were European (70% and 65%, respectively). Thus, the majority of children at each age exhibited a consistency between their geographical knowledge and their self-categorisation. Nevertheless, there was a substantial minority of children at each age (20%, 15% and 28%, respectively) who stated that England/Britain was a part of Europe but denied that they themselves were European people; this pattern of answering implies a dissociation between geographical knowledge and subjective self-categorisation among this subset of children. However, across the sample as a whole, there was a significant association between geographical knowledge and self-categorisation. In addition, specifically at the transitional age of ten years, the association between these two variables was highly significant.

The children were also asked for their feelings about being English/British and their feelings about being European. At all ages, the majority of children said that they were glad to be English/British (85%, 80% and 75% at each age, respectively). However, when it came to the category of European people, only a minority of the six-year-olds (30%) said that they were glad to be, or would like to be, European, whereas the majority of the ten- and fourteen-year-olds gave a positive reply to this question (80% and 65%, respectively). The difference between the six- and the ten-year-olds was significant, but that between the ten- and the fourteen-year olds was not. A similar finding emerged when the children's feelings were tapped in a comparative context using the question "Would you rather be European, American, Chinese or African?". The percentages of children at each age who said that they would rather be European were 18%, 65% and 58%; once again, the difference between the six- and the ten-year-olds was significant, whereas that between the two older age groups was not. The children were asked to explain their responses to both the non-comparative and the comparative question. The justifications which were provided were varied and diverse at all ages, and the analyses failed to find any trends or differences of any particular note.

The children's responses to the self-categorisation question "Are you a European person?" were cross-analyzed against their responses to the question concerning their feelings about being European. The majority of six-year-olds (70%) said that they were not a European person and that they would not like to be one, whereas the majority of both the ten-year-olds (63%) and the fourteen-year-olds (58%) said that they were European and were glad to be so. Overall, then, there was a significant association between self-categorisation and feelings concerning this self-categorisation. However, once again, there were substantial minorities of children at each age who did not show such a consistent pattern: the most striking asymmetry was that exhibited by 28% of the six-year-olds who said that they were not European but would like to be. Here, these children seemed to be placing a high positive value upon the membership of an outgroup.

The statistical analyses concerning the children's self-categorisations used not only age but also sex as a blocking variable. However, none of these analyses revealed any evidence for sex differences in this domain. This is an interesting outcome, given the consistency of the sex differences which were found in the children's geographic knowledge of Europe.

The Children's Beliefs and Feelings about European People

English children's beliefs and feelings about four specific target groups of European peoples (French, German, Spanish and Italian people) have already been investigated in a previous study (Barrett and Short, 1992). By contrast, one of the purposes of the present study was to look at English children's beliefs and feelings concerning the superordinate category of "European people". The questions tapping into this knowledge began with the general open-ended question, "What do you think European people are like? Can you tell me anything about them?" The percentage of children at each age who were able to offer any relevant information in response to this question was 38%, 83% and 78%, respectively. The difference between the six- and the ten-year-olds was significant, but that between the ten- and the fourteen-year olds was not. In response to the question "What do you think is good about being a European person?", the frequencies of children at each age who were able to offer any information were 38%, 68% and 58%; once again, the difference between the six- and the ten-year-olds was significant, whereas that between the ten- and the fourteen-year olds was not. (The converse question, concerning what the children thought was bad about being European, failed to produce any interesting findings, with 43%, 55% and 48% of children at each age offering some information in response to this question.) Thus, the majority of the six-year-olds did not appear to have a concept of European people which they could access when asked open-ended questions about Europeans in a non-comparative context, whereas the majority of ten- and fourteen-year-olds did appear to have such a concept.

In addition to these non-comparative questions, the children were also asked open-ended questions which required them to think about Europeans in three different comparative contexts: "In what ways do you think European people are different from Americans/from Chinese people/from Africans?" The American and Chinese context questions enabled the majority of children at all ages to offer some relevant information about European people (70%, 90% and 85% in the case of the American context, and 70%, 95% and 85% in the case of the Chinese context); however, once again, in both cases, the six-year-olds did so significantly less frequently than the two older groups of children, and there were no significant differences between the ten- and the fourteen-year-olds. With the African context question, a similar pattern occurred but, in this case, rather fewer six-year-olds were able to offer some information (the figures here being 40%, 88% and 100%, respectively). Nevertheless, the general picture which emerges is that the majority of the six-year-olds did have a concept of European people which they were able to access in response to questioning, but unlike the ten- and the fourteen-year-olds, many of the six-year-olds needed an explicit comparative context in order to be able to do so.

In order to look at the specific contents of the children's beliefs about Europeans, the children's replies to these open-ended questions (i.e. questions 11 to 16 in the interview schedule) were content-analyzed. This revealed three principal types of answers. Firstly, there were answers which referred to some aspect of the physical appearance of European people; e.g. "They're brown, sunburnt", "They all have different coloured hair". Secondly, there were answers which referred to the behavioural or psychological traits or customs of European people; e.g. "They're friendly", "They do dances when eating", "They're money grubbers", "They like sport a lot" (traits and customs were combined in a single category because it proved difficult in practice to differentiate reliably between references to traits and references to customs). And finally, there were answers which referred in some way to the languages of European people; e.g. "They can speak more than one language", "They talk differently from us". The relative frequencies with which these three different types of answers occurred in the responses of the children to questions 11 to 16 overall are shown in Figure 21.1. The difference between the frequencies with which the six- and the ten-year-olds referred to behavioural or psychological traits and customs was highly significant; this difference across these ages is, of course, fully consistent with the findings of previous studies on children's verbal descriptions of people (Livesley and Bromley, 1973; Yuill, 1993).

In addition to these open-ended questions, the children were also asked a series of closed questions about some of the possible characteristics of European people (questions 19 to 26). Analysis of the responses to these closed questions revealed two principal trends with age. Firstly, on all eight questions, the six-year-olds produced significantly more univalent responses (i.e. responses asserting that European people have just a single value on the dimension specified in the question; for example, that European people are friendly, are happy, etc.) than the

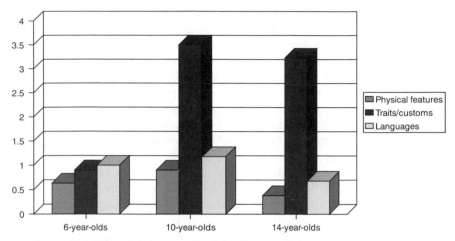

FIGURE 21.1   The relative frequencies with which the children referred to the physical features of European people, to the behavioural and psychological traits and customs of European people, and to the languages spoken by European people, in their answers to questions 11–16.

ten- and the fourteen-year-olds; the ten- and the fourteen-year-olds instead produced significantly more multivalent responses (i.e. responses to the effect that there is variability among European people on the dimension specified in the question; for example, that some European people are clean but some are dirty, etc.) than the six-year-olds. Averaging across all eight questions, the percentages of univalent responses at each age were 77%, 56% and 47%, and the percentages of multivalent responses were 16%, 43% and 53%, respectively; in both cases, the difference between the six- and the ten-year-olds is significant, but that between the ten- and the fourteen-year-olds is not.

The second general trend which occurred in the children's responses to these questions was a significant decline with age in the number of univalent negative responses produced to seven out of the eight questions (the exception here being the peaceful/aggressive question). Summing across all eight questions, the percentages of univalent negative responses produced by the children at each age were 26%, 12% and 3%; by comparison, the percentages of univalent positive responses were 51%, 44% and 44%.

Thus, when they made univalent judgements about European people, the children at all three ages tended to be positive rather than negative; with increasing age, fewer children expressed univalent negative comments about European people; and with increasing age, the children were more likely to acknowledge the existence of variability among European people.

The children's feelings about European people were also assessed by asking them whether they would like to have friends that came from lots of different parts of Europe. In response to this question, the majority of children at all three ages (78%, 95% and 100%) said that they would like to have such friends. The difference between the six- and the ten-year-olds was significant, whereas that between the ten- and the fourteen-year-olds was not. When asked to give a reason for their answer, the frequency with which the children were able to offer some explanation increased significantly with age (75%, 82% and 97%). The most common explanation that was given at each age was that having European friends would be a good learning opportunity of one kind or another (e.g. to find out about other countries, other peoples, other languages, etc.). The frequency with which this explanation was produced increased significantly with age (30%, 55% and 75%, respectively).

Thus, irrespective of the particular way in which the children's feelings were assessed, it appeared that the children felt fairly positively about European people at all ages. In order to examine whether such positive feelings only occurred when the children had categorised themselves as Europeans, the children's answers to question 21 (about whether Europeans are nice or not nice), question 24 (about whether Europeans are good or bad) and question 27 (about whether they would like to have friends from Europe) were cross-analyzed against their answers to question 7 (about whether or not the children categorised themselves as European). Among the six-year-olds, 97% of the children did not categorise themselves as European; of these 97%, 54% said that Europeans were nice, 51% said that Europeans were good, and 77% said that they would like to have European friends. Thus, the majority of the six-year-olds who viewed European people as an outgroup nevertheless still exhibited positive affect for this group. Among the ten- and fourteen-year-olds, because many more children expressed the more realistic view that European people could be either nice or not nice, and could be either good or bad, the results were rather less clear-cut. However, of the 30% of the ten-year-olds who did not categorise themselves as European, 83% of these children said that they would like to have European friends; and of the 32% of the fourteen-year-olds who did not categorise themselves as European, 100% of these children said that they would like to have European friends. Thus, overall, the children who participated in this study did seem to have positive feelings for European people, even when they perceived these people as an outgroup.

The data were also analyzed to see whether there were any sex differences in the children's beliefs and feelings about European people. However, these analyses failed to find any evidence for sex differences in this domain.

The Children's Sources of Information about Europe and European People

Finally, the children were asked about the sources from which they thought they had obtained their information about Europe and European people. To this end, the interviewer went through a checklist of possible sources with the children. Obviously, the accuracy of such self-reports from children must be interpreted with considerable caution as far as their veridicality is concerned.

TABLE 21.3   The five sources of information cited most frequently by each age group, listed in order of frequency (figures in parentheses denote the percentage of children at each age who cited that source)

Six-year-olds	Ten-year-olds	Fourteen-year-olds
Parents (83)	Television (90)	Television (95)
Television (73)	Parents (88)	Teachers (83)
Teachers (68)	Teachers (80)	Parents (80)
Books (53)	Books (53)	Newspapers (80)
Grandparents (53)	Grandparents (53)	Grandparents (78)

Nonetheless, the results obtained by this line of questioning are interesting for what they reveal about the children's own beliefs about the sources from which they thought they had obtained their information.

The five most frequently cited sources for each age group are shown in Table 21.3. As can be seen from this table, the children's responses at all three ages suggested that they believed their information came from: their communicative exchanges with other people, particularly their parents and grandparents (grandparents possibly served as a salient source of information because many of these children were of an age such that their grandparents would have been participants in the Second World War), from the media (television and newspapers), and from pedagogical sources (teachers and books). The older the children were, the more sources they were likely to cite. Holidays in European countries were only cited by 18%, 40% and 65% of the children at each age, respectively.

Discussion

The principal findings of this study can be summarised as follows. At all ages studied, the majority of children knew that they lived in England, categorised themselves as English, and were glad to be English. However, there was a significant increase in the children's basic geographic knowledge about Europe between six and ten years of age. Between these two ages, there was also a shift in the children's self-categorisations: from the age of ten onwards, they began to categorise themselves not only as English but also as European, and said that they were glad to be European. Thus, there appeared to be a fundamental shift in the children's awareness of the supranational group to which they belonged between six and ten years of age.

These findings accord with those of previous studies on the development of national identity in children. For example, Piaget and Weil (1951) and Jahoda (1963a, and 1964) both found that, before ten years of age, children have difficulty in understanding that they simultaneously belong both to a local geographical region and to a larger geographical region which subsumes the local one. But whereas these two previous studies focused upon children's understanding of the relationship between their regional identity and their national identity, the present study had a different focus, looking instead at the acquisition of a supranational identity by English children. Consequently, the present findings imply that: (i) by ten years of age, English children understand not only the relationship between their region and their country, but also the relationship between their country and their continent; and (ii) by ten years of age, English children have usually acquired, in addition to their national identity, a supranational identity.

As far as the children's beliefs and feelings about European people were concerned, the children at all three ages said that they would like to have European friends. The majority of six-year-olds viewed European people univalently and positively, even though European people were still perceived as an outgroup at this age. At ten years of age, there was an increasing recognition that European people have variable rather than univalent attributes. Nevertheless, at ten and at fourteen years of age, many children still ascribed a preponderance of univalent positive attributes to European people. The frequency with which univalent negative attributes were ascribed to Europeans, which was low even at six years of age, declined still further at ten and at fourteen years of age.

Once again, these findings accord with those of previous studies, in this case studies which have examined children's knowledge of groups of foreign people. For example, Lambert and Klineberg (1967), Johnson *et al.* (1970), Barrett and Short (1992) and Gimenez de la Peña and Barrett (1992) all found that, between approximately six and ten years of age, there is an increase in knowledge about groups of foreign people, and that this increase in knowledge is accompanied by a decline in the amount of negative affect which is expressed towards those groups. In addition, Barrett and Short (1992) found that, by ten years of age, children are more likely to admit that there is individual variation among the members of a group of foreign people than they are at six years of age. The present study shows that this pattern of changes occurs not only in relationship to the child's concepts of specific groups of European nationals, but also in relationship to the child's concept of the superordinate group of European people.

The pervasive lack of substantial differences between the ten-year-olds and the fourteen-year-olds in the present study is a surprising outcome, and one which was not anticipated at the outset. Fairly major cognitive and social-developmental changes would normally be expected to occur between these two ages. In addition, fourteen-year-olds in England should have received far more explicit teaching about Europe at school than ten-year-olds. The National Curriculum for Geography in England (Department of Education and Science, 1991) specifies that children who are at level 6 of the curriculum (i.e. the level which should be reached by the average fourteen-year-old) should have received considerable teaching about Europe, unlike children who are at level 4 (i.e. the level which should be reached by the average ten-year-old). This lack of substantial differences between the ten- and fourteen-year-olds may, of course, have been due to the fact that the questions in the interview schedule were not sufficiently taxing; thus, it may be the case that, had the children been asked more searching questions, differences in knowledge, beliefs and feelings would have emerged. An alternative possible explanation is that this study happened to use a biased sample of fourteen-year-olds. However, we do know from previous studies that children's affective responses to groups of foreign people do indeed have a tendency to become more positive between six and ten, and to then level out and remain relatively constant until fourteen years of age (see, for example, Lambert and Klineberg, 1967). This convergence of findings with other studies suggests that the findings of the present study are not merely artefactual.

Another finding which emerged from this study was that there were sex differences in the children's geographic knowledge of Europe, but no sex differences in either self-categorisations or beliefs and feelings about European people. This study replicates the findings of Barrett and Farroni (1993), who also found sex differences in a separate study which explored English and Italian children's knowledge of European geography. The reason for the existence of these sex differences is unclear at the present time. There is some evidence that girls in middle childhood show a particular disadvantage when compared with boys on tasks which involve spatial visualisation and the coordination of the position and configuration of locations relative to the self (see Harris, 1981 and Matthews, 1992 for useful reviews), and it may be the case that this disadvantage impacts upon girls' acquisition of geographical information. Alternatively, it may be the case that geographical knowledge about other countries is not so pertinent to girls' cognitive styles and concerns as other types of information about those countries. There is little evidence available at the present time to resolve this issue one way or the other. However, insofar as the present study failed to find any evidence for sex differences in the acquisition of a European identity, it would appear that girls' disadvantage in the geographical domain does not have any direct impact upon their identity development.

The overall developmental picture which emerges from this study can probably best be summarised in terms of the responses which were obtained from at least 50% of the children within each age group; these responses therefore represent the beliefs, the feelings and the values which were shared by a majority of the children at each age. These majority responses are summarised in Table 21.4.

Looking first at the six-year-olds, it appears that children acquire a national identity before they acquire a supranational identity: at six years of age, these children knew the name of their own country and were glad to be English, but they did not yet know that, *de facto*, they lived in Europe, they did not yet categorise themselves as European people, and they did not wish to be members of this category themselves. As we have seen already, it may be the case that children at this age have particular difficulty in appreciating that it is possible to have two geographically-based identities simultaneously. Nevertheless, these

TABLE 21.4   The responses produced by at least 50% of the children in each age group

Six-year-olds	Ten-year-olds	Fourteen-year-olds
Live in England	Live in England	Live in England
Europe bigger than England	Europe bigger than England	Europe bigger than England
England not in Europe	England in Europe	England in Europe
Not a European person	A European person	A European person
Glad to be English	Glad to be English	Glad to be English
Wouldn't like to be European	Glad to be European	Glad to be European
	Prefer to be European	Prefer to be European
European people are:	European people are:	European people are:
Friendly	Of variable friendliness	friendly
Happy	Happy	Happy
Clever	Clever	Clever
Nice	Of variable niceness	Nice
Good	Hardworking	Hardworking
Of variable goodness	Of variable cleanliness	Of variable peacefulness

children did share common beliefs about some of the characteristics of European people, and the six-year-olds generally felt very positively about this outgroup.

As far as the ten-year-olds are concerned, these children knew that, *de facto*, they lived in Europe. These children also identified with, and subjectively categorised themselves as, members of the group of European people. Knowledge that England is geographically a part of Europe, and self-categorisation as a European person, were significantly associated in this group of children (as they were in the children overall). This suggests that their geographical knowledge was integrated with their self-categorisations in this domain. In addition to this act of self-categorisation, the ten-year-olds also shared various beliefs about the characteristics of European people, and ascribed a mixture of positive and multivalent attributes to this group of people who were now viewed as an ingroup.

The fourteen-year-olds exhibited largely the same pattern as the ten-year-olds. The principal differences between the ten- and the fourteen-year-olds lay in the specific contents of the shared beliefs which the children held about the characteristics of European people.

Finally, it should be recalled that the children themselves reported that they had obtained their knowledge about Europe and European people from a variety of sources, including other people, the media, and pedagogical sources (see Table 21.3). Direct experience gained through travel in other European countries was mentioned as a source of information increasingly with age, but was only mentioned by a majority of children at fourteen years of age.

It may be tempting to view the contents of Table 21.4 as summary descriptions of the social representations of Europe and European people which are shared by six-, ten- and fourteen-year-old English children, respectively. However, to take such a view would be a considerable overinterpretation. It is important to bear in mind that the contents of this table merely summarise the majority responses which the children at each age gave to an adult during the course of a one-to-one interview. As such, these responses reflect the children's cognitive representations (as accessed from memory, and then encoded for linguistic expression, in the course of an adult–child conversation/ interview). In addition, the fact that it was possible to identify majority responses within each age group implies that many children at each age had acquired similar cognitive representations. However, in theoretical terms, a social representation is not simply a system of beliefs and feelings which is held in common across a group of individuals. It is crucially a system of beliefs, feelings and practices which enables the members of a community to communicate with one another, by providing them with a code for social exchange and a code for naming, classifying and making sense of the world and of their individual and group histories (see Moscovici, 1973, 1988). There is thus a considerable distance between what is shown in Table 21.4 as a convenient summary of the children's responses in an interview and what may be properly termed "social representations", particularly as no evidence has been presented here concerning whether or not these beliefs and feelings play any part in children's social exchanges and communications beyond the interview itself. And as a consequence, considerably more empirical work is required before it will be possible to say whether the contents of Table 21.4 should or should not be viewed as summary descriptions of the social representations of Europe and European people which are acquired by English children.

Although this study provides a useful starting point for mapping out the development of supranational identity in children, it has clearly raised far more questions than it has managed to answer. For example, we now need to find out about (among other things): how children's beliefs and feelings about European people, and how children's self-categorisations, change in the intermediate years between six and ten; the extent of the individual differences which obtain in this domain (for example, although the majority of children did appear to have integrated geographic knowledge and self-categorisations, there appeared to be a smaller subset of children at each age who asserted that although England was a part of Europe, they themselves were not European); whether there are any systematic intra-national differences in this domain (for example, whether there are any variations according to geographical region or social class); whether there are any cross-national differences across Europe in children's development in this domain; how children's cognitive representations of Europe and European people relate to the social representations which prevail in their community and to the representations which occur in media presentations; how children's beliefs and feelings impact upon their assimilation and acquisition of further information about Europeans (for example, the information which is encountered either through travel or through the educational process); how children's regional identities develop, and how this relates to the development of both national and supranational identities; and the circumstances under which one or other of the child's identities and associated set of beliefs, feelings and values are mobilised. Thus, there is still a very great deal which needs to be investigated. It is hoped that the present study has at least served to indicate that children's development in this domain is likely to prove an extremely interesting and fertile area for future research.

Acknowledgement

I would like to thank Jenny Maslin-Bird who helped to design the interview schedule and conducted the interviews with the children. An earlier version of this chapter was presented at the 5th European Conference on Developmental Psychology, University of Seville, Spain, September 1992, as a paper entitled "English children's knowledge of and attitudes towards Europe and European people".

References

Barrett, M. and Farroni, T. (1993). English and Italian children's knowledge of European geography. Paper presented at the Annual Conference of the Developmental Section of the British Psychological Society, Birmingham, September 1993.

Barrett, M. and Short, J. (1992). Images of European people in a group of 5–10 year old English schoolchildren. *British Journal of Developmental Psychology*, **10**, 339–63.

Barrett, M. and Wilson, H. (1994). The development of children's regional identity. Paper presented at the Annual Conference of the Developmental Section of the British Psychological Society, Portsmouth, September 1994.

Breakwell, G. and Canter, D. (eds) (1993). *Empirical Approaches to Social Representations*. Oxford: Oxford University Press.

Condor, S. (1993). The invisible nation: a social psychological investigation of "The English". Paper presented at the Conference on Changing European Identities: Social-Psychological Analyses of Social Change, Farnham, May 1993.

Connor, W. (1978). A nation is a nation, is a state, is an ethnic group, is . . . *Ethnic and Racial Studies*, **1**, 377–400.

Department of Education and Science (1991). *Geography in the National Curriculum*. London: HMSO.

Deutsch, K. (1966). *Nationalism and Social Communication*, 2nd edn. New York: MIT Press.

Farr, R. and Moscovici, S. (eds)(1984). *Social Representations*. Cambridge: Cambridge University Press.

Gimenez de la Peña, A. and Barrett, M. (1992). "They are red in summer": prototypes of Spanish people about their European neighbours. Paper presented at the Fifth European Conference on Developmental Psychology, Seville, Spain, September 1992.

Harris, L. J. (1981). Sex-related variations in spatial skill. In L. Liben, A. H. Patterson and N. Newcombe (eds), *Spatial Representation and Behaviour across the Life Span*. New York: Academic Press.

Hogg, M. and Abrams, D. (1988). *Social Identifications: A Social Psychology of Intergroup Relations and Group Processes*. London: Routledge.

Jahoda, G. (1962). Development of Scottish children's ideas and attitudes about other countries. *Journal of Social Psychology*, **58**, 91–108.

Jahoda, G. (1963a). The development of children's ideas about country and nationality, Part I: The conceptual framework. *British Journal of Educational Psychology*, **33**, 47–60.

Jahoda, G. (1963b). The development of children's ideas about country and nationality, Part II: National symbols and themes. *British Journal of Educational Psychology*, **33**, 143–53.

Jahoda, G. (1964). Children's concepts of nationality: a critical study of Piaget's stages. *Child Development*, **35**, 1081–92.

Johnson, N., Middleton, M. and Tajfel, H. (1970). The relationship between children's preferences for and knowledge about other nations. *British Journal of Social and Clinical Psychology*, **9**, 232–40.

Lambert, W. E. and Klineberg, O. (1967). *Children's Views of Foreign Peoples: A Cross-national Study*. New York: Appleton-Century-Crofts.

Livesley, W. and Bromley, D. (1973). *Person Perception in Childhood and Adolescence*. London: Wiley.

Matthews, M. H. (1992). *Making Sense of Place: Children's Understanding of Large-scale Environments*. Hemel Hempstead: Harvester Wheatsheaf.

Middleton, M., Tajfel, H. and Johnson, N. (1970). Cognitive and affective aspects of children's national attitudes. *British Journal of Social and Clinical Psychology*, **9**, 122–34.

Moodie, M. (1980). The development of national identity in white South African schoolchildren. *Journal of Social Psychology*, **111**, 169–80.

Moscovici, S. (1973). Foreword. In C. Herzlich, *Health and Illness*. London: Academic Press.

Moscovici, S. (1988). Notes towards a description of social representations. *European Journal of Social Psychology*, **18**, 211–50.

Oakes, P. J., Haslam, S. A. and Turner, J.C. (1994). *Stereotyping and Social Reality*. Oxford: Basil Blackwell.

Piaget, J. and Weil, A. (1951). The development in children of the idea of the homeland and of relations with other countries. *International Social Science Bulletin*, **3**, 561–78.

Smith, A. D. (1991). *National Identity*. London: Penguin.

Smith, A. D. (1992). National identity and the idea of European unity. *International Affairs*, **68**, 55–76.

Tajfel, H. (1981). *Human Groups and Social Categories*. Cambridge: Cambridge University Press.

Tajfel, H., Jahoda, G., Nemeth, C., Rim, Y. and Johnson, N. (1972). The devaluation by children of their own national and ethnic group: two case studies. *British Journal of Social and Clinical Psychology*, **11**, 235–43.

Tajfel, H., Jahoda, G., Nemeth, C., Campbell, J. and Johnson, N. (1970). The development of children's preference for their own country: a cross-national study. *International Journal of Psychology*, **5**, 245–53.

Turner, J. C. (1987). *Rediscovering the Social Group: A Self-categorization Theory*. Oxford: Basil Blackwell.

Yuill, N. (1993). Understanding of personality and dispositions. In M. Bennett (ed.), *The Child as Psychologist*. New York: Harvester Wheatsheaf.

22

In Search of the "Euro-manager": Convergences and Divergences in Event Management

PETER B. SMITH AND MARK F. PETERSON

CRICCOM, University of Sussex and Roffey Park Management Institute and Texas Tech University

In view of the increasingly international nature of commerce both within the European Union and more widely, one might expect that managers would be in the forefront of any convergences of identity which might be under way in Europe. It is certainly true that many managers within large business organisations have regular contact with colleagues from a variety of European nations, and that business organisations are increasingly assigning managers to posts located in countries other than their country of origin. There has been a good deal of rhetoric in the management-oriented media concerning the emergence of "Euro-managers", as well as more sceptical scholarly studies (e.g. Hickson, 1993; Eberwein and Tholen, 1993). Euro-managers are portrayed as managers unencumbered with the values or identities associated with their country of origin, and able to operate with equal effectiveness in whatever location they may be.

A promising location in which to search for "Euro-managers" might be the INSEAD business school in Fontainebleau near Paris. Over the past twenty years, it has attracted multilingual groups of ambitious managers from all over Europe to its programmes. Ratiu (1983) asked groups of managers attending INSEAD programmes to rate one another on "internationalness". Effective international managers were seen as more intuitive, more provisional in their judgments, more open in discussion of their experience of culture shock and how they handle it, and more concerned to understand specific experiences rather than to make global generalisations. There is thus some consensus on what makes an effective Euro-manager and the European identity which might be expected to go with it. However it should not be assumed that the path towards such an identity is a simple consequence of increasing contact. Another researcher at INSEAD compared the values of managers working in mono-cultural organisations with those working in multinationals. He found that those working in the multinationals had values which approximated more closely to the average of values for their country of origin (Laurent, 1983). Apparently for many managers the "culture shock" of working with a range of other Europeans can cause a resurgence of values associated with one's own primary source of identity.

The pioneering study in identifying cultural differences in values was that by Hofstede (1980, 1991), who focused upon what he called the "collective programming of the mind" among large numbers of employees of IBM located in many countries. He was of course concerned not so much with what IBM employees had in common with one another, but with the differences to be found between each of his national samples. The four dimensions of variation identified by him from responses obtained from his fifty-three different national samples have provided the conceptual framework of many subsequent cross-cultural studies. Of particular relevance to our present concern with European identities is Hofstede's finding, reiterated recently (Hofstede, 1993), that he found almost as much cultural diversity within Europe as he did within the entire world.

While Hofstede's dimensions, especially his distinction between individualism and collectivism, have given a rather firmer theoretical focus to cross-cultural social psychology, they have also attracted their share of both conceptual and methodological critique. At the methodological level, it has been pointed out for instance that Hofstede's data were all drawn from the same organisation, that they were collected rather long ago and that the respondents were mostly males working in marketing and servicing (Smith and Bond, 1993). Although the delineated nature of his sample can also be considered a virtue, its very precision means that the scores recorded on his scales for Individualism or Power Distance for example may give only a weak guide to the cultural values now predominating within a nation, and no guide at all to the values or identities of distinctive communities within that nation.

The purpose of the present study is to examine an alternative source of data from work organisations and see how far it does or does not characterise a group of nations in ways which are compatible with those adopted by Hofstede. More specifically it will seek to clarify whether the orientations of a wide sample of European managers are still as diverse as Hofstede found them to be or whether there is any evidence for convergence towards a more consensual, Europe-wide view of the tasks and roles of management.

In working towards this goal, this study defines cultures as systems of shared meanings placed upon events. The emphasis of this definition is upon sharedness of meaning as the central component of a cultural group. There are greater possibilities for valid analyses within such an approach than appear possible using data characterising cultural groups as a whole. This focus on shared meaning necessarily requires measures of the ways that individuals set about attributing meaning to events, focusing particularly on whether different individuals do so in similar ways. As a contribution towards that general goal, this chapter examines the case of how this process occurs within work organisations in six different national cultures located in Western Europe.

Event Management

Hofstede's project rested upon analysis of respondents' reactions to various aspects of the organisation's overall behaviour and their employment within it. The present project chose to focus instead upon rather specific events, as these should provide a better prospect that respondents will be able to characterise more precisely how they handle them. Utilising a framework developed by Smith and Peterson (1988), an organisational event is defined as any occurrence impinging upon the awareness of an organisation member. All events are seen as initially ambiguous, and requiring some kind of processing before the manager has a sense of how they might best be handled. Some may quickly be diagnosed as routine, while others will require sustained attention. A central element in a manager's effectiveness is likely to rest on the appropriateness of the meanings thus assigned.

A questionnaire was constructed whose purpose was to elicit not the actual meanings placed upon selected events, but the processes by which meanings are put on events. For each event the respondent is asked how much they rely upon each of eight sources of event meaning. For instance, faced with the need to appoint a new subordinate, does a manager consult other people, such as superiors, existing subordinates, colleagues at the same level or personnel specialists? Or, do they rely entirely upon their own experience and training? A further possibility is that they might be guided by more impersonal sources of guidance, such as books of formal rules and procedures, informal understandings about how things are usually done within the organisation, or systems of beliefs which are widespread in their society. The questionnaire asks for a rating on five-point scales of the extent to which each of these eight possible sources of meaning is used. Thus it is implied that the sources are not exclusive of another, and that one might well draw upon several.

The sources of meaning provided were intended to span the range of possible sources available to a manager as widely as could be, although they may omit sources that prove to be distinctively important within some specific national cultures. Nonetheless they permit an initial analysis of the degree to which similar or different sources are used in different parts of Europe. Within the present study, eight organisational events were selected on the basis that they would most probably occur frequently in all countries. Some of those selected were of primary importance within the work team, whereas others referred to relations with the wider organisation within which the team worked. The events were:

- appointing a new subordinate in your department;
- when one of your subordinates is doing consistently good work;
- when one of your subordinates is doing consistently poor work;
- when some of the equipment or machinery in your department seems to need replacement;
- when another department does not provide the resources or support you require;
- when there are differing opinions within your department;
- when you see the need to introduce new work procedures into your department;
- when the time comes to evaluate the success of new work procedures.

Research Methods

The questionnaire was constructed in English, and then translated into a variety of other languages, with checks on the validity of translation through back-translation and correction. It was then distributed to samples of middle managers in around thirty countries in all the continents of the world, including eleven within Europe. The present chapter is concerned only with the results for the six European countries from which data collection has currently been completed, namely Finland, Germany, Netherlands, United Kingdom, France and Portugal.

In each country a sample was sought which included managers from both public and private sector organisations, and which included respondents from at least several different organisations. Chief executives and first-line supervisors were not included. Respondents were also asked whether they had faced each of the events in recent months and data from those who had not was excluded from analyses. Finally, the fullest possible demographic details of respondents were obtained in order to facilitate subsequent comparisons of the datasets. These included age, sex, organisational ownership, organisational size, organisation's task, department's task, education, religion and ethnicity.

In order that responses to the questionnaire can be used to provide valid comparisons of event management in different national cultures a series of methodological hazards must be addressed. A first problem is that if one compares mean responses from subjects from different countries, often based upon different language versions of the questionnaire, spurious differences may be detected, based upon for instance differential response biases. To overcome this difficulty, the procedure outlined in detail by Leung (1989), and employed also in Hofstede's project, of using a within-subjects standardisation of scores was adopted. That is to say that when displaying how often a respondent uses a particular source of event meaning, the score for that source is made proportional to how much they report using all the other sources.

Secondly, the use of convenience samples from within each country clearly constitutes a risk. There is no way of knowing whether the sampling within a particular country is or is not representative of either the average way of handling events there, or of the range of variation in handling events. What can be done to render the samples rather more directly comparable is to undertake analyses of covariance, using demographic variables as covariates, thereby providing adjusted mean scores which discount the demographic variations across samples. This procedure cannot adjust however for the different social roles which managers in different countries may have. For instance advancement by age may be more rapid in some countries than others. Beyond this type of adjustment, the only possible checks on representativeness are further replications and comparisons of results with those arising from other relevant studies.

Finally, in order to characterise the manner in which managers utilise sources of event meaning, one needs to know how reliably they characterise what they do. Since the questionnaire refers to eight different events, there is some opportunity to test the consistency with which each source is utilised across all eight types of events. There is no obvious reason why they should be: it is intuitively equally plausible that a manager would rely on different sources of meaning when handling different types of events. However, if as postulated at the beginning of this paper, culture has to do with systems of widely shared meanings it is not implausible that there would be substantial consistency both within particular individuals and within groups of individuals in the sources which they report using most heavily.

Results

The size of samples of respondents varied between 76 from Germany and 130 from France. The average age for the Finnish managers was lowest at 28, with the Germans oldest at 42. All samples were predominantly male, with the greatest proportion of women (33%) being in the Portuguese sample.

Good reliability across events of which sources of event meaning were most employed was found. Forty-six of the 48 values of alpha (six countries × eight event management strategies) were at or above 0.60. This overall satisfactory level of reliability made it possible for the standard scores for each individual respondent to be averaged across events. These scores were then adjusted on the basis of demographic differences, through the use of analysis of covariance as described above, using six covariates, namely age, sex, organisation size, organisation ownership, organisation's task and department's task.

In order to gain the clearest possible picture of whether, as Hofstede found, the European countries varied as widely as did those for the rest of the world, the European means were compared with the means for sixteen non-European samples. Substantial evidence was found for a distinctive European approach. In the case of reliance on one's own experience and training as a way of handling events, the six European samples achieved the six highest ranks. Less marked but noticeable effects indicated a high reliance on consulting one's subordinates and low reliance on formal rules and procedures as well as on beliefs which are widespread in one's country. On the remaining scales the European scores were more widely spread. The similarities found between the six samples are striking, but they cannot be said to disprove Hofstede's assertion, since he sampled a total of eighteen European countries, and it is evident that the wider one's sample the stronger will be the evidence for diversity. Nonetheless, within the present predominantly West European sample, there is a strong hint of convergence on several of the scales.

Another way of comparing Hofstede's results and the present ones is to compare the way in which countries score along the respective dimensions employed in each study. Almost all of the countries in this study were also represented within Hofstede's sample. An earlier report using this type of analysis has shown that there are strongly significant correlations between the adjusted country means for each source of event meaning and Hofstede's characterisation of that country upon each of his four dimensions (Smith *et al.*, 1994). Managers in countries classed by Hofstede as relatively high on individualism and low on power distance (which includes most West European countries) report greater reliance on their own experience and training and on their own subordinates. Conversely, managers in countries classed by Hofstede as low on individualism and high on power distance rely more on formal rules and procedures. Both of Hofstede's remaining dimensions also show some linkage with reported event management procedures. In countries categorised by Hofstede as feminine there is greater reliance on "unwritten rules as to how we usually do things around here" and a trend towards greater reliance on specialists. In countries Hofstede classified as more masculine, there is a trend towards more reliance on formal rules. Finally there is also a trend towards more reliance on specialists in countries rated high on uncertainty avoidance.

Numerous authors have attached a good deal of weight to Hofstede's finding that his US respondents scored the highest of all his 53 samples on individualism. Despite the strong correlation between Hofstede's individualism scores and the present scores for reliance on own experience and training, it is notable that all six European countries scored higher than the US sample in their reliance on own experience and training. This result is consistent with the recent work of Schwartz (1994) who found samples of teachers and students from Western European countries to have more individualistic values than those obtained from several US samples.

While the relation of these results to Hofstede's earlier findings are of substantial interest, the principal point at issue in this chapter concerns the similarities and differences between the responses of the managers in the six European countries sampled. In addition to describing how they handled the eight selected events, respondents were also asked to describe how well those events had in fact been handled, both in the short-run and in the long-run. Ratings on the short-run and long-run scales proved to be strongly correlated and they were collapsed into a single score evaluating the effectiveness with which events had been handled.

Separate hierarchical regressions for each of the six European countries were computed. In each case, demographic variables were first entered, in order to discount their effect, followed by forward entry of whichever sources of guidance could best account for the manager's ratings of the effectiveness with which events had been handled.

The results gave an apparently rather clear picture. Within Northern European countries, well-handled events were seen as those in which subordinates were involved. Further to the South and to the West, reliance upon one's own experience and training and upon rules and procedures were more to the fore. A variety of plausible interpretations for these findings could be advanced, but before one does so, it is important to check whether or not the results are validly attributable to differences in national culture, or whether instead they derive from sampling differences between countries. It is notable for instance that the Finnish respondents were rather younger, and that rather more of the Portuguese managers worked in publicly-owned organisations.

In order to discount between-country differences in sampling, a single regression equation was constructed, entering first dummy variables for countries, secondly demographic variables, and then the four sources of guidance which the separate country regressions had shown to be crucial. Finally, interactions between guidance sources and countries were entered. This regression showed that, after differential effects due to overall country means and demographic differences had been discounted, four significant main effects remained but only two modest interactions were found.

The differences found between the separate country regressions must therefore be considered as mostly due to sampling differences, and a different set of conclusions drawn. It appears that managers in all six European countries are in agreement that well-handled events are those in which the manager relies primarily upon his or her own experience and training (R^2 change = 0.04; beta = 0.21; $p < 0.0001$), with some assistance also from rules and procedures (R^2 change = 0.02; beta = 0.17; $p < 0.0001$) and from subordinates (R^2 change = 0.01; beta = 0.09; $p < 0.0001$), while reliance upon unwritten rules is said to be detrimental (R^2 change = 0.01; beta = -0.09; $p < 0.0001$). The significant interactions obtained indicated that Portuguese managers also favoured reliance upon one's superior (R^2 change = 0.01; beta = 0.12; $p < 0.0001$), while Finnish managers evaluated reliance on one's own experience less positively than those in other countries, albeit still positively (R^2 change = 0.02; beta = -0.10; $p < 0.05$).

Discussion

The significance of these results is twofold. Firstly, we have the convergence between Hofstede's characterisations of managers and our own results. In this context, the weakness of the present project's use of convenience samples can be construed as a strength. Despite the fact that the samples in different countries varied in their demographic characteristics, consistent relationships are found with Hofstede's dimensions of individualism, power distance and masculinity. This outcome implies that the cultural differences which he sampled from within a single organisation are still readily detectable within a varied range of European and other organisations nearly thirty years later and must therefore be relatively stable and widely spread within the countries sampled. If we see culture as defined by shared meanings, then the degree to which particular ways of handling events are widely shared within a national culture is important. Only where this proves to be the case would it be defensible to consider nations or groups of nations as cultures. Our findings show only the mean scores obtained by each country sample, rather than the level of consensus within a given country. However, the robustness of the means obtained does provide encouragement that there are substantial and continuing differences between many nations as to the way in which the events in managerial environments may best be given meaning.

The second point of significance is that Hofstede's study did not include any measure of the way in which managers evaluated performance. Our results indicate that across a relatively diverse group of European countries, use of the same sources of guidance was approved, *even though the frequency of using those sources varied substantially.* Since this near unanimity as to how best to manage is not obtained in some of the non-European countries sampled, it does provide some support for the view that there is a distinctively European view of effective management. However the sample of countries from which data have so far been obtained is not sufficiently broad for such a conclusion to be firmly drawn.

Even if it proves to be the case that such a consensus is not in fact Europe-wide, there is value in examining within each country the divergence between how events are handled and the evaluations of effectiveness. For instance, Portuguese managers report relying very substantially upon their superiors, while favouring reliance upon their own experience and training rather more than reliance on one's superior. Such a pattern may well reflect the legacy of the past in conflict with the current Europeanisation of Portuguese management. In contrast, Finnish managers report extremely low reliance upon formal rules and procedures, even though they concur in the view that rules and procedures aid effective event management. Commentators do frequently describe Finnish interpersonal behaviour as relatively formal, but the present data indicate greater reliance on unwritten rules rather than on explicit procedures.

One final question to ask of the data is why reliance upon one's superior is not more positively evaluated by Europeans. Much of management theory is centred upon the focal role of superiors in guiding effective organisational performance. The most probable explanation is that managers choose to handle themselves those events which are non-problematic, and refer more difficult cases to their boss. Thus when asked to rate how effectively events have been handled they are able to assert that those handled by themselves went well, whereas those in which the boss was involved did not. We may have here an instance of the self-serving bias, which is widespread in individualistic Western cultures though not elsewhere (Nisbett and Ross, 1980; Smith and Bond, 1993).

In conclusion, it is evident that our study supports Hofstede's view that cultural differences in Europe as much as elsewhere are deeply-rooted and not readily susceptible to short-term change. Despite this we have been able to show also that some values concerning effective styles of management do transcend current European national boundaries, thus giving some substance to the emerging identity of the Euro-manager.

References

Eberwein, W. and Tholen, J. (1993). *Euro-manager or Splendid Isolation? International Management—An Anglo-German Comparison.* Berlin: De Gruyter.

Hickson, D. J. (ed.) (1993). *Management in Western Europe: Society, Culture and Organization in Twelve Nations.* Berlin: De Gruyter.

Hofstede, G. (1980). *Culture's Consequences: International Differences in Work-related Values.* Beverly Hills, CA: Sage.

Hofstede, G. (1991). *Cultures and Organisations: Software of the Mind.* London: McGraw Hill.

Hofstede, G. (1993). Intercultural conflict and synergy in Europe. In D. J. Hickson, (ed.), *Management in Western Europe: Society, Culture and Organization in Twelve Nations.* Berlin: De Gruyter.

Laurent, A. (1983). The cultural diversity of Western conceptions of management. *International Studies of Management and Organization,* **13**, 75–96.

Leung, K. (1989). Cross-cultural differences: Individual-level and cultural-level analysis. *International Journal of Psychology,* **24**, 703–19.

Nisbett, R. E. and Ross, L. (1980). *Human Inference: Strategies and Shortcomings of Human Judgment.* Englewood Cliffs, NJ: Prentice-Hall.

Ratiu, I. (1983). Thinking internationally: a comparison of how international executives learn. *International Studies of Management and Organization,* **13**, 139–50.

Schwartz, S. H. (1994). Cultural dimensions of values: towards an understanding of national differences. In U. Kim, H. C. Triandis, and G. Yoon, (eds), *Individualism and Collectivism: Theoretical and Methodological Issues.* Newbury Park, CA: Sage.

Smith, P. B. and Bond, M. H. (1993). *Social Psychology across Cultures: Analysis and Perspectives.* Boston, MA: Allyn and Bacon.

Smith, P. B. and Peterson, M. F. (1988). *Leadership, Organizations and Culture: An Event Management Model.* London: Sage.

Smith, P. B., Peterson, M. F., Akande, D., Callan, V., Cho, N. G., Jesuino, J., D'Amorim, M. A., Koopman, P., Leung, K., Mortazawi, S., Munene, J., Radford, M., Ropo, A., Savage, G. and Viedge, C. (1994). Organisational event management in 14 countries: a comparison with Hofstede's dimensions. In F. van der Vijver, P. Schmidt, and P. Boski (eds), *Journeys in Cross-cultural Psychology.* Amsterdam: Swets and Zeitlinger.

Acknowledgemement

We gratefully acknowledge the assistance of Pierre-Henri Francois, Jorge Jesuino, K. Hofmann, Paul Koopman and Arja Ropo in collecting the data analyses in this chapter.

23

Reality Changes Faster than Research: National and Supranational Identity in Social Representations of the European Community in the Context of Changes in International Relations

ANNAMARIA SILVANA DE ROSA

"La Sapienza" University of Rome, Italy

Introduction

The fall of the Berlin Wall, the collapse of the USSR, the whole restructuring of the relations between East and West and between Europe (as a geographical and political whole) and the European Community (Albert, 1984; Kaelble, 1987; Pollini, 1987; Cecchini, 1988; Dastoli, 1989; Dahrendorf, 1989; Dahrendorf *et al.*, 1992; Morin, 1988; Moscati *et al.*, 1989; Emerson, 1990; Braudel, 1992; Guarino, 1992; Losito and Porro, 1992): all these events are of great importance for a social psychology concerned with the study of social representations as dynamic socio-cognitive constructions linked to changes in intergroup relations and the expression of social identities (Etzioni, 1969; Inglehard, 1970, 1977; Lau and Sears, 1986; Flament, 1992). However, the rapidity of change in these situations is so searing that scientific research often cannot keep pace, with the risk that the instruments devised either become obsolete even before they can be used, or at the very least require modifications in the course of the research.

Having spent almost two years modelling the theoretical and methodological aspects of the project here presented, so many changes have taken place in the socio-political reality of Europe that the instruments have had to be updated frequently; particularly the maps which require each subject to identify national borders, capital cities and areas of political/social/ethnic conflict. Notably, the rapid changes in Eastern Europe have required redefinitions of capitals and borders which are themselves subject to local ethnic tensions, both schismatic and separatist. Further changes have occurred while I was revising this chapter, such as the change of the denomination of the EC into European Union and the transformation of the Twelve EC countries into Fifteen European Union Countries.

The research, which is on-going, will be presented analytically with regard to its methodological basis, both in terms of its theoretical background and the general objectives of the study.

Theoretical Background

This investigation is based on two theoretical paradigms of great importance for psycho-social research:

(a) the paradigm of Social Representations (Moscovici, 1981, 1984, 1986, 1988, 1991; Moscovici and Vignaux, 1994; Jodelet, 1984, 1989, 1991, 1992; Farr, 1984, 1987; Farr and Moscovici, 1984; Doise, 1993; Doise, Clemence and Lorenzi-Cioldi, 1992; Palmonari, 1989; Flament, 1989; von Cranach, Doise and Mugny, 1992; de Rosa, 1990a, 1991, 1992a, 1992b, and 1993; Duveen and de Rosa, 1992; Abric, 1994; Guimelli, 1994; Wagner, 1994) currently subject to lively critical debate both in terms of meta-theory and methodology: (for a review, see: de Rosa, 1994a), also in relation to other emerging perspectives, such as the "rhetorical approach" (Billig, 1991, and 1993);

(b) Social Identity Theory (following the original formulation by Tajfel, 1981, 1982, and the English School and the more recent developments in the work of Turner (1987) and Hogg and Abrams (1988) also taking in consideration the wider literature on Self-Identity in a social perspective (Gergen and Davis, 1985; Zavalloni, 1983; Zavalloni and Louis-Guerin, 1984; Rosenbergh, 1987; Rosenbergh and Gara, 1985; Lapsley and Power, 1987; Yardley and Honess, 1987; Neisser, 1988; Doise and Lorenzo-Cioldi, 1991; Breakwell, 1992).

A synthesis of these two approaches has so far been neglected in literature, at least at the level of theoretical formalisation, if not in research practice (where an example can be found in the work of Di Giacomo, 1985). However, fairly recently interest has been expressed in this direction by Breakwell (1993) and Vala (1992).

Breakwell's proposal is developed from the observations made by Doise (1993) who emphasises how researchers have up until now directed their theoretical efforts towards just one aspect of the theory of social representations. In fact, researchers have limited themselves either to describing the content of the representations with reference to the most varied objects of the social world, or to researching the way in which the processes of anchoring and objectification work. This focus has left unexplored Moscovici's hypotheses regarding the dynamics by which at the level of metasystem social groups generate representations as a function of the group's identity.

This suggests that intergroup dynamics and relationships could direct and channel the formation of every specific social representation.

In the light of this possibility, Breakwell suggests integrating Social Identity Theory and Social Representations theory: the first taken as a model which focuses attention on needs and motivations (the need for a positive social identity) considered as ways of explaining intergroup and interpersonal dynamics; the second which, by describing how people construct their model for interpreting the world, brings interpersonal communication processes to the fore as determining factors in the structuring and content of social representations.

Breakwell does not restrict herself to hoping for this integration, but identifies the ways in which group dynamics could influence:

(a)   the production, diffusion and functions of social representations;
(b)   the targets chosen for SRs;
(c)   the salience of SRs;
(d)   the relation between different SRs.

In this perspective, group interests would influence SRs, but the social representations in turn would contextualise, motivate and legitimate group actions.

Just as social identities are a product of group memberships, they similarly influence the involvement of the individual in the representational processes, determining to a large degree the exposure to, acceptance of and use of SRs (Breakwell, *ibid.*).

On the basis of empirical data from research currently in progress at the Social Psychology European Research Institute at the University of Surrey, Breakwell shows how individual psychological traits, taken as both subjective states and as self-consciousness or self-definition, also influence the exposure to, acceptance and use of SRs, as well as influencing the individual's disposition to participate in the production of SRs. Similar observations had also been made by Markova and Wilkie (1987), on the subject of the different emotional and cognitive anchoring of the SR of AIDS as a function of the proximity/distance in the experience that individuals have had of the illness.

Another attempt to find a way of integrating the theories of Social Identity and SR can be found in the empirical work of Vala (1992), who tries to show how (a) social groups, as cognitive products, represent the contexts in which SRs are constructed, and (b) representations of the social structure create categorisation systems which allow social groups to be formed.

The hypotheses formulated by Vala are born from consideration of the role of anchoring process in the formation of SRs and of the functional role played by the process itself at the level of the organisation of social relations.

The research outlined in this chapter differs from other work on the same theme (Hewstone, 1986; Magrin and Gheno, 1990) with respect to both the proposed theoretical framework and the multi-methodological approach (de Rosa, 1987, 1990b; Sotirakopoulou and Breakwell, 1992) which is designed to adapt methodological tools to the complexity of the social-representational construct with all its various sub-dimensional components (image, opinion, attitude, stereotype etc.) (Jaspars and Fraser, 1984; McGuire, 1986; Doise, 1989; de Rosa, 1993) and in its critical links with other social constructions, such as ideology (Aebischer *et al.*, 1991)

In previous articles (de Rosa, 1987, 1990b) I have proposed a multi-method approach to the study of Social Representations in order to adapt research instruments to the various levels and dimensions of analysis implicit in the complex construct of SRs. This proposal was made on the basis of the results of an articulated research programme on the SR of mental illness in both lay and expert populations. These results suggested a significant interaction between communicative codes (figurative and linguistic) activated as a function of different techniques (verbal or non-verbal) and of the level of the representations elicited (either more or less peripheral or central, variant or invariant). These representations emerged as more or less similar or differentiated not only as a function of the population variables under consideration but also as a function of the research instruments used.

Recently, the proposal for a multi-method approach has been taken up again in the literature (Sotirakopoulou and Breakwell, 1992) and discussed critically (Flick, 1992; de Rosa, 1993a, 1994). It is my intention that it should not be considered as a simple "*summing up*" of methods, but as a precise choice of methods as a function of the specific levels implicit in the representations under investigation, supported by definite hypotheses.

Furthermore, still on the theoretical-methodological question, the research presented here offers the opportunity to deepen fundamental aspects of the SR construct, which is still lacking adequate empirical proof from *field research*; for example, of the dynamic nature of SRs as processual and transformative. As has been said before, the literature shows that these aspects have mostly been approached with experimental or laboratory techniques (most notable in this respect is the work of the Aix-en-Provence school). In this research project, the choice of the object of enquiry (focused on dynamic processes that link *changing identities* and *social representations* within fast-changing socio-political contexts) and the decision to explore the extent of sharing and differentiation between two generations (young people and adults) together provide an interesting means of studying in the field the processes of transmission and changes in social representations—which are the vehicle for expressing identity.

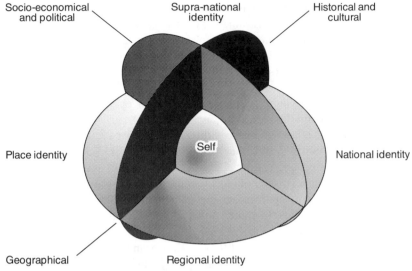

Socio-economical and political

Supra-national identity

Historical and cultural

Place identity

Self

National identity

Geographical

Regional identity

FIGURE 23.1   Multidimensional identity involved in social representation of the European Community

Objectives

The research aims to investigate European identity in adults and students (the adults of tomorrow). This identity is a synthesis of values, feelings of belonging and social representations, which together with cognitive/informative factors contribute to the structuring of identification processes with an object (the EC) which is particularly salient at a time characterised by wide-ranging and profound changes in international East—West relations.

The intention of the research is to identify the points of intersection between the levels of identity (supranational, national, social and personal) of the chosen subjects, also as a function of the generation gap between young people and adults (see Figure 23.1)

The ultimate goal of the research is a comparative analysis of the data collected in different European countries (Austria, France, Finland, Germany, Greece, Italy, Portugal, Spain, Switzerland and the UK) using the same methodologies.

Hypotheses

The research has been guided by a series of hypotheses concerning the likely influences of both the characteristics of the chosen sample and the methods used. The hypotheses were therefore articulated on the basis of a very detailed series of sub-hypotheses, connected to all the population variables involved as well as to the various sections of the instruments. Here—by way of synthesis—only the guiding hypotheses will be presented.

So far as the population characteristics are concerned, we particularly expect to see differences in the SRs of the EC:

1. Between adults and young people, with a greater openness towards themes related to the EC on the part of young people.
2. As a function of other variables of the sample groups considered, such as: subjects' familiarity with other European cultures (identified through information on frequency of travel abroad and length of stay, and knowledge of foreign languages); strength of commitment to/active participation in European integration, e.g. membership of political, cultural or study groups, and political tendencies. In short, all those variables that are salient for the social identity of the subjects.
3. Between sample groups from different European nationalities (this is the guiding hypothesis of the European project as a whole, of which the present paper forms a part), as well as between different groups within the same nationality group. So far as the Italian samples are concerned, we expect to find differences as a function of place of residence: urban-metropolitan areas (represented by Rome) are presumed to bring about openness to the process of internationalisation because of daily contact—praxis—with tourists and people from other parts of the world while provincial areas (represented by Trento and Cosenza) presumed to be more focused on the specifics of local matters. In addition border areas which have traditions of intercultural exchange and middle-European characteristics (Trieste) or which are subject to inter-ethnic and political tensions between linguistic minorities (Bolzano) are likely to have an effect on the expressed SRs.

As regards the influence of perceived conflict, we expect that a perceived conflict at an intra-national level (between regions of the same country) could be correlated with a high degree of identification with a supranational entity (EC), in agreement with Valencia et al. (1991) who argued that the identification with a third object (Europe, EC) is perceived as a place in which it would be possible to resolve the existing conflicts.

We also expect that a perceived conflict at an international level (between one's own country and a foreign country) could anchor the representation of the EC to a specific dimension, such as Economic Relations (for example in the case of perception of tension between Italy and the potent imposing Germany).

Concerning the impact of the methods used and their relationship between some of the selected variables or the designed dimensions and the expected data, on the basis of the above mentioned consideration about the multi-method approach to the study of SR (more analytically expressed in previous work: de Rosa, 1990b), we expect to find the following.

1. A significant interaction between the methods used and the results gained, in so far as the instruments of a more projective nature (such as the associative network, the projective use of space through the graphical map, and the semantic differentials) should allow the nuclei of the SRs expressed by the subjects to be singled out, as well as the components which are most closely anchored to their true identities (both personal and social). The more structured sections of the questionnaire will most probably elicit more peripheral dimensions of the representation, which are more sensitive to social preference effects.

    Because of these influences, we expect that both the verbal and non-verbal projective above mentioned instruments will reveal latent tendencies in the subjects to discriminate the "outgroup" (other countries and nationalities) and the "ingroup" (own country) both in terms of idealising them as well as devaluing them.

2. That in the category differentiation between outgroup and ingroup a central role will be played:

    2.1 by self-representation, discriminating between subjects with a very positive self-representation and those with a very negative self-representation – singled out by both the "associative network" and the "semantic differential" for the stimulus-word "self";

    2.2 by the degree of identification with different entities (such as own town, region, country, Europe, EC), identified by the section of the questionnaire focused on the multi-dimensional (local, national and supranational) levels involved in the identification processes.

    These dimensions are held to be so influential that at a later stage of data analysis they will no longer be treated as dependent variables, revealed through respective sections of the instruments, but as independent variables and as illustrative variables on the basis of which groups will ultimately be differentiated in order to show respectively the influences on the responses to other sections of the questionnaire, related to the evaluation of the process of European integration, and the relation with the structure and contents of the representations elicited by means of "associative networks".

3. That the evaluation of the process of European integration—as identified by the various sections of the questionnaire—are attitudinal dimensions somewhat external to the deepest nuclei of the sensitivity towards the EC, based on a more complex representational system characterised by an interweaving of various elements (the EC seen in relation to geographical Europe, to one's own country, to the other EC member countries, East/West, North/South, borders etc.)—as identified by both the semantic differential and the associative network of the different stimulus-words. We expect that on the one hand a higher level of information will be positively correlated

with a greater degree of sensitivity towards the process of European integration, and that in any case this will be strongly conditioned by the subject's perception of costs/benefits, with a strong downward trend in all those cases in which the process of European integration is seen as a disadvantage for one's own country and even more so if it is seen as a disadvantage for oneself.

Methodology

Population

In anticipation of a more extensive sampling technique (almost 4,000 subjects) which has been extended to parallel groups gathered from other European countries both EC member and not EC member, an Italian pilot sample of almost 400 subjects—residing in Rome—was taken for the explorative phase of the investigation. These subjects were chosen from 262 final-year students from the various types of Italian secondary schools (humanities, scientific, business, industrial, teacher-training) and 121 adults (fathers and mothers of adolescents of the same age of the students frequenting secondary schools).

The subjects were equally distributed in terms of sex and social status, and other variables were also controlled for, including political inclination; frequency of travel in Europe and choice of respective countries; knowledge of foreign languages; sources of information on and/or possible active involvement with the issue of the European Community.

So far as the adult sample was concerned, we would have preferred to have chosen it from the actual parents of the adolescents in our research project, rather than from the general population of parents of adolescents of the same age as those in our sample. In this way we could have controlled not just the "generation gap" variable but also the "family culture" variable, through membership of the same family nucleus.

The choice to explore the degree of sharing and differentiation between two generations (young people and adults), controlling for the variable of family culture (children and their parents), would have provided an interesting means of studying the processes of transmission and change in SRs and identity in natural primary groups which have a history (i.e. the family). However, it proved almost impossible to match the availability of both parents with the children who had been contacted via the schools, so we had to reorient the selection of the adult sample according to the criterion that they were parents of children of the same age as those who had agreed to participate in our research.

As regards the Italian sample, this pilot sample, consisting of residents of Rome, will be compared with analogous samples from Northern Italy (Trento), areas on the borders of Italy which are not marked by conflict (Trieste, Udine) and those that are (Bolzano), as well as Southern Italy (Cosenza), by other teams working on this project.

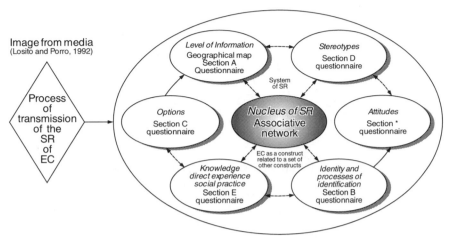

FIGURE 23.2   The different dimensions of S.R. of the E.C. as investigated by the multi-method approach

Instruments

In accordance with the multi-method approach to research required by social representations (de Rosa, 1990b; Sotirakopoulou and Breakwell, 1992), the following schedules were designed:

Projective Verbal Instruments

The "*associative network*", which is based on the technique of free associations with a series of stimulus-words, chosen as a function of the research objectives (de Rosa, 1993b, 1995). The stimulus-words were as follows, aimed at studying the EC not as an isolated representation, but as a system of SR, i.e. as a representation related to a set of other social representations:

1. European Community
2. North/South
3. East/West
4. nation
5. boundaries
6. myself
7. the twelve Members of the EC requiring three adjectives to be given for each country. (In the version of the associative network administered in new member countries of the EU, this stimulus included also Austria and Finland.)

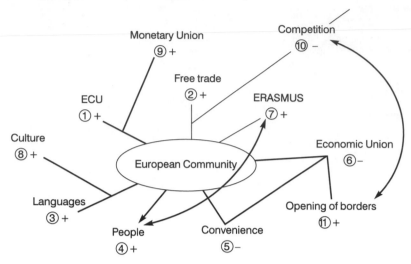

FIGURE 23.3   An example of an associative network

This instrument, which was specifically created for this and other research projects currently running, is aimed at investigating some of the latent and evaluative components of SRs. Similarly to the technique of free association, already widely used in research on SR (de Rosa, 1988), the "associative network"—despite making use of verbal code—allows some of the deep evaluative elements of representations to be captured due to its projective nature, thus avoiding the filter of social desirability that subjects often employ to orient their replies. I have called this instrument the "associative network" because—unlike traditional techniques of free association (Di Giacomo, 1985) which simply plot the constitutive elements of the semantic field activated by the stimulus-word (that is the whole vocabulary which constitutes the elicited representation)—the associative network enables subjects to specify the *structure of the semantic field* by establishing connections between the words they have written down. In traditional free association techniques, this stage is deduced post-hoc by the researcher on the basis of statistical techniques that identify clusters among the field elements.

The associative network gives this task to the subjects who are expressing the representation, by asking them to identify the *ramifications* between the words and any *further connections* between the words or groups of words written around the stimulus-word which appears at the centre of the page (see example, Figure 23.3).

In fact what is interesting is that with this technique the phenomenon of emergence of the words (common to all traditional associative tasks) is contextualised in a chain of words directly indicated by the subjects, through their ramifications and further connections. For example, in the associative networks that the subjects completed to the stimulus-word "European Community", the word "community" appears with different meanings according to the chain of ramification or connections in which it is included. It refers to at least three meanings:

1. to the *"EC as political institution"* when the word appears in the ramification such as "community-nations-government-politics" or in the connection "Strasbourg-parliament";
2. to the *"EC as economic union"*, when the word appears in the connection such as: "community-ecu-free trade-monetary union-common market";
3. to the *"community as social dimension"* when the word appears in the ramification such as: "community-solidarity-people-communication-friendship-cooperation".

Further information given by the associative network is the *order* in which the words were thought of, as an index of their *accessibility*.

Finally, it requires each word to be given a *polarity* by the subject, who is asked to place a sign by each word (+, – or 0) to show whether that term in the context of the test has a positive, negative or neutral valency for him/her (see in the following paragraph the criteria for coding and for weighing the polarity (positive, negative or neutral) on the basis of the total number of the associated words).

Non-verbal Instruments

A *map* which calls on wide-ranging graphical and spatial representations of the EC and of individual member countries (question 1 in the questionnaire) requiring:

1. identification of the geographical and political borders of the EC and of the individual EC member countries;
2. names of the EC member states and their capitals;
3. identification of the areas perceived by the subjects as foci of intense social or ethnic conflict.

Structured Verbal Instruments

A *questionnaire* structured around the following thematic areas:

A.   Level of Information

These questions are intended to supplement the information/knowledge component regarding geographical-political details of EC countries demonstrated by the Graphical Map, by ascertaining the degree of knowledge of political-institutional aspects of the EC, such as:

● the date of foundation of the EC and the reasons that led to its establishment;
● its constituent bodies;
● the most widely used currencies, languages and religions in the EC;
● information on possible future members of the EC;
● the Maastricht treaty and the changes made to the single market from 1 January 1993.

B. Identity and Processes of Identification

Various scales designed to measure:

● the *processes of identification/sense of belonging* felt by the subjects with their own town, region, home country, the EC and geographical Europe;
● their *value judgements of the different geographical-political entities* named above, with the objective of discerning the breadth and degree of inclusion of specific places in their personal identity;
● the *awareness of foci of tension or conflict* at a regional level, between neighbouring areas or between one's own country and other European countries (in the Italian version, only for subjects resident in border areas).

The questions in this section of the questionnaire were inspired by a study on "The images of Europe in the European" (Valencia *et al.*, 1991).

A *semantic differential* for the different geo-political entities (for example, city of residence, own country, the European Community etc) as well as for the stimulus "*yourself*", with the aim of revealing the links between the connotative aspects attributed to the identification objects and the Self.

The twenty-one adjectives used in the scales were selected after having analysed studies aimed at cross-cultural validation of the semantic differential in different countries (Capozza, 1977; Capozza *et al.*, 1981).

C. Evaluation of the European Integration Process in Various Areas and Degree of Confidence in Referring to a Supranational Entity such as the EC rather than a National one

The questions in this section are intended to reveal:

● the *evaluation of the EC* in reaching its goals and the evaluation of the success of the EC in various areas, as well as the length of time thought necessary to realise these goals completely;

- the *degree of confidence*—understood as willingness to turn to a supranational entity, i.e. the EC, rather than a national or regional entity, so far as decision-making processes of a political, economic or social nature are concerned; trust in the institutional and social set-up of the subject's own country is also investigated;
- the *perception of cost/benefit* derived from EC membership for some EC countries;
- the *perception of disparity* between members in terms of active participation in the unification process on an economic level, and confidence in a change of direction towards decreasing inequality.
- *Perception of equity/inequity* in cost-benefit terms derived from belonging to the EC both for one self and for one's own country

The questions in this section (not included in the Italian version used by the other research group working in North Italy) are intended to find out the subject"'s perception of whether EC membership brings advantages or disadvantages in various areas: Agriculture, Environment, Freedom of opinion, Economy, Education, Employment, Health, Science and Technology, National security, Tourism.

For each area the questions have been formulated (and equally distributed) in such a way that the criterion of advantage/disadvantage implicit in the statements takes on either an individual perspective (referring to oneself) or a collective perspective (referring to one's country).

D.   *Stereotypes Attributed to the EC Member Countries and their Populations*

In this section, the questions are designed to reveal nuclei of stereotypes in the evaluation of different EC member countries and their populations, to be compared to the image of own country (evaluated on the same scales by the semantic differential included in the section B) and self-image (section B) which forms the central criterion for making self-other comparisons.

The aim is to identify the articulations between stereotypical attributions to the out-group (and possible categorical differentiations) and attributions to the in-group (own Country) and self-categorisation.

E.   *Sociodemographic Data*

The questions which make up this section are intended to collect information related to population variables (such as age, sex, place of birth, place of residence, school, profession and level of education of the subject's family). It also asks about the subjects' direct experiences and familiarity with the EC (destinations and frequency of travel abroad, foreign languages spoken), their political identity and their major sources of knowledge about the EC and related matters.

Criteria for Coding Procedure and Analysis of the Dependent Variables

In view of the complexity of the instruments and the number of both dependent and independent variables, the design for coding the data is of necessity very detailed. As such, it allows the pool of variables to be divided up into parts, each of which is subjected to factor analysis, followed by a multidimensional analysis of the factorial scores which have emerged.

Notably, the *codebook for the questionnaire* alone provides for the codification of 798 variables which are recorded on fourteen sheets for each subject.

For the spatial indices singled out by the *graphical map*, a correction grid was prepared on a transparency, which allowed the exactness or inexactness (in terms of expansion or underestimation) to be judged for the boundaries drawn for each member state and the EC as a whole. We could also see if any countries had been included which are not currently members of the EC, from the different areas of geographical Europe.

For the *associative networks*, a separate database for each stimulus-word was created (using "Filemaker" on Macintosh) in order to record all the information obtained by this instrument: (a) associated words; (b) ramifications between the words; (c) connections between groups of words; (d) order of priority in words were written; (e) polarity both of each word (positive, negative or neutral) and of the total associated words.

In order to weigh the polarity (positive, negative and neutral) on the basis of the total number of words associated by each subject, two specific statistical indexes were created. In particular, the first is:

index of polarity (P)

$$= \frac{N° \text{ positive words} - N° \text{ negative words}}{N° \text{ total words associated}}$$

This index ranges between -1 and +1.

If P was between -1 and -.05, this means that most of the words were connotated negatively.

If P was between -.04 and +.04, this means that the positive and the negative words tend to be equal.

If P was between +.04 and +1, this means that most of the words were connotated positively.

The second index is:

index of neutrality (N)

$$= \frac{N° \text{ neutral words} - (N° \text{ positive words} = N° \text{ negative words})}{N° \text{ total words}}$$

This index too ranges between -1 and +1.

If N was between -1 and -.O5, this means that few words were connotated neutrally (i.e. = low neutrality).

If N was between -.O4 and +.O4, this means that the neutral words tend to be equal to the sum of the positive and the negative words (i.e. = medium neutrality).

If N was between +.04 and +1, this means that most of the words were connotated neutrally (i.e. = high neutrality).

Multistep strategies of statistical analyses

Step 1 (Analysis of Factorial Structures at Different Levels of Abstraction and of Communality of the Structures across Different Countries)

The questionnaire was analysed separately for each section, in order to single out dimensions of an intermediate level of abstraction. A series of factor analyses (Principle Component Analyses: PCA) were carried out for each country and the emerging factorial structures for each country were compared. Depending on the quality of the factorial structure (tightness, simplicity), a different procedure, ranging along a continuum from the most exploratory to the most confirmatory, was used each time. These procedures can be depicted as follows:

Simple visual comparison	Coefficients of congruence (Everett, Phi, etc.)	Procustes rotations	Simultaneous Component Analysis	MTMM Multi-sample Analysis

The first two procedures do not modify the factorial structure, they simply give insights into the comparability of the factorial structure between countries.

In some cases classical orthogonal (Varimax) or oblique (Oblimin) rotation, while in other cases Procustes orthogonal rotations (McCrae *et al.*, 1994) have been used. While the Varimax and Oblimin Rotations are well known and used in literature, it is useful to provide some more information about the less known Procustes Rotations.

This third procedure (Procustes Rotations) is aimed at lining up as much as possible, given the empirical results, one extracted factorial structure with another by using an algorithm of minimum squares under the bond of orthogonality. This rotation requires the identification of a *target* matrix, which acts as "anchor", towards which the extracted factorial solutions are rotated. In this case, the factorial structures emerging from the pilot study carried out in Italy were considered as the target matrices and the other countries' structures as pattern matrices to be rotated.

The fourth procedure is much more demanding from a computational point of view and is mostly useful with simple parsimonious factorial structures, given the length of computations. In other words, it could give an intermediate factorial structure between different countries and many indices of congruence.

Coefficients of congruence of factorial solutions or their stability (Everett, 1983) were also calculated. For both these coefficients, the values vary between 0 and 1, where 1 shows a perfect congruence or stability.

The fifth procedure is a strictly confirmatory procedure. The two sub-procedures are two submodels of the structural equation models and, depending on the quality of exploratory results, both of them could be used to gain different empirical information about the communality of the structures across different countries. Even in this case, the hypothesised structures should not be too complex, otherwise it would be quite difficult to find a numerical solution.

In some cases hierarchical cluster analyses were carried out.

Step 2 (Analysis of Differences and Positioning of Groups)

Depending on the findings in the step 1 analyses, at step 2 emphasis was given to the difference (or equality) in scores in the factors stemming from the previous analyses. The aim was to compare scores of similar factors between countries while also considering other potentially influencing variables (socio-demographic, etc.).

In this respect, a series of ANOVA and ANCOVA was performed. When major differences in the factorial structures between countries had been found in step 1, the emphasis was placed upon similar countries.

In other words, the point was to try to focus on the communalities between countries, as well as on the specificity of each country (or groups of countries, i.e. Northern vs Southern, subjects with high or low distal or proximal identification, etc.).

Step 3 (Cross-analysis of the Results Collected by Different Methods: Questionnaire and Associative Network)

A cross-analysis between both the set of representations related to the various stimulus-words used in the associative network (EC, National, Borders, South–North, East–West, EC Member States, Myself) and all the dimensions identified at different levels of abstraction (more detailed and descriptive vs more synthetic and supra-ordered) by analysing data of the questionnaire was carried out.

To this end, a series of SPAD-T was performed, by using as *active* variables all the associated words related to each stimulus and as *illustrative* variables not only the subjects' socio-demographic variables, but also all the dimensions extracted by the questionnaire relating to the following wide categories: informational and experiential knowledge of the EC, descriptors of self, evaluation of local, national and supranational objects of identification, degree of confidence in the EC, the evaluation of the EC Member countries (country by country), the evaluation of EC countries organised in clusters (Northern vs Southern, Powerful vs Weak, etc.), evaluation of the people of the various EC countries.

Furthermore, the indices of polarity and of neutrality as a composite measure of the evaluative dimensions linked to the representations associated with all the different stimulus-words were also included in the file of the illustrative variables in order to use them for a cross-analysis between the different files of the active variables (associated words) relating to other stimuli. The aim in this case was, for example, to analyse how subjects with a positive or negative index of polarity towards Nation were positioned on the representations referring to the EC, or again, how subjects with a positive or negative index of polarity towards North vs South were positioned when they produced representations of the EC countries perceived as belonging to Northern vs Mediterranean culture.

Factorial analyses aimed at identifying the latent structure between the indices of polarity expressed in relation to the different stimulus-words, and a correlational analysis between an index of polarity relating to a particular stimulus-word (such as Self) and the indices of polarity relating to all the other stimulus-words (previously regrouped by factor analyses) were also performed. The same was done to test the structure of the indices of neutrality.

Step 4 (Building General Structural Models)

As the final step, more than one general model will be built by trying to take into account the factorial dimensions emerging from the analyses of the questionnaire as well as the indices of polarity related to the representations emerging from the associative network.

A structuring equation modelling approach via LISREL has already been used to build and test one of the hypothesised general models.

Other general structural models—involving other flows of variables—will also be tested by this statistical strategy (Bollen, 1989), each time providing results on the total sample and the sub-samples country by country.

Status of the International Research Programme

In the first three years of this project, the following have been finalised:

1. *The theoretical model* (review of Italian and foreign literature; identification of the specific objectives and hypotheses within the general aims of the research project).
2. *Definition of the methodology* according to the multi-methodological design presented above, which required a lot of revision as work progressed, also a result of the continual changes in the political and institutional picture of Europe (particularly the East) in recent years.
3. *Collection and analysis of data related to the pilot study*
   The data related to the pilot study carried out in Italy has been analysed as far as the sample collected in Rome (both on adult and young people) is concerned, while the data is currently being processed as far as the sample

collected in the other areas of Italy is concerned. Preliminary reports on the results related to the pilot study have been presented at various international conferences (de Rosa, 1993c, 1994b, 1994c).

4. *Status of the cross-national programme*

The cross-national extension of the research project has involved the adoption of a common methodological research plan and the translation of the instruments into various languages and the identification of parallel sample groups in the ten European countries. English, Finnish, French, German, Portuguese, Spanish, Basque, Greek versions of the instruments have been realised. The data has already been collected and processed as far as the following European countries are concerned: Austria (Vienna), France (Aix-en-Provence and Paris), Portugal (Lisbon), UK (Cambridge), Spain (Barcelona and San Sebastian, on Spanish and Basque sample), Switzerland (French and Italian Regions), Greece (Patras). The data has already been collected also in Germany and in a new member country of the European Union (Finland), and is currently being processed.

Preliminary reports on the results related to the cross-national research programme have been presented during a symposium (de Rosa, 1995) and a summer school on Social Representations and Communication organised by de Rosa and Helkama in Finland (August–September 1995).

Acknowledgements

I would like to thank my ex-students Sergio Olivares, Roberta Covina, Greta Neri, who worked intensively with me on the construction of the questionnaire and the data collection for the sample of young people; and also Elena Clemente and Barbara Cavuto who gathered the data for the adult samples of the pilot study. I would also like to mention the group of the Erasmus students (ICP-I – 93/3074/14; 94–3074/14, coordinated by A. S. de Rosa, University of Rome "La Sapienza"), who have made it possible to extend this project on an international level and those foreign Erasmus partners who have welcomed them and supported their work (in particular, J. C. Abric, G. Breakwell, W. Doise, G. Duveen, F. Elejabarrieta, U. Flick, A. Hantzi, K. Helkama, J. Jesuino, D. Jodelet, E. Kirchner, K. Liebkind, S. Moscovici, and J. Valencia). Jaclyn Wallach worked on the translation of the preliminary version of this chapter.

References

Aebischer, V., Deconchy, J. P. and Lipiansky, R. (eds) (1991). *Idéologies et représentations sociales*. Fribourg: Delval.
Abric, J. C. (ed.) (1994). *Pratiques sociales et représentations*. Paris: P.U.F.
Albert, M. (1984). *Una sfida per l'Europa*. Bologna: Il Mulino.
Billig, M. (1991). Social representations and rhetoric. In M. Billig (ed.), *Ideology and Opinions*. London: Sage.
Billig, M. (1993). Studying the thinking society: social representations, rhetoric and attitudes. In G. Breakwell and D. Canter (eds), *Empirical Approaches to Social Representations*. Oxford: Oxford University Press.
Bollen, K. A. (1989) *Structural Equations with Latent Variables*. New York: Wiley.
Braudel, F. (1992). *L'Europa e gli Europei*. Bari: Laterza.

Breakwell, G. M. (ed.) (1992). *The Social Psychology of the Self Concept*. London: Academic Press/ Surrey University Press.

Breakwell, G. M. (1993). Social representations and social identity. *Papers on Social Representations*, **2**, 198–217.

Breakwell, G. M. and Canter, D. V. (eds) (1993). *Empirical Approaches to Social Representations*. Oxford: Oxford University Press.

Capozza, D. (1977). *Il differenziale semantico. Problemi teorici e metrici*. Bologna: Patron.

Capozza, D., Bonaldo, E. and Di Maggio, A. (1981). Problems of identity and social conflict: researches conducted on ethnical groups in Italy. In H. Tajfel (ed.), *Social Identity and intergroups relations*. Cambridge: Cambridge University Press.

Cecchini, P. (1988). *La sfida del 1992*. Sperling and Krupfer.

Dahrendorf, R. (1989). *Riflessioni sulla rivoluzione europea*. Bari: Laterza.

Dahrendorf, R., Furet, F. and Geremek, B. (1992). *La democrazia in Europa*. Bari: Laterza.

Dastoli, P. V. (1989). *Europa senza frontiere?*. Bologna: Il Mulino.

de Rosa, A. S. (1987). Différents niveaux d'analyse du concept de représentation sociale en relation aux méthodes utilisées. In G. Bellelli (ed.), *La représentation social de la maladie mentale*. Napoli: Liguori.

de Rosa, A. S. (1988). Sur l'usage des associations libres dans l'étude des représentations sociales de la maladie mentale. *Connexions*, **51**, 27–50.

de Rosa, A.S. (1990a). Considérations pour une comparaison critique entre les représentations sociales et la social cognition. Sur la signification d'une approche psychogénetique à l'étude des représentations sociales. *Cahiers Internationaux de Psychologie Sociale*, **5**, 69–109.

de Rosa, A. S. (1990b). Per un approccio multi-metodo allo studio delle Rappresentazioni Sociali, *Rassegna di Psicologia*, **3**, 101–52.

de Rosa, A. S. (1991). Idéologie médicale et non-médicale et son rapport avec les représentations sociales de la maladie mentale. In V. Aebischer, J. P. Deconchy and R. Lipiansky (eds), *Idéologies et représentations sociales*. Fribourg: Delval.

de Rosa, A. S. (1992a). Thematic perspectives and epistemic principles in developmental Social Cognition and Social Representation. The meaning of a developmental approach to the investigation of Social Representation. In M. von Cranach, W. Doise, and G. Mugny (eds), *Social Representations and the Social Bases of Knowledge*. Lewiston, NY: Hoegrofe & Huber Publishers.

de Rosa, A. S. (1992b). Social cognition e Rappresentazioni Sociali in prospettiva evolutiva: una doppia via alla conoscenza del mondo sociale? *Rassegna di Psicologia*, **1**, 41–94.

de Rosa, A. S. (1993a). Social Representations and Attitudes: problems of coherence between the theoretical definition and procedure of research. *Papers on Social Representations*, **2**, 178–92.

de Rosa, A. S. (1993b). The associative network: a new technique for studying projective and evaluative components of Social Representation. *Proceedings of EAESP General Meeting*, Lisbon 16–19 September.

de Rosa, A. S. (1993c). Building the E.C. puzzle. The "12" countries and their people in the Social Representations of the European Community. *Proceedings of EAESP General Meeting: Workshop on "National identities in Europe"*, Lisbon, 16–19 September.

de Rosa, A. S. (1994a). From the theory to the meta-theory of Social Representations: emerging trends. *Social Sciences Informations*, **33**, 273–304.

de Rosa, A. S. (1994b). Multi-dimensional identity and processes of identification in the social representations of the European Community in young Italian people. *Proceedings of the Conference of IAAP* (Madrid, July).

de Rosa, A. S. (1994c). Am I Italian and/or European? Multi-dimensional identity and processes of identification in the Social Representations of the European Community. *Proceedings of the British Psychology Society Social Psychology Section Annual Conference*, Cambridge, September.

de Rosa, A. S. (1995a) Le "réseau d'associations" comme méthode d'étude dans la recherche sur les représentations sociales: structure, contenus et polarité du champ sémantique. *Cahiers Internationaux de Psychologie Sociale*, **1** (in press).

de Rosa, A. S. (1995b) Putting together the European puzzle: Social representations of the Union, its countries and peoples. Invited paper presented at the "Social representations in the Northern context" symposium. Mustlio, Finland, August.

Di Giacomo, J. P. (1985). *Rappresentazioni sociali e movimenti collettivi.* Napoli: Liguori.

Doise, W. (1993). Debating social representations. In G. M. Breakwell and D. V. Canter (eds), *Empirical Approaches to Social Representations.* Oxford: Oxford University Press.

Doise, W. and Lorenzi-Cioldi, F. (1991). L'identité comme représentation sociale. In V. Aebischer, J. P. Deconchy and E. M. Lipiansky (eds), *Idéologies et représentations sociales,* Fribourg: Delval.

Doise, W., Clemence, A. and Lorenzi-Cioldi F. (1992). *Représentations sociales et analyses de données.* Grenoble: Presses Universitaires de Grenoble.

Duveen, G. and de Rosa, A. S. (1992). "Social Representations and the Genesis of Social Knowledge". *Ongoing Production on Social Representations,* **1**, 94–108.

Emerson, M. (1990). *La nuova economia europea.* Bologna: Il Mulino.

Etzioni, A. (1969). Social-psychological aspects of international relations. In G. Lindsey and E. Aronson (eds), *The Handbook of Social Psychology.* Mass.: Addison-Wesley.

Eurobarometro, Brussels, Commission of the European Communities.

Farr, R. M. (1984). Les représentations sociales. In S. Moscovici (ed.), *Psychologie sociale.* Paris: PUF.

Farr, R. M. (ed.) (1987). Social representations. Special Issue. *Journal for the Theory of Social Behavior,* **17**, 4.

Farr, R. and Moscovici, S. (eds) (1984). *Social Representations.* Cambridge: Cambridge University Press (Italian translation, 1989: *Le rappresentazioni sociali,* Bologna: Il Mulino).

Flament, C. (1989). Structure et dynamique des représentations sociales. In D. Jodelet (ed.), *Les représentations sociales.* Paris: PUF.

Flament, C. (1992). Request to all researchers in the field of social representations. *Ongoing Productions on Social Representations,* **1**, 137.

Flick U. (1992). Combining methods—lack of methodology: discussion of Sotirakopoulou and Breakwell. In W. Wagner, F. Elejabarrieta and U. Flick (eds), *Ongoing Production on Social Representations,* **1**, 43–8.

Gergen, K. J. and Davis, K. E. (eds) (1985). *The Social Construction of the Person.* New York: Springer-Verlag.

Guarino, G. (1992). *La libertà e le regole.* Bologna: Il Mulino.

Guimelli, C. (ed.) (1994) *Structures et transformations de représentations sociales.* Neuchâtel: Delachaux and Nestlé.

Hewstone, M. (1986). *Understanding Attitudes to the European Community: A Socio-psychological Study in Four Member States.* Cambridge: Cambridge University Press.

Hogg, M. and Abrams, D. (1988). *Social Identification: A Social Psychology of Intergroup Relations and Group Processes.* London/New York: Routledge.

Inglehard, R. (1970). Cognitive mobilisation and European Identity, *Comparative Politics,* **3**, 45–70.

Inglehard, R. (1977). *The Silent Revolution: Changing Values and Political Styles among Western Public.* Princeton: Princeton University Press.

Jaspars, J. and Fraser, C. (1984). Attitudes and social representations. In R. Farr and S. Moscovici (eds), *Social Representations.* Cambridge: Cambridge University Press (Italian translation, 1989: *Le rappresentazioni sociali,* Bologna: Il Mulino).

Jodelet, D. (1984). Représentation sociale: phénomènes, concept et théorie. In S. Moscovici (ed.), *Psychologie sociale.* Paris: PUF.

Jodelet, D. (ed.) (1989). *Les représentations sociales.* Paris: PUF.

Jodelet, D. (1991). L'idéologie dans l'étude des représentations sociales. In V. Aebischer, J. P. Deconchy and R. Lipiansky (eds), *Idéologies et représentations sociales.* Fribourg: Delval.

Jodelet, D. (1992). Mémoire de masses: le côte mural et affectif de l'histoire. *Bulletin de Psychologie,* 45, 239–56.

Kaelble, H. (1987). Auf dem Weg zu einer europäischen Gesellschaft: Eine Sozialgeschichte Westeuropas 1890–1980, München: Beck (Italian translation, 1990: *Verso una società europea,* Bari: Laterza).

Lapsley, D. K. and Power, F. C. (eds) (1987). *Self, Ego and Identity.* New York: Springer Verlag.

Lau, R. R. and Sears, D. O. (eds) (1986). *Political Cognition.* Hillsdale: Lawrence Erlbaum.

Lebart, L., Morineau, A. and Becue, M. (1989). *SPAD-T. Système portable pour l'analyse des données textuelles, Manuel de l'utilisateur.* Paris: Cisia.

Losito, G. and Porro R. (1992). *Le rappresentazioni giornalistiche dell' Europa e del 1992. Primi risultati di una ricerca pilota*. Roma: ed. RAI VQPT.

Magrin, M. E. and Gheno, S. (1990). La concezione dell'Europa in soggetti in età evolutiva: indagine preliminarye sugli attributi costitutivi, *V Congresso Nazionale della Divisione di Psicologia Sociale, Società Italiana di Psicologia* (Milan, 27–29 March).

Markova, I. and Wilkie, P. (1987). Representations, concepts and social change: the phenomenon of AIDS. *Journal for the Theory of Social Behaviour*, **1**, 389–409.

McCrae, R. R., Zonderman, A. B., Costa, P. T., Bond, M. H. and Paunonen, S. V. (1994). Evaluating replicability of factors in the Revised NEO Personality Inventory: confirmatory factor analysis and Procrustes rotation. Submitted for publication.

McGuire, W. J. (1986). The vicissitudes of attitudes and similar representational constructs in twentieth century psychology. *European Journal of Social Psychology*, **16**, 89–130.

Morin, E. (1988). *Pensare l'Europa*. Milano: Feltrinelli.

Moscati S. *et al.* (1989). *Europa: mito e realtà*. Roma: Editalia.

Moscovici, S. (1981). On social representations. In J. P. Forgas (ed.), *Social Cognition. Perspectives on Everyday Understanding*. London: Academic Press.

Moscovici, S. (1984). The phenomenon of social representations. In R. M. Farr and S. Moscovici (eds), *Social Representations*. Cambridge/Paris: Cambridge University Press and Editions de la Maison des Sciences de l'Homme.

Moscovici, S. (1986). L'ère des représentations sociales. In W. Doise and A. Palmonari (eds), *L'étude des représentations sociales*. Paris: Delachaux et Nestlé.

Moscovici, S. (1988). Notes towards a description of social representations. *European Journal of Social Psychology*, **18**, 211–50.

Moscovici, S. (1989). Des représentations collectives aux représentations sociales. In D. Jodelet (ed.), *Les représentations sociales*. Paris: PUF.

Moscovici, S. (1991). La fin des représentations sociales? In V. Aebischer, J. P. Deconchy, and R. Lipiansky, *Ideologies et représentations sociales*, Fribourg: DelVal.

Moscovici, S. (1992). The psychology of scientific myths. In M. von Cranach, W. Doise and G. Mugny (eds), *Social Representations and the Social Bases of Knowledge*, Lewiston, NY: Hogrofe & Huber Publishers.

Moscovici, S. and Vignaux (1994). Le concept de thèmata. In C. Guimelli (ed.) *Structures et transformations de représentations sociales*, Neuchâtel: Delachaux et Nestlè.

Neisser, U. (1988). Five kinds of self-knowledge. *Philosophical Psychology*, **1**, 35–59.

Palmonari, A. (1989). *Processi simbolici e dinamiche sociali*, Bologna: Il Mulino.

Pollini, S. G. (1987). *Appartenenza e identità*, Milano: Angeli.

Rosenbergh, S. (1987). Self and others: studies in social personality and autobiography. In L. Berkowitz (ed.), *Advances in Experimental Social Psychology*. New York: Academic Press.

Rosenbergh, S. and Gara, M. A. (1985) The multiplicity of personal identity. In P. Shaver (ed.), *Review of Personality and Social Psychology*. Beverly Hills: Sage.

Sotirakopoulou, K. P. and Breakwell, G. M. (1992). The use of different methodological approaches in the study of social representations. In W. Wagner, F. Elejabarrieta and U. Flick (eds), *Ongoing Production on Social Representations*, **1**, 29–38.

Tajfel, H. (1981). *Human Groups and Social Categories*. Cambridge: Cambridge University Press.

Tajfel, H. (1982). Social psychology of intergroup relations. *Annual Review of Psycholgy*, **33**, 1–30.

Turner, J.C. (1987). *Rediscovering the Social Group: A Self-Categorization Theory*. Oxford/New York: Blackwell.

Vala, J. (1992). Towards an articulation of social identity and social representations. In *1st International Conference on Social Representations* (Ravello, 3–5 October 1992)

Valencia, J. F. *et al.* (1991). Las imagenes de Europa en los Europeos, Donostia. *Publicaciones del Departamento de Psicologia Social de la UPV-EHU*, **5**.

von Cranach, M., Doise, W. and Mugny, G. (eds) (1992). *Social Representations and the Social Bases of Knowledge*. Lewiston, NY: Hoegrofe and Huber Publishers.

Wagner, W. (1994). *Alltagsdiskurs. Zur theorie sozialer Repräsentationen*. Göttingen: Hogrefe Verlag.

Wagner, W., Elejabarrieta, F. and Flick, U. (eds) (1992 onwards). *Ongoing Production on Social Representations*, 1–2.

Wagner, W., Elejabarrieta, F., Flick, U. and Guimelli (eds) (1993 onwards). *Papers on Social Representations*.

Yardley, K. and Honess, T. (1987). *Self and Identity*. Chichester, England: Wiley & Sons.

Zavalloni, M. (1983). Ego-ecology: the study of the interaction between social and personal identity. In Jacobson-Widding (ed.), *Identity: Personal and Socio-cultural*. Atlantic City: Humanities Press.

Zavalloni, M. and Louis-Guerin, C. (1984). *Identité sociale et conscience: introduction à l'égo-écologie*. Montreal: Presse de l'Université de Montréal. Toulouse: Privat.

Part Four

Coping with Social Change

24

Social Identity of East Germans: The Process of Unification between East and West Germany as a Challenge to Cope with "Negative Social Identity"

AMÉLIE MUMMENDEY, ROSEMARIE MIELKE, MICHAEL WENZEL AND UWE KANNING

Universität Münster

Introduction

Since the classic Sherif-Experiments in the 1950s there have been theories in social psychology which dealt especially with intergroup processes and emphasised the fundamentally different nature of interpersonal and intergroup behaviour. Examples are: Theory of Realistic Group Conflict (Sherif, 1966), Theory of Relative Deprivation (Gurr, 1970; Crosby, 1976; Runciman, 1966) and of course the well known Social Identity Theory (SIT); (Tajfel, 1978; Tajfel and Turner, 1986).

The study here deals with such intergroup processes. It focuses on the intergroup relations between East and West Germans after the unification of Germany in 1990.

For the last few years a new nationalism has been arising in Germany. Right wing radicalism has culminated in disgusting murders of foreign people seeking refuge or living in Germany for decades. Not only asylum seekers and guest workers have been the victims of violent attacks, but also members of other minorities and marginal groups—like the handicapped or homeless.

These nationalistic tendencies as well as the brutality in the name of a privileged race did not appear by coincidence just after an important political

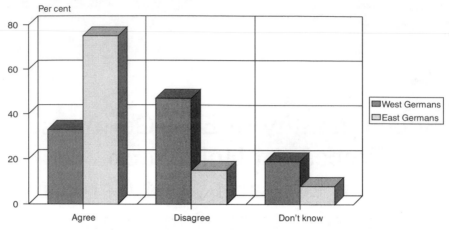

Per cent

FIGURE 24.1   Amount of agreement that East Germans are second-class citizens

change in Germany, i.e. the German unification process. This event and especially the way it was dealt with in the official political discussion generated a climate in Germany which fostered the salience of German identity and ethnocentric nationalism. The special pressure in this direction results from the currently enduring split of Germany in two parts—the East and West, which possibly will become even stronger. The physical wall has broken down, but has been replaced by a wall inside people's heads. In public opinion there is a clear status differentiation between East and West. In fact, with respect to the economic situation, East Germans are worse off than West Germans. But the downgrading of East Germans goes even beyond this material dimension. By attributing the economic misery in the East to particular personality characteristics of the East Germans—their inefficiency, laziness and low ambition—their position is rationalised.

Thus East Germans are assumed to experience a so called negative social identity resulting from negative comparison outcomes with West Germans on nearly every important evaluative dimension. Empirical evidence supports this assumption. According to poll studies East Germans felt like second-class citizens (Figure 24.1; Harenberg, 1991) and rate themselves much lower ($M = 4.9$) on a 10-point status-scale than West Germans ($M = 5.9$) (Noll and Schuster, 1992). To date there is a clear differentiation between the groups in economic power, living standards and unemployment rate. West Germans fare better on all these criteria than the East Germans. It would seem plausible that East Germans might be dissatisfied and would try to change the unpleasant situation of the negative evaluation of own group. But what will they do? What are the prerequisites for different kinds of coping behaviour? These questions lead us to the Social Identity Theory (SIT).

Theoretical Framework

Social Identity Theory (Tajfel, 1978; Tajfel and Turner, 1986) assumes that people strive to achieve or maintain a positive self-evaluation. In situations of social identity salience, group members evaluate their self by comparing the position of the ingroup with a relevant comparison outgroup on an important comparison dimension. If the ingroup holds an inferior position, according to SIT, members experience a "negative social identity". In order to achieve a positive self-evaluation these group members try to (re-) gain a positively distinct position for their own group.

There are several strategies for coping with a negative social identity. We suggest a 2 × 2 taxonomy presented in Table 24.1. First, according to Tajfel and Turner (1986), the distinction is made between *individual versus collective strategies*. Individual coping means that each group member tries to improve his/her position, with the status relationship between both groups remaining unchanged. The inferior as well as the superior group keep their former positions. Collective strategies on the other hand aim at improving the ingroup's position by changing the intergroup status relations.

Another differentiation of coping behaviours refers to their psychological means. Strategies can be *behavioural or cognitive*. Behavioural strategies lead to actual improvements for individuals or groups. Cognitive strategies lead to improvements which result from re-interpretations of an unchanged situation. The aim is that the re-interpretation will be socially shared by the in- and outgroup. In fact, of course, there is no change in the status differentiation between both groups. Generally it seems clear, that in most situations behaviour is related to cognition and vice versa. So both variables are not fully independent. Our differentiation means only an emphasis on behaviour or on cognition.

Table 24.1 gives some examples for strategies which fit this 2 × 2 model.

Social mobility: Members of an inferior group stop identifying with this group and join a higher status group. In this way they really improve their personal situation and gain a positive social identity. This strategy does not affect intergroup relations.

Social competition: Members of an inferior group try to improve the relative position of the own group on the most important comparison dimension. If they are successful, the formerly inferior group gets the superior position and members of this group really and collectively receive positive social identity.

TABLE 24.1   Taxonomy of strategies for coping with negative social identity

	Individual	*Collective*
Behavioural	Social mobility	Social competition
Cognitive	Individualization	Social creativity

Individualisation: Members of an inferior group shift individually from social identity to personal identity and try to get a positive self-evaluation in terms of personal identity (Ng, 1989). By this means they suppress their negative social identity without changing reality.

Social creativity: Members of an inferior group try to improve the position of their own group in different cognitive ways. They can do this by selecting a new comparison dimension, selecting a different comparison group or by re-evaluating the former comparison dimension. These strategies cannot improve the real situation but provide a positive social identity by changing the comparison process.

One important question refers to the prerequisites for selecting different coping strategies. According to SIT there are three variables which describe the structure of the intergroup relation and which can be related to the choice of coping strategies.

The first structure variable deals with the perception of boundaries between the inferior and superior group: perceived permeability versus impermeability. *Permeability* means the perception of the possibility of leaving the inferior group and joining the higher-status outgroup.

The second structure variable deals with the perceived variability of the given status differentiation between both groups: perceived stability versus instability. *Stability* means the perception of the impossibility to change the relative position of the groups on the most important comparison dimension.

The third variable refers to the justification of the status differentiation: perceived legitimacy versus illegitimacy. *Legitimacy* means the degree of acceptance of the status differentiation between both groups in terms of its justifiability.

Taken together we get a $2 \times 2 \times 2$ table which describes the different intergroup structure conditions in the view of SIT (Table 24.2).

Until now there has been a lack of systematic research on the influence of these types of intergroup structure on the selection of different coping strategies, especially in field settings. Often researchers focus only on one or two of the three structure variables (for example: Taylor *et al.*, 1987; Turner and Brown, 1978; Vaughan, 1978). We know of only two studies in which all three variables are combined: the laboratory study of Ellemers (1991; Experiment 5) and the

TABLE 24.2   Types of intergroup structure

	Permeability		Impermeability	
	Stability	*Instability*	*Stability*	*Instability*
Legitimacy				
Illegitimacy				

field study of Kanning and Mummendey (in preparation). When Tajfel (1978) formulated his theory, he especially had in mind real intergroup relations in society. So it may be interesting to test the SIT outside of the laboratory. This was one of our main intentions when starting the research on intergroup relations between East and West Germans.

At present for East Germans comparisons with West Germans are extremely salient and nearly inevitable in everyday life. Obviously East Germans perceive themselves as inferior when they compare themselves with West Germans. Hence, insofar as the grouping East German contributes to the individual's social identity, the lower status of the East Germans leads to a negative social identity. The idea behind this part of our research project was to investigate the main features of the intergroup situation between East and West Germans according to the structural variables identified in SIT and to analyse the predictive power of these variables with respect to the most important strategies for coping with a negative social identity. Insofar as the unification process is in progress, we assume that the intergroup situation will change during the coming years. The predictability models of our first data analyses will provide the basis for the predictions of the choice of strategies to cope with negative social identity when the intergroup situation is changed in the future.

Because of the process quality of the field situation, a longitudinal study is planned to find out in which way the unification process changes the social identity of East Germans. Our main interests focus on (1) the differential conditions for the choice of strategies to cope with negative social identity; and (2) testing social psychological theories of intergroup processes—such as social identity theory, relative deprivation theory and social comparison theory—in a process of social historical change.

In this chapter we will concentrate on the main assumptions of *social identity theory* (SIT) concerning strategies to cope with negative social identity.

General Assumptions

According to SIT the following assumptions about the predictability of strategies to cope with negative social identity by strength of social identification and structural characteristics of the intergroup relation can be stated.

Social identification

We assume that collective strategies to cope with negative social identity are favoured if the ingroup identification is strong. The more a person identifies with the ingroup the more he or she tends to engage in collective strategies. By means of enhancement of ingroup position, strongly identified persons enhance their self-esteem. Subjects with weak attachment to an ingroup are more likely to adopt individual strategies which aim to enhance their personal position, leaving the group's position unchanged.

Stability

If subjects perceive the relationship between the groups as stable, no alternatives to the existing status positions of the groups are perceived. Collective strategies aiming at change of the status relation between the groups seem to be impossible. Stability includes the stability of the evaluations of comparison dimensions. Social creative solutions like re-evaluation of comparison dimensions or invention of new dimensions (including changes of the ranking of the dimensions according to importance) are impossible in stable intergroup contexts. Subjects with close attachment to the group must be creative and think about changing the whole comparison situation for the group, e.g. to look for another comparison group. Stability of the intergroup status relation fosters individual solutions. Subjects may leave the lower-status group and join the higher-status group. Another possibility consists in leaving the group cognitively (turn to inner emigration) by reinterpreting the self-concept more in terms of personal characteristics.

Legitimacy

If there are no doubts about the legitimacy of the status relation between the groups, there is no basis for thinking of alternatives and for changing the status position. Strategies to change the status relation between the groups are more likely if the existing relationship cannot be justified. If both groups agree that the relationship is legitimate, collective actions to change the group's inferior position are unlikely. Similar to the predictions concerning stability, individual solutions for coping with negative social identity by leaving the group literally or cognitively (turn over to inner emigration), are fostered more if the relationships between the groups are perceived as legitimate.

Permeability

If group boundaries are perceived to be permeable and it is possible for persons to move from one group to the other, individual strategies will be preferred over collective ones. Collective strategies are unlikely to be used, because improvements in the group's position are difficult to realise, need a lot of effort and are associated with greater delays of gratification. Enhancement of self-esteem can be more easily attained by leaving the group. The possibility to leave the group makes social change unlikely because the individual solution is much easier to attain. If group boundaries are impermeable the group sticks closely together; that means, members are more strongly attached to their group when there is no possibility to move to the higher status group. If we consider this relationship between permeability and identification, we can assume that identification mediates the effect of permeability on the preference for different strategies: impermeability leads

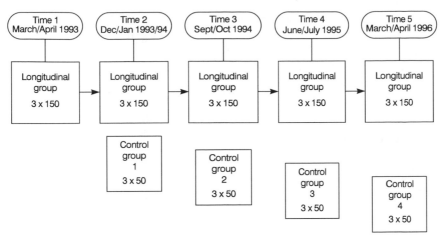

FIGURE 24.2   Longitudinal/cross-sectional sequences design

via strong identification to collective strategies. Permeability leads via weak identification to mobility.

Method

The main concepts of the above mentioned theories were operationalised in a questionnaire. The concepts of social identity theory which are of interest in this report about our project are operationalised by several items (see Appendix).

The questionnaire study is designed according to the following longitudinal/cross-sectional sequences design in order to control for effects of repeated measurement (Baltes, 1986) which covers about three years (see Figure 24.2).

With five measurement points in total, at nine-month intervals, data collection began in spring 1993 and will be finished in spring 1996. Subjects are recruited in three different ways and differ in the amount of heterogeneity within each sample. The first group of subjects are members of the municipal government of a medium sised town (about 50,000 inhabitants) in Sachsen-Anhalt. The second sample consists of bank clerks in four different towns and three different regions in the new lands of Germany. The third sample is the most heterogeneous one, subjects are recruited by supervisors who are paid for each person they recruit for the study. The only limitation is that the person who takes part has to be more than eighteen years old. The three longitudinal groups consist of 150 subjects each. The control groups at each measurement point consist of fifty subjects who are recruited in the same three ways as described above.

This report covers the data of our first homogeneous group which were collected in spring 1993. We analysed the data of 188 subjects. 93 per cent of the subjects perceived the situation of East Germans worse than the situation of West

Germans. To make sure that our sample consists only of subjects who perceive their social identity as "negative" in terms of negative social comparison outcomes, we excluded 13 subjects who perceived the situation between East and West Germans as equal. The reported results are based on 175 subjects, 49 of them were male and 98 female (28 subjects refused to answer this question). The age varied between 17 and 72 years, with a mean of 39.

Specific Assumptions and Results

Individual Strategies

The most important feature of individual strategies is that the status relation between the groups is not changed: the aim of these kinds of strategy is to achieve a personal not a group solution. These strategies consequently will be taken into account when the social identification with the group is low. If the social group is of minor importance for a person's self-concept he or she will find possibilities to dissociate from the group. This might be even more likely if the inferior status of the group is perceived to be stable and the status discrepancies between the groups are justified (legitimate status relation).

Behavioural Individual Strategies: Mobility

The most prominent individual strategy is to leave the group and try to join another more attractive group. One important prerequisite for changing the group is the perception of permeable group boundaries, that is, the membership in the higher-status group must be attainable. According to Tajfel and Turner (1986) "This strategy usually implies attempts, on an individual basis, to achieve upward mobility, to pass from a lower to a higher-status group" (p. 9). As long as the relationship between the groups is not questioned and there are justifications for the status relation, the situation is stable and social change is unlikely. The only solution seems to be an individual one. Individual mobility is assumed to occur if a subject is not strongly identified with the group, if the boundaries of the groups are perceived as permeable and the relationship between the groups is stable and legitimate.

These assumptions are tested in a structural equation model (by LISREL VII, Jöreskog and Sorbom, 1988) with direct paths from identification, stability, legitimacy and permeability to mobility, and indirect paths of the three structural variables via identification to the coping strategy. As can be seen in Figure 24.3 81 per cent of the variance of individual mobility can be explained by the tested model. The path from identification to mobility is extremely high ($\gamma = -.94$) and negative. As predicted: Individual mobility is a strategy which is the more preferred strategy to cope with negative social identity the less the person identifies with the group. As predicted, legitimacy has a significant positive effect ($\gamma = .24$) to mobility. Stability fails to contribute to the prediction of mobility. Contrary to our

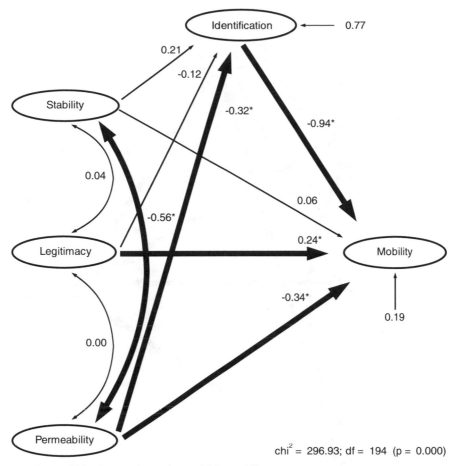

FIGURE 24.3   Structural equation model for mobility

prediction, impermeability leads directly to individual mobility ($\gamma = -.34$). This is difficult to interpret, as permeable group boundaries are the most plausible prerequisites for leaving the group and joining the higher-status group. The negative path from permeability to identification and from identification to mobility fits very well to the theoretical assumptions: impermeability fosters social identification which in turn leads to tendencies to remain within the group.

Cognitive Individual Strategies: Individualisation

The second kind of individual strategy is the shift from social to personal identity. This means that the person de-emphasises the membership to groups in general and stresses more his or her personal identity. This strategy has no

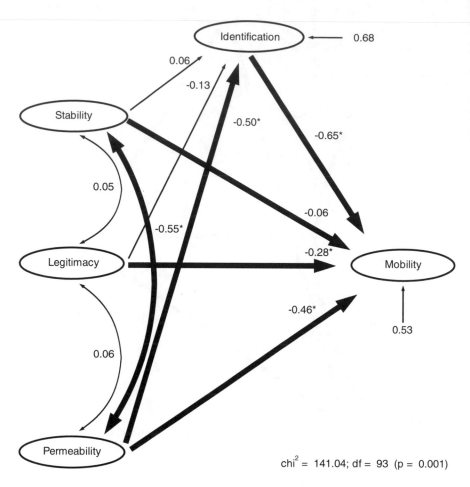

FIGURE 24.4   Structural equation model for individualization

observable consequences as the person does not move and the relationship between the groups remains as it is. We assume individualisation to occur if the group boundaries are perceived to be impermeable, while the individual strategy of mobility would be more likely to be chosen when group boundaries are perceived to be permeable. We also assume stable and legitimate status relations to be prerequisites for individualisation. Rather than individual mobility, *im*permeability makes individualisation more likely. If the status relation is stable and legitimate, tendencies to leave the group are expected to be fostered, but without permeable group boundaries the leaving of the group turns into a cognitive withdrawing from group ("inner emigration").

Individualisation should be best predicted by low identification, high legitimacy and high stability of the intergroup relation, and high impermeability of the group boundaries. The direct paths from the structural variables and identification to individualisation as well as the indirect paths from the structural variables via identification to individualisation are tested in a structural equation model. The results are presented in Figure 24.4.

Nearly half (47%) of the variance of individualisation can be explained by the structural variables and identification. All of the four concepts significantly take part in the explanation of this coping strategy. All direct paths to the strategy of individualisation are significant but only half of them are in the predicted direction. As in the case of individual mobility we can explain a great amount of the variance of individualisation by (low) identification (γ = -.65). As assumed, individualisation can be predicted by impermeable group boundaries (γ = -.46). Thus, individualisation is chosen as an individual solution of coping with negative social identity, when group boundaries are perceived as impermeable. Contrary to our predictions, individualisation is pursued under the conditions of perceived instability and illegitimacy of the status relation.

Collective Strategies

Collective strategies are by definition distinguished from individual strategies in that they aim at a more favourable evaluation of the *group as a whole*. Thus, the group member maintains his/her group membership, defines himself/herself still as a member of the group, and tries to achieve a more positive social identity by improving the group's image.

Thus, the main characteristic of collective strategies is the continuity of the social identity. The subject still identifies with the group, maybe because it is his/her own choice, but more probably because there is no alternative: *impermeable* group boundaries make it impossible to leave the own group and join the higher status group. (Other reasons which prevent a redefinition of the self as either a member of a different group or by relying on individual attributes and stressing the personal identity are: high salience of the relevant intergroup situation, and even less satisfying alternative identities.)

Behavioural Collective strategies: competition

Next to the maintenance of the identification with the ingroup, a specific characteristic of behavioural collective strategies—in contrast to cognitive ones—is that the original comparison situation is preserved: members of the lower status group continue to compare to the dominant group, to make comparisons along the same dimensions, and to evaluate these dimensions in the same way. The behavioural strategies aim at improving their group's status position, which derives from this specific comparison situation. The group members may try to reverse both groups' status relation or at least try to approximate the own group's status to the status position of the superior group.

However, to hold on to these comparisons to the superior group possibly being extremely different from the own group is not a simple matter. According to Festinger's (1954) theory of social comparisons, comparisons are restricted to other social units subjectively regarded as similar to oneself. But if this was the whole story, there would hardly be any social change in our world. Tajfel (1978, p. 74) resolves this question by assuming that groups will gain or maintain comparability if their status discrepancy is perceived as insecure. If the status relation is assumed to be questionable and one can rather easily think of alternatives to this situation, the current status inequality is not interpreted as a general dissimilarity. Instead, to question the group relation implies some dimensions of comparability. As Tajfel points out, the felt insecurity of the status relation can have two sources: first, the relation can be seen as unstable and easy to change, and, second, it can be viewed as illegitimate or unjustified. Both aspects as a rule interact with each other (Tajfel, 1978, 52).

Thus, these behavioural collective strategies are competitive strategies. In the first place, they are forms of social competition, as the group competes for a more favourable evaluation and members are motivated by a positive self-evaluation. Turner (1982) distinguishes this social competition from the realistic competition, for which—in the sense of the realistic group conflict theory (Sherif, 1966)—incompatible group goals are necessary and which means the rivalry for real resources.

To sum up, it should have become clear that the SIT states the following conditions encouraging the pursuit of social competitive strategies: high identification, impermeability, instability and/or illegitimacy.

The structural equation model used to test these assumptions considered again direct paths from stability, legitimacy, permeability, and identification to competition, as well as indirect effects of the structural variables via identification. For the strategy "social competition" the LISREL procedure yielded the path coefficients of the structural model as shown in Figure 24.5. As predicted, permeability has a significant negative effect on the strategy ($\gamma = -.51$): impermeability leads directly to the pursuit of the social competition strategy. Though, the remaining predicted effects on the social competition strategy are not confirmed. Particularly, identification attains an astonishing negative path coefficient ($\beta = -.28$); although it is non-significant, the path's direction contradicts our hypothesis that identification is a prerequisite of social competition. As in the foregoing models, permeability has an expected negative effect on identification ($\gamma = -.49$). But the negative direct effect of permeability on social competition is not significantly diminished by the positive indirect effect via identification.

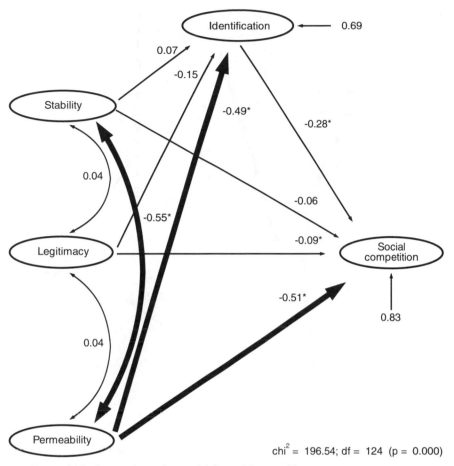

FIGURE 24.5   Structural equation model for social competition

Cognitive Collective Strategies: Social Creativity

The cognitive collective strategies imply—as they are collective (see above)—that the members still *identify* with their group. Possibly impermeable group boundaries force them, more or less, to do so. In addition and more specifically, these strategies are characterised by some change in the social comparison process. Some of the components of the social comparison are modified in order to secure a more positive comparison outcome and, thus, a more favourable evaluation of the own group. As Turner and Brown (1978, 204) defined: "Social Creativity—the group members may achieve PD (positive distinctiveness) through altering or redefining the elements of the comparative situation. This does not necessarily imply any change in the

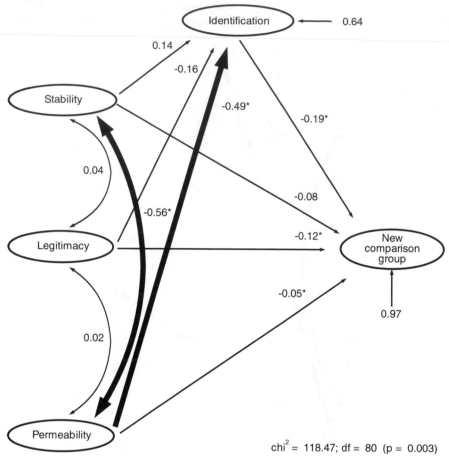

FIGURE 24.6   Structural equation model for "choice of another comparison group"

ingroup's objective social position." These authors give three instances (p. 205):

- changing the *outgroup* with which the ingroup is compared, in particular ceasing to use the dominant group as a relevant comparison group;
- comparing the ingroup to the outgroup on some *new dimension*;
- changing one's *values* so that previously negative comparisons are perceived as positive.

The first variant, which we call "choice of another comparison group", means to reduce the relevance of the dominant group as comparison group and, instead, to choose an even more inferior group compared to which the ingroup comes off

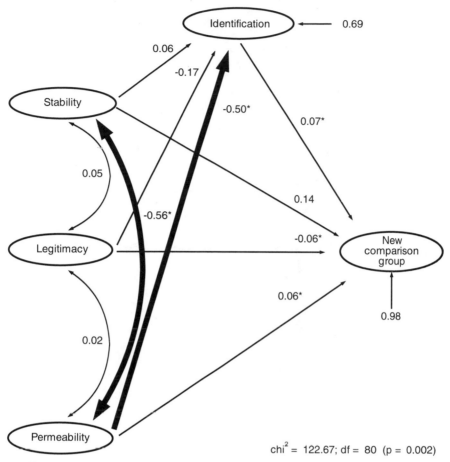

FIGURE 24.7   Structural model for "change of comparison dimensions"

well (downward social comparison). For this strategy we predict that with secure status inequality, which is subjectively considered *stable* and *legitimate*, the similarity of comparison subject and object decreases. In addition, similarity being the basis for social comparison processes, an exchange of the comparison object, i.e. the relevant outgroup, is expected.

We label the two remaining cognitive collective strategies "change of comparison dimensions" and "re-evaluation of comparison dimensions". In the first case, group members stress the importance of so far neglected group characteristics which could demonstrate the superiority of the ingroup over the currently dominant group. East Germans for example might refer to their traditionally satisfying social relationships and their emphasis on friendship as well as mutual help, which are supposedly weak in West Germany.

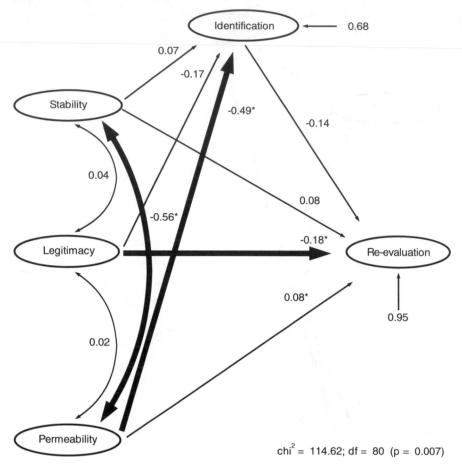

FIGURE 24.8   Structural equation model of "re-evaluation of comparison dimensions"

The third strategy encompasses changing the value connotations of those dimensions on which the ingroup currently experiences its inferiority, so that the ingroup's lower position on this dimension is actually redefined as superior. For example, the material situation, which is without doubt worse for the East than for the West Germans, could be re-evaluated by stating that wealth is strongly related to egoism, arrogance, etc., so that richness is in fact not desirable ("poor is rich and rich is poor").

In line with Tajfel (1978) and Turner and Brown (1978), for these two social creative strategies the following should hold: perceived *instability* and/or *illegitimacy* of the groups' status relation imply cognitive alternatives; and these are expected to support strategies redefining the intergroup relation, suggesting new criteria for its evaluation, etc.

Structural equation models equivalent to the former ones were used to test these predictions. As Figures 24.6 to 24.8 show, all three strategies considered were hardly predicted by the structural variables and the identification concept. The explained variances of the strategies range from unsatisfactory 2 to 5 per cent. The single significant path to one of these cognitive collective strategies leads from legitimacy to "re-evaluation of the material dimension" (γ =-.18). Its direction corresponds to our prediction: the more illegitimate the status relation is perceived, the more the re-evaluation strategy is pursued.

But on the whole our hypotheses concerning the cognitive collective strategies were not confirmed.

Discussion

In our longitudinal study we are concerned with strategies East Germans could pursue to overcome their negative self-evaluation which is assumed to follow the German unification process. There is evidence that this political development has made West Germans a salient comparison group for East Germans: West Germans are considered to have in many, especially—and undoubtedly—in economic, respects a higher status relative to the East Germans. Ingroup's negative comparison outcomes are assumed to threaten the members' social identity which they have to cope with.

One part of this study was presented here. We reported data from the first wave, which was analysed to test some hypotheses derived from Social Identity Theory (SIT). They concerned the predictability of some selected strategies by the group identification concept as well as the so called structural variables stability, legitimacy, and permeability. The strategies were chosen in order to represent each cell of our taxonomy consisting of the dimensions "individual-collective" and "behavioural-cognitive". Structural equation models were used to test our hypotheses.

The residuals of our strategy concept, i.e. the unexplained variance of these endogenous concepts, reveal that the predictabilities of the strategies considered here differ strongly. The best predicted strategy is mobility (81% explained variance), then individualisation (47%), social competition (17%), and—absolutely poorly predicted—the cognitive collective strategies (2% to 5%). On the whole, out of the predictors we implemented in our models here, social identification and permeability seem to have the strongest causal effects. The predictors and their causal effects are briefly discussed now.

To begin with *social identification*, it has the expected negative effects on mobility as well as on individualisation. On the one hand, as Tajfel and Turner (1986, p. 19) put it: "individual mobility implies a disidentification with the erstwhile in-group". On the other hand individualisation means reliance on personal attributes; the individual defines himself/herself less by group membership.

As regards the collective strategies – behavioural as well as cognitive—identification has no significant explanatory quality. For social competition there is even a remarkable, though insignificant, negative path of identification, this is counter-theoretical as well as counter-intuitive. To work for a better position for the group—possibly making personal sacrifices—should demand strong identification with that group.

Stability of the status relation is on the whole a poor predictor. There are no significant effects except for a negative path to individualisation. This finding is contrary to our hypothesis, we predicted that a reliance on personal identity and a restriction to intragroup comparisons would occur in particular within a strong and stable group stratification. However, of course, we have to admit that our reasoning was quite indirect: one can individualise despite stability, but that does not make stability a necessary condition for individualisation. But a negative causal effect of stability is hard to explain.

In the case of social competition as a group strategy, instability was thought to be one possible source—next to legitimacy—of perceiving the status relation as insecure and having alternatives in mind, which should motivate one to fight or argue against the status quo. Yet the effect of stability on social competition is negligible.

The same holds for perceived *legitimacy* of the status relation. On the one hand it has no significant effect on the social competition strategy, as was predicted. On the other hand legitimacy has an expected impact on mobility: only if one considers the superiority of the dominant group legitimate, can one try to join it without accusing oneself of supporting injustice.

Legitimacy, in addition, has the single significant effect on one of the cognitive collective strategies, to wit, the re-evaluation of the comparison dimension. As expected, illegitimacy implies cognitive alternatives to the status quo; one of these could be to reverse the value connotations of the dominant comparison dimension.

With regard to individualisation, there is again an unexpected path; perceived illegitimacy leads to individualisation. Considered together with the same unexpected effect of stability, one could conclude that individualisation is a favoured strategy when the status relation is thought to be insecure. One possible reason why under these conditions subjects tend to individualise instead of identifying with their group and competing collectively with the superior group could be their low trust in the ingroup's power, i.e. they have a low opinion of their groups' collective efficacy (Abrams, 1991, personal communication). This idea has to be tested in future analyses.

The third structural variable, *permeability*, has unexpectedly no significant impact on cognitive collective strategies. There are significant negative paths to the remaining three strategies.

The first one, impermeability leads to mobility, is contrary to our hypothesis. This seems to contradict one of the most plausible and self-evident assumptions of SIT. The only reasonable way for us to resolve this contradiction is to assume that especially those subjects who would like to become West Germans, i.e. to join the superior group, experience that it is impossible to do so very clearly. That means, while the permeability of group boundaries might be consistently perceived as low, subjects reacted differently to our permeability items due to being differently affected by this "fact". Of course, this is just a post-hoc interpretation, but it should be taken seriously.

On the other hand, there is an opposite indirect effect of permeability via identification on mobility. This fits the theory, as it predicts that impermeability yields stronger identification which in turn leads to reduced tendencies to leave the inferior ingroup.

The effects of permeability on the two remaining strategies are in accordance with our theory as well. Impermeability leads to individualisation. It is plausible that in the face of impermeable borders one restricts the view to subjects within the borders and compares to other individuals in the own group.

The causal path of permeability to social competition is also negative. It confirms our hypothesis that when group members are bounded to their group by impermeable group boundaries and their fates are identical with their group's fate they try to improve the situation of the whole group. But, more critically the theory at least implicitly suggests that this effect of impermeability operates via the intervening identification concept. According to our analysis this was not supported, as social identification has no positive effect on social competition (but rather a negative effect).

To sum up, no predictor concept is in accordance with our hypotheses in every respect. Stability particularly shows none of its predicted relations to the selected strategies or to the identification concept. In addition, the remaining predictors each have one effect contrary to our expectations (if one counts the insignificant effect of identification on social competition as such). But, on the other hand these concepts—identification, legitimacy, and permeability—each have at least two significant paths which are in line with our predictions. There is no clear pattern which would allow us to reject or accept a whole set of assumptions with regard to either one single predictor or one single strategy.

With regard to the concept of stability, there are some particularities in the natural setting, so stability in our study has a special meaning. Thus, the consequences of stability for the choice of coping strategies have to be reconsidered. The official policy as the broader social context for our particular intergroup situation provides an optimistic view of a quick integration of East and West Germans. Therefore instability gains a particular meaning implying improvements in the situation of East Germans. Perceived instability means that the subjects of our study place trust in the promised enhancement of their situation after unification. The more they believe that these changes will take place soon and the process of transformation will be successfully finished, the less they are motivated to engage in collective strategies to enhance the position of the group. Contrary to other natural situations the superior group is interested (or at last pretends to be) in the equalisation of both groups. Belief in the stability of the relation between the groups means that there are doubts concerning the realisation of this aim. Consequently, in this case the prediction of individual vs collective strategies by stability should be reversed. Social actions to enhance the position of East Germans are more likely the lower the trust in the political promise of a speedy equalisation of East and West Germans; we assume that persons who have reasonable doubts in the prospective equality of East Germans will score high on our stability items.

The critical point is that subjects who argue the situation is stable because they want to express that they do not believe that there are realistic chances of enhancing the situation of East Germans, cannot be distinguished from those who believe in stability because they are critical in their attitude towards the government and are doubtful about its willimgness to fulfill its political promise. The former kind of perception of stability would prevent the choice of collective strategies because enhancement of the position of the group is perceived as impossible. The latter kind of stability would foster collective actions because only the whole group is powerful enough to put pressure on the government to accelerate the unification process. Obviously there may be both kinds of stability perceptions in our sample so that we cannot decide if stability might prove to be a valid predictor for individual strategies in natural settings. We have to look for another concept which might differentiate between these two kinds of stability or perhaps between the two corresponding groups of subjects.

Possibly, future analyses considering further variables, especially those going beyond the frame of social identity theory like personality characteristics and social orientations, will help to clarify matters.

References

Baltes, P. B. (1986). Longitudinal and cross-sectional sequences in the study of age and generation effects. *Human Development*, **11**, 145–71.
Crosby, F. (1976). A model of egoistical relative deprivation. *Psychological Review*, **83**, 85–113.
Ellemers, N. (1991). Identity management strategies. Dissertation, Universität Groningen.
Festinger, L. (1954). A theory of social comparison processes. *Human Relations*, **7**, 117–40.
Gurr, T. R. (1970). *Why Men Rebel*. Princeton: Princeton University Press.
Harenberg, W. (1991). Vereint und verschieden. In Spiegel-Verlag Rudolf Augstein (Hrsg.) *Spiegel Spezial: Das Profil der Deutschen*. Hamburg: Spiegel-Verlag.
Jöreskog, K. G. and Sörbom, D. (1988). *LISREL 7: A Guide to the Program and Applications*. Chicago: SPSS, Inc.
Kanning, U. P. and Mummendey, A. (in preparation). Strategies for coping with negative social identity—a study in East Germany.
Luhtanen, R. and Crocker, J. (1992). A Collective self-esteem scale: self-evaluation of one's social identity. *Personality and Social Psychological Bulletin*, **18**(3), 302–18.
Ng, S.-H. (1989). Intergroup behaviour and the self. *New Zealand Journal of Psychology*, **18**, 1–12.
Noll, H.-H. and Schuster, F. (1992). Soziale Schichtung: Niedrigere Einstufung der Ostdeutschen. *Informationsdienst Soziale Indikatoren*, **7**, 1–6.
Runciman, W. G. (1966). *Relative Deprivation and Social Justice: A Study of Attitudes to Social Inequality in Twentieth-century England*. Berkeley: University of California Press.
Sherif, M. (1966). *Group Conflict and Cooperation: Their Social Psychology*. London: Routledge & Kegan Paul.

Tajfel, H. (1978). (ed.), *Differentiation between Social Groups*. London: Academic Press.

Tajfel, H. and Turner, J. C. (1986). The social identity theory of intergroup behaviour. In S. Worchel and W. G. Austin (eds), *Psychology of Intergroup Relations*, 2nd edn, Chicago: Nelson-Hall Publishers, 7–24.

Taylor, D. M., Moghaddam, F. M., Gamble, I. and Zeller, E. (1987). Disadvantaged group responses to perceived inequality: from passive acceptance to collective action. *Journal of Social Psychology*, **127**, 159–272.

Turner, J. C. (1982). Towards a cognitive redefinition of the social group. In H. Tajfel (ed.), *Social identity and intergroup relations*. Cambridge: Cambridge University Press, 15–40.

Turner, J. C. and Brown, R. (1978). Social status, cognitive alternatives and intergroup relations. In H. Tajfel (ed.), *Differentiation between Social Groups: Studies in the Social Psychology of Intergroup Relations*. London: Academic Press, 201–34.

Vaughan, G. M. (1978). Social change and intergroup preferences in New Zealand. *European Journal of Social Psychology*, **8**, 297–314.

Appendix

For each concept of our study considered in this presentation the operational-isations are given below. The items are translated from German to English. All items listed were finally selected due to confirmatory factor analyses as well as consistency analyses. In the case of multiple indicators, the α-coefficients for internal consistency are reported.

Social identification is a special case: sixteen items had been formulated according to four theoretically distinguishable aspects of identification, i.e. a cognitive, an evaluative, and an emotional component (see Tajfel, 1978) as well as an aspect called "relevance of membership for the self-concept" (cf. Luhtanen and Crocker, 1992—identity subscale). This theoretical structure was not confirmed empirically. Thus, these items were exploratorily factor analysed. The result revealed three orthogonal factors. For each factor three indicators were considered.

The response format was a five-point scale, on which subjects as a rule had to indicate how much they agree or disagree with the statements presented.

I. Social Identification

Factor 1: "relevance for the self-concept" (α = .54)

(a) Being East German is no important aspect of my personality. (-)
(b) My self-image is characterised by my membership (*Zugehörigkeit*) to the East Germans.
(c) On the whole, being East German has little to do with how I perceive myself. (-)

Factor 2: "declared belongingness" (α = .81)

(a) I consider myself as belonging to the East Germans.
(b) I frankly admit to be East German.
(c) I identify with the East Germans.

Factor 3: "emotional-reactive affiliation" (α = .83)

(a) I am annoyed about being East German. (-)
(b) I would be happy if I were not East German. (-)
(c) I often regret being an East German. (-)

II. Structural Variables

Stability (α = .57)

(a) For the next years I think that relations between East and West Germans will remain the same.
(b) The current relations between East and West Germany will just last a certain time. (-)
(c) The current relations between East and West Germany cannot change easily.

Legitimacy (α = .66)

(a) The West Germans are entitled to be better off than the East Germans.
(b) The East Germans have the right to demand to be as well off as the West Germans. (-)
(c) It is justified that the West Germans are currently doing better than the East Germans.

Permeability (α = .67)

(a) No matter what effort he makes, an East German can never become a West German. (-)
(b) In principle, there are no difficulties for an East German to be considered as a West German.
(c) There are plenty of examples that East Germans can integrate into West Germany.
(d) For an East German it is nearly impossible to be perceived as a West German. (-)
(e) West Germans do not tolerate me becoming one of them. (-)

III. Strategies

Mobility (α = .83)

(a) I make an effort to be considered as a West German.
(b) I try to live as a West German rather than as an East German.

(c)   Even if I moved to West Germany I would like to be perceived as an East German. (-)
(d)   I will never give up my East German identity in favour of a West German identity. (-)
(e)   In the future I would like to regard myself as a West German.
(f)   It is my very wish to belong to the West Germans.
(g)   I like to be considered as a West German, though I do not want to be a West German.
(h)   I would appreciate being hardly distinguishable from the West Germans, though I do not want to be one of them.

Individualisation ($\alpha = .53$)

(a)   I do not consider myself as belonging to any group.
(b)   I regard myself as a single person rather than a member of a certain group of people.

Social Competition ($\alpha = .67$)

(a)   We will make it clear to the West Germans that we are the more efficient Germans.
(b)   It is our goal not to be taught by the West Germans, but to teach them ourselves.
(c)   We from the *"neue Bundesländer"* will very soon show more initiative and engagement than the West Germans.
(d)   We East Germans have to work on enjoying a higher world-wide reputation than the West Germans.

Choice of different comparison group

This concept was measured by one single indicator constructed from the following three items:

In your opinion, how important is it for the East Germans to compare themselves with each of the following groups?

(a)   with West Germans
(b)   with a country belonging to the former Eastern bloc
(c)   with a developing country.

At first, two difference variables were built: $b - a$; $c - a$.

The maximum of these variables was chosen as an indicator of the strategic preference of a downward comparison.

Choice of other comparison dimensions

This concept was measured by one single indicator constructed from the following four items:

How important do you consider the following dimensions to be for a characterisation of the East Germans' situation?

(a)   material situation
(b)   social relationships
(c)   quality of life
(d)   opportunities for self-actualisation.

The "material situation" served as a baseline for three difference variables: $b - a$; $c - a$; $d - a$.

The maximum of these variables was defined as the indicator of the strategy to increase the relevance of other dimensions relative to the material one.

Re-evaluation of comparison dimensions

With regard to the dimension "material situation", this strategy was built from the following two items:

(a)   Please indicate how in your opinion the East Germans value the following dimensions.

The East Germans consider economic wealth as ...
... undesirable–desirable (5-point scale).

(b)   Now, please indicate how in your opinion the West Germans value the following dimensions.

The West Germans consider economic wealth as ...
... undesirable–desirable (5-point scale).

The difference, $b - a$, is defined to indicate the East Germans' devaluation of the material dimension, relative to the imagined view of the West Germans.

25

Alienation and Social Identity: The Bringing Together of Two Theoretical Paradigms

MARY HORTON

University of Hertfordshire

The similarities and differences between Social Identity Theory and Alienation Theory are reviewed with particular attention to their explanations of social change. A new "alienation" model of deep-structure attitudes to social systems is put forward. Some results from a study of attitudes to local government are shown, which demonstrate class and gender differences in the levels of conflict and alienation from the local authority. A possible use of this model to look at public attitudes to the EC is suggested.

Introduction

That the relation between the individual and the group is the fundamental question of social psychology is a truism, but profoundly true. That social psychology as a discipline lies poised between the devil of psychological reductionism and the deep blue sea of sociology is another truth. This chapter will argue that social psychology can use its position the better to address its fundamental question.

Social Identity Theory has been fruitful in providing satisfying explanation for social phenomena such as social influence, group cohesion, prejudice, discrimination, inter group hostility, crowd behaviour and even war. Why then, do we need to look at Alienation Theory, which has its roots—but, I will argue, neither its branches nor fruit—in sociology? One answer is that Social Identity Theory does not look in detail at the complex and sometimes contradictory nature of the relationship between the individual and the group as institution.

429

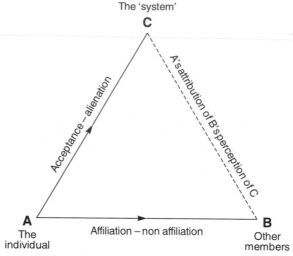

The 'system'

C

A's attribution of B's perception of C

Acceptance – alienation

A
The
individual

Affiliation – non affiliation

B
Other
members

FIGURE 25.1   The Triadic Model

The alienation model developed by Horton (1985) is primarily concerned with looking at this relationship in terms of perceived reciprocal understanding and perceived reciprocal power between the individual and the institutional structure (norm, rules, roles, rewards, values, goals). A combination of alienation theory and Social Identity Theory would see the group as a relation between three aspects—A the individual; B other members and C the group structure. Both A–B and A–C relations would be bi-polar. The A–B relation would be affiliative (wanted to be more or less like the others). The A–C relation would be one of agreement or acquiescence versus disagreement or alienation.

Thinking in terms of a Heiderian triadic relationship may be more use to social psychologists, than Social Identity Theory as it now stands. First it seems to relate more closely to the social actuality we are living in. Being in the European community, for example, does not simply mean finding (say) the Dutch more similar to us than are (say) the Swiss or Romanians—though that is part of it. It also means an individual agreement (i.e. a metaphorical personal contract with) or at least an acquiescence in (i.e. a disinclination to disobey) the rules of the institution. In particular, alienation theory seems useful in looking at emergent institutions such as the European community. That is, the difference between an emergent and an existent body is that, for the latter the first A–C relation is that of acquiescence, followed hopefully by agreement. For an emergent institution the first A–C relation would be that of agreement (if it is to emerge at all).

The need for a further explanatory dimension has been explicit for some time in work on Social Identity Theory. Rabbie and Horowitz (1988) in their reply to Doise's paper on "individual and social identities in intergroup relations" say:

> To assume that people perceive a group simply as a category of individuals obscures the fact that they also endow a group with the capacity to act and react as an organised entity, and will make attributions about the group's actions . . .

(p. 122)

Alienation theory would suggest that people have these perceptions, and make attributions, concerning their own group as well as the out-group.

The aim of this chapter is first to review briefly the development of alienation theory, especially in the context of the explanation of social change, then I want to describe my own model and its testing, and the inferences to be drawn from the findings. Finally, I hope to show how the alienation model combined with the social identity model could be used to structure further research—for example, research into attitudes to European Unity.

The Origins of the Concept of Alienation

Alienation is inherently a multi-disciplinary concept. Its origins lie deep in the history of religion and philosophy (Horton, 1985). But the three generally recognised roots from which contemporary thinking stems are those of Marx (Alienation), Durkheim (Anomie), and Freud (Discontent). All three theories can be conceived as process models and a meta-model comparison can be conducted by envisaging the three goals and the means by which the goals are reached in terms of the interactions of the components of each model. The three goals are:

For Marx: the overcoming of *Alienation* defined as the limitation on individual freedom and happiness imposed by the existence of private property and the social relations of labour (capitalism).

For Durkheim: the control of *Anomie* defined as the unbridled ambition of entrepreneurs set loose by the absence of social rules during periods of social change.

For Freud: the amelioration of *Discontent* defined as the inadequacy of civilised society to provide full individual satisfaction, as civilisation inherently demands a renunciation of instinct and the sacrifice of individual liberty.

The three conditions (Alienation, Anomie and Discontent) are similar in that they are thought of as general (to a class, a time or to humanity) and "bad", in that the goal in all three cases involves the overcoming, control or amelioration of the condition. The end-states envisaged, however, are sharply distinct, as is the function of social change within the models. For Marx and Freud, "social change" in prescribed directions is the goal, though for Marx the means is revolution and for Freud, evolution. For Durkheim, "social change" is the given, the uncaused causer, and the goal is the restitution of the status quo. The difference is that between an equilibrium or consensus model (Durkheim) and conflict models (Marx, Freud).

Looking now at the structure of the three models, three components can be seen to make up each model, and they are directly comparable:

1. *The System*: Capitalism (Marx), The Conscience Collective (Durkheim), Civilisation (Freud).
2. *Rational self-interest*: Loss of false consciousness (Marx), the individual conscience (Durkheim), the ego (Freud).
3. *The individual passions*: Needs (Marx), Desires (Durkheim), Libido (Freud).

The processes by which the components interact to achieve the goals can be described in the following way:

To Marx: The end of Alienation will be achieved through the overthrow of the capitalist system, by clear-sighted rational action (the scales of false consciousness having fallen from the eyes), mediated by individual passion (the desperation of the oppressed).

To Durkheim: The control of Anomie is through the moderation of the individual passions (entrepreneurial greed) by the collective conscience (social rules) mediated by the individual conscience (rationality).

To Freud: The alleviation of the Discontent inherent in civilised society is possible through the intrapsychic moderation of the super-ego, and the over-restrictive social rules it generates, by the ego, mediated by libidinal energy.

The crucial differences between the three models can be seen through a meta-level comparison:

Marx's   is a positive feedback model. Given the initial, and historically necessary change in social perception (the loss of false consciousness), the end (catastrophic change in the system itself) is inherently necessary.

Durkheim's   is a negative feedback model, where a balance is held between the extinction of the passions (anomic suicide), and their uncontrolled freedom (in the de-regulated society) by the operation of the Conscience Collective (seen as the meta-rule of moderation).

Freud's   model is more complex involving an explicit interaction between intrapsychic and social processes. Amelioration of intrapsychic conflict through increased self-understanding will free the individual to act in his own interest to ameliorate a repressive society.

To summarise: all three are describing a condition of misfit between the individual and society; to all three the situation is endemic and each explanatory model was designed to show how the condition would or could be altered. But there are fundamental differences between the two sociologists and the psychologist. To Freud, the generative force (similar, I believe, to what Breakwell (1993) after McDougall, calls the oretic process) is individual self-interest or the ego. To Marx and Durkheim, the generative force is social (Historical Necessity or the Conscience Collective). To them, change to a static and known future (the end of pre-history) or the regaining of a static and known past, were necessary processes, and their models are simply descriptions. Only to Freud was change merely a possibility, and the end unknown—that is, it is an explicitly falsifiable or scientific hypothesis—and only Freud uses a reductive model. It is my contention that the so-called "devil" of reduction (whether Freudian or not) may be to social psychologists, an angel in disguise, and the most fruitful way forward in the explanation of social processes.

Alienation in Social Psychology

A review of the use of the concept of alienation in social psychology from the 1950s to the present day (Horton, 1985) shows that its generative or change-producing property has been lost. It is seen as a hypothetical construct, describing the unrelated pole of a continuum of relatedness, operating on one of three distinct levels:

- between the self and the self (*intrapsychic*);
- between the self and others or the primary group (*interpersonal*);
- between the self and the generalised other or the system (*social*).

At *level one*, explanations for the "condition" are often given in terms of the operation of Freudian defence mechanisms. At *level two*, explanations are mainly in terms of defects in social personality, social motivation or social learning. At *level three*, alienation is generally described as a "social problem" and cause is variously attributed to aspects of the system or the individual. Overall, although there are a few notable exceptions (Averill, 1968; Goffman, 1961; Stokols, 1975), attempts to find relations between the three levels and to "generate a . . . theoretical framework which can specify the relational rules" (Breakwell, 1993) are lacking in the literature. Freud's own framework in *Civilisation and its Discontents* discussed above, remains, to me, the most fruitful alienation model to appear to date.

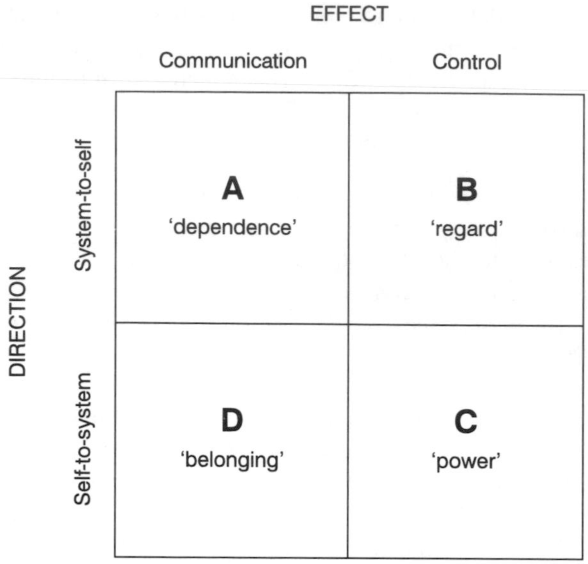

EFFECT

		Communication	Control
	System-to-self	**A** 'dependence'	**B** 'regard'
	Self-to-system	**D** 'belonging'	**C** 'power'

DIRECTION

A "my needs are understood/not understood by the system"
B "the system rules are for my good/not for my good"
C "I can/cannot influence the system"
D "I feel at one with/not at one with the system"

FIGURE 25.2   The Horton Alienation Model

The Horton Alienation Model

This model adopted from Seeman (1959) was developed and tested in my thesis (1985). It is not primarily a change model, though I will try to show how results derived from it, could be used to estimate the degree of conflict (and therefore potentiality for change) in a group's perception of the system in which it is operating. The model is an expansion and investigation of the level 1 relationship between self and system, using attitude measurement techniques to test a model of what I have called "deep-structure attitudes".

A latent process model was used—that of a within individual set of learnt and modifiable schemata acting to filter perception of a predisposed action towards a social object. The most general object possible was set—that of any social system seen from the inside, or the concept of authority itself. In that way the model aimed to be generalisable to the study of the attitudes of members towards the perceived authority of any group or institution to which they belong.

The model thus depends on an initial assumption by the individual that the system is a *legitimate* authority—that is, that a mutually agreed set of reciprocal relationships (rights and duties) between individual and system should be present. The individual's perception of the disconfirmation of these expectations is the core definition of the feeling of "alienation".

The deep-structure nature of the model was created by defining the minimum elements that needed to be present to describe a relationship between reciprocating entities—that of perceived *direction* and that of perceived *effect* (i.e. formal and efficient causality). Other questions such as how and why (i.e. material and final causality) were not considered essential to this minimal description. There were seen to be two categories of direction: system-to-self and self-to-system. A minimum of two theoretically distinguishable effects could be seen: that of communication (or a change in understanding) and that of influence (or a change in behaviour).

When these minimal definitions are modelled as an interactive quadrant and concretised in terms of the self's perception of the system, four bi-polar constructs defining each of the four cells of the quadrant can be created.

A   My needs are understood/not understood by the system *Dependence*.
B   The system rules (organisation) are for my good/not for my good *Regard*.
C   I can/cannot influence the system *Power*.
D   I am/am not "at one with" the system *Belonging*.

The model, at this deep-structure level, is clear and complete. It can be postulated that any belief about the nature of a self-system relationship, if reduced to a simple statement of efficient or formal causality, should fit into one of the cells of the quadrant, given the limiting factor that the relationship is desirable, i.e. Self is in the System.

This model was initially tested in a study of electors' attitudes to local government. The hypotheses were that four valid and reliable dimensions, interpretable in terms of the model would be found. These would be empirically distinguishable but not necessarily unrelated. A maximum-likelihood factor analysis using an oblique rotation procedure, was conducted on the data, followed by a convergent and discriminant construct validity matrix test, of the factors in order to test these hypotheses on a probability sample of 101 London electors. Factor reliability was tested on a volunteer sample of 750 members of a national organisation contacted by post.

Basically, the hypotheses were largely supported. My interest, in terms of this paper, is to show some of the differences in the pattern of results for different sub-samples. From these comparisons, inferences concerning differing levels of integration-alienation between self and system can be made. The indices used are the covariances of the factor scores.

The pattern produced by the general population sample of Londoners (largely working-class) shows that there is no perception of reciprocal identification with the local authority system. The covariances across Directions are low or negative. The perceptions of a "good" caring and controlling system are just related (.18). The perception of self as having any control is highly negatively related to the

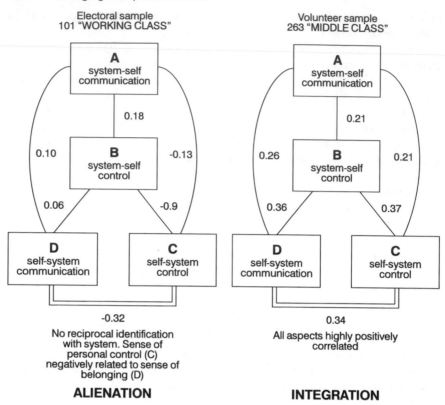

Electoral sample
101 "WORKING CLASS"

Volunteer sample
263 "MIDDLE CLASS"

FIGURE 25.3   Local government Londoner's self-system attitude pattern

perception of self as "belonging" was related to trade union membership, seen as in opposition to the local authority. This is a pattern that could be termed *Alienated*—conflicted and unintegrated. The volunteer middle-class sample of Londoners, on the other hand, shows a highly integrated pattern with covariances all positive and fairly high.

Figure 25.1 shows a comparison between male and female members of the national organisation (middle-class and educated). The female pattern suggests a position of partial identification, partial alienation. The covariances across Direction are high for the control effect—that is there is a perceived reciprocity. The sense of personal power and commitment are related, as is the sense of commitment and the perception of a benign control. But the perception of being understood and cared for by the system is unrelated to the other dimensions. The pattern for the males, on the other hand, is highly integrated. One can infer from these patterns that middle-class males see themselves as highly identified with the local government system (largely controlled by middle-class males), whereas the middle-class females do not.

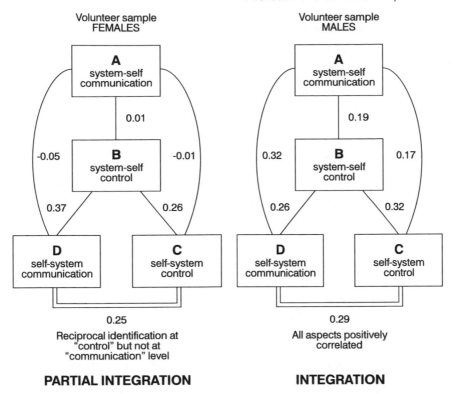

FIGURE 25.4   Local Government National self-system attitude pattern

However, the middle-class female pattern is not so starkly "alienated" as that of the working-class sample.

Alienation, Social Identity and Social Change

The descriptive, attitude structure model of alienation put forward above, defines the degree of alienation in a self-system relationship in terms of the lack of integration of the attitude dimensions as discovered in a representative sample of members of the system. This, it is hypothesised, should show up as a lack of perceived reciprocity of "positive" communication and control between self and system such that a *negative* perception of lack of control (powerlessness) and communication (isolation) from self to system, will be combined with a negative perception of over-control from system to self, and the perception of an alien value system. The value-conflict is posited as the pivotal dimension, in line with Billig (1976):

there may well be a mis-match between the social experience of a group and the elements of its professed ideology. This ideological tension may itself reflect the processes by which a group-in-itself becomes a group-for-itself.

(p. 375)

However, it is hypothesised that value conflict will act as a force for change only in combination with relevant positions on other dimensions of the overall attitude (the perceived impossibility of communication with and influencing of the system, and the perceived pressure to conform).

An additional and crucial measure is that of the perceived legitimacy of the system itself. The alienation attitude model is constructed on the assumption that self is inside the system. It is hypothesised that when a certain level of "alienation" is reached, as defined above, then the legitimacy of the system as an authority may be questioned. It would be difficult to posit stages in the development of alienation towards a final rejection of legitimacy, as a high degree of perceived value-conflict in a system with a high level of perceived communicability, a low pressure to conform and the hope of some degree of self-system influence (i.e. a democratic, open society) would, in terms of the model, not result in an overall de-legitimisation of the authority status of the system whereas a lower level of value-conflict in a more rigid system might well do so.

The influence of the system's own history on its members' perceptions, and events external to the system (economic, political, environmental?), would also need to be taken into account in any social analysis, but as a model on the social-psychological level of explanation, in alienation theory social change or social action is seen as an effect, not a cause. The possible actions of individuals or sub-groups resulting from a change in perceived legitimacy of the system can be conceptualised in terms of a development of Tajfel's (1978) conceptualisation of "negative social identity" as a force for social change, in the light of the work of others such as Billig, Lemaine and Breakwell.

Action Possibilities of Subordinate in Relation to Dominant Group

Inaction

1. *Acceptance* of negative social identity; authority perceived as legitimate; self-blame for own position: i.e. "false consciousness" (Billig, 1976)
2. *Apathy*: some perception of illegitimacy (i.e. discontent) but despair of ignorance of action possibilities.

Avoidance mechanisms

3. *Passing*: individual or group action to change or disguise one's identity so as to join the dominant group. This can involve a change of values (as in social mobility) or the adoption of a false or marginal identity.

4. *Exiting*: individual or group action to remove oneself from the "alien" system. Examples might be migration either towards acceptance or re-enculteration within a more positively perceived system, or towards the formation of a separatist community (such as the Amish or Doukhobours). The formation or joining of "fantastical" social movements, or some extremist political or religious cults would be forms of "avoidance by exiting".
5. *Scapegoating*: avoiding negative comparison with the dominant group by choosing an even more "inferior" group to compare oneself with (for example poor whites and blacks in the southern states).

Challenge mechanisms

6. *Voicing*: individual or group action to change out-group self-perception from negative to positive in attempts to influence the dominant group's perception of the out-group. Out-group refusal to accept in-group's labelling (as in Breakwell's "Quiet Rebel").
7. *Evolving*: changing individual or out-group perceptions of the comparison rules (the rules of the game itself) in attempts to reverse or ameliorate the relative positions of the subordinate and dominant groups (cf. Lemaine, 1974). This can be seen as a creative and change-oriented response to the recognition of inequality, which can result in new discoveries in science, originality in art or innovative developments in systems of social relations, i.e. progress.
8. *Revolving*: direct challenge and competition aimed at reversing the positions of in and out group. When seen as group action it leads to inherent social instability and an endemic state of conflict.

Underlying all these action possibilities in social identity theory is the individual motivational concept of the need for self-esteem acting through the process of self-categorisation as a group member to change a negative to a positive social identity. Inaction (as defined above) is difficult to explain in terms of social identity theory, and is usually not mentioned. It can, however, be accommodated in an alienation theory framework in terms of the multi-dimensional perception of self-system relations, already discussed.

Alienation theory, can be seen as complementing social identity theory explanations of social change. By concentrating on the perception of the relationship between self and other, at all three levels of relatedness (Intra-psychic, Interpersonal and Social), the explanation of social change (or its absence) would lie in the amount of perceived conflict and the manner of its resolution. The crucial or motivating conflict can be seen as one of value. Values, initially learnt from the group become internalised, i.e. the property of the self, and act to protect the self against "malign" change in the larger system—but only if the self is separate enough from the system to hear the sound of the "different drummer". Alienation theory would suggest that the growth of a strong self (i.e.

unalienated at level 1) is itself a precondition for the possibility of separation and change at level 3.

The sequence would be:

1. acquisition of group values at level 2 (Self-other, Interpersonal or the primary group);
2. internalisation of group values as level 1 (Self-Self or Intrapsychic);
3. leading to the possibility of separation from the system at level 3 (Selfsystem or Social);
4. leading to the possibility of social action at level 2 (i.e. group action in SIT terms).

An essential aspect of alienation theory, and where it does not seem to have a counterpart in social identity theory, is that it allows both for a distinction and a possible conflict between as well as within levels. For example, self-self integrity or self-other loyalty may necessitate self-system alienation (or vice versa). (For example: the assassination attempt on Hitler. Some combination of a renewed belief in internalised values (self-self integrative) together with loyalty to the primary group (the other conspirators) and disillusionment with the leader, allowed the conspirators to "act against the State".)

Alienation theory, as its name suggests, is primarily a theory describing, and hopefully going some way to explain, the disaffection of the individual and/or the group, from the larger system. Perceived "benign" changes in the larger system would not normally lead to disaffection—except, perhaps, in the limiting case where raised expectations due to the liberalising of a formerly repressive system, were to outrun the capability of the system to fulfil them—the possibility of which the new South African government will no doubt be well aware.

The main difference between alienation theory and social identity theory is that the primary motivating force is seen to lie in a conflict of values or goals (note "survival" or self-interest can be values in this sense) rather than a threat to social identity and its underlying motive force of a need for self-esteem. However, it does not seem that the two positions are irreconcilable.

A Proposal for Testing the Alienation-Identity Model

There are two essential attributes of a good theory or model—that it should be fruitful of ideas and that it should be testable. The fruitfulness of alienation theory, even in the embryo stage presented in this paper, I leave to the minds of the readers. Its testability I hope to demonstrate here.

There are actually three models presented in this chapter—the original "quadrant" model (Figure 25.3); the "triadic" model (Figure 25.1) which aims to combine the quadratic model of deep-structure attitudes of self to system with an affiliative model of self-other perceptions; and, finally, the "value-conflict" three-level model, the aim of which is the explanation of social change.

The 1985 deep-structure attitude model was designed to measure attitudes to any systematic authority or structured group to which the individual belonged. Its original testing in the political arena (local government) makes its application to the study of attitudes to European government particularly appropriate. Operational measures of self-other identifications, self-system value conflicts and legitimacy remain to be constructed but there is an ample literature from which ideas may be drawn (cf. Liebkind, 1993).

An initial study could be carried out on a twin-town basis comparing a probability sample of electors in a town from a country with evidence of a large popular support for the EC (for example, Ireland) and a "matched" town in a country with low population support (for example, England) and perhaps a third matched town from a country where pro- and anti- feeling is fairly evenly matched (for example, France or Denmark). A comparison of the results across countries may show differences in the patterns of response which might help to elucidate underlying factors in the acceptance or non-acceptance of the EC. Further questions could be asked of the data: for example, do those who identify themselves as Europeans at the A-B level of the triadic model, also feel a sense of reciprocal control and communication in their perceived relation with Europe as a political and economic institution, or is there a split between institutional and group identifications? Is there a link between this split (if it should be found) and the level of value-conflict between the intrapsychic, interpersonal and institutional levels? Can we predict the amount and direction of attitudes change at T2 from the response patterns at Tl?

A research programme of this nature would, I suggest, be of both theoretical value in testing and, hopefully, extending the model, and practical relevance in increasing our understanding of underlying public attitudes to the European Community. It could perhaps lead to suggestions for changes in the presentation of the community's views and values, to its members—the public.

References

Averill, J. R. (1968). Grief: its nature and significance. *Psychological Bulletin*, **70**(6), 721–48.

Billig, M. (1976). *Social Psychology and Intergroup Relations*. London: Academic Press.

Breakwell, G. M. (ed.)(1983). *Threatened Identities*. Chichester: Wiley.

Breakwell, G. M. (1985). *The Quiet Rebel*. London: Century Publishing.

Breakwell, G. M. (1993) Introductory paper read at conference on "Changing European Identities" Farnham, 7 May 1993.

Durkheim, E. (1970). *Suicide: A Study in Sociology*. Translated by J. A. Spaulding and G. Simpson. London: Routledge & Kegan Paul.

Freud, S. (1969). *Civilisation and its Discontents*, ed. J. Strachey. London: Hogarth Press.

Goffmann, E. (1961). *Asylums*. New York: Anchor Books.

Hogg, M. A. and Abrams, D. (1988). *Social Identifications*. London: Routledge.

Horton, M. (1985). The nature of alienation: a theoretical review and empirical test of Seeman's hypothesis. PhD Thesis, University of London.

Lemaine, G. (1974). Social differentiation and social originality. *European Journal of Social Psychology*, **4**(1), 17–52.

Liebkind, K. (in press) Vietnamese refugees in Finland—Changing cultural identities. In G. M. Breakwell and E. Lyons (eds), *Changing European Identities: Social-psychological Analysis of Social Change*. London: Butterworth-Heinemann.

Marx, K. (1972). *Early Texts*. Trans. and ed. D. McLellan. Oxford: Blackwell.

Rabbie, J. M. and Horowitz, M. (1988). Categories versus groups as explanatory concepts in intergroup relations. *European Journal of Social Psychology*, **18**(2), 117–24.

Seeman, M. (1959). On the meaning of alienation. *American Sociological Review*, **24**(6), 783–89.

Stokols, D. (1975). Toward a psychological theory of alienation. *Psychological Review*, **82**(1), 26–44.

Tajfel, H. (1978). *Differentiation between Social Groups: Studies in the Social Psychology of Intergroup Relations*. London: Academic Press.

Author Index

Subject Index